The Economics of Infrastructure Provisioning

CESifo Seminar Series
edited by Hans-Werner Sinn

Perspectives on the Performance of the Continental Economies, Edmund S. Phelps and Hans-Werner Sinn, editors

Industrial Policy for National Champions, Oliver Falck, Christian Gollier, and Ludger Woessmann, editors

Illicit Trade and the Global Economy, Cláudia Costa Storti and Paul De Grauwe, editors

The Continuing Evolution of Europe, Thiess Buettner and Wolfgang Ochel, editors

The Evolving Role of China in the Global Economy, Yin-Wong Cheung and Jakob de Haan, editors

Critical Issues in Taxation and Development, Clemens Fuest and George R. Zodrow, editors

Central Bank Communication, Decision Making, and Governance, Pierre L. Siklos and Jan-Egbert Sturm, editors

Lessons from the Economics of Crime, Philip J. Cook, Stephen Machin, Olivier Marie, and Giovanni Mastrobuoni, editors

Firms in the International Economy, Sjoerd Beugelsdijk, Steven Brakman, Hans van Ees, Harry Garretsen, editors

Global Interdependence, Decoupling and Recoupling, Yin-Wong Cheung and Frank Westermann, editors

The Economics of Conflict, Karl Wärneryd, editor

Climate Policy and Nonrenewable Resources, Karen Pittel, Frederick van der Ploeg and Cees Withagen, editors

Taxation and Regulation of the Financial Sector, Ruud de Mooij and Gaëtan Nicodème, editors

The Mobility of Students and the Highly Skilled, Marcel Gérard and Silke Uebelmesser, editors

Political Economy and Instruments of Environmental Politics, Andrea Kollmann, Johannes Reichl, and Friedrich Schneider, editors

Emissions Trading Systems as a Policy Instrument, Marc Gronwald and Beat Hintermann, editors

The Economics of Infrastructure Provisioning, Arnold Picot, Massimo Florio, Nico Grove, and Johann Kranz, editors

See http://mitpress.mit.edu for a complete list of titles in this series.

The Economics of Infrastructure Provisioning

The Changing Role of the State

edited by
Arnold Picot, Massimo Florio, Nico Grove, and Johann Kranz

CESifo Seminar Series

The MIT Press
Cambridge, Massachusetts
London, England

This book was set in Palatino LT Std by Toppan Best-set Premedia Limited. Printed and bound in the United States of America.

Library of Congress Cataloging-in-Publication Data

The economics of infrastructure provisioning : the changing role of the state / edited by Arnold Picot, Massimo Florio, Nico Grove, and Johann Kranz.
pages cm. — (CESifo seminar series)
Includes bibliographical references and index.
ISBN 978-0-262-02965-0 (hardcover : alk. paper) 1. Infrastructure (Economics)—Government policy. 2. Public goods. 3.
Public works. I. Picot, Arnold.
HC79.C3E23 2015
363.6--dc23

2015011450

10 9 8 7 6 5 4 3 2 1

Contents

Series Foreword

This book is part of the CESifo Seminar Series. The series aims to cover topical policy issues in economics from a largely European perspective. The books in this series are the products of the papers and intensive debates that took place during the seminars hosted by CESifo, an international research network of renowned economists organized jointly by the Center for Economic Studies at Ludwig-Maximilians-Universität, Munich, and the Ifo Institute for Economic Research. All publications in this series have been carefully selected and refereed by members of the CESifo research network.

I Introduction

1 Public Infrastructure Provisioning: Foundations and Challenges

Arnold Picot, Massimo Florio, Nico Grove, and Johann Kranz

1.1 The Rediscovery of Infrastructures as an Economic Challenge

Infrastructures have again become a topical issue in economics and management. For quite some time it seemed that the functioning of markets in all fields of our economies would be the dominant perspective for economic reasoning and empirical or theoretical analysis. However, those once unaware know today that infrastructures are a vital precondition for economic and societal well-being and that the provisioning of infrastructures poses problems of its own that are only partly coincidental with traditional market-based approaches. There are several factors that drive the economic policy debate on infrastructure: the pressing need for the repair, renewal, and expansion of classic infrastructures, such as roads, bridges and railways, not only in developing regions; the demand for new and innovative infrastructures, such as broadband, smart grids, and large-scale research infrastructures; and the growing insight that market forces alone are not able to bring about the necessary investment for and the sustainable maintenance of infrastructures but rather that some form of collective and public responsibility is needed to complement private activities. It is against this background that the editors of this book organized a CESifo conference in Venice in summer 2013, bringing together researchers from various parts of the globe specializing in infrastructure economics and policy. This book is a collection of a set of papers initially presented at that conference. The introductory chapter sets some of the ideas around which the conference was organized, introduces the papers presented and discussed, and adds the perspective of the editors in the current debate on infrastructure provisioning.

1.2 Economic and Political Importance

The Republic of Panama recently proclaimed a new record of one billion USD in net earnings from the Panama Canal (dpa 2013). The respective contribution to the national budget of 9.2 billion USD accounts for nearly 11 percent of total government revenues. Although today, the Panama Canal is celebrated as a big success, more or less the opposite was true before, that is, both during and after construction in 1914. Critics were abundant, not only targeting the economic success but also because of the high complexity of the project due to political and military instability (Grove 2014).

It is common knowledge that a correct decision in infrastructure can cause tremendous developments and effects thereafter. Wrong decisions in infrastructure, in contrast, can lead to massive losses and eventually prohibit development of other competing systems, possibly precluding superior solutions. Furthermore infrastructure and service systems are often specifically intertwined, which may result in huge losses of infrastructure investment if the related service system is eventually not accepted by users. For example, remember the history of the great dirigible airship infrastructures. In its flowering stage before World War II, airships were regarded as the future of air and flight travel worldwide. An international network of airship harbors with accompanying ground infrastructure, with halls and ground facilities, was created and operated. However, massive construction-related security risks existed. The entire airship era ended with the "Hindenburg" disaster, when the Zeppelin LZ 129 exploded while landing at Lakehurst in the United States. As a consequence the entire industry sector collapsed because there was no alternative uses foreseen for the specific airship facilities that existed (Grove 2014).

This book aims to create renewed understanding of the importance of the economics of infrastructure provisioning but also to show that the subject is intrinsically interdisciplinary. It is this interdisciplinary perspective—the historical lessons, institutional and legal developments, and the cultural environment around the public discourse on infrastructure—that makes the topic so challenging and fascinating. The editors hope that the contributions selected for the book will convey to economists the need to pay attention to such a broad research agenda.

1.3 Definition

In general, there is no consistent definition of "infrastructure" across the economic literature. Some ideas were reviewed twenty years ago in a much cited paper (Gramlich 1994), but not much progress in the taxonomy has been achieved in more recent years (Torrisi 2009). From the broadest perspective, infrastructure can be defined "as the sum of material, institutional and personal facilities and data which are available to the economic agents and which contribute to realizing the equalization of the remuneration of comparable inputs in the case of a suitable allocation of resources, that is complete integration and maximum level of economic activities" (Jochimsen 1966: 100). Hence infrastructure represents general public facilities that are often essential prerequisites for economic life (see Gabler 1993; Esfahani and Ramírez 2003; Frischmann 2012; Florio 2013) and can be differentiated into tangible, intangible, and institutional infrastructure (Witte 2002; Klodt 2009):

- *Tangible infrastructure* Traffic systems, including streets, railways, and transportation roads, as well as utilities such as energy, water, sewer, and communication networks
- *Intangible infrastructure* Education, research, health and social services, and endowments at the country or local level
- *Institutional infrastructure* Additional legal, economic, and social systems

In a wider scope, culture and traditions are also regarded as fundamental infrastructure.

Torrisi (2009: 8) describes public infrastructure as a capital good, "originated by investment expenditure and is characterized by long duration, technical indivisibility and a high capital–output ratio," on the one hand. On the other, infrastructure is regarded as a public good, creating external effects.

This definition suggests that it is the responsibility of the public to spur economic growth through upgrading the quality and efficiency of public infrastructure (Portland Development Commission 2002). Del Bo (2011) referred to the classic questions about how and to what extent public investment is related to growth. To determine an optimal level of infrastructure provision, Gramlich (1994) considered the question of a shortage of infrastructure capital. In figure 1.1 we take a closer look at the provision of infrastructure.

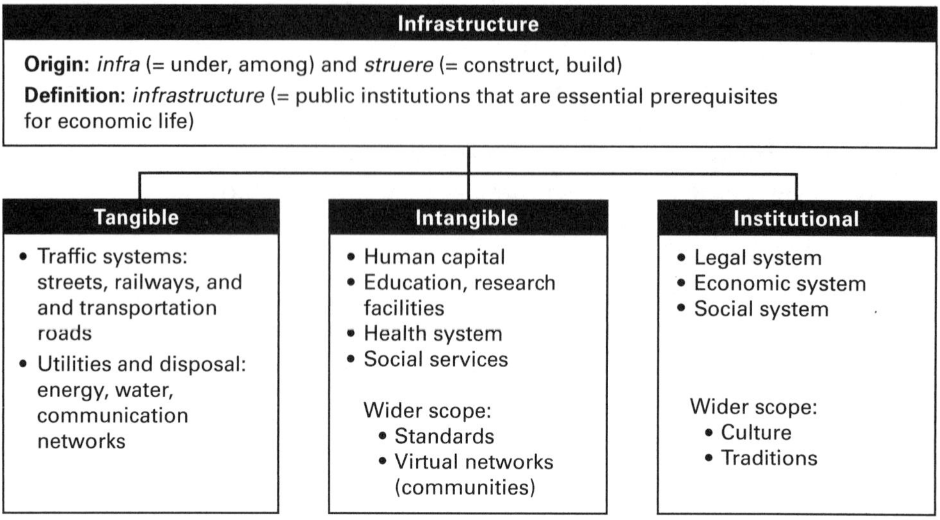

Figure 1.1
Infrastructure defined

1.4 Provision of Public Goods

Infrastructure in fact is often referred to as a public good (Aschauer 1989; Grimsey and Mervyn 2004). However, this rather holistic approach is missing important details. Public goods are described by Samuelson as goods, "which all can enjoy in common in the sense that each individual's consumption of such a good leads to no subscriptions from any other individual's consumption of that good …." (Samuelson 1954: 387). Public goods are characterized by their nonrivalry in consumption and their low excludability from consumption (Olson 1965; Musgrave 1959).

As figure 1.2 shows, the consumption of a public good by an individual does not exclude a third individual from its consumption, nor does its (concurrent) use lower the benefit of its use for another individual. Traditional examples range from national defense to public TV. However, infrastructures such as networks of hiking trails or public water dispensers bear some characteristics of public goods. "Common goods," in contrast, refer to goods where use is not restricted to a specific group but can lead to rivalry for consumption by different groups. Typical examples include roadways, natural resources, and some public

Diminishability (rivalry) in consumption \ Excludability from consumption	High	Low
High	**Private goods** (e.g., food, cars)	**Collective or common goods** (e.g., road system, natural resources)
Low	**Club goods** (e.g., private schools, pay TV)	**Public goods** (e.g., national security, public TV)

Figure 1.2
Categorization of public goods

institutions. Looking at a motorway, it is theoretically accessible for everyone. However, in practice, too many road users, or cars, can lead to traffic jams, decreasing the individual and hence overall road use for everyone. "Club goods" are nonrival, but their consumption is exclusionist. This is the practice of private schools or pay TV where access is granted by a payment scheme. Also among infrastructures there are some that have aspects of club goods; for example, only people who buy flight tickets can enjoy aircraft transport, which in turn relies on specific infrastructures such as airports and air traffic control.

The political discourse on public goods often mentions "common goods" despite being theoretically incorrect. This use of the term contradicts the prerequisite of nonrivalry in consumption for pure public goods. Nevertheless, infrastructure investments are generally regarded politically as public provisions, as roads, culture, education, and health care, for example. Public provision can thus result from a semantic confusion in the qualification of merit goods. This, in the public discourse, is perhaps a symptom of the perceived criticality of merit goods in shaping the economic performance and the social welfare of the community. After all, labeling "things" or "goods" is never a purely value-free process, and the oscillations on how to classify infrastructures are most likely a reflection of the changing attitudes of policy makers and citizens toward their provision. This issue is better illustrated in what follows.

1.5 Merit and Demerit Goods

"Merit goods" are sometimes closely related to public goods. They are defined as goods underestimated in value by individuals (Musgrave 1959). Hence these goods tend to be consumed in a lower quantity than would be beneficial for the entire society. This lower demand leads to a lower production capacity in the free market economy. Merit goods are therefore supplied by the government or with public financial aid to fulfill a socially desirable higher supply. Examples include compulsory education, compulsory health insurance, and public museums. Classic physical infrastructures share some properties of merit goods. It is, for instance, not at all clear from the outset what level of infrastructure rollout is necessary to bring about a flourishing economy. Value-based decision-making, and thus political processes and interests, are at work when deciding, for example, whether road or telecommunication networks should be knit more or less densely and with more or less capacity. Considering infrastructures as public goods, Torrisi (2009) refers to them as merit goods because economic agents show their "real" preferences with regard to individual willingness to pay for their provision. This argument is convincing where the individual user of an infrastructure has alternative solutions and can decide whether to pay based on his or her individual willingness (e.g., toll roads). If the financing of an infrastructure, such as urban road work or public safety work, occurs indirectly via general taxes, the connection between the individual demand and public provision of the merit good infrastructure is hardly traceable and thus more subject to political discretion.

In contrast to merit goods, "demerit goods" (or demerit "bads") are socially undesirable in consumption for the individual and hence for the entire society. The unregulated market does not lead to the optimal quantity of demerit goods from the perspective of social welfare. As a result governments have to support and fund the appropriate containment of demerit goods to increase overall social welfare—again, a much discussed public issue and a matter of divergent evaluations and discretion. In addition infrastructures might involve negative external effects that are valued differently by users and other social groups. The consumption of land, the emission of smog, noise, radiation, gases, and the like, generated by specific infrastructures and related services are examples in which the political struggle against demerit goods comes into play and must be balanced with the expected benefits of the relevant infrastructure.

1.6 Provisioning Mechanisms

Against this rather uncertain background in terms of definition and analytical classification, the actual forms of infrastructure provisioning can be roughly divided into four distinct categories: government-based provisioning, market-based provisioning under public procurement, regulated market-based provisioning, and private provisioning.

In a system of government-based provisioning, infrastructure is provided directly by the government. In many countries this includes most intangible and institutional infrastructures such as the health system, the education system, social services, and the legal system. It requires, in principle, a certain degree of independence from political influence, and a long-term commitment from the government to the sustainability of the systems. Direct government provision initially includes a large share of tangible infrastructures such as roads and ports but less so in later years.

In a system of market-based provisioning under public procurement, the government buys infrastructure from private companies and provides it to the citizens at no cost or at subsidized prices. When there are considerable external effects on goods, by such an approach the cost of provisioning can be justified. Examples include tangible infrastructures, such as railways and communication networks, and also systems for public safety.

A system of regulated market-based provisioning rests on the assumption that there are significant economies of scale to the infrastructure good, so leaving the provisioning to the market will lead to suboptimal prices. In such cases governments provide monopoly powers to a single company, which will then be overseen by a regulatory authority. Examples include the telecommunications, energy, and railway sectors.

Private companies provide ever more infrastructures that once were publicly owned. This liberalization is aimed at improving the quality of service, decreasing costs, and encouraging innovations, but it simultaneously raises concerns with respect to sufficient investments, security of supply, social affordability, and sustainable growth (Finger and Künneke 2011; Florio 2004, 2013).

Since the late 1970s and early 1980s, governments all over the world have shifted away from government-based provisioning and public procurement to either regulated market-based provisioning or complete privatization. This has affected important sectors of the economy such as the telecommunication, electricity, post, and railway systems. The shift was triggered by the rejection of the postwar Keynesian consensus and the emergence of neoclassical economics as the new mainstream as well as increasing budget constraints. One important manifestations of this shift has been the rise of hybrid arrangements between government and markets, with the most prominent form being public–private partnerships (PPPs; see Engel et al. 2013; Hart 2003; Yescombe 2011). Such arrangements involve a contract between a private company and a public sector entity that includes the provision of a predefined public infrastructure, it's financing and risk-sharing. It can include contracts on the transnational level, such as the construction of a tunnel between two countries, or on the local level, such as the maintenance of a sewage plant. PPPs constitute the market-based provisioning of infrastructure formerly provisioned by the government or regulated monopolies.

Recently public–private partnerships have been heavily affected by the global financial crisis: Between 2007 and 2009 the total volume of PPP transactions in Europe decreased by almost 50 percent (European Investment Bank 2010). Public–private partnerships have been the subject of considerable controversy: whereas its proponents argue that such partnerships can increase the efficiency of infrastructure provision, critics note that the allocation of risks is often unfavorable to both the private sector and the public sector. In finding a viable balance between the diverging interests and incentives among the partners involved in PPPs, several studies (Brinkerhoff and Brinkerhoff 2011; Forrer et al. 2010) note that governing PPP projects requires that partners agree upon governance rules and unambiguously specify accountability. To ensure public accountability, Goldsmith and Eggers (2004) conclude that governing PPP projects requires (1) properly aligning incentives, (2) routinely measuring performance, (3) building trust in the network, and (4) appropriately sharing risks.

1.7 Financing

Governments have many options as to financing public infrastructure. Broadly speaking, their choices fall into two categories: "Pay-as-you-go" (cash flow) financing, based on direct revenues resulting from the project or budget appropriations from the public sector, and capital-market financing, based on borrowings or equity contributions from private sources. The use of budget appropriations or capital-market financing can vary considerably among countries, and moreover can affect the temporal distribution of the government's financial burden: for instance, in the United States, 70 percent of the infrastructure projects is financed through bonds that shift the tax load to subsequent generations; in the United Kingdom, budget appropriations account for 74 percent of public infrastructure investment, amounting to nearly two-thirds of the tax burden borne by the present generation (Chan et al. 2009).

In the past two decades major innovations were introduced to project financing in terms of credit enhancement and securitization. More efficient use of financing resulted from an increased use of a combination of debt and equity financing from both private- and public-sector sources. The specific decision of governments on how to finance a certain infrastructure now depends on a number of factors, with infrastructure characteristics, fiscal and macroeconomic conditions, institutional arrangements, and prevailing views on government control being among the most important considerations (Florio and Colautti 2005).

The financing vehicles differ in accord with the extent of market discipline, incentives for project risk management, and transaction costs. For instance, budget appropriation is subject only to parliamentary discipline; incentives for project risk management are low but so are transaction costs. A public–private partnership, on one hand, entails higher transaction costs but, on the other, if designed appropriately, brings market discipline and incentives for adequate risk management of the infrastructure project. Another tool, which is especially common in the United States and Canada, is the issuance of special purpose bonds whereby repayment depends on the performance of the underlying asset.

The success of a particular financing vehicle will depend on its ability to allocate risks to those best suited to manage it, reduce the market risk for investors by diversification, or reduce transaction costs. Making the decision as to which financing vehicle is best suited is a nontrivial issue; for innovative way to quantify these factors at the municipal level, see Warner (2013).

1.8 Regulation

The aim of government regulation is to ensure an optimal supply of public and merit goods (Picot 2009). Where public infrastructure is a natural monopoly due to immense irreversible costs and economies of bundling (Joskow 2005; Picot 2009; Viscusi et al. 2005), governments impose regulation to curb monopoly power, facilitate competition, and promote maximum efficiency—not only for traditional infrastructural utilities but also for newly emerging infrastructures, such as smart grids (Kranz and Picot 2011).

Such regulations can take a variety of forms, with the most common being the following:

- *Price regulation* Governments can regulate the prices monopolies or quasi-monopolies can charge from their customers. For instance, electricity prices are heavily regulated in most countries.
- *Access regulation* Governments can force private companies maintaining an infrastructure to provide access to competitors. For instance, in many countries, providers of telecommunication services are forced to provide equal access to competitors to avoid discrimination.
- *Rules for supply to settlements* For instance, providers of electricity and water are forced to provide services to every community within a country.

From the end of WWII until the late 1970s, public infrastructure services experienced a period of stability in their modes of organization and regulation in many Western countries (Millward 2005). During this period public ownership was dominant and justified by arguments on the presence of market failures (e.g., natural monopolies), the strategic and economic importance of public services, as well as concerns about social justice (Clifton et al. 2004; van de Walle 2009). Since the late 1970s, however, public services became subject to substantial reform. In the European Union, for instance, these reforms intensified during the 1990s, particularly due to market integration processes and liberalization policies in the public services sectors (Bauby 2008; Bognetti and Obermann 2008). In parallel, member states embarked upon the privatization of many of these services.

Reform of public infrastructure services, particularly liberalization, deregulation, and privatization, was founded on neoclassical economic theory, which rested on two critical sets of assumptions: The first assumption was that exposing firms to competition would result in lower prices and increased service choices for consumers. From the theoretical perspective (Armstrong and Sappington 2006) and ex post empirical analysis of price and choice (Fiorio and Florio 2013; Florio

2013), it has been shown that these reforms did not necessarily always deliver the promised results. The second assumptionwas that citizens, cast as rational consumers, would be positioned to benefit universally from these developments (EC 2004). From the outset of reform, however, concern was expressed by some agents about whether, under market-driven rules, the traditions of public service obligations and universal access would be undermined and citizens would end up receiving lower quality services (CEEP and ETUC 2000).

1.9 Path Dependency and Endurance of Infrastructure

As we noted earlier, the endurance of infrastructure should not be underestimated. Decisions made once are not easily reversible after systems have been established in a substantial way. This issue is mainly linked to the technological, organizational, and cultural specificities of infrastructures, preventing them from use for purposes other than the initial service purpose (e.g., see Berkhout 2002; Sydow et al. 2009; Korpi 2001). A good example is today's private transport sector, dominated heavily by combustion engine-based vehicles. Changing the system toward alternative mobility concepts such as electric or hydrogen vehicles is a massive challenge. The drawbacks are manifold: There is not only a need for the development of alternative technologies; systemic adaptions or entire system changes are required. Although technological solutions have arisen in recent decades, the real breakthrough that has to be made is departing from the established ecosystem based on the automobile. This process includes streets, petrol stations, parking systems, city architecture and planning, manufacturers and suppliers, as well as upstream and downstream service providers. Furthermore all current new concepts and ideas have one thing in common: They do not have access to a functioning, area-wide infrastructure, such as the one represented by the current individual car vehicle-based traffic system. Therefore it is once more important to note the necessity of prompt and "right decisions" in infrastructure to implement politically, socially, or ecologically desired changes.

In most situations decisions to implement infrastructural enable new industries to emerge and thus raise the wealth potential for society at large, but as a consequence there may be long-lasting restrictions on future decision-making, constricting the freedom to adopt fundamentally better solutions. This unavoidable path dependency has to be kept in mind when evaluating infrastructural alternatives.

1.10 Current Challenges for the Provision of (Public) Infrastructure

The brief overview of the fundamentals of infrastructure and its provision above shows the complexity of relationships and decisions required for financing, installing, implementing, and regulating (public) infrastructure. In the past, governments or at least governmental bodies dominated the provision of public infrastructure. In recent years this position has changed, and belief in the free market has solidified. In many areas, market competition leads to high levels of choice, low prices, and hence consumer benefits. However, especially in infrastructure markets, we observe that initial successes sometimes turn into the opposite over time. The free market in principle does lead to optimal solutions in product and service markets from the perspective of individual players (as stated in its "DNA"). However, for the underlying infrastructure—being in general the enabler for the mentioned free markets—this self-organizing mechanism does not necessarily work in an optimal way for society. Especially for merit and demerit goods, the free market approach does not lead to the optimal required provision of infrastructure. By definition, the quantity of merit or demerit goods is decided by normative political values and not by demand or the willingness to pay of individual consumers. As a result we are dealing now with the questions of a "right" quantity of provisioning and the "right" level of provisioning for infrastructure and related investments. Additional questions include the optimal quality and form of providing infrastructure to the society. A phenomenon going along is the observation of a "changing role of the state." This term refers to the governmental shift from a general provider of infrastructure toward a "provision manager." Former governmental executions, including the selection, financing, implementation, and management of public infrastructure, have shifted more toward a governmental responsibility for infrastructure provision. In recent decades PPPs were developed to overcome the mentioned problems. However, it has turned out that many contracts discriminate against the public interest. In hindsight, most of the deals were done to achieve the best for both sides, but this position has neglected the fact that a negative business case will not become positive simply by renaming it a PPP.

The new role of the state includes pure governmental market management in every direction possible to achieve the optimal desired quantity and level of infrastructure from private market players.

In summary, a new research agenda on infrastructure provisioning should include the different perspectives that have been mentioned. There is no shortcut offered by a simplistic reliance on free-standing market mechanisms with only soft regulation. The analysis should instead carefully consider, on one hand, the interplay between political processes (including the definition of what is a "merit" or "demerit" good, what is an essential facility and what is not so essential, and the roles of regulation and of public finance) and, on the other hand, the incentives and constraints of private agents (financial actors, contractors, and partners of PPPs, oligopolistic service providers, etc.).

1.11 Contribution Offered by This Book

To illustrate some aspects of the new research agenda on infrastructure provisioning and the role of the state, the contributions included in this volume pick up a variety of questions regarding the provision, development, management, and impact of different types of facilities. The editors have selected papers that cover a broad range of methodological approaches, including historical and empirical research; analytical models; theoretical insights from political economics, development economics and other perspectives; and sector and regional case studies.

In what follows we show how the book contributes to a research agenda on the future of infrastructure provisioning and how some themes are recurrent, albeit from different perspectives, across the chapters. We do not strictly follow the sequence of the chapters in the book; rather, we show possible relationships between each chapter under the above-mentioned broad themes (public and merit goods and the role of the state, regulation, provision mechanisms, financing) from different perspectives.

1.12 Historical Perspective

The innovative impacts, the financing, the institutional preconditions of infrastructures, and the roles of government are addressed in chapter 2.In the chapter, Hugh Goldsmith draws a far-reaching historical picture of the economic and social roles of infrastructures. Goldsmith shows that large and complex technological systems that deliver water, transportation, communications, and energy services have evolved over hundreds and sometimes thousands of years. He describes not only the pivotal role of the state as a regulator, contracting authority, and default investor in public infrastructure but also the involvement of the private sector in some countries and industries.

Complementary to chapter 2, but taking a more general historical perspective, is chapter 8 in which Markus Hofmann provides a comprehensive and stimulating evolutionary view of the development of infrastructures over time, coining the concept of "infraculture," as societal development in the future is imprinted by digitalization. Hofmann also considers the deep changes in the patterns of human infrastructures, interpreted as the "operating system of society," due to digitalization.

Yet another historical perspective is offered in chapter 16 by Olivier Crespi Reghizzi on the provisioning and financing of urban water and sewer infrastructure at the turn of the twentieth century using the example of Milan. Reghizzi considers how water and sanitation infrastructure was financed by Italian municipalities, the financing tools implemented to cover the huge investments' costs, and the end-payers involved. His detailed analysis of the rolling-up phase of Milan's modern water and sanitation services (1888 to 1924) offers insight on the cost allocation of the chosen financing schemes by way of a basic overlapping generation model he uses to explore how infrastructure costs were allocated between generations.

1.13 Public–Private Finance Perspective

The relationship between public and private finance is a recurrent theme in a number of chapters. In particular, public–private partnerships sometimes are seen as the definitive solution for failures of government finance when governments face hard budgetary constraints. In chapter 4, Martina Santandrea, Stephen Bailey, and Marco Giorgino consider the funding and financing of infrastructure and analyze the functions and shortcomings of PPPs. In chapter 5, Daniel Danau and Annalisa Vinella focus their analysis on the contractual design of the interrelations between financing and incentives may help bring about a successful PPP solution. Santandrea, Bailey, and Giorgino suggest how the repayment of funding-related liability could be financed as governments seek to reduce their debts. Within that context, their contribution broadens the "value for money" options appraisal framework for infrastructural PPPs by taking into simultaneous consideration their upfront funding and subsequent financing requirements. The perspective of the analysis by Danau and Vinella is different. Their research focuses on information and incentive issues whereby a private firm may be in a better position to assess an infrastructure project than the government.

Contractual arrangements between the public and the private sectors are the central considerations in the empirical analyses provided in chapters 10 and 11. The bidding for toll road concessions (chapter 10) is at the center of the analytical and empirical work of Laure Athias and Antonio Nunez on the behavior of private firms bidding for infrastructure contracts when they discount some risk of renegotiation. The authors study the bidding behavior in the context of auctions for toll road concessions on 49 worldwide toll road concession auctions, for which the number of bidders was publicly known, the bidding procedure was the same. Julio Aguirre (chapter 11) studies relationships between electoral cycles and the renegotiation of a transport infrastructure concession contract. Aguirre combines the topic of contract renegotiation with political cycles using a unique database from Peru, and finds that electoral cycles significantly affect the hazard of renegotiation of those contracts. He provides a perspective on the importance of enforcing the institutional and regulatory supervisory activities of infrastructure concession contracts to minimize possible political influences on the contractual stability of these contracts. Taken together, these four chapters on PPPs and public procurement, two more theoretical and two more empirical, suggest that the relationship between government and the private sector as infrastructure providers is far from yielding a robust contractual model that can avoid the challenges of inadequate public accountability, information asymmetry, strategic behavior in bidding, renegotiation, and political influence.

1.14 Ownership Perspective

Two more chapters address the issue of infrastructure provisioning from the point of view of ownership. In chapter 13, Michael Pollitt tackles a classical question of infrastructure economics: What is the optimal ownership form in a particular country at a particular time? His analysis considers the factors that influence ownership positions (e.g., competition, regulation, technology, and institutions) and the increasing role of mixed ownership. Pollitt revisits the debate about ownership in the modern context in which the energy sector finds itself, where policy makers across the world want some combination of secure, low-carbon, and cheap energy but consider this "trilemma" impossible to solve. The author suggests what the elements of the "general" theory of public ownership might look like and the implications for the energy sector. In chapter 14, Federico Boffa and Lynne Kiesling analyze how competitive joint ventures may be an alternative to natural monopoly regulation in the distribution of energy. Boffa and Kiesling suggest, as less prone to information problems, a competitive joint venture (CJV) institution as an alternative to traditional natural monopoly regulation of the distribution wires portion of the electricity supply chain.

1.15 Growth Perspective

The relevance of infrastructure for growth is a classic theme that is addressed in this book by applying new research perspectives. In chapter 9, Stéphane Straub reviews lessons from the recent literature on transport infrastructure development using spatially disaggregated microeconomic data. He discusses the impact of transport infrastructure on outcomes, including production, population movements, and firm entry and exit, and the policy lessons for developing countries. In chapter 3, Sumit Deole presents a comprehensive model to study the impact of transportation infrastructure on economic growth in India, taking into account the population density and contrasting the analytical results with data from India. In chapter 7, Sumedha Bajar also uses regional data from India to show regional growth impacts as well as dynamics with respect to disparity stemming from infrastructure development. In chapter 15, Stephan Fretz considers the connection between fixed broadband access and economic growth in developed economies as new types of infrastructure, based on data for the OECD countries. Fretz examines the productivity data at the industry level for a sample of 21 OECD countries over the period of 1997 to 2006 and analyzes whether industries with strong broadband dependence experienced more proportional productivity growth as broadband diffusion progressed. Deole argues that an optimal distribution of infrastructure can boost the transition of an economy from economic stagnation toward a developing phase provided that population-induced productivity improvements and the provision of optimal infrastructure are already present in a region as the necessary conditions for this transition.

1.16 Regulation and Policy Perspectives

Institutions and policy are at the core of infrastructure economics. In chapter 12, Bhattacharyay provides a perspective from Asia on the financing needs for 32 Asian economies at the national and regional levels until the year 2020 in transport, energy, telecommunications, water, and sanitation as well as the financing gaps. Asia needs $2.6 trillion (or $236 billion per year) during the period of 2010 to 2020 for national transport infrastructures. In addition Asia's investment needs for the identified 1,202 regional or cross-border transport projects are estimated at approximately $229 billion (or 20.8 billion per year) during the period of 2010 to 2020. Last, in chapter 6, Égert reviews the role of policy and regulation from a broad regional perspective in the network industries of OECD economies. Contrary to previous empirical work, Égert finds that rate-of-return regulation does not result in overinvestment, and incentive regulation in underinvestment. Égert uses Bayesian averaging and a new dataset on price regulation to show that incentive regulation implemented jointly with an independent sector regulator has a strong positive impact on investment in network industries.

We hope that this collection of research stimulates discussion regarding the provisioning, management, and evolution of infrastructures and provides guidance for scholars and policy makers alike in their orientation for future priorities in research and politics.

Acknowledgments

The editors want to thank all those who made possible the 2013 CESifo conference in Venice on the beautiful Island San Servolo and who helped to bring about this volume. Above all, we are grateful to CESifo, Munich, especially to its Director, our esteemed colleague Hans-Werner Sinn, and his staff, particularly Olga Zudova and Dr. Michael Stimmelmayr. Their financial and personal support was decisive for the launch and the realization of this project. We would like to thank the MIT Press for its very delightful cooperation, particularly Dana Andrus, John Covell, and Emily Taber, and five anonymous referees who have provided several valuable comments. We thank Joachim Sedlmeir for his relentless organizational and editorial assistance in putting together the numerous versions of the manuscripts and in maintaining contact with authors and partners of the conference. Last, but not least, we are very thankful to all the authors, discussants, and participants of the conference, who provided the intellectual basis for this undertaking. Witnessing the high relevance in real life, we hope that the economic analysis of infrastructures and related decision making will continue to be a prominent topic in economics and other social sciences.

References

Armstrong, M., and D. E. M. Sappington. 2006. Regulation, competition, and liberalization. *Journal of Economic Literature* 44 (2): 325–66.

Aschauer, D. 1989. Is public expenditure productive? *Journal of Monetary Economics* 23 (2): 177–200.

Bauby, P. 2008. L'européanisation des services publics. *Téléscope* 14 (1): 11–22.

Berkhout, F. 2002. Technological regimes, path dependency and the environment. *Global Environmental Change* 12 (1): 1–4.

Bognetti, G., and G. Obermann. 2008. Liberalization and privatization of public utilities: Origins of the debate, current issues and challenges for the future. *Annals of Public and Cooperative Economics* 79 (3–4): 461–85.

Brinkerhoff, D. W., and J. M. Brinkerhoff. 2011. Public–private partnerships: perspectives on purposes, publicness, and good governance. *Public Administration and Development* 31 (1): 2–14.

CEEP and ETUC. 2000. Proposal for a charter for services of general interest. http://www.etuc.org/documents/etucceep-proposal-charter-services-general-interest#.U20T0ceJhmo.

Chan, C., D. Forwood, H. Roper, and C. Sayers. 2009. Public infrastructure financing: An international perspective. Staff working papers 0902. Productivity Commission, Government of Australia.

Clifton, J., C. Francisco, and D. Diaz-Fuentes. 2004. Nationalisation, denationalisation and European integration: Changing contexts, unfinished debates. *Entreprises et histoire* 3: 24–52.

Del Bo, C. 2011. Recent advances in public investment, fiscal policy and growth. In M. Florio, ed., *Public Investment, Growth and Fiscal Constraints: Challenges for the EU New Member States*. Cheltenham: Edward Elgar, 25–48.

dpa. 2013. Kanal bringt Panama Gebührenrekord. http://www.manager-magazin.de/politik/weltwirtschaft/kanalgebuehren-bringen-panama-fast-eine-milliarde-dollar-ein-a-935644.html.

EC. 2004. Horizontal evaluation of the performance of network industries providing services of general interest. Commission staff working paper 866. SEC.

Engel, E., R. Fischer, and A. Galetovic. 2013. The basic public finance of public–private partnerships. *Journal of the European Economic Association* 11 (1): 83–111.

Esfahani, H. S., and M. T. Ramírez. 2003. Institutions, infrastructure, and economic growth. *Journal of Development Economics* 70 (2): 443–77.

European Investment Bank. 2010. Capital markets in PPP financing: Where we were and where are we going?" European PPP Expertise Centre, EIB, Luxembourg.

Finger, M., and R. W. Künneke. 2011. *International Handbook of Network Industries: The Liberalization of Infrastructure*. Northampton: Edward Elgar.

Fiorio, C. V., and M. Florio. 2013. Electricity prices and public ownership: Evidence from the EU15 over thirty years. *Energy Economics* 39: 222–32.

Florio, M. 2013. *Network Industries and Social Welfare: The Experiment That Reshuffled European Utilities*. Oxford: Oxford University Press.

Florio, M., and S. Colautti. 2005. A logistic growth theory of public expenditures: A study of five countries over 100 years. *Public Choice* 122 (3–4): 355–93.

Florio, M. 2004. *The Great Divestiture: Evaluating the Welfare Impact of the British Privatizations, 1979–1997*. Cambridge: MIT Press.

Forrer, J., J. E. Kee, K. E. Newcomer, and E. Boyer. 2010. Public–private partnerships and the public accountability question. *Public Administration Review* 70 (3): 475–84.

Frischmann, B. M. 2012. *Infrastructure: TheSocial Value of Shared Resources*. Oxford: Oxford University Press.

Gabler. 1993. *Gabler-Wirtschafts-Lexikon*,13th ed. Wiesbaden: Gabler.

Goldsmith, S., and W. D. Eggers. 2004. *Governing by Network: The New Shape of the Public Sector*. Washington, DC: Brookings Institution Press.

Gramlich, E. M. 1994. Infrastructure investment: A review essay. *Journal of Economic Literature* 32 (3): 1176–96.

Grimsey, D., and L. Mervyn. 2004. *Public Private Partnerships: The Worldwide Revolution in Infrastructure Provision and Project Finance*. Northampton: Edward Elgar.

Grove, N. 2012. Einführung in die Infrastrukturwirtschaft. Lecture materials.

Grove, N. 2014. Infrastrukturökonomie: Neue Herausforderungen für Gesellschaft und Staat. In D. Klumpp, K. Lenk, and G. Koch, eds., *Überwiegend Neuland: Zwischenbilanzen der Wissenschaft zur Gestaltung der Informationsgesellschaft*. Berlin: Sigma.

Hart, O. 2003. Incomplete contracts and public ownership: Remarks, and an application to public–private partnerships. *Economic Journal* 113 (486): C69–C76.

Jochimsen, R. 1966. *Theorie der Infrastruktur. Mohr*. Tübingen: Paul Siebeck.

Joskow, P. 2005. Regulation of natural monopolies. MIT Center for Energy and Environmental Policy Research. http://dspace.mit.edu/bitstream/handle/1721.1/45038/2005-008.pdf?sequence=1.

Klodt, H. 2009. Wettbewerbspolitik. In W. Weidenfeld and W. Wessels, eds., *Jahrbuch der europäischen Integration*. Baden-Baden: Nomos, 215–18.

Korpi, W. 2001. Contentious institutions: An augmented rational-action analysis of the origins and path dependency of welfare state institutions in Western countries. *Rationality and Society* 13 (2): 235–83.

Kranz, J., and A. Picot. 2011. Why are consumers going green? The role of environmental concerns in private Green-IS adoption. Proceedings of the 19th European Conference on Information Systems (ECIS).

Millward, R. 2005. *Private and Public Enterprise in Europe: Energy, Telecommunications and Transport, 1830–1990*. Cambridge, UK: Cambridge University Press.

Musgrave, R. A. 1959. *Theory of Public Finance*. New York: McGraw-Hill.

Olson, M. 1965. *The Logic of Collective Action: Public Goods and the Theory of Group*. Cambridge: Harvard University Press.

Picot, A. 2009. Unternehmen zwischen Markt und Staat—Regulierung als Herausforderung. *Schmalenbachs Zeitschrift für betriebswirtschaftliche. Forschung* 61 (6): 655–78.

Portland Development Commission. 2002. *Economic development strategy for the city of Portland*. Summary Report of the Blue Ribbon Committee.

Samuelson, P. A. 1954. The pure theory of public expenditure. *Review of Economics and Statistics* 36 (4): 387–89.

Sydow, J., G. Schreyögg, and J. Koch. 2009. Organizational path dependence: Opening the black box. *Academy of Management Review* 34 (4): 689–709.

Torrisi, G. 2009. Public infrastructure: Definition, classification and measurement issues. *Economics, Management, and Financial Markets* 4 (3): 100–24.

van de Walle, S. 2009. International comparisons of public sector performance: How to move ahead? *Public Management Review* 11 (1): 39–56.

Viscusi, W., J. Harrington, and J. Vernon. 2005. *Economics of Regulation and Antitrust*, 4th ed. Cambridge: MIT Press.

Warner, M. E. 2013. Private finance for public goods: social impact bonds. *Journal of Economic Policy Reform* 16: 303–19.

Witte, E. 2002. Regulierungspolitik. In V. Jung and H.-J. Warnecke, eds., *Handbuch für die Telekommunikation,* 2nd ed. Springer, Heidelberg: Springer, ch. 6, 58–71.

Yescombe, E. R. 2011. *Public–Private Partnerships: Principles of Policy and Finance*. Amsterdam: Butterworth-Heinemann.

2 Actors and Innovations in the Evolution of Infrastructure Services

Hugh Goldsmith

2.1 Introduction

Adequate provision of infrastructure is a sine qua non of economic development. Despite some ambiguous econometric findings, it is generally acknowledged that infrastructure matters for growth, institutions matter for the effectiveness of infrastructure, and availability of finance is a major constraint to developing infrastructure (Estache 2004; Esfahani and Ramírez 2003). Innovation is about change and change is not necessarily growth. There is an emerging consensus that long-run economic change needs to be understood as the co-evolution of technologies and the institutional frameworks within which they are applied (Nelson 2008). The complexity of modern infrastructure as a "system of systems" invites a multi-domain, multi-disciplinary approach (Hansman et al. 2006).

The linkage between infrastructure and economic growth has been the subject of intense theoretical and econometric investigation for over twenty years, both from the perspective of macroeconomic production functions using time-series or cross-sectional data, and through microeconomic studies of individual sectors. Ever since Aschauer (1989) kicked off the debate by claiming large positive growth impacts from public infrastructure investment, the arguments have raged back and forth, with claim and counterclaim about econometric methodologies and the significance, sign, and magnitude of results. Esfahani and Ramírez (2003) extended the analysis to include institutional factors, concluding not only that the contribution of infrastructure services to GDP was substantial and generally exceeded the cost of provision but also that institutional capabilities lending credibility and effectiveness to government policy play a critical role. Good summaries of the evidence and state of play at the time are given by

Gramlich (1994), Romp and de Haan (2005), Straub (2008), and Égert et al. (2009).

While econometrics struggles to find robust evidence, the need for basic infrastructure is manifest throughout the developing world. In cities hit by natural disasters, infrastructure services are the first priority to get back online. Current infrastructure technologies are extremely large, complex, capital-intensive network industries, usually managed as regulated monopolies and not renowned for their innovation. Despite innovation now being seen as a critical to the engine of growth, the challenge of changing the way we "do" infrastructure continues to be posed either in a development context or in terms of a need to introduce market forces through privatization, liberalization, and public–private partnerships (PPP).

The role of the private sector in delivering infrastructure services is particularly topical in the current economic climate. The financial crisis that started in 2007 left many Western governments with a dilemma. They can't afford to pay for infrastructure, but they also can't afford not to build it. On the one hand, infrastructure projects are seen as a way to provide a short-term Keynesian stimulus by creating employment in construction while, at the same time, offering the potential to stimulate long-term growth through productive efficiency and competitiveness. On the other hand, the impact of the crisis on public finances has left many rich nations struggling to pay their debts while continuing to meet current spending commitments. The "fiscal space" for maneuver by governments to undertake major infrastructure investment is heavily constrained. So private-sector infrastructure investment is high on the policy agenda in both the developed and developing world. Yet infrastructure networks involve massive fixed costs that, when combined with the political sensitivity of user charges, can make them appear very risky for private investors. How to raise finance is often the binding constraint.

There is still no consensus on exactly what should be included in a definition of infrastructure, how to measure it, and who should be responsible for building, owning, financing, and operating it. Does private or public ownership of infrastructure matter for its long-run development? What are the roles of government and of private companies and markets in driving innovation in infrastructure services?

There is a growing interest both in what Niall Ferguson calls "big picture" history (Ferguson 2012) and in exploring historical parallels as a way to inform contemporary policy debates (e.g., see Reinhart and

Rogoff 2009; Guldi 2012). The invention, deployment, and worldwide diffusion of clean water supplies, railways, electricity, and the Internet are some of the most profound innovations in the history of technology. Does history have anything to tell us about how infrastructure systems evolve and the role of public and private actors in driving change?

In this chapter I seek to throw some light on these questions by developing a long-run narrative of infrastructure service innovations. I will use these observations on how services have developed in different sectors and contexts to examine how well different economic theories match with the stylized facts. In particular, in my interpretations I apply the explanatory power of the evolutionary economic models of Grübler (1990) and Perez (2002).

The World Bank has commissioned a number of think pieces on the lessons that history might bring to current debates about infrastructure policy. From Eichengreen (1995) and Jacobson and Tarr (1995) the main conclusion is that although historically private actors have at times played an important role, the political influence on decisions about infrastructure are never far from the surface. Government always needs to play its part, not just through effective regulation but also through guarantees and other forms of public sector support to attract foreign investment. The parts of public and private actors have played out very differently in different countries, with the United States being something of an anomaly in how little government has been involved as an owner or investor in infrastructure. Whether infrastructure investment decisions have been growth or welfare maximizing, or simply the result of pork barrel politics, is a valid question for many nations to ask themselves (Cadot et al. 2006; Golden and Picci 2008).

Economic historians have gone more in depth to look at how specific technologies have evolved in different countries. Most accounts start with the great nineteenth-century innovations of railways, electricity, the telegraph and telephone. The classic works are Foreman-Peck and Millward (1994) and Millward (2005) on the development of network industries (water, gas, electricity, transport, and telecoms) in the United Kingdom and Europe from 1830, and Hausman et al. (2008) on the role of multinationals in the development of the global electricity industry from the 1880s. The series of monographs on the history of infrastructure by Friedlander (1995a, b, 1996, 2005) give an excellent overview of the roles of public and private actors in all sectors, but she focuses mainly the United States and does not specifically look at innovation. A more eclectic approach is taken by the large technical systems (LTS) theory school, following the pioneering work of Hughes (1983) on electricity systems, who stress the evolutionary dynamics of LTS development and the critical role played by system builders like Thomas Edison. Even more general sociotechnical system theories encompass infrastructure, technology, society, regulation, markets, user practices, and cultural meaning (Geels 2004). Kaijser (2004) sees what he terms "infrasystems" as sociotechnical systems in which institutional frameworks and system cultures are as important as the technical components. He contends that the "soft" parts of infrasystems are poorly understood by policy makers who tend to focus on finding technical fixes to problems.

I contend that by looking only at specific sectors, countries, or periods, there is a risk that a bigger picture is missed. My argument is that infrastructure is fundamental to how a society and its economy evolve over time and that this needs to be understood from a multidisciplinary systems perspective of change, not just economic growth. Although at times it may appear that infrastructure services are simply part of the market economy, such as late-nineteenth-century Britain and the United States, there is also a deeper underlying reality: the power of positive feedback between infrastructure, economic activity and financial systems.

The rest of the chapter is organized as follows. Section 2.2 defines the characteristics of infrastructure, its institutions, and the key factors influencing planning, delivery, and operation that will need to be traced back through time. This is followed, in section 2.3, by a novel historical sketch of the key developments in several infrastructure systems (urban, water, transport, communications, and energy) from their origins through to the present day. In each period I try to identify the key technological, financial, and institutional innovations by public and private actors that had a lasting impact on how infrastructure developed. My discussion focuses on what got built, why, how, by whom, and what was the long-term fate of the system. Very early infrastructure systems are treated in some depth, as this is an area where there has been relatively little academic investigation. Many later examples are taken from the United Kingdom, in part because there are good data but also because many key infrastructure innovations in the nineteenth century initiated there. In section 2.4, I identify the different forms of innovation relevant during each stage of infrastructure system development and diffusion. In sections 2.5 to 2.6, I show how well current economic theories fit the stylized historical facts, outline where more efforts are needed, and set out a simplified model of the phases of infrastructure innovation over the long run.

After a discussion of the linkages between the evolution of the financial system and infrastructure, in section 2.7, I conclude with a reflection on whether 11,000 years of infrastructure history offer any lessons to today's decision makers.

2.2 What Is Infrastructure and What Functions Does It Serve?

There is no commonly accepted definition of infrastructure. The *Oxford English Dictionary* (OED) defines it as: "the basic physical and organizational structures and facilities (e.g. buildings, roads, power supplies) needed for the operation of a society or enterprise: the social and economic infrastructure of a country." Infrastructure is a relatively new word in English, with a first entry in the OED in 1927. It was rarely used before the 1960s other than in a military context. The *Proceedings of the Institution of Civil Engineers*, published continuously since 1826, has a first citation for "infrastructure" in 1933, in connection with ports and public works in India. "Public works" was the term used by classic economists from Smith to Marshal to describe roads, bridges, canals, docks, and water supplies.

The essential physical and economic characteristics of infrastructure that we will be looking for as we go back in time are as follows:

- *Immobility* Fixed in space and needs to be designed for a specific geography
- *Longevity* Takes a long time to build and lasts a long time if well maintained
- *Expensive* Costs a lot of resources to construct, operate and maintain
- *Public service* Provides a basic service that is of value to a community

A defining characteristic of infrastructure is that it is designed to meet a need in a particular geographical context. Although occasionally components can be dismantled and sold, such as when London Bridge was bought by an American oil entrepreneur in 1968 and rebuilt in the Arizona desert, this is the exception. Roads are not traded like used cars. Arguments about whether infrastructure provides public, merit, or demerit goods are largely academic: infrastructure provides lasting public services in a specific location.

Table 2.1
Infrastructure service sectors

Sector/service	Typical physical works
Urban	Public buildings; streets; street lighting; leisure facilities
Social	Universities; schools; hospitals; social housing; prisons
Water	Irrigation canals; water supply networks; dams; drainage; flood defenses
Transport	Roads; bridges; ports; canals; railways; tramways; airports
Communications	Telegraph; telephone; wireless; TV; Internet; broadband
Energy	Gas; electricity; oil; nuclear; renewables
Environmental	Wastewater treatment; waste disposal; green infrastructure

Source: Author's elaboration based on typical investment project categories

There is no unique way of classifying the different physical infrastructure sectors. Table 2.1 proposes a classification based on the function served, seeking to avoid major overlaps, and reflecting the major types of contemporary projects presented for financing. In simplistic terms, individual projects are either buildings with different functions or different components of a network. "Health" and "Education" could be made separate categories. Water, transport, energy, and communications are frequently jointly referred to as "economic infrastructure," while hospitals and schools are deemed "social infrastructure."

In practice, all such classification systems need to be treated rather flexibly. Urban infrastructure includes all other categories to some extent, such as public transport and sewerage, but here is restricted to the urban fabric of public buildings and streets that create the urban environment. Some infrastructures can be multipurpose, such as a dam intended for water supply but that also functions for flood defense, hydroelectricity, and control of navigation upstream or downstream. A potable water supply can be both a resource input to a production process like brewing beer and play a vital role in public health and firefighting.

Even the functions of infrastructure can change over time. A London power station is now an art gallery. A railway line has become a cycle way. Today it may be meaningful to speak of "knowledge infrastructure," of which the Internet, education system, and libraries all form part. Some authors include military and even financial infrastructure in their definition. The infrastructure sectors that I focus on in this chapter are the traditional economic infrastructure sectors of transport, water, communication, and energy.

A useful clarity brought about by the recent push to get more private sector involvement in infrastructure was the need to define the services that private owners or operators should make available to the public. This required a refocus from physical assets to services. Long-term private infrastructure contracts need to specify service outputs rather than construction inputs. In other words, it is not the existence of a road that matters but that all its lanes are open for traffic, that it is well maintained, and that it is safe. Using a framework of delivering services rather than focusing on the assets turns out to be very powerful.

The next step in the argument is to realize that demand for the services infrastructure provides has always been around. Although as technology advances our expectations of those services changes, the need has always been there. Occasionally a new technology comes along that seems to create new markets, such as the mobile phone with Internet connection. But equivalent services were already there in 1900 if you sent a letter, installed a telephone, and visited the public library. They just weren't as fast, convenient, or integrated. Electric lightbulbs provide interior lighting services that previously came from gas mantles, lamps, candles, and originally burning torches. A household water supply means we no longer need to walk for hours to the nearest river. So new infrastructure services are always substitutes for how that need was already being met. The critical question is whether the new service is better and/or more affordable.

Another important feature of infrastructure services is that they are public, in the sense that they can be used by governments, firms, or households alike. Whether the poor have access or can afford to pay for the services is another matter, unless of course access is provided free. Military infrastructure is not public access, even if it does provide a public service of defense.

Finally, what institutions are relevant for infrastructure? Using the metaphor of a game, the term "institution" can used to describe the players of the game (e.g., private companies, public administrations, independent regulators, and the judiciary) as well as the formal and informal rules of the game (e.g., contracts, regulation, property rights, legal system, and acceptance of corruption) and the current state of the game (e.g., ownership structures and effectiveness of legal enforcement). Most authors in the new institutional economics tradition treat institutions and organization/hierarchies as different. Over the long run, organizations themselves are subject to change. For example, they can change ownership from public to private, or they can change their structure from national to multinational. In what follows, I refer to organizations as actors. Institutions and actors can then be considered functionally in terms of different rules, roles, and influences they have in the infrastructure project and service delivery cycle: planning, financing, constructing, and operating.

2.3 A Brief History of Infrastructure Innovations

What follows is a sketch of some of the key innovations in the history of infrastructure systems. The periodization is deliberately broad brush, and events highly selective in order to illustrate the bigger picture. I occasionally add a fast-forward to illustrate how events from the past may be relevant today. The purpose is to identify key innovations and actors that launched the infrastructure services that, with hindsight, evolved to take on global significance. The narrative is not just about technological invention, it also looks at the evolving institutions and financial innovations that allow technological innovations to be deployed on a large scale. Maddison (2007) gives an economic narrative and quantitative estimates of key macroeconomic data that provides a backcloth to the period starting from the Roman empire. Figure 2.1 shows our journey of infrastructure discovery in the context of rising real global incomes, both the global average and for the leading nation in any period. Over such a long time span, national borders and even the notion of the state itself have evolved. Countries mentioned in the text refer to the modern name of the geographical area, with historically fluid boundaries and related institutions.

A few explanations and disclaimers are necessary before embarking on this journey. First, a relatively long section is dedicated to the ancient world. This is because many of the fundamental ideas about what infrastructure is and what its role is in society were developed by older civilizations. This is the period where the economic history literature is sparsest, so I try to fill a gap. Later technological advancement just brought new ways of solving old problems and made solutions cheap enough to be shared by society more widely.

The narrative is primarily focused on the West, mainly due to lack of space. This is not to deny the importance of Eastern civilizations for infrastructure innovation. For example, Morris (2010) argues that in periods such as the fourteenth century, China was far more developed in technology and markets than was Europe. Last, it is not the purpose

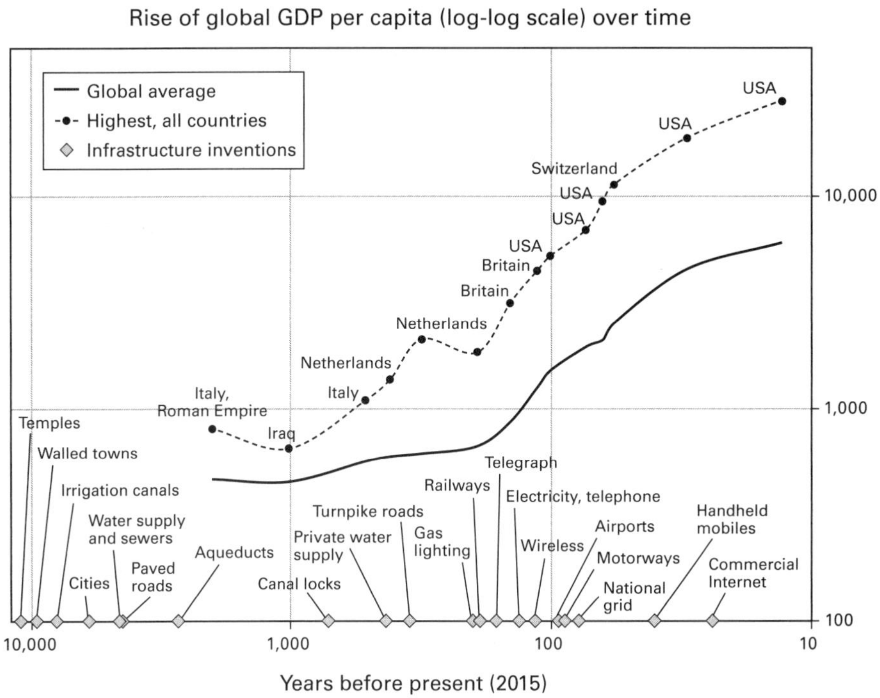

Figure 2.1
Timeline of infrastructure innovations and economic growth. After 1920 country maximum values exclude small oil states.
Source: Author's own elaboration for infrastructure invention dates; GDP/capita data in Geary Khamis dollars from Maddison (2007)

here to consider the claims and counterclaims of which country or individual was "first" with some innovation or invention. Nonetheless, it is worth noting that it is rarely one person or one place that gives birth to a new technology and that, in any case, diffusion of good ideas is usually rapid.

2.3.1 9500 BCE to 2500 BCE: Building Civilizations

On the basis of current archeological knowledge, the starting point of any infrastructure time trip back to the present must be Göbekli Tepe, a complex of early Neolithic structures on the hilly flanks along the northern rim of the Mesopotamian plain (Schmidt 2000). Göbekli Tepe is the world's first temple. The earliest structures date to before 9000 BCE, pre-dating Stonehenge in Britain by some 6,000 years. The partially buried buildings are circular, 15 to 25 m in diameter, with monumental T-shaped limestone pillars set regularly within dry stone walls. Each building contains two central free-standing pillars decorated with carved animals and human forms, some of which are 6 m high and weigh 20 tons. Up to 500 workers must have worked at the construction site, and the early Neolithic hunter gatherer society clearly generated sufficient surplus to feed them. The group effort and skills needed to conceive, quarry, transport, erect, and carve these megalithic structures using Stone Age tools is astonishing. As far as we know now, there was nothing like it before.

So here it is, the first, large-scale, permanent structure to serve a community, involving an innovative technology and built to last. The idea of constructing massive, monumental stone buildings as inspirational infrastructures for religious worship spread slowly across the globe over the following 10,000 years, with a last great flowering in the golden age of gothic cathedrals and grand mosques. Despite the lack of direct economically productive function, these first social infrastructures bound communities together, often became centers of learning, and the cities that grew up around them regularly spent huge amounts of resources to rebuild and enlarge them.

Our next stop is the first walled town at Jericho around 7000 BCE and the invention of safe urban living. Jericho had massive defensive walls 3.5 m high and a taller tower with an internal staircase. Inside the walls, some 70 dwellings occupied 0.025 km^2. The walls had to be rebuilt several times, but they functioned until around 1500 BCE. Inside the protected town, new forms of urban living developed along with domestication of cereals and animals. The idea spread, and the scale of urban infrastructure grew. The need to build city walls to protect cities from the enemy without lasted well into the late Middle Ages.

Figure 2.2 illustrates the growth in the world's largest cities from ancient times. These cities were usually the capitals of the most advanced state of the day. The need to support the increasing scale of urban living, to connect cities to each other, and to bring resources into cities for life support was a major driver of infrastructure growth, both in scale and in the complexity of organizations needed to manage systems.

Uruk is situated on the banks of the Euphrates River in modern day Iraq. By the end of the fourth millennium BCE it covered an area of 2.5 km^2 within 9 km of massive city walls of clay bricks, made famous by the first surviving work of world literature, the *Epic of Gilgamesh*. By now, urban living was on a far grander scale, with laid out gardens,

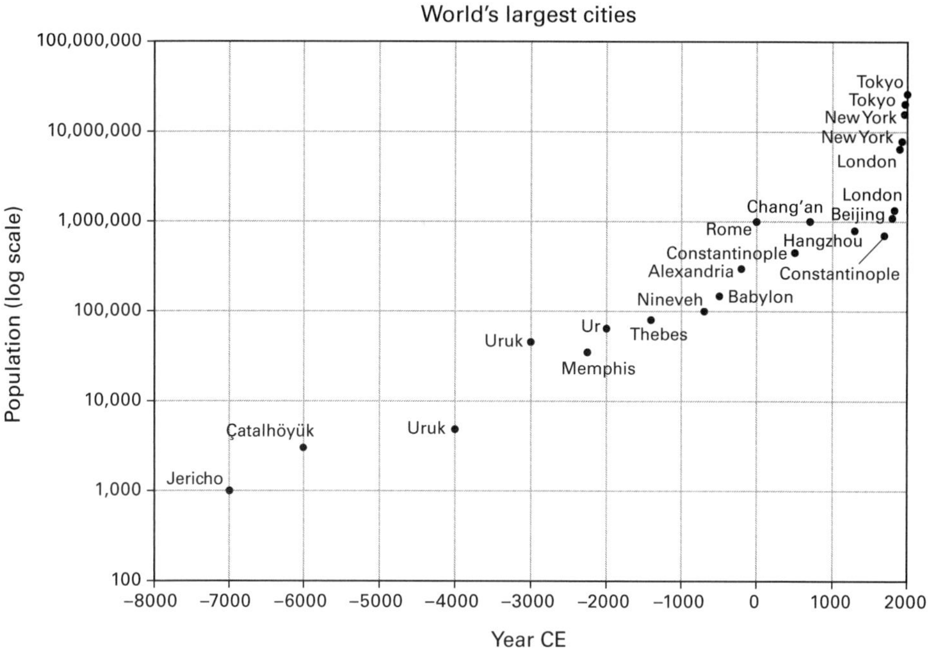

Figure 2.2
Long-run growth of infrastructure's biggest customer
Sources: Author's elaboration based on selected data in Morris (2010) and Chandler (1987—Chandler's updated data available at The Institute for Research on World Systems website at http://irows.ucr.edu/research/citemp/citemtoc.htm (accessed November 27, 2013). Population estimates, and when they reached "world's largest" status, vary between authors.

streets, residential areas, temples, and a library for the newly invented communication and knowledge storage system using clay tablets: writing. There was a palace for another institutional innovation: the King. Uruk was the first of a succession of autonomous city states being established across Mesopotamia, characterized by new elements of social, economic, and religious complexity.

The other great infrastructure innovation of Mesopotamia was irrigation. Earliest archeological remains are simple irrigation channels from around 6000 BCE (Bagg 2012). By 2100 BCE, large-scale construction and maintenance of irrigation channels is well documented in cuneiform records showing that it is organized by the state. Although the original ideas of Wittfogel (1957) that public administration and the state arose as a social construct in order to manage complex hydraulic systems are now largely discredited, the fact remains that irrigation can more than double crop yields compared to rain-fed agriculture. The resulting rapid population growth and urbanization in an essentially arid environment depended on irrigation systems. Here the infrastructure is a direct input to economic production and growth is measured in biomass of people, plants, and animals. We also see the first conflicts over water rights between cities. Mithen (2012) argues convincingly that water infrastructure and control of water resources were central to securing and maintaining power in the ancient world … and that in water scarce regions the same dynamic continues today. Similar large-scale hydraulic technologies started to appear across Mesopotamia, Egypt, India, and China, including massive masonry dams to divert rivers and new land reclamation projects combining diversion, irrigation, and drainage. Some authors claim that climate change and failure to manage the agricultural production systems sustainably led to the collapse of whole civilizations (Diamond 2005). Yet there are also examples of water supply and irrigation systems still in use today that have functioned continuously for over 2,500 years, such as those around Lake Van in Turkey (Garbrecht 1980).

2.3.2 2500 BCE to 200 BCE: The Age of Empires

As cities vied to dominate each other, professional armies were established and empires rose and fell. A biblical story of Sumerians, Akkadians, Assyrians, Hurrians, and Hittites follows. By the time of the Akkadian empire of Sargon the Great (2250 BCE), it is considered meaningful to talk about a state rather than just a city. The law was codified for the first time as a formal institutional framework, such as the "eye-for-an-eye" Code of Hamurabi (1790 BCE), which covers land tenure, rent, marriage, divorce, inheritance, contracts, public order, administration of justice, wages, and labor conditions.

Banking and debt were invented around this time, with richer merchant families making grain loans to traders carrying goods between cities and specific regulations related to debt included in the Code of Hamurabi. By 500 BCE professional bankers had appeared such as the Babylonian House of Egibi (521–487 BCE). But there is no evidence of debt finance being used to pay for large scale public infrastructure projects. Infrastructure was directed and built by the state and paid for by taxes, with military supervision of construction. Forced or slave labor made up the majority of the input into large-scale construction projects into modern times. As late as the 1860s, forced labor from fishing villages was still being used to build the Suez Canal until pressure from investors and international public opinion forced the company to curtail the practice, and to import modern steam-powered dredgers and excavators from specialist French contractors to complete the project (Bonin 2010).

Labor markets started to develop around infrastructure projects. Adams (2010) describes a recent cuneiform translation of records from a construction project for the city of Ur around 2030 BCE that provides evidence on how work was organized and paid for. The project was overseen by a military general and his assistants, but carried out by a mixture of hired laborers and slaves. By this time slavery was well established. Slaves could be inherited, bought and sold, freed, taken as war prisoners, or given as payment for debt. However, women, mostly unskilled brick-carriers, made up two-thirds of the hired free laborers and were paid in barley, although they received only 60 percent of the male wage.

Household water supply and sanitation systems were first developed in this period. Some authors point to the Indus Valley civilization as a "first," with towns like Mohenjo-daro having sophisticated water supply and sanitation systems for every house by around 2450 BCE (Jansen 1993). Other contenders are the Minoan civilization, with the Queen's bathroom in the Palace at Knossos demonstrating an extremely high degree of knowledge about internal plumbing systems. In any case, piped water supply and wastewater systems were understood well before the Romans.

By 700 BCE, the new King Sennacherib of Assyria had accumulated enough wealth to embark on the biggest urban project seen to date to make Nineveh the most spectacular city on earth. He diverted the river, built new temples, gardens, street layouts, and constructed the world's first masonry raised aqueduct to bring drinking water into the city from Jerwan, 40 km away. The city walls enclosed an urban area of 7.5 km^2 and the population swelled to nearly 100,000. As the Assyrian empire collapsed, Nineveh was sacked and raised to the ground in 625 BCE.

There is something of a pattern emerging. Infrastructure is built by the state. Economic activity and trade develops. Then the whole thing is raised to the ground by another state that steals the gold, any useful assets and takes the population into slavery. It was an evolutionary socioeconomic process that lasted several thousand years. What also lasted was knowledge about the deeds of great kings and the wonders they built. This knowledge was codified in marble inscriptions and in the texts of Greek and Roman historians. The gist is that good kings built cities, irrigation canals, and roads for the benefit of their people, whereas bad ones waged unnecessary wars and built large palaces for themselves.

Between 550 and 450 BCE, three generations of Persian kings, Cyrus, Darius, and Xerxes, expanded the Achaemenid empire, to become the largest state up to that time. It had a population of some 50 million and covered an area of 8 million km^2. Darius divided up the empire into governorates and raised huge amounts in taxation, which he then spent on building a new city at Persopolis and undertaking major civil works, notably in transportation.

Darius built the largest road network seen to date, the backbone of which was the 2,700 km Royal Road from Sardes to Susa. The earliest paved roads date to around 2500 BCE in Egypt and were used to connect quarries to the Nile. The Royal Road was not built as a single engineered structure but joined existing roads into a network. As well as the trade cities along the route, there were additional postal stations every 20 to 40 km where fresh horses had to be kept. The main purpose of the road network was to ensure swift communication throughout such a vast empire. Trade was secondary and moved at a slower pace. Herodotus states that "there is nothing in the world that travels faster than these Persian couriers," who could carry a message from Sardes to Susa in seven days. The Royal Road was the fiber-optic cable of its day, though traveling at the speed of a horse rather than of light. The communication system relied not just on the existence of the road, but the messengers, postal stations and administrative rules that allowed it all to function. Darius is also credited with completing the first Suez Canal, inscriptions from which were discovered during the construction of the modern version in the 1860s.

An important system of water infrastructure generally credited to the Achaemenid empire was the spread of qanats (Goblot 1979). These are long subterranean galleries dug at an upward slope into rock to intercept a source of underground water. The regular outflow is channeled for irrigation. Such small-scale sustainable water sources were dug throughout the Arabian Peninsula and Persia. Over 18,000 have been identified in modern Iran, many still working. According to the Greek historian Polybius, a Royal Decree granted any private individuals/families who dug and maintained a qanat the right to all profits for 5 generations (Lightfoot 2000). Such works entailed a high risk of tunnel collapse or of not producing a reliable flow of water. Once built, they could be operated and maintained for centuries. Sometimes they fell into disrepair or were abandoned as empires rose and fell, but when calmer times returned they were repaired and brought back into productive use. This is one of the earliest references to private infrastructure development based on a time-limited, risk-sharing contract with the state.

After a succession of wars between Greece and Persia, Alexander the Great conquered the Persian empire in 330 BCE. The Greeks made huge advances in scientific knowledge, law, philosophy, and government, but they were not large-scale infrastructure builders outside of their own cities, partly because the local geography favored sea-based transport.

An exception was water engineering. Koutsoyiannis and Angelakis (2003) document how the ancient Greeks furthered hydraulic engineering in a number of areas, including land drainage and tunneling. The Greeks established a legal framework for water services in cities. Solon was elected Officer of the Fountains of Athens by public vote in 594 BCE. This made him responsible for the operation and maintenance of the city's water system, including enforcement of regulations to ensure fair distribution of water. At that time the city had a mixture of public and private wells. He passed a law that owners of private wells should maintain them in good condition to be ready for use in case of war. He also rationalized the system, by decreeing that citizens could only drill a new private well when there was not a public well within a distance of a hippicon, that is 710 m.

One of the most astonishing ancient documents about infrastructure to come down to us is the contract from 318 BCE, carved on a marble *stele*, between the independent Greek city of Eretria and a foreign contractor called Chairephanes (Knoepfler 2001). The contract details the engineering works planned in order to drain a lake at Ptechai. It has all the features of a modern project finance contract in terms of risk allocation, including:

- the contractor to meet all expenses plus pay a lump sum of 30 talents to the city;
- the contractor is granted exclusive right to cultivate and retain the products of the reclaimed land for ten years;
- an exemption from local taxes and certain laws;
- a four-year construction schedule, which could be extended in case of war;

- an obligation on Chairephanes heirs/collaborators to complete the works in case of his death;
- extreme sanctions against anyone attempting to cancel the contract;
- the contract was "signed" by 230 citizens with six named Eretria-citizens as guarantors.

For transparency, the marble contract was to be on public display and a copy deposited at Delphi. Unfortunately, other than the inscription, the exact location of the lake and whether the contract was ever executed are unknown. Concession contracts of a similar form were used by the Romans for works related to public services and continued to form the legal basis for a 2000 year history of public–private partnerships in France (Bezançon 2004).

By 200 BCE, as Rome was starting to build the greatest empire seen to date, the technology and institutions for managing water, transportation, communications, and urban infrastructure services were well established.

2.3.3 200 BCE to 500 CE: What the Romans Did for Us

The Romans took the idea of infrastructure as a driver of development to a whole new level. They militarily conquered and culturally subsumed much of the known world, and in the process they shamelessly borrowed technology and ideas from others, notably the Greeks, Persians, Carthaginians, and Etruscans. They also did everything on a grander scale and with a greater purpose. For lesser nobles from conquered tribes, they offered the seduction of civilized life and access to goods from global markets. The roads, aqueducts, sewer systems, civic spaces, and public baths that came in the wake of the legionnaires were as much what built the empire as the laws, language, and common currency. In civil engineering, the invention of concrete using slaked lime and a volcanic ash known as *pozzolana* allowed them to create durable water-proof structures, many still functional today.

From the end of the second Carthaginian war in 201 BCE, Rome embarked on a period of expansionist empire building that reached its largest geographical extent in 117 CE, at which point the Emperor Trajan ruled over an area of 6.5 million km^2 and a population in excess of 70 million. Temin (2006) claims that at this pinnacle of economic and social achievement, Rome was a market economy built on a long period of stable government, with well-functioning market institutions, including financial intermediation. It also possessed transport and urban infrastructure that would not be matched again in Europe until after 1800.

In terms of infrastructure services, Rome was the largest and most sophisticated city in the world. Even the poor living in the great cities of the Roman empire were rich in the public goods available to them. The urban poor, often freed slaves, lived in great poverty in the slums, but had access to reliable water supplies, the great public baths, public squares, parks, and forums (Griffin 1986).

The Romans left a recipe book for building the physical infrastructure of civilized life. Vitruvius's (c. 70–10 BCE) ten books on architecture set out the public and private works required to construct a city in their natural order: selecting the site, building city walls, creating the layout of streets and public buildings, housing, materials, temples, forum, basilica, treasury, prison, senate, theater, public baths, palaestra, harbors, breakwaters, shipyards, aqueducts, wells, cisterns, and finally machinery (Vitruvius 1914). This is literally a procedures manual of how to construct civilized life based on the six Greek principles of Order, Arrangement, Eurythmy, Symmetry, Propriety, and Economy. Vitruvius's opus is dedicated to the Emperor Caesar whom he lauds as giving "attention not only to the welfare of society in general and to the establishment of public order, but also to the providing of public buildings intended for utilitarian purposes."

Even in Vitruvius's day, good practices from the past were being forgotten. Vitruvius records that the Romans completely lost the disciplines of the Greeks in controlling the cost of public works. He cites a law in the Greek city of Ephesus that required architects, when entrusted with a public works project, to lodge a cost estimate with a magistrate. The architect's property was held as security until the work was finished. On completion, if the final cost did not exceed the estimate, he was celebrated with decrees and honors. When the cost exceeded the estimate by no more than a quarter of the original estimate, it was defrayed by the public purse and no punishment inflicted. But when the cost overrun was more than 25 percent, the architect was required to pay the excess out of his own pocket. He bemoans: "Would to God that such a law existed among the Roman people, not only in respect of their public, but also of their private buildings, for then the unskillful could not commit their depredations with impunity" (Vitruvius 1914: 281).

Knowing roughly how much a big infrastructure project will cost is fundamental to making a decision about whether to go ahead. If the cost turns out to be double the original estimate, then the economic rationale for doing the project in the first place may be weak or nonexistent. Flyvbjerg et al. (2003) show that large infrastructure cost overruns caused by "optimism bias" are still a curse today.

The Roman empire developed the most sophisticated large-scale transportation and communication system the world had seen. The paved road network at its peak was slightly in excess of 80,000 km with a further 320,000 km of unpaved minor roads that reached to the furthest corners of the empire. Road sizes and the legal status of public rights of way were already standardized by 450 BCE in the Law of the Twelve Tables. The right of the population to use public roads was protected by law. Paved roads were constructed on the principle of economy to be as straight as possible and built to last according to standards that minimized long-term maintenance needs.

Roads were subjected to an evolving system of governance and financing. Although the state financed road construction through taxes, longer term maintenance was devolved. Road building was part of empire building and logically was organized under the military responsibility of a consul outside the city walls. Each municipality was responsible for the roads within its boundaries. Although the majority of funding continued to come from taxes, some consuls such as Julius Caesar spent considerable amounts from their own resources to maintain roads under their personal responsibility. Gifts to fund infrastructure such as bridges or buildings by wealthy citizens were common, although of minor overall significance. De Luca and Lorenzini (2013) explain how Roman systems of infrastructure finance lasted well into the medieval period.

A major reform took place under Augustus, who first made himself supreme head of the empire's road network and then created a commission of senators, the Supervisors for Roads, with personal responsibility for their upkeep (Eck 2007). In practice, the Supervisors worked with local officials and contractors to organize regular repairs. Although travel on roads was free, charging tolls at bridges and town gates to vehicles transporting goods was a standard way to raise local taxes, but these were not directly applied to road maintenance.

Augustus also reorganized the legal responsibilities for water supplies and sewerage. We know from Frontinus, who took over as Commissioner for the Aqueducts of Rome in 95 CE that the system was in a poor state of maintenance and repair, with a lot of fraud and many illegal connections. Citizens had the right to collect free water from public fountains distributed evenly throughout the city. Private supply connections to an individual villa could only be authorized by the emperor and had to be paid in proportion to use as estimated by the size of pipe. Water rights were personal and did not automatically pass to the heirs or purchasers of a property.

Frontinus took over a public company dedicated to the operation and maintenance of Rome's water supply system with 700 workers, mainly slaves. Its costs were covered by the imperial budget, against which was offset some income from payment for water rights. In short, there was a complex system in place for operation and maintenance of services with a small income from private connections, but the service was predominantly public and paid from general taxation.

Finally, there was a good communications network throughout the empire using the roads and ports. The *Cursus publicus*, founded by Augustus, carried official mail by relay throughout the Roman road system. This replaced a dual system of public mail used by officials and private citizens alike and a private postal system for wealthy citizens carried by *tabellarii*, who were slaves and free citizens paid to carry private messages or letters. Archaeologists have found the letters of Roman legionnaires posted at Vindolanda fort on Hadrian's wall at the outer fringes of the Roman empire in Britain written to their families in Gaul requesting warm clothing to cope with the harsh weather.

While it is important not to slip into anachronism, it is equally important not to underestimate how similar some aspects of everyday life, including commerce, were in the ancient world. Toutain (1930) explains the complexity and evolution of economic activity through antiquity until the end of the Roman empire in the West. He describes the impressive scale of Roman trade and its dependence on transport and other forms of infrastructure. Commercial traffic had to pay a number of duties and taxes, collectively referred to as *portorium*, at the frontier of a province, on entering or leaving a town, and a toll for passing certain points such as bridges (Toutain 1930: 312). Pliny reports that goods from India, such as highly valued pepper, increased in price a hundredfold by the time they reached their destination. Thus, while the state provided the transport system, it also extracted a large part of its revenues from taxes on the trade using the transport network.

Although urbanization increased significantly during the Roman empire, the society remained predominantly rural with the majority employed in agriculture to feed themselves, the landowners, and the cities. Maddison (2007) estimates that about 14 percent of the population in peninsular Italy lived in urban areas by 150 CE, which was similar to the degree of urbanization in 1800. With the exception of Britain and the Netherlands, urbanization remained below 20 percent until after the 1850s. The main benefits from infrastructure were therefore only experienced by a minority of the population. Better roads and communication directly benefited the state, including the army, and an elite of private merchants. The need for infrastructure was in part driven by the scale of cities, empires, and markets.

2.3.4 500 CE to 1500 CE: Castles, Cathedrals, and the Rebirth of Cities

In the fifth century the Roman empire in the West collapsed. Rome was sacked by Alaric the Goth. Britain was abandoned in 410 CE. Roman infrastructure continued to function, but in a state of slow deterioration. Popes funded the rebuilding of Rome's aqueducts whenever the system looked in real danger of collapse. Mirroring the priorities of those who controlled resources at the time, the main type of new infrastructures built were castles and cathedrals.

The following centuries were extremely turbulent in Europe, with invasions and military conflicts as the Roman empire fragmented, was reunited under Charlemagne and then fragmented again. Feudalism and serfdom became the dominant economic production system. Compared to the past, it is hard to point to any great achievements in infrastructure before 1000 CE. In 793 CE Charlemagne built a new canal, the Fossa Carolina, to connect the Rhine with the Danube basins, but it was only 3 km long. During this period China was carrying out gigantic engineering works using forced labor, including the completion of the Chinese empire's new superhighway: the 1700 km Grand Canal. In the Muslim world, Baghdad grew to become the largest city on earth and a center of multicultural learning.

In Europe, a shift started after 1000 CE, with old and new cities in Italy and Flanders emerging as powerful commercial centers. Venice established a trading monopoly with the East and used the resulting wealth to build an extraordinary city in the middle of a lagoon. This relaunch of commerce was closely bound up with continued trade links with Byzantium (Pirenne 1956). The Roman empire in the East continued until the fall of Constantinople in 1453, which remained one of the largest cities in the world.

Land reclamation projects using dyke and drain infrastructure started to create new wealth and new landowners, with the first polder recorded in Flanders in 1150 (Pirenne 1956: 81). A new merchant class grew and established itself as new town "burghers" around fortified strongholds. The new cities were given powers to make their own laws and tax local markets. Any serfs who lived within city walls for a year and a day could earn their freedom. Flanders merchants introduced new textile manufacturing and dying techniques, such that by the twelfth century they came to dominate the northern European cloth market. Toll collection (*teloneum*) on roads and canals grew again as an important source of taxation. This new found economic surplus found expression in the great cathedrals built across Europe from the twelfth to sixteenth centuries and in the public and private infrastructure of towns like Ghent and Bruges.

In the Middle Ages, water remained the responsibility of city councils (Magnusson 2003). Cities improved water supplies by building "conduits," funded by taxes and frequently developed in collaboration with local monasteries or with royal support. The church maintained the old Roman knowledge of hydraulic engineering. One of the earliest surviving maps of a piped water distribution system comes from Canterbury Cathedral in the United Kingdom. Construction of London's Great Conduit in 1237 relied on a grant of land and springs from the king and contributions from merchants in cities such as Amiens who received trading privileges in return. In 1340 Sienna funded new drinking water fountains from a tax on its dependent territories. In Paris, Dublin, and Southampton the town council collaborated with the local monks to develop and maintain water supply systems.

2.3.5 1500 to 1800: Private Water, Roads, and Canals

From 1500 onward, private rather than public investment started to play a significant role in infrastructure investment with Britain in the lead. This coincided with the age of European voyages of exploration, the start of a scientific revolution following the discoveries of Copernicus, and formation of the earliest joint shareholder corporations. The various companies trading with the East Indies and beyond were established with private capital, often with the heavy involvement of European monarchs.

Water

Water supply led the first in a succession of institutional innovations in Britain's infrastructure. The first private company was the London

Bridge Waterworks Company, which opened in 1582. Its success relied on the application of new technology, a force pump operated by a waterwheel in an arch of old London Bridge, the legal protection of Letters Patent signed by Queen Elizabeth I, and a 500-year lease contract with the Corporation of London for a bridge arch (Goldsmith and Carter 2015).

By far the most important private company was New River Company, incorporated in 1619. It required an enormous capital investment for the time in order to build a 60 km new river (actually a canal) to bring an additional fresh water supply to the city and then distribute it via wooden pipes. The technology was barely Roman. The real challenge was the scale of private financing, which was raised through thirty-six "Adventurers" shares. In reality, the project was driven by the private wealth and vision of a single man, Hugh Middleton. His brother was the mayor of the city. Certain innovative clauses in the Royal Charter helped to overcome difficulties in expropriating the land for the project. When construction costs started to spiral over budget, the king injected an additional 50 percent of new capital to complete the project. A clause was added to its charter that gave it a legal monopoly over water supply to the city. The early years were financially challenging, but after a few decades it had paid back original investors many times over. It went on to be described as "the most remunerative and successful of all the trading corporations of the world" (Ward 2003: 228). All water services in London were consolidated into municipal ownership by 1904 and later reprivatized in 1989.

Bridges

Charging tolls to cross bridges goes back to Roman times. The earliest bridge in London was Old London Bridge, which took over thirty-three years to build, through the reigns of three kings, before completion in 1209 under King John. To finish it, he had to borrow heavily from City Merchants and in return granted land to fund its upkeep. As well as tolls, it was decided to develop property on the bridge for extra income. The bridge became the tidal limit of the River Thames as its narrow arches blocked the flow. The buildings on the bridge had to be substantially rebuilt after the Great Fire in 1666, but it was not until 1754 that an Act was passed to remove all the buildings. As a result of a Royal Charter from 1282, Old London Bridge was operated and maintained by the Bridge House Estates Trust, under the control of the Corporation of London. Owning land in the capital city, the Trust became so wealthy from property and other investments that it was able to remove all tolls on its bridges. Today the Trust maintains five central London bridges at no charge to the public purse. If one of them collapsed, it would be rebuilt by the Trust.

Iron Bridge, over the River Severn in Shropshire, England, was the world's first large span structure made entirely of cast iron. The bridge was promoted by its builder Abraham Darby, who owned the local iron foundry. It opened in 1781 after two years' construction. It was pure project finance, with construction funded from the sale of sixty shares at £50 each, to be paid back entirely from toll revenues. It was a financial success. The tolls were set by an Act of Parliament of 1776 and thereafter couldn't be increased other than by amending legislation, which is why pedestrians were charged a halfpenny to cross for nearly two hundred years until the toll was eventually removed in 1950. Similar project finance techniques for bridges were used in France before and after the Revolution in 1789. By 1843, there were five bridge companies listed on the London Stock Exchange. From the 1850s onward, bridge project finance based on tolls disappeared in the British Isles as road and bridge construction became publicly funded. It was reinvented in the 1960s for the new Severn Bridge and used for later estuary crossings.

Turnpikes

The next revolution was in the British roads system. Turnpikes were primarily a financial and institutional innovation that created a financing vehicle for road maintenance and improvements. Predating the Industrial Revolution by nearly a century, the first Turnpike Act was passed in 1663 affecting 48 km of the Great North Road in Huntingdonshire, on the country's main north–south transport link. The Act was approved following a petition by local parishes claiming that they could no longer adequately maintain the road with local *corvée* statute labor, because traffic was so heavy.

The next Turnpike Trust Act was not until 1695, after which there were several a year. Up to 1706, turnpike trusts were always controlled by local magistrates. In 1707, the first Turnpike Act with trustees who were not local Justices of the Peace was approved and this became the standard model. This institutional adaptation had important consequences as it allowed local landowners, farmers and businesses who would directly benefit from road improvements to promote a new Trust.

Turnpike Acts authorized a not-for-profit Trust to levy tolls on road users and to use that income to repair and improve the road. Legal arguments prevented the King's Highway becoming a for-profit private company and the Trust was a convenient solution to avoid a burden on general taxation. The "turnpike" was the gate that blocked the road until the toll was paid. The Trustees could purchase property to widen or realign existing roads and were authorized to borrow against future toll revenues.

The turnpike road network grew organically, radiating out from the main cities, following the directions of heaviest traffic and trade (Pawson 1977). By 1750 virtually all of the main roads from London were turnpiked. The peak for new turnpikes occurred in a "turnpike mania" between 1752 and 1772, when 413 new trusts were created. By the time the last Act was passed in 1836, there had been almost 1,000 Acts for new turnpike trusts in England and Wales, and turnpikes controlled about a fifth of the national road network.

Many Trusts were well run, but financial mismanagement and fraud were not uncommon (Albert 2007). A survey in 1824 found that the average ratio of outstanding debt to annual income before expenditure was 4.5, but for some trusts it was above 20 and clearly unsustainable. Most turnpike trusts were wound up under General Acts of Parliament between 1873 and 1878. By the Local Government Act of 1888, the maintenance of main roads went full cycle by being entirely passed back to County Councils. Road building and maintenance was financed out of local government taxation, and then from 1919 by an annual Road Fund Tax on vehicles, which was later subsumed into the government's general tax income. Once roads were free, government found it very difficult to reintroduce user charges, in contrast to the concession finance model used to fund motorways in France and Italy. A classic example of institutional path dependency.

Ironically, the first important technological innovation in roads for 2000 years came almost at the end of the turnpike era. In 1819 the general surveyor for the turnpike trusts in Bristol, John McAdam, published a new method for "the Scientific Repair and Preservation of Public Roads." His techniques, not just of using graded stones for construction, but also his overall approach to the organization and professionalization of road maintenance, became standard practice throughout the world. A century later, when asphalt (a by-product of the oil industry) became widely available, tarmacadam road surfacing created another technological revolution. In the United Kingdom, road upgrading using the new technology was carried out by local authorities. Private companies made money from efficient contracting and owning patents on the surfacing technology.

Canals

The last private transport infrastructure revolution of this era was the construction of a private canal network across the industrial heartlands of Britain. Acts to improve river navigations on the Thames and the Lea date back to the sixteenth century. The key technological invention that made an inland canal network possible was the invention of the pound lock to allow boats to go up a relatively steep land gradient in steps using a chamber between two lock gates. Reputedly invented by a Chinese engineer on the Grand Canal in the tenth century, the technology was first used in Europe by the Dutch at Vreeswijk in 1373. The system was further refined technically with the addition of miter gates, probably designed by Leonardo da Vinci, for the canals built in 1458 to transport the marble for building Milan Cathedral. The first use of a pound lock in Britain was on the Exeter canal in 1563.

It was not until the privately funded Bridgewater Canal opened in 1761 and effectively halved the cost of transporting coal to Manchester that private finance and business became interested in canals. Like the New River for London water supply and the Canal du Midi in France, this was a large-scale infrastructure engineering project funded from the personal wealth of an individual, in this case the third Duke of Bridgewater. The commoner engineer on the project, James Brindley, developed a number of techniques to overcome construction difficulties, including linings made from puddled clay and an aqueduct over the river Irwell worthy of the Romans. Brindley formed an alliance with influential early industrialists, including Josiah Wedgewood the pottery manufacturer, and developed a plan for a network of canals linking the great rivers of England: the Mersey, Trent, Severn, and Thames in a "Grand Cross" (Corble 2011). Brindley went on to build over 580 km of canals himself. Independent private canal companies financed by local landowners, merchants, and industrialists built the network piecemeal in a "canal mania" frenzy of construction between 1793 and 1820. The network length grew to over 6,400 km and joined all corners of the country. To keep costs down, it was built to a "narrow" gauge, which ended up limiting its future capacity for expansion to take larger barges, unlike the network constructed later in mainland Europe.

The invention of railways spelled financial disaster for Britain's canals and most turnpike trusts. Although a few trusts managed to increase revenue by acting as feeder roads for railways, most were in direct competition.

Ports

A lesser researched topic is the substantial investment that Britain put into her ports from 1535 onward. This was primarily funded by Parliament, since ports also had a military purpose due to the strategic importance of Britain's navy. However, docks and harbors were granted powers to raise loans against their harbor fees. As commercial interests in shipping grew rapidly in the late eighteenth century, some commercial ports and harbors raised additional private funding via listings on the London Stock Exchange.

2.3.6 1800 to 1900: Pipes, Rails, and Wires

The nineteenth century saw the most dramatic changes in infrastructure since the Roman empire. The new boom was fueled by private capital in the heyday of laissez faire, but ultimately driven by changes in society, rapid urbanization, and expanding markets as railways shrank the world. For primarily intra-urban infrastructure, such as gas lighting, water supply, and trams, municipalities were the critical actors—either developing services themselves or awarding concessions to private companies. In the latter half of the nineteenth century, a trend of (re-)municipalization saw many private municipal services being taken back into public ownership.

For primarily inter-urban infrastructure, such as railways and telegraphs, national governments had the dominant role in granting concessions to private promoters who needed to know how to play the political game in order to get their projects approved. Over time, many services that started as local were pushed by economies of scale toward becoming an integrated national service.

Gas

The first in a century of new infrastructure innovations was piped gas for street and domestic lighting. After several technical and commercial false starts, including litigation over rival patent claims and parliamentary opposition, the London and Westminster Chartered Gas-Light and Coke Company became the world's first gas company in 1810. It started life selling services to private clients, notably mills in the rapidly industrializing north of England, but then switched to selling street lighting to cities. The company's chief engineer, Samuel Clegg, invented the first practical gas meter and patented various technical improvements to coal gas manufacture. Gas distribution used the cast iron pipe technology already in use for water supply. Britain was abundant in coal, the raw material needed to manufacture the gas.

The requirement to light city streets can be traced back to 1417, when the mayor of London ordered householders to hang out lanterns on winter evenings. Paris followed suit in 1524. By 1700 the residents of most cities were required to hang out a lamp every night as soon as it got dark. So the demand for the services that gas lighting could provide were already well established.

When applied at a commercial scale, gas lighting halved the cost and quadrupled the light output compared to candles. In the United States the first gas lighting was opened in Baltimore in 1816. Paris adopted gas street lighting in 1820, using a rival French technology developed by Lebon. Brussels became the first city to be entirely lit by gas in 1825. Gas lighting companies rapidly spread throughout the then developed world as a symbol of progress. The reported reductions in crime rates made street lighting a "must have" for the modern mayor.

To be economic, gas lighting was limited to larger cities with relatively dense distribution networks. Once the mains were in place to light the streets, normally in the wealthier parts of town, additional connections to private premises could be hooked up quite cheaply. From the start, British companies and households paid for use rather than just for the connection as was the case for water. Internal fittings to take gas mantles into each room remained a significant private expense that only wealthier households could afford. Cities paid for street lighting based on metered consumption using funds raised from municipal taxation. Private individuals paid on the basis of consumption. Factories were major early adopters of gas lighting as the new technology lowered costs and improved working conditions. Gas companies often applied lower rates to the municipality to avoid political difficulties and would charge higher tariffs to households and businesses.

Millward (2005) describes how different patterns of private or municipally owned gas companies became the dominant model for expanding services in different countries. In Germany and Scandinavia, the tradition was more for municipal ownership. Once initial investment costs were depreciated, services were invariably money making "cash cows." This provided a useful form of additional income to keep municipal taxes low. In the United States, private gas companies became highly profitable. Friedlander (1996) reports that over 70 percent of revenues were available for dividends. The extremely high profitability of gas lighting was one of the factors that attracted J. P. Morgan to invest in a competitor technology when he backed Edison's research into electric lighting. Returns from the London Stock Exchange confirm the high profitability of gas companies by 1882.

Gas lighting was eventually substituted by cheaper and more reliable electricity. The gas companies had huge sunk costs and perfectly viable networks to exploit. After WWI, they increasingly turned their efforts to innovation to develop new markets, first for cooking and then for heating. The industry went through some natural consolidation as larger private companies took over adjoining smaller ones, but the service remained a patchwork of public and private interests. In 1948 the government nationalized the UK gas industry by merging the 1,062 private and municipal owned gas companies into twelve area gas boards. These were further consolidated in 1972 into a single public company, British Gas, which was privatized again in 1986.

Railways

The next infrastructure revolution changed everything. The *Stockton & Darlington Railway* was the pioneer in 1825, but the railway age really began in 1830 with the success for passengers as well as freight of the *Liverpool & Manchester Railway Company.* The story of the engineers, promoters, contractors, and financiers that turned a local project into a global industry is well documented.

Railways heralded a transport revolution with far reaching ramifications for communications, finance, and corporate organization. In Britain, railway investments were entirely privately financed. The two separate British "railway mania" financial bubbles in railway shares in the 1830s and 1840s destroyed many small investors' savings. The second of these has been called the "greatest bubble in history" (Campbell and Turner 2010). As with canals, early railway investors represented local interests. By 1844, as the benefits of industrialization spread wealth more widely, whole new classes of investors were supplying capital for railways (Reed 1975). The battle to establish technical standards was won by Stephenson with the "standard gauge." Network consolidation was achieved through acquisition of different lines by private financial investors such as George Hudson. Starting with the

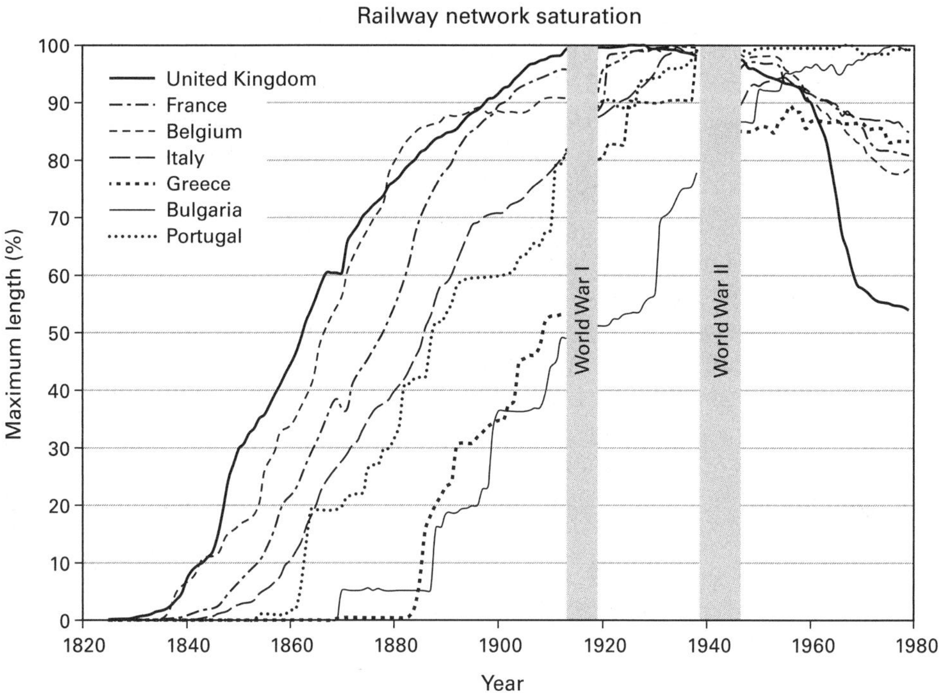

Figure 2.3
Growth and diffusion of railways across Europe
Source: Author's analysis based on data in Mitchell (1992)

1844 Railways Act, government regulations were introduced on pricing, timetabling, and coordination to compensate for market failures.

Within twenty years the railway network length in Britain grew from zero to 6,500 km. But the real story was the growth of railways around the world to 38,152 km by 1850, accelerating to 765,222 km by 1900. The largest network in the world was in the United States, which literally built its nation along with the railways. Railway infrastructure went global in less than seventy years. Even Africa had 16,319 km of railways by 1900, although primarily for exporting natural resources from colonies. Britain was also the main source of investment finance, especially after 1870 when foreign investments started to offer far higher returns than domestic stocks.

Figure 2.3 shows the relative rate of diffusion of railway infrastructure across Europe. Britain led the world in railway technology and its contractors, engine manufacturers, engineers, and entrepreneurs benefited from the resulting export boom. Britain had built 50 percent of its eventual maximum network length by 1863. Using this degree of network saturation as a benchmark, we see that the rate of "catch up" with Britain by other European countries varied by up to fifty years. The government in each country played a critical role in the technology diffusion process. The government was variously owner, guarantor, contracting authority, and concession grantor. The private sector was always involved as contractor and usually as operator. Many private companies formed to build railway lines were listed on the London Stock Exchange, which was the main source of private capital, followed at some distance by the Paris Bourse.

Belgium was the first follower country to decide launch a national program of railways as part of a government-led industrialization policy. The government launched new lines according to a plan to link the main industrial areas and ports. Railways were seen as strategically important both for military reasons and to help bind together the newly created nation. Only after the main East–West and North–South axes were complete in 1843, were private companies allowed to construct and use their own railroad systems. By 1867, Belgium had built half its eventual network, less than five years after Britain. Belgium continued to lead the Industrial Revolution in continental Europe until France and Germany started to catch up.

In stark contrast, Bulgaria did not reach 50 percent saturation until 1915. In 1850, Bulgaria was still part of the Ottoman empire, which prioritized development of railways in Turkey. The Turkish government was permanently short of funds. In the 1860s, they managed to attract British investors to build a line from Varna on the Black Sea Rustchuk on the Danube. The Turkish government then signed a concession with an Austrian, Baron Hirsch, to build 2,500 km of railways all over the region, including Bulgaria, Serbia, and Bosnia. To attract the concessionaire, the government promised a subsidy per kilometer of construction, guaranteed revenues per kilometer when operational and handed over the proceeds of a national lottery bond to start construction (Feis 1930: 293–12). The plan progressed very slowly. Northern Bulgaria achieved independence in 1878, but the south remained an autonomous Turkish province. Only 224 km of railway line existed in the new country. Railways became a strategic piece in the game of diplomatic chess in the region. Even after independence, Bulgaria remained largely agricultural and suffered a succession of wars that made investors unwilling to support large capital investments like railways. The lines that were built were government owned or had a full government guarantee.

Across Europe, different patterns of government-owned and privately owned companies emerged to build the networks. There was no simple "model" of railway ownership and development. Political, economic, and cultural traditions were too diverse. Nations that built railways and industrialized fastest ended the century with the highest GDP per capita (Millward 2005).

The United States also decided to use railways as a strategic technology to build its nation. But, like Britain, it decided to let private companies own and build the entire network. This was achieved using subsidies and incentives on a massive scale, the most important of which were land grants. In the case of the first transcontinental line, high-level corruption ensued via bribes to Congress to secure favorable treatment in the 1864 Railroad Act. As well as soft loans, the two competing companies building the line from opposite ends were given a land grant of 12,800 acres for every mile they built, and received full mining rights. The owners of the railway companies became extraordinarily rich. The line that joined the nation from coast to coast was completed in 1869, fueled by competition, cash incentives, land grants, and government bonds based on performance. Despite the subsidies, the government made a net profit on the deal once loans were repaid (Rohatyn 2009: 49–73).

Telegraph

Next came the wire-based communications revolution started by the telegraph and continued by the telephone. The telegraph was invented more-or-less simultaneously by William Fothergill Cooke and Charles Wheatstone in Britain and Samuel Morse and Alfred Vail in the United States in 1837, with similar technologies but different coding systems. Cooke and Wheatstone's system was immediately put into operation by the Great Western Railway Company and telegraph wires run along the railway network as a way of signaling messages faster than the trains. In the United States, Morse believed his invention should be owned by the federal government. But the US Postmaster General declined to purchase his patents, considering that the technology would never pay for itself (Friedlander 1995b). In the United States, the news service, stockbrokers, and eventually railways became major private clients of a highly competitive communications industry.

By 1861 the first transcontinental telegraph system was established across North America. In 1866 a US–British company laid a telegraph cable across the Atlantic establishing the first intercontinental communication system. In the same year, Western Union bought out its rivals creating a de facto monopoly for telegraph services throughout the United States. By this time, railway magnates like Jay Gould and Cornelius Vanderbilt had realized the potential and synergies of the new communications technology and were ploughing profits from railways into buying ownership of telegraph companies. In the United Kingdom, the private telegraph company using the Cooke and Wheatstone patents was nationalized in 1869 and became another service of the General Post Office (GPO), a publicly owned national monopoly of postal services for Britain established in 1643.

Telephone

In 1876 Alexander Graham Bell patented the first commercially viable telephone. He had started out working on the problem of increasing the capacity of existing telegraph lines but had realized that sending messages with multiple frequencies would allow him to transmit the sound of a human voice. Western Union declined to buy Bell's patents in 1876. As his first companies struggled for lack of capital, Bell drew further investment from William Forbes, son of another railroad financier looking for new investment opportunities. Further technological breakthroughs came with the invention of the switchboard exchange in 1877 and the loading cell in 1899. A change from charging per connection to charging for each call helped establish a viable business model. Bell used its patent monopoly and profits to expand both nationally and internationally and to buy up rival technologies. Bell established one of the first corporate R&D laboratories that went on to become a model of how in-house R&D can solve business problems (e.g., the loading coil) and help retain a competitive advantage. The company was restructured to separate long distance from local services and AT&T became the holding company for a series of regional operating companies. It took time, but the telephone would eventually kill off the telegraph.

Globally, household connection rates for the telephone progressed slowly compared to water and sanitation, gas, or electricity. Connections were expensive and the fewer people connected, the less valuable was the service. The market penetration rate, expressed as the percentage of households with a fixed line telephone connection, only reached

50 percent of households in the United Kingdom in the mid-1970s, some thirty years later than the same level was reached in the United States. However, from 1920 onward the GPO ensured that the service was widely available across the United Kingdom by gradually installing "public" pay-per-call telephone boxes throughout the nation.

Competition in telephone services continued in the United States up to at least 1920, but a careful corporate strategy by AT&T and the growing influence of regulation eventually allowed it to establish an effective national monopoly by 1924. The 1907 Public Utilities Act placed gas, heat, electricity, and telephone services under the Railroad Commission, which had powers to set prices based on the cost of service. The US government briefly took over the telephone system during WWI. After returning it to private ownership, government seemed to accept the argument that public services could be provided by a private sector monopoly as long as there was a system of strong regulatory controls to protect the public interest (Friedlander 1995b). AT&T's monopoly of local and long distance telephone services was finally broken up in 1982 in a compromise deal with the US Antitrust Authorities.

The first European company formed to exploit the Bell patents was established in England in 1878 after Bell personally demonstrated the telephone to Queen Victoria. However, the GPO rapidly obtained a legal judgment that telephone conversations came within its remit and required licensing. The private National Telephone Company consolidated its service by buying up any smaller companies. By 1896 the UK telephone service had been nationalized and brought within the ambit of the GPO. The strategic importance of all forms of communications would be confirmed by the outbreak of war. Telephone services were separated from the GPO in 1981 as British Telecom, and then re-privatized in 1984.

Electricity

The other world-changing infrastructure system to be invented in the nineteenth century was electricity. In 1879, Thomas Edison registered a patent for an "economic" electric lighting system that envisaged a power-generating station, a network of conductors, a meter, and several high-resistance filament lamps. Unlike his earlier British competitor Joseph Swan, Edison was not just looking to manufacture lightbulbs, he was developing an integrated lighting system to compete with the gas lighting companies. Other systems for electric arc lighting and the incandescent electric filament lamp had achieved some commercial success between 1879 and 1884. In 1882, Edison demonstrated the world's first integrated generating station and lighting system at the offices of his financial backers on Pearl Street in New York. From 1880 onward, Edison formed a series of companies to control patents and deal with different aspects of the business, notably manufacture and distribution, both in the United States and overseas. His major financial backer was J. P. Morgan, who had started out financing railways and went on to gain financial control of telephones as well.

Edison's business model was to gain a technical monopoly through patents, license local utility operating companies, equip them from his own manufacturers, and accept payment in shares from the new utility. The US financial panic and crash of 1893 left many stocks near worthless and left the company in a crisis. J. P. Morgan engineered the split of the manufacturing equipment arm of the company to become General Electric. Edison remained wedded to the idea of a utility company supplying services.

Overseas, the various Edison companies founded between 1882 and 1885 went on to become dominant players in national electrical industries (Hausman et al. 2008). Deutsche Edison Gesellschaft was formed in 1883 to construct the first generating stations in Berlin. The company was reorganized in 1887 as the *Allgemeine Elektrizitats-Gesellschaft* (AEG). The *Comitato per le Applicazioni dell'Elettricita Sistema Edison* in Italy constructed the first central generating station in Milan in early 1883 and is still a powerful presence in the Italian energy sector as Montedison. National networks were rolled out at a pace dictated by both economics and by political considerations. Electricity started out as a local municipal service like water and gas, but the economies of scale argued for consolidation and eventually the need to construct integrated networks at a national scale.

In the United Kingdom, the world's first National Grid connecting the network to all major power stations was established in the 1926 Electricity Supply Act. It was complete by 1935. The industry was nationalized in 1947, and the Central Electricity Generating Board set up in 1958. The world's first full-scale nuclear power station was opened in Cumbria in 1956. The network was privatized again in 1989.

In the United States, the networks remained mainly private, but increasingly heavily regulated at the state level and from 1935 at the federal level. By the 1920s the rapidly growing US electricity utility companies were making extensive use of opaque holding company structures to raise large amounts of debt finance to fund expansion, but with very low amounts of equity, a technique learned from railways. A number of highly leveraged companies collapsed during the Great Depression, leading to tighter financial regulation. A persistent problem in the United States was that power companies would not expand services to the rural poor because they saw high costs and potentially low revenues per customer.

The electrification of rural America was pursued as one of Roosevelt's New Deal policies. This was achieved with an innovative mix of supply and demand side measures relying on cheap power from the government backed Tennessee Valley Authority (TVA) hydroelectric scheme, construction of municipally owned power stations, and loans and loan guarantees to support small-scale electricity cooperatives. The Rural Electrification Authority combined cheap long-term loans for electrification with household loans to purchase the farm and household equipment that ran on electricity. In fifteen years, the rate of rural electrification went up from 10 to 50 percent. This was a classic example of using cheap government loans to kick-start the economy with everyone winning. TVA sold more power, the equipment manufacturers sold their products, and the quality of life of rural farmers improved, overcoming a market failure caused by the reluctance of big private electricity utilities to invest despite the longer run social benefits.

Tramways

The last transport boom of the nineteenth century came from combining rail technology with the power of electric motors, offering a solution to the growing problems of urban transport in rapidly growing cities. The use of horse-drawn, then steam-powered and cable-pulled vehicles on rails for public transport predated railways by several decades. The first horse-drawn tramway opened in 1804 in South Wales, UK. US cities led in developing the early technology before electricity, with New York starting a regular horse drawn tramway service in 1832. But until 1862 only France, Britain, and the United States had cities big and rich enough to afford tramways. Starting in the 1880s with a line built by Ernst Werner Siemens in Berlin, an electric tramway boom spread versions of the technology to almost every major city in the world. Versions of the technology proliferated but soon became a specialization of Belgian investors and contractors.

Belgium had been the first country after the United Kingdom to industrialize, and from 1870 its bankers and industrialists were starting to be interested in foreign investments. A tramway investment boom occurred in Belgium between 1895 and 1900, with 62 overseas tramway companies formed and successfully floated on the Brussels' stock market. In 1900 there were 105 Belgian companies operating foreign tramways. The vast majority operated in towns in Italy, Russia, and Spain. They were formed following successful tenders for concessions, with or without competition, and relied heavily on Belgian capital and Belgian manufactured equipment (López 2003). The industrial and financial links were closely intertwined, particularly in the companies owned by Édouard Empain, who had multiple infrastructure interests, such as the Paris Metro and building a new city in Egypt at Heliopolis. The tramway financial bubble burst with the onset of WWI.

2.3.7 1900 to 2000: Back to the Present

In the Age of Extremes between 1914 and 1945, two World Wars, antitrust legislation, the end of the gold standard, hyperinflation, and the Great Depression saw many private companies go bankrupt. Changing social and political values resulted in nationalizations or government-led initiatives. State provision became the dominant model for "natural monopolies." Much financial paper became near worthless as inflation ate away value, local politicians were reluctant to raise tariffs, and foreign owners of basic services were not very welcome. In the midst of the Depression, Roosevelt's New Deal used infrastructure investment as a positive force to restore jobs, growth, and prosperity. Post–WWII, the Marshall Plan helped rebuild Europe's shattered infrastructure.

After WWII and a long period of infrastructure being owned and run by governments, the pendulum swung back in favor of privatization in the 1980s with United Kingdom in the vanguard. Summing up the experience of the UK privatizations in utilities and other infrastructure between 1980 and 1997, Parker concludes: "The lesson of the history of both nationalisation and privatisation in the UK is that the propensity of Governments to intervene in industries is a function of the performance of the industry and its consequences for public welfare, both when it is publicly owned and when it is privately owned" (Parker 2012: 528).

Government went from being an owner to being a regulator and contracting authority for infrastructure services. The independent regulators had to learn from their mistakes, but the new systems of incentive-based regulation delivered investment. Services improved due to more investment and better management. Efficiency gains were most likely when there was increased competition or more effective regulation and measurable productivity improvements were greatest in those sectors subject to some form of competition, notably telecoms and gas (Newbery 2002). Newbery concludes that all modern network industries, whether private or publicly owned, must operate under rules set by government due to the implicit tension between the political interests of investors and those of consumers in industries with both high sunk costs and high welfare sensitivity. Overall, Parker (2012) concludes that it is difficult to pass a judgment about whether performance improved more than it would have under continued public ownership because of the lack of a counterfactual.

Wireless

Guglielmo Marconi patented the first wireless communications device in 1896 and then demonstrated that he could transmit a signal without wires over several kilometers. In 1901 he transmitted a signal across the Atlantic. Over the coming decades public broadcasting was established in most advanced countries for oneway mass communication. The technology continued to evolve until the mobile phone allowed telephones to escape the fixed wiring, with the first chord-free handheld device offered to the public in 1973.

Building out mobile phone networks has been led primarily by private capital. This works because of the relatively low capital cost of establishing the network and what turned out to be a high willingness to pay, first by business then by private users. Once spatial network coverage is established, rich and poor are covered alike and can simply choose a different level of service and user device to reflect their needs and budget. The diffusion of low-cost and reconditioned mobile phones into the developing world, combined with pay-as-you-go services, has meant that mobile phones have achieved the fastest global network expansion in the history of infrastructure. However, those who claim that mobile technology can teach something to those worrying about basic public health services in Africa fail to understand the weight difference and resultant cost implications of distributing a cubic meter of water compared with a gigabyte of digital data.

Airports

Airports are a recent form of transport infrastructure driven by technological innovation. Following the Wright brothers first powered flight in 1903, takeoff and landing facilities moved modestly on from a field to an engineered strip with ancillary facilities. Major advances occurred during the two world wars.

There are several contenders for the first commercial airport as sites established during WWI were later converted to civilian use. Maryland, Bremen, Rome, and Paris all have a claim. Hounslow Heath Aerodrome near London was the first airport to operate scheduled international commercial services in 1919. Both public and privately owned airports were established over the coming decades. All were converted to military use during WWII. Many technological innovations were introduced after WWII, but the real boom occurred after 1970 with the introduction of low-cost, mass-market international charter flights to support the growing tourism industry. Britain's airports were privatized in 1987.

Motorways

By far the largest capital investment in new infrastructure networks since WWII has gone into building motorway networks. These have either been financed by government directly or through concessions, with or without tolls charged to road users (see the country papers in Ragazzi and Rothengatter 2005).

The world's first public motorway opened to traffic in 1924 in Italy. The 40 km *Autostrada dei laghi* linked Milan to Varese and was later extended to Como. It was privately financed and introduced tolls from the start. The early Italian fascist government had a policy of privatization and using private concessions for public works, including motorways (Bel 2011). Italy completed five other major motorways before WWII. Germany followed the Italian lead and completed its first autobahn between Cologne and Bonn in 1932. In 1933 the newly elected Nazi party launched an ambitious autobahn construction program that built 3,300 km of motorways by 1939. As well as developing a national network that served military as well as commercial purposes, it employed over 100,000 laborers during construction and supported the nascent German car industry.

Post–WWII, building motorways became part of the postwar reconstruction of Europe. A common European specification for motorways was agreed in 1957. By 2010, the total length of motorways in the European Union was 68,000 km. This represents less than one-third of the length of railways and is still less than the maximum length of the paved Roman road network. Since the 1990s, experimentation with various forms of PPP arrangements for private financing of motorways has been popular.

Internet, Broadband, and the Worldwide Web

The latest global network grew organically out of initial projects funded by the US military such as ARPANET and the eventual enthusiastic uptake by academics around the world as a way to share information. The key technological breakthrough was a concept called packet switching, rather than a piece of physical kit. Whether these technologies should be called physical infrastructure and whether the services they provide are communication, information, or knowledge is a matter for debate. In documenting the evolution of the technology and networks, Abbate (2000) argues persuasively that the Internet was shaped by social and cultural factors that defy simple narratives of production and use.

Broadband is a way of delivering far greater capacity to the Internet and other digital services and can involve wired, wireless, or optical technologies. Rolling out coverage of high-speed broadband to rural areas is reawakening all the old challenge about how to overcome the reluctance of private companies to invest in areas of high cost but low potential revenues, challenges that were already faced by water, gas, and electricity and overcome by regulation, subsidies, or public ownership.

2.4 Technological, Financial, or Institutional Innovation?

With the historic narrative presented, we can now explore the relative importance of technological, financial, and institutional innovation in driving the major changes in transport, water, energy, and communications infrastructure services.

In the ancient world the city, and then the empire state, was the major driver of all infrastructure projects. Command-and-control policies built civilizations. The economic role of slavery was important for major works, but paid labor was also used. A legal framework evolved that dealt with risk and contractual debt. The benefits of infrastructure were shared to some extent with the population, but at far lower standards of service than the king, emperor or social elites. With the exception of the Indus Valley civilization, water and sanitation services to private households remained the preserve of a privileged few. However, water was a public good available for free at public fountains throughout the city. The needs within cities and the need to connect cities defined infrastructure. Large amounts of resources went into temples, pyramids, and other monumental public buildings with no immediate economic purpose, even if in the very, very long run they generate employment in archeological tourism!

The Persians and Greeks introduced many institutional innovations that improved infrastructure services, including the use of private contractors for public works. There is evidence of project finance having been used for the first time by Greek city states and the first large-scale private infrastructure program was for qanats across Persia. Legal provisions covered both public and private rights and obligations in relation to infrastructure. A long-distance road transport and communication system was in place by around 500 BCE, but the major user was the state itself. Taxes on the transport of goods were an important source of state revenues.

The Romans developed a military- and infrastructure-led model of conquest and development that created an empire lasting over a thousand years, at least in the East. Trade flourished. The government led all major infrastructure construction with funding from general taxation. Once built, each city was supposed to maintain the infrastructure services within its walls. The road network was built by the military and private contractors. The system of maintenance for roads and aqueducts was completely reorganized by Augustus to concentrate power and clarify responsibilities. Private contractors for civil works flourished on a diet of construction and maintenance contracts. Slaves made up a significant part of the workforce building and operating networks. Technological innovation was more about scale and ambition rather than invention, although waterproof concrete was an important advance. At the high watermark of the Roman empire around 120 CE, the diffusion, scope, and quality of infrastructure services reached a highpoint that would not be regained until the nineteenth century.

From 1500 onward, private capital started to play a part in infrastructure. All of the water supply and transport revolutions over the coming 400 years had private investment playing a leading role. There was very little in the way of "technological revolution." Canals and pipes used old technologies, often inferior to that employed by the Romans. In road construction and maintenance, the focus was on efficiency rather than building to last. The first new road technology was not introduced until 1830, well after the turnpike mania years. The new materials of cast and then wrought iron transformed the technology for bridge construction, pipes and above all machinery with the invention of the steam engine.

Often there were huge lags, literally hundreds of years, between first use of an innovative infrastructure technology and its wider adoption. The turnpike mania started 90 years after the first turnpike. The UK canal mania started 260 years after the first pound lock at Exeter. The New River Company was formed nearly 30 years after the first new water supply to London. The necessary condition for take-off to attract private investors appears to be a combination of suppressed demand and a financial "success story" to create a bandwagon effect. Private investments needed to be financially viable. The vision of individual system builders, such as Hugh Myddleton, James Brindley, Robert Stephenson, Thomas Edison, or Guglielmo Marconi combined with the willingness of their financial backers to take the initial risks played a critical role in the start-up phase for each new system.

The picture changed dramatically with the railways. The new technology was adopted very rapidly and started a construction boom that covered the entire United Kingdom with railways within 20 years and the world within 70. What really facilitated the diffusion of railways globally was finance and the joint stock company. However, it is important to recognize the important groundwork that had been laid by turnpikes and canals.

Private financing of infrastructure was a major factor in industrial take off in England after 1750 (Trew 2010). This involved a combination of financial innovation and institutional reform involving standardization in the way in which infrastructure finance was regulated through Parliament. The repeal of the restrictions of the Bubble Act in 1824 and creation of limited liability joint stock companies completed the transformation in time for the railway revolution. In finance, a positive feedback loop was established among savings, investment, and growth. Early industrialists, mainly in Lancashire, funded local infrastructure from which they benefited directly. Then slowly as the capital needs grew, the center of fund raising gravitated toward London. As the limited liability company format became successful, it expanded the range of individuals trading in shares. Finally, the emergence of large railway companies with huge capital needs facilitated the emergence of a centralized London stock market, which in turn began to direct surplus savings into all forms of profitable industry and then to investment opportunities overseas.

To underline this point, excluding domestic and foreign government debt, of the 70 companies whose stocks and shares were listed in the *London Gazette* in July 1817, there were 29 canals, 3 docks, 9 bridge/road, 7 water, 1 gas, 10 insurance, and only 8 companies that could be considered commercial, including 3 mines. The stock exchange was dominated by government debt and infrastructure. This is a pattern that persisted into the 1850s (see figure 2.7). The companies busy delivering the industrial revolution were privately or family owned and did not need to raise capital on the stock market. The capital markets were delivering the infrastructure for industry to run on.

Competition started to play a critical part in the early stages of all new private infrastructure services where there was a potentially lucrative market. Competition could either be between alternative technologies or for the monopoly of a service area. The New River Company's legal monopoly and high profitability allowed it to buy up several smaller rivals within its service area. New water companies were formed to exploit services for new areas of development as London grew. It was generally the new companies that were more innovative as they had less sunk cost and could adopt the newest technologies. Hence it was the newly founded Chelsea Waterworks that was the first to use cast iron pipes and the first to introduce water treatment to improve quality. Even in water supply, a dynamic market developed with 29 private companies supplying Greater London at different times until consolidation reduced this to 8 local private monopolies and finally a single publicly owned service provider after 1903 (Goldsmith and Carter 2015).

In the railway sector, where companies faced competition from canals they would frequently purchase the canal and either let it run down or *in extremis* fill it in and build a railway on top. Competition between companies was fierce to capture travelers. But there was no interest in collaboration and coordination on issues like timetables or through ticketing until either companies merged or cooperation was imposed through regulation.

In the gas sector, the negative effects of competition in London led to government regulation from 1860, first to allocate service area boundaries to keep streets from being dug up multiple times and then in 1868 to allow takeovers, amalgamations, and fewer restrictions on companies' abilities to raise debt. In return, a cap on profits was agreed at 10 percent, and government imposed increased financial scrutiny. In many other cities the local councils bought out the gas company and ran the service themselves as a cash cow.

Fueled by competition and financial frenzy, Britain overbuilt its railway network until it became the densest in the world. Huge amounts of capital were wasted due to duplication of lines and inefficiency caused by weaknesses in government regulation and defects in policy (Casson 2009). Several authors contrast the extreme laissez faire in Britain with France or Belgium where the government took the lead in planning the core network on a rational basis. In Belgium, this was linked to a conscious plan to catch up with Britain in industrialization and to help unify a new nation. In Britain, it was left to the market.

In the case of gas, electricity, and telephone utilities, most were consolidated and then nationalized by 1950, and the main investment drivers became efficiency, safety, network coverage, national strategic goals, and building new capacity to meet ever rising demand. On top of that, in public ownership they were under political pressure to limit rises in user charges. Technological innovations were adopted insofar as they helped achieve those objectives, such as the switch to natural gas or the construction of nuclear power stations. Millward (2005) explains how contradictory, multiple objectives placed on managers of state-owned enterprises (SOEs) were one of the factors that eventually led to privatization and deregulation.

From 1800 onward, revolutions in infrastructure services became technology driven and almost exclusively led by private entrepreneurs. Once a new infrastructure technology had been invented, the problem was always how to raise the funds for service expansion and diffusion. Once a technology had taken off in one country, competitor nations were quickly looking at how to follow the leader. If a new infrastructure was perceived as strategic, the state would try to get it built, first with private capital and then, if that failed, with guarantees, other incentive mechanisms, or eventually public ownership.

A similar dynamic of competition and follow the leader occurred with municipal services, but with very different development paths in each country. Once one city had introduced gas lighting, water supply, or electricity others rushed to follow suit, either via private concessions or municipally owned companies. The variety of public, private, and mixed ownership models for municipal enterprises across Europe is remarkable for its diversity. The different legal frameworks for municipal services in each country also played an important part in directing the trajectory of ownership and scale of development. In Germany, publicly owned, semi-autonomous, multi-utility companies,

Stadtwerke, became the dominant model for citywide utility services that persists into modern times. In France, fragmented autonomous communes let out their municipal water services to private companies, first through concessions and then *gestion déléguée* contracts. Economies of scale were achieved by the private concessionaires, with industry consolidation eventually leading to the creation of the two French multinational companies that dominate the international private municipal service business to this day.

Telegraph, telephone, and electricity were all technology-driven innovations based on a better scientific understanding of the potential of wired electricity to transmit signals and power. Patents became a key instrument for gaining commercial advantage in the early years of network building. Competition between standards, such as the AC versus DC current wars or the broad versus narrow gauge on railways were common in the early years, but each industry trended toward standardization followed by economies of scale. The United States managed to retain a vibrant private competitive market in telegraphy and telephony, until Western Union maneuvered a national monopoly. By contrast, in most of Europe communications was considered a strategic sector and was immediately taken over by governments.

To illustrate this story from start to finish, figure 2.4 shows the birth, expansion, growth and decay of the main inland transport technologies in the United Kingdom. The length of the Roman paved road network in Britain was 3,400 km at its peak, a length the modern motorway network only achieved in 1999. Each transport service revolution had its own actors and logic. Roman roads were state financed, built, and maintained. Turnpikes were not-for-profits representing local commercial interests, paid for through tolls and raising debt from local investors by pledging future toll revenues. Canals repeated the financing model used for turnpikes, but this time with local investors as owners rather than trustees and providing mainly equity rather than debt. Railways rapidly became mass shareholder owned with equity and debt funds raised through the capital markets in London. Motorways were publicly owned and funded with no user charges, but a tax on vehicle ownership. Of the four transport revolutions shown, only railways could be considered as technology led. A perhaps surprising feature of figure 2.4 is that the pace of network expansion toward saturation is remarkably similar over time.

What figure 2.4 does not portray is that the road network built by the Romans, paved and unpaved, never really went away. Certainly

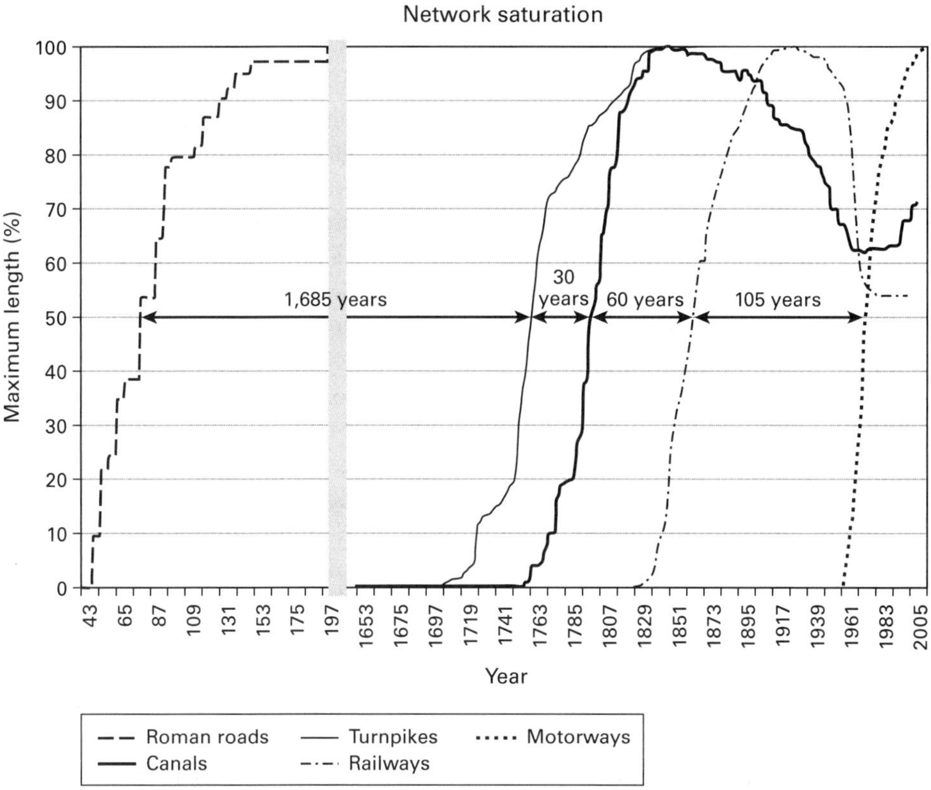

Figure 2.4
Growth and decline of UK inland transportation networks
Sources: Author's elaboration combining different sources. Length of UK railways from Mitchell (1992); Roman roads from Sitwell (1981); turnpike data from Albert (2007); motorways from Charlesworth (1984); where available, data updated with recent figures from Transport Statistics Great Britain at https://www.gov.uk/government/collections/transport-statistics-great-britain.

much paving material was stolen for other building projects over the centuries. However, many turnpikes were built along the line of existing Roman roads. When the turnpikes were wound up in the 1880s, it was only ownership that changed, not the network. The roads transferred to local authorities who maintained and upgraded them, including a major trunk road upgrading program starting in the 1920s using labor from high unemployment areas. When the motorway network was added starting in the 1950s, it only added capacity to the existing main roads, many of which were already dual carriageway.

The rail network has been reduced by almost 50 percent from its maximum length in 1920. Although rail use in terms of passenger-kilometer increased year on year until WWI, thereafter it suffered a continuous slow decline as road traffic substituted rail. Demand only started to climb again after 1994. The smaller lines that no longer made economic sense were slowly closed until a major rationalization and closures took place from 1965 onward. The latest capacity enhancement—high-speed railway lines (HSL)—is not shown in the graphic. The United Kingdom has only one line at present. The leader for HSL in Europe is France. HSL adds speed and capacity to the rail network, just as motorways did for the road system.

When the privatized rail infrastructure company Railtrack failed financially in 2002 as a consequence of safety problems, the government stepped in to ensure continuity of service and a transfer of assets to a new not-for-profit entity, Network Rail. Infrastructure assets last, even if ownership changes or companies go bust, and the public sector always has to step in to keep the services running. The government is de facto the infrastructure service provider of last resort.

The canal network suffered an even worse fate than the railways, with what looked like a terminal decline. The network was taken into national ownership as British Waterways Board (BWB) in 1962 with virtually zero commercial traffic. Many canals were derelict. From the 1950s onward, leisure boating on the old canals started to become popular and a nongovernmental organization of enthusiasts started a campaign to keep canals open and restore them using volunteer labor. The length of the network open for pleasure boats has been increasing since 1977. BWB has recently been transferred to a not-for-profit Trust. Should restoration of old canals with volunteer labor be seen as social innovation? In terms of infrastructure service to the public, the scale and quality of service is improving.

In the country that started the modern transport revolution with not-for-profit Turnpike Trusts 350 years ago, two of its earliest major networks, canals, and railways, are now owned by not-for-profit entities. At the same time major new projects are being structured on a project finance basis, with or without sovereign guarantees. The importance of innovation is increasingly being factored into public procurement of infrastructure, with the latest underground station refurbishment contract in London awarded through a competitive tender in which the degree of innovation was a significant factor in winning the bid. So while old infrastructures with declining attraction are allowed to gracefully decline, new investment projects are either managed by corporate utilities or contracted out to encourage innovation and efficiency.

2.5 Phases of Infrastructure Innovation

Adapting Freeman's categories of innovation (Freeman 1992; Freeman and Louçã 2001) to infrastructure services, we can identify four distinct types of innovation by their scale and speed of diffusion: *incremental innovations* that bring minor improvements to a part of the overall system, *radical innovations* involving a reconfiguration of existing technological systems, *disruptive innovations* that introduce a whole new way of providing the service, and changes in overall *technoeconomic paradigm* leading to new forms of production, consumption, and economic organization.

Incremental innovations are the small-scale changes that improve the performance of a system in terms of efficiency, capacity, quality, and/or cost. For physical infrastructure, incremental innovations are closely linked with the day-to-day processes of replacing existing components with new ones rather than replacing like with like. Central to the decision whether to innovate is the life and serviceability of the existing asset. Optimized asset management planning has become a central concern of public and private infrastructure operators alike. Examples would be changes to road surfacing materials to improve ride quality or replacing old wooden pipes with cast iron ones to reduce leakage and increase durability. An efficient operator should always be looking to adopt innovations of this type, especially if they are cost saving. However, if they are financially constrained to invest in asset replacement, there can be a tendency to "sweat the assets" rather than modernize. Moreover, where infrastructure operators are in a monopoly supply position, they may be less motivated to make changes, particularly if changes are more on the side of quality or safety.

While technological innovations are the most visible, in a world of high labor costs, changes to the "soft systems" of how infrastructure is operated can potentially bring big savings or improve user satisfaction. An example would be help lines to allow the public to report potholes in roads that need to be repaired or evidence of leaking water mains. Making infrastructure "smarter" is another hot topic, such as the smart electricity grid to manage decentralized generation from renewable sources. Another important way of gaining efficiencies is through economies of scale or scope. Examples include consolidation of railway companies in the nineteenth century or water companies in the twentieth century and the emergence of the private multi-utility model in the 1990s.

Radical innovations involve major changes to the way a system is configured or operates. An example would be the introduction of nuclear power plants for electricity generation in the USSR, United States, and United Kingdom in the 1950s and 1960s. For users of electricity, the source of power generation is not directly experienced, so it has no immediate impact on the quality of service. There must be an economic or other strategic driver to adopt innovations at a large scale. Historically such radical innovations are often associated with new regulatory requirements or major policy shifts, such as France's decision to go for nuclear energy production after the 1973 oil price shock or the current switch to renewable energy sources. Environmental infrastructure investments in wastewater treatment and solid waste have largely been driven by tightening environmental regulations. Economic factors signaled by relative prices can also be major drivers, such as the "dash-for-gas" switch to cheap gas-fired power generation in the 1980s. So such changes can be technology driven, regulatory, or price driven.

Disruptive innovations are the invention of a whole new way of meeting a basic infrastructure service need. The classic examples would be railways replacing canals, cars and tarmac roads replacing railways, electric lighting replacing town gas, and mobile phones replacing fixed lines. These are innovations that have systemic implications as they open up whole new ways delivering services. Of course, the pattern of use does not change overnight. It takes time to build out the new networks, and the old incumbents can respond with aggressive price competition to try and survive.

Not all disruptive innovations are competitive and ultimately destructive to existing infrastructure systems, but can actually trigger new waves of innovation. Canals were partially complementary to turnpike roads as they only took the heavy freight traffic for bulk materials or bulk manufactured goods off the roads and were not used for short journeys or for passengers. Similarly the invention of the Internet gave a respite to the fixed telecoms operators faced with competition from mobiles as they could now offer new ADSL services over phone lines. In fact the survival strategies of "old" infrastructures faced with new competition can lead to a new wave of innovation. When the town gas monopolies were faced with being made redundant by the invention of electric lighting, they responded by reinventing themselves as suppliers of gas for cooking and heating.

Diffusion refers to the expansion of the application of a technology in space over time. Rogers (1962) theory of the diffusion of innovations has gone through various refinements over the decades, but the essential story remains the same. Invention of new technologies is followed by an S-curve growth in market uptake, which starts slowly with a few innovators, reaches a take-off point of rapid market expansion through take-up by early adopters, after which it accelerates with growing profitability and market penetration, followed by a final phase of the slow tail of laggard late adopters. Finally the innovation becomes outdated and is replaced by a new cycle of innovation. This model needs to be adapted for infrastructure services, since adoption is dependent on the physical network being expanded over a geographical area rather than the sale of a product. Infrastructure customers are not just individuals, but cities and even nations.

The institutional and financial regimes governing how infrastructure is planned, built, and services delivered have a direct impact upon the socioeconomic efficiency of investments (Prud'homme 2005). The potential channels of influence are many. Without an adequately functioning financial system of banks, capital markets or access to development grants, potentially beneficial projects simply won't get built. If public authorities are incompetent or corrupt, they may build the wrong project or choose a shoddy contractor in order to maximize bribes rather than welfare. Planning delays or inefficient procurement may endlessly delay the investment. A public utility with inadequately trained staff may not operate the assets well. If user tariffs are kept too low for political reasons, the service may enter a vicious spiral of insufficient revenues leaving insufficient funds for maintenance leading to deteriorating services and an even lower willingness to pay by users. The quality of infrastructure investment is important, not just the amount spent.

Figure 2.5 presents a synthesis of the innovation cycle for a typical infrastructure network expansion and diffusion. Each stage of the cycle has different innovation drivers. The cycle starts with a new technological, financial, and/or institutional innovation that challenges the existing way of delivering services. At the start, either an existing mature network provides the service, as with canals prior to railways,

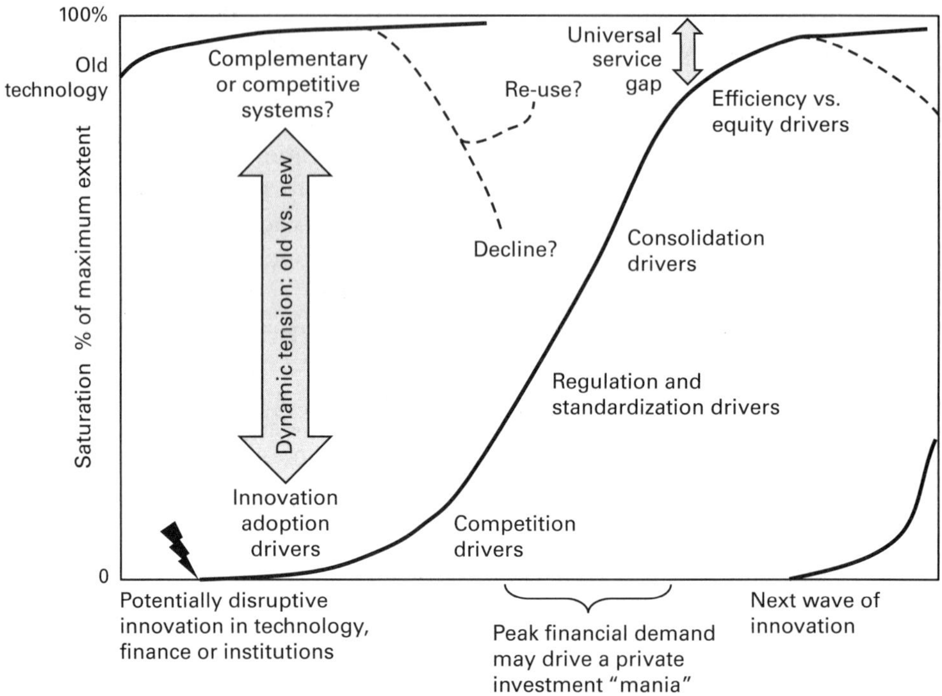

Figure 2.5
Infrastructure innovation cycle

or the need is met by a non-network solution, such as oil lamps prior to the invention of gas lighting. An innovative technology opens up new possibilities to meet that demand at lower cost. If the cost savings are significant (or could be if the network achieved scale), then it would make sense to build the network. If the existing service is private and operated for profit, then there will be strong incentives to develop the new technology to capture profits. Sometimes the new technology is not competitive, but complementary, such as canals with turnpikes or broadband with fixed telephone lines. A pilot project goes ahead and demonstrates viability. Success attracts investors, but also potential competitors. As we have seen, the lags between invention and large-scale deployment can be very long.

The drive to expand services proceeds through six phases. The first stage starts with a disruptive innovation that can be technological, financial, or institutional. In a leader country or city, this stage is often driven by a new technology. In a follower country or city, the existence of the new technology is known so the innovation can become a policy choice for the public sector. If private actors are already proposing the new technology, then it may make sense to "leave it to the market." This is what happened with mobile phones in Africa. But, if the market is not working, then governments may decide to intervene either to encourage private investors or as an owner in its own right.

Next comes the period for competition if there are competing technologies or if other private firms are competing for the service. Then comes the onset of a need for standardization and regulation. Historically regulation has been a major driver of innovation as it forces service providers to meet tougher quality standards and imposes costs.

There follows the period of most rapid expansion and peak demands on the financial system to fund investments. The dynamics here are very different for a private investment opportunity, when indeed a speculative bubble may develop, or with public promoters, who may struggle to raise funds. The critical point is that the period of peak financial demand is constrained by the ability to raise finance, whether public or private sector. This phase has played out different in different contexts. In the United Kingdom, for canals and railways it was possible to raise private investment funds. In Bulgaria, this required a sovereign guarantee and other incentives to attract private capital. Toward the end of this stage, there is usually a strong push toward consolidation to reduce costs.

At this point, the network is largely built and two new dynamics come into play. First, there are the ongoing efficiency drivers to generate higher profits or to keep user tariffs low. The network operator should have incentives to innovate. The other driver is toward universal service, whereby even the poorest or most remote areas are given access to the service. Innovative ways to achieve this may involve adapting service standards in low-income areas, or providing subsidies. Last, the next disruptive technology comes along and the cycle starts again.

2.6 Confronting Theories

How well does economic theory fit the stylized narrative above? Neoclassical economics is focused on markets, competition, choice, relative price, and the behavior of rational optimizing economic agents. It is essentially a static theory, despite new growth theorists having used the magic of log-difference equations and the strange economics of knowledge to explain growth. As an economic theory it does not capture the complexity, innovation, and adaptation we see in the real world (Nelson 2005).

Nonetheless, the neoclassical tradition remains powerful, and new endogenous growth theories have sought to internalize infrastructure and human capital accumulation as important variables in the aggregate economy-wide production function, usually paid for through taxation (Barro 1990; Agénor 2007). Agénor (2012) further develops the feedback between human and infrastructure capital to explore the policy choices of growth or welfare optimizing governments. A recent review of the infrastructure and endogenous growth literature concludes that "the theoretical studies modelling infrastructure within endogenous growth models, whether as a flow or a stock variable, tend to disregard the indirect effect that infrastructure has on some measure of output via TFP" (Dissou and Didic 2013: 42).

In all such models, growth is essentially more of the same not long-term change in the structure of the economy. The change in the world economy between 1820 and 1870, between 1870 and 1920, and between 1920 and 1970 is not simply a growth in the amount or output of the same old stuff but rather a fundamentally different pattern of production of new as well as old things, supported by radically new infrastructure systems.

In this chapter I have sought to demonstrate that infrastructure services change dynamically in tandem with the real economy, but that change occurs slowly over decades and sometimes centuries. For socio-political reasons, infrastructure services have frequently been provided at zero price to users, thus falling outside the realm of price-based market clearing mechanisms. Many of the benefits of infrastructure, such as quality of life, are hard to quantify in market terms, but they do affect well-being and have a measurable effect on welfare and behavior. Prud'homme (2005) makes a strong case that the concept of capital was never designed to be applied to infrastructure and that the standard production function is inappropriate for modeling it.

What of new institutional economics (NIE), and particularly transaction cost economics (TCE)? North pioneered the view that economic change needs to be seen in a long-run perspective where institutional innovations are as important as technological progress (North and Thomas 1976; North 1990, 2006; North and Wallis 1994). NIE is an eclectic tradition that embraces institutions, property rights, contracts, regulation, politics, asset specificity, and so on. Different infrastructure sectors have been examined by a range of authors who try to go beyond "institutions matter" to look at systems of government, contract and regulatory design, and their impact on outcomes. They find a huge variety of outcomes in terms of the structure of vertical and horizontal integration of network industries providing infrastructure services, even when there are a common set of rules. History and path dependency play an important role in determining how industries are organized and regulated.

Given the importance of regulation, doing it well should be a major concern of governments. History offers many clues as to how and how not to regulate private infrastructure services. Gómez-Ibáñez (2009) argues that credible long-term commitments are at the heart of the regulatory bargain between private investors and government. Without such credibility, there may be an inevitable cycle of oscillations between public and private ownership.

An important insight from the TCE tradition is that running markets has a cost and therefore that anything lowering those costs will increase the efficiency of markets in solving resource allocation problems. At a macro-level this is where infrastructure really gains traction as a driver of efficiency. Lower transportation, energy, water, and communication costs feed through to all aspects of economic activity. For firms, it lowers the costs of inputs and the costs of getting their goods or services to market. Better transportation enlarges markets. For households, it can lower prices and increase the choice of goods available, since they can come from wider markets. It lowers the costs of traveling to work and the effort needed for household work, thus freeing more time for productive activity or leisure. Safe drinking water in the home saves time, reduces mortality, and brings a huge improvement to quality of life. Environmental infrastructure makes our cities more livable. For governments, it can make the cost of administration and coordination lower. And then there are the systemic long-term benefits to human capital resulting from better education and health care that school and hospital infrastructure supports.

Of course, you can have too much of a good thing and infrastructure is not immune to the law of diminishing returns. So saying "no" to the unjustified incremental investment project is an important role for private investors, governments, and development banks.

The evolutionary growth-substitution economic models of Grübler (1990, 2003) offer the closest fit with the details of innovation, growth, diffusion, saturation, and decay cycles that we see in history. He emphasizes how infrastructure expands, has to find new forms of organization to deal with the coordination problems of scale and also how institutions have to adapt to the new economic reality. He found similar patterns of infrastructure growth in socialist USSR as in the United States, which for him confirmed that infrastructure services were independent of a particular economic system for organizing society. The longer term historic perspective presented here supports that view. China currently has some of the fastest expanding infrastructure networks anywhere on the planet because it can afford to spend and its people expect better infrastructure services, not because there was a new technological breakthrough.

There are a number of features where Grübler's model is less convincing. First, he underplays the importance of relative price and quality of services both to firms and households as being decisive in early stage adoption of potentially disruptive innovations. The price-quality advantage was the critical factor that launched the canal and then the railway booms in Britain and the telegraph in the United States. Making transportation cheap and convenient from Manchester to Liverpool suddenly made a weekend at the seaside a possibility for those inland factory workers. Railways literally created new markets, first locally, then nationally, and then globally.

Second, Grübler also claims that the regularity of major transport innovations provides support to the idea of 55-year Kondriatev wave long cycles. The longer term perspective presented here does not support this type of technology driven determinism; see figure 2.4. Many of the early infrastructure network revolutions were effectively reinventing the technology well known to the Romans. Moreover the turnpike revolution grew more slowly than is portrayed, starting well before the Industrial Revolution and beginning with an innovation in financing not with technology.

Fouquet (2008) has expanded the earlier analysis of Nordhaus on the long-run cost of providing lighting services to estimate changes in costs and the corresponding prices of services for both energy and transport in the United Kingdom over the last 700 years. He demonstrates that new energy sources and transport systems develop in response to changing price signals. It is the relative cost of one technology over another than drives the long-run substitution effect. But crucially, this only applies when infrastructure is charged for and market forces are at work. Thus electricity replaced gas that had replaced whale oil that had replaced candles as a source of light. The impact of

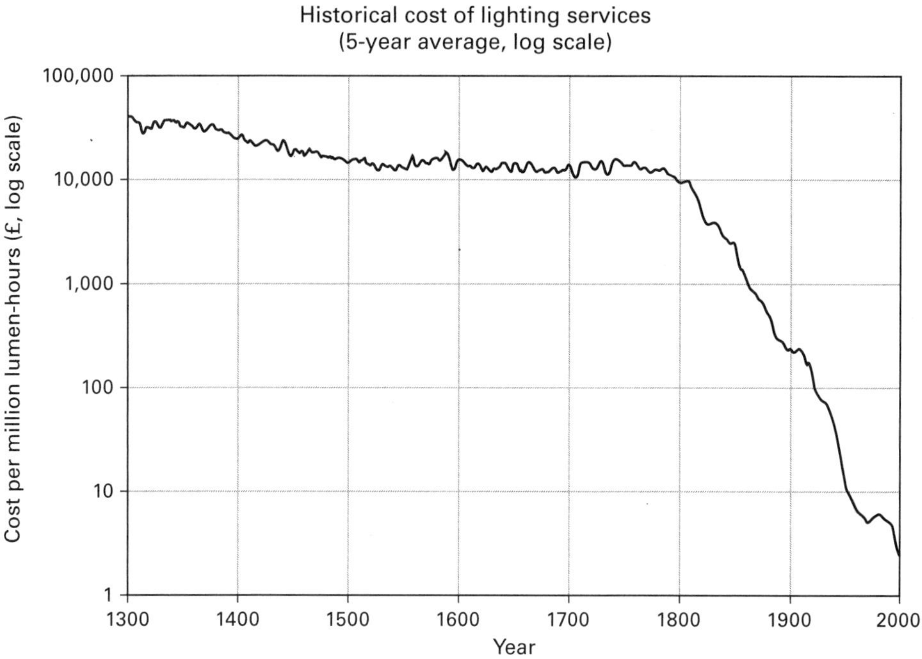

Figure 2.6
Long-run trends in the cost of lighting services
Source: Data in Fouquet (2008)

this technological progress on the price of services is illustrated in figure 2.6. Starting in 1800, the cost of lighting services fell due to the substitution of gas for oil lamps. The trend continued with the substitution of gas by electricity and further through increasing efficiency and scale economies in electricity generation and distribution.

Fouquet traces a similar pattern for the reduction in the price of transport services based on energy and time considerations as the truck replaced the train, which had replaced the barge, which had replaced the horse-drawn cart, and so on. Bogart (2012) found that freight charges in Britain decreased by 95 percent in real terms from 1700 to 1870 implying an annual total factor productivity gain of more than 2 percent.

In a simplistic version of this story, technological progress drives the whole process, and network infrastructure is just a particular way to provide low-cost services by exploiting economies of scale. That would fit the recent mobile phone story very well. But it does not explain why canals, a technology that had been known in the United Kingdom for over 200 years were not deployed sooner. It also doesn't explain why, once the advantages of a particular infrastructure technology are known, all nations don't immediately adopt it. One answer is that nations, like households, face a budget constraint. Finance determines what infrastructure gets built and is the key factor missing from Grübler's analysis.

Perez (2002) takes a neo-Schumpterian view of long-run change in technoeconomic systems. She adds the role of speculative finance to the technological innovation story. In her model, infrastructure is portrayed as a supporting actor in the drama of successive great surges of development (GSDs) driven by the interaction of technological progress and financial speculation in the capitalist market economy. She identifies five technological revolutions and resulting GSDs starting with the first industrial revolution and ending with the age of information and telecoms. Her model involves four phases of irruption, frenzy, synergy, and maturity. Financial capital plays a critical role during the frenzy phase as it determines the speed of diffusion of the technology or infrastructure.

Perez view of the role of infrastructure is somewhat ambivalent. On the one hand, she clearly sees infrastructure as both an enabler and integral to the process of each technological revolution, quoting turnpike, canal, and railway mania as examples of the frenzy stage. But she also sees advances in infrastructure as an "externality," to such an extent that the index to her book Technological Revolutions and Financial Capital has the entry: "Infrastructures … *see also* Externalities" (Perez 2002: 189). Each GSD has "given rise to a whole set of new industries along with a set of new organisational principles and externalities of infrastructure and knowledge that enable the modernisation of practically all of the existing industries" (Perez 2010: 4). In this model, infrastructure is an externality that arises to support industry.

Perez model has all the crucial ingredients and positive feedback dynamics that we observe in the history of infrastructure development, but she considers it a theory of the overall technoeconomic paradigm, not individual sectors. New technoeconomic paradigms involve systems of innovation that affect the entire economic system and open up entirely new possibilities for economic activity based on a new "common sense" about how the economy works. Perez sees the interactions and particularly the positive feedback among technological systems of production, infrastructure, finance, and institutions as the driving force of economic development in the long run.

A deeper look at the functioning of early capital markets suggests a rather more prominent role for infrastructure. I would claim that the evolution of capital markets from funding sovereign debt to finance wars or excessive consumption of the king to a system of risk-based financing of infrastructure was one of the most important innovations in the history of economic development. By channeling the savings of the industries and workers who were directly benefiting from the lower transaction costs and overall increased efficiency of the system back into creating more infrastructure, a positive feedback developed that underpinned the growth shift we see starting in the 1800s.

2.7 Co-evolution of Infrastructure and Financial Systems

The historic linkages between infrastructure investments and the development of capital markets are not stressed in the literature, although Reed (1975) and Michie (2006) refer to the importance of railways in the history of the global securities markets. The worldwide investment boom in railways, particularly from 1870 to 1914, could only be financed through a global capital market with Europe as the world's banker. For net debtor countries the huge investments required for infrastructure had to come from foreign savings. The relationship played out differently over time in different nations, depending on the level of domestic savings, the appetite of foreign investors, government policy, and the state of national and international capital markets. France, Netherlands, Germany, and Belgium quickly managed to copy the British industrial system and mobilize domestic savings to fund the development of their own networks. They all then became net capital exporters for infrastructure projects in their own niche sectors and countries of influence. Belgium specialized in tramways, especially in Russia and Italy. France specialized in railways, notably in Spain and Portugal. Once the United States became a net capital exporter, it specialized in its home-grown technologies of telecoms and energy. The highly capital-intensive nature of infrastructure investments meant that huge amounts of capital were needed to grow the global networks already in place by 1914. Events thereafter put a strong break on global integration, until the re-launch of project finance for infrastructure in the 1960s. The following synthesis draws heavily on Michie (2006), Kindleberger (1993), and Feis (1930), plus other sources referred to in the text.

Until the mid-eighteenth century most publicly held and traded securities were forms of sovereign and, to a far lesser extent, municipal debt. Origins go back to the Venice forced loan of 1171. Such paper debt instruments became relatively widely traded in Italian city states. By the 1600s Amsterdam was the main center for trading the debt of Dutch and foreign nations. Defaults or arbitrary changes of terms were common, such as with French *Rentes*. The first private companies listed on stock exchanges were the great trading companies established in the sixteenth and seventeenth centuries, such as the East India Company founded in London in 1600 and Dutch East India Company founded in Amsterdam in 1602. The Netherlands, France, Great Britain, and Italian city states were the main suppliers of savings. Britain successfully privatized its national debt in 1694 through the formation of the Bank of England, a private company until 1946. The first major financial bubble and crash occurred in 1720, with almost simultaneous speculation driven excesses in France with John Law's Compagnie des Indes and in Britain with the South Sea Company.

As Britain embarked on the industrial revolution, it started to generate additional surpluses for investment and rapidly eclipsed Amsterdam as the world's leading exchange for securities. Despite strict regulation of private company formation by Parliament under the Bubble Act, which was passed in 1720 and only repealed in 1824, many new joint stock companies continued to be formed, raising private equity by subscription. The private Acts of incorporation for canal and water companies specified both the capital structure of the enterprise, which was mainly equity, and the tariffs that could be charged to users. Equity returns to infrastructure were usually limited to a maximum of 10 percent, above which the user tariffs should be reduced. The cap appears to be a legacy of the old usury laws restricting the ability to profit from purely financial transactions. Throughout this early period the reference rate for interest bearing paper was typically 3 to 5 percent.

In 1820, there were no railways. Foreign and domestic government securities made up over 90 percent of the value of traded securities on the London Stock Exchange. Corporate securities were predominantly financial undertakings (banks and assurance companies whose assets were also government securities) and infrastructure companies (canals, water supply, docks, bridges) plus a variety of smaller mining, trading, and other commercial companies. By 1850, over 10,000 km of railways had been built and railway stocks and shares represented the largest single category of private securities. The 1830s and 1840s saw two major financial bubbles in railway share prices. Over the following 50 years, the capital invested in the world's railways grew by a factor of four as railways became the global transport network across all continents. By 1910, 90 percent of all listed stocks and bonds on the New York Stock Exchange were railways. The net source of funds for global investments were a few countries in Western Europe, predominantly the United Kingdom, France, and the Netherlands.

This shift in the nature of capital market structure is illustrated in figure 2.7. By 1853, over 70 percent of the value of securities on the London Stock Exchange (LSE) was domestic public sector debt, 20 percent was infrastructure stocks and shares, mainly in railways, canals, and water supply, with the remainder 10 percent financial and manufacturing companies. By 1913, domestic debt was down to 12 percent and dwarfed by foreign securities, both government debt, mainly to British colonies and Latin America, and corporates. Domestic and foreign railways alone represented almost 40 percent of the total value of all securities. The old infrastructures of canals and water supplies had all but disappeared as securities on the LSE to be replaced by the new industries of energy, telecoms, and tramways. As markets and company cash flows matured, bonds replaced equity as the financial instrument of choice for raising new funds. After WWI, domestic public sector debt rose again due to war bonds.

Across Europe the rules of the game for domestic investment varied. While many countries followed the British lead in looking to the securities markets for capital, in Germany, the Austro-Hungarian empire and Eastern and Southern Europe infrastructure promoters also looked to German-style "universal banks" for funding. France largely financed its infrastructure investments from domestic savings. The communes and municipalities borrowed through direct contact with government-controlled credit institutions such as *Caisse des Dépôts et Consignations*. Abroad, each nation had its own networks and sphere of influence. Britain was focused on the United States, its own colonies, and Latin America. France was focused on Russia, Turkey, Spain, and Portugal, primarily through direct involvement in French-owned railway concessions. German capital was concentrated on Austria-Hungary, Russia, and its African colonies. In all cases the dominant securities were government bonds and railways.

As Michie (2006: 86) notes "Instead of borrowing for unproductive military purposes, governments were bequeathing to later generations ownership of profitable assets like railways, docks, and public utilities

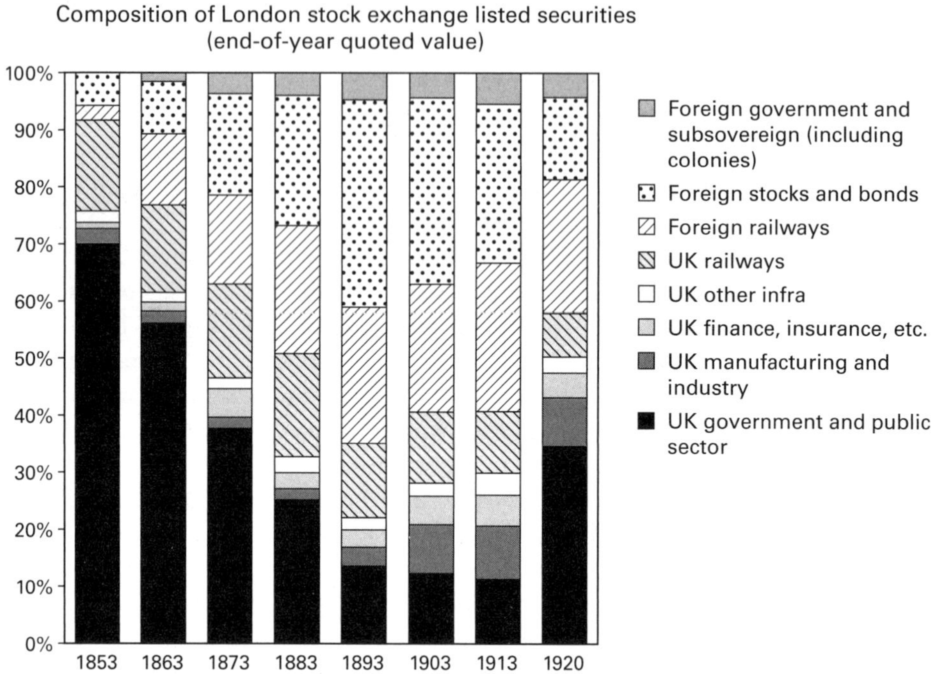

Figure 2.7
Changing structure of UK stock market investments, 1853 to 1920
Source: Percentages derived from table 5 in Goetzmann and Ukhov (2006) based on original data in Morgan and Thomas (1962)

and contributing to the means of paying these debts through rising national incomes." Finance had shifted from a negative feedback loop of converting savings into the destructive intent of war into the positive feedback loop of reinvesting profits and savings into infrastructure that lowered the costs of transport, increased the size of markets, speeded up information flows and increased overall welfare and quality of life. But it didn't last.

WWI caused a complete disjuncture in the global financial system. It marked the end of the first age of globalization. All major stock exchanges closed or operated in a very restricted way for all or part of the war. Public finances of all the major world economies went into reverse. National debt increased 20-fold in Germany and the United States, 10-fold in Britain, and 5-fold in France and Italy. Economies became less interdependent as foreign debt held abroad was repurchased by domestic savers. Much overseas private investment in infrastructure had to be written down or written off completely. French investors were particularly affected as both the Russian and Ottoman empires collapsed and public and private debts were repudiated. The biggest beneficiary was the United States, which transformed most of its foreign held debt into domestic holdings. New York rapidly eclipsed London as the world's largest financial center, and US investors started investing abroad to support their electricity, telephone, and emerging petrochemical industries. The locus of economic and financial power shifted across the Atlantic.

With the financial turmoil of the following decades as the gold standard collapsed, hyperinflation took hold in Germany and Hungary, the Great Depression in United States spread worldwide, and then nationalism increased in the run up to WWII, global capital markets were mobilized only sporadically for infrastructure projects and usually required sovereign guarantees. Most new infrastructure investment was funded from domestic savings, sovereign debt or by large multinational corporates, notably in energy.

At the end of WWII, the United States funded the infrastructure and industry reconstruction programs in Europe through soft loans and grants from the Marshall Plan and via the newly created International Bank for Reconstruction and Development, later renamed the World Bank. By now, most infrastructure services in Europe were managed by SOEs, so borrowing for investment usually implied some form of sovereign support. Infrastructure providing public services like water and electricity was subsidized in order to keep tariffs to the public low. Infrastructure finance to the developing world was dominated by the World Bank and the regional Multilateral Development Banks that followed its model.

The re-launch of the global capital markets is often attributed to the first dollar-denominated eurobond in 1963 for the Italian motorway operator Autostrade. As capital could increasingly ignore borders, investment managers focused on government fixed income securities, corporate debt, and equities. Financing for infrastructure investments came either direct from governments or through the corporate debt market for firms specialized in infrastructure, notably the big energy companies. The project finance market started anew in the 1980s, again for energy projects. From the 1980s a new wave of interest in private infrastructure started after the United Kingdom privatized its energy, telecoms, and water utilities, which again became star performers on the London Stock Exchange. The Private Finance Initiative extended the new financing trend into harder to privatize sectors such as transport, hospitals, and schools via PPP contracting arrangements. In developing nations an agenda of infrastructure privatization was pushed as a way to bring both foreign investment and improved efficiency to public services. Today, getting more private investment into infrastructure, for example, from pension funds, is seen as an important policy goal (Croce 2011).

A critical issue for achieving "financial sustainability" of infrastructure service providers is pricing policy. Getting the right balance between user charges and taxes is high on the policy agenda in many countries and sectors. Historically, whether a service was provided free to all, like water fountains or road access in Rome, or had to cover its costs from the start, like the telegraph, had a critical influence on how services developed. Many nineteenth-century innovations led by private capital started out only affordable to private companies that could pay for the improved services. A core of public and private customers need to be willing to pay enough to justify building out the network, as with the early years of gas lighting, until in time services become affordable to all. Today the necessity of making users at least cover operational costs is widely recognized, while carefully designed tariff structures can protect the poorest consumers. Regulation becomes the key policy instrument to balance economic, social, environmental, and service quality expectations of different stakeholders.

2.8 Conclusions

The physical infrastructure systems that underpin everyday life in a modern economy have evolved over hundreds and sometimes thousands of years. The basic elements of urban, water, sanitation, transportation, and communication systems were well developed by the late Roman empire. These large-scale public works required not only engineering knowledge, but also the institutions to operate, contract, and provide a legal framework for critical matters like using public rights of way, charging for services, and enforcing contracts. After a pause of several centuries, a new generation of private infrastructure projects started in Britain after 1500 with an acceleration in the early 1800s that has sustained two centuries of unparalleled increase in wealth and well-being. Infrastructure was at the core, not the periphery of this story.

Throughout history, the pivotal role of goverment as regulator, contracting authority, and default investor in public infrastructure is self-evident. In contrast, the involvement of the private sector has waxed and waned over millennia, although at times it has been pivotal in bringing innovation, taking risks, and driving efficiency. Evaluating the merits of different theoretical frameworks in explaining such long-run dynamics, only a multidisciplinary, systems approach that embraces innovations in technology, finance, and institutions can capture the positive feedback among infrastructure, industry, and finance that has characterized the last 200 years.

We have been on a strange journey. We started out looking for the origins of infrastructure and of the innovations that have driven its evolution over the centuries. We ended up with the origins of modern capital markets. Perhaps this is not so surprising. I contend that the revolution that started in Britain in the eighteenth century was not just an industrial revolution; it was also an infrastructure revolution and a capital markets revolution, and I contend that all three were interdependent. It built positive feedback among industry, infrastructure, and finance that spread from local to national to global scale. The positive feedbacks were among different sectors, between product and labor markets, and between public and private actors. The capital-intensive nature of infrastructure means that savings have to be mobilized from somewhere. And savings put to the constructive use of reducing economy-wide transaction costs, must be better than the negative cycles of human and physical capital destruction that categorized the first half of the twentieth century and many centuries before.

Innovation does not stop with the big bang moment of inventing the railways or electricity. It goes on through competition between rival systems to establish a standard for the new technology, through finding new organizational models and financing systems to deliver rapid expansion, through regulation or social ownership to ensure that benefits are extended to all through universal service. It requires incentives through competition and regulation to keep grinding out the efficiency gains that deliver improvements to quality at lower costs. Infrastructure needs to be central to the development of a "national system of innovation."

Does history have anything useful to tell us about our current infrastructure challenges? Perhaps. Spotting the historic parallels and understanding how particular projects and policies played out in the past will surely help us make better decisions today. Of course, the context will always be different. The art is to appreciate the differences as well as the similarities and use them to enrich our understanding of the risks and opportunities we face.

Just as Vitruvius lamented that the Romans had forgotten Greek contracting practices, with a better grasp of history, there are rich seams of past practices to re-explore. "New" approaches to infrastructure finance using land grants or performance-based subsidy competitions among firms to complete different components of a network were all successful experiments in the past that researchers and practitioners could fruitfully examine for inspiration today.

Meanwhile the next technoeconomic paradigm may already be with us in the form of "sustainability" and all that it implies for renewables, green infrastructure, and decoupling growth from wasteful exploitation of natural resources. The role of infrastructure systems in enabling or constraining the transition to a new, more sustainable economy will be critical (Kaijser 2003; Loorbach et al. 2010). In any case, infrastructure needs to be understood as more than an input into a growth optimization game: it literally underpins civilized life.

Note

The author is Economic Advisor at the European Investment Bank (EIB), Luxembourg, and sponsor of the EIB Institute funded History of European Infrastructure Finance research project. An earlier version of this chapter appeared as CESifo Working Paper Series No. 5073, The Long-Run Evolution of Infrastructure Services. Disclaimer: This chapter should not be reported as representing the views of the EIB. The views expressed are those of the author and do not necessarily represent those of the EIB or EIB policy.

References

Abbate, Janet. 2000. *Inventing the Internet*. Cambridge: MIT Press.

Adams, Robert McC. 2010. Slavery and freedom in the third dynasty of Ur: Implications of the Garshana Archives. *Cuneiform Digital Library Journal*: 2. http://www.cdli.ucla.edu/pubs/cdlj/2010/cdlj2010_002.pdf (accessed October 4, 2014).

Agénor, Pierre-Richard. 2007. Fiscal policy and endogenous growth with public infrastructure. *Oxford Economic Papers* 60 (1): 57–87.

Agénor, Pierre-Richard. 2012. Infrastructure, public education and growth with congestion costs. *Bulletin of Economic Research* 64 (4): 449–69.

Albert, William. 2007. *The Turnpike Road System in England: 1663–1840*. Cambridge, UK: Cambridge University Press.

Aschauer, David Alan. 1989. Is public expenditure productive? *Journal of Monetary Economics* 23 (2): 177–200.

Bagg, Ariel M. 2012. Irrigation. In Daniel T. Potts, ed. *A Companion to the Archaeology of the Ancient Near East*. Hoboken, NJ: Wiley, 261–78.

Barro, Robert J. 1990. Government spending in a simple model of endogenous growth. *Journal of Political Economy* 98 (5, pt. 2): 103–25.

Bel, Germà. 2011. The first privatisation: Selling SOEs and privatising public monopolies in Fascist Italy (1922–1925). *Cambridge Journal of Economics* 35 (5): 937–56.

Bezançon, Xavier. 2004. *2000 Ans d'histoire du partenariat public-privé: pour la réalisation des équipements et services collectifs*. Paris: Presses de l'École nationale des Ponts et chaussées.

Bogart, Dan. 2012. The transport revolution in industrializing Britain: A survey. Working paper. Department of Economics, UC Irvine. http://www.socsci.uci.edu/~dbogart/transport_revolution_surveyjan2013.pdf (accessed October 4, 2014).

Bonin, Hubert. 2010. *History of the Suez Canal Company, 1858–1960: Between Controversy and Utility*. Genève: Droz.

Cadot, Olivier, Lars-Hendrik Röller, and Andreas Stephan. 2006. Contribution to productivity or pork barrel? The two faces of infrastructure investment. *Journal of Public Economics* 90 (6): 1133–53.

Campbell, Gareth, and John David Turner. 2010. The greatest bubble in history: Stock prices during the British railway mania. MPRA paper 21820. University Library of Munich; http://mpra.ub.uni-muenchen.de/21820/ (accessed November 27, 2013).

Casson, Mark. 2009. *The World's First Railway System: Enterprise, Competition, and Regulation on the Railway Network in Victorian Britain*. Oxford: Oxford University Press.

Chandler, Tertius. 1987. *Four Thousand Years of Urban Growth: An Historical Census*. Lampeter, Wales: St. David's University Press.

Charlesworth, George. 1984. *A History of British Motorways*. London: Thomas Telford Ltd.

Corble, Nick. 2011. *James Brindley: The First Canal Builder*. London: Faber and Faber.

Croce, Raffaele Della. 2011. *Pension Funds Investment in Infrastructure: Policy Actions*, no. 13. Paris: OECD Publishing.

De Luca, Giuseppe, and Marcella Lorenzini. 2013. A taxonomy of infrastructure financing in Europe on the long run (12th–18th century). *Entreprises et histoire* 1: 10–36.

Diamond, Jared. 2005. *Collapse: How Societies Choose to Fail or Succeed*. London: Penguin.

Dissou, Yazid, and Selma Didic. 2013. Infrastructure and Growth. In John Cockburn et al., eds., *Infrastructure and Economic Growth in Asia*. New York: Springer Open International Publishing: 5–45.

Eck, Werner. 2007. *The Age of Augustus*. Hoboken, NJ: Wiley-Blackwell.

Égert, Balázs, Tomasz J. Kozluk, and Douglas Sutherland. 2009. Infrastructure and growth: Empirical evidence. Working paper 685. OECD Economics Department. http://ssrn.com/abstract=1360784 (accessed November 27, 2013).

Eichengreen, Barry. 1995. Financing infrastructure in developing countries: lessons from the railway age. *World Bank Research Observer* 10 (1): 75–91.

Esfahani, Hadi Salehi, and María Teresa Ramírez. 2003. Institutions, infrastructure, and economic growth. *Journal of Development Economics* 70 (2): 443–77.

Estache, Antonio. 2004. *Emerging Infrastructure Policy Issues in Developing Countries: A Survey of the Recent Economic Literature*, vol. 3442. Washington, DC: World Bank.

Feis, Herbert. 1930. *Europe: The World's Banker, 1870–1914*. New Haven: Yale University Press.

Ferguson, Niall. 2012. *Civilization: The Six Killer Apps of Western Power*. London: Penguin.

Flyvbjerg, Bent, Nils Bruzelius, and Werner Rothengatter. 2003. *Megaprojects and Risk: An Anatomy of Ambition*. Cambridge, UK: Cambridge University Press.

Foreman-Peck, James, and Robert Millward. 1994. *Public and Private Ownership of British Industry, 1820–1990*. Oxford: Clarendon Press.

Fouquet, Roger. 2008. *Heat, Power and Light: Revolutions in Energy Services*. Cheltenham, UK: Elgar.

Freeman, Christopher. 1992. *The Economics of Hope: Essays on Technical Change, Economic Growth and the Environment*. London: Pinter.

Freeman, Chris, and Francisco Louçã. 2001. *As Time Goes By: From the Industrial Revolutions to the Information Revolution*. Oxford: Oxford University Press.

Friedlander, Amy. 1995a. *Emerging Infrastructure: The Growth of Railroads*. History of Infrastructure Series, vol. 1. Reston, VA: Corporation for National Research Initiatives.

Friedlander, Amy. 1995b. *Natural Monopoly and Universal Service: Telephones and Telegraphs in the US Communications Infrastructure, 1837–1940*. History of Infrastructure Series, vol. 2. Reston, VA: Corporation for National Research Initiatives.

Friedlander, Amy. 1996. *Power and Light: Electricity in the US Energy Infrastructure, 1870–1940*. History of Infrastructure Series, vol. 3. Reston, VA: Corporation for National Research Initiatives.

Friedlander, Amy. 2005. *Communications and Content: Radio Technologies in the US Infrastructure, 1865–1976*. History of Infrastructure Series, vol. 5. Reston, VA: Corporation for National Research Initiatives.

Garbrecht, Günther. 1980. The water supply system at Tuşpa (Urartu). *World Archaeology* 11 (3): 306–12.

Geels, Frank W. 2004. Understanding system innovations: A critical literature review and a conceptual synthesis. In Boelie Elzen, Frank W. Geels, and Kenneth Green, eds., *System Innovation and the Transition to Sustainability: Theory, Evidence and Policy*. Cheltenham, UK: Elgar, 19–47.

Goblot, Henri. 1979. *Les Qanats: Une technique d'acquisition de l'eau*, vol. 9. Paris: Editions de l'Ecole des Hautes Etudes en Sciences Sociales.

Goetzmann, William N., and Andrey D. Ukhov. 2006. British investment overseas 1870–1913: A modern portfolio theory approach. *Review of Finance* 10 (2): 261–300.

Golden, Miriam A., and Lucio Picci. 2008. Pork-barrel politics in postwar Italy, 1953–94. *American Journal of Political Science* 52 (2): 268–89.

Goldsmith, Hugh., and Dan Carter. 2015. Financing the evolution of London's water services: 1582 to 1904. DEMM Working paper 2015-02. Italy: Università degli Studi di Milano. https://ideas.repec.org/p/mil/wpdepa/2015-02.html (accessed April 26, 2015).

Gómez-Ibáñez, José A. 2009. *Regulating Infrastructure: Monopoly, Contracts, and Discretion.* Cambridge: Harvard University Press.

Gramlich, Edward M. 1994. Infrastructure Investment: A Review Essay. *Journal of Economic Literature* 32 (3): 1176–96.

Griffin, Jasper. 1986. Introduction. In John Boardman, Jasper Griffin, and Oswyn Murray, eds., *The Oxford History of the Classical World.* Oxford: Oxford University Press, 1–13.

Grübler, Arnulf. 1990. *The Rise and Fall of Infrastructures: Dynamics of Evolution and Technological Change in Transport.* Heidelberg: Physica-Verlag.

Grübler, Arnulf. 2003. *Technology and Global Change.* Cambridge, UK: Cambridge University Press.

Guldi, Joanna. 2012. *Roads to Power: Britain Invents the Infrastructure State.* Cambridge: Harvard University Press.

Hansman, R. John, Christopher Magee, Richard De Neufville, and Renee Robins. 2006. Research agenda for an integrated approach to infrastructure planning, design and management. *International Journal of Critical Infrastructures* 2 (2): 146–59.

Hausman, William J., Peter Hertner, and Mira Wilkins. 2008. *Global Electrification: Multinational Enterprise and International Finance in the History of Light and Power, 1878–2007.* Cambridge Studies in the Emergence of Global Enterprise. Cambridge, UK: Cambridge University Press.

Hughes, Thomas P. 1983. *Networks of Power: Electrification in Western Society, 1880–1930.* Baltimore: Johns Hopkins University Press.

Jacobson, Charles David, and Joel Arthur Tarr. 1995. Ownership and financing of infrastructure: Historical perspectives. Policy Research working paper 1466. World Bank.

Jansen, Michael. 1993. *Mohenjo-daro: City of Wells and Drains, Water Splendour 4500 Years Ago.* Frontinus Society Publications.

Kaijser, Arne. 2003. Redirecting infrasystems towards sustainability. In *Individual and Structural Determinants of Environmental Practice*, ed. Bengt Hansson et al., 152–79. Williston, VT: Ashgate.

Kaijser, Arne. 2004. The dynamics of infrasystems: Lessons from history. *Proceedings of the 6th International Summer Academy on Technology Studies: Urban Infrastructure in Transition.* IFF/IFZ Graz, Austria: 153–65.

Kindleberger, Charles P. 1993. *A Financial History of Western Europe.* New York: Oxford University Press.

Knoepfler, Denis. 2001. Le Contrat d'Eretrie en Eubée pour le drainage de l'étang de Ptéchai. In Pierre Briant, ed., *Irrigation et drainage dans l'Antiquité. Qanats et canalisations souterraines en Iran, en Égypte et en Grèce.* Paris: Thotm éditions, 41–79.

Koutsoyiannis, Demetris, and Andreas N. Angelakis. 2003. Hydrologic and hydraulic science and technology in ancient Greece. In Bobby Alton Stewart and Terry A. Howell, eds. *Encyclopedia of Water Science.* New York: Dekker, 415–17.

Lightfoot, Dale R. 2000. The origin and diffusion of qanats in Arabia: New evidence from the northern and southern peninsula. *Geographical Journal* 166 (3): 215–26.

Loorbach, Derk, Niki Frantzeskaki, and Wil Thissen. 2010. Introduction to the special section: Infrastructures and transitions. *Technological Forecasting and Social Change* 77 (8): 1195–1202.

López, Alberte Martínez. 2003. Belgian investment in tramways and light railways: An international approach, 1892–1935. *Journal of Transport History* 24 (1): 59–77.

Maddison, Angus. 2007. *The World Economy*. Vol. 1: *A Millennial Perspective*. Vol. 2: *Historical Statistics*. New Delhi: Academic Foundation.

Magnusson, Roberta J. 2003. *Water Technology in the Middle Ages: Cities, Monasteries, and Waterworks after the Roman Empire*. Baltimore: Johns Hopkins University Press.

Michie, Ranald. 2006. *The Global Securities Market: A History*. Oxford: Oxford University Press.

Millward, Robert. 2005. *Private and Public Enterprise in Europe: Energy, Telecommunications and Transport, 1830–1990*. Cambridge, UK: Cambridge University Press.

Mitchell, Brian R. 1992. *International Historical Statistics: Europe 1750–1988*. New York: Stockton Press. .

Mithen, Steven. 2012. *Thirst: For Water and Power in the Ancient World*. Cambridge: Harvard University Press.

Morgan, Edward Victor, and William Arthur Thomas. 1962. *The Stock Exchange*. Schweinfurt, Germany: Elek Books.

Morris, Ian. 2010. *Why the West Rules–For Now: The Patterns of History, and What They Reveal about the Future*. New York: Farrar, Straus and Giroux.

Nelson, Richard R. 2005. *Technology, Institutions, and Economic Growth*. Cambridge: Harvard University Press.

Nelson, Richard R. 2008. What enables rapid economic progress: What are the needed institutions? *Research Policy* 37 (1): 1–11.

Newbery, David M. 2002. *Privatization, Restructuring, and Regulation of Network Utilities*, vol. 2. Cambridge: MIT Press.

North, Douglass C., and Robert Paul Thomas. 1976. *The Rise of the Western World: A New Economic History*. Cambridge, UK: Cambridge University Press.

North, Douglass C. 1990. *Institutions, Institutional Change and Economic Performance*. Cambridge, UK: Cambridge University Press.

North, Douglass C., and John J. Wallis. 1994. Integrating institutional change and technical change in economic history: A transaction cost approach. *Journal of Institutional and Theoretical Economics* 150 (4): 609–24.

North, Douglas C. 2006. *Understanding the Process of Economic Change*. New Delhi: Academic Foundation.

Parker, David. 2012. *The Official History of Privatization*, vol. 2. London: Routledge.

Pawson, Eric. 1977. *Transport and Economy: The Turnpike Roads of Eighteenth Century Britain*. New Delhi: Academic Press.

Perez, Carlota. 2002. *Technological Revolutions and Financial Capital: The Dynamics of Bubbles and Golden Ages*. Cheltenham: Elgar.

Perez, Carlota. 2010. The financial crisis and the future of innovation: A view of technical change with the aid of history, no. 28. Tallinn: Tallinn University of Technology, Ragnar Nurkse School of Innovation and Governance. http://hum.ttu.ee/wp/paper28.pdf (accessed April 26, 2015).

Pirenne, Henri. 1956. *Medieval Cities: Their Origins and the Revival of Trade*. Princeton: Princeton University Press.

Prud'homme. Rémy. 2005. Infrastructure and development. In François Bourguignon and Boris Pleskovic, eds., *Lessons of Experience: Proceedings of the 2004 Annual Bank Conference on Development Economics*. New York: World Bank/Oxford University Press, 153–81.

Ragazzi, Giorgio, and Werner Rothengatter, eds. 2005. *Procurement and Financing of Motorways in Europe*, vol. 15. Philadelphia: Elsevier.

Reed, Malcolm C. 1975. *Investment in Railways in Britain, 1820–1844: A Study in the Development of the Capital Market*. Oxford: Oxford University Press.

Reinhart, Carmen M., and Kenneth Rogoff. 2009. *This Time Is Different: Eight Centuries of Financial Folly*. Princeton: Princeton University Press.

Rogers, Everett M. 1962. *Diffusion of Innovations*. New York: Free Press.

Rohatyn, Felix G. 2009. *Bold Endeavors: How Our Government Built America, and Why It Must Rebuild Now*. New York: Simon and Schuster.

Romp, Ward E., and Jakob De Haan. 2005. Public capital and economic growth: a critical survey. *EIB Papers* 10 (1): 41–70.

Schmidt, Klaus. 2000. Göbekli Tepe, southeastern Turkey: A preliminary report on the 1995–1999 excavations. *Paléorient* 26 (1): 45–54.

Sitwell, Nigel H. 1981. *Roman Roads of Europe*. New York: Cassell.

Straub, Stephane. 2008. Infrastructure and development: A critical appraisal of the macro level literature. Policy Research working paper 4590. World Bank.

Temin, Peter. 2006. The economy of the early Roman empire. *Journal of Economic Perspectives* 20 (1): 133–51.

Toutain, Jules. 1930. *The Economic Life of the Ancient World*. London: Kegan Paul, Trench, Trubner.

Trew, Alex. 2010. Infrastructure finance and industrial takeoff in England. *Journal of Money, Credit and Banking* 42 (6): 985–1010.

Vitruvius (Marcus Vitruvius Pollio). 1914. *Vitruvius Pollio, The Ten Books on Architecture*. Morris Hicky Morgan, transl. Cambridge: Harvard University Press.

Ward, Robert. 2003. *London's New River*. London: Historical Publications.

Wittfogel, Karl A. 1957. *Oriental Despotism: A Comparative Study of Total Power*. New Haven: Yale University Press.

II Investment, Growth, Policy Issues

3 Population Density, Optimal Infrastructure, and Economic Growth

Sumit S. Deole and Asmae El Gallaa

3.1 Introduction

The contributions of different growth-enhancing policies in the aggregate development of an economy has been the central question in the literature on economic growth. Accordingly, public education, foreign investments, domestic financial markets, and international trade have been considered important engines of economic growth. Domestic human and physical capital development do form the initial conditions for the above-mentioned growth engines, and hence literacy and infrastructure improvements are usually set as primary goals. Yet, even though human capital formation in a country is important for economic growth, in the absence of optimal infrastructure (physical capital), there is often outward migration of educated people to the developed world.[1] Likewise infrastructure development alone can further regional inequality within a country.

In this chapter we study the impact of available infrastructure on the fertility and education decisions of individuals, hence on human capital formation, and then at the macro level, on the economic growth of a country. Our main motivation for this study are the socioeconomic changes in post-independence India during the years 1961 to 2012. In India, the region around river Ganga, mainly consisting of states like Bihar and Uttar Pradesh (UP), accounts for almost 35 percent of the population of India, but its GDP is not in that proportion to the national GDP.

Since India's independence this region has faced problems similar to those in other parts of the country, namely inequality, poverty, and illiteracy, but unlike other regions, the lack of infrastructure development has led it into a poverty trap and the severity of these problems has magnified. As shown in the figure 3.1, the population density of

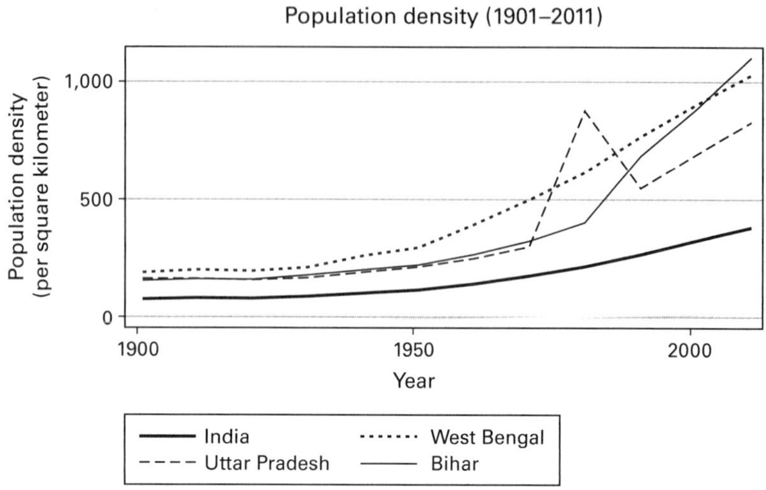

Figure 3.1
Population density

this region has diverged from that of the aggregate Indian population density. One cause of this divergence may be the asymmetric effect of international and interregional trade of this region with the other parts of the country and with other countries, resulting in the channeling of trade gains into population growth (Galor and Mountford 2008). Nevertheless, the lack of per capita available infrastructure has induced the working population to migrate out of Bihar and UP to other Indian states.[2]

In a study of India's physical capital, the crucial role played by railways in the aggregate transportation infrastructure cannot be ignored. The ticket prices of Indian railways are under the control of the central government, and there is a relatively infrequent change in the price structure. Moreover, unlike the city and interstate bus systems, the rail system lacks proper ticket checking at stations, and a separate compartment for the poor (general class) makes it a reliable source of transportation. Successive selections of the Ministers of Railways from this poor region comprised of the Bihar and UP states, and also West Bengal, has made it a political priority to get an increased share of the infrastructure to these states. If connected with other growing parts of the country, the region's poor could easily receive care at better health facilities and seek out job opportunities.[3] As shown in figure 3.2, since the independence of India, there has been a slow increase in the construction of

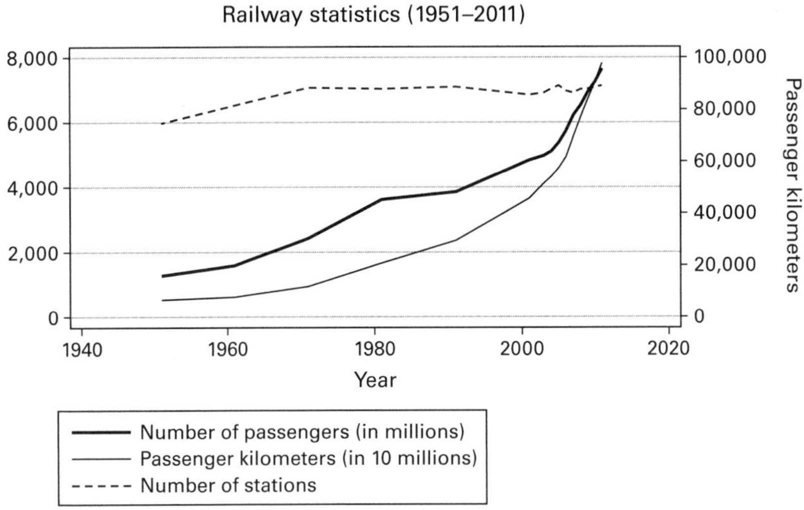

Figure 3.2
Indian railway statistics

railway stations and also in the number of passengers traveling the country. But there has been a rapid increase in passenger-kilometers traveled, indicating tendency of passengers to travel long distances. One good reason for this shift may be the geographic restructuring of the country that took place in the post-independence era, whereby different states were formed on the basis of different languages. Subsequently people have had to travel long distances for economic gain and for education purposes, and this in turn has contributed to an out-migration and dense metropolises.

Studies of the growth-enhancing effects of infrastructure provision go back to Rosenstein-Rodan's (1943) call for a big push, by which huge infrastructure investments would alleviate poverty and stimulate economic growth. More recently Agénor (2010) has pursued this theory of investment in public infrastructure as the main engine of economic growth. According to Agénor, infrastructure investments have a positive effect on GDP and are not restricted to the capital stock creation, via economies of scale, but are competition enhancing for the economy via network externalities.

Another strand of literature analyzes the causality link between infrastructure investments and population shifts. Does infrastructure investment lead to densely populated cities? The obvious answer is yes. Beyzatlar and Kuştepeli (2011) in their empirical study on Turkish annual data from 1950 to 2004 point out that there is a short-term as well as long-term positive relationship between the length of a railway infrastructure and population density. As is well understood, higher population density can lower the construction costs and facilitate the construction of more infrastructure (Fujita 2002).

An early study by Glover and Simon (1975) indeed showed that dense populations bring in more infrastructure per worker in a region. An indirect effect of dense populations, as argued by Becker, Glaeser, and Murphy (1999), is that large populations have specializations that encourages greater specialization in the form of assimilation of ideas. Along similar lines, Galor and Weil (2000) discuss the positive impact of population density on technological progress. But such an effect only shows up through an increase in the profitability of the infrastructure-providing facility with the increase in population density (Boucekkine et al. 2007). Thus an economic contraction or underperformance of an economy would be due to failure of government to provide the optimum level of infrastructure.

Hence in this chapter we attempt to show how population density and profitability of an infrastructure-providing facility can explain the economic growth of a country. From the description given above, we draw two necessary conditions for policy-making that would take an economy from stagnation to economic development: (1) population-led productivity improvements and (2) extensive investments in a region's infrastructure. In modeling population-induced productivity improvements to infrastructure allocation, Boucekkine et al. (2007) note an important deficiency having to do with exogenous demographics. But to endogenize fertility in a model à la Boucekkine et al. (2007) is a very complicated task; hence we use here an overlapping generations model (OLG) à la Croix and Doepke (2003). The micro-foundations of geographical interpretation of economic growth are also considered by Boucekkine et al. (2007), and here too they augment the Croix and Doepke (2003) model as well as the later model of Galor (2005). However, the computations involving micro-foundations of geographical interpretations in presence of the OLG model are very complicated, and thus we incorporate simplified versions in our study by omitting computations for the optimal number of public facilities, namely the number of railway stations.

We test the main theoretical predictions of the model by using time-series data on India for years 1961 to 2012. We use a three-variable equations system and both Granger causality and Wald tests to investigate the effects of population density and transportation infrastructure on economic growth. Our main result indicates that population density and profitability of the infrastructure-providing facility do contribute to economic growth of a region.

The rest of the chapter is organized as follows. Section 3.2 provides an overview of the theoretical model. In this section we describe the overlapping generations model we use to study the impact of population-induced productivity improvements and infrastructure provision on economic growth of the model economy. In section 3.3 we test the important theoretical predictions using time-series data for years 1961 to 2012 in India. In section 3.4 we offer some concluding remarks.

3.2 Theoretical Exploration

Our model economy is populated with overlapping generations of people, and the basic infrastructure provided is public in nature.[4] Time is discrete and goes from 0 to ∞. Individuals make all their decisions in their adulthood. These decisions include a decision related to the number of children they should beget (i.e., fertility decisions) and education decisions for their progenies. Parental decisions are related to the location of their residences, so household location is assumed to be exogenously determined. In order to provide geographical interpretations of the economic growth of the model economy, three location possibilities are considered: (1) residence near the workplace or (2) near the school or (3) between the school and the workplace.

3.2.1 Residing near Workplace

In this setting, parents decide to reside near their workplace and the location of the school for their children is a secondary decision on their part. As a result there are no transportation costs for parents to go to work, but children incur transportation costs for their daily commute to the school.

Model Specifications

In our model we consider an economy consisting of individuals who live for two periods: childhood and adulthood. Adults make all the decisions. The utility of a household depends on consumption (c_t), number of children (n_t), and the human capital of their children (h_{t+1}):

$$U = \max\{\ln(c_t) + \beta \ln(n_t h_{t+1})\},$$

where $\beta(>0)$ represents the degree of altruism. A largevalue of β indicates that family earns more utility from investing in next generation. In this model parents care about both the quantity (n_t) and the quality of schooling delivered to their children (h_{t+1}). Our formulation of the utility function allows us to study the quantity–quality trade-off that a household faces (see proposition 1).

The representative adult parent uses his/her time in two activities—rearing children and working (so that the total time endowment of an adult is assumed to be 1). The fraction of time spent in rearing one child is assumed to be constant at $\phi \in (0, 1)$; hence, in order to rear n_t children, the adult spends, in total, the time equivalent to ϕn_t (a nonwage earning activity). The total wages earned are spent on consumption, education, and transportation costs of the children. Hence the budget constraint that a parent faces is

$$c_t + e_t w_t \bar{h}_t n_t + k_t w_t \bar{h}_t n_t = w_t h_t (1 - \phi n_t), \tag{1}$$

where the term on the right-hand side of equation (1) indicates the total labor income (earned from wage-paying activities) of an adult calculated in efficiency units,[5] whereas the term on the left-hand side indicates all expenses incurred by the adult for consumption and for their children's education.[6] Variable w_t represents wage per unit of human capital, e_t represents the schooling time per children, $\bar{h}_t$ represents average human capital of the society, and hence the term $w_t \bar{h}_t$ represents the average labor income measured in efficiency units. Because basic services of education and transportation are provided by a central authority by construction, the per child costs for education and transportation (e.g., bus tickets) are determined centrally and denoted in terms of average labor income measured in efficiency units. Henceforth the term $e_t w_t \bar{h}_t$ denotes the education cost of one child and $k_t w_t \bar{h}_t$ denotes the transportation cost for that child, where variable k_t is the fraction of the labor income devoted to pay for the child's use of public services to travel from home to the school. This study also takes into account the fact that up to certain age, children have to be accompanied by an adult to be able to take the bus. So, even if the nominal price of the ticket is zero, the real price of the ticket is not zero. Hence it is assumed that k_t is never zero in this setting.

Following Croix and Doepke (2003), we assume that given the public nature of the education system, teachers rather than parents provide education. In addition we assume that the average human capital of teachers (their education or ability to teach) equals the average human capital of the population (i.e., $\bar{h}_t$). Another assumption entails that there is an intra-family transmission of human capital whereby educated parents create a positive externality on their children's human capital level. This transmission is called an externality as the level of human capital of parents in first place is not their decision but is considered as given. Thus the human capital of a child develops according to the following equation:

$$h_{t+1} = B_t(\theta + e_t)^{\eta}(h_t)^{\tau}(\bar{h}_t)^{\kappa}, \tag{2}$$

where parameter θ captures the positive human capital of a child, in the circumstances when the child is not in school, η represents the accumulation of human capital due to schooling, τ represents the inter-generational transmission of human capital within the household, κ represents the quality of the educational system or a teacher's ability to teach, and B_t is the efficiency parameter of the human capital function defined as

$$B_t = (1 + \rho)^{(1-\tau-\kappa)t}. \tag{3}$$

As in Rangazas (2000), we introduce endogenous growth in the model, by a compatible condition on $\kappa = 1 - \tau$. Parameters B, θ satisfy the positivity condition, that is, $B, \theta > 0$.

The human capital of the individuals is distributed by the function $F_t(h_t)$. Given the fertility decision of each individual, the total population of the economy evolves as

$$P_{t+1} = P_t \int_0^{\infty} n_t dF_t(h_t), \tag{4}$$

where P_{t+1} is the total population at time $(t + 1)$ and n_t is the fertility rate. The distribution of human capital function evolves according to

$$F_{t+1}(h) = \frac{P_t}{P_{t+1}} \int_0^{\infty} n_t I(h_{t+1} \leq h) dF_t(h_t), \tag{5}$$

where $I(.)$ is a typical indicator function. Similarly the average human capital, $\bar{h}_t$ is given by

$$\bar{h}_t = \int_0^{\infty} h_t dF_t(h_t). \tag{6}$$

There is a unique consumption good that is produced by a single representative firm. The production technology used by this firm is

$$Y_t = AL_{t,} \tag{7}$$

where L_t is the aggregate labor supply. Firms do not need capital for the production of the consumption good. Because infrastructure is assumed to be provided by the government, it is used by the individual laborers but not by the firms. By this assumption, we keep to our prime motivation of this study, to analyze the accumulation of human capital. The profit function of the firm is given by $Y_t - w_tL_t$.

Definition 1 *For given initial distribution of human capital* $F_0(h_0)$ *and for an initial population size* P_0, *an equilibrium consists of wages* $\{w_t\}$, *aggregate quantities* $\{L_t, \bar{h}_t, P_{t+1}\}$, distributions $\{F_{t+1}(h_{t+1})\}$, *and decision rules* $\{c_t, n_t, e_t, k_t, h_{t+1}\}$.

1. The decision rules of the household maximize utility subject to the constraints explained in equations (1) and (2).
2. Firms producing a unique consumer good maximize profits by hiring labor inputs.
3. The wages of labor inputs, w_t, clear markets.
4. Human capital distribution follows equation (5).

Now let's solve the households' decision rules c_t, e_t, n_t, h_{t+1}, and d_{t+1} in order to maximize the utility subject to constraints (1) and (2). We substitute these constraints into the Lagrange equation to get

$$\begin{aligned}\mathcal{L} = {} & \ln(w_t h_t(1-\varphi n_t)-(e_t+k_t)n_t w_t \bar{h}_t) \\ & + \beta(\ln n_t B_t + \eta\ln(\theta+e_t)+\tau\ln h_t+\kappa\ln\bar{h}_t).\end{aligned} \tag{8}$$

For computational simplicity and sectional analysis of the population with distributed human capital, we make the different parameters form to the condition that parents with higher human capital level are identified by the condition: $x_t > (\theta - k_t\eta)/\varphi\eta$ and those with lower levels of human capital are identified by the condition $x_t \leq (\theta - k_t\eta)/\varphi\eta$. Where x_t is relative human capital and is given by $x_t = h_t/\bar{h}_t$. At equilibrium, these conditions become $(\phi + k_t)\eta > \theta$ for parents with higher levels of human capital and $(\phi + k_t)\eta \leq \theta$ for parents with lower levels of human capital.

There is an interior solution for the optimal level of education, and this is obtained by solving the optimization problem for the household with higher human capital $\{x_t > [(\theta - k_t\eta)/\varphi\eta]\}$. Now solving for the equation for e_t, we have

$$e_t = \frac{\phi h_t \eta + k_t \eta \overline{h}_t - \overline{h}_t \theta}{\overline{h}_t (1-\eta)}.$$

Taking $\overline{h}_t$ out from numerator and denominator, we can rewrite the equation above in terms of x_t and obtain the relative human capital of a household:

$$e_t = \frac{\phi x_t \eta + k_t \eta - \theta}{(1-\eta)}. \tag{9}$$

This equation shows that the transportation cost as a fraction of labor income is complementary to the schooling time. Similarly we can write the equation for number of children as

$$n_t = \frac{\beta h_t (1-\eta)}{(1+\beta)(k_t \overline{h}_t - \overline{h}_t \theta + \phi h_t)}.$$

Then n_t expressed in terms of x_t is

$$n_t = \frac{\beta x_t (1-\eta)}{(1+\beta)(\phi x_t - \theta + k_t)}. \tag{10}$$

From the equation derived above for n_t, it is clear that the number of children or the fertility rate of the parent is nonincreasing with the transportation costs as a fraction of labor income. Thus parents have to pay to educate their children.

The labor market condition required for equilibrium analysis is

$$L_t = P_t \left(\int_0^\infty h_t (1 - \phi n_t) dF_t(h_t) - \int_0^\infty n_t e_t \overline{h}_t dF_t(h_t) \right). \tag{11}$$

On the right-hand side of the equation is aggregate labor demand, and also on the right-hand side is labor supplied by households in efficiency units. At equilibrium the human capital of individuals is equal to the average human capital of the society, so we can rewrite the labor market condition as

$$L_t = P_t \left(\int_0^\infty \overline{h}_t (1 - \phi n_t - n_t e_t) dF_t(\overline{h}_t) \right). \tag{12}$$

In other words, as equation (12) shows, time devoted to teaching is not available for working parents. Based on the conditions above, we have again equilibrium of the economy defined as in section 2.1.2.

Proposition 1 (*Quantity–quality trade-off*[7]) *Skilled workers invest more in quality than quantity of offspring, that is, investment in education of offspring increases with the relative human capital of parents and number of offspring decreases with the relative human capital of parents.*

Proposition 1 is a well-documented fact, and we can prove it by taking simple derivatives of equation (9) and (10) with respect to x_t. That is, parents with higher relative human capital spend more on the education of their children and at the same time have a smaller number of children. Hence the quality–quantity trade-off is another way of saying that rich people end up improving the quality of their children's lives and poor people end up procreating more children whose lots in life they cannot improve ($\partial e_t/\partial x_t > 0$ and $\partial n_t/\partial x_t < 0$). In fact this trade-off suggests that the cost of education is fixed while the time cost of rearing many children increases with income.

Proposition 2 *Transportation costs negatively impact fertility decisions of the parents.*

To prove proposition 2, we use equation (10). The fertility decisions obtained in equation (10) are derived with respect to transportation costs. Hence there is a negative impact of transportation costs on the number of children parents give birth to.

Balanced Growth Path

The balanced growth path (BGP) is used to study the dynamic behavior of the economy. To do so, we can express the equilibrium conditions in terms of the variables that are kept constant. We can write the growth rate of average human capital, the population growth rate N_t, distribution of relative human capital levels, and deflated level of average human capital $\tilde{h}$ as

$$g_t = \frac{\bar{h}_{t+1}}{\bar{h}_t}, \quad N_t = \frac{P_{t+1}}{P_t}, \quad G_t(x_t) = F_t(x_t\bar{h}_t), \quad \tilde{h} = \frac{\bar{h}}{(1+\sigma)^t}.$$

We then use these variables to rewrite equations (4), (5), and (6) as follows:

$$N_t = \int_0^\infty n_t dG_t(x_t), \tag{13}$$

$$G_{t+1}(x) = \frac{1}{N_t}\int_0^\infty n_t I(x_{t+1} \le x) dG_t(x_t), \tag{14}$$

$$1 = \int_0^\infty x_t dG_t(x_t). \tag{15}$$

At equilibrium, at the firm level, marginal costs equalize marginal productivity. So we have from equation (7),

$$w_t = A \quad (16).$$

To find the range of fertility rate, we use equation (9), which denotes the fertility rate of parents with higher human capital level. Parents with low human capital levels, end up producing more number of children instead of attending to the education quality of the children. The fertility rate of the parents with low human capital level is given by

$$n_t = \frac{\beta}{\phi(1+\beta)}.$$

The range of fertility rates in terms of x_t is

$$n_t = \text{Min}\left[\frac{(1-\eta)\beta x_t}{(\varphi x_t + k_t - \theta)(1+\beta)}, \frac{\beta}{\varphi(1+\beta)}\right]. \tag{17}$$

From equation (2) and proposition 2, we can derive the equation of human capital of the children as

$$x_{t+1} = \frac{Bx_t^{\tau}}{g_t}\left(\theta + Max\left[0, \frac{\eta(\varphi x_t + k_t) - \theta}{(1-\eta)}\right]\right)^{\eta}(\tilde{h})^{\tau+\kappa-1}. \tag{18}$$

The labor market-clearing condition, as expressed in (11), then becomes

$$\frac{L_t}{P_t \bar{h}_t} = \int_0^{(\theta - k_t\eta)/\eta\varphi} \frac{(1+\beta)x_t}{1+\beta+\gamma} dG_t(x_t) + \int_{(\theta - k_t\eta)/\eta\varphi}^{\infty} \left(1 - \gamma\frac{\varphi(1-\eta)x_t + (\eta\varphi x_t + k_t - \theta)}{(\varphi x_t + k_t - \theta)(1+\beta+\gamma)}\right) x_t dG_t(x_t). \tag{19}$$

Now we can apply the balanced growth path analysis to study the long-run behavior of the economy.

Proposition 3 *In the long run, for given k, every individual in the economy has the same level of human capital ($dG(1) = 1$) and also ($\phi + k$) > θ; then there is a balanced growth path and growth factor of output growth and human capital is given by* $g^* = B(\eta(\varphi + k - \theta)/(1-\eta))^{\eta}$.

By the conditions mentioned in proposition 3, every individual is endowed with same level of human capital, that is, $h_t = \overline{h}_t$. Hence relative human capital of each individual is $x_t = \overline{h}_t / \overline{h}_t = 1$. In words, every child will be able to attend school, so we have a maximum schooling effect. Based on the condition that there is endogenous growth ($\kappa = 1 - \tau$) and using equations (13), (14), (15), (17), and (18), we can write

$$1 = \frac{B1}{g^*}\left(\theta + \frac{\eta(\varphi x_t + k) - \theta}{(1-\eta)}\right)^{\eta} (\tilde{h})^0,$$
$$g^* = B\left(\frac{\eta(\varphi + k - \theta)}{(1-\eta)}\right)^{\eta}. \tag{20}$$

Hence we have proved proposition 3. By assumption then, at $(\phi + k) > \theta$ at equilibrium, there is a positive growth in this setting. To interpret the results, it is important to remember that k is introduced to account for the transportation spending of parents on their children's travel from home to school. In other words, k captures in this model the importance of population mobility in terms of more schooling, and that as more and more children attend school, growth is achieved. The proportional relationship of k with g represents importance of getting individuals educated for economic growth of the economy.

Corollary 1 *Steady-state growth rate is positively impacted by k.*

Following on the derived formula for growth factor of output growth in proposition 4, $g^* = B(\frac{\eta(\varphi+k-\theta)}{(1-\eta)})^{\eta}$. Now deriving g^* with respect to k gives

$$\frac{\partial g^*}{\partial k} = \frac{\partial B\left(\frac{\eta(\varphi + k - \theta)}{(1-\eta)}\right)^{\eta}}{\partial k},$$
$$\frac{\partial g^*}{\partial k} > 0.$$

Hence steady-state growth is positively impacted by k and proved.

3.2.2 Residing in a School District

As we mention above, our study investigates the various ways that residential location can impact parental fertility and child education decisions, and hence the economic growth of an economy. We start with an example where parents pay transportation costs to reach their workplaces, but for children going to school, no transportation costs are incurred. In the real world this is the practice in Belgium where children are exempted from paying for transportation. In this situation there is no change in the optimizing utility equation and constraints other than the budget constraint, which becomes

$$c_t + k_t\bar{h}_t w_t + e_t\bar{h}_t n_t w_t = w_t h_t(1-\phi n_t - q),$$

where q is a constant representing the time it takes for an individual to reach his/her workplace. Solving the optimization program using the Lagrangian technique, we obtain the following effective equations for education and number of children:

$$e_t = \frac{\phi h_t \eta - \bar{h}_t \theta}{\bar{h}_t(1-\eta)}, \tag{21}$$

$$n_t = \frac{\beta(h_t(1-q) - k_t\bar{h}_t)(1-\eta)}{(\phi h_t - \bar{h}_t\theta)(1+\beta)}. \tag{22}$$

Equation (21) shows that education costs are independent of the transportation costs incurred by parents. Equation (22) shows that the transportation costs incurred by parents and the time they spend in travel negatively impact the number of children they beget.

Proposition 4 *In the long run, for given k, every individual in the economy has the same level of human capital ($dG(1) = 1$) and also $\phi > \theta$; then there is a balanced growth path and growth factor of output growth and human capital given by*

$$g^* = B\left(\eta\left(\frac{\varphi-\theta}{1-\eta}\right)\right)^{\eta}. \tag{23}$$

The proof of proposition 3 can be used to prove this formula as well. By assumption of proposition 4, at $\phi > \theta$ there is a positive growth in this setting. Unlike the results obtained in the section 2.1, here economic growth is independent of transportation costs. This is because, by proposition 4, parents have already decided to reside near a school, so the schooling decision is independent of the transportation costs incurred by parents.

3.2.3 Parents as well as Children Incur Transportation Costs

Suppose that parents choose instead to reside away from their workplaces as well as from schools. These parents would need to pay for transportation costs incurred both by them as well as and by their children. But as the case before, there is no change in the optimizing utility equation and other constraints except for the budget constraint, which becomes

$$c_t + k_t \bar{h}_t w_t + (e_t + k_t) n_t \bar{h}_t w_t = w_t h_t (1 - \phi n_t - q).$$

Solving the optimization program using the Lagrangian technique, we obtain the following effective equations for education and number of children:

$$e_t = \frac{\eta(h_t \phi + k_t \bar{h}_t) - \bar{h}_t \theta}{\bar{h}_t (1-\eta)}. \tag{24}$$

$$n_t = \frac{\beta(1-\eta)(h_t - q h_t - k_t \bar{h}_t)}{(h_t \phi - \theta \bar{h}_t + k_t \bar{h}_t)(1+\beta)}. \tag{25}$$

From equation (24), we see that education costs are dependent on the transportation costs incurred by parents but strictly because of the commuting by the children to school. From equation (25), it is clear that transportation costs incurred and time spent by parents in traveling impact the number of children negatively.

Proposition 5 *In the long run, for the given k, every individual in the economy has the same level of human capital* ($dG(1) = 1$) *and also* ($\phi + k$) > θ*. Thus there is a balanced growth path and growth factor of output growth and human capital given by*

$$g^* = B\left(\frac{\eta(\varphi + k - \theta)}{(1-\eta)}\right)^{\eta}. \tag{26}$$

The proof of equation (26) is the same as that which we used to prove proposition 3. The difference in this setting is that the parental decision to educate their offspring impacts economic growth.

3.2.4 Station Location Policy

For the infrastructure allocation policy we consider a location in continuous space. The cohort of individuals born at the same date are distributed uniformly throughout this space. The individuals in each cohort have different human capital h, given by the distribution $F_t(h_t)$. The migration of households is only acceptable when people are optimizing the distance for commuting and decide to reside near school or near work.

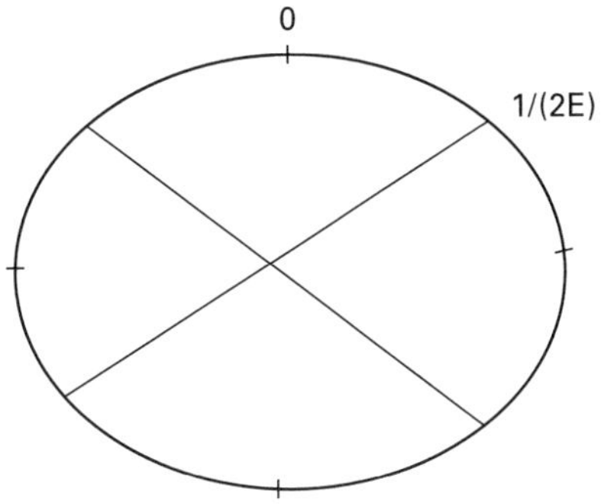

Figure 3.3
Station location policy

We assume the existence of a central authority that determines the optimal number of transport stations to be built in this space. The setup cost for implementing a new transport facility (train station) is C. If no station is created, the transportation costs are infinite. The first assumption comes from the logical realization that building cost of the new station is inversely proportional to total population present in each area. At each date, a number E of stations are created to serve the population. The framework we use follows that of Bos (1965) and Boucekkine et al. (2007). We further assume that the population is heterogeneous with respect to human capital level and is distributed not only uniformly in the space but also uniformly around the stations. This way we consider the transportation costs to be a function of distance, so as the distance from a destination is reduced, the transportation costs will decrease as well.

Now, because the population is evenly spaced, the optimal setting is for stations to be equidistantly and uniformly distributed. To avoid indeterminacy, we can assume that there is a station located at 0 and other locations given by $(j - 1)/E$, where $j = 1, \ldots, E$. The potential catchment area of the station is shown in figure 3.3. The circular segment in the figure is denoted by $[-1/(2E), 1/(2E)]$.

By assumption, a population with higher level human capital will use the station facility, and a similar assumption can be applied for the residential distance from a station. As the distance increases, fewer people (those with high-level human capital) will use the facility. To keep calculations simple, we will impose a homogeneity condition on the population's human capital level wherever feasible. But first we will consider the important factors/conditions for the erection of single station also in terms of a simple geographical interpretation.

Population Dynamics

Let us assume that the rate of growth of population is equal to the fertility rate, so that the total population can be treated as endogenous in this model. Then the equation for total population from equation (5) is

$$P_{t+1} = P_t \int_0^\infty n_t dF_t(h_t), \tag{27}$$

where P_{t+1} is the total population present at time $t + 1$, P_t is the population present at time t, and n_t is total fertility rate at time t.

Incentive for Central Authority to Build Infrastructure

Every individual in the population uses the transportation facility. Since there is heterogeneity in the human capital of the population, it is important for the central authority to determine how to profitably distribute the station facility. To make calculations simple, we will suppose that central authority foresees the demographic growth and can accordingly decide on the transportation costs to charge individuals and the number of stations to be built. So in this instance of perfect foresight by central authority as to demography, we have a population $t + 1$ to consider for transportation costs at time t. The nominal benefits brought about by each station are thus

$$\int_0^\infty k_t A h_t P_{t+1} dF_t(h_t),$$

where P_{t+1} is the population at time $t + 1$, h_t is the human capital at time t, and A is introduced to control for technological progress. And hence the profit function of the facility becomes

$$\Pi(k_t) = \int_0^\infty k_t A h_t P_{t+1} dF_t(h_t) - C, \tag{28}$$

and after substituting equation (5), we have

$$\Pi(k_t) = \int_0^\infty k_t A h_t P_t \int_0^\infty n_t dF_t(h_t) dF_t(h_t) - C. \tag{29}$$

Proposition 6 *Given a homogeneity of human capital in the population, no stations will be built in the region if* $P_{t+1} < C \Big/ \left[\int_0^\infty k_t A\overline{h}_t dF_t(\overline{h}_t)\right]$; *that is, if the costs of building stations are not covered by aggregate benefits, then no stations are built.*

As proposition 6 states, given a population that is homogeneous in human capital (i.e., at human capital level $\overline{h}_t$), equation (28) on the profitability of the facility can be rewritten as

$$\Pi(k_t) = \int_0^\infty k_t A\overline{h}_t P_{t+1} dF_t(\overline{h}_t) - C.$$

For any loss-making station facility, we would rewrite the equation above as

$$\int_0^\infty k_t A\overline{h}_t P_{t+1} dF_t(\overline{h}_t) - C < 0.$$

After rearranging for P_{t+1}, we have

$$P_{t+1} < \frac{C}{\int_0^\infty k_t A\overline{h}_t dF_t(\overline{h}_t)}. \tag{30}$$

Thus proved, proposition 6 can be used to determine the threshold level on the populationthat would make the station facility profitable.

Lemma 1 *At* $k_t \cong 0$, *the facility, with given benefit function, turns into the loss-making entity.*

As explained earlier, benefit function is a linear function of transportation cost as a fraction of labor income, which is, k_t, written as

$$\Pi(k_t) = \int_0^\infty k_t A h_t P_{t+1} dF_t(h_t) - C.$$

At $k_t \cong 0$, the equation becomes

$$\Pi(k_t) = [0 - C]$$
$$= -C.$$

Hence lemma 1 is proved.

Lemma 2 *Properties of* $\Pi(k)$

1. $\Pi(k)$ is obviously a continuous function.
2. Limits on the profit function as k_t grows infinitely are

$$\lim \Pi(k_t) = -C,$$

$$k_t w_t \bar{h}_t \to 0;$$

$$\lim \Pi(k_t) = indefinite\ (-C \text{ or } \infty),$$

$$k_t w_t \bar{h}_t \to \infty.$$

Lemma 3 *The optimization problem of* $\Pi(k_t)$ *at* $E > 0$ *admits a solution* K, *such that for all* $k > K$, *the profit of the entity enters into a loss,* $\Pi(k_t) < 0$.

By lemma 3, we have an assumed level of transportation cost as a fraction of labor income; that is, K denotes the affordability of the availed facility for the population. With the ticket set at $k > K$, no one uses the facility and the facility turns into a loss-making entity. Affordable levels of ticket pricing based on population income is well explained in Boucekkine et al. (2007) and is useful to recall here.

It can also be said that the optimization problem admits a maximum at $k \in [0; K]$.

$$\frac{\partial \Pi(k)}{\partial k_t}(0) = \int_0^\infty A h_t P_{t+1} dF_t(h_t),$$

$$\frac{\partial \Pi(k)}{\partial k_t}(0) > 0.$$

This is also a global maximum because of the condition already obtained: $\Pi(k_t = 0) = -CE$ for all $k > K$.

Proposition 7 *In the case where* $\bar{k} = \bar{k}(E)$, *a unique and global optimal solution for* (k) *exists and the maximized profit is necessarily nonnegative.*

By proposition 7, the optimal transportation cost is assumed to be a fraction of labor income $\bar{k}$ and independent of the fixed cost incurred; that is, C, which is a function of the number of stations available in the region, E. The condition of positive profitability of the facility suggests the necessity of condition $\int_0^\infty \bar{k}(E) A h_t P_{t+1} dF_t(h_t) \geq C$. As it could be derived from implicit theorem, $\bar{k}(E)$ is a differential function, and as a result of which, $\xi(E) = \int_0^\infty \bar{k}(E) A h_t P_{t+1} dF_t(h_t)$ is also a continuous and a differential function. But because we have $E \rightarrow \infty$, the rate at which population uses a station facility, its use goes to almost zero, since $\bar{k}(E) < \bar{k}$, where $\bar{k}$ is the optimized transportation cost for maximum profit. Hence our study requires a boundary condition to be set on the number of stations being built in order to achieve a positive or zero-profit condition, that is, nonnegative profits. Yet a nonzero condition on the number of station facilities will still hold because the positive profitability condition will not hold for $E = 0$. Hence we can state the optimization problem with respect to (E) mathematically as

$$S = \{k \in R^2 : 0 \le E;\ \xi(E) \geqslant C;\ 0 \le k \le \bar{k}\}.$$

The set S is a compact subset of R^2, and because $\Pi(k)$ is continuous in (k), it must reach a maximum in S. The nonnegativity of the profit comes immediately from the above-mentioned definitions of $\bar{k}$ and $\xi(E)$.

Alternative Specifications

Besides studying the optimal behavior of the central authority for static profits, we construct two alternative specifications, as we describe next.

Case I (Intertemporal Profits) The profit function in equation (31) is a problem of static optimization. But it can be used to study the intertemporal profits for each public infrastructure facility by considering all the sequences of transportation costs and the profit function:

$$\Pi = \int_0^\infty \delta^t \Pi(k_t)dt,$$
$$\Pi = \int_0^\infty \delta^t \left(\int_0^\infty k_t A h_t P_t \int_0^\infty n_t dF_t(h_t) dF_t(h_t) - C\right)dt, \tag{31}$$

where Π is the intertemporal profits of the public facility, and δ is the discount factor.

Case II (Zero Profits) Although it does not occur in reality, the zero-profit condition on the central authority is considered here as welfare enhancing. The mathematical specification of the model at zero profits thus becomes

$$\Pi(k_t) = 0,$$
$$\int_0^\infty k_t A \overline{h_t} P_{t+1} dF_t(h_t) - C = 0, \tag{32}$$

which implies that

$$\int_0^\infty k_t A\overline{h_t} P_{t+1} dF_t(h_t) = C.$$

While it may not be possible to impose welfare-enhancing zero-profit conditions on a central authority in fast-growing countries like India, where investment funds for infrastructure are so crucial, it is nevertheless a conceivable outcome.

3.2.5 Equilibrium Analysis with Endogenous Transportation Costs

After determining station locations and exogenous transportation costs in our model, we attempted to endogenize the transportation costs. To do so, we relaxed our assumption of heterogeneity in the level of human capital of the population. Hence we assumed a simplified economy filled with a homogeneous level of human capital.[8] Then we solved the equation for the first-order condition with respect to k_t, and obtained

$$k = \frac{\phi - \theta}{\beta}. \tag{33}$$

The result for the homogeneous human capital level condition proved that transportation costs would amount to a fraction of labor income. After substituting this value of k, we recalculated the growth rate for endogenous transportation costs as

$$g^* = B\left(\frac{\eta\left(\varphi + \frac{\varphi - \theta}{\beta} - \theta\right)}{(1-\eta)}\right)^\eta. \tag{34}$$

Note that the growth rate calculated above, although constant, is for endogenous transportation costs as well as endogenous demographics.

3.3 Empirical Evidence

Last we investigate the dynamics involving per capita GDP, population density, and net revenues of railways. We begin our analysis by reviewing the descriptive statistics of our three variables, and we apply a Granger causality test to verify if population density and net revenues significantly affect per capita GDP.

Table 3.1
Descriptive statistics for India, 1961 to 2012

Variables	1961–2012	1961–1971	1972–1982	1983–1993	1994–2004	2005–2012
GDP per capita	14195.38 (19969.07)	654.7165 (171.257)	1707.113 (538.0808)	5674.375 (2226.622)	19447.53 (5621.257)	54479.82 (17529.69)
Population density	276.261 (81.38411)	171.6948 (12.1807)	219.8414 (16.86065)	280.5388 (19.37357)	344.7019 (19.22815)	397.6283 (12.86031)
Net revenues of railways	2.32e+10 (3.61e+10)	1.23e+09 (2.05e+08)	2.07e+09 (1.13e+09)	8.74e+09 (5.05e+09)	3.10e+10 (1.00e+10)	9.19e+10 (4.52e+10)

Note: Mean and standard deviation (in brackets) are of per capita GDP, population density, and net revenues of railways over five decades, 1961 through 2012. Variable population density is measured in terms of number of people per square kilometer square of area. Variable total fertility rate is the number of children per woman. Net revenue of Indian railways is measured in Indian rupees. Similarly GDP per capita is measured in local currency units (Indian rupees).

3.3.1 Data Description

We gathered data on per capita GDP (in rupees) and population density (per square kilometer of land area) from the World Bank database for India. The data of net revenues (in rupees) earned by Indian railways were collected from the statistical reports on Indian railways' website. All time series used were at annual frequency. Based on data availability, we restricted our analysis to the 1961 to 2012 period. Table 3.1 gives the descriptive statistics of the time series we had in hand.

Table 3.1 shows that the means of per capita GDP, population density, and net revenues of railways did evolve over the five decades of the period 1961 to 2012. Note that per capita GDP only gradually increased over the sample period, with a significant increase beginning in the 1980s. Population density progressively increased through the sample period, whereas the net revenues of railways significantly fluctuated over the entire sample period.

3.3.2 Testing the Causality

We next transform the data into logs and perform augmented Dickey–Fuller (ADF) and Philips Perron unit root tests to check for evidence of nonstationary data. Both tests confirm that the time series of per capita GDP, population density, and net revenues of Indian Railways are nonstationary and integrated of order 1; I(1) series. As a result we base our causality testing on first-difference (i.e., stationary) data.

For the causality test, we used a three-equations system whereby each variable, GDP per capita, population density, and net revenues of railways, is expressed by lagged values of that variable and lagged values of two additional variables. The information criteria we used to select the optimal number of lags in our system was set at a number 4. This way we could use data in first difference, the variation of per capita GDP, population density, and net revenues of railways, with variations of their value levels over the past four years, as is consistent with their nature as low-frequency variables and with the policy cycles. We estimate the following three equations model:

$$GDP_t = \alpha + \sum_{i=1}^{p=4} A_1^i GDP_{t-i} + \sum_{i=1}^{p=4} A_2^i PopDens_{t-i} + \sum_{i=1}^{p=4} A_3^i NetRev_{t-i} + \epsilon_t^{GDP}, \tag{35}$$

$$PopDens_t = \beta + \sum_{i=1}^{p=4} B_1^i PopDens_{t-i} + \sum_{i=1}^{p=4} B_2^i GDP_{t-i} + \sum_{i=1}^{p=4} B_3^i NetRev_{t-i} + \epsilon_t^{PopDens}, \tag{36}$$

$$NetRev_t = \gamma + \sum_{i=1}^{p=4} C_1^i NetRev_{t-i} + \sum_{i=1}^{p=4} C_2^i GDP_{t-i} + \sum_{i=1}^{p=4} C_3^i PopDens_{t-i} + \epsilon_t^{NetRev}. \tag{37}$$

Since our aim is to investigate the dynamic relationships among per capita GDP, population density, and net revenues of railways, we want to learn the extent of causality among these three variables. That is, we want to see if population density and net revenues of railways Granger-cause per capita GDP in order to test our main hypothesis underlying the theoretical model we presented at the beginning of this chapter. We thus performed the following Wald causality test:

- For the GDP equation, the null hypothesis we tested is $H_0 : A_2^i = A_3^i = 0$.

That is, we are interested in testing whether the variations in population density and net revenues do not Granger-cause variations of per capita GDP, and that variations in per capita GDP can be explained only by its past variations. The rejection of this hypothesis implies that population density and net revenues of railways do Granger-cause GDP per capita, and that their past variations significantly explain the variation of per capita GDP.

- For the equation of population density, the null hypothesis we tested is $H_0 : B_2^i = B_3^i = 0$.

Table 3.2
Granger causality and Wald tests

Equation	Excluded	(Chi2)	#(lags)	Prob>Chi2
D.lGDP	D.lPopdens	4.0826	4	0.395
D.lGDP	D.lNetRev	8.4099	4	0.078**
D.lGDP	ALL	16.773	8	0.033***
D.lPopdens	D.lGDP	3.8182	4	0.431
D.lPopdens	D.lNetRev	3.9024	4	0.419
D.lPopdens	ALL	8.9155	8	0.349
D.lNetRev	D.lGDP	3.522	4	0.475
D.lNetRev	D.lPopdens	6.5784	4	0.160
D.lNetRev	ALL	9.3466	8	0.314

Note: *, **, and *** indicate the rejection of the null hypothesis at 1, 10, and 5 percent significance, respectively.

That is, we are interested in testing whether the variations in per capita GDP and net revenues do not Granger-cause variation of population density, and that variations in population density can be explained only by its past variations. The rejection of this hypothesis implies that per capita GDP and net revenues of railways do Granger-cause population density, and that their past variations help explain the variation of population density.

- For the equation of net revenues of railways, the null hypothesis we tested is $H_0 : C_2^i = C_3^i = 0$.

That is, we are interested in testing whether the variations in per capita GDP and population density do not Granger-cause variation of net revenues of railways, and that the variation of net revenues of railways can be explained only by its past variations. The rejection of this hypothesis implies that per capita GDP and population density do Granger-cause GDP per capita, that their past variations affect the variation of net revenues of railways, that is, profitability of the railway lines.

Results and Discussion

In table 3.2 we present the results of the Granger causality and Wald tests that we applied to our three-variables system. In the equation of per capita GDP, past values of population density proved not to Granger-cause per capita GDP variation; however, net revenues of railways proved to have statistically significant explanatory power for per capita GDP variation. Overall, the variation of per capita GDP were well explained by past values of population density and past values of net revenues of railways; that is, population density and net revenues of railways do Granger-cause per capita GDP variation. The Granger causality test for the equations of population density and net revenues of the railways show that each of these variables is significantly explained by only its past values; hence we accept the null hypothesis underlying the test of the equations of population density and net revenues.

The results we obtained are consistent with the theoretical predictions of our model. They basically suggest that profitability of the infrastructure providing facility (net revenues of Indian Railways) should drive more investment in infrastructure for the denser population. These new investments in infrastructure should result into improved access of basic services such as education and health for the population, and hence translate into economic growth of the region via population-induced productivity improvements. However, our analysis did encounter some limitations. The first and foremost is that we could not find any causal impact of population density on income growth. This result somewhat undermines the claims of human capital theory, but it does support our theoretical claim that population density alone does not translate into income growth unless basic infrastructure is provided. Indeed, over the years 1961 to 2012, while a substantial increase in population density occurred, there was no complementary increase in infrastructure-providing facilities. Another limitation was that our study could not benefit from the availability of data on actual infrastructure indicators, such as length of railway tracks, road density, and number of stations. For example, we could not take into account the road transportation infrastructure significantly enlarged since the 1950s (35 percent of total share of transportation in 1950s, 85 percent in 2000s).

3.4 Conclusion

The existing literature on factors influencing economic growth is broadly distinguished by two strands of theory: human capital theory and physical capital theory. In models of human capital theory, economic growth is achieved through accumulation of human capital resulting in productivity improvements; in models of physical capital theory, economic growth is based on huge infrastructure investments leading to creation of the capital stock required for growth. In this chapter we argued that for economic growth, both contributions of population-induced productivity improvements and optimally available infrastructure are essential.

Our main contribution is that we show the importance of the microfoundations of geographical interpretations in studying the effect of population density on growth. In our model setting, the location of transport facility is chosen optimally either to maximize the profit of the infrastructure providing facility or to increase the welfare of the society. As a result higher population density increases the number of facilities, and given the higher returns to education, individuals invest in schooling to reduce the distances children need to travel to schools. This development can stimulate an economically stagnated economy. An important limitation of theoretical model is that the parental decision to reside, that is, to choose where to locate, is assumed as given. This is a crucial issue when considering the massive rural–urban migration that takes place during the development phase of a country.

Second, we tested our predictions using a three-variables equations system and both Granger causality and Wald tests on the time-series data for the years 1961 to 2012 in India. We find that population density, and the profitability of infrastructure-providing facility, did indeed induce economic growth in the region.

Notes

We would like to thank two anonymous referees, and Raouf Boucekkine (GREQAM, AMSE and CORE, UCL), Patrick Pintus (AMSE), Michel Lubrano (AMSE), and Asim Afridi (INSERM) for their reviews and useful comments. We would also like to thank attendees for their comments at the RCEF conference (University of Toronto), CSAE conference (Oxford University) and CESifo Workshop at Venice.

1. Please see brain drain literature such as Fan and Stark (2007).

2. Please see http://www.unicef.org/india/1_Overview_(03-12-2012).pdf for more information suggesting that leading source states of interregional migration in India are Uttar Pradesh and Bihar.

3. This might have also resulted into increase in urbanization. According to World Bank estimates, urban share of total population was nearly 18 percent in 1961, which increased to 31 percent in 2010.

4. The term infrastructure, of course, refers any public facility provided by a central authority, but for simplicity, we have restricted the use of the term to the education and transportation facilities.

5. The wage in terms of efficiency units here indicate that the wages are measured in output per worker per hour.

6. Following De la Croix and Doepke (2003), the price of the consumption good is assumed to be normalized to 1.

7. Quality–quantity trade-off is between family size and child education quality, originally introduced in Becker (1960). Simply speaking, a rise in family size raises the cost of providing an average child with education, such as would induce parents to reduce per capita monetary and time investment in their children.

8. This makes all the integrations in the profit function vanish.

References

Agénor, P. 2010. A Theory of infrastructure-led development. *Journal of Economic Dynamics and Control* 34 (5): 932–50.

Becker, G. 1960. An economic analysis of fertility. In NBER, ed., *Demographic and Economic Change in Developed Countries*. Princeton: Princeton University Press, 209–40.

Becker, G., E. Glaeser, and K. Murphy. 1999. Population and economic growth. *American Economic Review* 89 (2): 145–49.

Beyzatlar, M. A., and Y. Kuştepeli. 2011. Infrastructure, economic growth and population density in Turkey. *International Journal of Economic Sciences and Applied Research* 4 (3): 39–57.

Bos, H. C. 1965. *Spatial Dispersion of Economic Activity*. Rotterdam: Rotterdam University Press.

Boucekkine, R., D. Croix, and D. Peters. 2007. Early literacy achievements, population density, and the transition to modern growth. *Journal of the European Economic Association* 5 (1): 183–226.

Croix, D., and M. Doepke. 2003. Inequality and growth: Why differential fertility matters. *American Economic Review* 93 (4): 1091–1113.

Fan, C. S., and O. Stark. 2007. The brain drain, "educated unemployment," human capital formation, and economic betterment. *Economics of Transition* 15 (4): 629–60.

Fujita, M., and J. F. Thisse. 2002. *Economics of Agglomeration: Cities, Industrial Location, and Regional Growth*. Cambridge, UK: Cambridge University Press.

Galor, O., and D. N. Weil. 2000. Population, technology, and growth: From Malthusian stagnation to the demographic transition and beyond. *American Economic Review* 90 (4): 806–28.

Galor, O. 2005. From stagnation to growth: Unified growth theory. *Handbook of Economic Growth* 1: 171–293.

Galor, O., and A. Mountford. 2008. Trading population for productivity: Theory and evidence. *Review of Economic Studies* 75 (4): 1143–79.

Glover, D. R., and J. L. Simon. 1975. The effect of population density on infrastructure: The case of road building, economic development and cultural change. *Economic Development and Cultural Change* 23 (3): 453–68.

Rangazas, P. 2000. Schooling and economic growth: A King–Rebelo experiment with human capital. *Journal of Monetary Economics* 46 (2): 397–416.

Rosenstein-Rodan, Paul N. 1943. Problems of industrialization of Eastern and South-eastern Europe. *Economic Journal* 53 (210/211): 202–11.

4 Infrastructure Funding and Financing: Safeguarding Value for Money in Public–Private Partnerships

Martina Santandrea, Stephen J. Bailey, and Marco Giorgino

4.1 Public–Private Partnerships in Infrastructure Provisioning

The strategy undertaken by the public sector to procure infrastructures and related services has impacts on its short- and long-term financial exposure no matter whether assets are accounted for on or off the public sector balance sheet. Through conventional public procurement, the public sector treats infrastructure investments as capital expenditures. Alternatively, the public sector can contract out the infrastructure provision to a private contractor and pay the private partner for such a provision.

Public–private partnerships (PPPs) exemplify the latter case, since they are a model for procuring infrastructures and related services through a long-term regulated contract between the public sector (i.e., buyer) and private sector (i.e., seller). The contract bundles the infrastructure building and subsequent service provision so as to secure the private sector's return on investment. The public sector is committed to pay unitary charges to compensate the private sector for the infrastructure provision, operations, and management.

PPPs have been studied as a means to maximize the value for money (VfM) of infrastructure provision through an effective risk-sharing between the public and private sectors (HM Treasury 2006). Theoretically PPPs are preferred to conventional public procurement when the investments in efficiency enhancement are relatively cheap (Bentz et al. 2005) and when the quality of services can be easily specified ex ante while the quality of the building cannot be (Hart 2003). Indeed, when the bundling of infrastructure building and operation generates positive externalities, the builder has incentives to make more productive investments ex ante so as to decrease the costs of the subsequent service provision (Bennett and Iossa 2006; Iossa and Martimort 2008;

Martimort and Pouyet 2008). As such, advocates stress that PPPs are more often delivered on time and on budget compared to conventional procurement (HM Treasury 2003; National Audit Office 2009). If the private sector has higher skill, expertise, and innovative capacity than the public sector, PPPs can promote cost-savings and efficiency strategies in the delivery of infrastructures and services. Nevertheless, critics of PPPs note that risk transfer to the private sector can be set so as to be sufficient to demonstrate VfM of PPPs, disguising the real risk exposure of the public sector (Froud 2003). This has raised concern about a questionable allocation of risk, possibly biased in favor of PPPs (Shaoul 2005). Further, in cases of poor accounting standards, renegotiation of PPP contracts allow governments to elude spending caps, since neither the additional investments nor the future obligations are accounted on balance sheet (Engel et al. 2009).

The impact of PPPs on the public sector's financial exposure has also been considered in the literature (Spackman 2002; Engel et al. 2013). PPPs have been used as a means for levering private-sector funding in infrastructure procurement so as to address public budget constraints. In cases where PPPs are used to accommodate administrative budget rules, they do not generate additionality[1] because costs are merely shifted from the capital to the revenue account (Quiggin 2004; Winch and Onishi 2012). The public sector has no formal capital expenditures and instead has to pay the ongoing unitary charges in the current expenditures that do not have to be capitalized. As such, the cost–benefits of the short-term avoidance of capital investments can be offset by future current expenditures (Engel et al. 2010, 2013). Overall, PPPs could potentially increase the efficiency of procurement and enable the cost of infrastructures to be repaid over time through unitary charges, though not alleviate the pressure on public finances "because all debts must be repaid in the end" (Hodge and Greve 2009: 34).

Despite these different views in the literature on VfM, evidence on the VfM of PPPs compared to conventional public procurement is still inconclusive. Empirical results are not comparable nor are they generalizable due to the wide use of case study research and to the difficulties in assessing the counterfactual alternative (Hodge and Greve 2009; Roehrich et al. 2014). Nonetheless, the actual public finance constraints require a closer look at the long-term financial implications of PPPs. Governments facing increased costs of borrowing are finding it ever more difficult to raise up-front capital investments for infrastructures. In particular, public investments for infrastructures in overindebted eurozone countries are constrained by public spending limits required by the EU Fiscal Compact.[2] Eurozone countries have had to reduce their liabilities and to ensure that their public budgets are kept in balance or in surplus (Masera 2012), thus favoring the use of those PPPs accounted off balance sheet.

In order to consider the long-term financial implications of PPPs, we extend the VfM framework to draw a conceptual distinction between funding and financing PPPs. We first discuss the mismatch between funding and financing and its different implications on short- and long-term public spending, and we provide an anecdotal example from the UK PPP policy field. The VfM framework is further explained in terms of additionality, economy, efficiency, effectiveness, and equity of procurement options. The framework is then applied to the public financial tools for the delivery of infrastructures.

4.2 Funding and Financing in Public–Private Partnerships

The conceptual distinction between funding and financing in PPPs makes clear the actual financial exposure of the public sector and the subsequent implications for public spending, regardless of the way liabilities are accounted on or off balance sheet.

In this chapter we use *funding* to refer to up-front investments for the provision of infrastructures and *financing* to refer to the revenues required to reimburse the providers/investors for the debt and operating costs they incur in providing the infrastructure and related services (Nuscheler and Roeder 2014; Biggar Economics 2014; Bailey 2013).[3] Consistent with this definition, the private sector is involved in PPP funding such that it provides debt-based (but with some relative minor equity) resources for the provision of public works. PPPs are thus considered to enhance the delivery of public services through private-sector investments and expertise, and the public-sector investments complement rather than substitute for private-sector funding. Financing of PPPs includes the financial resources used to remunerate the private sector for the provision of the infrastructure and related services. Since most infrastructure is not self-financing (i.e., revenues are not sufficient to repay the financiers), the public sector is often responsible for complementing the revenues of the private sector through current expenditures. As an example, user-pays PPPs occur when users pay directly for the facility or services (e.g., toll roads). The public sector can complement such revenues by paying shadow tolls (i.e., subsidizing all or part of the users' charge, the latter being a case of matching financing). The public sector may also guarantee a minimum level of payment if tolls do not generate sufficient revenues for the private sector. Unitary charge PPPs occur when the public sector pays the private sector for the availability of a given infrastructure facility and the services related to it (e.g., hospitals and health care services) through a single unified payment incorporating both payments for infrastructure and services. Unitary charges are set to pay back the capital investment (i.e., availability fee) and to remunerate the private sector for the service delivered (i.e., facilities management fee).

4.2.1 Mismatch of Funding and Financing

The conceptual distinction between funding and financing has diverse implications for the short- and long-term public spending in PPPs. PPPs allow the public sector to avoid short-term funding of infrastructures (i.e., capital investments). Nevertheless, the public sector is still contractually committed in the long-term financing of PPPs through unitary charges accounted as current expenditures.

Figure 4.1 shows the temporal mismatch occurring between funding and financing infrastructures via PPPs. The private sector provides funds during the planning and construction phases (phase A and phase B) while the public sector finance back the infrastructure over the whole operational phase (phase C) through unitary charges. Indeed, even if revenues are generated by user charges during the operational phase C, they can be insufficient to remunerate the private sector, and moreover their stability depends on the nature of the project. For example, health infrastructures tend to have stable returns due to both stable demand for health services and public financing which may complement any private revenue. Stable revenues are also associated with market regulation and the stability of incentives. For example, power generation is usually regulated by the national authority and may generate more stable returns when market cash flows are complemented by public financing. Otherwise, stability of cash flows depends on the economic situation. For example, road infrastructures may generate less toll revenues when oil prices are high if people switch to public transport, so reducing private transport.

Finally, the terminal value phase (phase D) identifies the end of the infrastructure's life and implies the decision to repurchase or dismantle it. Whether infrastructure's terminal value is positive depends on whether infrastructure assets can be sold (e.g., land) to generate

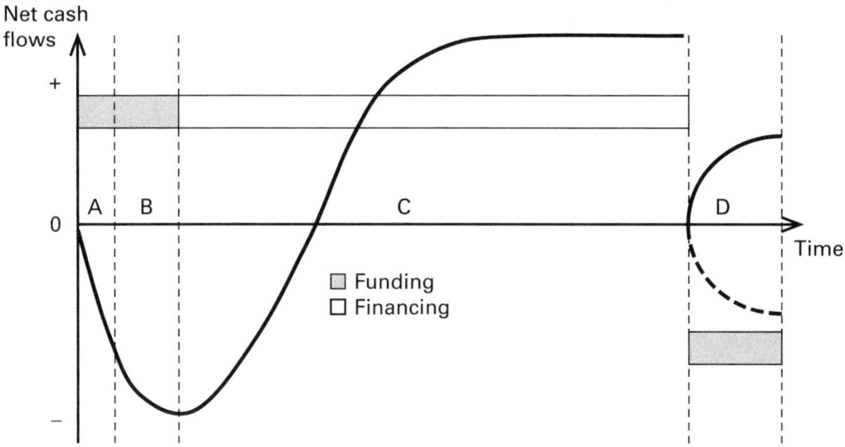

Figure 4.1
Purely illustrative net cash flow pattern of infrastructure projects. (A) Planning phase; (B) construction phase; (C) operational phase; (D) terminal value. "Time" refers to the duration of a PPP contract. The duration of phases A and B relative to each other depends on the type of infrastructure. The illustrated cash flow pattern applies for greenfield projects (i.e., new projects that have to be built and thus include the construction phase) rather than brownfield projects (i.e., projects that are already built but need to be renewed) for which the amount of expenditures is usually lower than for greenfield.

positive cash flows. In principle, the more adaptable the infrastructure, the higher is the probability it can be adapted for other uses (e.g., buildings with movable internal walls can be more easily made suitable for other uses) or sold and, ceteris paribus, the higher is the terminal value. When infrastructure's terminal value is negative, the infrastructure cannot be sold. In this case, phase D of the project bears dismantling costs whose amount depends on the type of project (e.g., dismantling costs for schools are lower than for nuclear plants which include the treatment of radioactive material). The dismantling costs imply new funding needs that are not covered by the project revenues, thus causing further mismatching between the funding and financing requirements and further financial obligations on the part of the public sector.

To provide a case example of the mismatch between funding and financing, we analyze the aggregate funding and financing requirements of the PPP policy in the United Kingdom. The dataset comprises PPP projects (725) signed in the United Kingdom from 1995 to March 2013.[4] We consider 695 projects after adjusting for missing data on capital value, unitary charges, and date of financial close. Descriptive

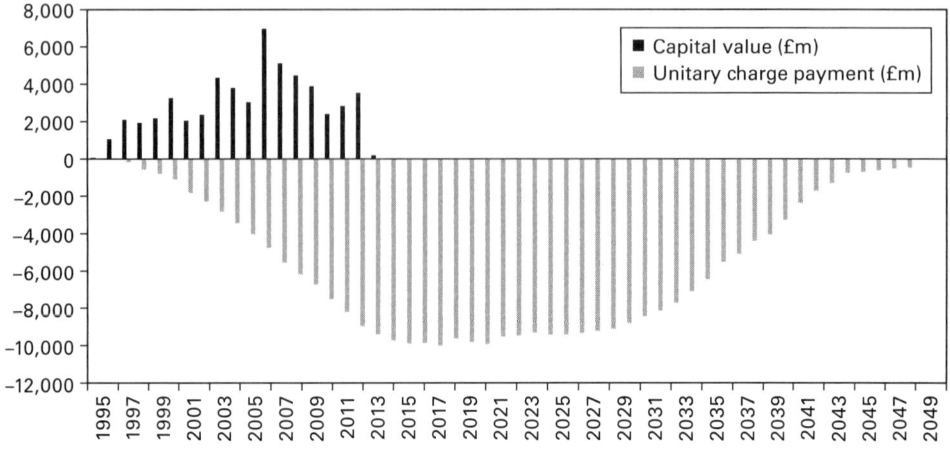

Figure 4.2
Capital investments and unitary charges

statistics are reported in table A4.1 in the appendix. The aggregate capital value of the analyzed projects is £53,163m that corresponds to the funding requirements of PPPs. In figure 4.2 we show the capital value of projects at the year of financial close and the unitary charges to be paid by the public sector to remunerate the projects over years. Total payments of unitary charges are increasing and will have the highest impact over the next decade. In the figure the effect is underestimated since it does not include the pipeline of new projects and the projects currently under procurement.

The mismatch between finding and financing makes PPPs affordable in the short term, shifting the burden of liabilities from capital to future current expenditures and leaving it unclear whether they will be sustainable in the long term (Hellowell and Pollock 2007). Indeed it is claimed in the literature that contracts lock in the public sector and decrease its ability to respond to financial and social changes occurring over the whole duration of the PPP contracts (Froud 2003; Lonsdale 2005), thus decreasing the democratic accountability of public resources (Flinders 2005; Shaoul 2011; Toms et al. 2011). For example, the public-sector partner might be committed to repay its private-sector partner even in times of unexpectedly severe budget constraints and spending limits and/or to guarantee a contractually defined return to the private sector for infrastructures that are underutilized. Nonetheless, in a comparative fashion, through conventional public procurement the public

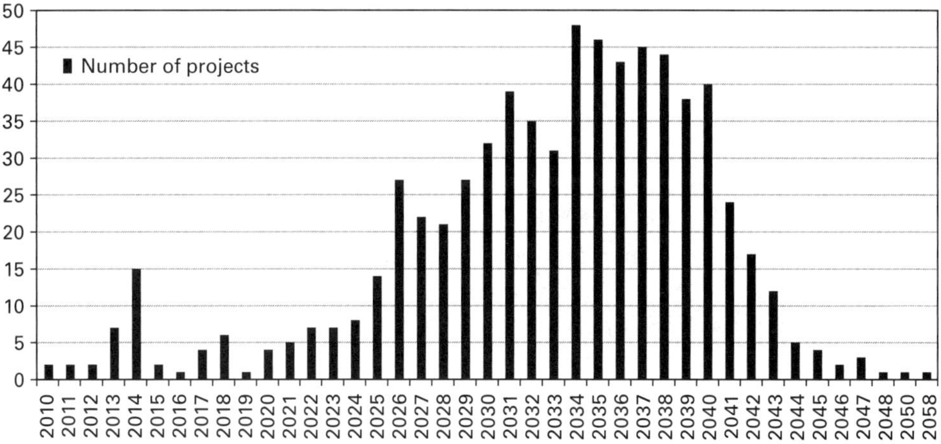

Figure 4.3
Year of contracts termination. The year of contract termination is computed as the first date of operation and the contract duration. If the first date of operation was not available (169 project), year of contract termination is computed as the date of financial close and the contract duration, thus underestimating the date of contract termination.

sector does still have to pay for the operations and management of infrastructures through current expenditures. As such, to assess the long-term implications for public spending, it is important to consider not only the amount spent for an infrastructure's operations and management but also its flexibility to respond to public finance constraints.

Finally, the PPP contract termination can lead to new funding requirements in cases where, for example, the infrastructure needs to be dismantled. As in conventional procurement, it is especially critical that there be forward planning of a PPP contract termination (figure 4.3 shows the termination year of PPP contracts), as along with the burden of operational contracts and managing a pipeline of new projects, time-expired contracts can be expected to have an impact on public budgets.

Overall, the avoidance of short-term capital expenditures does not directly imply a rationing of public spending, since the public sector must remain committed to financing infrastructure. Yet the use of conventional public procurement can be potentially unfeasible in cases of severe public finance constraints and spending limits. The decision-making between conventional public procurement and contracting out via PPPs has therefore to include the long-term financing implications of short-term funding so as to sustain VfM over time.

4.2.2 Value for Money in Infrastructure Provisioning

In the UK approach, PPPs are preferred to conventional public procurement in cases where they deliver higher VfM (HM Treasury 2006). The rationale for developing PPPs has been grounded in a 3Es approach comparing PPPs with conventional procurement in terms of economy (i.e., minimizing the costs of inputs), efficiency (i.e., maximizing the output given a specified amount of inputs), and effectiveness (i.e., the extent to which outputs deliver service objectives at minimum cost).

Although the 3Es approach had the potential to increase the efficiency of public procurement, it did not include long-term financing of accrued public-sector liabilities. For example, as noted by Winch and Onishi (2012), a purely cost-efficient strategy for funding infrastructures allowed the public sector to use private funding for immediate budgetary needs without regarding the full lifetime of the infrastructure so funded. The public sector would have had to continue to secure funds for financiers (through contractually required unitary charges) even in times of unexpectedly severe budget constraints and spending limits, thus raising equity issues about the intergenerational distribution of public resources (Mayston1999; Shaoul 2005). Inequity would arise because the contractually required unitary charges would commandeer public financing and so divert it from other services whose budgets are constrained.

In fact the 3Es approach failed to address equity issues (i.e., delivery of goods and services addressing the different levels of needs) since it focused on the *average* citizen's needs (i.e., the delivery of public services is standardized and homogeneous among all social groups) while not dealing with social issues such as unemployment and disadvantaged social groups (Norman-Major 2011; Andrews and van de Walle 2012).

The 4Es approach adds the concept of equity to the 3Es approach and considers *for whom* an organization is efficient, economical, and effective (Frederickson 2010). Equity refers to the distribution of public resources to different social groups within the current generation (i.e., intragenerational equity) and among different generations (i.e., intergenerational equity). Therefore, in contracting out infrastructures and related services, the 4Es approach to VfM has the potential to address the equity implications of different procurement options.

Intragenerational inequity may occur when the benefits of public services are concentrated on the few while their tax costs are spread over the whole population (Bailey 2004). The public interest test applied to PPPs can address intragenerational equity, since it is designed to ensure an adequate level of access to services, transparency, and disclosure of information to the general public, security of provision, and the achievement of the service requirements (Department of Treasury and Finance 2001). For intergenerational equity, it is instead necessary to assess the long-term equity implications of financing infrastructure. For intergenerational equity, future generations will need to make a contribution to the repayment of long-lived infrastructures from which they too will benefit. Requiring the current generation to pay the full capital cost would, of course, lead to intergenerational inequity. Intergenerational inequity can also occur in cases of cost and time overruns during the infrastructure delivery that are likely to impact not only within a generation but also on future generations. Time and cost overruns have occurred predominantly in conventional procurement rather than in PPPs (HM Treasury 2003; National Audit Office 2009).

Consideration of equity issues requires long-term predictions of not only who will be using the infrastructure but decisions on future financing.

4.2.3 Sustainability of Value for Money

Table 4.1 shows the analytical framework of VfM that we developed to distinguish funding and financing requirements for infrastructures as well as their equity implications for the sustainability of VfM. In making our distinction between funding and financing, we attempt to make explicit not only *who* provides funds for the delivery of infrastructures but also *who* is liable for financing the liquidation of those funds. Funding decisions require a short-term assessment of cost-efficient/effective strategies for infrastructure investment whereas financing decisions require longer term orientation since debt and equity obligations (i.e., contractual and noncontractual) have to be addressed until the end of the infrastructure's lifetime or PPP contract.

Additional public funding may be due, for example, when the public sector guarantees recovery of some minimum part of private funding or matches private funding at some percentage (i.e., indirect funding) rather than providing up-front payments (i.e., direct funding). Funding additionality can be achieved in the short term when a balancing of public and private capital expenditures is used to provide infrastructures and related services. Likewise VfM in the financing of infrastructure and related services can be achieved when public finance creates additionality in terms of additional net positive externalities generated when public financing complements private financing, such

Table 4.1
Analytical framework for VfM appraisal

		Public governance	
		Funding	Financing
	Additionality	Private-sector investment complements public-sector funding only when it creates additionality (and vice versa)	Public-sector financing complements user financing only when it creates positive externalities (and vice versa)
4Es	Economy	Minimize input and process cost of private and public funding	Economize/minimize the use of public financing
	Efficiency	Maximize outputs	Relate public financing with service delivery
	Effectiveness	Improve outcomes	Ensure public financing improves VfM of outcome objectives
	Equity	Implications of funding on both intergenerational and intragenerational equity	Implications of financing on both intergenerational and intragenerational equity

as in subsidizing fares levied on passengers using public transport schemes provided by PPPs. A related example would be the positive externalities that arise from decongestion of roads as people switch to trains and buses in response to subsidized fares. Financing additionality is a long-term consideration because it implies the balancing of future current expenditures so as to remunerate the private sector. Neither funding nor financing additionality is achieved through conventional public procurement since there is no integration between the public and private sectors' financial resources in infrastructure provision.

In the 3Es approach, benefit maximization is achieved when users pay the lowest price possible for the efficient and effective provision of goods and services. For example, funding a new road is determined by a mix of funding resources, provided at the lowest cost (e.g., kilometers of the new road or railway) for a given quality (e.g., of the road surface or track). In financing transport infrastructure, users would pay a transit toll or fare that should cover the costs they impose on the transit system and should be "fair." Both efficiency and fairness could be promoted by adoption of peak-load pricing so that those who determined the required capacity of the infrastructure would pay more than off-peak users. Within that tariff structure, low-income groups could qualify for subsidized fares or tolls so that fairness would be achieved both in paying for discretionary use and ability to pay and/or need for service so as to promote social inclusion (e.g., supporting the costs faced by disabled travelers). The same discourse on financing could be applied to conventional public procurement. Nonetheless, with conventional procurement the desired output can be achieved only through public resources, thus not providing the cost-efficient incentives characterizing PPPs.

The 4Es approach for VfM facilitates the assessment of how economy, efficiency, and effectiveness can be moderated to accommodate intergenerational and intragenerational equity. It addresses the issue that 3Es optimization of financing and funding would come at the cost of an increased intragenerational and/or intergenerational inequity. For example, it adds the consideration of *who* is liable for toll payment: users paying a real toll, taxpayers financing a shadow toll, or a combination of both forms of financing, now as well as in the future. The same equity consideration holds for the public-sector provision of infrastructure fully funded from current taxes because this causes intergenerational inequity in that the current generation subsidizes the future generation of users of that infrastructure. Moreover this holds for the reverse case where repayment of debt is repeatedly postponed by the use of further borrowing to refinance (i.e., refund), rather than liquidate, debt with the result that the current generation makes no contribution to financing, and all of the cost falls on future generations. There are even further equity issues relating to the distribution of the individual and social benefits (i.e., positive externalities) to different socioeconomic and demographic groups. Overall, equity depends not only on who has access to and uses that infrastructure but also on who pays for it.

Finally, public governance refers to the process through which the perception of VfM is determined, achieved and legitimized within an evolving multidimensional context. Indeed, because of this normative aspect, the concept of VfM cannot be universally and unequivocally defined. VfM is context-specific in being related to cultural, social, and economic contingencies. That is to say, what is perceived as VfM in one country may not be valued in other countries and what is currently perceived to be VfM may differ from what was considered value in the past or will be in the future. Hence perception of VfM evolves over time and so is a dynamic and contested normative concept.

4.3 Public Funding and Financing

Building on the previous section, we discuss the potential limitations to the sustainability of VfM within the VfM framework (see table A4.2 in the appendix). We apply the framework also to the public financial tools used for infrastructure and related service provision, and we consider their separate implications for safeguarding VfM.

The role of the public sector in funding and financing PPPs is claimed to potentially enhance private investments by increasing the confidence of potential financiers due to a "signaling effect" (EPEC 2011). Public support would signal to the private sector that the projects are valid investments, since the public sector is financially exposed on the project and/or bears the downside risk. By the signaling effect, the public sector will have been assumed to have run a grounded due diligence audit (i.e., sound evaluation and monitoring) and will bear the costs of the downside risk of projects, should it be required to do so. In this regard the effectiveness of the signaling effect and the ability to bear the downside risk depend on the public sector's creditworthiness (i.e., its ability to repay liabilities) that may impact both issues of additionality and economy. Nevertheless, public budget constraints can limit the ability of the public sector to fund and finance infrastructures. For example, since 2010 the eurozone public finance crisis has decreased the creditworthiness of certain countries (i.e., Greece, Portugal, Spain, Ireland, and Italy), hindering their financial stability. In general, public-sector investments in infrastructures can decrease due to the austerity measures implemented by the Fiscal Compact. These constraints can in turn limit the capability of the public sector to provide funding and financing and can further impinge on its capacity to provide for additionality.

Public spending constraints can also limit the ability of the public sector to provide contractually required financing and so lower the public sector's creditworthiness. This in turn can limit access to sources of private-sector funding and cause public-sector partners to pay higher risk premiums on PPP debt. Furthermore, many infrastructure projects are closely related to government creditworthiness since they depend on public funding and financing (e.g., land concessions, regulated tariffs). As such, the decreased creditworthiness of a government then negatively impacts the creditworthiness of the special purpose vehicle (SPV) established to provide and operate the service infrastructure (Moody's 2012) and impacts a project's VfM because the interest rate on debt used for the PPP will rise in line with the market premium. Finally, the public sector's capacity to support user-pays PPP infrastructure schemes will affect intragenerational and intergenerational equity because of such consequential reductions in the public sector's ability to spend on infrastructure. This can result in debt being repaid too quickly by the current generation of users through charges rather than being spread more equitably over the lifetime of the infrastructure.

The different VfM approaches to public funding and financing of infrastructures could be considered as a balance of power sharing between the private and public sectors. In cases where private partners have the greatest influence in PPP organizations, they can exert significant influence in the decision-making process, since any decision ultimately relies on the availability of funds (Asenova and Beck 2010; Toms et al. 2011). In such cases financiers could even keep the PPP hostage, and the contractor will collaborate with the private rather than the public sector (Barlow and Köberle-Gaiser 2008).

The power of lenders can impact the economy in both funding and financing. First, lenders may charge high interest to "secure" the bankability of the project. There have been cases where returns for PPP financiers were set too high for the risks they had eventually borne (HM Treasury 2012). For example, in 2008 the additional cost for private finance relative to public finance for twelve PPP hospitals in the UK was higher than expected at financial close (Shaoul et al. 2008). In Italy there is similar evidence that shows investors in Italian PPP hospitals to have gained unexpectedly high returns (Vecchi et al. 2010, 2013). Second, public-sector intervention can lead to moral hazard and opportunistic behavior by private-sector partners exercising monopoly power after the PPP has been established (the latter being deliberate and the former being the result of weak incentives and weak penalties), thus lowering both the efficiency and effectiveness of any funding. Indeed public monetary intervention can reduce the private sector's incentives to perform efficiently when the public sector bears the greatest quota of the downside risk, and weak incentives may result in organizational slack due to a decrease of the private sector's commitment. Third, conflict of interests between the public and private sectors can cause a

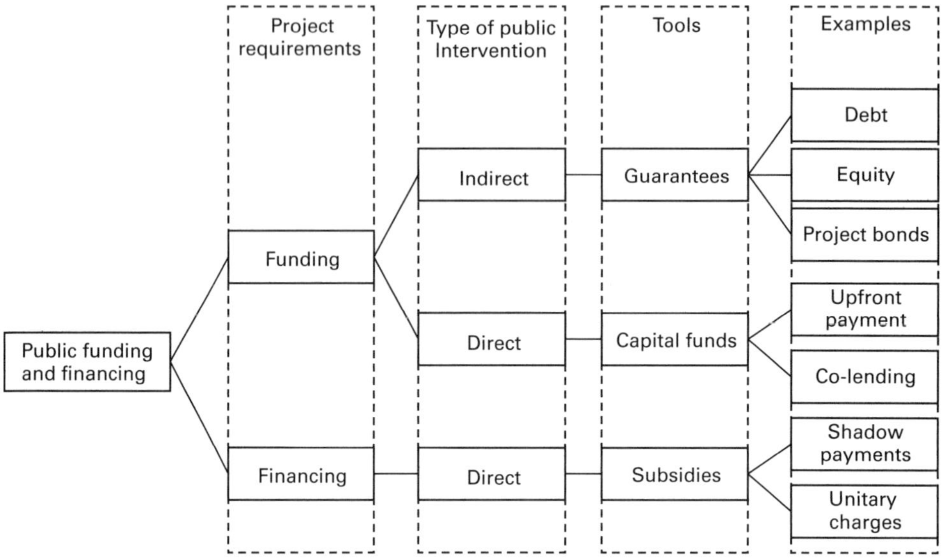

Figure 4.4
Public funding and financing for infrastructures

misalignment of incentives, thus affecting the public governance of PPPs. In cases where PPPs are promoted only to hide the public sector's long-term liabilities, accountability issues and political biases can constrain theVfM of the funding. Basing on these differences between funding and financing in PPPs it is possible to classify public financial tools in funding and financing tools, as we show in figure 4.4.

4.3.1 Funding Tools

With indirect funding the public sector's provision of funds is conditional on the occurrence of certain events that are contractually identified. Through public guarantees, the public sector agrees to bear some of the downside risk of the project. The degree of risk-sharing between the private and public sectors is highly controversial and its optimal allocation is claimed to be a fundamental driver for VfM (Grimsey and Lewis 2007). It is claimed that even if risks are best allocated between the private and public sector, certain risks (e.g., default risk) cannot be hedged by the private sector, and therefore it is up to the public sector to bear these risks. As for VfM implications:

- Guarantees can alter the PPP risk allocation if the public sector takes on most of the project's risks (EPEC 2011). Moreover full guarantees that cover all the downside risk can lead to opportunistic behaviors whereby the private-sector partners, set up within the SPV to run the PPP project, deliberately underperform because their returns are secured. Therefore it is suggested that the portion of the debt that is not guaranteed should be sufficient to ensure that the SPV will bear enough risk to ensure that it has the incentives to perform (Farquharson et al. 2011).

- Since guarantees are recorded only when they are called, they can be used to elude spending limits (Engel et al. 2009). In cases of default of strategically important infrastructures, the public sector would bear the greatest risk anyway because it would have to bail out the project (Bailey at al. 2009). Hence no matter what the contract specifies, by default the public sector bears the risk and so should insist on a warranty being lodged with an independent financial institution in order to safeguard their VfM in the event of a project failure (Bailey 2013).
- Guarantees can incentivize loan funding. For a given cost of capital, they can increase the project's bankability (i.e., decrease the riskiness for financiers) and/or decrease the project bond funding's risk by securing the coupon payment (i.e., fixed interest) and the par value (i.e., bond's invested capital) repayment. And this can result in excessive leverage (i.e., debt to equity).
- Guarantees can also affect the cost of capital. First, the presence of a guarantee is claimed to reduce risks for debt holders, and it can therefore decrease the cost of debt (EPEC 2011). Second, if the project is perceived as less risky, it is possible to increase the leverage (e.g., attract financiers to provide additional debt), and therefore decrease the exposure on equity. Nevertheless, increasing the leverage does not mean minimizing the cost of capital. Ceteris paribus, a high leverage results in a higher cost of debt because the higher is the bank's perceived risk. This offsets the benefits of a lower exposure to equity. Therefore guarantees are expected to alter the cost of capital of a project (and may impact on the VfM) because they effectively influence the leverage.

Through direct capital funding, the public sector is directly committed to infrastructure funding by the investment in up-front payment or co-lending. Unlike guarantees, capital funding involves direct monetary disbursement of the public sector that directly invests in the SPV's capital. Up-front payments by the public sector partner are funds that usually do not have to be repaid nor bear interest. But these funds can still impact VfM:

- Up-front payments represent sunk costs (i.e., cost that cannot be recovered) by the public sector and therefore have to be provided after a grounded due diligence assessment of eligible projects so as to evade a private partner's opportunistic behavior.
- If the public sector's up-front payments constitute a substantial part of the total project's investment, then in reducing the total financing needs, they can alter the balance of risk (Farquharson et al. 2011). If funding needs are wholly covered by the private sector, then it does not share the debt's risks with the public sector and as a consequence should require higher interest payments. Therefore, it could be argued, to attain VfM, the benefits of up-front payments by the public sector (with no required repayment interest and capital) must not lead to increased private funding costs and should instead reduce those costs.
- Private funding costs may increase in cases where lenders seek to appropriate some of the benefit of up-front payments. This likely would occur if the lenders have monopoly power (as a rule, monopoly power will be greater the less globalized the debt funding market is). If monopoly power exists, then public sector up-front payments do not improve the VfM.

Co-lending refers to loans provided by the public sector to complement private-sector loans. Unlike up-front payments, such loans are remunerated and repaid; therefore, in theory, the public sector recovers the investment. As for VfM impacts:

- These forms of funding can improve a project's creditworthiness in that they decrease the private sector's portion of debt and therefore its risk and cost (Farquharson et al. 2011).
- The decreased private sector's cost of debt does not necessarily imply a decreased cost of capital. Ceteris paribus, the cost of capital depends also on the amount of interest to be paid by the SPV to the public sector. As noted above, the cost of public funding in many eurozone countries has increased, and this can negatively impact on the cost of capital in co-lending arrangements.
- In the prioritization of co-lending by the public sector, subordinated debt takes priority over equity funding but is repaid after senior debt. Hence its interest rate is expected to be higher than the senior debt because of the higher risk. In cases of default, subordinated debt can be

refunded only when all the senior debt holders have been repaid and so can alter the risk-sharing between the public and private sectors.

- Co-lending can lead to a potential conflict of interest between the public and private sectors due to a misalignment between the incentives of the private sector, which is more profit oriented, and those of the public sector, which, by contrast, are more social oriented. Strong inter-creditor agreements can overcome these conflicts (EPEC 2010) but they imply negotiation costs (i.e., costs associated with the setting of arrangements and agreements between the private and public sectors). The higher these costs, the lower is the VfM, ceteris paribus.

4.3.2 Financing Tools

Subsidies are provided to complement project's revenues and usually do not have to be repaid or bear interest. These forms of direct intervention comprise, first, tariffs (e.g., shadow tolls) to be paid when revenues are subjected to demand risk and are below a predefined level. Second, unitary charges with a minimum floor amount compensate the private sector for the availability of a given facility regardless of the number of users, such as for health care services (Gatti 2008). Third are subsidies for financing infrastructures. As for VfM implications:

- Tariffs do not deal with the demand-side risk. A decrease in the demand for services causes a decrease of revenues for the private sector because revenues are not ensured by a minimum floor amount by the public sector. The private sector bears the uncertainty that demand may not generate enough revenues during the term of the contract to meet debt payments on schedule and expected equity remuneration (Engel et al. 2010). The private sector might ask for a higher return to compensate for higher risk and so affect VfM.
- Unitary charges with a minimum floor are less risky for the private sector since they guarantee a minimum level of return that, as a consequence, has to be secured by the public sector. It has been claimed that returns to PPPs' equity investors have usually been too high for the risks they have borne and the public sector has gained low margins (Shaoul 2005; HM Treasury 2012) while bearing also the default risk (Bailey et al. 2009) and so lower VfM.
- Subsidies can lock in the public sector, since they commit to the payment of contractually defined liabilities over the whole lifecycle of the project, thus affecting VfM (Lonsdale 2005).

4.4 Conclusion

In this chapter we have reframed the existing literature on VfM used to assess the relative merits of PPPs by considering the differences between funding and financing. Going beyond the terminological debate around funding and financing, we have stressed the diverse implications for public spending and the need for both funding and financing to be taken into consideration in VfM appraisals. Our conceptual and analytical framework provides a new way of the understanding of PPPs and safeguarding VfM over time.

Overall, the assessment of funding and financing requirements is a prerequisite to safeguarding VfM over time. The evaluation of VfM has predominantly been focused on a 3Es approach applied to initial funding requirements and subsequent operating costs. This conventional approach to assessing VfM fails to some extent to deal with equity issues on the use of infrastructures and their financing, whether by taxes to finance unitary charges, increased fares, or any combination of taxes and charges. The methods of financing the repayment of debt arising from funding have implications for both intragenerational equity (vertical and horizontal equity) and intergenerational equity. A funding and financing approach allows a much more comprehensive analysis of the liabilities of the public sector in a VfM perspective, regardless of whether they are accounted on or off balance sheet.

We have argued that the focus on cost of funding is much too narrow a perspective for the assessment of VfM. With the implementation of a 4Es approach to VfM, we consider both the up-front funding and subsequent financing of the infrastructure, and provide a much more holistic approach that can surmount the increasingly stringent funding constraints in both the public and private sectors. The constraints within the banking system arose subsequent to the 2007 to 2009 credit crunch, and the eurozone sovereign debt crisis, 2010 onward, has caused severe funding and financing constraints in the eurozone countries potentially defaulting on repayment of government debt.

These public and private financial constraints exacerbate the risks associated with the considerable temporal mismatch between funding and financing requirements over the lifetime of infrastructure projects and this can affect both private commercial and public social value of PPP contracts. This mismatch cannot be fully accommodated within contracts between public- and private-sector partners and, possibly, within the SPV itself. Contracts cannot regulate all possible future eventualities. Hence VfM over the long life of a PPP contract (25 to 30 years) cannot be ensured at financial close, and it will be affected by ongoing changes in funding and financing during the period the PPP is in operation. Instead, achievement and safeguarding of VfM over time requires a robust governance framework. Since short-term up-front funding implies long-term financing requirements, it has been argued that they have to be considered together for a credible VfM appraisal. VfM is a dynamic (rather than static) feature of long-lived infrastructures both because of the considerable mismatch between funding and financing and because of changing economic, social, political and institutional context within which infrastructure operates over its lifetime. Hence one-off static VfM assessments are inadequate to gauge the safeguarding of VfM over time. The arguments developed in this paper have to be considered in light of the evolving normative nature of the VfM concept within a dynamic governance model for achievement of VfM.

The dynamic governance model should focus on enhancing the flexibility and adaptability of PPPs to cope with new conditions so as to safeguard a PPP's relative VfM over the long term. Indeed, considering the normative nature of VfM, the growing complexity of public procurement, the changing role of the public sector in the provision of goods and services and its diminishing financial capacity for expensive infrastructure projects, it becomes virtually impossible to assess or predict with a reasonable degree of accuracy at their establishment whether PPPs will achieve VfM in the long term or, at least, deliver higher VfM than other alternative methods of public procurement.

Notes

This work was supported by Fondazione Cariplo, grant 2011-0788.

1. Additionality refers to the positive net results associated with an additional economic or financial stimulus (e.g., construction of a new local hospital), in terms of differential outputs (e.g., increase in the amount of services delivered) and differential outcomes (e.g., increase of the average health of the community).

2. The Fiscal Compact was ratified on January 1, 2013, and it defines budget rules whose aim is the containment of EU member state's general government deficits and debts. The Compact imposes the debt brake on all 25 of the 27 EU countries signed up to it. These countries are committed to progressively reducing their gross public-sector debt by 1/20th of the difference between the current level of debt and the 60 percent of GDP Maastricht limit.

3. The use of the terms funding and financing is not unequivocal. For example, both the Urban Land Institute (2013) and Project Finance International (2014) use the term financing to indicate the infrastructure capital investments while funding as the subsequent repayment of liabilities. Instead, the UK Chartered Institute of Public Finance and Accountancy's online Technical Information Service use the same definition provided in this work (TISonline: http://www.tisonline.net/glossary/default.asp?index=C accessed on October 2014). In this chapter we do not posit which is the correct use of the two terms and do not take part in the terminological debate around funding and financing. Our aim is rather to make clear that they pertain to two different points in time and they have separate implications for public spending and VfM.

4. Current Projects as of March 31, 2013 (Private Finance Initiative Projects: 2013; last accessed August, 2014). https://www.gov.uk/government/publications/private-finance-initiative-projects-2013-summary-data.

References

Andrews, Rhys, and Steven van de Walle. 2012. New public management and citizens' perceptions of local service efficiency, responsiveness, equity and effectiveness. Working paper 7. COCOPS.

Asenova, Darinka, and Matthias Beck. 2010. Crucial silences: When accountability met PFI and finance capital. *Critical Perspectives on Accounting* 21: 1–13.

Bailey, Stephen J. 2004. *Strategic Public Finance*. Basingstoke, UK: Palgrave Macmillan.

Bailey, Stephen J. 2013. *Guide to Finance Infrastructure and Basic Services*. Nairobi: UN-HABITAT Urban Economy and Social Development Branch.

Bailey, Stephen J., Darinka Asenova, and Matthias Beck. 2009. UK public private partnerships and the credit crunch: a case of risk contagion? *Journal of Risk and Governance* 1 (3): 1–11.

Barlow, James, and Martina Köberle-Gaiser. 2008. The private finance initiative, project form and design innovation The UK's hospitals programme. *Research Policy* 37: 1392–1402.

Bennett, John, and Elisabetta Iossa. 2006. Building and managing facilities for public services. *Journal of Public Economics* 90 (10–11): 2143–60.

Bentz, Andreas, Paul A. Grout, and Maija L. Halonen. 2005. What should governments buy from the private sector—Assets or services? Mimeo. University of Bristol.

Biggar Economics. 2014. *Scotland's Infrastructure—Delivering Firm Foundations for the Future*. Edinburgh: N-56.

Department of Treasury and Finance. 2001. *Practitioners' Guide*. Melbourne: Partnership Victoria Guidance.

Engel, Eduardo, Ronald Fisher, and Alexander Galetovic. 2009. Soft budgets and renegotiation in public–private partnerships. Working paper 15300. NBER.

Engel, Eduardo, Ronald Fisher, and Alexander Galetovic. 2010. The economics of infrastructure finance: Public–private partnerships versus public provision. *EIB PAPERS* 15 (1): 40–69.

Engel, Eduardo, Ronald Fisher, and Alexander Galetovic. 2013. The basics of public finance of public–private partnerships. *Journal of the European Economic Association* 11 (1): 83–111.

EPEC. 2010. *Capital Markets in PPP Financing*. Luxembourg: European PPP expertise Centre.

EPEC. 2011. *State Guarantees in PPPs A Guide to Better Evaluation, Design, Implementation and Management*. Luxembourg: European Expertise Centre.

Farquharson, Edward, Clemencia Torres de Mastle, Edward Yescombe, and Javier Encinas. 2011. *How to Engage with the Private Sector in Public–Private Partnerships in Emerging Markets*. Washington, DC: World Bank.

Flinders, Matthew. 2005. The politics of public–private partnerships. *British Journal of Politics and International Relations* 7 (2): 215–39.

Frederickson, George H. 2010. *Social Equity and Public Administration: Origins, Developments and Application*. Armonk, NY: M.C. Sharpe.

Froud, Jean. 2003. The private finance initiative: Risk, uncertainty and the state. *Accounting, Organizations and Society* 28 (6): 567–89.

Gatti, Stefano. 2008. *Project Finance in Theory and Practice*. Burlington, MA: Academic Press/Elviser.

Grimsey, Darrin, and Mervyn K. Lewis. 2007. Public private partnerships and public procurement. *Agenda, Journal of Policy Analysis and Reform* 14 (2): 171–88.

Hart, Oliver. 2003. Incomplete contracts and public ownership: Remarks and an application to public–private partnerships. *Economic Journal* 113 (486): C69–76.

Hellowell, Mark, and Allyson M. Pollock. 2007. New development: The PFI: Scotland's plan for expansion and its implications. *Public Money and Management* 27 (5): 351–54.

Treasury, H. M. 2003. *PFI: Meeting the Investment Challenge*. London: Stationery Office.

Treasury, H. M. 2006. *Value for Money Assessment Guidance*. London: Stationery Office.

Treasury, H. M. 2012. *Equity Investment in Privately Financed Projects*. London: Stationery Office.

Hodge, Graeme A., and Carsten Greve. 2009. PPPs: The passage of time permits a sober reflection. *Economic Affairs* 29 (1): 33–39.

Iossa, Elisabetta, and David Martimort. 2008. The simple microeconomics of public–private partnerships. Research Paper 139. CEIS.

Lonsdale, Chris. 2005. Post-contractual lock-in and the UK private finance initiative (PFI): The cases of national savings and investments and the Lord Chancellor's Department. *Public Administration* 83 (1): 67–88.

Martimort, David, and Jerome Pouyet. 2008. To build or not to build: Normative and positive theories of private–public partnerships. *International Journal of Industrial Organization* 26 (2): 393–411.

Masera, Rainer. 2012. Infrastructure financing in Europe and the Fiscal Compact approach. *Bancaria* 6: 2–21.

Mayston, David J. 1999. The private finance initiative in the National Health Service: An unhealthy development in new public management. *Financial Accountability & Management* 15: 249–74.

Moody's. 2012. *How Sovereign Credit Quality May Affect Other Ratings: Credit Policy, Rating Implementation Guidance*. Boston: Moody's Investors Service.

National Audit Office. 2009. *Private Finance Projects*. London.

Norman-Major, Kristen. 2011. Balancing the four Es; or can we achieve equity for social equity in public administration? *Journal of Public Affairs Education* 17 (2): 233–52.

Nuscheler, Robert, and Kerstin Roeder. 2014. Financing and funding health care: Optimal policy and political implementability. Working paper 4893. CESifo.

Project Finance International. 2014. *PFI Yearbook 2014*. New York.

Quiggin, John. 2004. Risk, PPPs and the public sector comparator. *Australian Accounting Review* 14 (2): 51–62.

Roehrich, Jens K., Michael A. Lewis, and Gerard George. 2014. Are public–private partnerships a healthy option? A systematic literature review. *Social Science and Medicine* 113: 110–19.

Shaoul, Jean. 2005. A critical financial analysis of the private finance initiative: Selecting a financing method or allocating economic wealth? *Critical Perspectives on Accounting* 16: 441–71.

Shaoul, Jean. 2011. "Sharing" political authority with finance capital: The case of Britain's public private partnerships. *Policy and Society* 30: 209–20.

Shaoul, Jean, Anne Stafford, and Pam Stapleton. 2008. The cost of using private finance to build, finance and operate the first 12 NHS hospitals in England. *Public Money and Management* 28 (2): 101–108.

Spackman, Michael. 2002. Public–private partnerships: Lessons from the British approach. *Economic Systems* 26: 283–301.

Toms, Steven, Matthias Beck, and Darinka Asenova. 2011. Accounting, regulation and profitability: The case of PFI hospital refinancing. *Critical Perspectives on Accounting* 22: 668–81.

Urban Land Institute. 2013. *Infrastructure 2013. Global Priorities, Global Insights*. Washington, DC.

Vecchi, Veronica, Mark Hellowell, and Stefano Gatti. 2013. Does the private sector receive an excessive return from investments in health care infrastructure projects? Evidence from the UK. *Health Policy (Amsterdam)* 110: 243–70.

Vecchi, Veronica, Mark Hellowell, and Francesco Longo. 2010. Are Italian healthcare organizations paying too much for their public private partnerships? *Public Money and Management* 30 (2): 125–32.

Winch, Graham M., and Masamitsu Onishi. 2012. The private finance of public infrastructure. In Graham M. Winch, Masamitsu Onishi, and Sandra Schmidt, eds., *Taking Stock of PPP and PFI Around the World*. London: ACCA, 11–15.

Appendix

Table A4.1
Descriptive statistics

	Number of projects	Capital value (£m)	Median capital value (£m)	Mean capital value (£m)
All projects	695	53,163	36	76
Region				
England	508	37,773	36	74
Scotland	88	5,843	46	66
Northern Ireland	37	1,657	24	45
National/More than one region	32	7,167	69	224
Wales	30	723	14	24
Sector				
Schools	193	10,377	44	54
Hospitals and acute health	143	13,078	36	91
Offices	46	3,767	14	82
Waste	40	4,767	94	119
Other	40	7,175	26	179
Emergency services	38	1,042	19	27
Housing	36	1,831	43	51
Street lighting	32	1,427	36	45
Roads and highway maintenance	28	4,339	97	155
Social care	23	266	9	12
Leisure facilities	15	296	17	20
Military facility	13	1,362	64	105
Prisons	12	637	46	53
IT infrastructure and communications	11	867	51	79
Courts	8	195	25	24
Libraries	7	158	20	23
Secure training centers (YJB)	4	68	17	17
Underground/train/light rail	3	1,275	475	425
Equipment	2	194	97	97
Energy	1	43	43	43

Table A4.2
Summary of limitations on the fulfillment of VfM criteria in public funding and financing

	Funding	Financing
Additionality	• Public sector's creditworthiness impacts on the ability to complement funding • Public sector's spending limits impact on additionality of public funding	• Public sector's creditworthiness impacts on the ability to complement financing • Public sector's spending limits impact on additionality of public financing
Economy	• Public sector's creditworthiness impacts on cost of funding • Power of lenders impacts on cost of funding	• Power of lenders impacts on the amount of financing • Public sector's spending limits impact on the ability to provide financing
Efficiency	• Moral hazard and opportunistic behavior impact on productivity of funding	
Effectiveness	• Moral hazard and opportunistic behavior impact on efficacy of funding	
Equity	• Public sector's spending limits impact on intragenerational equity requiring diversion of public finance from other uses in order to pay the contractually enforced unitary charges • Public funding tools affect risk-sharing by reducing financial risks faced by the special purpose vehicle	• Public sector's spending limits impact on intergenerational equity by postponing repayment of debt • Public financing tools affect risk-sharing via default risk
Public governance	• Transparency of public sector's budgets diminished by off-balance-sheet debt • Conflict of interest between the public and private sectors	

5 On the Financial Structure and the Contractual Length of Public–Private Partnerships

Daniel Danau and Annalisa Vinella

5.1 Introduction

Infrastructure projects have two main characteristics. First, the realization of the infrastructure involves huge investments. Second, the project unfolds essentially in two phases, namely construction and operation, between which synergies are very often present. In projects like transport, hospital, and prisons, building the infrastructure diligently may indeed lead to a reduction in the maintenance and operating costs. The contracts between governments and private firms for infrastructure projects display in turn three core features. To begin with, they have a long duration, especially when a large part of the investment is financed with private capital, namely own funds of the firm and bank loans. In that case the operation must remain private for a sufficiently long period of time so that the private investment can be fairly remunerated "as time goes by." In addition, as the projects are long termed and include two phases, the conditions under which the firm will operate are unknown, when the parties meet at the contracting table. Once the parties become aware of the actual operating conditions, each of them is able to evaluate how convenient it is to honor the contract, as compared to any alternative option faced at that time. As the parties lack the ability to commit to particular actions, in general, the contracts are vulnerable to renege, on the initiative of either one or the other party. Lastly, informational asymmetries arise between governments and firms. Although this is standard in agency relationships, peculiar to the contracts for infrastructure projects is that informational asymmetries are related to the very circumstance that such projects include different activities, between which synergies are present.

Many theoretical articles have recently been published, focusing on the desirability of involving private firms in infrastructure projects, as well as on the design of suitable contracts for bringing those projects to efficient outcomes. However, little effort has been made to account for all the aspects aforementioned in a comprehensive manner, hence to investigate how the contractual performance is thereby affected. Once those elements are considered altogether, one realizes that for efficiency to be attained, it is essential to adopt contractual instruments which are not usually thought of. These instruments are the financial structure of the project and the length of the contract. Concerning the latter, two options are available. The length of the contract can either be fixed or it can be tailored to the specific realization of the operating conditions. The ways in which these two instruments enhance the contractual performance are complex and not easily approachable. Resting on these considerations, the goal of the present work is to offer an intuitive, little technical explanation of the reasons why decision makers should pay much attention to the choice of the financial structure and the contractual length of infrastructure projects.

Before elaborating further on the analysis to be developed in this work, it is useful to say a few more words on the existing studies. A *first stream of literature* looks at the issues that ensue from the presence of informational asymmetries between governments and firms. The focus is on the presence of moral hazard in construction and the consequences it has on the operating conditions. Specifically, studies like Bennett and Iossa (2006), Martimort and Pouyet (2008), Iossa and Martimort (2015), investigate the desirability of delegating both construction and operation to a single private consortium, rather than relying on two distinct firms, each in charge of one activity. The former kind of arrangement, which is identified as a public–private partnership (PPP), is more and more frequently adopted in practice.[1] According to those authors, the PPP attains a more efficient outcome, as compared to traditional procurement, in which the tasks are separated, because the private consortium internalizes the synergies between construction and operation. *Other studies* focus on the opportunity of involving private capital in the realization of public projects. In particular, Engel, Fischer, and Galetovic (2013) argue that by resorting to private capital, governments can save on the administrative and agency costs associated with the disbursement of funds from the public budget. In practice, it is very often the case that politicians justify the reliance on PPPs as a way to develop infrastructure projects without burdening the public budget. As a matter of fact, involvement of private investment in infrastructure projects has first appeared in the United Kingdom in the form of a private finance initiative (PFI), despite that there was no rationing experienced on the credit market to raise funds for public investment. In Danau and Vinella (2015a, b), we consider the issue of limited commitment, which leads either to the suboptimal renegotiation or to the early termination of PPP contracts. We find that the private investment as well as the contractual length are effective instruments at fostering cooperation between the partners. In this work, we provide a "ready-for-use" description of some of the lessons ensuing from those studies.

The issue of a suboptimal renegotiation of PPP contracts has received much attention in the literature, though not necessarily with regard to frameworks of limited commitment. Engel, Fischer, and Galetovic (1997, 2001) focus on renegotiation resulting from contractual incompleteness, in the tradition of the studies on transaction costs and incomplete contracts. Their preoccupation is that, if the contract is incomplete, then the firm will seek to obtain a better deal, in the event that it faces unfavorable conditions. As a remedy to this problem, they suggest that the contract stipulate a certain return, which the firm will cumulate during the development of the project, regardless of the operating conditions. Hence the contract would be complete and contractual frictions would not arise. An important implication of this policy is that the termination date, which is not a contracting variable, will be contingent on the actual state of nature. That is, the termination date will be adjusted during the execution of the contract, in such a way that the firm obtains the return stipulated in the contract, regardless of the realized state of nature. Contracts of this kind are known as *flexible-term contracts*.[2]

While the mechanism proposed by Engel, Fischer, and Galetovic (1997, 2001) is appealing in incomplete-contracting frameworks, it is not necessarily the best solution under limited commitment. In the latter perspective, one can think of the flexible-term contract as being motivated by the possibility of the government being "weak," that is, prone to avoid that the firm incurs financial difficulties, when the project generates a poor cash flow. Situations in which the government has a limited ability to enforce the contract with a reticent firm can be associated with one side of the limited-commitment problem, namely *limited enforcement* (see Estache and Wren-Lewis 2009 for this terminology).

In other situations, as represented in Danau and Vinella (2015a, b), the government may not be weak, and yet it may welcome renegotiating the contract, after the firm reneges on it because the breakup of the partnership would be costly. In its turn the firm may want to renege, regardless of the insurance received at the contracting stage, simply because it expects to reach a better deal. Moreover a strong government may itself take the initiative to renege, thus exposing the partnership to early breakup. The possibility that the government will behave opportunistically, during the operation phase of the project, mirrors the second side of the limited-commitment problem, namely *noncommitment*. Considering noncommitment together with limited enforcement is in fact rather natural. In institutional environments where one party is unable to commit to contractual obligations, it is very plausible that the other party will not commit in turn. Once it is recognized that the government is not necessarily weak, so that renegotiation may also result from the government's opportunism, it becomes apparent that offering a flexible-term contract does not need to be the best remedy under limited commitment. As long as there is some extra benefit to retain from the government in a new negotiation, the firm will attempt to return to the contracting table, regardless of the insurance it receives under the initial deal. In addition, as soon as informational issues, which are also pervasive in PPPs, are accounted for, one would expect the firm to be transferred some risk and, hence, to receive different compensations in different states of nature, at odds with the flexible-term approach. Engel, Fischer, and Galetovic (1997, 2001) rely on an incomplete contracting approach to model the vulnerability of PPP contracts. In line with the studies following Laffont (2003), the focus is here on situations where the vulnerability of the contract follows from the lack of enforcement mechanisms in the economy.

The findings in Danau and Vinella (2015a) confirm that when the government is not necessarily weak and information issues are present, the firm's profits should be differentiated across states of nature, indeed. Actually, in that framework, not only the compensation scheme, but also the role that the duration plays, in affecting the contractual performance, differs from the role pointed out in Engel, Fischer, and Galetovic (1997, 2001). This reflects, first, the need to tackle information issues and, second, the circumstance that ex post opportunism is not bound to concern the sole firm but can also arise on the government's side. To catch the relationship between the contractual length and the partners' incentives to renege on the contract, it is essential to consider that for either partner, the convenience to renege, at each moment in time, depends on the residual duration of the partnership and ultimately on the termination date stipulated in the contract. In addition the convenience to renege depends on what is at stake, for either partner, at each moment in time. In turn this is related to the exact kind and amount of funds invested in the project up-front, which determine what the investors can gain or lose during the development of the project. It follows that not only the duration of the contract but also the financial structure of the project affects the incentives of the two partners to abide by the respective obligations.

As far as the contract duration is concerned, Danau and Vinella (2015b) highlight another important aspect. In situations where either partner may be reticent to honor the contract, it is useful to make the contractual length contingent on the realized operating conditions. Unlike in Engel, Fischer, and Galetovic (1997, 2001), the reason is that some of the incentive problems are relevant in the good state and the others are relevant in the bad state. Because the state-dependent approach yields additional flexibility in the determination of the contractual length, as compared to the fixed-term approach, it makes it easier to reconcile information problems and commitment problems across states of nature. Hence the desired outcome is more likely to be attained.

5.1.1 Outline

We proceed in two main steps, following the literature review. We first highlight how to address asymmetric information issues under full commitment (section 5.2). We then focus on a limited-commitment framework. After offering a few relevant examples of limited-commitment problems in practice, we move back to the formal analysis in order to explain why, under limited commitment, the duration of the contract and the financial structure of the project are essential contractual instruments. We show how they should be set in order to induce the two partners to abide by their contractual obligations (section 5.3). To conclude, we discuss the practical implications of the theoretical predictions (section 5.4).

5.1.2 Literature Review

It is now recognized that the poorness of enforcement mechanisms is a serious issue in the execution of long-term contracts. While this issue has been recently investigated in the literature on relational contracts (see Levin 2003), it is still underexplored with regard to PPP contracts.

Relational contracts are cast on repeated relationships. In PPPs, instead, the relationship is unique and its duration is endogenous to the contract. From the analysis in Danau and Vinella (2015a, b), it is apparent that the contractual length is an essential instrument to have PPP contracts executed, in the absence of enforcement mechanisms. The issue of commitment being limited, in the development of public projects, is also considered in the studies of Laffont (2003) and Guasch, Laffont, and Straub (2006, 2008). These authors are mainly concerned with concession contracts and focus on either government-led or firm-led renegotiation. The results presented in this work evidence that making a proper choice of the contractual length is especially important, and poses more challenges, when *both* the firm and the government, not only one of them, lack the ability to commit.

Among the studies in which contractual frictions stem from contractual incompleteness, most related to our analysis are those of Engel, Fischer, and Galetovic (1997, 2001). They show that, by adjusting the contractual length in the different states of nature, it is possible to eliminate the discrepancy between the discounted streams of profits, which the firm will cumulate, during the development of the project, in those states. They argue that this contractual policy, which fully insures the firm, should be adopted in order to avoid ex post renegotiation. In line with this, one of our findings is that under limited commitment, the firm should be exposed to little risk. In particular, for the partners' opportunism to be lessened, the wedge between the discounted streams of profits, which the firm will obtain through the termination date, in the two states, should be set as low as possible. The lower bound to that wedge is such that the firm is just indifferent between exerting effort and shirking when building the infrastructure. However, unlike in Engel, Fischer, and Galetovic (1997), the amount of risk transferred to the firm does not need to change as the contractual length is adjusted in the different states. This is because in our framework the per-period profits of the firm are endogenous. Thus a certain (desirable) risk transfer can be maintained, when inducing changes in the contractual terms, by compensating those changes with variations in the wedge between the per-period (rather than the cumulated) profits. This possibility proves dramatically useful to discipline the partners in environments in which commitment problems coexist with information problems.

Renegotiation issues in principal–agent relationships have been investigated by Dewatripont (1989), Hart and Tirole (1988), and Rey and Salanié (1996). They consider situations in which the contract is signed at *interim*, that is, when the agent is privately informed, and the contractual parties have an interest in coming back to the contracting table ex post, that is, when information is revealed and the principal no longer needs to incentivize the agent. In those models the contract must be made robust to renegotiation. Similarly in our framework the contract must be made robust to renege. Yet this involves that not only renegotiation but also early breakup be made unattractive to the parties. This task is more complex and subtle in that the desirability to the parties of the allocation resulting from the contractual frictions depends on the relative convenience of the two outside options (renegotiation and breakup). We argue that, by relying on credible third parties, such as export credit agencies, debt liabilities can be used strategically to eliminate any benefit from renegotiation, thus ruling out one of those options. This facilitates the task of making the contract self-enforcing.

5.2 Information Issues under Full Commitment

We begin by considering a situation in which the two partners to an infrastructure project, namely a government and a private consortium (henceforth, the firm, for the sake of brevity), commit to their contractual obligations. However, the government suffers from an informational gap vis-à-vis the firm. Albeit full commitment is a hypothetical situation, this approach is useful, as a first step, to enucleate information issues and to discuss their implications. Consistent with previous studies, we will show that the government needs to transfer some risk to the private partner, in order to tackle those issues. To assess how much risk should exactly be transferred to the firm, we refer to the simple analytical framework described hereafter.

5.2.1 Analytical Framework

The construction of the infrastructure involves a cost of $I > 0$. The subsequent provision of the service involves an inner marginal cost of $\theta > 0$ linked to the very characteristics of the infrastructure. To capture the real-world circumstance that the operating conditions are unknown when contracts are signed, we take the value of θ to be uncertain initially. It will be revealed after the investment cost is sunk and the infrastructure is built, at the outset of the operation phase. The operating marginal cost can take a value of θ_l or θ_h. We require that $\theta_l < \theta_h$ so that θ_l represents the good state of nature (the service is less costly) and θ_h represents the bad state of nature (the service is more costly). In addition, to capture the synergies between construction and operation, we assume that the probability of facing the low cost depends on whether or not the firm exerts an effort in construction. If it does, then the probability is v_1. Otherwise, it is v_0, with $0 < v_0 < v_1 < 1$. The firm may not be willing to exert effort because this causes a disutility of $\psi > 0$.

5.2.2 Information Issues and Financial Structure of the Project

Moral Hazard in Construction

Assume that $\tilde{\mathbb{E}}_i[\theta_i] - \mathbb{E}_i[\theta_i] > \psi$, where $\tilde{\mathbb{E}}_i[\theta_i]$ (resp. $\mathbb{E}_i[\theta_i]$) is the expected operating cost without (resp. with) effort provision. It means that the reduction in the expected operating cost, which effort provision grants, overcompensates for the disutility of that effort. Thus effort is socially desirable and the government should motivate the firm to exert it. Denote $\Pi_{i,0}$ the present value, at the contracting stage (date 0), of the stream of profits that the firm is supposed to obtain, during the operation phase, when the true cost is θ_i, $i \in \{l, h\}$. Further denote $\Delta v = v_1 - v_0$.

Result 1 *Effort is exerted in construction, if and only if*

$$\Pi_{l,0} - \Pi_{h,0} \geq \frac{\psi}{\Delta v}. \tag{1}$$

Condition (1) expresses a standard prescription in moral-hazard problems. A wedge must be induced between the compensation in the good state of nature and the compensation in the bad state of nature, as expressed in discounted terms. The wedge must be more important the higher the disutility of effort, and the lower the benefit in terms of enhanced probability of facing the good state. When the compensation scheme is structured according to this prescription, any incentive to shirk in construction is eliminated.

Adverse Selection in Operation

In addition to having an exclusive control on the effort to be provided when building the infrastructure, the firm is in a better position, as compared to the government, to assess the true value of the operating cost. Thus the firm will have an incentive to exploit this informational advantage to raise its return from the partnership, unless that incentive is eliminated by means of a properly designed compensation scheme. Denote T_i and q_i, respectively, the duration of the contract (i.e., the length of the operation phase) and the level of production chosen by the government, in the event that the cost is θ_i, where $i \in \{l, h\}$. Obviously the government prefers to recommend more production in the good state, so that $q_l > q_h$. Also let r be the discount rate and $\Delta\theta = \theta_h - \theta_l$.

Result 2 *Private information is revealed at the outset of the operation phase, if and only if*

$$\Pi_{l,0} - \Pi_{h,0} \geq \Delta\theta \int_0^{T_h} q_h e^{-rx} dx, \tag{2}$$

$$\Pi_{l,0} - \Pi_{h,0} \leq \Delta\theta \int_0^{T_l} q_l e^{-rx} dx. \tag{3}$$

Conditions (2) and (3) embody two additional prescriptions for a suitable design of the compensation scheme. On the one hand, according to (2), the profit in the good state must be large enough, as compared to the profit in the bad state. If it were not so, then the firm would have an interest in pretending a high cost, when the true cost is low. In exchange for receiving a lower compensation, the firm would appropriate the difference between the claimed total cost ($\theta_h q_h$) and the incurred total cost ($\theta_l q_h$), at each instant during the operation phase through the termination date T_h. On the other hand, according to (3), the profit in the good state must not be excessively larger than the profit in the bad state. Otherwise, the firm would have an incentive to claim a low cost, when the true cost is high. The compensation that the firm would receive, at each instant during the operation phase through the termination date T_l, would be so high to offset the penalty simultaneously incurred, as given by the difference between the incurred total cost ($\theta_h q_l$) and the claimed total cost ($\theta_l q_l$).

Interpreted together with result 1, result 2 conveys a neat message. Information issues call for transferring risk to the firm. Nonetheless, risk transfer must be limited.

Irrelevance of the Financial Structure of the Project

Inspection of (1), (2), and (3) evidences that the ability of the government to tackle moral hazard and adverse selection is not affected by the magnitude of the cost of investment (I), hence by the specific way in which this is covered. From this standpoint, the financial structure of the project does not matter. That is, under full commitment, any combination of public funds and private capital (i.e., own funds of the firm and borrowed funds) can be chosen to finance the project.

5.2.3 Information Issues and Contractual Length

From (1), (2), and (3) it is apparent that the way in which the contractual length is set, in the two possible states of nature, is essential to provide desirable incentives to the firm. The shorter the contract duration when the cost is low, the smaller the opportunity cost, for the firm, of pretending θ_l when the cost is high, hence the stronger the incentive to do so. If T_l is set short, then this incentive cannot be eliminated, unless a sufficiently high compensation is granted to the firm for correctly announcing θ_h. However, when this strategy is followed, it becomes difficult, for the government, to tackle the moral-hazard problem. A firm that receives a high compensation when faced with a high operating cost, is little motivated to exert effort in order to increase the likelihood of facing a low cost. Furthermore the longer the contract duration in the bad state, the more important the benefit that the firm obtains by pretending θ_h, when the cost is low, hence the stronger the incentive to do so. Once these elements are considered altogether, the intuitive conclusion is that restrictions will appear on how little the government can set T_l and, for any given T_l, on how big it can set T_h in order to solve the two information problems at once. We will state this result in a moment, after making the following assumption on the magnitude of the disutility of effort, which will be maintained all throughout:

$$\psi \leq \Delta\nu\Delta\theta\frac{q_l}{r}. \tag{4}$$

To see why we impose (4), suppose that this condition is violated. The disutility of effort is so big that shirking cannot be prevented, unless the firm is exposed to much risk. This involves making the compensation to the firm substantially higher in the good state, relative to the bad state. However, in that case it is impossible to persuade the firm to release information in state h, even if the contract has an infinitely long duration in state l. Hence (4) must hold. We are now ready to state the result.

Result 3 *Moral hazard and adverse selection are both addressed, only if*

$$T_l \geq \frac{1}{r} \ln \frac{\Delta v \Delta \theta q_l}{\Delta v \Delta \theta q_l - r\psi}, \tag{5}$$

and when

$$T_l \leq \frac{1}{r} \ln \frac{q_l}{q_l - q_h},$$

$$T_h \leq \frac{1}{r} \ln \frac{q_h}{q_h - q_l\left(1 - e^{-rT_l}\right)}. \tag{6}$$

We previously explained that when structuring the compensation scheme in order to address the different information issues, the government faces two potential conflicts. We also said that the first conflict, between moral hazard and adverse selection in state h, can be avoided only if (4) holds. We can now further specify that, for that conflict not to arise, T_l must be set large enough to satisfy (5). Additionally, in order to avoid also the second conflict, between preventing cost exaggeration in state l and preventing cost understatement in state h, T_h must be set below the threshold identified in (6).

A Particular Case: The Fixed-Term Contract

There is a very natural question that arises after drawing result 3, namely whether conditioning the duration of the contract on the true cost, as in the analysis developed so far, does deliver any benefit and is thus to be preferred to the fixed-term option. The relevance of this question becomes apparent as soon as it is observed that, in practice, most PPP contractual agreements have a fixed term.

Result 4 *Assume that $T_l = T_h \equiv T$. Moral hazard and adverse selection are both addressed, only if*

$$T \geq \frac{1}{r} \ln \frac{\Delta v \Delta \theta q_l}{\Delta v \Delta \theta q_l - r\psi}. \tag{7}$$

Result 4 echoes the content of proposition 1 in Danau and Vinella (2015a). It evidences that, when the contract has a fixed term, there is only one possible conflict between information problems, namely that between inducing effort in construction and eliciting information in state h. As from result 3, avoiding this conflict requires choosing a sufficiently long contractual term. The other potential conflict, between preventing cost exaggeration in state l and preventing cost understatement in state h, never arises with a fixed term. The insight that we can retain is that eliciting information in either state is not an issue, as long as the firm cannot pick, with a false cost claim, more convenient a contract duration than the one corresponding to the true cost.

Irrelevance of Whether the Contractual Term Is Fixed or State Dependent

From results 3 and 4, it ensues immediately that under (4), a suitable contractual length can be found to tackle both moral hazard and adverse selection, whether the term is conditioned on the cost realization ($T_l \neq T_h$) or is fixed ($T_l = T_h \equiv T$). In other words, anything the government can achieve, by offering a contract such that (5) and (6) are met, can also be achieved by means of a fixed-term contract that complies with (7). Thus, as long as the performance of the PPP is challenged by information issues only, there is no loss of generality in sticking to the usual practice of offering a fixed-term contract to the firm.

5.3 Contractual Length and Financial Structure under Limited Commitment

Under limited commitment the issue of identifying the optimal PPP contract is more complex. As will become apparent in the sequel of the analysis, the two "irrelevance" conclusions, which we drew concerning the financial structure of the project and the fixed or state-dependent duration of the contract, no longer hold. To fix ideas, before making further progress with the formal analysis, we provide a few relevant examples of limited-commitment problems in real world.

5.3.1 Limited Commitment in Practice

Limited Enforcement

Examples of limited enforcement and firm-led renegotiation are pervasive in PPPs. In institutionally weak contexts (developing countries, in general), strong rules of law seldom exist and renegotiation is frequent. Estache and Wren-Lewis (2009) recall that in Ghana the incumbent monopoly for fixed telephony entered the mobile business despite the explicit interdiction to do so. In Tanzania the regulator failed to enforce regional mobile license, and the dominant operator began to expand at the national level. Guasch (2004) and Guasch, Laffont, and Straub (2006, 2008) provide further examples in Latin America and in the Caribbean regions. Although less often, firms renege on contracts also in frameworks where institutions are solid (typically, developed countries) and contracts should be, in principle, more easily enforced, say, by fining firms reluctant to produce. Gagnepain, Ivaldi, and Martimort (2009) detect a progressive increase in the subsidies paid to French urban transport concessionaires through the contract execution. In the controversial London underground project, the service was taken in house when Metronet, the consortium in charge of the project, filed for bankruptcy (House of Lords 2010a, b). This suggests that governments are not prone to engage in costly and time-consuming litigations to enforce contracts.

Noncommitment

In developing countries government failure to honor contractual terms is even more problematic than limited enforcement. In those countries, large-scale investments are desperately needed, especially in utilities. However, they are unlikely to take place at all if governments cannot warrant investors' remuneration.[3] In Central and Eastern Europe repeated changes in the political attitude toward partnerships with private firms have challenged and slowed down the development of various infrastructure projects over the last decades. As an illustration, Brench et al. (2005) document the case of transportation projects in Hungary.

5.3.2 Governmental Guarantees under Limited Commitment

Under limited commitment the contract between the government and the firm is vulnerable to the risk of not being executed. Additionally, if the firm takes out a loan to fund (a part of) the initial investment, then also the credit contract is exposed to the risk of not being executed, provided that the firm cannot be compelled to return money to the lender. In turn the firm may be unable to borrow on the credit market. To circumvent this difficulty, the lender should receive a guarantee that the debt will be paid back. We will now explain which kind of guarantees can actually be provided in a PPP. Given the relevance that the participation of external financiers is attached in PPP projects, this aspect has very important practical implications, and yet it is still little explored in the economic literature.

Collateralized and Unprotected Debt

It is sometimes argued that either the assets of the firm or those created through the PPP project should be used to pledge debt collateral (e.g., see Engel, Fischer, and Galetovic 2013; Guasch, Laffont, and Straub 2006). However, the effectiveness of collateralizing debt in PPP projects is questionable. To clarify this point, let us first consider a private firm that takes a loan to run a private project. The assets pertaining to the new project are used to collateralize the debt. If the debt is not paid, then the creditor has the right to either liquidate the assets or use them to reorganize the activity. When a private firm takes out a loan to run a public project, rather than a private one, things are quite different. In the event of default, the activity is undertaken by the government and, possibly, delegated to a new firm. Because most of the assets are sunk in the project, they cannot be liquidated in favor of the creditor. However, even if there are assets that could be liquidated, without compromising the continuation of the project under the new management, the collateral is likely to be ineffective. Under limited commitment any claim by the government that it would not expropriate the creditor is indeed little credible.[4]

Governmental Guarantees and Their Limits in Practice

The government can use "external" means to commit to abide by the obligations acquired with the firm's lender. For instance, one could think of the government as depositing resources with a reliable third party. Such resources should then be released to the lender, in case the firm stops making repayments and the government does not step in to complete the repayments in the firm's place. In practice, a strategy of the kind just described is adopted when a government mandates an export credit agency (ECA) to act as an intermediary, providing cover in the event of any default in payment by a borrower (or its guarantor) under some loan agreement. Originally created as government entities to promote, facilitate, and support the exports of goods and services, starting from the 1990s, ECAs have begun to operate in project financing as well. This practice is now widespread.[5] Moreover in developing countries the World Bank and other multilateral development banks (e.g., the Inter-American Development Bank) provide guarantees that are less subject to project and country limits, as compared to insurance, and are intended to cover debt up to 100 percent of principal and interest. Irwin et al. (1997) stress that if properly managed, these guarantees are crucial at reinforcing governments' resolve to abide by their commitments.

Once it is clear that there is a way, for governments, to tie their hands and honor the guarantees provided to the firms' lenders, it is still to be clarified which practical effect governmental guarantees will have. When a firm defaults and the government intervenes to bail out the activity, debt responsibilities are passed onto taxpayers, with nonnegligible consequences. A particularly good example is the 2002 to 2003 London underground maintaining-and-upgrading project, which we recalled above. At the time when the project was launched, the public sector was uncertain over whether Metronet could raise enough funds to cover the investment. To boost the banks' appetite, during the bidding stage, Transport for London guaranteed 95 percent of Metronet's debt obligations. Eventually Metronet failed and the Department for Transport had to make a £1.7 billion payment to help Transport for London meet the guarantee (House of Lords 2010a, b). The National Audit Office (2008, 2009) reports that in addition to facing the failure of the partnership, taxpayers incurred a direct loss of between £170 million and £410 million. Something similar occurred in Mexico in 1990s, when the government embarked on an ambitious road building program, awarding more than fifty concessions for 5,500 km of toll roads. The concessions were highly leveraged. Debt financing for the projects was provided by local banks. Several such banks were government owned and faced government pressure to sponsor the concessionaires. Thus the government acquired a substantial amount of implicit liabilities. Eventually the government had to bail out twenty-five financially distressed concessions in order to avoid a disastrous bank collapse. This involved assuming $7.7 billion in debt, to the detriment of taxpayers (Ehrhardt and Irwin 2004).

A Remedy: Conditional Guarantees

The tales described above highlight one main weakness in the practical use of governmental guarantees. The latter come into force, despite that the partnership breaks down, following to the firm's default. There is thus an obvious way to avoid the double damage of the PPP failing and the debt burden relapsing to taxpayers. That is, the provision of governmental guarantees should be conditioned on the continuation of the partnership. It should be contractually stipulated that governmental guarantees will assist external financiers only in the event that the private partner does remain in the project, whether the original contract is honored until the termination date or it is, at some point, renegotiated. Importantly, the reliance on *conditional* guarantees of this kind is coherent with the project finance technique, which requires making the project legally and economically self-contained. This task is accomplished in two ways. First, a stand-alone firm (the special purpose vehicle) is created to undertake no other business than building and operating within the concerned project. Besides, the firm is endowed with the sole assets pertaining to the project, which are kept separated from the assets of the parent firm. Second, lenders are provided no guarantees beyond the right to be paid out of the resources generated within the project (i.e., user fees and, possibly, governmental transfers). This involves forgoing any repayment guarantee in the event that the firm abandons the activity.

5.3.3 Private Investment: Loan Guaranteed by the Government and Own Funds of the Firm

We now move back to the formal analysis in order to explain why involving private funds in the project, in the double form of funds belonging to the firm and funds borrowed by the firm on the credit market, plays an essential role in the execution of the contract under limited commitment. To this end, we need to describe what may motivate the partners to renege on the contract, foreseeing either renegotiation or breakup of the partnership.

Incentives to Renege Anticipating Renegotiation: The Role of the Governmental Guarantees

Suppose that in some state $i \in (l, h)$, at some date $\tau \in (0, T_i)$, either the firm or the government reneges on the contract. If the two partners are unable to reach a new agreement, then the government replaces the firm with a new operator. This occasions a "cost of replacement" of R_{δ_i}, where $\delta_i \equiv T_i - \tau$ is the residual contractual period. The replacement cost is basically a loss of reputation or credibility for the government. It is thus reasonable that it is bigger the longer the residual period through the termination date initially stipulated. To capture this circumstance, we assume that $R'_{\delta_i} > 0$. However, when replacing the firm, the government enjoys a benefit. This is measured by the value of the guarantee $D^{rn}_{i,\tau}$, which the government provides to the firm's lender at the contracting stage, with the agreement that it will come into force in case of renegotiation. The guarantee being conditioned on the continuation of the partnership, the government saves that money when the PPP is broken up. Therefore the net opportunity benefit of the government from continuing the partnership is $R_{\delta_i} - D^{rn}_{i,\tau}$.[6] Anticipating the government's convenience to appropriate that benefit, the firm might renege opportunistically. Its goal would be to induce the government to renegotiate and share the benefit. Recalling that $D^{rn}_{i,\tau}$ is one of the variables that the government chooses when the initial contract is drawn up, we can state the following result.

Result 5 *The firm's incentives to renege on the contract opportunistically, anticipating renegotiation, are eliminated, if the governmental guarantees, provided for the renegotiated contract, are set as*

$$D^{rn}_{i,\tau} \geq R_{\delta_i}, \quad \forall i \in \{l, h\}, \tau \in (0, T_i). \tag{8}$$

According to (8), the government should provide so high a guarantee, for the renegotiated contract, that any benefit from renegotiation would be eliminated. Then there would be nothing to share with the firm. Consequently the firm would have no interest in reneging on the contract in the prospect of reaching a new profitable agreement. Nor would the government attempt to renegotiate. Indeed replacing the firm would be less costly for the government than paying the amount guaranteed to the lender. Therefore the guarantees represent a powerful tool to eliminate the partners' incentives to renege on the contract.

Incentives to Renege Anticipating Breakup

Assume that (8) is satisfied. Then the only remaining concern is to ensure that under the initial contract, each partner attains a higher payoff than would be obtained if the partnership were to break up. To illustrate how this concern can be addressed, we need to formalize the partners' payoffs under the initial contract and in the event of breakup.

When the partnership is terminated, the firm obtains its best outside opportunity, which we take to be zero: $\Pi^{rp}_{i,\tau} = 0$. A new firm steps in and runs the activity. Denote $S_{i,\tau}$ the social benefit from the activity from date τ to date T_i, regardless of who runs it. Thus, when the partnership is terminated, the government obtains $V^{rp}_{i,\tau} = S_{i,\tau} - R_{\delta_i}$. Next let $\Pi_{i,\tau}$ and $V_{i,\tau}$ the values, at date τ, of the partners' payoffs under the initial contract. To eliminate the incentives to renege on the contract, anticipating breakup, it is necessary and sufficient that for all $i \in \{l, h\}$,

$$\Pi_{i,\tau} \geq 0, \tag{9a}$$

$$V_{i,\tau} \geq S_{i,\tau} - R_{\delta_i}. \tag{9b}$$

In what follows, we show that any temptation to renege on the contract, anticipating breakup of the partnership, is eliminated by making a suitable choice of the financial structure of the project. The latter includes the loan to be taken out by the firm and guaranteed by the government, as well as the funds to be provided by the firm.

Governmental Guarantees and Size of the Loan

Let us begin with the government. When the contract is executed, its payoff in state i, at date τ, is given by the gross social benefit generated by the activity from date τ to date T_i, namely $S_{i,\tau}$, net of the compensation that the government owes to the firm, namely $\Pi_{i,\tau}$, and net of the debt guaranteed to the lender, denoted $D_{i,\tau}$. Thus

$$V_{i,\tau} = S_{i,\tau} - (\Pi_{i,\tau} + D_{i,\tau}).$$

Recalling (10), we deduce that the government has no incentive to renege, with the purpose of terminating the partnership, if and only if the amount of debt, which is induced and guaranteed by the government in the initial contract, is not too large. That is,

$$D_{i,\tau} \leq R_{\delta_i} - \Pi_{i,\tau}, \quad \forall i \in \{l, h\}, \tau \in (0, T_i). \tag{10}$$

Setting $D_{i,\tau}$ as low as (11) requires is not an issue because any amount of debt, which is suitable to make the contract self-enforcing, can freely be chosen.

Once it is clear how $D_{i,\tau}$ should be set, one can deduce how much money the government should instruct the firm to borrow up-front and to use in the project in order to make the contract self-enforcing. For the sake of simplicity, we assume that the credit market is competitive. Hence the loan conceded to the firm, denoted C, is such that $C = \mathbb{E}_i[D_{i,0}]$. This means that the expected repayment, for the lender, is exactly equal to the loan taken out by the firm. Moreover, from the expected payoff of the government at the contracting stage, which is given by $\mathbb{E}_i[V_{i,0}] = \mathbb{E}_i[S_{i,0}] - \mathbb{E}_i[\Pi_{i,0}] - C$, where $\mathbb{E}_i[\Pi_{i,0}]$ is the expected stream of future operating profits, we see that giving up a rent to the firm is socially costly. Thus the government attempts to retain as much surplus as possible from the firm. The best outside opportunity of the firm being zero, this amounts to saturating its ex ante participation constraint. That is, the compensation scheme is such that $\mathbb{E}_i[\Pi_{i,0}] = M + \psi$, where $M \in [0, I]$ is the monetary contribution made by the firm up-front. Taking all this into account, we find an upper bound to the admissible size of the loan:

$$C \leq \mathbb{E}_i[R_{T_i}] - (M + \psi). \tag{11}$$

Result 6 *To eliminate the government's incentive to renege on the contract opportunistically, anticipating breakup, the governmental guarantees* ($D_{i,\tau}$) *provided to the lender, in the event that the initial contract is honored, must be small enough to satisfy* (10). *Moreover the firm should take out a loan* (C) *small enough to satisfy* (10).

To ensure that results 5 and 6 are completely clear, we make the following remark.

Remark *The governmental guarantees* ($D_{i,\tau}^{rn}$) *provided to the lender, in the event that the initial contract is renegotiated, are only relevant off equilibrium in the renegotiation game between the government and the firm, given that the contract is never actually renegotiated in equilibrium. Consequently it is not an issue to set those guarantees as large as* (8) *requires, regardless of the magnitude of the loan. By contrast, the governmental guarantees* ($D_{i,\tau}$) *provided to the lender, in the event that the initial contract is honored, do reflect the amount of money that the firm is to borrow on the credit market in order to enter the PPP. This is why, for* $D_{i,\tau}$ *to be set small enough to satisfy* (10), *the loan of the firm must comply with* (11).

Own Funds of the Firm

To determinate the appropriate amount of own funds (M) that the firm should invest in the project, it is first necessary to complete the analysis of the government's incentives to renege on the contract. To this end we notice that there exists no value of the guarantee $D_{i,\tau}$ such that those incentives are eliminated, unless the cost of replacing the firm at date τ is at least as large as the present value, at that date, of the stream of future operating profits of the firm, that is, $R_{\delta_i} \geq \Pi_{i,\tau}$. It turns out that this is more a concern in the good state, in which the firm is assigned a higher compensation. Thus we only need to consider the case of $i = l$, hence the condition $R_{\delta_l} \geq \Pi_{l,\tau}$. Recall that the ex ante participation constraint of the firm is saturated, so it must be the case that $\Pi_{l,0} = M$

$+ \psi + (1 - v_1)(\Pi_{l,0} - \Pi_{h,0})$. Thus the value, at date $\tau \in (0, T_l)$, of the stream of future profits is given by

$$\Pi_{l,\tau} = [M + \psi + (1 - v_1)(\Pi_{l,0} - \Pi_{h,0})]\frac{1 - e^{-\delta_l}}{1 - e^{-rT_l}}.$$

This yields an upper bound to the admissible magnitude of M:

$$M \leq R_{\delta_l}\frac{1 - e^{-rT_l}}{1 - e^{-\delta_l}} - \psi - (1 - v_1)(\Pi_{l,0} - \Pi_{h,0}). \tag{12}$$

For the government not to be willing to renege on the contract, anticipating breakup of the partnership, the firm should not be required to invest more own funds than is necessary to satisfy (12). A larger contribution would boost the appetite of the government, which would then terminate the relationship and appropriate the firm's investment. Under (12), for the government to honor the contract, it is necessary and sufficient that the guarantee it provides satisfies (10), as result 6 states.

We can now turn to consider the firm. Recall, from results 1 and 2, that $\Pi_{l,0} > \Pi_{h,0}$. It is thus immediate to deduce that the firm is more prone to abandon the partnership when it faces unfavorable operating conditions. That is, (9a) is relevant in state h only: $\Pi_{h,\tau} \geq 0$. Provided that the contract is such that the firm breaks even in expectation, we can write its profit in state h as

$$\Pi_{h,0} = M + \psi - v_1(\Pi_{l,0} - \Pi_{h,0}). \tag{13}$$

Therefore the firm has no incentive to renege as soon as it starts operating (i.e., when τ is very close to 0), if and only if it is required to invest a sufficiently high amount of money:

$$M \geq v_1(\Pi_{l,0} - \Pi_{h,0}) - \psi. \tag{14}$$

Inspection of (14) prompts us to make two interesting points. First, the minimum admissible size of M is smaller the higher the disutility of effort. This is intuitive. The firm's monetary contribution (M) plays the same committing role as the nonmonetary contribution (ψ). They act as substitutes, from this standpoint. The more costly effort is for the firm, the more prone the firm is to honor the contract in order to recover that cost "as time goes by," hence the less necessary it is to use the funds of the firm as a commitment device. Second, the minimum admissible size of M is bigger the higher the profit wedge at date 0.

This is also very plausible. The more the firm is exposed to risk, the less motivated it is to remain in the contract when the operating conditions are unfavorable. As those conditions are unchanged through the termination date, the firm is assigned the same profit in every operating period. Hence, once it is ensured that the firm is motivated to honor the contract at the outset of the operation phase, as is the case when (14) holds, it is ensured that it is also motivated to do so at any other instant through the termination date.

Result 7 *The incentives of the government to renege, anticipating breakup, are eliminated (i.e.,* (10) *holds), only if the investment of the firm* (M) *is large enough to satisfy* (12). *The incentives of the firm to renege, anticipating breakup, are eliminated, if and only if its own investment is small enough to satisfy* (14).

We explained that, for the firm to be willing to honor the contract, it must put on the table a sufficiently large amount of own funds, and that this amount must be higher the bigger the profit wedge is set. Clearly, this requirement cannot be met unless the firm is wealthy enough to begin with. Recall that the profit wedge cannot be narrower than required in (1). Together with (14), it follows that the firm must hold a minimum admissible amount of funds in order to participate in the PPP project. Letting $E \geq 0$ denote the endowment of the firm, and knowing that $M \leq E$, the following result can be stated.

Result 8 *The firm's incentives to renege on the contract can be eliminated, together with the firm's incentives to shirk in construction, only if the amount of own funds that the firm can invest in the project is such that*

$$E \geq v_0 \frac{\psi}{\Delta v}. \tag{15}$$

The need to motivate the firm to exert effort in construction is somewhat at odds with the need to eliminate the firm's incentives to renege on the contract. As we know, the former task is accomplished by transferring enough risk to the firm, which is done by differentiating the profits sufficiently between states of nature. The desire to extract all surplus from the firm, in expectation, involves that the profit must be low in the bad state and high in the good state. However, the lower the profit in the bad state, the more difficult it is to induce the firm to abide by the contractual obligations during the operation phase. To ensure that the state-h profit is high enough for the firm to honor the contract, the initial investment of the firm, hence its wealth, must be sufficiently important.

5.3.4 Contractual Length

General Case: State-Dependent Duration

Based on results 5 to 7, one may deduce that once the financial structure of the project and the guarantees are properly set, neither the firm nor the government will have any incentive to renege on the contract and to terminate the partnership. One may thus conclude that having the contract honored is no longer an issue. However, the picture is not yet complete. To see this, from result 7 notice that it might be impossible to find a value of M, since it is little enough to make renege unattractive for the government and, at the same time, big enough to make renege unattractive for the firm. The temptation of the government can be eliminated, together with that of the firm, only if the replacement cost, which the government faces in state l, is sufficiently high and/or the profit wedge $\Pi_{l,0} - \Pi_{h,0}$ is sufficiently small, that is,

$$R_{\delta_l} \geq (\Pi_{l,0} - \Pi_{h,0})\frac{1-e^{-\delta_l}}{1-e^{-rT_l}}, \quad \forall \delta_l \in (0, T_l). \tag{16}$$

Let us first focus on the cost of replacement. When this is large, the government is unwilling to break up the partnership, even if the monetary contribution of the firm is important. Therefore the firm can be required to invest as much as necessary to be discouraged from reneging, in turn, on the contract. Let us next consider the profit wedge. To see why under limited commitment it is helpful to keep it small, recall that the incentive of the government to renege is stronger in the good state, in which the compensation to the firm is high. By contrast, the incentive of the firm is stronger in the bad state, in which the compensation is low. Setting the profit wedge small involves that the compensation to the firm is not very different in the two states. That is, neither the state-l compensation is high nor the state-h compensation is low to the point that renege is convenient, respectively, for the government and for the firm.

Once the logic behind (16) is well understood, knowing that R_{δ_l} depends on the residual contractual period, from date τ to date T_l, and that, given the need to address the information issues, the profit wedge depends on T_l and T_h (results 1 to 3), one further deduces that it might be possible to eliminate the temptations to renege with an appropriate choice of the two termination dates. We hereafter explore this aspect.

Let us begin by checking how small the profit wedge can be set, consistently with (1) to (3), in order to relax (16). Hinging on results 1 to 3, the wedge is smallest when, for any pair of termination dates $\{T_l, T_h\}$ satisfying (2) and (3), (1) is saturated. Accordingly, we can rewrite (16) as

$$R_{\delta_l} \geq \frac{\psi}{\Delta v} \frac{1-e^{-r\delta_l}}{1-e^{-rT_l}}, \quad \forall \delta_l \in (0, T_l). \tag{17}$$

Then, for (2) and (3) to be satisfied, T_l must be set according to (5). In addition, whenever $\psi \leq \Delta v \Delta \theta (q_h/r)$, T_h must be set such that

$$T_h \leq \frac{1}{r} \ln \frac{\Delta v \Delta \theta q_h}{\Delta v \Delta \theta q_h - r\psi}. \tag{18}$$

Result 9 *The information issues are addressed, together with the commitment issues, only if T_l can be chosen in such a way that* (5) *and* (17) *are simultaneously satisfied and, whenever $\psi \leq \Delta v \Delta \theta (q_h/r)$, T_h is set to satisfy* (18).

From (5) we learned that the duration of the contract cannot be too short in the good state. If the firm were not allowed to enjoy the benefits of the effort exerted in construction, in the state in which they appear, for a sufficiently long period of time, then the firm would not be motivated to try and make that state more likely. The smaller the disutility of effort, the lower is the profit wedge for which shirking is avoided; hence the harsher is the adverse-selection problem in state *h* relative to the moral-hazard problem. The former problem is tackled, together with the latter, by ensuring that the contract has a sufficiently long duration in state *l*. From (6), we also know that the contract cannot have too long a duration in the bad state. Otherwise, it would be impossible to elicit information in the good state, as the firm would be able to obtain an important benefit, through date T_h, by pretending a high cost. The requirement on T_h stated in (18) is a particular case of the requirement stated in (6). It arises because the profit wedge is downsized to saturate (1). With (1) saturated, the profit wedge is smaller the lower the disutility of effort. This makes it more difficult to eliminate the incentive of the firm to cheat, when the cost is low, relative to preventing the firm from shirking. Condition (6) mirrors this circumstance. On the opposite, when exerting effort is costly for the firm, $\psi > \Delta v \Delta\theta(q_h/r)$, the moral-hazard problem remains important, relative to the adverse-selection problem in state h. It is thus unnecessary to set T_h in compliance with (18).

Fixed versus State-Dependent Duration: Which Approach Should Be Taken?

Result 9 does not evidence any necessity of choosing a different termination date in the two states of nature. This raises, again, the same question that was asked in the full-commitment framework, that is, whether conditioning the duration of the contract on the true cost delivers any benefit, as compared to the usual practice of designing fixed-term contracts. We investigate this issue referring to a specific replacement-cost function, namely

$$R_{\delta_l} = 1 - be^{-r\delta_l},$$

where $0 < b < \min\{1;\ \psi/\Delta v\}$. Notice that for all positive values of T_l, we have

$$R'_{\delta_l} = rbe^{-r\delta_l} < \frac{\psi}{\Delta v}\frac{re^{-r\delta_l}}{1-e^{-rT_l}}.$$

Thus all over the range of possible values of δ_l, (17) is tightest as δ_l approaches T_l. Provided that $\psi \le \Delta v/r$, (17) is rewritten as

$$T_l \ge \frac{1}{r}\ln\frac{b\Delta v}{\Delta v - r\psi}. \tag{19}$$

Recall that T_l must satisfy (5). In addition, if $\psi \le \Delta v\Delta\theta(q_h/r)$, then T_h must satisfy (18). Thus, combining (5) with (19), it is clear that there is no upper bound to the choice of T_l. Noticeably (5) might not hold jointly with (18), if the contract had a fixed term ($T_l = T_h \equiv T$). The following result can be drawn.

Result 10 *Suppose that* $\Delta\theta q_h > 1$ *and that*

$$b > \frac{\Delta v - r\psi}{\Delta v - (r\psi/\Delta\theta q_h)}.$$

Then (18) *is satisfied, together with* (17) *(rewritten as* (19)*), only if* $T_l > T_h$.

There is an important practical implication to result 10. In environments where, in addition to the firm holding private information, either contractual party lacks the ability to commit, the usual practice of setting a fixed contractual term may be inappropriate. It may fail to ensure that the contract is, indeed, executed. Decision makers should regard as a useful tool the possibility of modulating the duration of the contract according to the specific operating conditions. This rests on the circumstance, previously illustrated, that some incentive issues are relevant in the good state (i.e., the incentive of the government to renege and that of the firm to pretend a high cost), others are relevant in the bad state (i.e., the incentives of the firm to renege and to pretend a low cost). When the state-dependent approach is preferred to the fixed-term approach, the extra flexibility, which the government enjoys in the determination of the contractual length, can be exploited in the attempt to reconcile the different incentive issues across states of nature. Hence making the duration state-dependent facilitates the task of addressing those issues all at once.

5.4 Discussion and Conclusion

Taking together all the results presented in this work, one can see that various instruments can be used to attain efficient contractual outcomes in PPP arrangements and that ultimately they involve a proper choice of contractual length (results 9 and 10). Without the latter, it would be impossible to set the debt guarantees and the firm's investment in such a way to satisfy the conditions in results 6 and 7. Consequently the contract would not be enforceable. Therefore an important practical lesson to retain is that when designing the contract, it is essential to account for the financial structure of the project together with the contractual length rather than considering each of these separately. Indeed this is intuitive, given that the compensation to the firm, which drives the incentives of either partner to honor or to abjure the contract, does depend on the size of the debt, the firm's own contribution to the project, and the contractual length, all at once.

We found that the best strategy to deal with the opportunistic behavior of the partners is to let the contract have a longer duration in the good state of nature, a result that is at odds with the literature on flexible-term contracts. Although, to facilitate the exposition, we only provided an illustrative example, result 10 is in fact general, as the analysis in Danau and Vinella (2015b) shows. For practical use, setting a longer duration in the good state comes as a novel proposal. Indeed

PPP contracts have, in the majority, a fixed term and, in some instances, a flexible term. However, looking closely at real-world experiences, such as the Metronet case in London, it is evident that early terminations of PPPs follow often a default by the firm. By contrast, when contractual renege occurs on the initiative of the government, a new deal is usually reached, as was the case in Argentina, where many PPP contracts, signed during the 1990s, were subject to government-led renegotiations, even repeatedly (Guasch 2004). What result 9 suggests is that these issues, particularly the different incentives that the partners would display in the different states, should be accounted for in contractual design, and be addressed by choosing a longer duration in good states than in bad states.

We identified an important role for financial institutions such as the ECAs. One may wonder whether, without such institutions, the intended outcome could still be attained and, if so, which benefit could be obtained, in that case, by setting a longer contractual term in the good state. As from result 6 and the subsequent remark, the reason why it is useful to involve a credible financial institution in the government–firm relationship is that the payment from the government to the lender, to be enforced in the event of a renegotiation, is perceived by the government as a penalty, to be borne if deviating from the original contract to a new deal. Therefore institutions like ECAs are helpful when renegotiation is an attractive option. Their intervention is precisely intended to reduce the attractiveness of that option, thus lessening opportunism. Without that intervention, the commitment problem would be more difficult to tackle (formally, the conditions in result 9 would be tighter). Then, a fortiori, a longer duration in the good state would be useful, making a better job than a fixed duration.

Notes

We gratefully acknowledge comments from participants at the CESifo Summer Institute Workshop on The Economics of Infrastructure Provisioning: The (Changing) Role of the State (Venice).

1. In Europe, between 1990 and 2005/2006, PPPs experienced a sixfold increase, on an annual basis, being used in defense, government buildings, hospitals, ICTs, municipal services, schools, tourism, water, and, above all, transportation. Many such initiatives display local dimensions as municipalities are responsible for infrastructure provision in many countries (Allain-Dupré 2011). In the United States, PPPs became very popular a bit later, in the immediate aftermath of the recession (Engel, Fischer, and Galetovic 2011).

2. Although arguments are sometimes provided in favor of a more systematic adoption in toll-road concessions (e.g., see Albalate and Bel 2009), so far flexible-term contracts have received a limited support in practice.

3. From a cross-country analysis, Banarjee, Oetzel, and Ranganathan (2006) conclude that governments' opportunistic behavior does not propitiate private investment (see also Estache and Wren-Lewis 2009).

4. According to The EPEC PPP Guide (2012), in the event of PPP company default, the lenders should be allowed to step in to rescue the project. The PPP contract should be terminated and the government should appropriate the assets, only if the lenders renounce to this possibility. In fact this is a likely option, particularly in complex projects. However, even if the lenders were eager to undertake the activity, providing for their right to step in would require entering into a direct agreement with the government and the firm. Under limited commitment, the government would not commit to this agreement, just as it does not commit to the PPP contract.

5. Most European governments have set up ECAs for the purposes described in the text. All countries that have official ECAs are now party to the "Arrangement on Guidelines for Officially Supported Export Credits," which provides specific rules for project finance. Examples of European ECAs are Compagnie Française d'Assurance pour le Commerce Extérieur (Coface), Euler Hermes Kreditversicherungs (Hermes), Istituto per i Servizi Assicurativi del Credito all'Esportazione (SACE), and Office National du Ducroire (ONDD).

6. To be more rigorous, spending one unit of public funds requires collecting more than one unit of money from taxpayers. To capture this circumstance formally, we would need to introduce some parameter $\lambda > 0$, expressing the shadow cost of public funds. Then the net benefit of the government would amount to $R_{\delta_i} - (1+\lambda)D_{i,\tau}^{rn}$. However, because this would have no qualitative impact on results, we prefer to keep the formulation simple and to neglect the shadow cost of public funds.

References

Albalate, Daniel, and Germà Bel. 2009. Regulating concessions of toll motorways: An empirical study on fixed vs. variable term contracts. *Transportation Research Part A, Policy and Practice* 43: 219–29.

Allain-Dupré, Dorothée. 2011. Multi-level governance of public investment: Lessons from the crisis. Regional Development working paper 2011/05. OECD.

Banerjee, Sudeshna G., Jennifer M. Oetzel, and Rupa Ranganathan. 2006. Private provision of infrastructure in emerging markets: Do institutions matter? *Development Policy Review* 24 (2): 175–202.

Bennett, John, and Elisabetta Iossa. 2006. Building and managing facilities for public services. *Journal of Public Economics* 90: 2143–60.

Brench, Andreas, Thorsten Beckers, Maria Heinrich, and Christian von Hirschhausen. 2005. Public–private partnerships in new EU member countries of Central and Eastern Europe. European Investment Bank 10, no. 2.

Dewatripont, Mathias. 1989. Renegotiation and information revelation over time: the case of optimal labor contracts. *Quarterly Journal of Economics* 104: 589–619.

Danau, Daniel, and Annalisa Vinella. 2015a. Public–private contracting under limited commitment. *Journal of Public Economic Theory* 17 (1): 78–110.

Danau, Daniel, and Annalisa Vinella. 2015b. From fixed to state-dependent duration in public–private contracts. Working paper 201504 CREM.

Ehrhardt, David, and Timothy Irwin. 2004. Avoiding customer and taxpayer bailouts in private infrastructure projects: Policy toward leverage, risk allocation, and bankruptcy. Policy Research working paper 3274. World Bank.

Engel, Eduardo, Ronald Fischer, and Alexander Galetovic. 2013. The basic public finance of public–private partnerships. *Journal of the European Economic Association* 11 (1): 83–111.

Engel, Eduardo, Ronald Fischer, and Alexander Galetovic. 2011. Public–private partnerships to revamp U.S. infrastructures. Discussion paper 2011–02. The Hamilton Project, Brookings Institute.

Engel, Eduardo, Ronald Fischer, and Alexander Galetovic. 2001. Least-present-value-of-revenue auctions and highway franchising. *Journal of Political Economy* 109 (5): 993–1020.

Engel, Eduardo, Ronald Fischer, and Alexander Galetovic. 1997. Highway franchising: Pitfalls and opportunities. *American Economic Review* 87 (2): 68–72.

EPEC. 2012. *The Guide to Guidance: How to Prepare, Procure and Deliver PPP Projects*. Luxembourg: European Investment Bank.

Estache, Antonio, and Liam Wren-Lewis. 2009. Towards a theory of regulation for developing countries: Following Laffont's lead. *Journal of Economic Literature* 47 (3): 729–70.

Gagnepain, Philippe, Marc Ivaldi, and David Martimort. 2009. Renégociation de contrats dans l'industrie du transport urbain en France. *Revue Economique* 60 (4): 927–47.

Guasch, Jose L. 2004. *Granting and Renegotiating Infrastructure Concessions: Doing It Right*.Washington, DC: World Bank Institute.

Guasch, Jose L., Jean-Jacques Laffont, and Stéphane Straub. 2006. Renegotiation of concession contracts: A theoretical approach. *Review of Industrial Organization* 29: 55–73.

Guasch, Jose L., Jean-Jacques Laffont, and Stéphane Straub. 2008. Renegotiation of concession contracts in Latin America: Evidence from the water and transport sectors. *International Journal of Industrial Organization* 26 (2): 421–42.

Hart, Oliver, and Jean Tirole. 1988. Contract renegotiation and Coasian dynamics. *Review of Economic Studies* 55: 509–40.

House of Lords. 2010a. Private finance projects and off-balance sheet debt. First Report of Session 2009–10, vol. I: Report, HL paper 63-I.

House of Lords. 2010b. Private finance projects and off-balance sheet debt. First Report of Session 2009–10, vol. II: Evidence, HL paper 63-II.

Levin, Jonathan. 2003. Relational incentive contracts. *American Economic Review* 93: 835–57.

Iossa, Elisabetta, and David Martimort. 2015. . The simple micro-economics of public–private partnerships. *Journal of Public Economic Theory* 17 (1): 4–48.

Irwin, Timothy, Michael Klein, Guillermo E. Perry, and Mateen Thobani. 1997. *Dealing with Public Risk in Private Infrastructure*. Washington, DC: World Bank Latin American and Caribbean Studies.

Laffont, Jean-Jacques. 2003. Enforcement, regulation and development. *Journal of African Economies* 12: 193–211.

Martimort, David, and Jérôme Pouyet. 2008. To build or not to build: Normative and positive theories of public–private partnerships. *International Journal of Industrial Organization* 26 (2): 393–411.

National Audit Office. 2008–2009. The failure of Metronet. HC512. London.

Rey, Patrick, and Bernard Salanié. 1996. On the value of commitment with asymmetric information. *Econometrica* 64: 1395–1414.

6 Infrastructure Investment in Network Industries: The Role of Incentive Regulation and Regulatory Independence in OECD Countries

Balázs Égert

6.1 Introduction

Opening up network industries, through liberalization or privatization and the introduction of incentive regulation, has often been viewed as a way to promote infrastructure investment. For example, the separation of electricity generation and transmission in the United States was intended to boost investment by encouraging more entry into the market (Ishii and Yan 2006). Yet problems arising after the opening up of network industries have often been attributed to falling investment in network infrastructure. For example, a series of fatal train accidents in the United Kingdom (Southall in 1997, Paddington in 1999, and Hatfield in 2000) was widely blamed on underinvestment, while the blackouts in California in 2001 and in New York, London, Italy, Denmark, and Sweden in 2003 were largely blamed on underinvestment in electricity generation or transmission grids (Bialek 2004; Pollitt 2007; Hirschhausen et al. 2004; Joskow 2006).

Part of the divergence between ex ante expectations and ex post outcomes can be explained by incoherencies in the overall framework of the reforms. For example, in the electricity sector, Jamasb and Pollitt (2005) argue that introducing sustainable competition in electricity generation and distribution requires action with respect to liberalization, privatization, and regulation. First, vertical unbundling of generation, transmission and distribution (and horizontal splitting in generation) is necessary to ensure competition by preventing a vertically integrated company acting strategically to curb competition and to prevent new entry. Second, public incumbents in generation and distribution should be privatized to ensure a level playing field, which may result from their easier access to capital than for new entrants. Finally, setting up an independent regulator is needed to supervise the transmission network operator.

Against this backdrop, this chapter investigates the extent to which the consistency of the regulatory framework influences sectoral investment behavior in network industries in a sample of OECD countries. The outline of the chapter is the following: Section 6.2 reviews the theoretical arguments with regard to the relation between the regulatory framework and investment in network industries. Section 6.3 provides an overview of the empirical literature. Sections 6.4 and 6.5 discuss the methodology and data issues and then present the results. Finally, section 6.6 presents the results, and section 6.7 provides concluding remarks.

6.2 Investment Behavior under Different Regulatory Regimes

It is well known that an unregulated monopoly tends to produce lower quantities and charges higher prices than welfare maximizing would imply. This may imply that the monopolist's investment in network capacity does not correspond to that which is consistent with welfare maximization. Furthermore the monopolist will invest later than is socially optimal because it compares the costs related to its investment only with producer surplus and fully ignores consumers' surplus.

One way of raising social welfare is to introduce competition in network industries that are dominated by a monopolist.[1] However, parts of the vertically integrated network industries remain natural monopolies and will remain dominated by a single firm because of large fixed costs and economies of scale or scope relative to demand. But even if competition can be introduced in other parts of the industry, the state may want to regulate the market in the face of the possibility of market failure due to market power resulting from too few market participants, especially in the initial stages of liberalization. Furthermore, when competition is not feasible, appropriate regulatory frameworks can, nonetheless, simulate a competitive environment. The question is therefore to what extent these different regulatory regimes influence investment incentives.

Differences in price regulation have often been seen as particularly important in determining investment incentives. While cost-based or rate-of-return regulation is generally thought to bring about overinvestment (Averch and Johnson 1962), incentive price regulation is often considered as introducing the risk of underinvestment in the longer run (Armstrong and Sappington 2006). However, this characterization is too stark as the extent to which a particular regime supports investment depends considerably on the overall setup of the regime. In this context the next subsections discuss the factors that will result in over- and underinvestment.

6.2.1 Rate-of-Return Regulation and Overinvestment

Under rate-of-return regulation, prices are set to account for the production costs of the firm and the margin (the "plus factor") that is allowed by the regulator or agreed on between the regulator and the firm.[2] The "plus factor" can specifically relate to the return the firm is allowed to earn on its capital. This return, often coined "fair" rate of return, should allow the firm to recover investment costs. The prices are adjusted upon the initiative of the regulated firm, the regulator or consumers if production costs increased or decreased after the last regulatory review.

Rate-of-return regulation may encourage the regulated monopoly to overinvest in network capacity and lead to allocative inefficiency. Overinvestment occurs if the regulated fair rate of return exceeds the cost of capital leading the regulated monopoly to substitute capital for labor in order to increase profit. At the same time, the high capital–labor ratio will result in a production structure that is not cost efficient (Averch and Johnson 1962). Overinvestment due to high capital–labor ratio will result in higher levels of quality if service quality is a function of capital intensity.[3] More generally, overinvestment and the ensuing excess capacity may be used as a strategic tool to deter potential entrants and empire-building managers who tend to be ambitious may be tempted to increase investments because a larger company size results in higher status and material rewards (Starkie 2006).

6.2.2 Incentive Price Regulation and Underinvestment

The underlying idea of price cap regulation is to simulate conditions of perfect competition by imposing a price cap over the regulatory period adjusted for changes in (exogenous measures of) input prices, quality and efficiency targets imposed by the regulator. The possibility that costs and prices can diverge during the regulatory period provides firms incentives to implement cost-reducing investment and innovations aimed at improving operating efficiency to outperform the efficiency target.

Incentive regulation, such as a price cap that does not account for quality changes appropriately, encourages the regulated firm to increase profit by reducing service quality at unchanged prices. And typically there have been complaints that service quality declines shortly after price caps were introduced.[4] In order to prevent the firm reaping extra profit by reducing quality, the regulator may wish to adjust the regulated price by some measure for quality.

6.2.3 Regulatory Features Affecting Investment Behavior

There are a number of additional features of regulation besides the basic pricing regime that can result in underinvestment.[5] These include basically, the so-called regulatory asset base, the timing of regulatory reviews and uncertainty about the regulators actions ("regulatory opportunism").

The Regulatory Asset Base and Cost Disallowances

The so-called regulatory asset base or "rate base" is a critical regulatory parameter that constitutes the base for the calculation of the rate of return. If the rate base includes all assets of the firm, the firm may be tempted to invest imprudently. To avoid this problem, regulators may select investments that they allow to be included in the rate base.[6] Such "cost disallowances" may lead firms to cut back or reschedule investment plans (Guthrie 2006). If the regulator assesses a firm's investment ex post rather than ex ante, it will use information that was not available at the time the investment decision was made. Consequently the regulator may not allow the inclusion of the whole investment to the rate base.

A regulated firm that faces possible cost disallowance because the regulator relies on ex post information will be more prudent and will pick only those investment projects that are subject to low future shocks. In particular, a long time lag between the decision and the completion of an investment project makes investment vulnerable to future shocks. Hence investors will act with caution in selecting projects with long lead time, and smaller projects involving less sunk costs will be chosen over large projects that offer economies of scale. Industries with fast technological progress are also more likely to be hit by demand shocks and by a fall in capital costs. An ex post evaluation of investment by the regulator would make incumbents in these sectors overly cautious.

Timing of the Regulatory Review

When the regulatory cycle is sufficiently long relative to investment, firms will invest to benefit from cost-reducing investments in the case of incentive price regulation and because all costs are passed onto consumers under rate-of-return regulation. If the firm can choose the timing of the investment and if the timing of the regulatory reviews is exogenous, the firm will invest after the regulatory review to maximize payoff. The closer to the next review, the more likely that investments will be delayed for the next regulatory period and that the firm will seek to lower costs. If prices are reviewed in reaction to the profitability of the firm operating under rate-of-return regulation, the firm will refrain from implementing investments as the firm's rate of return approaches the upper bound. Instead, it will invest right after the review when the rate of return is reset.[7] When the regulatory cycle is too short, firms operating under a price cap regime will not be able to benefit from improved efficiency and will have less incentive to invest. Under price caps, regulatory reviews are often scheduled every 4 to 5 years. Industries subject to comparatively slow technological progress and a low-volatility environment such as the water industry can have longer review periods of eight years with an option to request an early review (Guthrie 2006).

The Regulator's Decision-Making and Uncertainty

In cases where the regulator is unduly influenced by politicians or the public, it may be tempted to set prices or the rate of return too low. Obviously the regulated firm may choose to reduce investment if the rate of return a firm can earn on its investment is seriously constrained. This may discourage high-return and, thus, more risky investments. In addition the move from rate-of-return to incentive price regulation shifts risk from consumers to shareholders and consequently raises the cost of capital for the regulated firm. The implications are that if the regulated firm is not allowed to earn a return on its capital that incorporates the higher risk (the implicit rate of return determined by the price cap), it will not invest in new assets (Alexander and Irwin 1996).

Uncertainty about the regulator's actions poses a nonnegligible threat to investment in network industries. If the regulator is unable to make a credible commitment that it will not change prices after the firm invests, the firm will tend to underinvest.[8] The regulated firm may either delay investment or invest sequentially to see the outcome at the next regulatory review. Regulatory uncertainty does not only generate underinvestment but will also affect the composition of the investment, as the regulated firm may choose a technology with lower fixed costs (Spiegel 1996). The regulated firm can also react to the lack of commitment by issuing more debt. A rise in the regulated firm's leverage (debt-to-equity ratio) increases the probability of future financial distress which may in turn induce the regulator to allow higher prices.[9] However, higher prices may not eliminate the underinvestment bias because the firm also faces the risk and costs of bankruptcy stemming from higher leverage (Spiegel and Spulber 1994).

Underinvestment resulting from regulatory uncertainty can be mitigated by establishing independent regulatory bodies.[10] For example, credibility can be achieved through financial, political, and institutional independence from the government while being accountable to a mandate. This can enhance the time consistency of policy and minimize uncertainty about future actions. This sort of regulatory uncertainty can be alleviated by implementing ex ante profit-sharing schemes that stipulate that the regulated firm must pay back part or the totality of the excess profit to consumers.[11]

Regulatory uncertainty may not be fully eliminated, however. For example, under incentive price regulation the potential efficiency gains may not be fully exploited if the regulated firm expects the regulator to impose price caps at the next regulatory review that are partly based on its past performance.[12] Under rate-of-return regulation, what is included in the regulatory asset base is likely to be a persistent area of uncertainty for the regulated firm.

Implications for the Different Pricing Regimes

In sum, the differences in investment behavior between rate-of-return and incentive price based regulation can rest on features of the regulatory regime. As firms under rate-of-return regulation are comparatively unresponsive to changes in demand, the regulator needs to play an important role in determining what investment is needed. Furthermore, due to the inherent tendency of investment being allocatively inefficient, there will always be a conflict between the firm and the regulator over what is included in the regulatory asset base. To some extent, this conflict will be ex post and regulatory decisions may not adequately reflect ex ante risks. In this light the regulator needs to be well informed to minimize allocative inefficiency and ensure that investment is sufficiently reactive to changes in demand and technology. By contrast, firms operating under incentive price regulation regimes will have higher levels of allocative efficiency and will have incentives to invest in cost-saving technology. Such firms, however, face higher ex ante market-driven risk, and other things being equal, this requires a higher rate of return. To the extent that regulatory risk and uncertainty are present (e.g., driven by the timing of the reviews and changes to the implicit rate of return during pricing reviews), investment will also be affected. Regulatory uncertainty and risk can be potentially mitigated by granting the regulator independence and a suitable mandate.

6.3 Empirical Evidence

6.3.1 Rail

Some of the problems following the liberalization in the 1990s of rail tracks in the United Kingdom have been blamed on massive underinvestment. A more detailed analysis of the underlying figures suggests however no systematic underinvestment in comparison with the previous system at the sectoral level. Pollitt (2000) finds that in constant 1995 prices between 1981 and 1995 investment increase significantly in British Rail (as well as airports and the water industries, while no significant changes took place in telecommunications, electricity, and gas industries). Investment in rail transportation did not drop but rather increased in 1999 following privatization in 1997. Furthermore, the investment rate was high in historical terms after privatization (compared to the 1970s and 1980s) and the introduction of incentive regulation (Clark, Elsby, and Love 2001).[13] Overall, incentive regulation did not appear to cause a major disruption in sectoral investments of the regulated sectors. The overall investment figures in the British railway sector until 1999 mask, however, a steady increase in investment in the railway network and a fall in investment in rolling stock (Affuso and Newbery 2000).[14]

6.3.2 Telecommunications

There are a number of studies that show a strong positive relationship between investment and incentive price regulation in the US telecommunication industry. For instance, Ai and Sappington (2002) note that past research has shown that incentive regulation was more powerful than traditional rate-of-return regulation during the late 1980s and early 1990s for the deployment of new technology. They then demonstrate that different forms of incentive regulation helped encourage the deployment of fiber optic cable during the 1990s. However, the different forms of incentive regulation they considered were not generally more conducive to raising overall investment relative to firms operating under rate-of-return regulation.[15] Greenstein, McMaster, and Spiller (1995) also find strong econometric evidence in favor of the investment promoting effect of price cap regulation in the US telecommunication sector. In particular, when controlling for local demographic and economic factors, firm-specific financial indicators, and the general regulatory environment, the authors unravel that investment in fiber-optic cable deployment, ISDN, and software updates during the late 1980s and early 1990s was substantially higher under price cap regimes. They estimate that in the United States at the end of the period under study, fiber-optic cable deployment would have been by 75 percent higher if price cap regimes had been in place everywhere.

A two-way causal link seems to exist between the incumbent's and facilities-based entrants' decisions to deploy fiber ring in the same city (Woroch 2000).[16] On the one hand, incumbents react swiftly to the deployment of fiber rings by new entrants. This can be interpreted as a predatory response or because new entry is viewed as signaling new profit opportunities. On the other hand, new entrants invest in their own network as a result of the incumbent's investment decisions. Furthermore the estimation results reveal that the incumbent's level of investment does not depend on the regulatory policy with regard to the access of their network by new providers, while new entrants invest more if they can access the incumbent's network.

Other evidence is less supportive of the role of incentive regulation in promoting the deployment of new technology. For example, Floyd and Gabel (2003), using a cross-sectional dataset for 2001, find that some types of incentive regulation are associated with both lower and higher investment rates for four kinds of new technologies, relative to rate-of-return regulation.[17] To some extent these findings may also reflect other differences in the regulatory regime. For instance, empirical evidence for the US telecommunication sector suggests that regulators tend to set lower access prices and more liberal entry conditions in price-cap regimes than in rate-of-return regimes (Lehman and Weisman 2000).

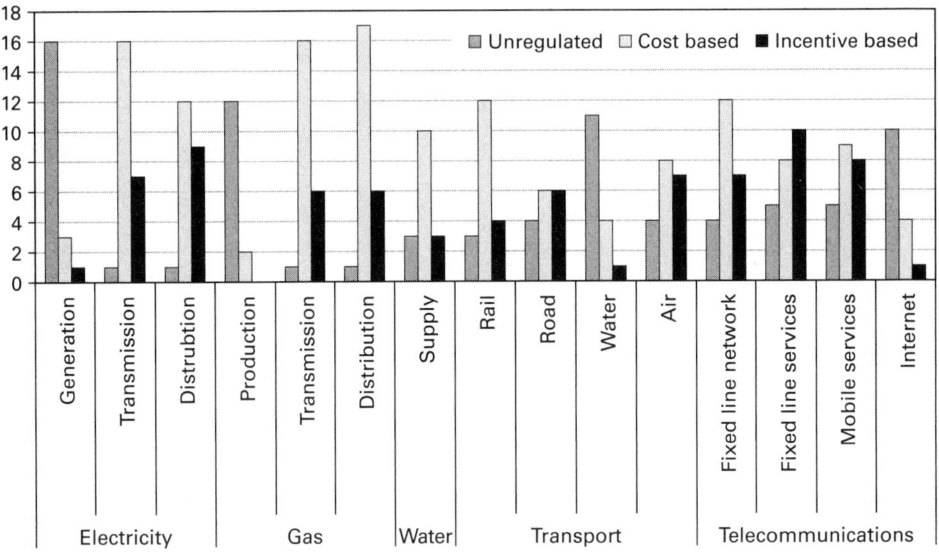

Figure 6.1
Regulatory regimes (late 2007 or early 2008)
Source: OECD infrastructure questionnaire responses

6.4 Data Issues

The primary interest of the empirical work lies in assessing the impact of the regulatory setup on investment decisions in electricity, gas, and water supply; road, rail, water, and air transportation; and telecommunications. Information on the type of regulatory regime and the independence of the sectoral regulator was derived from ad hoc surveys concerning infrastructure regulation and investment in OECD member countries. Regulatory regimes are divided into three broad categories: cost-based regulation (rate-of-return regulation), incentive price regulation; and no regulation (or where pricing has been deregulated).

Questionnaire responses indicate that cost-based regulation is the most popular form of regulation (figure 6.1). Out of the 15 sectors covered, 9 sectors are dominated by cost-based regulation, 4 sectors are mostly deregulated (electricity and gas generation, water transportation, and Internet services), while incentive regulation is the most popular form of regulation in fixed-line telecommunications services. Furthermore incentive regulation has a nonnegligible role in other seven sectors (electricity and gas transmission and distribution, road

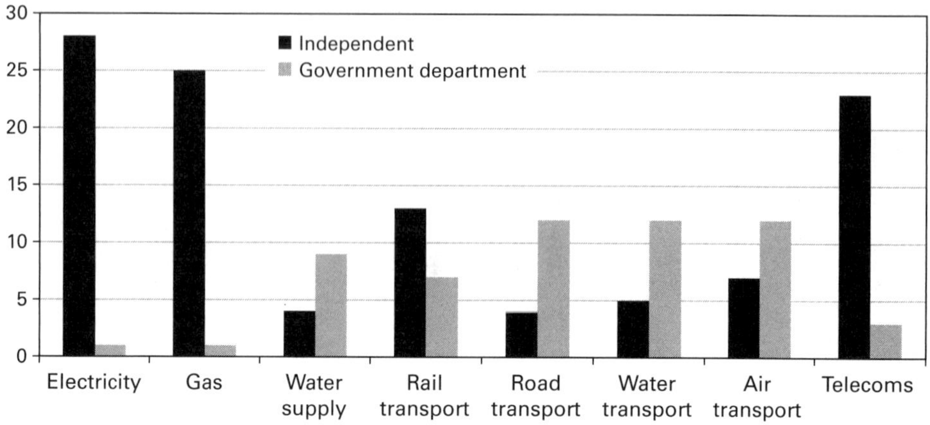

Figure 6.2
Regulatory independence (late 2007 or early 2008)
Source: OECD infrastructure questionnaire responses

and air transportation and fixed-line networks). For the empirical work, two variables are used that compare incentive regulation against cost-based regulation and deregulation or the absence of regulation against cost-based regulation.

Figure 6.2 shows that regulators are overwhelmingly independent in the electricity, gas, and telecommunications sectors, while regulators tend to be part of government agencies or ministries in transportation and in the water industry. Two measures of regulatory independence were constructed. The first was whether the regulator was independent of the government. The second measure was a gauge of de facto independence assessing the extent to which the executive can influence the regulator's decisions and operation (using responses from the OECD infrastructure questionnaire).[18] The two variables are not significantly different. The type of price regulation regime was interacted with the regulator's independence variable to see whether the consistency of the general policy framework matters for sectoral investment.

As questionnaire responses only provide a snapshot of regulation in late 2007 and early 2008, the data on the type of regulatory regime do not have a time dimension. For this reason, only cross-sectional regressions are carried out in the analysis (with sectoral investment being the dependent variable). In addition to the regulatory variables, other explanatory variables include lagged investment (I_{t-1}),lagged long-term sectoral real interest rate (r), and (lagged) variables capturing the general regulatory environment: entry barriers (*entry*),[19] public ownership (*po*),[20] whether there is incentive regulations (*inc*), whether prices are unregulated or have been deregulated (*dereg*), and whether the regulator is independent (*ri*). This gives the general form:

$$I_t = f(I_{t-1}, r_{t-1}, entry_{t-1}, po_{t-1}, inc, dereg, ri, inc * ri). \quad (1)$$

Investment data are obtained from the OECD's STAN and SNA (Sectoral National Accounts) database. These two databases have two serious shortcomings. First, the level of disaggregation is limited to three broad categories: electricity, gas, and water supply; transportation (road, rail, water, air, and associated storage); and telecommunications (which also includes postal services). Second, capital stock data needed to calculate the investment-to-capita stock ratio are available only for a limited number of OECD countries and are not fully comparable across countries. In principle, one could compute capital stock series using investment flows and the perpetual inventory method, but these estimates are extremely sensitive to the underlying assumptions. Given long asset lives, one often still needs an estimate of the value of the capital stock to anchor the series, which is not readily available. As a result sectoral value added is used to construct the investment ratio at the sectoral level. Overall, the sectoral dataset covers 13 countries for the three sectors.

6.5 Estimation Method: Bayesian Averaging of Classical Estimates

The main empirical approach is Bayesian averaging of classical estimates of the possible explanatory variables (applied to growth regressions in Sala-i-Martin et al. 2004).[21] For comparison purposes, results of OLS estimates are also reported. Bayesian averaging is a comprehensive analytical tool to check the extent to which any given explanatory variable improves the explanatory power of the estimated models when it is included. In other words, it investigates the probability with which any given variable would be included in the estimated models. This approach requires the estimation of all possible combinations of the candidate explanatory variables (of number K) that is usually quantified as 2^K.

Bayesian averaging of classical estimates (BACE) first determines the posterior probability attributed to each single model M_i that includes the given variable and conditioned on the underlying dataset y ($P(M_i|y)$).

$$P(M_i|y)=\frac{P(M_i)T^{-k_j/2}SSE_i^{-T/2}}{\sum_{i=1}^{2^K}P(M_i)T^{-k_i/2}SSE_i^{-T/2}}, \tag{2a}$$

where SSE is the sum of squared residuals, T is the number of observations, k denotes the number of explanatory variables included in the specific model, and K is the number of all explanatory variables considered. Expression (2a) shows the extent to which any given model contributes to explaining the dependent variable as compared to the other models. Expression (2a) is then summed up for the models that contain the variable of interest to obtain the posterior inclusion probability of this variable.

$$P(X_m|y)=\sum_{j=1}^{n}\frac{P(M_j)T^{-k_j/2}SSE_j^{-T/2}}{\sum_{i=1}^{2^K}P(M_i)T^{-k_i/2}SSE_i^{-T/2}}, \tag{2b}$$

where $P(X_m|y)$ is the posterior inclusion probability of a given variable, j denotes the models that include variable X_m, and n equals $2^K/2$. If the posterior inclusion probability is higher than the prior inclusion probability, one can conclude that the specific variable should be included in estimated models. We estimate all possible combinations of the explanatory variables. In this case the prior inclusion probability is 0.50.

The posterior mean conditional on inclusion ($E(\beta|y)$) is the average of the individual OLS estimates weighted by $P(M_j|y)$. Note that the unconditional posterior mean considers all regressions, even those without the variable of interest. Hence the unconditional posterior mean of any given variable can be derived as the product of the conditional posterior mean and the posterior inclusion probability. The posterior variance of β ($\mathrm{Var}(\beta|y)$) can be calculated as follows:

$$\mathrm{Var}(\beta|y)=\sum_{j=1}^{2^K}P(M_j|y)\mathrm{Var}(\beta|y,M_j)+\sum_{j=1}^{2^K}P(M_j|y)\left(\hat{\beta}_j-E(\beta|y)\right)^2. \tag{3}$$

The posterior mean and the square root of the variance (standard error) conditional on inclusion can be used to obtain t-statistics and to determine the significance of the individual variables upon inclusion.

Model averaging is vulnerable to the violation of the basic assumption of homoscedasticity and to the presence of outliers (Doppelhofer and Weeks 2007). Thus White's heteroscedasticity-corrected standard errors are used not only for the full sample but also for subsamples that

Table 6.1
Estimation results, sectoral investment data with country and industry fixed effects

	OLS		Bayesian model averaging		
	Coefficient	*p*-Value	Posterior inclusion probability	Posterior mean conditional on inclusion	Posterior standard error conditional on inclusion
Lagged investment	0.865	**0.000**	**1.000**	**0.880**	**0.166**
Real interest rate	0.009	0.130	**0.654**	**0.006**	**0.003**
Barriers to entry	-0.046	**0.008**	**0.998**	**-0.043**	**0.012**
Public ownership	0.004	0.701	0.151	0.000	0.002
Regulatory independence	-0.026	0.556	0.184	-0.004	0.006
Incentive regulation	-0.003	0.866	0.141	0.000	0.002
No price regulation	-0.016	0.133	0.975	-0.015	0.008
Independence and incentive Regulation interaction term	0.060	**0.002**	**0.996**	**0.053**	**0.014**
Adj. R-squared		0.741			
Regression runs			256		
Prior inclusion probability			0.5		

Notes: Posterior inclusion probability measures the extent to which any given model contributes to explaining the dependent variable as compared to the other models. Bold figures for the posterior inclusion probability indicate that it is higher than the prior inclusion probability of 0.5. The posterior mean conditional on inclusion is the mean of the individual OLS estimates weighted by the posterior inclusion probability of the individual models including a given variable.

exclude one country at a time. This makes it possible to evaluate the impact of individual countries on the robustness of the results and to eliminate potential outliers.

6.6 Empirical Results

Regressions results obtained for the 13 countries with 3 sectors each show that lagged investment, barriers to entry and the interaction term including regulatory independence and incentive regulation are significantly correlated with contemporaneous investment (table 6.1).[22]

Barriers to entry are found to influence investment negatively. The coefficient estimate of −0.043 indicates that a one-step change in the barriers to entry variable would be associated with a 4.3 percent increase in the investment ratio. This finding is broadly in line with results reported in Alesina et al. (2003).[23] When taken separately, neither regulatory independence nor incentive regulation seems to have an effect on investment. This suggests that a right policy mix is important in determining investment.

As a robustness check to the simple OLS results, Bayesian model averaging is carried out. Table 6.1 reports the main results for the different regulatory variables. If both country and industry fixed effects are used, the most robust findings are that for the whole sample and all subsamples (where one country at a time is dropped) posterior inclusion probabilities are always higher than 0.50 in the case of entry barriers and the interaction term combining incentive regulation with regulatory independence. Table 6.1 also indicates that in the cross section under consideration public ownership is not an important driver of investment rates and that the absence of price regulation tends to lower investment. This latter result suggests that price regulation in network industries has to be preferred over price deregulation. Yet this result seems to be driven by the observations for the United States, since it vanishes once the United States is dropped from the sample

The size of the coefficient estimates for the different subsamples suggests that on average a one-step change in the interaction term (e.g., a change from 1 to 2) would induce an average increase of the investment ratio by 4.9 percentage points. The lowest and highest coefficient estimates give a lower and higher bound of the increase in the investment ratio of respectively 1.6 percentage points and 6.5 percentage points. A move from the bottom to the top in the observed distribution of the interaction term—from 0 to 4.5—would on average increase the investment ratio by 22.2 percentage points, with the lower and upper bounds being 7.2 percentage points and 29.3 percentage points.

6.7 Conclusions

Theory suggests that none of the existing regulatory regimes is immune to the danger of over- or underinvestment in network infrastructure. Whether a particular regime incentivizes firms to invest depends to a large extent on the particular setup of the system. While rate-of-return regulation is traditionally thought to result in overinvestment, the more recent literature emphasized that underinvestment can also occur under certain circumstances. The regulated firm may choose to underinvest if the timing of the regulatory cycle is too short to recoup investment costs, or it may also decide not to invest, delay investment, or invest sequentially (or to increase its leverage) in the case of regulatory uncertainty. The regulated firm may also cut back investment in the face of uncertainty arising from the use of ex post rather than ex ante information with regard to the inclusion of investment to the rate base.

While it is widely accepted that incentive price regulation is a powerful tool to eliminate short-run cost inefficiencies, it is also thought to incite regulated firms to under-invest in network infrastructure with a view to increase short-term profits. Like rate-of-return regulation, incentive regulation may depress investment if the regulatory cycle is not long enough to break even, if the regulator revises efficiency targets before the next review period, if it sets unrealistic efficiency targets or if the rate base is evaluated with the wisdom of hindsight. The fact that risk is shifted back from consumers to shareholders implies higher risk and higher cost of capital translating into less investment.

Regulated firms may nevertheless want to increase investment spending because incentive price regulation offers more opportunities to increase revenue and profit by investing in cost-reducing technologies. A regulated firm will engage to upgrade its existing infrastructure if it decreases operating costs, if it permits the launch of new profitable services or to improve service quality.

The empirical literature suggests that shifting away from traditional rate-of-return regulation did not generally cause underinvestment in network industries. For instance, overall investment in the UK railway sector did increase in the aftermath of privatization and the introduction of incentive regulation. Empirical studies also highlight that incentive regulation was very helpful in promoting the deployment of new technologies in the US telecommunications sectors in the late 1980s and early 1990s.

The empirical results in this chapter suggest that the introduction of incentive price regulation or the establishment of an independent sector regulator do not have a positive influence on investment by themselves. However, once these policies are implemented jointly, they are associated with a significant increase in investment. This result highlights the importance of the overall coherence of the general regulatory environment in supporting investment incentives. Furthermore the empirical results show that lower entry barriers encourage investment in the network industries.

Notes

1. Liberalization and competition can bring large efficiency gains in industries with lower economies of scale and scope (e.g., telecommunications), but efficiency gains may be more limited in the presence of large economies of scope (e.g., the railway sector; Pittman 2005).

2. The costs of a regulated firm can be split into operating costs, the rate of return on the firm's capital, and the depreciation of the firm's capital. In this context the regulator sets the prices so that expected revenues for the period ahead equals expected operating costs for the next period, the rate of return on the firm's capital plus the depreciation of the capital stock.

3. The oversupply of service quality may be exacerbated if firms anticipate a change from a low-powered (rate-of-return) to a high-powered (incentive) regulatory price regime if they believe that they can continue to provide the same service quality relying on equipment installed before the regime change (Sappington 2005).

4. This has been reported in the UK and US telecommunication sectors, for example (Laffont and Tirole 2001).

5. Other factors, not considered here that can influence investment include difficulties in obtaining environmental licenses and planning permission or complying with health and safety requirements.

6. While this is primarily a concern for rate of return regulation, the regulator may take into account planned investment plans during regulatory price reviews in incentive price regulation. For example, Hern (2001) reports that the water regulator in the United Kingdom allowed generous capital expenditure programs until 1999, at which point it set more ambitious efficiency targets with lower implied rate of returns.

7. Rate-of-return regulation could be viewed as a system where the rate of return of the regulated firm fluctuates in a range. If the actual rate of return drops below the "fair" rate of return, the firm will request a review for an upward price adjustment, whereas if the firm's profitability increases beyond the "fair" rate of return, well-organized consumers may request a review to decrease prices or the regulated firm itself can ask for lower prices in anticipation to the consumers' reaction. As a result the realized dates of reviews are determined endogenously as a function of the firm's profitability (Joskow 1974). Endogenous timing has the advantage for the firm that it can shift some of the risks onto consumers by requesting an early review if cost shocks arise.

8. The academic literature often uses the term "regulatory opportunism."

9. For instance, Bradley, Jarrell, and Kim (1984) and Bortolotti et al. (2007) report evidence that regulated firms have high debt to equity ratios in the United States and in Europe.

10. This is similar to the problem of a central bank that seeks to reduce inflation but that cannot fully commit itself to its final objective (Kydland and Prescott 1977; Stern and Trillas 2003).

11. Profit sharing was introduced in 1987 in the US telecommunication sector and by 1993 almost half of US states adopted this regime (just to switch to price cap from the mid-1990s). Under profit sharing, several rates of return may be specified. Below a given rate of return (e.g.,10 percent), the regulated firm can keep all profits, for a range of rates of return (e.g., between 10 and 15 percent), it can retain part (e.g., 50 percent) of the profits, whereas above a specific level (e.g., 15 percent), excess profit has to be disbursed to consumers. Threshold rates of return, the shares to be paid above the threshold and the regularity with which profit rates are monitored have implications on the extent to which profit sharing reduces or increases incentives for cost efficiency and investments (Greenstein, McMaster, and Spiller 1995).

12. This is known as the "ratchet effect," which creates an upper bound on the regulated firm's efficiency gains (Freixas, Guesnerie, and Tirole 1985) and lowers the firm's cost-reducing investment.

13. Measuring investment at constant prices or as a percentage of GDP may not appropriately capture the quality dimension of investment. For instance, Clark, Elsby, and Love (2001) show that while being stable over the 1980s, total investment in roads in the United Kingdom picked up between 1990 and 1994 and then sharply declined from 1994 to 1999, in part because road maintenance became more efficient over time. Kinnunen (2006) argues that the declined in real investment in Finnish electricity distribution after liberalization is not necessarily an indication of lower volumes of physical investment. The same amount of network can be built from less money if new technology or the implementation of it becomes less costly.

14. Affuso and Newbery (2000) point out two possible reasons for a decline in rolling stock investment. First, contracts awarded to the train operation companies shorter than the lifetime of the rolling stock discourages investment. Second, in accordance with real option theory, train operators may postpone investment in the face of uncertainty with regard to future demand. Affuso and Newbery (2000) analyze the determinants of discretionary investment (investment other than committed to the regulator) of 25 train operators between 1997 and 1999. Their estimation results indicate that shorter contracts promote discretionary investment and that higher demand uncertainty and higher profits are positively correlated with discretionary investment.

15. The results of Ai and Sappington (2002) also provide some weakly significant and not very robust evidence that incentive regulation and competition may reinforce each other's effect on investment. Their approach controlled for multicollinearity in a large pool of possible explanatory variables and they accounted for potential endogeneity of the regulatory regime.

16. The sample contains firm level data concerning 128 US cities from 1983 to 1992.

17. The types of new technologies were packet switching, digital signal 1, digital signal 3, and optical carrier.

18. The de jure measure of independence was adjusted for the possibility of the executive overruling the regulator's decisions. The de facto measure of independence was calculated as the average of the de jure independence and the possibility of overruling.

19. The definition of entry barriers differs across sectors to reflect sector-specific characteristics. For more details, see Conway and Nicoletti (2006).

20. Entry barriers and public ownership was used in Alesina et al. (2003) who performed a panel data analysis of sectoral investment.

21. See also annex 2, where this method and other alterative approaches to assessing variable robustness are described.

22. The estimations use both country-fixed effects and then country- and industry-fixed effects as well as the explanatory variables lagged one period. An exception is the variable capturing incentive regulation because observations are only available for the most recent period.

23. Using panel data estimation methods, Alesina et al. (2003) find that coefficient estimates for the barriers to entry variable ranges from −0.009 to −0.01 depending on various model specification.

References

Affuso, L., and D. Newbery. 2000. Investment, re-procurement and franchise contract length in the British Railway Industry. Discussion paper 2619. CEPR.

Ai, C., and D. E. M. Sappington. 2002. The impact of state incentive regulation on the US telecommunications industry. *Journal of Regulatory Economics* 22 (2): 133–60.

Alesina, A., S. Ardagna, G. Nicoletti, and F. Schiantarelli. 2003. Regulation and investment. Working paper 9560. NBER.

Alexander, I., and T. Irwin. 1996. Price caps, rate-of-return regulation and the cost of capital, public policy forum for the private sector. World Bank Group.

Armstrong, M., and D. E. M. Sappington. 2006. Regulation, competition and liberalization. *Journal of Economic Literature* 44 (2): 325–66.

Averch, H., and L. L. Johnson. 1962. Behavior of the firm under regulatory constraint. *American Economic Review* 52 (5): 1052–69.

Bialek, J. W. 2004. Recent blackouts in the US and Continental Europe: Is liberalization to blame? Cambridge working paper in economics 0407.

Bortolotti, B., C. Cambini, L. Rondi, and Y. Spiegel. 2007. Capital structure and regulation: Does ownership matter? Working paper 94/2007. Fondazione Eni Enrico Mattei.

Bradley, M., G. A. Jarrell, and E. H. Kim. 1984. On the existence of an optimal capital structure: Theory and evidence. *Journal of Finance* 39 (3): 857–78.

Clark, T., M. Elsby, and S. Love. 2001. Twenty-five years of falling investment? Trends in capital spending on public services. Briefing note 20. Institute for Fiscal Studies.

Conway, P., and G. Nicoletti. 2006. Product market regulation in the non-manufacturing sectors of OECD countries: Measurement and highlights. Economics Department working paper 530. OECD.

Doppelhofer, G., and M. Weeks. 2007. Jointness of growth determinants. Working paper 1978. CESifo.

Floyd, E., and D. Gabel. 2003. An econometric analysis of the factors that influence the deployment of advanced telecommunications services. MIT Internet and Telecommunications Convergence Consortium, August 31.

Freixas, X., R. Guesnerie, and J. Tirole. 1985. Planning under incomplete information and the ratchet effect. *Review of Economic Studies* 52 (2): 173–91.

Greenstein, S., S. McMaster, and P. T. Spiller. 1995. The effect of incentive regulation on infrastructure modernization: Local exchange companies' deployment of digital technology. *Journal of Economics and Management Strategy* 4 (2): 187–236.

Guthrie, G. A. 2006. Regulating infrastructure: The impact on risk and investment. *Journal of Economic Literature* 44 (4): 925–72.

Hern, R. 2001. Competition and access pricing in the UK water industry. *Utilities Policy* 10 (3–4): 117–27.

Hirschhausen, C., T. Beckers, and A. Brenck. 2004. Infrastructure regulation and investment for the long-term: An introduction. *Utilities Policy* 12 (4): 203–10.

Ishii, J., and J. Yan. 2006. Does divestiture crowd out new investment? The "Make or buy decision in the US electricity generation industry. *Rand Journal of Economics* 38 (1): 185–213.

Jamasb, T., and M. G. Pollitt. 2005. Electricity market reform in the European Union: Review of progress. Toward liberalization and integration. Working paper 05–003. Center for Energy and Environmental Policy Research.

Joskow, P. I. 1974. Inflation and environmental concern: Structural change in the process of public utility price regulation. *Journal of Law and Economics* 17 (2): 291–327.

Joskow, P. I. 2006. Competitive electricity markets and investment in new generating capacity. Working paper 06–14. AEI-Brookings Joint Center.

Kinnunen, K. 2006. Investment incentives: Regulation of the Finnish electricity distribution. *Energy Policy* 34 (7): 853–62.

Kydland, F., and E. Prescott. 1977. Rules rather than discretion: The inconsistency of optimal plans. *Journal of Political Economy* 85 (3): 473–91.

Laffont, J.-J., and J. Tirole. 2001. *Competition in Telecommunications*. Cambridge: MIT Press.

Lehman, D. E., and D. I. Weisman. 2000. The political economy of price cap regulation. *Review of Industrial Organization* 16 (4): 343–56.

Pittman, R. 2005. Structural separation to create competition? The case of freight railways. *Review of Network Economics* 4 (3): 1–16.

Pollitt, M. G. 2000. The declining role of the state in infrastructure investments in the UK. Cambridge working paper in economics 0001.

Pollitt, M. G. 2007. The arguments for and against ownership unbundling of energy transmission networks. Cambridge working paper in economics 0737.

Sala-i-Martin, X., G. Dopperhofer, and R. I. Miller. 2004. Determinants of long-run growth: A Bayesian averaging of classical estimates (BACE) approach. *American Economic Review* 94 (4): 813–35.

Sappington, D. N. 2005. Regulating service quality: A survey. *Journal of Regulatory Economics* 27 (2): 123–54.

Spiegel, Y., and D. Spulber. 1994. The capital structure of a regulated firm. *Rand Journal of Economics* 25 (3): 424–40.

Spiegel, Y. 1996. The choice of technology and capital structure under rate regulation. *International Journal of Industrial Organization* 15: 191–216.

Starkie, D. 2006. Investment incentives and airport regulation. *Utilities Policy* 14 (4): 262–65.

Stern, J., and F. Trillas. 2003. Independence and discretion in telecommunication regulation: Lessons from independent central banks. *Utilities Policy* 11 (4): 191–201.

Woroch, G. A. 2000. Competition effect on investment in digital infrastructure. Mimeo. University of California at Berkeley.

7 Infrastructure–Output Nexus: Regional Experience from India

Sumedha Bajar

7.1 Introduction

Achieving balanced economic growth among the Indian states has been a persistent aim of the Indian government and the planners since Independence. Economic policies that helped in promoting economic growth with equity and minimizing interregional disparities formed the major thrust of planning process. But despite having common political institutions and national economic policies, state governments have not realized these objectives and considerable interstate disparities remain in India (e.g., Cashin and Sahay 1996; Nagaraj, Varoudakis, and Veganzones 2000; Rao, Shand, and Kalirajan 1999).

Although India's growth performance during the first thirty years of Independence had been lackluster (the term "Hindu rate of growth" was disparagingly used to refer to the modest growth rate experienced during this period), the pace of growth started to show change in 1980s with partial liberalization of the economy and more so with the wide-ranging reforms that followed the balance-of-payment crisis in 1991. Gross domestic product (GDP) grew on average at 5 percent in the 1980s and increased further in the 1990s and touched the 9 percent mark in the second half of 2000s.

Even with these fast evolving changes at the national level, regional inequalities have persisted. In 1980 to 1981, an average citizen of Punjab was four times richer than the average citizen of Bihar. The situation has not changed much since. In 2009 to 2010, the per capita income level in Bihar (the poorest state in India) was still one-fourth that of Maharashtra (the richest state) and one-third that of Punjab. Of the five initially poor states (Bihar, Madhya Pradesh, Uttar Pradesh, Rajasthan, and Andhra Pradesh) in 1980 to 1981, four still remained among the poorest (in per capita terms) in 2009 to 2010 with the exception of

Andhra Pradesh. Interestingly, Maharashtra which had 8 percent of total national population contributed 16 percent of the aggregate net state domestic product (NSDP) in 2009–10, while Bihar with more than 10 percent of population contributed only 4.5 percent of the aggregate NSDP (see table 7.1). Rising regional inequalities can have several repercussions on both economic and political stability in the country (Nagaraj, Varoudakis, and Veganzones 2000).

While reducing interstate disparities in growth and income remain avowed objectives of Indian planning for balanced regional development, reducing the real interest rate in the economy and ensuring long-run sustainable growth by reducing the fiscal deficit is of utmost importance for both the regional and national economy. The present system of fiscal federalism mandates increased transfers from central government to the less developed states, making it even harder to reduce the federal deficit. In addition, with the rise in coalition politics, the stability of central government is highly dependent on support from regional political parties. Thus achieving balanced growth and reducing regional disparities is a major challenge that the Indian government faces.

In view of such challenges it should be important to understand the determinants of development of subnational regions. The literature points to various sets of strategies through which the objective of balanced regional development can be accomplished. Infrastructure provision is seen as an instrument for promoting regional development in which the governments have an important role because of the public goods nature of infrastructure facilities. Services provided by infrastructure capital stock—power, transport, and telecommunication—are, of course, fundamental to economic activity. These services are considered intermediate inputs to production processes. Availability of this infrastructure can influence location decisions of firms or industries and thus, by facilitating market transactions and creating positive externalities among firms or industries, stimulate long-term economic growth (Jumenez 1995).

In this chapter I examine the precise economic relation of infrastructure and output with respect to the Indian states. I analyze a panel of 17 major Indian states over the time period 1980 to 2010 (excluding telecommunications, for which data are available from 1991 onward). The focus in this chapter is on physical capital stocks in network sectors: transport (roads and railways) and nontransport (electricity, telecommunications). All these sectors can be expected to have network externalities and large economies of scale. I begin my analysis using basic descriptive statistics followed by panel econometric techniques.

The chapter is structured as follows: A brief review of the literature presented in section 7.2 serves to position this study. An overview of inequalities in per capita income and growth performance of Indian states is presented in section 7.3. The same section summarizes the evolution of infrastructure availability at the state level. Section 7.4 presents the empirical results obtained from the panel cointegration and Granger causality tests, which help in accounting for direction of causation among the variables. Section 7.5 focuses on nature and strength of the relationship between infrastructure and per capita net state domestic product (PCNSDP) for the three decades of 1980s, 1990s, and 2000s. The last section offers concluding remarks.

7.2 Brief Review of Literature

Until the late 1980s little attention was paid by economists to the role of infrastructure in either theoretical or empirical studies (Gramlich 1994). Starting with the seminal work by Aschauer (1989), public capital (or infrastructure) formed an element in the aggregate production function. He examined the relation between aggregate productivity and the stock and flow government spending variable for the US economy for the time period 1949 to 1985 and concluded that nonmilitary public capital stock yields very high returns (in the range of 60 to 100 percent per annum). This sparked off a debate in the empirical literature focusing on the technical issues such as the form of the production function used. Probably the first study that included public capital in an empirical cross-country growth model was by Easterly and Rebelo (1993), who ran pooled regressions (using decade averages for the 1960s, 1970s, and 1980s) of per capita growth on (sectoral) public investment and conditional variables for 36 countries(see Sturm et al. 1998 for a summary). They found that the share of public investment in transport and communication infrastructure is correlated with growth. Likewise Gwartney et al. (2004) consider 94 countries during the time period 1980 to 2000 and find a significant positive effect of public investment, although its coefficient is always smaller than that of private investment. However, other studies using the public investment share of GDP as a regressor report different results. For instance, Sanchez-Robles (1998) explores empirically the relationship between infrastructure and economic growth by including the data of expenditure in infrastructure as a share of GDP in traditional growth cross-country regressions and find a negative growth impact of infrastructure expenditure in a sample of 76 countries. In addition Sanchez-Robles elaborates on some new indicators of investment in infrastructure employing physical units of infrastructure. Devarajan et al. (1996) report evidence for 43 developing countries, indicating that the share of total government expenditure (consumption plus investment) has no significant effect on economic growth. Their empirical analysis makes use of annual data on 43 developing countries from 1970 to 1990 to examine the connection between components of government expenditure and economic growth. Devarajan et al. attribute their results to the fact that excessive amounts of transport and communication expenditures in those countries make them unproductive. Prichett (1996) suggested another explanation, arguing that public investment in developing countries is often used for unproductive projects. As a consequence the share of public investment in GDP can be a poor measure of the actual increase in economically productive public capital.

Other important studies that have made use of either Cobb–Douglas or trans log production function, with different types of infrastructure as separate factors of production alongside private physical capital and labor, at either the cross-country or national level, are by Easterly and Rebelo (1993), Everaert and Heylen (2004), Bonaglia et al. (2001) Cadot et al. (1999), Canning (1999), Canning and Bennathan (2000), Charlot and Schmitt (1999) Calderon and Severn (2002), and Esfahani and Ramíres (2002), and they report output elasticities of infrastructure between 0.1 and 0.2. More recently Egert et al. (2009) find that investment in network infrastructure can boost long-term economic growth in OECD countries. Their study is especially important because it considers the time-series properties of data and concludes that the contribution of infrastructure to long-run output levels and growth are not homogeneous across countries and sectors and over time.

The patterns of growth of the group of developed countries and a group of developing nations have been found to be quite different. The study by Straub and Terada-Hagiwara (2010) presents the state of infrastructure in developing Asian countries and applies two approaches: growth regressions and growth accounting in order to understand the link between infrastructure growth and productivity. They find that growth rate of infrastructure stocks has a positive and significant impact on per capita GDP average growth rates in these countries while the impact on productivity was inconclusive.

While income differentials between countries are extremely large, income differentials within regions of a given country can also be significant. In case of India, Nair's (1982) pioneering analysis covers 14 major states of India and finds that the interstate disparities in per capita NSDP, as measured by coefficient of variation (CV), had declined over the period 1950–51 to 1964–65 but increased between 1964–65 and 1976–77. Study by Mathur (2001) reports a steep acceleration in the coefficient of variation of per capita incomes in the post-reform period of 1991 to 1996. The study also concludes that within the middle-income states there was a tendency toward convergence, while divergence was evident within the groups of high- and low-income states. A comparative analysis of 15 major states in respect of a variety of indicators is attempted by Kurian (2000). His study also draws attention to interstate disparities by presenting data for states on demographic characteristics, poverty ratio, magnitude and structure of state domestic product (SDP), developmental and non-developmental revenue expenditure, indicators of physical infrastructure development, and indicators of financial infrastructure, among other variables.

A large part of the mainstream economic research on infrastructure (as mentioned above) has concluded that the impact on growth is substantial and significant. In this context it will be worthwhile to look at the case of Indian states and consider the patterns and impact of factors like infrastructure development in explaining interstate differences in growth rate in India. Ghosh and De (1998) try to identify the role of infrastructure in regional development over the plan periods from 1971–72 to 1994–95. They test the impact of public investment and physical infrastructure on both private investment behavior and regional economic development using OLS regression. For this purpose a physical infrastructure development indicator is formulated by them using the principal component analysis. The results of their study are significantly conclusive for the time period studied, and they find that the increasing regional disparity in India and regional imbalances in physical infrastructure are responsible for the rising income disparity across the states.

A related study by Ghosh and De (2000) tries to find the linkage between a composite index of infrastructure development and income across Indian states. The index is constructed using principal component analysis and includes ten infrastructural variables for four different years across 26 Indian states. The years are 1971–72, 1981–82,

1991–92, and 1994–95. This study concludes that the rising inequality in ten important infrastructure facilities is responsible for widening income disparity. Planned disbursement of funds by the government had failed to cure this disparity.

Another study on the same lines by Ghosh and De (2004) tests the relationships of physical, social, and financial infrastructure with per capita income across states. Three separate indexes are created—Physical Infrastructure Development Index (PIDI), Social Infrastructure Development Index (SIDI), and Financial Infrastructure Development Index (FIDI). They conclude that infrastructurally better endowed states have remained in the same position relative to their poorer counterparts and this sets limits to growth.

The study by Nagaraj, Varoudakis, and Veganzones (2000) examines the growth performance of Indian states during 1970 to 1994. They start by grouping the states according to differences in the availability of physical, social, and economic infrastructure using principal component analysis and assess the contributions of various infrastructure indicators to growth performance using PCA and panel data estimation techniques. Instrumental variable estimation technique is applied to tackle the endogeneity issue in the provision of infrastructure. Their study finds persistent income inequalities among states and accounts for these due to differences in the structure of production, infrastructure endowments, and state-specific fixed effects in growth regression.

Along a different line, Lall (1999) had tried to examine the relationship between public infrastructure investments and regional development in India. He concludes that leading, intermediate and lagging states are structurally different and infrastructure investments influence growth in these regions through different pathways. This study covers time period 1980–81 to 1993–94 and examines the development process of 15 states. Instead of using physical indicators of infrastructure, the dependent variables in the study are—public investments in economic infrastructure (transport, power, telecom, and irrigation), public investment in social infrastructure (education, water supply and sanitation, medical and public health), and private investment and private employment. A common result that emerged across all states is that investments in social infrastructure have positive effects on regional growth. This study failed to show any positive linkage between economic infrastructure investments and regional economic growth. This could be due to the use of a simple unidirectional causal model that fails to capture the multiple impact path potentials between infrastructure and growth.

In the following two sections, after providing evidence for existence of regional disparities in per capita NSDP in India, identification of the role that differences in infrastructure endowment have played in per capita income level and its growth in Indian states is attempted.

7.3 Economic Features of Indian States and Regional Disparities

There are big disparities in economic development and growth performance among states in India. Understanding these disparities is important for determining the factors that account for long-run Indian growth trends. Attention is called to inequalities in real per capita net state domestic product (in 2004–05 prices) and analysis is presented below. The present study intends to examine the effect infrastructure has on the level of state output. For this purpose certain infrastructure variables were selected as indicators of infrastructure development and their trend analyzed over time and across states. Most of these indicators are either absolutely government controlled or are regulated either by central or state government. It must be noted that supply of infrastructure is a stock available over discrete time points.

7.3.1 Data, Coverage of States, and Time Period

India is a union of 28 states and 7 union territories, but the analysis in this chapter is confined to 17 major states—Andhra Pradesh, Assam, Bihar, Gujarat, Haryana, Himachal Pradesh, Jammu and Kashmir, Karnataka, Kerala, Madhya Pradesh, Maharashtra, Orissa, Punjab, Rajasthan, Tamil Nadu, Uttar Pradesh, and West Bengal. These 17 states account for about 90 percent of national net domestic product, 92 percent of national gross fixed-capital formation (GFCF), and 93.5 percent of total labor force in 2009–10 and are therefore representative.

For the purpose of this chapter, data series for PCNSDP, PCNSDP in the secondary sector, and PCNSDP in the tertiary sector in 2004–05 constant prices was created for the above-mentioned 17 Indian states. These data were obtained from the Central Statistical Organisation (under MOSPI, government of India) website. The state-wise and sector-wise worker's data were compiled from NSSO rounds on employment and unemployment for the years 1987, 1993, 1999–2000, 2003 (gives sector-wise distribution of workers), and 2009–10 (for details on employment data series, please contact the author). Data for electricity consumption (kWh per capita), surfaced road density (km of surfaced road per 1,000 km^2 of geographical area), Rail density (km of rail length per 1,000 km^2 of geographical area), Teledensity (per 10,000 people), number of schools, primary health centers, and community health centers (all figures in per 100,000 population) was compiled from Statistical Abstract of India, CMIE database on infrastructure, and respective ministries of the government.

In order to understand the impact of infrastructure on different regions in India, the states were grouped as high-income, medium-income, and low-income states in each of the three time periods. The basis for this stratification was states with average PCNSDP above (national average PCNDP – 0.5 * (standard deviation of national income)) were classified as high income, those less than this were categorized as low income, and states with average PCNSDP between the two ranges were put in the middle-income category.

Time Period

The basic strategy employed in this chapter is to divide the entire time period into three decades: 1980 to 1989, 1990 to 1999, and 2000 to 2010 and to discern the impact of infrastructure variables on levels of PCNSDP in the respective time period. The same was repeated with sectoral PCNSDP—secondary and tertiary sector PCNSDP—to examine the differences in the impact of infrastructure development on levels of the respective sectoral PCNSDP.

The decision to divide the time period into three phases was inspired by policy. These three decades are characterized by stark differences in terms of the infrastructure development policies that were shaped, in large part, by the changing political priorities of governments in each decade (Lall and Rastogi 2007). At the beginning of the 1980s, following the second oil crisis, concentration was mainly on rural India, and the sixth Five Year Plan (FYP) was characterized by massive public investment in sectors like rural roads, groundwater irrigation, and a system of procurement prices. Rural electrification did not mean electrification of rural households, but grid extensions were provided to farms to meet the demand for irrigation. There was great politicization of fiscal policy, and this was an era of bigger government and public spending. The entry of Rajiv Gandhi in 1984 is characterized by two noteworthy features with respect to infrastructure development. The development of telecommunication sector acquired a position of significance and large amounts of investments were made for the same. The Centre for Development of Telematics was established in 1987 to cultivate and improve India's telecom sector and help it catch up with the rest of the world, thus setting the stage for takeoff of the Indian IT industry during the 1990s. Second, the build-out of infrastructure for groundwater irrigation and electricity supply for irrigation purposes continued; however, the financial situation of State Electricity Boards deteriorated and there appeared chronic shortages of power for commercial and urban use. The development of critical transportation and urban infrastructure continued to be neglected.

In the post-1991 period the emphasis was on fiscal consolidation, and investment in infrastructure became a major casualty when the aim of central government was to reduce fiscal deficit from 8.4 percent of GDP in 1990–91 to 5 percent 1992–93. Although the decline in infrastructure spending and putting on hold almost all infrastructure projects should have impacted the GDP growth adversely, the marked improvement in targeting of infrastructure spending and telecom-related reforms had a positive impact on productivity. Until 1994 Telecom was a government monopoly. In 1994 National Telecom Policy was released by the government and it stressed upon the need to liberalize the telcom sector and recognized the telecom sector as an important component of the infrastructure. The second half of 1990s saw an upsurge in recognition of the shortages in infrastructure. The *India Infrastructure Report* (Government of India 1996) was the first of its kind and many of the recommendations in it found their way into government policy. *World Development Report* (World Bank 1994) brought to the attention of policy makers the initiatives followed globally to induce greater private-sector participation in infrastructure development, and would later become part of many of the policies crafted by Indian policy makers. With the ninth Five Year Plan debate over private-sector participation entering into infrastructure sector was initiated and steps taken to encourage the same, and there was an emergence of a strategic focus on infrastructure policy. It also emphasized the disproportionate reliance on congested national highways compared to railways.

The decade of 2000s saw the above-mentioned policy suggestions and initiatives take shape. There was targeted spending on national highways network and build-out of Golden Quadrilateral and related North–South and East–West road corridors under the tenth Five Year Plan. Policies to create enabling conditions for the private-sector financing of infrastructural projects were initiated. With the Electricity Act of

2003 the policy framework was brought in place to draw private investment in the sector. In order to provide direction to the effort to prioritize infrastructure development, especially the public–private partnerships (PPP) effort, the government organized a Committee on Infrastructure (CoI) in August 2004. . The eleventh Five Year Plan envisaged stepping up the gross capital formation in infrastructure from 5 to 9 percent of GDP. Despite the emphasis placed on PPP by plan documents, the response of private sector has been lukewarm. Several reasons have been highlighted such as overlapping regulatory jurisdiction, improper design, bidding transparency issues, project costs, and time overruns.

Thus it can be gauged that each of the three decades of 1980s, 1990s, and 2000s were characterized by different policy foci, infrastructure policies, and developments of infrastructure sectors. This then becomes the motivation to divide the entire time period into three phases.

7.3.2 Regional Disparity in Per capita NSDP

There is a vast body of literature dealing with economic growth and its pattern in Indian states (e.g., Nair1982); Raychoudhary 1993; Cashin and Sahay 1996; Rao, Shand, and Kalirajan 1999; Das and Barua 1996; Mathur 2001; Kurian 2000). In this section, data from 1981 to 2010 were selected and state-wise disparities in PCNSDP and its growth rate in the above mentioned 17 states were computed. A single time trend will not adequately characterize the evolution of PCNSDP over time as instability and phases in growth rates over time is a reality in India. To begin with, figure 7.1 presents the trend in level of PCNSDP in the following years: 1980–81, 1990–91, 2000–2001, and 2009–10. There can be seen an increase in PCNSDP across all states and time period. Maharashtra had the highest PCNSDP followed by Haryana and Gujarat in 2009–10, whereas Bihar, Uttar Pradesh, and Madhya Pradesh were among the "poorest" states in per capita NSDP terms in India in all the four years.

The share of India's population living with per capita NDP less than half the aggregate per capita NDP for India has increased marginally from 10.2 percent in the 1980s to 10.7 percent in the 2000s (assuming all households within a state are the same). Interestingly, the proportion of India's population that earned more than half but less than the aggregate per capita NDP for India first increased in the 1990s and then fell even below the 1980s level (49 percent in 1980s to 51 percent in 1999s to 44 percent in 2000s). Almost the same set of states fell in this category in all the three decades—Uttar Pradesh, Madhya Pradesh,

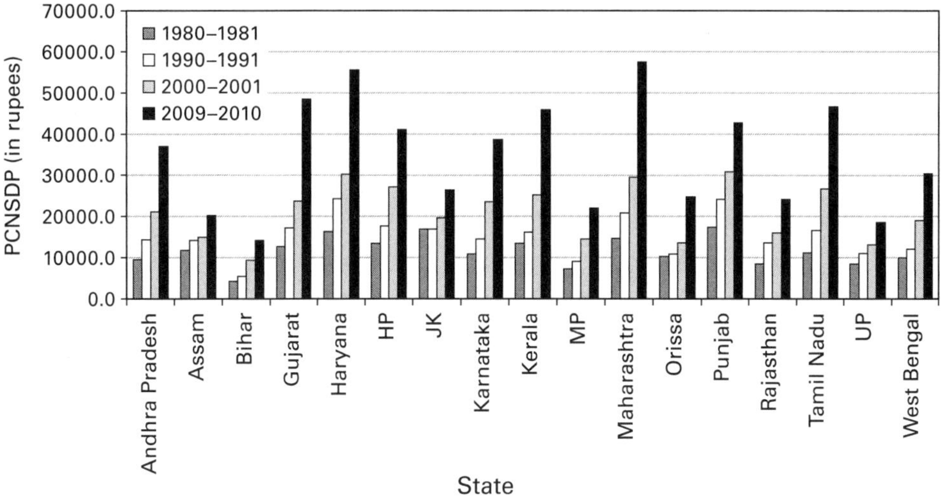

Figure 7.1
Per capita net state domestic product in 2004–05 prices

Orissa, Rajasthan, and West Bengal, with the exception of Andhra Pradesh that saw an improvement in its NSDP, which led to its exit from this group in the decade of 2000s, and this is significant as it constitutes around 7 percent of the population in India. The states that earned more than the aggregate India's PCNDP have remained consistent—Gujarat, Haryana, Punjab, Maharashtra, Tamil Nadu, Karnataka, and Kerala

It is important to note that states like Uttar Pradesh, Madhya Pradesh, Bihar, and Rajasthan, which have a large population base, seem to perform badly in per capita terms. In 2009–10 Uttar Pradesh produced 9.15 percent of India's NSDP (following only Maharashtra's contribution), but almost 17 percent of India's population lived in this state, which brings the per capita NSDP of the state down to second lowest in the country (following Bihar). Then again, states like Punjab, Haryana, and Kerala, considered the rich[1] states of India, contribute 3 to 4 percent of India's NDP but have low population base thus raising their per capita income. Maharashtra (a highly industrialized state) had the highest NSDP trend growth rate for the entire period. In the 1980s it was Haryana, Maharashtra, and Punjab that had high NSDP growth rates. The success story of Punjab and Haryana in this period rests mainly on their high growth of agricultural output productivity. The situation changed drastically after the 1991 reforms and opening up of the economy, which had adverse impact on the growth of agriculture sector in India after mid-1990s (Chand and Parapurrathu 2012) leading to a big drop in the ranking of Punjab and Haryana's NSDP growth rate. Surprisingly, Bihar grew at close to 10 percent in the 1990s and the trend continued in the 2000s as well. The growth of Bihar is primarily from a lower base and supported mainly by the construction sector. The huge growth in construction activities was largely propelled by public investment in the last few years, which included construction of roads, bridges, and government buildings. The majority of the growth is occurring in the tertiary sector, whereas agriculture and allied sectors, on which about 80 percent of the state's population depends, have registered very low growth rates.

As can be gathered from the analysis above, the growth pattern of the 17 major states has been quite diverse. In table 7.1 an attempt is made to group the states based on their average level of PCNSDP and trend growth rate of NSDP for the three time periods: 1980s, 1990s, and 2000s into poor/middle income/rich states and low/middle/high growth states. Over the entire time period Punjab, Haryana, Maharashtra, Himachal Pradesh, Gujarat, Kerala, and Tamil Nadu are the high-income states and remain so in each of the three decades except for Tamil Nadu in the 1980s. Bihar, Madhya Pradesh, Uttar Pradesh, Orissa, Rajasthan, and Assam are the poorer states in India and have lower growth rates. Interestingly, Punjab and Haryana, which were in the high-income, high-growth category, fared worse in the 1990s and fell to low-growth (but still remain in high income) category, whereas Kerala, Karnataka, West Bengal, and Madhya Pradesh improved their growth record. States that fared better in terms of growth rate in the 1990s compared to their performance in the 1980s are Bihar, Madhya Pradesh, Karnataka, Gujarat, and Maharashtra. Some interesting results that can be seen is that in the 1990s states like Madhya Pradesh and Bihar fell into the high-growth category even if they still remain in the low-income group. West Bengal fell to the poor-income category but with a high growth rate. States that remained in the high-growth, high-income group in 1990s and 2000s are Maharashtra and Gujarat. Among the low-income states, Uttar Pradesh continued with its low-growth performance.

Figures 7.2 to 7.4 illustrate the variations in per capita output for the initially (1981 to 1990) rich and poor states in India over the period 1981 to 2010. Among the six initially poor states, Bihar and Madhya Pradesh (and to some extent Uttar Pradesh) that were growing at a very slow

Table 7.1
Classification of states based on income and growth

Growth 1981 to 1990	*PC income in 1980–81*		
	Poor	Medium	Rich
Low	MP,	WB, AS	KER, JK
Medium	Bih, UP, RJ, AP	OR, KAR, GJ	HP, MAH
High		TN	HR, PJ
Growth 1991 to 2000	*PC income 1990–91*		
Low	OR,UP	AS, JK	PJ, HR
Medium		RJ, AP	
High	Bih, MP, WB	KAR, KER,TN	HP, MAH, GJ
Growth 2001–10	*PC income 2000–01*		
Low	UP, MP, AS, RJ	JK	PJ
Medium	Bih,	WB, KAR	HP,
High	OR	AP,	GJ, KER, TN, MAH, HR

Source: Author's calculations
Notes: *States are classified as rich if their average PCNSDP is more than (India's mean PCNDP+0.5(std dev)), poor if it is less than (India's mean PCNDP-0.5(std dev)), and middle income if it lies in between. **A state is said to have high (or low) growth rate if the NSDP trend growth rate for the state is more (or less) than 0.5*(India's trend NDP growth rate) for that time period. In this table, AP—Andhra Pradesh, AS-Assam, Bih—Bihar, GJ—Gujarat, HR—Haryana, HP- Himachal Pradesh, JK—Jammu & Kashmir, KAR—Karnataka, KER—Kerala, MP—Madhya Pradesh, MAH—Maharashtra, OR—Orissa, PJ—Punjab, RJ—Rajasthan, TN- Tamil Nadu, UP—Uttar Pradesh, WB—West Bengal.

pace, suddenly picked up their growth in 1993–94 and have been growing at a high rate since then. Assam failed to pick up its growth rate throughout the thirty-year period and displayed a sluggish growth performance. However, Rajasthan and Orissa displayed considerable variation in their growth performance. Orissa took off to be part of the high-growth states in the 2000s based on a commendable performance in the registered manufacturing sector that grew at very high rate (close to 30 percent by the end of 2009–10).

Of the seven initially rich Indian states (Haryana, Himachal Pradesh, Punjab, Maharashtra, Gujarat, Tamil Nadu, and Kerala), Punjab had a high-growth rate in the 1980s, but it almost stabilized and there were not much variations in its growth rate. Himachal Pradesh has been benefiting greatly from Centre-State grants and steadily improving its growth path. Maharashtra and Gujarat present motivating examples with substantial improvement in growth rates on already vast base, especially post-1991 reforms. This is due to expanding industrial

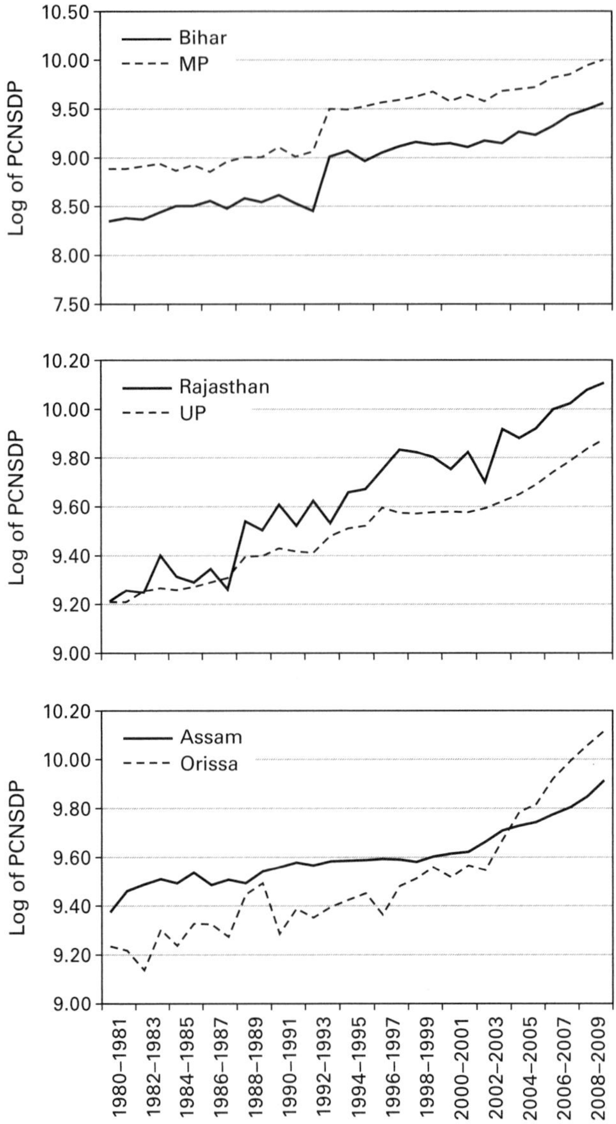

Figure 7.2
Per capita NSDP in 2004–05 prices: Six initially poor states, 1981 to 2010

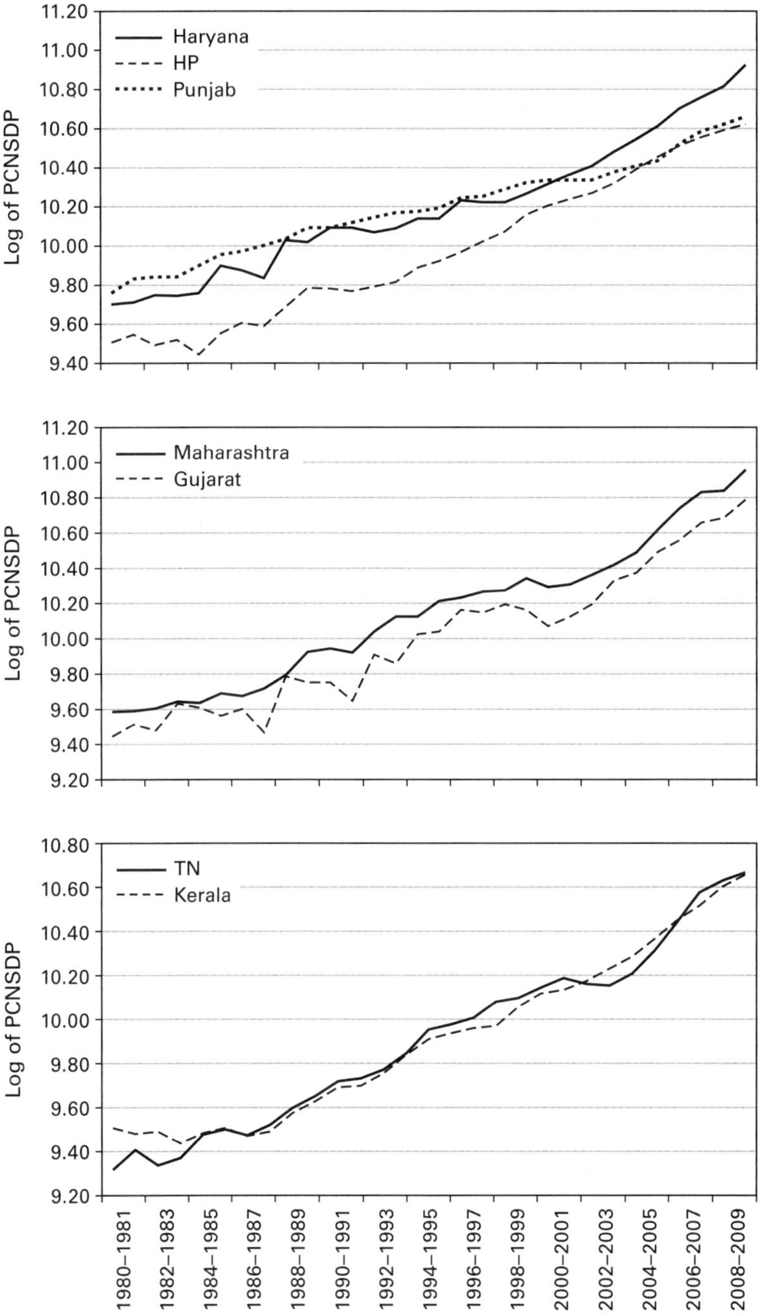

Figure 7.3
Per capita NSDP in 2004–05 prices: Seven initially rich states, 1981 to 2010

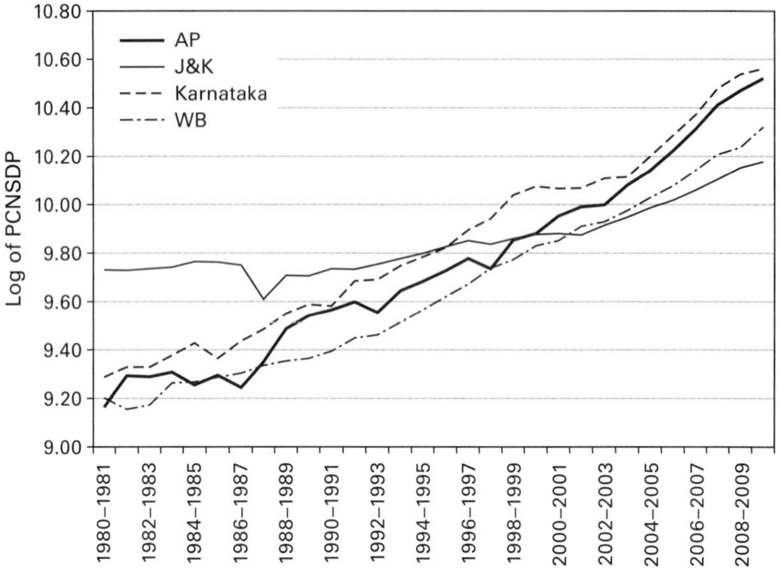

Figure 7.4
Per capita NSDP in 2004–05 prices: Four initially middle-income states, 1981 to 2010

production and rising share of manufacturing in state's NSDP and exports. The south Indian states of Tamil Nadu and Kerala always had income level and its growth much above the Indian average and the trend has continued into 2000s. The services sector continues to dominate Tamil Nadu's economy and is the main contributor to the state's growth performance. Kerala's very low population growth rate along with growing service industry and tourism is responsible for this exemplary performance in recent years. Among the middle-income groups, Karnataka and Andhra Pradesh have benefited from the emergence and growth of information technology sector, making these states as the IT hubs and riding on the wave of services growth in this sector.

As a first step toward achieving a better understanding of differences or similarities among the states with respect to their economic performance (for the purposes of this chapter, PCNSDP), let us look at the development in infrastructure sector in various states. Availability and status of infrastructure is considered as an important pre-condition for a region to develop and grow and it thus serves as a mechanism by which differences in cross-regional per capita incomes can be reduced within the national economy.

7.3.3 Comparison of Infrastructure Facilities across Indian States

The major economic variables used for this study are net state domestic product (and PCNSDP) and physical infrastructural variables—per capita electricity consumption (KwH), road density (surfaced road per 1,000 km^2 of geographical area), rail density (rail length per 1,000 km^2 of geographical area), and tele-density (per 10,000 population). The data were compiled from Ministry of Statistics and Programme Implementation (MOSPI); Ministry of Road Transport and Highways, Government of India; various issues of *Statistical Abstract of India*, Government of India , and *Economic Intelligence Service* (various years) published by CMIE. For tele-density state-wise data are available only from 1991 onward, and Indiastats was accessed for the compilation of the same. Number of schools, primary health centers, and community health centers (all figures in per 100,000 population) were compiled from *Statistical Abstract of India*.

In table 7.2 the state-wise trend growth rate of PCNSDP and availability of infrastructure variables are shown as calculated for the three time periods: 1981–90, 1991–2000, and 2001–10; for the three categories of states: rich, middle, and poor income states. The classification is based on the results presented in the previous section.

We observe that the initially poor states Bihar, Madhya Pradesh, Rajasthan, Uttar Pradesh, Orissa, and Assam had a very high growth rate for electricity consumption in the 1980s (table 7.2b). This is mainly because of the low base they started off with. The richer states like Punjab, Gujarat, Haryana, and Maharashtra had per capita electricity consumption as high as 300, 224, 200, and 225 KwH, respectively, in 1981, whereas the electricity consumption of Bihar—54, Madhya Pradesh—88, Rajasthan—87, Orissa—95, and Uttar Pradesh—74 KwH was far below the national average (data available upon request).

Similarly road density in these initially poor states was considerably below the national average in all the three decades. In fact the gap between road density of the rich and poor states was so high that the average road density of poor states in 2001 to 2010 was still lower than that of the rich states in 1981 to 1990 (see tables 7.3a and 7.3b). Rail density was high to begin with in Bihar and Uttar Pradesh as the British left a well-developed railway system in these states. But an increase in rail density in Madhya Pradesh, Rajasthan, Orissa, and Assam was observed as new rail routes were laid to improve access to reserves of natural resources in these states.

Among the rich income states, Haryana, Punjab, and Tamil Nadu had the highest PCNSDP growth rates in the decade of 1981 to 1990 and were also the best endowed with infrastructure facilities (table 7.2a). Punjab had the highest road density (757 km^2) followed by Tamil Nadu (736 km^2) and Haryana had the fourth highest road density during the period of 1981 to 1990. These states were also found to have the highest per capita electricity consumption, and a significant trend growth rate of more than 5 percent was registered by them despite the relatively wide base that already existed (see table 7.2a).

The other two rich income states, Maharashtra and Gujarat, also had higher infrastructure availability in the beginning of the period under consideration (1980–81), and they continued to build upon it with electricity consumption growing at 7.4 percent in Gujarat and 7 percent in Maharashtra between time period 1981 to 1990, and the consumption kept growing at the rate of 4 to 5 percent even in 1990s and 2000s. These states also succeeded in building up their roads infrastructure with highest trend growth in road density reported in 1980s and by 2010 road density of Maharashtra (1,091 km^2) and Gujarat (719 km^2) was fairly high but was still below that of Kerala (state with highest road density of 2,839 per 1,000 km^2 in 2010), Punjab, West Bengal, and Tamil Nadu.

Another interesting feature that the data indicate is that for all three categories—rich-, poor-, and middle-income states—the trend growth rate of electricity consumption was higher in the decade of 1980s than in 1990s (except for Kerala and West Bengal), and it picked up again in 2000s (tables 7.2a, 7.2b, and 7.2c). For the road networks, rich states had a higher trend growth rate in the 1980s and 2000s than in 1990s, but in both poor- and middle-income states the trend growth rate of road density was steadily rising and highest in 2000s, indicating continuous attempts to catch up with the rich states (exceptions are Orissa and Andhra Pradesh). However, despite this consistently increasing growth rate in road density, the average road density in the poor income states (except Uttar Pradesh) in 2001 to 2010 was still lower than the average road density of the rich states in 1981 to 1990, which indicates the scale of catching up that these states are still left to do.

Performance of middle-income states was only slightly better than that of poor-income states. Both electricity consumption and rail density average trend growth rate was worst in 1990s. Average per capita electricity consumption and road density are always found to be between that of rich- and poor-income states in all the three decades—1981 to

Table 7.2a
Trend growth rate of PCNSDP and infrastructure variables in the rich states

	PCNSDP			Elec			Road			Rail			Tele	
State	1981–90	1991–2000	2001–10	1981–90	1991–2000	2001–10	1981–90	1991–2000	2001–10	1981–90	1991–2000	2001–10	1991–2000	2001–10
Haryana	3.72	2.25	6.98	5.73	1.91	7.37	2.12	0.98	3.95	−0.35	0.55	−0.29	20.16	35.64
Punjab	3.49	2.48	4.11	9.85	4.44	5.50	2.07	2.88	4.01	0.13	−0.23	0.22	22.21	30.62
Tamil Nadu	3.46	5.25	7.69	6.38	5.25	6.73	2.11	-1.98	2.76	0.38	0.56	−0.36	21.84	33.88
Maharashtra	3.21	4.71	8.28	7.04	3.94	4.91	6.38	3.68	3.87	0.35	−0.02	0.32	15.13	25.60
Gujarat	2.77	6.00	8.53	7.42	6.56	5.83	6.16	4.51	1.23	−0.39	0.07	−0.50	16.38	31.90
HP	2.67	4.43	5.16	12.74	6.89	12.86	6.16	4.37	3.34	0.24	0.16	1.20	25.84	35.24
Kerala	1.14	4.83	7.16	4.45	4.87	3.58	3.62	3.19	10.04	0.51	0.43	0.00	22.00	30.46
Mean	2.92	4.28	6.84	7.66	4.84	6.68	4.09	2.52	4.17	0.13	0.22	0.09	20.51	31.91

Source: Author’s calculations

Table 7.2b
Trend growth rate of PCNSDP and infrastructure variables in the poor states

	PCNSDP			Elec			Road			Rail			Tele	
State	1981–90	1991–2000	2001–10	1981–90	1991–2000	2001–10	1981–90	1991–2000	2001–10	1981–90	1991–2000	2001–10	1991–2000	2001–10
Assam	1.10	0.33	3.20	8.51	0.16	5.44	2.51	2.53	10.50	0.95	0.05	−0.78	21.44	44.78
MP	1.17	7.68	4.23	10.38	4.99	6.75	3.99	0.50	4.84	0.56	−0.05	0.21	16.36	37.61
UP	2.40	2.31	3.70	9.11	1.73	2.99	3.27	5.90	5.61	0.20	0.00	0.18	19.95	42.88
Bihar	2.53	7.84	5.08	8.17	2.81	6.54	0.82	0.95	9.85	0.65	−0.24	0.92	19.15	45.73
Orissa	2.92	2.38	7.43	8.47	1.95	8.10	1.85	17.16	0.59	0.28	2.04	0.47	21.59	44.38
Rajasthan	3.22	4.03	4.98	10.35	5.51	6.72	5.52	4.56	8.31	0.27	0.28	−0.22	21.44	42.71
Mean	2.22	4.09	4.77	9.16	2.86	6.09	2.99	5.27	6.62	0.48	0.35	0.13	19.99	43.01

Source: Author's calculations

Table 7.2c
Trend growth rate of PCNSDP and infrastructure variables in the middle-income states

	PCNSDP			Elec			Road			Rail			Tele	
STATE	1981–90	1991–2000	2001–10	1981–90	1991–2000	2001–10	1981–90	1991–2000	2001–10	1981–90	1991–2000	2001–10	1991–2000	2001–10
Andhra Pradesh	3.03	3.69	7.09	10.14	4.79	6.66	2.78	4.38	2.65	0.26	0.09	0.04	22.21	35.16
J & K	−0.60	1.72	3.67	9.71	5.05	9.99	1.31	3.58	6.46	1.09	0.63	13.63	14.46	54.23
Karnataka	3.18	5.38	6.55	6.52	3.13	7.36	2.86	2.27	4.74	0.97	−0.50	0.28	19.79	35.68
West Bengal	2.33	5.04	5.25	3.52	4.36	7.07	1.01	5.92	7.54	0.16	−0.40	0.73	13.62	44.96
Mean	1.99	3.96	5.64	7.47	4.33	7.77	1.99	4.04	5.35	0.62	−0.05	3.67	17.52	42.51

Source: Author's calculations

1990, 1991 to 2000, and 2001 to 2010. Surprisingly, rail density of most of the middle-income states was lower than the rail density in poorer states, and the rail density of poor-income states was not much lower than that of the rich-income states.

A telecommunication revolution is evident in India from the sheer trend growth rate figures for all states—rich, poor, or middle income especially in the time period 2000 to 2010. But even so, it was the rich states that had better tele-density to begin with followed by the middle-income and poor-income states. Moreover, though, on average, the poorer states had a higher growth rate (average 43 percent for poor-income and 32 percent for the rich-income states), followed by the middle-income group, the average tele-density was still much higher in the richer states.

Thus the main conclusion that can be drawn from this brief look at the data is that the initially rich states were also the ones best endowed with infrastructure facilities—roads, electricity, railways, and telecommunication infrastructure. These states continued to remain in the rich-income category in the decade 2001 to 2010 with average PCNSDP much above India's average PCNSDP. These states managed to grow in terms of their infrastructure endowments, which is noteworthy considering that these states had a relatively wider base to begin with. This can also imply that although infrastructure facilities were better developed in these states compared to the poor- or middle-income states, in absolute terms there still is a huge scope for development and that with an increase in availability of infrastructure, these states would continue to further increase and grow their PCNSDP.

Second, as mentioned in the previous section, poor states like Bihar, Madhya Pradesh, and Orissa improved their growth performance in the later decades, mainly due to the low base they started off with, and also managed to increase their infrastructure endowments (some of these states were the worst endowed states in the country). The trend growth rate of electricity, road, and even tele-density has been among the highest for most of these initially poor states, but they still lag much behind the rich in income and the rich in infrastructure availability states.

7.4 Econometric Methodology and Analysis

A multivariate panel approach, based on panel cointegration and error correction techniques, proved useful in showing the long-run linkages

Table 7.3a
Average PCNSDP and infrastructure availability in the rich states: 1981 to 1990, 1991–2000, 2001–10

	PCNSDP			Elec			Road			Rail			Tele	
State	1981–90	1991–00	2001–10	1981–90	1991–00	2001–10	1981–90	1991–00	2001–10	1981–90	1991–00	2001–10	1991–00	2001–10
Punjab	20512.8	26981.6	35214.5	436.7	750.6	1350.3	756.7	945.1	921.8	42.7	42.1	42.1	2.6	31.3
Haryana	18756.5	25811.5	40610.8	262.5	485.3	1045.1	492.3	570.1	674.0	33.1	34.2	35.3	1.6	20.6
MH	16180.5	25773.9	40686.0	298.7	503.3	893.7	338.6	626.0	716.6	17.2	17.7	18.0	3.0	19.0
Gujarat	14637.7	22145.1	34743.2	298.3	643.9	1278.4	271.8	409.9	670.0	28.4	27.1	26.7	2.0	22.0
HP	14443.1	20479.8	33753.5	117.4	269.0	805.7	95.7	254.5	303.2	4.6	4.8	5.1	2.0	26.8
Kerala	13474.8	19986.1	34022.6	127.6	235.0	419.3	670.6	1086.6	2482.4	23.8	26.8	27.0	2.6	30.5
TN	12978.7	20819.9	33954.3	217.6	423.5	943.3	735.9	921.9	1076.0	30.5	31.3	31.8	2.6	31.3
Mean	15854.9	23142.6	36140.7	251.2	472.94	962.26	480.2	687.72	977.72	25.76	26.28	26.57	2.35	25.94

Source: Author's calculations

Table 7.3b
Average PCNSDP and infrastructure availability in the poor states: 1981 to 1990, 1991 to 2000, 2001 to 2010

State	PCNSDP			Elec			Road			Rail			Tele	
	1981–90	1991–00	2001–10	1981–90	1991–00	2001–10	1981–90	1991–00	2001–10	1981–90	1991–00	2001–10	1991–00	2001–10
Bihar	4779.4	7628.5	10938	80.1	129.5	213.1	169.2	190.4	313.9	32.3	30.2	30.8	0.3	7.2
MP	7526.2	12616.8	17338	147.4	330.2	621.7	140.5	223.0	287.8	13.3	13.4	13.7	0.8	9.7
UP	9298.8	12057.1	15059	108.9	190.0	343.8	262.8	448.9	719.8	30.6	30.3	30.4	0.6	10.7
RJ	9915.7	14848.4	19655	132.5	278.2	588.7	132.2	217.0	335.2	16.5	17.2	17.0	1.0	15.8
Orissa	10986	12385.4	18400	135.2	317.5	649.3	114.5	330.3	230.1	12.9	13.8	15.0	0.6	10.7
Assam	13223	14503.7	17085	50.5	97.3	168.3	113.2	145.8	307.5	28.7	30.8	30.7	0.5	9.1
Mean	9288.5	12340.0	16412	109.1	223.8	430.8	155.4	259.2	365.7	22.4	22.6	22.9	0.6	10.6

Source: Author's calculations

Table 7.3c
Average PCNSDP and infrastructure availability in the middle income states: 1981 to 1990, 1991 to 2000, 2001 to 2010

	PCNSDP			Elec			Road			Rail			Tele	
State	1981–90	1991–2000	2001–10	1981–90	1991–2000	2001–10	1981–90	1991–2000	2001–10	1981–90	1991–2000	2001–10	1991–2000	2001–10
J & K	16732.5	18155.1	22409.2	128.1	220.8	684.8	33.4	38.1	64.2	0.3	0.4	0.7	0.8	14.6
Karnataka	12362.0	18730.9	29639.5	188.8	342.7	706.9	375.5	501.2	742.5	16.7	15.9	15.8	1.8	22.8
A.P.	11254.6	16445.9	27720.8	165.1	346.5	759.5	240.6	361.2	481.3	17.5	18.5	18.9	1.2	19.0
West Bengal	10651.2	14939.8	23841.0	122.0	179.9	395.1	295.3	444.5	657.6	42.1	42.6	43.2	0.8	9.6
Mean	12750.1	17067.9	25902.6	151.0	272.5	636.6	236.2	336.3	486.4	19.2	19.3	19.7	1.1	16.5

Source: Author's calculations

between infrastructure and per capita NSDP. To achieve econometrically appropriate results, three steps were followed for a panel of 17 states in India. First, the stationarity property of individual series in the panel was examined using panel unit root tests. Second, the unit root tests were followed by testing for a long-term cointegration relation between the main variables. Appropriate panel long-run estimates (fully modified OLS) were then developed to describe each long-run relationship. Finally, a panel VEC model was estimated to study the Granger causal relationship.

7.4.1 Panel Unit Root and Cointegration Tests

This study uses several panel unit root testing methodologies to determine the order of integration of all the variables. If the order of integration is zero, the series is considered to be stationary and thus free from a unit root. The more reliable and well-behaved panel unit root tests (as opposed to traditional DF or ADF tests that suffer from low power in rejecting the null hypothesis of a nonstationary series as well as limiting distributions) such as those developed by Levin, Lin, and Chu (2002)—LLC—Im, Pesaran, and Shin (2003)—IPS—and Breitung (2000) were applied. These econometricians all show that panel unit root tests are more powerful than unit root tests applied to individual series because the information is enhanced when adding cross-sectional dimension to time-series data. The IPS, LLC, and Breitung tests have the null hypothesis of a unit root. Table 7.4 reports the panel unit root tests on the relevant variables. As the results show, all data are integrated of order one when in levels (all variables are in logarithm). It can also be seen that the null of nonstationarity is rejected at first difference at the 1 percent level of significance for all the variables.

The results of the panel unit root tests suggest that all the relevant variables in levels are integrated of order one. If the presence of a unit root is detected in the variables, then it is necessary to check for cointegrating relationship between the variables.

From econometric theory we know that if any two variables X or Y are integrated of same order, and if we estimate them by OLS and their residuals are found to be stationary, then they are said to be cointegrated and have a long-run equilibrium relationship (Engle and Granger 1987). A similar approach of testing the nonstationarity properties of the residual for a panel data setting was developed by Pedroni (1999, 2004). In this paper panel cointegration for the time period 1980

Table 7.4
Panel unit root tests result

		NSDP	SecNSDP	ServNSDP	Elec	Road	Rail	Tele
LLC	level	0.02 (0.50)	2.31 (0.98)	0.21 (0.58)	15.1 (1.00)	2.65 (0.996)	−0.02 (0.49)	0.36 (0.64)
	Δ	−20.5* (0.000)	−22.1* (0.000)	−16.3* (0.000)	−21.3* (0.000)	−12.7* (0.000)	−14.3* (0.000)	−9.38* (0.000)
Breitung	level	4.73 (1.00)	1.52 (0.93)	5.51 (1.00)	−4.44* (0.00)	2.85 (0.997)	−0.65 (0.25)	6.24 (1.00)
	Δ	−8.23* (0.000)	−10.3* (0.000)	−13.02* (0.000)	−12.8* (0.000)	−5.14* (0.000)	−6.42* (0.000)	−7.4* (0.000)
IPS	level	2.00 (0.97)	5.63 (1.00)	4.68 (1.00)	4.13 (1.00)	2.7 (0.996)	0.94 (0.82)	5.14 (1.00)
	Δ	−21.4* (0.000)	−22.2* (0.000)	−16.9* (0.000)	−20.3* (0.000)	−12.4* (0.000)	−14.7* (0.000)	−9.4* (0.000)
ADF Fisher	level	22.7 (0.92)	33.4 (0.49)	11.1 (0.99)	0.02 (1.00)	22.0 (0.94)	27.1 (0.79)	12.6 (0.99)
	Δ	382.5* (0.000)	364.7* (0.000)	268.1* (0.000)	347.4* (0.000)	205.5* (0.000)	236.2* (0.000)	138.1* (0.000)

Notes: All variables are in natural logarithms. Δ is the first-difference operator. The null hypothesis of Breitung, LLC, and IPS tests examines nonstationary. Lag selection (automatic) is based on Schwarz Information Criteria (SIC). * denotes statistical significance at the 1 percent level (*P*-values are presented in parentheses). NSDP = ln(per capita NSDP); SecNSDP = ln(per capita NSDP from secondary sector); ServNSDP = ln(per capita NSDP from services sector); Elec = ln(electricity generation); Road = ln(road density); Rail = ln(rail density); Tele = ln(tele-density).

to 2010 were estimated to determine the long-run relationships among the following variables: log of PCNSDP, log of per capita electricity generation, log of road density, log of rail density, and log of tele-density employing residual-based cointegration tests suggested by Pedroni (1997). He proposed seven test statistics, four of them (panel v, panel rho, panel PP, panel ADF) show in-group test statistics and the other three (group rho, group PP, group ADF) show between-group test statistics (if the null is rejected in the panel case, then the variables are cointegrated for all states, whereas if null is rejected in the group panel case, then cointegration among the relevant variables exists for at least one of the cases).

The results of these tests are presented in table 7.5 for time period 1980 to 2010. Out of the seven tests, four test statistics are significant and reject the null of no-cointegration, suggesting the existence of a

Table 7.5
Pedroni panel cointegration test results

	Panel with PCNSDP		Panel with SecNSDP		Panel with ServNSDP	
	Test statistic	Probability	Test statistic	Probability	Test statistic	Probability
Within dimension						
Panel v-statistic	−0.632	(0.736)	−2.655	(0.996)	−1.111	(0.996)
Panel rho-statistic	0.595	(0.724)	2.202	(0.986)	2.938	(0.998)
Panel pp-statistic	−3.868***	(0.000)	−5.557***	(0.000)	−1.834***	(0.000)
Panel ADF-statistic	−4.089***	(0.000)	−7.770***	(0.000)	−2.641***	(0.004)
Between dimension						
Group rho statistic	2.717	(0.996)	3.885	(0.999)	4.630	(1.000)
Group pp-statistic	−3.963***	(0.000)	−9.555***	(0.000)	−5.854***	(0.000)
Group ADF statistic	−3.967***	(0.000)	−6.037***	(0.000)	−5.087***	(0.000)

Notes: The null hypothesis of Pedroni test examines the absence of cointegration. Lag selection (Automatic) is based on SIC with a max lag of 5. *, **, and *** denote statistical significance at the 10, 5, and 1 percent levels, respectively. PCNSDP = ln(per capita NSDP); SecNSDP = ln(per capita NSDP from secondary sector); ServNSDP = ln(per capita NSDP from services sector).

long-run equilibrium relationship among the relevant variables. Thus the tests show that for the 17 states there seems to be a long-run equilibrium relation between per capita NSDP and the given infrastructure indicators. The next step is to obtain the long-run coefficients of individual variables using the fully modified ordinary least squares (FMOLS) estimation technique, which will provide long-run elasticities. FMOLS was originally designed by Phillips and Hansen (1990) to provide optimal estimates of cointegrating regressions. This method modifies the least squares method and accounts for serial correlation effects and for the endogeneity in the regressors that result from the existence of a cointegrating relationship.

Table 7.6
Panel FM-OLS results

Long-run elasticity	*Independent variables*				
	Elec	Road	Rail	Tele	
NSDP	0.135***	0.368***	2.206***	0.082***	
	(2.95)	(5.37)	(17.35)	(4.75)	
SecNSDP	0.043	0.395***	1.732***	0.108***	
	(0.74)	(3.87)	(9.03)	(4.46)	
ServNSDP	0.237***	0.416***	1.537***	0.124***	
	(5.38)	(6.8)	(12.23)	(8.13)	
Short-run elasticity	ΔElec	ΔRoad	ΔRail	ΔTele	ECT_{t-1}
ΔNSDP	0.02	−0.04	−0.19*	0.15***	−0.27***
	(0.9)	(−0.97)	(−2.3)	(11.4)	(−7.6)
ΔSecNSDP	0.02	−0.05	0.08	0.16***	−0.003*
	(0.66)	(−0.75)	(0.58)	(7.13)	(−1.7)
ΔServNSDP	−0.01	0.06*	−0.38*	0.12***	0.01
	(−0.84)	(1.77)	(−1.7)	(9.67)	(−0.86)

Notes: *t*-statistics are in parentheses. ***Indicates that the estimated parameters are significant at 1 percent level.). NSDP = ln(per capita NSDP); SecNSDP = ln(per capita NSDP from secondary sector); ServNSDP = ln(per capita NSDP from services sector); Elec = ln(electricity generation); Road = ln(road density); Rail = ln(rail density); Tele = ln(tele-density).

7.4.2 Panel FMOLS Estimation

Table 7.6 provides the results of panel FMOLS and all the variables expressed in natural logarithms. The estimated coefficients from the long-run cointegration relationship can be interpreted as long-run elasticities. In all cases the parameters are quite significant at the 1 percent level for the overall economy. From the table we can conclude that there is a strong and positive long-run relationship between output (PCNSDP, secondary sector's PCNSDP and services sector PCNSDP) and the infrastructure variables. The results indicate that a 1 percent increase in electricity generation is correlated with an increase in PCNSDP by 0.13 percent (and 0.23 percent for the service sector). In the long run the elasticity of output with road infrastructure is also significant, with a 1 percentage point increase in road density contributing approximately a 0.4 percent increase in output. The long-run elasticity from both rail and tele-density is likewise significant and positive for the overall economy as well as for the industry and services sector. However, the short-run elasticities, as estimated from an OLS regression with all variables in first differences and including a lagged error correction term (ECT) that is the residual from the long-run cointegration relationship (residuals from FMOLS equation estimated above) and is interpreted as the speed to which the system adjusts toward its long-run trends when subjected to a shock, provide different result. The short-run elasticities are smaller (in absolute terms) than the long-run estimates, but most of them are insignificant except the result for tele density. Thus we can conclude that infrastructure sector has positive and significant elasticity with output over the long run.

7.4.3 Panel Granger Causality Test Results

While the existence of cointegration implies long-run Granger causality in at least one direction (Granger 1988), cointegration says nothing about the direction of the causal relationship among the variables. As is common practice a panel VECM is estimated to perform Granger-causality tests (Pesaran et al. 1999). The panel short- and long-run Granger-causality results conducted are reported in table 7.7. The statistical significance of the coefficients associated with the ECT (error correction term) provides evidence of an error correction mechanism that drives the variables back to their long-run relationship. According to the coefficient on the lagged ECT (negative and significant), there exists a long-run relationship among the output and infrastructure variables. However, in the short run the results indicate that there does not exist bidirectional Granger causality between all variables. There is evidence of unidirection causality running from electricity, railways, and telecommunication toward output. In the short run the PCNSDP (industry and service sector) is Granger-caused by the electricity and telecommunication infrastructure.

7.5 Period-wise Analysis of Impact of Infrastructure on Output

The preceding analysis was done using the entire thirty-year period from 1980 to 2010. Attempt was made to understand the nature of relation between infrastructure and output and to look at the issues of possible endogeneity among the variables that may arise due to reverse causality. In this section we divide the entire thirty-year period into three decades and analyze the impact of infrastructure (after controlling for other factors) on output. As is mentioned in section 7.3, the

Table 7.7
Panel causality test results

Dependent	Source of causation (independent variable)					
variables	Short run					Long run
ECONOMY	ΔNSDP	ΔElec	ΔRoad	ΔRail	ΔTele	ECT
ΔNSDP	–	−1.94***	0.26	1.58*	−0.28*	−0.11***
ΔElec	−0.51	–	−0.13	−0.81***	0.14***	−1.23***
ΔRoad	3.81	−7.41	–	6.05***	−1.09	−0.012
ΔRail	0.63	−1.22***	0.16	–	−0.18	−0.13***
ΔTele	−4.49	14.9	−1.77*	−4.35	-	−0.012
INDUSTRY	ΔNSDP	ΔElec	ΔRoad	ΔRail	ΔTele	ECT
ΔNSDP	–	−0.67***	0.32	0.42	−0.17***	−0.62***
ΔElec	1.49***	–	0.48***	0.62***	−0.26***	−0.65***
ΔRoad	−0.46	−5.5	–	4.30***	−0.53	−0.02
ΔRail	0.10	−1.29***	0.23	–	0.12	−0.12***
ΔTele	−0.87	10.3	−1.8	−8.0*	–	−0.004***
SERVICES	ΔNSDP	ΔElec	ΔRoad	ΔRail	ΔTele	ECT
ΔNSDP	–	−4.9***	0.94	−4.05	−0.65*	−0.02***
ΔElec	−0.20	–	−0.19***	−0.8***	0.13	−1.33***
ΔRoad	1.05	−5.25	–	4.26***	−0.69	−0.02
ΔRail	0.24	−1.23***	0.23	–	−0.16	−0.13***
ΔTele	−1.51	7.57	−1.44	−6.14*	–	−0.01

infrastructure policy in India has incurred several developments that differ over the decades depending on the nature of the overall economic policy. In order to gauge the varying impact of different infrastructure variables in each of these three decades, I estimate separate equations and present the results in the following sections.

In this regard I estimate the following equation using the panel of 17 Indian states for the time period 1980 to 2010:

1) $\ln(y) = \ln(a) + \beta \ln(w) + \gamma \ln(\text{Credit}) + a_1 \ln(\text{El}) + a_2 \ln(\text{RR}) + a_3 \ln(\text{Tele}) + a_4 \ln(\text{Schl}) + a_5 \ln(\text{Health})$,

where $\ln(y)$ = log of per capita net state domestic product, $\ln(w)$ = log of worker to population ratio, $\ln(\text{Credit})$ = log of per capita credit disbursed by all scheduled commercial banks, ln(El) = log of per capita electricity consumption, ln(R) = log of density of surfaced road per 1,000 km^2 (alternatively, the variable ln(RR) = log of density of total density of surface transport and includes surfaced road and rail density was used with similar results—results not shown but available upon request), and ln(Tele) = log of tele density per 10,000 people. To augment the model, human capital is treated as an additional factor of production and has been included as number of schools per 100,000 population and number of health centers per 100,000 population: ln(schl) and ln(health).

7.5.1 Empirical Results

In order to coherently present the results from panel data analysis, they have been segregated and presented for 1980 to 1990, 1990 to 2000, and 2000 to 2010 time periods. The relationships of PCNSDP, secondary and tertiary sector PCNSDP, and infrastructure variables for the states are described for each of these periods along with the regional impacts of infrastructure. Regressions were run using pooled OLS, fixed effects, and random effects but only the more econometrically correct results are shown (based on Hausman's specification test for fixed and random effects and the Breusch–Pagan test for relations between random effects and the pooled OLS; see Hausman 1978 and Breusch and Pagan 1979). Postestimation tests for heteroscedasticity and autocorrelation were conducted and only the corrected estimates along with robust standard errors are presented in this chapter.

Aggregate Output and Infrastructure

For the period 1980 to 1989, the impact of the energy infrastructure indicator—electricity generation—was found to be significant and positive, even after correcting for heteroscedasticity and serial autocorrelation. Electricity has a huge impact on output and a one percentage increase in electricity consumption increases output by 0.14 percent. The elasticity for transport infrastructure was not high, and a percent increase resulted in 0.10 percent increase in output, which was not found to be significant. Human capital was added in the form of number of schools and health centers, and the number of schools was negative and significant, whereas the elasticity for health centers was 0.08 and significant (table 7.8, column 1).

For the period 1990 to1999, to the equation was added a variable for the telecommunication infrastructure; see table 7.8, column 2. The

Table 7.8
Dependent variable: ln(PCNSDP) and for sample of 17 Indian states

Independent variables	(1)	(2)	(3)
	FE (Robust) 1980–89	FE(Robust) 1990–99	FE(Robust) 2009–10
Constant	9.7 (1.00)***	4.77 (1.12)***	6.18 (1.3)***
Ln(credit)	0.05 (0.02)	0.14 (0.01)***	0.25 (0.07)***
Ln(*W/P*)	0.37 (0.14)***	0.32 (0.11)***	-0.39 (0.16)***
Ln(elec)	0.14 (0.06)***	0.40 (0.08)***	0.03 (0.06)
Ln(road)	0.10 (0.10)	0.08 (0.10)	-0.06 (0.09)
Ln(tele)		0.12 (0.02)***	0.10 (0.04)***
Ln(school)	-0.44 (0.21)**	0.16 (0.07)***	-0.05 (0.74)
Ln(health)	0.08 (0.02)***	-0.11 (0.10)*	-0.03 (0.06)
Observations	120	151	150
R^2	0.56	0.85	0.91
Hausman test	0.05	0.000	0.000
F-statistic	72.2(0.000)	57.2(0.00)	0.000
Breusch–Pagan			
Modified Wald	0.00	0.000	0.000
Test for serial AC	0.99	0.20	0.18

Notes: Numbers in parenthesis below the coefficient estimates are standard errors. *P*-values for the null hypothesis of the usual diagnostic tests are also reported in parenthesis. *,**, and *** indicate that the variable is significant at 10, 5, and 1 percent level. Dependent variable is the log of per capita NSDP; or log of per capita secondary sector NSDP; or log of per capita tertiary sector NSDP And ln(*W/P*) = log of worker population ratio; ln(credit) =log of per capita credit given by SCBs; ln(elec) = log of per capita electricity consumption; ln(road) = log of road density per thousand km^2 area; ln(tele) = log of tele-density per ten thousand people; ln(school) = log of number of school per 100,000 population, ln(health) = log of number of health centers per 100,000 population. Hausman test used to decide between fixed effect and random effect. Modified Wald test used for heteroscedasticty. The null of homoscedasticty and Wooldridge test used for first-order serial autocorrelation: the null of no autocorrelation.

impact of electricity infrastructure increased and was positive and significant. The transport infrastructure contribution declined and was not significant. The elasticity of tele-density was around 0.12, indicating the increasingly important role played by this sector for output generation. Surprisingly, the health infrastructure showed a negative and significant relation with output for this period. For most states during this period there was a decline in government spending on health (the public expenditure elasticity with respect to NSDP for this period was less than one, which was among the lowest in the world); however, there were definitional changes in what services are encompassed under primary health centers, community health centers, and hospitals, which led to several discrepancies in the data. Apart from the low level of access to health facilities in terms of number of health centers per capita, there were many unfilled vacancies for doctors and paramedical staff in many states of India. One reason for the large number of vacancies could have been the low number of health workers. These are among the several factors that the data were unable to capture and that could have had an indirect impact on overall output.

The results for the time period 2000 to 2010 indicate that only tele-density was important for output generation (table 7.8, column 3). Yet for the first time the worker–population ratio had a negative sign. The explanation for this phenomenon is well noted in the literature as in this time period, especially in the latter half of the decade, employment growth rate was very low while output was increasing at a high rate. The service sector whose share in the aggregate output had been increasing steadily saw high employment in this period, but it was not commensurate with its output growth, which led to a decline in employment elasticity especially beginning in 2004–05. The primary sector and in some years even the manufacturing sector actually registered a negative employment elasticity (Papola and Sahu 2012). All these reasons substantiate the results we obtained for worker–population ratio.

Another observation that can be made from this table is the insignificant and negative contribution of transport infrastructure during this period. Possible explanations for this phenomenon that stem from the literature and are based on existing theories are the following: (1) according to the political business cycle theory (e.g., Rogoff 1990; Dixit and Londregan 1996), the geographic distribution, timing, and composition of infrastructure development is decided upon in such a manner that they coincide with elections and their geographical distribution is directed toward those areas that are considered critical for re-election bid rather than based on development criterion, which could mean that roads were built in more visible and electorally important areas (Calderon and Chong 2004); (2) the investment decisions to build roads are politically driven and depart from efficiency criterion, resulting in over accumulation of stock resulting in negative returns; or (3) although the roads exist, their quality is dubious, and so it may not have the expected impact on increasing access to productive opportunities or productivity. These are explanations for the observed result, however, could not be proved with the existing dataset.

Sectoral Output and Infrastructure

In this section relation between the per capita NSDP from secondary sector or tertiary sector and various infrastructure sectors is presented. The secondary sector includes manufacturing; construction; electricity, gas, and water supply; and mining and quarrying. Similarly the tertiary sector comprises of transport, storage, and communication; trade, hotels, and restaurants; banking and insurance; real estate, ownership of dwellings and business services; and public administration and other services. The worker–population ratio for these respective sectors excludes Assam, Jammu, and Kashmir due to unavailability of data.

Starting with 1980 to 1989 time period for both secondary and tertiary sector per capita net state domestic product, the Hausman test suggests the use of a fixed-effects model. Hetersokedasticity and first-order autocorrelation is a problem, and to correct for the same, Driscoll and Kraay standard errors were used (Hoechle 2007).The elasticity for electricity consumption (0.24) is significant and almost the same for both PCNSDP of secondary and tertiary sector. But the transport infrastructure elasticity is higher and significant for services sector than it is for the secondary sector (tables 7.9 and 7.10, columns 1). In the 1990s electricity contributed the highest to secondary sector PCNSDP than in any other period or to any other sector (table 7.9, column 2). Mid-1990s had also witnessed the highest manufacturing sector output growth.

The tele-density elasticity was significant for secondary sector as well as for tertiary sector and as expected the elasticity was higher for the latter. The results for 2000s for the secondary sector suggest that only tele-density contributed significantly to its output, whereas transport and electricity infrastructure seem to have a negative contribution but not significant. Services sector output shows positive but decreasing elasticity with electricity over the three time periods. Tele-density

Table 7.9
Dependent variable: ln(secondary PCNSDP) and for sample of 17 Indian states

	(1)	(2)	(3)
Independent variables	FE (Discoll and Kraay)1980–89	Random effect 1990–99	FE (Discoll and Kraay)2000–10
Constant	5.23	1.00	6.88
	(1.09)***	(0.94)***	(0.83)***
Ln(PCSec credit)	0.03	0.27	0.17
	(0.06)	(0.12)***	(0.05)***
Ln(*W*/*P*)	0.03	0.03	0.15
	(0.15)	(0.01)**	(0.02)***
Ln(elec)	0.24	0.69	−0.01
	(0.10)**	(0.09)***	(0.07)
Ln(road)	0.19	0.16	−0.17
	(0.13)	(0.09)**	(0.06)
Ln(tele)		0.08	0.16
		(0.02)***	(0.01)***
Ln(school)	−0.04	0.24	−0.04
	(0.13)	(0.08)***	(0.07)
Ln(health)	0.07	0.18	−0.13
	(0.02)***	(0.09)**	(0.1)
Observations	119	150	149
R^2	0.63	0.79	0.87
Hausman test	0.000***	0.70	0.000***
Breusch–Pagan		0.000***	
F-statistic	0.000***	0.000***	0.000***
Modified Wald	0.000***		0.000***
Test for serial AC	0.000***	0.60	0.000***

Notes: Numbers in parenthesis below the coefficient estimates are standard errors. P values for the null hypothesis of the usual diagnostic tests are also reported in parenthesis. *, **, and *** indicate that the variable is significant at 10, 5, and 1 percent level. Dependent variable is the log of per capita NSDP, or log of per capita secondary sector NSDP, or log of per capita tertiary sector NSDP. ln(*W*/*P*) = log of worker population ratio; ln(credit) =log of per capita credit given by SCBs; ln(elec) = log of per capita electricity consumption; ln(road) = log of road density per thousand km^2 area; ln(tele) = log of tele-density per ten thousand people; ln(school) = log of number of school per 100,000 population, ln(health) = log of number of health centers per 100,000 population. Hausman test is used to decide between fixed effect and random effect; modified Wald test for heteroscedasticty, the null of homoscedasticity; and Wooldridge test for first-order serial autocorrelation, the null of no autocorrelation.

Table 7.10
Dependent variable: ln(tertiary PCNSDP) and for sample of 17 Indian states

	(1)	(2)	(3)
Independent variables	FE (Driscall) 1980–89	Random effects 1990–99	FE (Driscall) 2000–10
Constant	2.99 (1.2)***	5.04 (0.52)***	5.73 (0.44)***
Ln(*W*/*P*)	0.16 (0.03)***	0.27 (0.08)***	−0.02 (0.07)
Ln(PCserv credit)	0.04 (0.02)**	0.11 (0.03)***	0.22 (0.04)***
Ln(elec)	0.25 (0.03)***	0.17 (0.04)***	0.08 (0.03)***
Ln(road)	0.26 (0.08)***	0.08 (0.05)	0.02 (0.05)
Ln(tele)		0.23 (0.01)***	0.13 (0.01)***
Ln(school)	0.36 (0.17)*	0.12 (0.06)***	−0.07 (0.06)
Ln(health)	0.08 (0.02)***	−0.12 (0.06)***	−0.09 (0.02)***
Observations	119	150	149
R^2	0.85	0.91	0.93
Hausman test	0.000	0.55	0.05
Breusch–Pagan		0.000	
F-statistic	0.000	0.000	0.000
Modified Wald	0.000		0.000
Test for serial AC	0.04	0.001	0.005

Notes: Numbers in parenthesis below the coefficient estimates are standard errors. *P*-values for the null hypothesis of the usual diagnostic tests are also reported in parenthesis. *, **, and *** indicate that the variable is significant at 10, 5, and 1 percent level. Dependent variable is the log of per capita NSDP; or log of per capita secondary sector NSDP; or log of per capita tertiary sector NSDP And ln(*W*/*P*) = log of worker population ratio; ln(credit) =log of per capita credit given by SCBs; ln(elec) = log of per capita electricity consumption; ln(road) = log of road density per thousand km^2 area; ln(tele) = log of tele-density per ten thousand people; ln(school) = log of number of school per 100,000 population, ln(health) = log of number of health centers per 100,000 population. Hausman test is used to decide between fixed effect and random effect; modified Wald test for heteroscedasticty, the null of homoscedasticity; and Wooldridge test for first-order serial autocorrelation, the null of no autocorrelation.

also had positive significant but decreasing elasticity with output, from 0.23 to 0.13. As expected, the elasticity of tele-density on service sector output was the highest and highly significant. Health infrastructure, however, showed a negative and significant elasticity with services output in 1990s and 2000s.

As a separate exercise dummies were created according to high-, low-, and medium-income group, and these were interacted with infrastructure variables to determine the regional differences in the influence of infrastructure on output. All such dummies were found to be not significant except for high-income states (results available upon request).

7.6 Conclusion

In this chapter an attempt was made to provide an empirical evaluation of the impact of infrastructure development—measured by stocks of individual physical infrastructure—on economic output across 17 Indian states over the 1980 to 2010 time period. The analysis was first done for aggregate PCNSDP, followed by a sectoral impact of infrastructure on secondary and tertiary sector PCNSDP. Data were gathered from panel cointegration results that suggest a long-term relationship between infrastructure variables and output. However, the obtained results do not support this relationship in the short run. Whereas electricity and telecommunication infrastructure are found to Granger-cause output, the same could not be said regarding transport infrastructure. This has serious implications because we know from both theoretical and empirical literature that transport infrastructure plays a crucial role in contributing toward output growth through both direct and indirect channels. It could either be that there are issues with roads statistics or that an alternate indicator for transport infrastructure needs to be applied as it's not just the quantity of road but also its quality that matters, and as such is not captured entirely by data on surfaced road density.

From the analysis undertaken on shorter time period (the thirty-year period was divided into three decades) the main conclusions drawn are that physical infrastructure variables did not have a uniform influence on output. The relationship not just differed for aggregate output, and for secondary and tertiary sector output, there was also distinct difference in the impact infrastructure had on the same sector for different time periods. For aggregate PCNSDP there were observed positive and significant elasticities of electricity and health infrastructure variables but negative for schools. However, transport infrastructure was not significant throughout the three time periods. Elasticity of electricity was highest during the 1990s and number of schools had a positive elasticity with output. Electricity had the highest elasticity for the secondary sector output in the 1990s and tele-density had highest elasticity for services sector during the same period. The impact of social infrastructure—education and health—also showed similar pattern. Where the education infrastructure had a significant contribution to secondary sector output only in the 1990s, for tertiary sector, it had positive elasticities in 1980s and 1990s.

Road Infrastructure variable are a major factor in determining output, was found to have insignificant and even negative elasticity with output, and this can be perceived as an indicator that although roads are built and network exists, the quality of roads is such that they are not having the desired impact on output. . When different regions were interacted with infrastructure variables, high-income regions were found to have an edge over the low-income regions in their impact on output, but the results were not conclusive.

Nevertheless, these results do not point to any uniform relationship between infrastructure availability and output. This possibly is due to the fact that infrastructure development in the country has not been uniform. India has seen in each decade patterns of infrastructure buildup that correspond to different political-economy eras. The corresponding Five Year Plans were shaped in large part by the changing political priorities of the governments.

An important question for further examination is that even as growth rates in real infrastructure development have declined, output growth rates have tended to accelerate. This could be explained, first, by the buildup of infrastructure stock up to 1990–91, which was sufficient to support the growth surge that occurred, and, second, by the post-1991 reforms, when the drivers of growth changed and were more significant than the declining infrastructure growth. All in all, as was observed, the long-term effects of infrastructure on output in India cannot be undervalued. Although this analysis found no immediate impact, the development of infrastructure is critical to economic growth.

Note

I would like to acknowledge here that an earlier version of this chapter was published as Working paper 319 at the Institute for Social and Economic Change, 2014.

1. In this chapter, states are considered as rich (or poor) if their PCNSDP is more (or less) than mean NDP (India)+ Standard Deviation (or (mean–std dev)India NDP).

References

Aschauer, D. A. 1989. Is public expenditure productive? *Journal of Monetary Economics* 23 (2): 177–200.

Bonaglia, F., E. La Ferrara, and M. Marcellino. 2001. Public capital and economic performance: Evidence from Italy. Working paper 163. IGIER.

Breitung, J. 2000. The local power of some unit root tests for panel data. In *Advances in Econometrics: Nonstationary Panels, Panel Cointegration, and Dynamic Panels*. vol. 15. Ed. B. H. Baltagi, 161–178. Amsterdam: JAI Press.

Breusch, T. S., and A. R. Pagan. 1979. A simple test for heteroscedasticity and random coefficient variation. *Econometrica* 47 (5): 1287–1294.

Cadot, O., L. H. Röller, and A. Stephan. 1999. A political economy model of infrastructure allocation: An empirical assessment. Discussion paper 2336. CEPR.

Calderon, C., and L. Serven. 2002. The output cost of Latin America's infrastructure gap. Working paper 186. Central Bank of Chile.

Calderon, C., and A. Chong. 2004. Volume and quality of infrastructure and the distribution of income: An empirical investigation. *Review of Income and Wealth* 50 (1): 87–106.

Canning, D., and E. Bennathan. 2000. The social rate of return on infrastructure investments. Working paper 2390.World Bank.

Cashin, P., and R. Sahay. 1996. Internal migration, centre-state grants and economic growth in the states of India. *IMF Staff Papers* 43 (1): 123–71.

Chand, R., and S. Parapppurathu. 2012. Temporal and spatial variations in agricultural growth and its determinants. *Economic and Political Weekly* 47 (26/27): 55–64.

Charlot, S., and B. Schmitt. 1999. Public infrastructure and economic growth in France's regions. ERSA conference paper ersa99pa142. European Regional Science Association.

Das, S. K., and A. Barua. 1996. Regional inequalities, economic growth and liberalisation: A study of the Indian economy. *Journal of Development Studies* 32 (3): 364–390.

Devarajan, S., V. Swaroop, and H. F. Zou. 1996. The composition of public expenditure and economic growth. *Journal of Monetary Economics* 37 (2): 313–44.

Dixit, A., and J. Londregan. 1996. The determinants of success of special interests in redistributive politics. *Journal of Politics* 58: 1132–55.

Easterly, W., and S. Rebelo. 1993. Fiscal policy and economic growth: An empirical investigation. *Journal of Monetary Economics* 32, (3): 417–58.

Economic Intelligence Service. Various years. Centre for Monitoring Indian Economy. Mumbai.

Egert, B., T. Kozluk, and D. Sutherland. 2009. Infrastructure and growth: Empirical evidence. Working paper 957. William Davidson Institute.

Engle, R. F., and C. W. J. Granger. 1987. Cointegration and error correction: Representation, estimation, and testing. *Econometrica* 55: 251–76.

Esfahani, H., and M. T. Ramíres. 2003. Institutions, infrastructure and economic growth. *Journal of Development Economics* 70 (2): 443–77.

Everaert, G., and F. Heylen. 2004. Public capital and long-term labour market performance in Belgium. *Journal of Policy Modeling* 26 (1): 95–112.

Ghosh, B., and P. De. 2000. Linkage between infrastructure and income among Indian states: A tale of rising disparity since Independence. *Indian Journal of Applied Economics* 8 (4): 391–431.

Ghosh, B., and P. De. 2004. How do different categories of infrastructure affect development? Evidence from Indian states. *Economic and Political Weekly* 39 (42): 4645–4657.

Ghosh, B., and P. De. 1998. Role of infrastructure in regional development: A study over the plan period. *Economic and Political Weekly* 33 (47/48): 3039–48.

Granger, C. W. J. 1988. Some recent developments in a concept of causality. *Journal of Econo-metrics* 39(1–2): 199–211.

Government of India. Various years. *Statistical Abstract of India*. Central Statistical Organisation, Ministry of Statistical and Programme Implementation. Delhi.

Government of India. 1996. *India Infrastructure Report: Policy Imperatives for Growth and Welfare. Report of Expert Group on the Commercialisation of Infrastructure Projects (Dr. Rakesh Mohan, Chair) for The Ministry of Finance*. vol. 1–3. Delhi: Thomson Press.

Gramlich, Edward M. 1994. Infrastructure investment: A review essay. *Journal of Economic Literature* 32: 1176–96.

Gwartney, J., R. G. Holcombe, and R. Lawson. 2004. Institutions and the impact of investment on growth. Presented at the Conference of the Association Private Enterprise Education, APEE, Bahamas.

Hausman, J. A. 1978. Specification tests in econometrics. *Econometrica* 46: 1251–71.

Hoechle, D. 2007. Robust standard errors for panel regressions with cross sectional dependence. *Stata Journal* (3): 281–312.

Im, K. S., M. H. Pesaran, and Y. Shin. 2003. Testing for unit roots in heterogeneous panels. *Journal of Economics* 115: 53–74.

Jumenez, E. 1995. Human and physical infrastructure: Public investment and pricing policies in developing countries. In *Handbook of Development Economics, vol. 3B. Amsterdam*, ed. Jere R. Behrman and T. N. Srinivasan, 2773–2843. North Holland: Elsevier Science.

Kurian, N. J. 2000. Widening regional disparities in India: Some indicators. *Economic and Political Weekly* 35 (7): 12–18.

Lall, R., and A. Rastogi. 2007. Political economy of infrastructure development in post-Independence India. Occasional paper 2007/1. IDFC.

Lall, V. Somik. 1999. Role of public infrastructure investments in regional development: Experience of Indian states. *Economic and Political Weekly* 34 (12): 717–25.

Levin, A., C. F. Lin, and C. Chu. 2002. Unit root tests in panel data: asymptotic and finite sample properties. *Journal of Economics* 108: 1–24.

Mathur, A. 2001. National and regional growth performance in the Indian economy: A sectoral analysis. Presented at National Seminar on Economic Reforms and Employment in Indian Economy, IAMR.

Nagaraj, R., A. Varoudakis, and M. A. Veganzones. 2000. Long-run growth trends and convergence across Indian states. *Journal of International Development* 12 (1): 45–70.

Nair, K. R. G. 1982. *Regional Experiences in a Developing Economy*. New Delhi: Wiley Eastern.

Papola, T. S., and P. Sahu. 2012. *Growth and structure of employment in India: Long-term and post reform performance and the emerging challenge. Study prepared as part of research programme, Structural Changes, Industry and Employment in the Indian Economy*. Indian Council of Social Science Research.

Pedroni, P. 1997. Panel cointegration; asymptotic and finite sample properties of pooled time series tests, with an application to the PPP hypothesis: New results. Working paper. Indiana University.

Pedroni, P. 1999. Critical values for cointegration tests in heterogeneous panels with multiple regressors. *Oxford Bulletin of Economics and Statistics* 61: 653–70.

Pedroni, P. 2004. Panel cointegration: Asymptotic and finite sample properties of pooled time series tests with an application to PPP hypothesis. New results. *Econometric Theory* 20 (3): 597–627.

Pesaran, M. H., Y. Shin, and R. Smith. 1999. Pooled mean group estimator of dynamic heterogeneous panels. *Journal of the American Statistical Association* 94: 621–34.

Phillips, P. C., and B. E. Hansen. 1990. Statistical inference in instrumental variable regression with I (1) processes. *Review of Economic Studies* 57: 99–125.

Pritchett, L. 1996. Mind your P's and Q's: The cost of pubic investments in not the value of public capital. Policy research paper 1660. World Bank.

Rao, M. Govinda, R. T. Shand, and K. P. Kalirajan. 1999. Convergence of incomes across Indian states: A divergent view. *Economic and Political Weekly* (March 27): 769–78.

Raychaudhuri, A., and P. De. 2010. Trade, infrastructure and income inequality in selected Asian countries: An empirical analysis. Working paper 8210. Asia-Pacific Research and Training Network on Trade (ARTNeT), an initiative of UNESCAP and IDRC, Canada.

Rogoff, Kenneth. 1990. Equilibrium political budget cycles. *American Economic Review* 80: 21–36.

Sanchez-Robles, B. 1998. Infrastructure investment and growth: Some empirical evidence. *Contemporary Economic Policy* 16 (1): 98–108.

Straub, S., and A. Terada- Hagiwara. 2010. Infrastructure and growth in developing Asia. Asian Development Bank Institute. Economics working paper 231. Tokyo.

Sturm, J. E., G. H. Kuper, and J. de Haan. 1998. Modelling government investment and economic growth on a macro level: A review. In S. Brakman, H. van Ees, and S. K. Kuipers, eds., *Market Behaviour and Macroeconomic Modelling*. London: Macmillan.

World Bank. 1994. *World Development Report: Infrastructure for Development*. New York: Oxford University Press.

8 Connecting People—An Evolutionary Perspective on Infraculture

Klaus Markus Hofmann

8.1 Introduction

The rise and fall of cities and entire civilizations can be linked to development of local, predominantly urban and transurban, infrastructures.[1] Infrastructures enabled comprehensive networks of communication that were, broadly speaking, connecting people, delivering public services for the state and its population, accumulating cultural surplus, and safeguarding empires. Regardless of their vital functions for society and indispensability, infrastructures were neither induced by an act of a divine creator nor are end products in themselves. Infrastructure systems do not simply happen, and neither can they be meaningfully considered an act of an individual. Infrastructure evolves and requires a social and cultural context, a mental and institutional framework, an initial intent shaped by an effort of interaction and communication, and an allocation of labor, capital, energy, and other resources.

My discussion in this chapter focuses on three infracultural aspects of infrastructure: (1) systemic and transdisciplinary functions and dimensions of infrastructure networks, (2) historical development of infrastructure systems, and (3) present-day infracultural advancements toward digitalization. The concept of infraculture presented here was developed in a transdisciplinary research project comparing governance principles of renewable socioecological systems ("common pool resources"; see Ostrom 1990) with sociotechnical systems, represented by large-scale infrastructure networks, examined in that context as "modern commons."[2]

8.2 A Systemic Approach toward Functions of Infrastructure

The central source of alimentation in human society has been agriculture since the Neolithic period. Hard human labor went into the struggle for survival. Time was scarce. The efficient use of time and the effective allocation of social and physical resources were key to a socio-economic evolution forming urban agglomerations. Infrastructures, facilitated human interaction and trade and thereby productivity, creativity, and cultural diversity typical for cities. Yet, while evolution is not an economic concept, it does in this infrastructural context underlie innovation cycles and sociotechnical development. Infrastructures are multifunctional, designed to increase the efficiency of human labor, transportation, and the multipurpose use of resources. "Infrastructure resources enable many systems (markets and nonmarkets) to function and satisfy demand from many different users. Infrastructure resources are not special-purpose resources. … Instead they provide basic, multipurpose functionality. … Users determine what to do with the capabilities that infrastructure provide" (Frischmann 2012: 65).

Every road has a destination. Infrastructure rarely produces tangible products nor is the infrastructural resource platform itself consumed by individual users. Rather, infrastructure connects sources and drains, or creates supply and demand for a wide range of services. As a sociotechnical resource system (STS), a specific infrastructure, like socioecological resource systems (SES) whose principles are described by Ostrom (2012: 73), produces a number of resource units that are consumed by groups or individuals according to a specific framework of arrangements for access, use, maintenance, and compensation. According to organic renewal and reproduction rates, the number of resource units can be boundless in an SES. "The challenge instead is to develop a social-ecological systems (SES) framework to multiple ecological problems in a variety of settings. … to discover the principles of—what I have called the design principles—that are at work in sustainable ecological and social systems" (Ostrom 2011: 22). Although the production of the various resource units of an STS is tied to permanent input investments such as energy, labor, and communications that can limit the units of output, some of the *commons principles* applied in SES can offer insight as to the challenges of sustainable infrastructure provisioning.

There is no question that access to infrastructure is closely connected with cultural rules formed by economic and interdependent social developments. From an institutional economy perspective, infrastructure costs occur the same way in society as transactions costs do in any firm (Coase 1937). Infrastructure investments could in fact be considered *societal transaction costs* in that they foster an economically cooperative and communicating society. Open access prevents exclusive monopolies or holdups, and any special infrastructure can be financed by either private or public institutions to meet an identified societal or economic objective. A functioning infrastructure system is necessary, but rarely is it alone a sufficient precondition for a sustainable economic development.

Again, every road has a destination. Infrastructure systems can be immobile and provide multiple services to meet a narrow set of social, economic, and ecological objectives or a collective set of objectives with widespread impact. From the socioeconomic perspective, the four functions of physical infrastructure platforms are (1) to protect, (2) to provide, (3) to support, and (4) to connect groups or individuals. To these four basic functions there should be added two complementary sociocultural functions: (5) to contain and (6) to include. This set of *infrafunctions* can be applied to almost any type of infrastructure. Of course, separately, some of these functions can be met by industrial products, investment goods, or specific needs services, but the full set of six functions does not apply to the primary or secondary level of production to the extent that they do to infrastructural systems.

From the evolutionary perspective, infrastructure systems can be considered intermediary infracultural platforms, where all kind of services within a society can occur. These six complementary infracultural functions (*infrafunctions*) persist, as do the fundamental needs and the basic communication mechanisms of a society; although the *services* offered like energy supply, communication devices, and means of transportation have changed throughout the centuries, responding to changes in culture and technology. This transition is inherent to infrastructure networks, and it has been taking place according to a set of governing principles, established and lasting over very long periods of time, exceeding the lifespans of human beings. Infrastructure systems thus should be considered part of an intergenerational cultural heritage, which I have called *infraculture*. From a systemic perspective on societal functions, infraculture can be regarded an emergent urban response to agriculture in rural communities.

The discussion in this chapter follows the sociologist perspective on infrastructure and technology of Popitz (1989) and Toynbee (1976),in describing distinct epochs of infracultural co-evolutionary development in socioeconomic history. The infracultural analysis of Europe with its Mediterranean foundations will not be limited to technological changes. There are strong influences of institutions and belief systems, as Parsons (1951) called it, as well as the shifting roles of individuals, states, markets, and civic society networks that connect urban centers across the European continent. Fundamentally, infrastructure can be linked to the knowledge and technology of its time, as a collective effort by individuals or a group toward a desired benefit. Indeed infrastructure investments can be considered not only social capital but societal intent and collective knowledge frozen in time.

A lot of research has been conducted on local infrastructure developments; this chapter will therefore address the challenges facing the wide area infrastructure networks that facilitate communications, energy transmissions, and transportation between metropolitan centers, the *transurban networks*, and corresponding supra-local economic and social effects. Together, communicating networks form the foundation of a collaborative society and as such, from an economic, social, and evolutionary perspective, could be considered as *one interdependent infracultural system*. Of course, without an energy source, there would be no transportation; without communication, there would not be any cultural use of energy or transport; and without transportation, there would be no media for conveying human culture, be it for use of energy or long-distance communication. This chapter argues that any sociocultural transformation requires and induces corresponding developments of infrastructure, though the transformation process may be expansive or contractive in character.

Infrastructures are not only important physical resources of urban settlements, facilitating transportation systems and the flow of traffic between urban clusters; infrastructure networks of energy, transportation, water, and communications are essential in the exchange of services, information, and wealth[3] in modern society. The emergence of these networks has led to socioeconomic patterns and spatial-cultural developments that reach beyond boundaries of clans, communities, cities, and countries. *Transurban infrastructure networks* could indeed be regarded as sociotechnical hybrid systems linking cultural progress with economic development through technical innovation, and to interdependent and self-supportive relationships.

Figure 8.1 presents a schematic illustration of how generic infracultural functions can be allocated to three complementary areas of activity: social interaction, physical flows, and economic transactions. The basic social function of infrastructure is to connect people, to include every living being within a societal context of working or worshiping together. Intent and collective effort are needed to establish any social

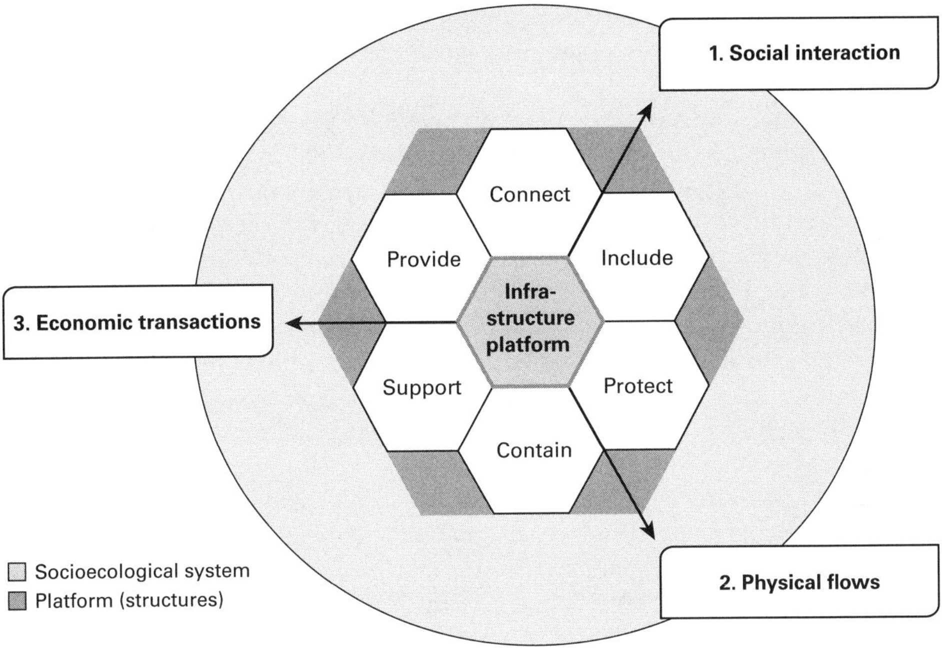

Figure 8.1
Infrafunctions and infracultural context

and physical infrastructure for communication, and at the same time to stimulate a sense of common identity and belonging (Tomasello 2008: 192). Usually social exchange of information and local community life takes place in a marketplace or a community building. In German villages the *Dorflinde*, a traditional village lime tree, had traditionally served as a multipurpose platform where public meetings were convened, marriages arranged, carriages and news arrived, and trials held, long before public buildings were erected to house the same functions.

Culture forms the invisible and fluid foundations for social and economic infrastructure. Technology, as such, is always a product of culture, shaped by knowledge and governed by social institutions. Thus infraculture determines the physical interfaces of material flows and transformation taking place in the natural environment, in a perpetual and highly adaptive exchange process of all biological forms of being. Physical protection and shelter against nature or adversaries have fostered community spirit from prehistoric caves to modern suburbs—and all the flows of exchange with biological and ecological systems, by waters, forests, or fields, have set natural boundaries for civilization that can contain or increase welfare through shortages, rivalries, and crises. The local pub where villagers meet for nourishment and social exchange is yet another such example of an infracultural platform for multifunctional exchange. Then there are such collective efforts and adopted schemes as irrigation, energy production, and transportation that determine the ecological efficiency and the environmental impacts of a society. In effect infrastructural networks shape the very "shoe sole" of the collective ecological "footprint" that socioeconomic development inflicts on the natural environment in the long term. Frischmann (2012) has described this as *societal metabolism,* a concept he derived from Fischer–Kowalski (1997).

In economic terms, infrastructure is what enables a multitude of human activities and transactions of commercial and noncommercial character. Systems of infrastructure are used for combining, transforming, and transporting goods; planning, delivering, and rendering services; recording, storing, and transmitting documents, funds, and other intellectual capital. These systems create transmitting platforms for modern societies in contracting employment of labor, generating wealth, and ensuring the provision of agricultural products to urban agglomerations and for the exchange of goods, labor, and capital in real or virtual marketplaces, thus enabling a multipurpose platform for provisioning in an interdependent and collaborative economic system.

The infrastructure systems we have today were never planned as entireties; they are the outcome of a polycentric cultural and economic development process over many decades and determined by the governing socioecological framework, technologies, innovations, and available resources. Over long decades more or less well-balanced institutions for collective action were created, and individual choices and preferences could be expressed in consumption patterns or politically at ballot boxes, or even vocalized in street demonstrations. Once established, infrastructure becomes part of the path-dependent development process and acquires a reflexive self-energizing role. Transgenerational cultural roots and an existential dependency on functioning infrastructure systems can explain the ambiguous emotional involvement of residents when changes to habitual infrastructures are imminent, be they planned improvements or new infrastructure obstructing familiar territory.

Such evolving transformation processes, as can best be described as *infracultural evolutions*, that is, as the fundamental mechanisms and principles of a holistic approach in specific social, economic, and ecological contexts. The underlying structural platforms may be public goods or common pool resources, depending on their degree of subtractability (Ostrom 1990), supplied to all participants of the system without a required specific contribution. Individual choices and action may nevertheless be necessary to obtain benefit from a public good, a common pool resource, a club good, or a private good as these functions would depend on rules of supply and excludability of access. In a systemic perspective, infrastructural platforms enable a community to produce desirable infracultural functions and services for a multitude of economic and noneconomic purposes.

We need also to consider the fast technical and economic development of various infrastructure industries, since a process of convergence can be observed for the transurban infrastructure networks. Convergence, as it has been defined by Messerschmitt (2000: 570), occurs when "structures that were considered independent become competitive or complementary." In the transportation sector, roads, railways, and shipping can be competitive as well as mutually dependent in an intermodal complementary transportation chain. Across the three infrastructure sectors mutual dependence existed from the beginning. Convergence of infrastructure systems is accelerated by digitalization (Branscomb and Keller 1996: 280), transforming the vertically integrated value generation process in all sectors of economy into large infrastructure systems, where economic value is added in each horizontal layer as shown in the infrastructure development framework in figure 8.2.

Infrastructure requires major investments over very long periods of time and therefore can never be an end in itself. Infrastructures always evolve based on spatial and economic conditions, and also on cultural context and societal expectations. The physical networks develop in mutual exchange with the ecosystem, especially the local natural environment and an accessible economic, physical, and social resource base.

In his *Theorie der Infrastruktur* (translates: Theory of infrastructure) Jochimsen (1966: 100) establishes three complementary types or *dimensions of infrastructure*—material, institutional, and personal infrastructure—that are widely used, though critics like Frey (1972) have doubted the benefit of an institutional dimension for infrastructure in highly integrated economies of well-developed countries in Europe. The sociologist Talcott Parsons established a concept of *structural functionalism*, where open systems of interacting environing systems and human beings influence the functions and the cultural dynamics of societal change (1961: 412ff), and the same could be applied to infrastructure. Expanding on Parsons's work, the American economist and human ecologist Roy E. Allen (2008) has added to the ecological complex of human development, the interacting factors of population, environment, and technology, that is, more explicitly, the *social organization*. This includes competences, institutions, collective problem-solving capacities, and belief systems as equally important resources, such as would confirm the reflexive role of infraculture. More recently Frischmann (2012) emphasizes the *social and intellectual dimensions* and the noneconomic social value of infraculture. An additional dimension can be found in the notion of *mental infrastructure* due to Welzer (2011), which widens the scope of institutional infrastructure in social arrangements earlier suggested by Jochimsen (1966). Welzer's more inclusive approach integrates the subconscious and emotions, corresponding to the intuitions of behavioral economics and recent brain research.

These complementary types of infrastructure, described as five dimensions with corresponding *infrafunctions*, are listed, along with some general contemporary examples, in table 8.1.

The table gives no direct hierarchy to these complementary dimensions, but their normative aspects occur together. To illustrate this infracultural concept, imagine a group of players kicking a ball on a *meadow* on a Saturday afternoon. To better enjoy their outdoor game, they follow a set of rules: they mark the field and put up goal posts, thus creating an *institutional infrastructure*. They agree that each team have eleven members, of which one is allowed to use his hands, and they also appoint one referee and one person to look after their field during the week. This forms a *personal infrastructure*, addressing a set of duties. As more people come to watch this event, benches are built, a kiosk serving drinks and snacks, and finally a toilet, all these to attend to bodily needs. This demand-driven *technical infrastructure* is soon complemented by showers for the players, floodlights, and raised seating for the audience, so that a modern stadium is erected. To cover the initial investment and the operating budget, visitors are willing to pay entry fees, and buy merchandise; radio broadcast stations acquire media rights. All follow an economic logic: as team loyalty transforms random support groups into commercially valuable soccer fans, the marketing, and common goal of winning matches, a tournament, or championship infuses the team with credibility and thus a *mental infrastructure* along with a lucrative sport business. A casual bystander may find it difficult to recognize the *natural infrastructure* from the outset.

Table 8.1
Complementary infrastructure—dimensions and infrafunctions

Functions/ dimensions	Protect	Support	Provide	Connect	Include	Contain
Mental infrastructure	• Security • Shelter • Self-esteem	• Values • Common Spirit • Personal resources	• Performance • Progress • Innovation	• Freedom • Solidarity • Responsibility	• Belief Systems • Identity • Belonging	• Justice • Barrier determined
Social and personal infrastructure	• Community • Service for public • Police, Defense	• Neighborhood • Platform • Social access • Welfare	• Community • Basic provisioning • Workforce	• Networks • Communication • Interaction • Travel	• Society • Access rights • Art, sports • Culture	• Laws, rights • Cultural bound. • Social, public Acceptance
Technical infrastructure systems	• Livingspace • Physical protection • Fences • Fortification	• Platforms • Transportation • Vehicles • Devices	• Transport • Water • Sewage system • Energy grid	• Telecoms, ICT • Telematics • Broadcast, TV • Broadband	• Physical protection • Access media • Devices	• Capacity • Standards • Borders • Capital
Institutional infrastructure	• Defense • Healthcare • Service for public	• Education • Knowledge • Legal system	• Service for public • Trade • Property	• Democracy • Markets • Competition • Cooperative	• Culture • Education • Service for public	• Property • Regulation • Financing • Jurisdiction
Natural infrastructure	• Physical protection • Shelter • Topography	• Water, Air • Sun, Wind • Land, Topsoil	• Global commons • Forests, • Agrarian areas	• Waterways • Valleys • Resources	• Landscape • Biosphere • Habitat	• Topography • Ecosystem • Climate • Resources

In general, investments in infrastructure will be economically sustainable and not controversial as long as the sum of benefits for states, markets, and the population exceeds the foreseeable deficits for the public, environment, and future generations. This is a simplification, of course, of the very long phases of infrastructure investments: planning, construction, operation, and conversion or demolition of outdated infrastructure; these phases, by their longevity, exceed the management, fiscal, and electoral planning periods of infrastructure. From an economist's perspective, in today's Europe, it is not possible to evaluate an infrastructure project separate from its systemic effects in relation to existing structures, the natural environment, and economic and social structures, that is, its entire cultural context (Mayntz 2009). Depending on the social framework and specific roles, public and private actors tend to externalize social costs or to discount costs to future generations. To characterize infrastructure as the *operating system for perpetuity* shifts the attention beyond the initial investments toward a more complete perspective on life-cycle cost. Regular and preventive maintenance updates and strategic migration, which are common in telecommunications, can add a more sustainable infracultural perspective to business models of private and public infrastructure operations in the energy and transportation sectors, where re-investments are induced by obsolesce. Such costs are often neglected in initial investments or the necessity of innovation and technical upgrades to avoid obsolescence is underestimated in the long run.

Interdependent infrastructure systems, designed and operated as one interacting complex adaptive system (CAS), may better meet future requirements if the financial means are available from private and public sources. Infracultural governance issues of property rights, access to network platforms, allocation of public resources, externalitites, the quality of services produced (resource units), as well as maintenance of infrastructure resource systems are inherent challenges, a point addressed early on by Adam Smith (1776) in his inquiries and comments on *publick works*. While an infrafunction may be detached from a platform technology, it remains embedded in a cultural context. A sound and balanced infraculture provides a flexible and multidimensional framework for financing, planning, and burden sharing. The intensely debated ownership issue remains a question of minor importance, provided that governance is polycentric and effective at the local, regional, and national level.

8.3 A Historical Perspective—A Multidimensional Analysis of the Transition Pathway

To explain the infracultural dynamics of infrastructure networks better the historical development of people over a period of approximately 8,000 years and their infrastructural platforms will be contextualized from a social, ecological, and economic perspective to indicate the validity of the infracultural approach. Without a comprehensive understanding of the sociocultural framework of a specific period, it is difficult to recognize the interacting patterns of societal challenges, innovation, and collective action. Looking at infrastructural development, we are faced with complex adaptive sociotechnical and sociocultural hybrid systems. Complex adaptive systems are systems typically characterized by high interdependency and a large number of agents that interact, adapt, and learn over a given period of time: if a CAS does not succeed in doing so, it gets replaced (Miller 2007). Beyond the classic asymmetry of information in transactions, infrastructure development undergoes asynchronous planning, building, and usage periods along timelines exceeding the lifespans of individuals. Hence infrastructure development (as discussed by Goldsmith in chapter 2 of this volume) can be considered a mirror image of societal expectations—rational or irrational—regarding the corresponding or contradicting goals on wealth, social values, and the expected quality of life.

The demand side, historically represented by a sovereign, required certain services to achieve specific objectives and for the populace to build an appropriate infrastructure for those purposes. Obvious examples are streets for rapid movements of troops, relay messengers, and civil servants to collect taxes (Fuchs 1911). Other ancient infrastructures to be noted are temples and cathedrals for religious observances, often used as social control mechanisms, markets and storage facilities for foods, lighthouses and harbors for trade and exchange of goods, hospitals and monasteries for teaching skills and preserving knowledge. Once in place, the demand for more services from other stakeholders would arise. Thus common people could acquire specific terms of access. Migration, marital arrangements, and pilgrimage were strong cultural factors that would lead to the demand for means of travel.

Beginning around 6000 BC, nine epochs of infraculture can be distinguished by the development of dominant belief systems, cultural skills of communication, means of transportation, and technology, primarily information and the contemporary use of energy (Fouquet

2008). The development of culture enables economic development and wealth, which in return stimulates the development of more culture, with infrastructure forming the stabilizing and at the same time a binding between the two spheres.

Most sources mark the Neolithic period as the beginning of civilization and the creation of infrastructure. However, it can be assumed that before fixed settlements and anthropogenic infrastructure was erected, humans utilized infrastructure provided by nature to meet their basic needs: lakes and rivers for fishing and transport, caves and cliffs for protection and housing, and springs and creeks for drinking water. In a wider sense the commons—topsoil, forests, and oceans alike—could be classified as environmental infrastructure supporting human development. The provisional and recreational aspects of natural infrastructure have been discussed extensively by Aschauer (1990) and Frischmann (2012), whereas environmental boundaries and nature seem of no specific interest in early works of Jochimsen in the 1960.

The first "roads" besides natural waterways and fords were probably stamped out by animals and shared by groups of hunters-gatherers to connect their dispersed settlements. The four basic functions of physical infrastructures—to protect, to provide, to support, and to connect in creating common benefit—were regarded as basic human needs long before anthropogenic infrastructure was brought into being. Individuals alone hardly had a chance to survive in harsh circumstances, but local groups had the resources necessary to enhance natural infrastructure and thus improve their living conditions by a collective investment of labor, creativity, and capital. Infrastructure development was likely closely linked to the rise and fall of local communities, social capital, and communication and cultural exchange of goods and skills, all of which are the building blocks of civilization.

The priorities in the development of physical infrastructure can be derived using Maslow´s hierarchy of needs (Maslow 1954) as well as inferences based on human evolution and infracultural functions. The physical needs come first, and thus wells for the provision of fresh water and crop growing and livestock for foodstuffs. Improvement of food quality followed as means of appropriate storage, cooking, and access to energy were acquired.

8.3.1 First Infracultural Epoch: Agrarian Communities

Our infracultural beginnings came eons ago as *agrarian communities* gained control over the use of fire, a basic technological skill that added physical protection from cold and poor weather, and advanced such cultural skills as forging of tools, weapons, and production of other useful artifacts. Safety was increased by light fortifications that, when closed at nightfall, protected inhabitants from wild animals and bands of hostile humans. Living in groups offered safety and support structures to individuals who could not have survived alone. Palisades were erected first and made clear who belonged and who did not belong to the local clan or community. Together, the inhabitants could defend themselves, their families, and property better against intruders or possible attacks. The process of constructing a common infrastructure brought into the emerging social community system people who could prove their value to the group and gain respect from its members. Thus, beyond safety, the physical encampment increased a spatial and mental sense of belonging to group members. The functional collective with its reliable infrastructures became a social prerequisite for reproduction and the formation of social identity.

Beyond mere technical functions all anthropogenic infrastructure can be characterized as social arrangements. While the social and economic benefits of the vital infrastructure functions are obvious, in the early days burdens of infrastructure to fellow humans and nature were likely neglected or dealt with locally. Likely, too, groups were small and arable land abundant, so the impact of agrarian communities on the natural environment was limited. Of course, we depend on artifacts to document these first settlements as no written testimony exists.

8.3.2 Second Infracultural Epoch: Urban Melting Pots

The rise of expansive metropolises along the riverbeds of Euphrates and Tigris or, further west, the Nile, also called the hydraulic civilizations (Wittfogel 1957), marks the second infracultural epoch of *urban melting pots*. A lot of research has been conducted on the ancient cities of Uruk and Babylonian Mesopotamia and early Egyptian kingdoms. These ancient kingdoms developed trade, acquired wealth, and practiced a religious culture beyond attending to mere safety and survival. As archeologists have shown, the ancient metropolises attracted labor and traders from distant regions and formed a rich cultural synthesis. The economical and infrastructural backbones of these hydro-agrarian societies were the rivers supplying a *natural infrastructure* for irrigation, both water and wind used as agro-technical energy sources, scriptures and written laws, thorough accounting and communication (e.g., Hammurabi codex), organizing sophisticated divisions of labor and

Table 8.2
Infracultural epochs of infrastructure development

Network-epochs/ periods	People, infracultural belief systems	Infrastructure platforms	Products and services
First infracultural revolution →writing (technology-driven spatial expansion)			
1.Agrarian communities 6000 BC	• Local groups/ villages • Clans/chiefs • Subsistence economy	• Fire, boundary fences • Springs/wells • Fields/forests	• Shelter, potable water • Defense/ safety • Alimentation
2. Urban melting pots 3000 BC	• Kingdoms • Migration • Scripture/crafts • Surplus economy	• Bricks, buildings • Temples, forts • Boats, harbors • Fireplaces, forging	• Division of labor • Trading/ shipping • Tools/ irrigation
3. Transurban networks 2000 BC–AD 600	• Regional empires • Central authority • Nobility/slave labor	• Transport (roads) • Letters, messengers • Water/heating	• Military dominance • Laws, cults, scriptures • Property rights/taxes
Second infracultural revolution →copying (knowledge-driven scalability)			
4. Infracultural network nodes AD 600–1450	• Migration period • Crusades/ feudalism • Nation building	• Monasteries/ hospitals • Wind/water mills • Universities, theaters	• Education, knowledge • Medicine/ health • Rights/ commons
5. Intellectual networks 1450–1750	• Renaissance • Reformation • Mercantilism, banking	• Movable type printshops • Mining/gold • Postal monopoly	• Research, navigation • Discoveries, sciences • Books/ newspapers • Shops, school, stocks
Third infracultural revolution →transmitting (power-driven distribution)			
6. Industrialized networks 1750–1900	• Wealth of nations • Industrialization • Imperialism, capitalism	• Canals/ railways • Steel, chemistry, Sewage management • Cables/ Telegraphs	• Bulk shipments • Commuting, factories, healthcare • Metropolitan centers

Table 8.2 (continued)

Network-epochs/ periods	People, infracultural belief systems	Infrastructure platforms	Products and services
7. Automation networks 1900–1970	• Rise of superpowers • Oil/nuclear age • Free-trade doctrine	• Electricity, coal, gas • Highways, pipelines • Telephony, broadcasting	• Mass production/cars • Agrochemicals • Mass media
8. Interactive networks 1970–near future	• "Welfare democracy" • Postwar/proxy wars • Reflexive modernism	• Microelectronics • Computers/ satellites • Renewable energies	• Global internet access • Converging networks • Quest for sustainability
Fourth infracultural revolution →calculating (analytic algorithms)→outcome uncertain			
9. Transformative networks midterm future	• Postmodernism • Climate change • Dematerialized growth	• Smart grids • Big Data dynamics • Gene technology, bionics	• Renewable transports • Resilience/ Cyber security • Cyborgs, nano robotics

Note: For the focus on Europe, see Fouquet (2008), Popitz (1995), Toynbee (1976), and Parsons (1951).

transportation. Innovation was likely driven by scarcity, population pressure, and necessity; investment in infrastructure was likely stimulated by the creative friction between human ingeniousness, protection of vested rights, and the readiness to assume the risks of transformation (Serbser 2008). The visual expression of unifying belief systems treating nature as a powerful godhead, and the cultural skills to write and organize, manufacture bricks and build effective irrigation systems fostered rich architecture and temples, pyramids, fortifications, and canals whose remains can still be visited today.

8.3.3 Third Infracultural Epoch: Transurban Networks

Transurban networks of impressive scale grew in the ancient Mediterranean with the emergence of military-dominated regional empires. Slave labor, tax money, and extensive military forces enabled Egyptian pharaohs, Hellenic tyrants, and Roman emperors to shape the infrastructures of their realms. Their empires were vast and governed with efficient information (relay messenger services) and administrative systems. The *tekton* (carpenter or builder) marks the birth of the engineering profession (Greek root also used in "technic," "architecton"). The Roman road system, producing the largest transurban infrastructure networks in Europe, was differentiated into four categories of national (*viae consularis* or *publicae*), military (*viae militaris*), regional (*viae vicinales*), and local (*viae rusticate* or *private*) roads. The Roman administration provided a detailed manual for road construction, priority usage, and regular maintenance (Morlet 1861). The major roads had drainage, and foundations one meter deep on artificial dams, were fortified with clay, chalk stone, and mortar (*statumen*), and covered with fist gravel (*ruderatio*) and pebble (*nucleus*). Depending on climate and usage, the physical substructure (lit: infrastructure) was paved (Presch 2012). Well-documented laws and quality standards are one reason why this infrastructure still forms the dominant lifelines of Europe and shapes the administrative structure in most European countries.

The Roman period is also connected with the first international taxation system and laws establishing and regulating private property rights, both infracultural achievements persisting in modern states, followed by a wide range of institutional infrastructure. With regard to the shadow of infrastructure it should be noted at this point that the Roman writer Tacitus (AD 60) complains about the shadows of urbanization and infrastructure, the sickening stench and lack of hygiene in the streets of Rome accompanied by extensive noise during night caused by fast driving wagons.

8.3.4 Fourth Infracultural Epoch: Infracultural Network Nodes

With the decline of the Roman empire, Europe went through an intense period of barbarian migration and political instability. Monasteries and convents sharing strong belief systems of Christianity developed into influential *infracultural network nodes* in which important scriptures were preserved and copied manually. In these guarded infracultural repositories (*stabilitas loci*), country youths learned to read and write, about husbandry, healing herbs, and all kinds of crafts in addition to the compulsory religious education. The Roman Church and its orders rose to become a trusted economic and cultural stronghold supporting and competing with secular rulers, depending on the regional politics. Although physically of local character, the spatial effects of these *belief grounded networks* were impressive, spanning centuries of central governance from Rome but also encompassing missions of Irish-Scottish monks reaching from Scotland to Germany, France, Switzerland, and Italy to establish a decentralized spiritual, cultural, and legal network throughout the Frankonian empire (Hage 1993).

With the Crusades, cultural infrastructure, medicine, geography, astronomy, and engineering were updated with imported knowledge from the Orient. (Prutz 1964: 452).The first European universities were founded and established a tradition of research institutions. Mechanical technologies like milling used both water and wind as renewable sources of energy. Written contracts and laws made institutional arrangements tangible. The Magna Charta Libertatum (1215) documented the oldest written constitutional law in the era of nation building complemented by the less famous Charter of the Forest (1217), establishing the first rights of the commons and guarding sustainable use of natural infrastructure as a resource systems based on Commons rules, guaranteed by the state (Chomsky 2012).

8.3.5 Fifth Infracultural Epoch: Intellectual Networks

The Renaissance of the 1400s marked a historic shift of power from the eastern Mediterranean to continental Europe. To finance the ventures, alliances were formed between merchants and banks, later between wealthy bankers (e.g., Medici, Fugger) and states to support imperial expansion. The invention of printing, especially the successful innovation of movable type printing by Johannes Gutenberg (1395–1468), *marks the beginning of the digital production principles* resulting in the *scalability of knowledge*. Valuable content entities are first disaggregated into single characters, restructured into readable lines, and reassembled into pages to be imprinted with ink on paper. Content management was split from the mechanical reproduction process in the printing stock, thus information; intellectual capital of great value was made scalable ad infinitum by a social and technical communication infrastructure. Books and papers became the media de jour, spreading news, philosophy, and (technical) knowledge to an anonymous audience unprecedented in speed, quality, and cost.

This groundbreaking cultural technology was quickly adopted and fueled the first media-based revolution of European belief systems, the Reformation. The first printers were trained goldsmiths and engravers who moved with their new skills to vital humanistic communities where their craft could prosper. The map of print shops across Central Europe correlates closely with the activities of the Reformation preachers a few decades later in these same cities (e.g., Straßburg, Basel,

Nürnberg, Augsburg, Leipzig, and Erfurt). A contemporary artist and early media tycoon and himself a trained goldsmith and printer, Albrecht Dürer (1471–1528) contributed to the first encyclopedia, *Schedel's World Chronicle*, in 1493[4] and wrote an architectural manual in 1527 on infrastructure design advising the Emperor Maximilian I and the city council of Nürnberg on fortifications, the latter also on urban planning of how to reduce stench and pollution in the ideal city.

The importance of the control of media and information systems can be emphasized through the postal infrastructure monopoly granted to the Thurn and Taxis families by Emperor Maximilian I. around 1500. This *infrastructure privilege* lasted until the end of the twentieth century, persisting in a constant transformation of infrastructural platforms from written letters to signal telegraphs, typewriters, radio, telephony, telex, satellites, and the digital convergence of voice, data, and mobile communication. The monopoly in Germany was terminated in a period when the technology of communications infrastructure had reached the stage of multimedia and almost unlimited global Internet services.

The second infracultural revolution, covering epochs 3 through 5 was knowledge driven, facilitating urban expansion and the social networks of its time, using the scalability of written culture. The third infracultural revolution is tied to the beginning of industrialization, and a dramatic reduction of economic distance by modern telecommunications and transport technologies, described in epochs 6 through 8.

8.3.6 Sixth Infracultural Epoch: Industrialized Networks

Industrialization and transportation were and are carbon driven up to the present day. Large *industrialized networks* for transportation and the perpetuation of decentralized access to power supplied by steam increased productivity and proved a tipping point in mechanized manufacturing. Weaving, mining, and all kinds of mills and factories applied this unprecedented source of efficiency to increase their both quality and quantity of output at decreasing costs per unit produced. A semantic analysis of the English term "mill" shows that it persists as cultural synonym almost generic for any factory (Webster 1966: 934). Raw materials from domestic agriculture and generic mining or foreign colonies were monetarized at high speed, using fast-growing infracultural inventions like canals and railroads that offered efficient and affordable transportation networks for bulk shipments. Markets moved from the traditional market places to virtual trading across vast distances. Industrialization created wealth and offered paid employment. A competition of nations and social development accelerated urbanization, creating strong coal- and steel-based economies as well as demand for communications and improvements in public services such as sewage systems and health services. Rising social pressure and social innovation demanded and incubated sociocultural institutions like hospitals, orphanages, and poorhouses. The mechanisms and drawbacks of the capitalist economy were observed early by sociologists like Karl Marx (1818–1883) and Max Weber (1864–1920), starting an ongoing debate on base- (infrastructure) and superstructure, whether the one dominates the other's development. Infrastructure development was received with enthusiasm by a large majority comparable to the new economy euphoria and commented by few warning skeptics.

The actual term "infrastructure" was probably coined early during this period by accountants and sophisticated canal engineers in France, to describe the subconstruction (infrastructure) and superstructure necessary for building a railway track. The first evidence of the use of infrastructure is indeed the call for tenders for the railway construction between St. Petersburg and Warsaw, published in the *Gazette de la Bourse* (Paris 1857), and in the financial reports from the Conseil d´Oise, 1866, followed by many other Conseils accounting for infrastructure expenditure preparing their railway tracks. The term superstructure was utilized by scientists and engineers in Europe since 1700 for technical constructions, mainly foundations for canals, bridges, roads, and railways. In 1842 a law was passed by the French parliament, later to be called the "infrastructure law" (*loi d´infrastructure*). The invention of the railway was expected to be a threefold blessing to increase the levels of wealth, intellectuality, and morals (Deharme 1874). Canal engineers building tracks, English engineers moving to the continent to run railways, and investors to finance private turnpikes, canals, and railroad undertakings prove the importance of *personal infrastructure* as well as the role of capital and infracultural institutions in the transitional concept of path-depending innovation.

8.3.7 Seventh Infracultural Epoch: Automation Networks

The epoch that marks the beginning of the twentieth century will be called the age of *automation networks*, with know-how and technology spreading fast powered by electricity and oil. Europe was to become politically torn by democratic experiments, economic depression, and two world wars, leading to a cascade of innovations followed by the rise of two global superpowers. The conveyer belt taylorized production, first in the slaughterhouses of Chicago and then fast carried to automotive production in Detroit. Agrochemicals and land machines increased the productivity of farming to the extent that a fast-growing industrial workforce came to populate the assembly lines and was absorbed by modern cities. Fordism paved the road for mass motorization as well as mass production, laying the foundations for consumerism. The economic ideals of this period being steady growth, high employment and the *social engineering* of progress (Etzemüller 2009) were confronted with the Great Depression in the 1920s. This in turn generated public investment programs like the New Deal in the United States, the social democratic concept *Folkhemmet* in Sweden, and the national socialist RAD (*Reichsarbeitsdienst*) in Germany, funneling large public investments into the modernization of infrastructure networks of highways, airports, canals, and housing projects. Postwar reconstruction efforts (ERP), financed mainly by the American government, continued to improve infrastructure, remaking the economic base and thus enhancing industrial productivity in Central Europe.

8.3.8 Eighth Infracultural Epoch: Interactive Networks

With the invention of telecommunications, computers, and microelectronics, there has emerged a new form of global mass media and digital *automation networks* that exceed the prospects of increased productivity expected from the nuclear age. The incarnation of the ARPANET served as the nucleus for the World Wide Web financed by Department of Defense (Whitney and Mottl 1996: 34). This digital legacy from cold war research coincided with the cultural changes of the 1970s, to which could be traced a common quest for sustainability, aimed at resolving the conflict of interests between people, industry profits, and the welfare of the planet (Diederichsen and Franke 2013). Universal access to the global Internet via mouse click connects *Netizens* (Hauben 1996) and billions of smart devices worldwide, accelerating global exchange of knowledge. Converging networks enable data analysis by algorithms and knowledge-based value creation, changing every area of life, science, and business. The resource-imposed limits to growth may be overcome using more efficient technologies; the idea of achieving ecological balance and climate goals has set ambitious infracultural objectives for the *Energiewende*, proclaimed by German Parliament in reaction to Fukusihma events of 2011, effecting infrastructure developments in the entire European Community.

8.3.9 Ninth Infracultural Epoch: Transformative Networks

While the future remains uncertain, *transformative networks* using Big Data dynamics will no doubt shape the culture far beyond today's globalized economy. Smart grids, people always in touch with real-time management of demand, and an increasing diversity of supply formats offer a promising vision of a connected real-time society and global economy. The Internet of things, connecting and controlling almost every device in real time, with sensors measuring algorithms optimzing and micro motors manipulating automated systems, will subsequently transfer more decision-making power to machines, using artificial intelligence to compute and analyze trillions of data records, options like anticipative social control, gene manipulation, and biorobotics. The ethical issues as new infracultural frontiers arise will need to be addressed in a democratic infracultural forum bringing together corporations, states, and societal networks.

8.4 Digitalization Requiring an Update of Infraculture

Every society has the infrastructure it deserves. Infrastructure has to be paid for initially, and it earns its worth multiply over time, according to economic theory. To receive more value from every single euro or dollar invested in infrastructure, the decision-making process, tools, and financing instruments for all actors have to be recalibrated. To achieve the transformation necessary to meet the international political commitments in time requires not only a transgenerational coalition for infracultural priorities and an immediate change of investment policies toward sustainability; the investment has to be enforced by an orchestrated transdisciplinary initiative for systemic research of the infrastructure system and comprehensive infracultural education for engineers and economists in the sector.

Digitalization is one major driving force of convergence, followed by spatial synergies, economic efficiency, as well as social and environmental synergies. Infrastructure networks have developed following settlements and economic and social patterns of behavior. Synergies can be created by physical bundling of land use for construction, for example, of highways, railroads, and electrical overland lines. Physical synergy sources will further reduce distances and costs for construction, operation, and decentralized maintenance structures. Substantial social and administrative synergies can already be identified in planning, financing, and management of infrastructures, accompanied by leveraged risks for investors, political budget committees, and public acceptance as well as by facilitating access to infrastructure services at affordable prices. Ecological synergy could be developed so as to minimize physical impacts of infrastructures systems on the immediate natural environment, the physical protection of critical infrastructures against natural or anthropogenic risks, and the long-term effects to the local and global ecosystems and climate. Efficiency resulting from these will contribute to the societal acceptance of infrastructure development. The catalyst for infrastructure development is, of course, shared social capital, such as knowledge, belief systems, and cultural patterns, documented and transferred among individuals, groups, and generations by cultural communication channels (i.e., verbal chants and narratives, symbols and pictures, written documents and scriptures, printed mass-media, electronic platforms and devices; see table 8.1). Leaps in infrastructural technology require innovative rethinking of established patterns on how to communicate, design sustainable businesses, and manage energy use efficiently.

The infracultural development framework (IDF) in figure 8.2 shows a complex adaptive system of infrastructure management and the main feedback loops within this system. It explains in a schematic flow how sociocultural and economic objectives influence the development framework for infrastructure in reaction to global economic dynamics, a threatened natural environment, and societal change. Although infrastructure networks may be spread across a wide area, they are physically a local occurrence and bound to specific spatial, socioeconomical, and international governance frameworks and contemporary conditions. Investment in infrastructure development, regardless whether private or public, always reflect expectations of wealth and quality of life in the foreseeable future. Convergence in connection with increased global awareness of climate change and exhaustion of resources could open a window of opportunity to reorganize the infrastructure industry, shaped by spatial, national and sectoral monopolies, for the common benefit of users, environment, suppliers, and operators alike.

Additional synergies can be expected in the near future with the increase of backend intelligence in systems connecting users, suppliers, and other commercial or noncommercial institutions. The demand and supply sides of the infrastructure service would be linked in real time using data analytics to optimize the efficiency of an infrastructural

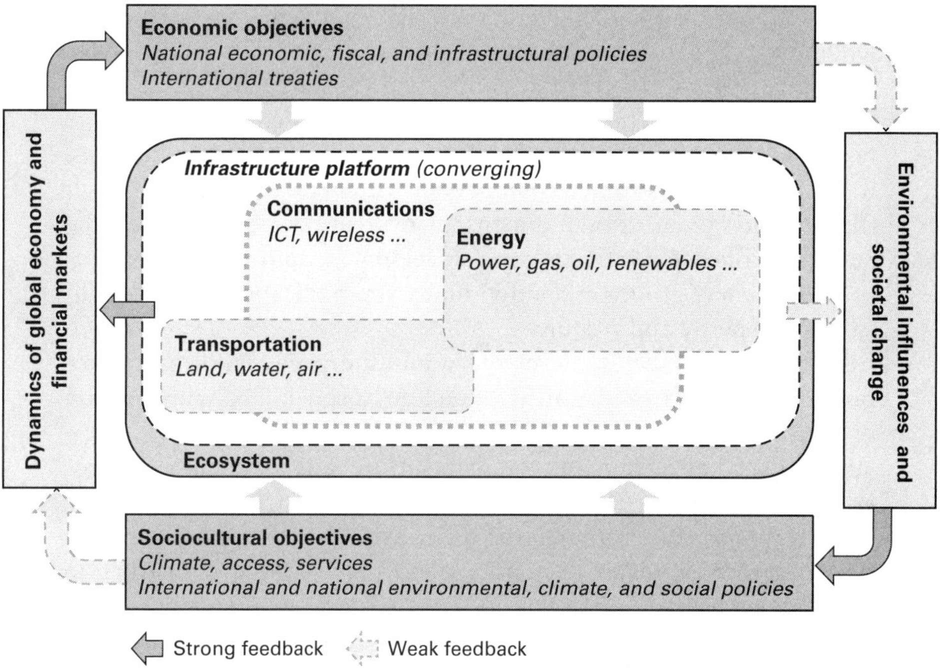

Figure 8.2
Infracultural development framework (IDF)

resource system, such as a traffic scheme for public transport, for electric vehicles charging from and delivering power to smart grids. Future infrastructure services may and will be offered across the traditional sector borders by one-stop suppliers (Weijnen, Herder, and Bouwmans 2008), overcoming path-dependent options of a specific industry. This technical opportunity will encourage new entrants, some of them disruptive game changers, to compete with established infrastructure actors in more than one sector at a time and, if successful, redefining paradigms of entire markets and existing regulations. Current examples of this infrastructure based, cross-sectoral transformation are Tesla, supplying energy free of charge to its customers across Europe; Skype, disrupting the value chain of telecommunications; Google, generating value from ubiquitous data, building proprietary search-based business models; and iTunes or Spotify, changing the paradigms of music industry.

Considering recent progress in technical convergence, it has to be considered that none of the three vital infrastructure networks for civilization and collaborative economy could have developed in the first place without the parallel evolution of the complementary structures (communication, transportation and energy). Digitalization accelerates the infrastructural convergence far beyond the interactive surface of a customer interface. This supports a systemic approach to infrastructure networks because, if one component in the network structure changes, it has effects on the other components within the system. Although digitalization opens a new dimension for real-time convergence, the cultural context for infrastructure development remains that of purposeful intent of groups and individuals, communication, and the skillful use of energy and resources.

Infrastructure creates intermediary, multipurpose platforms for economic and social activities and is therefore closely linked with creation of wealth and common well-being. The systemic effects make infrastructures a key sector and prerequisite for any national economy, which makes a comprehensive evaluation of benefits and burdens evoked by infrastructure measures necessary. On one hand, a minor project can cause major adaptations and impose large infrastructure externalities on the population in one area (e.g., excessive noise and emissions) but, on the other hand, have important quality and capacity effects on the level of Trans-European Networks. Major public investments in one specific project do not always serve the common interest in the best possible way, given the opportunity cost of other projects that will consequently not be pursued. Access to the ubiquitous data could be restricted by technical barriers to open exchange by certain suppliers. An early and comprehensive stakeholder discussion of the purpose and means for adequate infrastructure development could foster transparency and social acceptance, if it is motivated by the social value that would hence be created (Frischmann 2012). As traditional and digital infrastructure has become a kind of mortar for real bricks and virtual building blocks of today's global society, policies determining social and economic priorities have to be well grounded in today's societal narrative and belief systems.

Infrastructure development has to meet future economic requirements as well as serve political and social expectations. Most engineers in the infrastructure sector in Germany have a clear understanding of the concept of sustainability and consider intergenerational responsibility important. However, infrastructure development seems to have experienced both market failure and state failure. In consequence the infrastructure actors position their businesses right in the middle between state-granted services and free-market principles.

Infrastructure industry in Germany today calls for a reliable political frameworks of predictable requirements, financial state support, and in return will accept an adequate degree of market regulation. Affordable and sustainable institutions are an infracultural prerequisite to social acceptance of infrastructure development, enabling civic society to regain control over infrastructure development, as financed and upheld mainly in service to the public (*Daseinsvorsorge*) and thus made possible by public expenditure.

Following the logic of the Internet, technology will change the role of consumers, converting them into interactive prosumers, contributing in smart transformative infrastructure networks to the provisioning of energy, transportation, and communications. The time may have come for private and public actors in the infrastructure arena to rethink their provisioning in an infracultural system of a *modern commons*, mobilizing citizens to become *Netoyens* (Net Citoyens comp. Fr.: *citoyens*) with granted rights and obligations in reciprocity still to be defined, becoming empowered and conscious co-designers of the networks that determine their every life, their social and economic perspectives, and will shape the environmental conditions for their offspring and generations to come. Balanced infracultural institutions will result in a more sustainable development of infrastructural resource systems.

Notes

1. Infrastructure in this context is defined as the large networks for transport, energy, and communications. The comprehensive meaning: physical, institutional, and personal infrastructure is compressed within infraculture.

2. Modern Commons is an interdisciplinary research project of the NETWORK Institute in cooperation with Leipzig University, Institute for Infrastructure and Resource-Management. The concepts of infrafunctions and infracultural epochs presented here are first published in this volume, with further results forthcoming in *Eine Theorie der Modern Commons*, Hofmann (2016 Berlin).

3. "Wealth" will be used in its comprehensive meaning of both well-being and prosperity.

4. The printed encyclopedia of its time.

References

Allen, Roy. E. 2008. *Human Ecology Economics.* London, Routledge, p. 9.

Aschauer, David Alan. 1990. *Why Is Infrastructure Important?* Boston: Federal Reserve Bank of Boston.

Branscomb, Lewis M., and Keller, James. 1996. *Converging Infrastructures*. Cambridge: MIT Press.

Chomsky, Noam. 2012, *Destroying the Commons: How the Magna Carta Became a Minor Carta*. http://www.chomsky.info/articles/20120722.htm.

Coase, Ronald. 1937. The nature of the firm. *Economica (new series)*4 (16): 386–405.

Deharme, Ernest. 1874. *Les Merveilles de la locomotion*. Paris: Hachette.

Deharme, Ernest. 1890. *Chemin de fer: Superstructure*. Paris: Baudry.

Diederichsen, Diedrich, and Anselm Franke. 2013. *The Whole Earth*. Berlin.

Etzemüller, Thomas. 2009. *Die Ordnung der Moderne*. Bielefeld: Transcript.

Fischer-Kowalski, Marina. 1997. *Gesellschaftlicher Stoffwechsel und Kolonisierung von Natur*. Berlin: Fakultas.

Frischmann, Brett. M. 2012. *Infrastructure: The Social Value of Shared Resources*. Oxford. Oxford: University Press.

Fuchs, Eduard, and Kreowski, Ernst. 1911. *Die Straße. Vom Urwald bis zur Eisenbahn*. Berlin:Verlag Neues Leben, Wilhelm Borngräber.

Frey, René. 1972. *Infrastruktur. Grundlagen der Planung öffentlicher Investitionen* Tübingen: Mohr.

Fouquet, Roger. 2008. *Heat, Power and Light. Revolutions in Energy Services*. Cheltenham, UK: Elgar.

Gazette de la Bourse. 1857. *Commerce, industrie, finance*. No 1857/03/08 (N4).

Hauben, Michael. 1996. *The Net and Netizens: The Impact the Net has on People's Lives*. Columbia University. http://www.columbia.edu/~rh120/ch106.x01.

Hage, Wolfgang. 1993. *Das Christentum im frühen Mittelalter*. Göttingen: Vandenhoeck Ruprecht.

Hofmann, Klaus Markus. 2016. *Eine Theorie der Modern Commons*. Berlin/Leipzig, forthcoming.

Jochimsen, Raimund. 1966. *Theorie der Infrastruktur*. Tübingen: Mohr.

Kingdom of England. 1982. *King John, Magna Charta and Charta of the Commons, and The First Forrest Charter*. London: Legal Classics Library.

Maslow, Abraham. 1954. *Motivation and Personality*. New York: Harper.

Mayntz, Renate. 2009. *Über Governace. Institutionen und Prozesse politischer Regelung*. Schriften aus dem Max-Planck Institut für Gesellschaftsforschung. Frankfurt: Campus Verlag.

Messerschmitt, David. 2000. *Understanding Networked Applications*. San Francisco: Morgan Kaufmann.

Miller, John H., and Scott E. Page. 2007. *Complex Adaptive Systems*. Princeton: Princeton University Press.

Morlet, de Beaudet Charles Gabriel. 1861. Notices sur les voies romaines. *Bulletin de la Société pour la Conservation* 4.

Ostrom, Elionor. 1990. *Governing the Commons: The Evolution of Institutions for Collective Action*. Cambridge, UK: Cambridge University Press.

Ostrom, Elionor, Roy Gardner, and James Walker. 1994. *Rules, Games, and Common-Pool Resources*. Ann Arbor: University of Michigan Press.

Ostrom, Elionor. 2011. *The Challenges of Achieving Conservation and Development. Annual Proceedings of the Wealth and Well-being of Nations*, vol. 4. Bloomington: Indiana University Press, 21–27.

Ostrom, Elionor. 2012. *The Future of the Commons: Beyond Market Failure and Government Regulation*. London: Institute of Economic Affairs.

Parsons, Talcott. 1951. *The Social System*. New York: Free Press of Glencore.

Parsons, Talcott. [1961] 2007. *An Outline of the Social System*. In Craig Calhoun, ed., *Classical Sociology Theory*. Malden, MA: Blackwell.

Popitz, Heinrich. 1989. *Epochen der Technikgeschichte*. Tübingen: Mohr.

Presch, Katharina. 2012. *Einführung in die provinzialrömische Archäologie, Thema: Römische Straßen*. Ruhr Universität Bochum.

Prutz, Hans. 1964. *Kulturgeschichte der Kreuzzüge*. Hildesheim: Georg Olms Verlag.

Serbser, Wolfgang H. 2008. *Zur Genese der gesellschaftlichen Institutionen*. In Karl-Siegbert Rehberg, ed., *Die Natur der Gesellschaft*. Frankfurt am Main: Campus Verlag, 2847–2959.

Smith, Adam. [1776] 1998. *An Inquiry into the Nature and Causes of the Wealth of Nations*. Oxford: Oxford University Press, 412–15.

Tomasello, Michael. 2008. *Origins of Human Communication*. Cambridge: MIT Press.

Tacitus.1911. Histories and annals. In Eduard Fuchs and Ernst Kreowski, eds., *Die Straße—Vom Urwald bis zur Eisenbahn*. Berlin: Verlag Neues Leben.

Toynbee, Arnold J. 1976. *Mankind and Mother Earth: A Narrative History of the World*. Oxford: Oxford University Press.

Weijnen, Margot, Paulin Herder, and Ivo Bouwmans. 2008. Designing complex systems. In Mick Eekhout, Ronald Visser, Ronald and Tetsuoeds Tomiyama, eds., *Delft Science in Design*. Delft: University of Delft, 235–54.

Welzer, Harald. 2011. *Mentale Infrastruktur*. Berlin: Schriften zur Ökologie Heinrich Böll Stiftung.

Whitney, David A., and Thomas O. Mottl. 1996. Assessing federal roles. In *Converging Infrastructures*, ed. Lewis M. Branscomb and James Keller, 24–58. Cambridge: MIT Press.

Wittfogel, Karl August. 1957. *Oriental Despotism: AComparative Study of Total Power*. New Haven: Yale University Press.

III Sector: Transport

9 Policy Lessons from the Recent Literature on Transport Infrastructure Development

Stéphane Straub

9.1 Introduction

Since the late 1980s a large empirical literature has explored the link between economic development and infrastructure investment, and in particular, transport infrastructure, which is understood to include roads, railroads, ports, and airports.[1] Until recently most of that literature has been based on macro-level data, namely cross-country or cross-state data.

As argued in Straub (2011), however, this literature has often performed simple cross-country estimations without clearly specifying the theoretical questions to be addressed, and without addressing in a convincing way the endogeneity issues at the core of infrastructure investment decisions. Moreover this literature has tended to ignore the fact that most relevant policy issues, such as the impacts of different investments on the spatial allocation of population and activity, can simply not be meaningfully addressed with macroeconomic data. This is a major flaw of this body of academic work.

Localized microeconometric studies, however, have brought a wealth of insights on the effects of transport infrastructure on local development outcomes.[2] Nevertheless, though these contributions stand out in terms of the identification techniques they use, the results are too small scale and location specific for wider use across both space and time.

In the last few years a growing number of contributions have started to apply geocoded data at a fine enough level of spatial disaggregation to bring new insights to the topic. The main contribution here has been the application of micro-level data within a global framework to account for the spatial, sectoral, and macroeconomic linkages of investments in infrastructure. These studies have succeeded in broadening the identification techniques from microeconometrics to the macro level, combining strong internal validity with better external validity.

This chapter reviews this new literature and draws from it some specific policy lessons. Section 9.2 briefly summarizes the limitations of previous approaches and the challenges of working with transport infrastructure data. Section 9.3 presents the core studies reviewed in this chapter. Section 9.4 discusses the specific identification challenges linked to the use of spatially disaggregated transport data. Section 9.5 then offers an overview of the progress made using this approach, with a particular focus on developing countries. It summarizes the results found in terms of the impact of transport infrastructure on population, growth, trade, and firms' entry and exit rates. Section 9.6 concludes.

9.2 The Transport Infrastructure Research Challenge

When it comes to assessing the impact of large-scale transport networks, the main endogeneity issues encountered in macro studies using transport infrastructure data revolve around the three common econometric issues stressed, for example, in standard econometric textbooks,[3] namely reverse causality, unobserved effects, and measurement errors.

Reverse causality concerns arise from the fact that infrastructure investments may follow output growth rather than the contrary. This is likely to be the case if higher growth fosters bigger investments in infrastructure, and the implication is an upward bias in the estimates of infrastructure impact on growth. Aschauer (1989), which is often considered the seminal paper in the macro literature on infrastructure, found an output elasticity of infrastructure of 0.30, corresponding to a scenario in which investments would pay for themselves in around one year, an implausible result that subsequent contributions have attributed mostly to reverse causality.

Unobserved effects are relevant if there are country-, state-, or region-level characteristics that are unobserved to the econometrician but are causing growth (or productivity) and the observed level of infrastructure development. Such unobserved effects may be both time invariant and time variant. In the case of time-invariant effects, the problem may be solved by the use of fixed effects, as in the case of Holtz-Eakin (1994), who shows that the state-level impact of public capital can be entirely attributed to state-level time-invariant unobserved effects. In the case of time-variant effects, however, this strategy will not solve the problem.

Finally, most transport infrastructure proxies used in the macro literature suffer from serious measurement error problems.[4] As for monetary measures of investment, such as public capital, they are questionable for at least two good reasons. First, they fail to account for the fact that since the 1990s a nonnegligible and nonrandom part of transport investments is made by the private sector. Second, cumulative investment flows do not adequately proxy for effective capital stocks, as Pritchett (2000) has argued quite convincingly.

In consequence an alternative way of measuring transport infrastructure stock, using physical indicators, has come to dominate in the literature. Yet some issues remain. The measurement error problem mentioned above has not been solved because of the coarseness of the indicators being used, as these generally take the form of aggregate kilometers of roads or railroads and do not account for aspects such as quality, usage, and spatial distribution.

All three issues could be addressed by the use of adequate instrumental strategies. However, as is also the case in the cross-country literature on growth, researchers have struggled to find convincing instruments. The main approach has been to use the lagged values of independent variables as instruments. Although these techniques have already generated a large downsizing of the average estimates found in the previous literature,[5] these instruments are generally quite weak and their use limited by the relatively small sample sizes of the studies.

In that regard the use of spatially disaggregated and geocoded data has two main advantages.[6] First, by allowing researcher to handle microeconomic data, often produced through household or firm censuses or surveys, with a level of aggregation not higher than the municipality or county level, it produces richer datasets capturing local-level availability of transport infrastructure, often over several decades, and allowing for the crossing of these data with local socioeconomic characteristics.

Second, it makes it possible to apply neat and sophisticated identification techniques, ensuring a high-level of internal validity. As a result, thanks to the spatial and time scope of datasets spanning large geographical areas over periods of ten to thirty years, the new studies produce important lessons based on medium to long-term development processes with significant external validity.

The next section reviews some recent studies using these new techniques and the type of datasets and outcomes analyzed.

9.3 Recent Contributions

Table 9A.1 in the appendix shows the main characteristics of the most relevant studies surveyed in this chapter, indicating the country, time period, and spatial level used, and the outcomes analyzed.[7]

Contribution concerning the impact of road infrastructure in developing countries, include Banerjee, Duflo, and Qian (2012), Baum-Snow et al. (2012), Ghani, Goswami, and Kerr (2012, 2013), Bird and Straub (2014), Faber (2012), Storeygard (2012), and Volpe et al. (2012). Large developing countries with a good availability of data are overrepresented, as three of the papers study China, two are on India, and one on Brazil. They cover two to three decades, from the 1970s to the 2000s, and their spatial level of analysis is the municipality / district / county level. Storeygard (2012), and Volpe Martincus, Carballo, and Cusolito (2012) stand out as considering different spatial units, namely cities and regions. Finally, outcomes studied are wide-ranging and include population, output, housing value, firm-level outcomes, and trade outcomes.

We also consider contributions addressing the impact of road infrastructure in developed countries, where the quality of data is sometimes better. These include Duranton and Turner (2012), Gibbons et al. (2012), Baum-Snow (2007), Chandra and Thompson (2000), Michaels (2008), and Duranton, Morrow, and Turner (2014).

All the papers included here concern the United States, with the exception of Gibbons et al. (2012), who study the United Kingdom. The time periods are generally longer than for developing countries due to data availability, and the unit of analysis is again the municipality/ level, with the exception of Baum-Snow (2007) and Duranton, Morrow, and Turner (2014), who look at cities. A wide array of outcomes is again studied.

Finally, we also review a set of studies looking at the impact of railroads development in an historical context, which includes Jedwab and Moradi (2012), Atacket et al. (2010), Donaldson and Hornbeck (2013), Atack and Margo (2011), and Donaldson (forthcoming). All these studies are concerned with the (possibly long-term) impact of the first wave of railroads development that occurred in the second half of the nineteenth century and at the beginning of the twentieth century. While three of them use US data, there is also evidence from developing countries, namely India (Donaldson 2012) and Ghana (Jedwab and Moradi 2012). The level of analysis is again counties/districts, and outcomes studied include population, land value, agricultural production, as well as trade-related variables.

The next section discusses the identification concerns specific to this new type of data.

9.4 Spatially Disaggregated and Geocoded Data: (Paved) Roads to Identification

The key point that we address in this section is the fact that the use of spatial data implies a fundamental change in the nature of the endogeneity issue that researchers face. Indeed, it becomes a variant of standard microeconometrics identification issue of the type encountered in labor or development applications using microeconomic data.

In a nutshell, the main issue is now one of endogeneous placement of infrastructure works, in the sense that roads or railroads, for example, are generally allocated to specific locations according to (un)observed characteristics not orthogonal to their development potential. Three main possibilities arise. First, roads are often built to cater in priority to the need of locations with above average growing potential or with favorable geographic characteristics. Second, the polar case where they are planned to serve lagging regions is also relevant. Finally, a growing number of contributions reveal that political reasons, therefore orthogonal to economic determinants or potential, are frequently behind infrastructure investment choices (e.g., see Cadot, Röller, and Stephan 2006 or Burgess et al. 2013). While in the first case, we expect simple OLS estimates of the effect of infrastructure on growth for example to be biased upward, in the other two cases, the expected bias is toward zero.

These specific endogeneity motives have motivated a few identification techniques, which we will group in three categories. First, a number of contributions have used historical maps of early networks or exploration routes, as well as network extension plans drafted in the past, as instruments for current transport corridors location. Second, some studies have argued for the quasi-exogeneity of locations situated "along the way" to obtain unbiased estimates. Third, authors have superimposed straight lines connecting specific points onto the maps showing transport corridors, arguing again for the exogeneity of the distance between intermediate locations and these lines. Finally, recent contributions have used this technique to generate distance to lines measures as an instrument for more sophisticated access measures. We now review each of these approaches in turn.

9.4.1 Historical Maps and Plans

Examples of studies that use historical maps and plans as instruments are Baum-Snow et al. (2012) on China, Duranton and Turner (2011) on the United States, and Volpe Martincus, Carballo, and Cusolito (2012) on Peru.[8] The underlying logic is that these maps should reflect the priorities of earlier periods, and that these should not be affected by contemporary economic outcomes such as changes in population, employment, or output.

For example, in the case of the United States, Duranton and Turner (2012) state that the 1947 plan was first drawn to "connect by routes as direct as practicable the principal metropolitan areas, cities and industrial centers, to serve the national defense, and to connect suitable border points with routes of continental importance in the Dominion of Canada and the Republic of Mexico." Similarly in Peru Volpe Martincus, Carballo, and Cusolito (2012) show that the Inca roads served religious, military, and administrative and communication purposes whereas trade was nonexistent.

The conditions for validity are twofold. First, the instruments should have predictive power, in the sense that some contemporary infrastructure should match the early blueprint. This is a standard condition that can be verified through the first stage significance of the instruments and the overall F-test.[9]

Second, it is necessary that the instruments affect the outcomes of interest only through their effect on initial stock of roads. This means that early maps or plans should not be correlated with unobservables that influence the subsequent evolution of both the transport network and the outcomes. A standard answer to this requirement has been to add a set of controls at the initial date, in order to obtain orthogonality of the dependent variable and the instruments conditional on these controls. The suitability of this procedure can then be assessed by comparing the result from an over-identification test with and without the controls.

To determine the appropriate set of controls, one needs to understand how early maps or networks were established, to assess their stated or hidden objectives and to understand how this relates to contemporary channels affecting outcomes. In particular, it is often the case that locations that got more roads earlier on are larger and later have different growth paths. This observable fact advocates for using early values of local population, employment, and output. We know also that historically early roads tended to cater to the needs of the agricultural sector, which calls for the inclusion of early agricultural population and output as controls. Finally, most studies also include geographic and geologic variables to address the concern that these might affect changes in outcomes directly. This is, of course, relevant when location fixed effects are not included, that is, when only two periods are available.[10]

9.4.2 Quasi-exogeneity of Locations "Along the Way"

The exogeneity of locations approach was introduced as by Chandra and Thompson (2000) to consider the effects on nonmetropolitan regions of the US interstate highway network. More recently a similar approach is at the core of the works by Michaels (2008) using US data and by Ghani et al. (2013) on India.

Identification consists in comparing "nonnodal" locations that are more or less close to the roads being built or improved. For example, Ghani et al. (2013), following Datta (2011), study the impact on the manufacturing sector of the Golden Quadrilateral highway project, which upgraded the quality and width of 5,846 km of roads in India. They compare nonnodal districts located in the 0 to 10 km range from the Golden Quadrilateral (GQ) network to districts located 10 to 50 km away.

In this study the identification of the effect of roads requires that the roads connect nodes only in a direct way and not deviate to connect important intermediate cities, so the distance to the line is no longer exogenous. Because this condition is unlikely to apply to important intermediate urban areas, most such studies focus on rural districts.

9.4.3 Straight Lines Connecting Two Points

A variation on this theme was originally introduced in an early 2004 version of the work by Banerjee, Duflo, and Qian (2012) on China. They superimpose straight lines onto the country's map and compare outcomes between locations at different distances from the lines. A similar approach is used by Atack et al. (2010) in their study of the impact of railroads on the US midwest between 1850 and 1860.

As they make clear in the description of their empirical strategy, the use of distance to the lines as a direct regressor to explain per capita GDP does not allow Banerjee, Duflo, and Qian (2012) to rule out the possibility that large GDP gains were due to the roads, but the distribution of these gains was not significantly related to the distance to the transportation corridor. Indeed they find that their results can be reconciled with a model in which labor does not move, and capital movements are costly, a scenario consistent with Chinese stylized facts.

To avoid this problem, in a study of the impact of the road network development in Brazil, Bird and Straub (2014) use the distance to similar straight lines as an instrumental variable for the location-specific cost of access to the country's main economic centers, namely the local state capital Sao Paulo.

A number of requirements are in order for the straight line strategy to be valid. The lines chosen connect points of importance when (or before) the network was built, such as large cities and ports. The identification strategy is based on comparing nonnodal locations that are more or less close to the lines, assuming that the only difference between them is their distance to the line. That is to say, this strategy is valid if the nodes were not chosen so that the line between them would run through economically important regions; the choice was dependent on the lines' end points and not locations along the lines.

The studies addressed this matter in different ways. Banerjee, Duflo, and Qian (2012) chose only historical points (historically important cities and Treaty ports) as the lines nodes, whereas Bird and Straub (2014) use the ex nihilo creation of the capital city Brasilia at the end of the 1950s as a "natural experiment" and draw lines between this city and the eight more important cities and ports that had to be subsequently connected. Additionally both studies had to control for the distance to the nodes (which is correlated with the distance to the lines) and to other infrastructure modes (rivers, railroads).

While this is enough when the estimates use distance to the lines as an explanatory variable, the use of this distance as an instrument for change in a market access measure due to the extension of a transport network requires, first, the use of an interaction with some time-varying variable to be able to use the panel dimension of the data. . Potentially, such time-varying variable could be any aspect interacting with distance in shaping the degree of connectedness of locations. In examples of related research, Storeygard (2012) uses variations in the price of oil, and Duflo and Pande (2007) use the number of dams in a district as the time-varying variable.[11]

When locations and region-year fixed effects are included, the first stage then captures, within each region (states in the case of Brazil), the share of improvement in road access over the period under study, which can be attributed to each location (district) according to its distance to the closest exogenous straight line. Similarly to the case of early network plans, excludability of the instrument is required; that is, it should affect the outcome of interest only access to the transport network, conditional on the controls, which could include any location time-invariant factors, captured by location fixed effects, as well as the time-variant factors already discussed above.

9.5 New Results

In this section we summarize the key results in recent studies using the techniques described above.

9.5.1 Population

Early studies focused on urban areas and the impact on population of the development of major transport corridors, such as highways that reduced commuting time between city centers and suburbs, and also ring roads.

This generation of studies first assessed the contribution of road networks to the suburbanization phenomenon. In a study of the 1950 to 1990 population distribution in the United States, Baum-Snow (2007) finds highway construction to be responsible for a 17 percent aggregate population decline in central cities, despite a 72 percent growth in metropolitan areas as a whole.

A similar decentralization effect, with people leaving city centers as new roads make commuting easier, is found in China by Baum-Snow et al. (2012). Each radial highway is shown to displace 4 to 5 percent of the central city population to surrounding regions, while the existence of a ring road displaces an additional 20 percent. Moreover, against a backdrop of large increase in urban populations, the Chinese migration process shows characteristics that differ significantly from those of the United States. Indeed a large share of the population settling in suburbs is likely to be composed of both rural people living near central cities, who are prevented from moving to city centers, and of rural migrants coming from the hinterland to settle in suburbanizing areas.

Another set of studies has focused on the distribution of population over the whole country (or large regions). For example, Atack et al. (2010) show that railroads development in the US midwest in 1850 had little impact on population densities but led to urbanization. Their estimates indicate that half of the increase in the fraction of urban population in the 1850s can be related to railroads.

Then again, Faber (2012) finds that China's National Trunk Highway System (NTHS) had no discernible effect on county-level population growth, a result that he attributes to the rigid rules governing Chinese migration policy.[12]

In the case of Brazil, Bird and Straub (2014) find a different pattern, in which road development spurs important migratory movements over the 1970 to 2000 period. In particular, they find evidence of differentiated patterns of population growth within the country. On the one hand, in the south (south, southeast) historically the most developed part of the country, roads account for the growth of population in large circles, up to 360 km, around the main centers.[13] This development goes together with some evidence of suburbanization, whereby locations near the main urban centers grow and become more urbanized. On the other hand, the north (north, northeast, and center-west) displays exactly the reverse pattern. Road-related reductions in travel cost appear to have caused a population decline in the main urban centers leading to an emergence of secondary urban centers in the hinterland.

9.5.2 Output Growth

Growth of output, as Faber (2012) shows, appears to be due to the reduction of trade costs between large and small markets, which generates a "home market effect" that translates into a reduction of industrial and total output growth in peripheral regions. Thus, instead of diffusing economic activity across the country, road development can lead to a concentration of activity in the most developed areas. These findings on China are consistent with Baum-Snow et al. (2012), who find that railroads and ring road developments have led industrial production to relocate to the suburban areas of large cities.

Similar evidence from clusters of light in satellite pictures, as a proxy for economic activity, is presented by Storeygard (2012) who considers the effects of road connections in Africa. He shows that when transport cost increases, based on oil price changes, the income of cities near major ports increases relative to otherwise identical cities farther away.

For Brazil, Bird and Straub (2014) find increasing GDP around the major cities in the south, together with a relative decrease of industry and an increase of services. Again, this pattern is reversed in the north. Bird and Straub also consider how these patterns of growth correspond to the prediction of the urban literature. Indeed the paper shows that improvements in the transport infrastructure have a positive effect on GDP growth around urban areas that are above given thresholds in terms of size (as proxied by initial population or GDP), quality of amenities (as proxied by the share of population with access to the water network), human capital (as measured by the average level of education of the population), and industrialization (captured by the industry to service ratio). In contrast, urban areas that are at a low level of development along these dimensions actually suffer from better access.

For China, Banerjee, Duflo, and Qian (2012) find no or small effects of road development on per capita GDP in Chinese counties between 1986 and 2003, a result that they attribute to the fact that the gains were not much greater for locations near the roads because of a lack of factor mobility, despite high potential overall gains. The results of Bird and Straub (2014), who find little or no effect on per capita GDP in Brazil, alternatively suggest that another reason might be the fact that GDP gains in specific locations subsequently spurred migration, an so partly canceled the gains in output.

This raises the question of how to evaluate the overall growth effect of transportation improvements. A first way to approximate the growth dividend may be simply to compare the estimated difference in impact between locations close and far from newly constructed corridors to the overall growth observed over the periods under study.

In doing so, and comparing locations in the 25th and the 75th percentiles in terms of distance to the main roads, Banerjee, Duflo, and Qian (2012) conclude that for China over the period 1986 to 2003, 7.9 percent of per capita GDP growth can be attributed to the causal effect of roads. In their similar computation for Brazil over the 1970 to 2000 period, Bird and Straub (2014) conclude that roads explain one-third of the population changes, 7.6 percent of GDP, and 7.3 percent of GDP per capita changes.

Bird and Straub (2014) further provide a counterfactual estimate of what fraction of overall per capita GDP growth can be attributed to roads connecting Brasilia to the main state capitals over the three decades they study. They conclude that the absence of such roads would have divided overall growth by almost a factor of 2. This is, of course, an extreme counterfactual. Going beyond this would require having a general equilibrium model of alternative road construction scenario. Using a market-access approach, Donaldson and Hornbeck (2013) provide such a counterfactual and conclude that removing all US railroads built between 1870 and 1890 would have decreased the total value of US agricultural land by 64 percent.

9.5.3 Trade Outcomes

Some studies have looked at the effects of transport corridors on trade volumes and prices. Donaldson (forthcoming) analyzes the impact of nineteenth-century railroads in colonial India. Looking, in particular, at the price of salt, he finds that railroad connections "decreased trade costs and interregional price gaps; increased interregional and international trade; [and] increased real income levels."

Looking at US counties, Michaels (2008) shows that highways generated an increase in trade-related activities such as trucking and retail sales in rural counties that they crossed, and that they raised the relative demand for skilled manufacturing workers in skill-abundant counties.

Last, concentrating on the impact of roads on trade among US cities, Duranton, Morrow, and Turner (2014) show that highways have a large effect on weight but little effect on the total value of exports, in that better connected cities tend to specialize in heavy goods. These results are confirmed in developing countries cases, such as the paper by Volpe Martincus, Carballo, and Cusolito (2013) on Peru, which shows, using the Inca road network as an instrument for the development of the modern road system, that it fostered increased exports and employment. Specifically, they find a distance elasticity of export of 1.8 and argue that the main channel behind this is an increase in the number of shipments, due to the increased quantities shipped, rather than a change in the value of exports.

9.5.4 Firms

Several studies have used firm-level surveys to assess the impact of transport infrastructure on the spatial pattern of firms. They all find that the location of the network has a significant impact on firms' entry and exit patterns.

For China, Banerjee et al. (2012) show that counties close to the constructed lines have a higher number of firms and higher average firm profits. For India, Ghani et al. (2013) find substantial growth in firms' entry rates, as well as increase in labor productivity and TFP, in nonnodal districts within 10 km of the GQ network after the roads upgrades.

For the United Kingdom, Gibbons et al. (2012) look at the impact of road network improvements between 1998 and 2007 and find evidence of firm entry in locations that connectedness improved. There are also important effects on employment at the geographical area level, an effect that derives from firms' entry rather than changes at the plant level.

9.6 Conclusion: What We Have Learned and the Way Forward

The literature on the economic impact of infrastructure, through to the combination of technological improvement, thanks to the generalization of large-scale geocoded data and of researchers' creativity, has recently generated a large amount of new findings.

A growing set of contributions has improved significantly on the previous established knowledge by enabling a better understanding of the impact of transport corridors development on the spatial reorganization of population (suburbanization, hinterland patterns) and production (output growth and production mix), and of the mechanisms through which locations gain or lose. These studies have also shed light on the impact of transport infrastructure on the location choices of firms, on the effects on incumbent producers, and on input choices and employment patterns evolution.

The contributions reviewed in this chapter show that roads have important effect on all these decisions. With regard to growth, the few results available point to a large effect of long-term road development programs in countries such as Brazil, China, and India.

By allowing for conclusions that are directly policy relevant for population growth, output, trade, and firm spatial patterns, this new literature represents a big step forward. In the future, improved data availability, covering such factors as usage and quality of infrastructure, will allow for better and more relevant research results.

Appendix: Papers Reviewed

Table 9A.1
Roads (developing countries)

Authors	Country	Time period	Spatial unit	Outcomes
Economic development				
Banerjee, Duflo, and Qian (2012)	China	1986–2003	County	Per capita GDP / firm count and profit (manufacturing surveys)/income (household surveys)
Baum-Snow et al. (2012)	China	1990–2010	Prefectures / cities	Satellite data on lights/GDP/ population
Ghani, Goswami, and Kerr (2013)	India	1994–2007	Districts	Plant count, output, productivity and employment (manufacturing surveys)
Ghani, Goswami, and Kerr (2013)	India	1989–2007	Districts	Plant count, output, productivity and employment
Bird and Straub (2014)	Brazil	1970–2000	Municipalities (1970 MCA)	Population/GDP/ sector GDP/per capita GDP
Faber (2012)	China	1997–2006	Counties	GDP and value-added/GDP and value-added by sector/population
Storeygard (2012)	Africa (15 coastal countries)	1992–2008	Cities (287)	Satellite data on lights
Volpe Martincus, Carballo, and Cusolito (2013)	Peru	2003–2010	Regions	Firms' export value and volume, employment

Table 9A.2
Roads (developed countries)

Authors	Country	Time period	Spatial unit	Outcomes
Economic development				
Duranton and Turner (2012)	United States	1983–2003	Cities	Employment / population
Gibbons et al. (2012)	United Kingdom	1997–2008	Electoral wards (10,300)	Plant count, productivity and employment
Baum-Snow (2007)	United States	1950–1990	Metropolitan areas (139)	Population/ population density
Chandra and Thompson (2000)	United States	1969–1993	Counties (1,781)	County-level earnings, by industry
Michaels (2008)	United States	1950–2000	Counties	Wage bill, by industry
Trade				
Duranton, Morrow, and Turner (2014)	United States	1956–2003 (2007 data only for trade)	Cities (66)	Weight and value of exports and imports

Table 9A.3
Railroads (historical)

Authors	Country	Time Period	Spatial unit	Outcomes
Economic development				
Jedwab and Moradi (2012)	Ghana	1901–2000	GIS cells (11 × 11km)	Cocoa production/ population
Atack et al. (2010)	United States	1850–1860	Midwestern counties (278)	Population density, urbanization
Donaldson and Hornbeck (2013)	United States	1897–1890	Counties (2,161)	Land value
Atack and Margo (2011)	United States (midwest)	1850–1860	Counties (278)	Area of improved farm land
Trade				
Donaldson (forthcoming)	India	1870–1930	Districts (235)	Salt price/ exports value/ agricultural income

Notes

I thank the Agence Française de Développement (AFD) and CESifo for Financial support. Comments from participants at the 2013 CESifo Venice Summer Institute workshop on "The Economics of Infrastructure Provisioning: The (Changing) Role of the State" are gratefully acknowledged.

1. Examples of recent surveys of the broader literature on infrastructure include those by Romp and de Haan (2005), Estache (2010), and Straub (2008, 2011).

2. See, for example, Van de Walle (2009) for a review of contributions on rural roads.

3. See, for example, Wooldridge (2010).

4. See Straub (2008) for a more detailed treatment of this issue.

5. Estimates were reduced to output elasticity of infrastructure levels of around 0.10 (Romp and de Haan 2005).

6. See Gibson and McKenzie (2007) for an early survey on the use of GPS data in economic research.

7. Note that similar techniques have also been applied to study the impact of other types of infrastructure, such as electricity. See, for example, Dinkelman (2011) and Lipscomb et al. (2013).

8. For a variation on this theme, see Faber's (2012) least-cost path-spanning tree network, which amounts to artificially generating the map to be used as instrumental variable.

9. See Stock and Yogo (2005).

10. A similar argument applies when the instrument is least-cost routes. For example, Faber (2012) includes geographical characteristics used in the construction of his instrumental variable, province fixed effects, distance to the nearest targeted city region, administrative status, and county-level economic conditions in 1990 as controls.

1. The two last papers do not use straight lines as indicated above.

12. Note that he excludes counties in a 50 km radius around the main city centers.

13. Again, end points (i.e., main urban centers) are excluded from the estimations. These are also robust when larger circles around the urban centers are excluded.

References

Aschauer, D. A. 1989. Is public expenditure productive? *Journal of Monetary Economics* 23: 177–200.

Atack, J., and R. A. Margo. 2011. The impact of access to rail transportation on agricultural improvement: the American midewest as a test case. *Journal of Transportation and Land Use* 4 (2).

Atack, J., F. Bateman, M. Haines, and R. A. Margo. 2010. Did railroads induce or follow economic growth? Urbanization and population growth in the American midwest, 1850–1860. *Social Science History* 34 (2): 171–97.

Banerjee, A., E. Duflo, and N. Qian. 2012. On the road: Access to transportation infrastructure and economic growth in China. Working paper 17897. NBER.

Baum-Snow, N. 2007. Did highways cause suburbanization? *Quarterly Journal of Economics* 122 (2): 775–805.

Baum-Snow, N., L. Brandt, V. Henderson, M. Turner, and Q. Zhang. 2012. Roads, railroads and decentralization of Chinese cities. Working paper. Brown University.

Bird, J., and S. Straub. 2014. Road access and the spatial pattern of long-term local development in Brazil. Policy Research working paper 6964. World Bank.

Burgess, R., R. Jedwab, E. Miguel, A. Morjaria, and G. Padró i Miquel. 2013. The value of democracy: Evidence from road building in Kenya. Mimeo. LSE.

Cadot, O., L. H. Röller, and A. Stephan. 2006. Contribution to productivity or pork barrel? The two faces of infrastructure investment. *Journal of Public Economics* 90: 6–7.

Chandra, A., and E. Thompson. 2000. Does public infrastructure affect economic activity? Evidence from the rural interstate highway system. *Regional Science and Urban Economics* 30: 457–90.

Datta, S. 2011. The impact of improved highways on Indian firms. *Journal of Development Economics* 99 (1): 46–57.

Dinkelman, T. 2011. The effects of rural electrification on employment: New evidence from South Africa. *American Economic Review* 101 (7): 3078–3108.

Donaldson, D. (forthcoming). Railroads of the Raj: Estimating the impact of transportation infrastructure. *American Economic Review*.

Donaldson, Dave, and Richard Hornbeck. 2013. Railroads and American economic growth: A "market access" approach. Working paper 19213. NBER.

Duflo, E., and R. Pande. 2007. Dams. *Quarterly Journal of Economics* 122 (2): 601–46.

Duranton, G., and M. Turner. 2012. Urban growth and transportation. *Review of Economic Studies* 79 (4): 1407–40.

Duranton, G., P. Morrow, and M. Turner. 2014. Roads and trade: Evidence from the US. *Review of Economic Studies* 81 (2): 681–724.

Estache, A. 2010. A survey of impact evaluations of infrastructure projects: Programs and policies. Working paper 2010-005. ECARES.

Faber, B. 2012. Trade integration, market size, and industrialization: Evidence from China's National Trunk Highway System. Mimeo. LSE.

Ghani, E., A. Goswami, and W. Kerr. 2013. Highway to success in India: The impact of the Golden Quadrilateral project for the location and performance of manufacturing. Policy Research working paper 6320. World Bank.

Gibbons, S., T. Lyytikäinen, H. G. Overman, R. Sanchis-Guarner. 2012. New road infrastructure: The effects on firms. SERCDP0117.

Gibson, J., and D. McKenzie. 2007. Using global positioning systems in household surveys for better economics and better policy. *World Bank Research Observer* 22 (2): 217–41.

Holtz-Eakin, D. 1994. Public-sector capital and the productivity puzzle. *Review of Economics and Statistics* 76: 12–21.

Jedwab, R. and A. Moradi. 2012. Revolutionizing transport: Modern infrastructure, agriculture and development in Ghana. Mimeo. LSE.

Lipscomb, M., M. Mobarak, and T. Barham. 2013. Development effects of electrification: Evidence from the topographic placement of hydropower plants in Brazil. *American Economic Journal. Applied Economics* 5 (2): 200–31.

Michaels, G. 2008. The effect of trade on the demand for skill: Evidence from the interstate highway system. *Review of Economics and Statistics* 90 (4): 683–701.

Pritchett, L. 2000. The tyranny of concepts: CUDIE (cumulated, depreciated, investment effort) is not capital. *Journal of Economic Growth* 5 (4): 361–84.

Romp, W., and J. de Haan. 2005. Public capital and economic growth: A critical survey. *European Investment Bank Papers* 10 (1).

Stock, J., and M. Yogo. 2005. Testing for weak instruments in linear IV regression. In D. W. K. Andrews, ed., *Identification and Inference for Econometric Models*. New York: Cambridge University Press, 80–108.

Storeygard, A. 2012. Farther on down the road: Transport costs, trade and urban growth in sub-Saharan Africa. Mimeo. Tufts University.

Straub, S. 2011. Infrastructure and development: A critical appraisal of the macro-level. *Journal of Development Studies* 47 (5): 683–708.

Straub, S. 2008. Infrastructure and growth in developing countries: Recent advances and research challenges. Policy Research working paper 4460. World Bank.

Van de Walle, D. 2009. Impact evaluation of rural road projects. *Journal of Development Effectiveness* 1 (1): 15–36.

Volpe Martincus C., J. Carballo, and A. Cusolito. 2013. Routes, exports and employment in developing countries: Following the trace of the Inca roads. Mimeo. Inter-American Development Bank.

Wooldridge, J. M. 2010. *Econometric Analysis of Cross Section and Panel Data*, 2nd ed. Cambridge: MIT Press.

10 Effects of Uncertainty and Opportunistic Renegotiations on Bidding Behavior: Evidence from Toll Road Concessions

Laure Athias and Antonio Nunez

10.1 Introduction

Public–private partnerships (hereafter designated as PPPs) have generated keen interest in recent decades in a number of countries, including both developed and developing countries. PPPs, which bundle construction and operation into a single contract,[1] encompass two main types of contract: (1) contracts where the stream of revenues for the private partner consist of user fees (e.g., concession contracts) and (2) contracts where the stream of revenues for the private partner consist of payments from the procuring authority (e.g., availability contracts). Concession contracts account for most PPPs around the world. According to the World Bank PPI database, between 1990 and 2000, overall 65 percent of the projects in Latin America and the Caribbean were adjudicated as concessions. More generally, they account for 54 percent of all the PPPs developed in low- and middle-income countries, and for most PPPs in the road sector (57 percent of the projects in the road sector in the World Bank PPI database are concession contracts). Toll road concessions should also deserve a special attention because they are particularly prone to the difficulties inherent to PPPs. In these contracts, concessionaires undertake the design, building, financing, and operation of the relevant facility, and their main source of revenue are the tolls that they can charge to users for the whole length of the concession. Concessions are long-term contracts (often over thirty years) involving large upfront specific investments, and a degree of uncertainty that is much greater than in most ordinary contracts. Indeed traffic forecasts are notoriously imprecise, making toll road concessions very risky (Flyvbjerg, Bruzelius, and Rothengatter 2003). This fact, combined with informational asymmetries, implies that the winner's curse, an adverse-selection problem that arises because the winner tends to be the bidder with the most overly optimistic information concerning the auctioned contract value, may be particularly pronounced within toll road concession auctions. These features of toll road concessions make them prone to opportunism and renegotiation. For instance, Guasch (2004) found, in a study on more than 1,000 concession contracts awarded during the 1990s in Latin America, that 53 percent of the concessions in the transport sector were renegotiated, and this took place on average only 3.1 years after the signing of the contract.

Thus, while there is a large literature highlighting that the profitability of public–private partnerships, and in particular of toll road concessions, is ex post affected by uncertainty and opportunistic renegotiations, much less is known on the impact of such features on firms' bidding behavior ex ante. The aim of this chapter is to fill in this gap and hence to study how such features influence bidding behavior, and to quantify their bid effects. We collected original data, although very difficult to obtain, on the actual traffic and the traffic forecast included in the winning bids, for 49 worldwide toll road concession contracts. We argue that the ratio between the actual and forecasted traffic is a good proxy for firms' ex ante bidding behavior. We show that bidders bid less aggressively in toll road concession auctions when they expect more competition; that is, the internalization of the winner's curse by bidders is particularly strong in toll road concession contract auctions. In addition we find that this internalization is stronger in auctions with a greater degree of common uncertainty (measured by the length in kilometers of the infrastructure) but weaker when future profitable renegotiations are more likely, as in weaker institutional environments. This last result questions the theoretical predictions of the winner's curse effects in common-value auctions. Thus we stress the necessity to improve the theoretical framework by considering the transaction as a whole, that is, considering the impact of not only the ex ante but also the ex post conditions on bidding behavior.

The chapter is organized as follows: Section 10.2 presents the particular features of toll road concession auctions. To formalize the effects of uncertainty and opportunistic renegotiations on bidding behavior in such auctions, we present in section 10.3 a simple model of competitive bidding with common-value components, and state our three theoretical propositions. Section 10.4 provides a description of the data while section 10.5 reports the econometric results. In section 10.6 we provide a robustness analysis of our results, and in section 10.7 we discuss the policy implications of our work and offer some concluding comments.

10.2 Auctions for Toll Road Concessions

10.2.1 First-Price Sealed-Bid Auctions

In this chapter we study bidding behavior in first-price sealed-bid auctions, using data on road concessions. In a first-price sealed-bid auction, each bidder independently and privately picks a price and offers to buy the contract at that price. The one who bids the lowest price wins (most of toll road concession contracts are awarded via low-bid auctions with adjudication criteria going from the lowest toll, to the lowest public subvention required, or to the shortest length of the concession).

Concession contracts are most often awarded in two stages. In the first stage, private consortia submit their technical qualifications, following the rules defined by the public authority. In the second stage, qualified consortia (i.e., the consortia selected after the first step) are allowed to bid. The concession is then awarded to the consortium with the best bid (sometimes there is an additional stage between the second stage and the selection of the best bid, which consists in selecting the two best bidders and asking them to submit in a third stage their best and final offer). Except in exceptional cases, the number of bidders qualified to bid is published by the public authority as a matter of transparency. It is therefore a known variable to the participants.

10.2.2 Common-Value Auctions

We assume that toll road concession auctioning environment fall exclusively in the common-value category. Although most real-world auctions are not exclusively common value or private value (Laffont 1997), we consider that this is not a too restrictive assumption to the extent that in the road construction sector, it is now well known that firms have the same technology, so that private value differences do not arise.

The common-value element is induced by the fact that the concession contract being bid for will not be fulfilled immediately and bidders have heterogeneous information about future states of the world—such as market conditions or the supply and demand for substitute objects. Traffic forecasting errors and associated risks are characteristics of transport infrastructure projects. Studies of such errors (Trujillo, Quinet, and Estache 2002; Flyvbjerg, Bruzelius, and Rothengatter 2003;

Standard and Poor's 2005) show that future traffic is most often overestimated, by large amounts.

The sources of traffic forecast inaccuracy can be classified in three main groups. First, there is the pure uncertainty effect. Economic, social, environmental, and technological changes can affect the previsions, especially in the long run, making forecasts uncertain by their nature. Another important source of traffic forecast errors and biases stems from methodological or scientific sources, including data, models, and hypotheses. Third, there are the behavioral sources, which include optimism and opportunism. Optimism comes from the overconfidence that analysts and project promoters place in the project and in themselves. Opportunism refers to the strategic manipulation of traffic forecasts. In fact uncertainty in forecasts induces the possibility of manipulation that is exacerbated by the information asymmetries in concession projects.[2]

Bidders also have access in such an environment to different information. A bidder might conduct her own traffic forecast survey of a toll road concession or might learn about market conditions from her own customers and suppliers. Furthermore, even if bidders have access to the same market data, they might follow different methods or rules-of-thumb for using this information to form beliefs about the contract's value. The outcome of one bidder's model (her signal) might then be useful to another bidder in assessing her own valuation even after seeing the output of her own model (Athey and Haile 2007). In such cases it is appropriate to model bidders as having different private information of a common-value nature.

Thus each bidder's traffic appraisal represents just an estimate, subject to error. No bidder knows the future level of traffic and each realizes that the other bidders may possess information or analyzes that the bidder would find useful for her own traffic forecast. As a result in toll road concession auctions, the winning bidder may be the one who most overestimates future traffic. This is all the more true that under first-price sealed-bid auctions, bidders have less information on other bidders' estimates of project value.[3]

10.2.3 Auctions with Differing Levels of Common Uncertainty

There are two main factors that can reduce the level of contract valuation common uncertainty in the first-price sealed bid toll road concession auctions: the public release of information about future traffic and the characteristics of the facility.

The impact of the public release of information on bidding behavior in auctions with common-value uncertainty begins to be studied in the experimental or empirical literature (Kagel and Levin 1986; De Silva et al. 2008). Such studies show that in first-price sealed-bid auctions, public information reducing item valuation uncertainty can lead to more aggressive bidding behavior[4] and that this effect can be more pronounced in auctions with larger common uncertainty. While the auction format for toll road concessions is quite similar across auctions, a feature that varies across auctions is the information provided to bidders regarding the procuring authority's internal forecast of the future traffic. Some procuring authorities release this information prior to bidding and others do not, so the level of information dispersion varies across auctions in the sample. This effect is all the more important that governments negotiators juggle with multiple concerns and more general expertise than private partners with focused specialized negotiators and advised by deal specialists with insufficient sectoral and macro vision. This variation helps identify the effect of changes in information dispersion on bids. For example, in a study of computer auctions on eBay, Yin (2006) examines the effect of value dispersion and seller reputation on prices. She finds that the seller's reputation complements information provided in the auction descriptions by lending more credibility to that information. Thus we can expect that the level of common uncertainty also varies with the procuring authority's reputation when the latter chooses to release her own traffic forecast.

Another way to distinguish toll road projects regarding their common traffic uncertainty is to account for their differing uncertainty-leading characteristics, in particular, the physical length.[5] In fact, based on the preceding literature on this sector and on discussions with some private concessionaires, we believe that there is less uncertainty associated with traffic forecasts of longer facilities. Although none study (as far as we know) has focused on the relationship between the physical length and the methodological problems associated with the forecasting exercise, we can give at least three arguments supporting this hypothesis. First, the law of large numbers: since the number and size of zones involved (possible origin–destination—OD—pairs) is much higher in long interurban transport facilities than in short ones, misspecification or error prediction on some ODs has less impact in equilibrium. Second, if the value of travel time savings increases with the travel length, misspecification should occur for small savings because studies on stated and revealed value of travel time savings usually evaluate large time

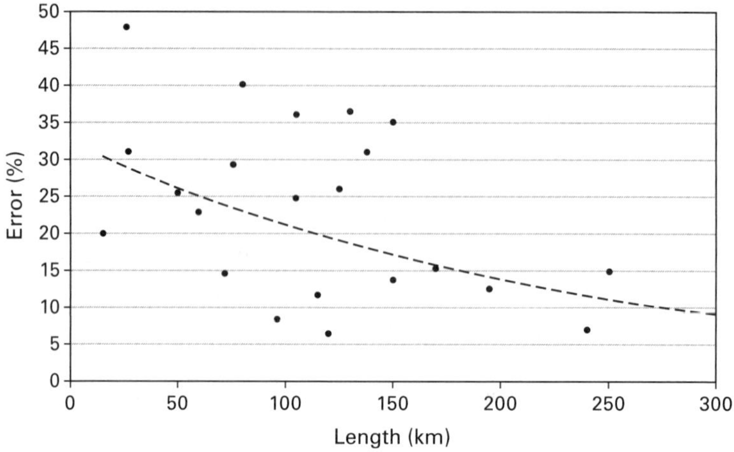

Figure 10.1
Length and forecast error

savings. Third, short-distance travels do not follow the traditional relationship between GDP and mobility and are determined by life patterns. In particular, in urban transport, demand growth is strongly impacted by urban land-use, and transport policy (Schafer 2000).

Moreover, using an external sample (22 motorway sections in France, with forecast errors ranging from 5 to 50 percent, which are not included in our analysis), we can corroborate this hypothesis (figure 10.1). Although the coefficient of determination is low (due to the fact that only a portion of the error is correlated with the length), there is evidence of a decreasing relationship.

10.2.4 Renegotiation in Toll Road Concessions

A particular characteristic of toll road concession auctions is that they are public–private contracts with particularly high potential for renegotiation in less developed countries (Estache 2006; Guasch 2004; Laffont 2005; Guasch, Laffont, and Straub 2003, 2007), but also in developed countries (Gomez-Ibanez and Meyer 1993; Engel, Fischer, and Galetovic 2003, 2006a, b; Athias and Saussier 2007).

Some renegotiation is often desirable and is to be expected as contracts are, in practice, necessarily incomplete. Unforeseen events that are not induced by either the government or the operator (e.g., currency devaluation) can significantly affect the financial equilibrium of firms, and can be used as an opportunity to redistribute rents. However, a high incidence of renegotiations, particularly in early stages, would be beyond expected or reasonable levels, and would raise concerns about the validity of the concession model in which renegotiations are not taken into account (Guasch, Laffont, and Straub 2003). Such a case might induce excessive opportunistic behavior by the operators, or by the government, in detriment to the efficiency of the process and overall welfare. Once an enterprise has been granted a concession in an infrastructure sector—and the eventual bidding competitors are gone—that enterprise may correspondingly be able to undertake actions that "hold up" the government, for example, through insisting on renegotiating the contract ex post. The inherent contractual incompleteness, the potential incentives for political incumbents to use renegotiation to anticipate infrastructure spending and thereby increase the probability of winning an upcoming election (Engel, Fischer, and Galetovic 2006), and the perceived leverage of the enterprise vis-à-vis the government in a bilateral negotiation might constitute a powerful motivation to seek renegotiation of the contract and secure a better deal than the initial one.

Thus, when bidders expect a high likelihood of renegotiation that renders it possible to avoid any losses, they have strong incentives to submit bids containing promises difficult to satisfy, with the sole purpose of being awarded the tender (Spulber 1990). Uncertainty in forecasts is then used in a strategic way by bidders, and this could be exacerbated by information asymmetries in concession projects. For example, traffic overestimation (up to the constraint of credibility) may represent equilibrium in the short run. While candidates submit opportunistic bids to increase their probability of success, the more aggressive the bids, the better it would be for the public procuring authority, since it is more cost saving in the short run. Moreover financial agencies and lenders, suspecting that traffic forecasts are strategically increased, may find a risk-sharing agreement that cushions them against any losses.

10.3 Bidding for Toll Road Concessions: A Simple Model

We now present a simple model of competitive bidding that takes into account the various features highlighted above.

10.3.1 Model Framework

For concreteness, let us assume that firms bid on lowest toll. We assume that there exists a one-to-one, decreasing, relation between the traffic forecast and the toll included in the bid. First, this boils down to assuming that the costs (global investments and operation costs) are independently and identically distributed—this assumption is standard in the literature on PPP (e.g., Engel, Fischer, and Galetovic 2013)—and that costs underestimation cannot be used strategically; this assumption is realistic to the extent that concessionaires cannot complain ex post about cost underestimation when there are very few exogenous components in the cost estimation, and the uncertainty and information asymmetry between bidders and procuring authorities regarding construction costs are low. Second, it implies that rates of return are the same across firms. Again, this does not seem to be a too restrictive assumption because it is well known that procuring authorities expect a range of values for the financial rate of return of a particular project.

Thus the firm decides the toll it wants to bid on and then puts pressure on the forecaster so that she approves the traffic forecast consistent with this bid. As already discussed, it is possible for firms to have some margin to adjust the traffic forecasts, since the uncertainty associated with forecasts (exogenous and methodological) makes it very easy to manipulate the forecasts. For instance, considering that the project will produce higher time savings or using higher rate of economic growth than should be expected can lead one to overestimate demand.

In a recent survey, Nunez (2007) asked a sample of 178 forecasters whether they were pressured to manipulate traffic forecasts. Few forecasters (25.6 percent) declare that they are rarely if ever pressured for forecast results. Nunez (2007) also asked them about the role and sense of strategic manipulation of forecasts. For around 46 percent of forecasters, the strategic manipulation of forecasts plays either a very important or an important role in the final traffic estimations. Another 42 percent considered that strategic manipulation plays a somewhat important role. Only 12 percent of the forecasters judged this concern inconsequential (i.e., even where strategic manipulation exists, the final estimations are not affected in a significant way).

In addition, while most forecasters affirm that such pressure may cause traffic overestimation, bidders do not have an unbounded margin to adjust traffic forecasts. There is primarily the margin of credibility. Procuring authorities have an expectation, though inaccurate, of what level the future traffic may be, so the bidder is not able to manipulate disproportionately traffic forecasts. Second, the margin is bounded by the other bidders' tenders. Procuring authorities are able to compare the traffic forecasts of different bidders and hence spot a forecast differing largely from all others. Such a case occurred in France where one bidder was asked for an audit to justify some overly high traffic forecasts compared to those submitted by other bidders.

By our central assumption, there is additionally the fact that procuring authorities have information provided by firms on costs, rates of return, traffic forecasts, so that they can do consistency checks on the bids. This seems realistic to the extent that, first, a financial model is often required with a bid; second, whenever international development banks are involved, they have the responsibility to assess all bids; third procuring authorities have internal resources to check the consistency of the bids.[6]

Finally, strategic bidding behavior is function of the possibility for bidders to renegotiate the contract. As mentioned in the previous section, there is a high incidence of renegotiation in toll road concessions, mainly because actual traffic is known not to always meet the forecasts due to changing exogenous factors.

10.3.2 Model Setting

Consider the future actual traffic D^A. This actual traffic is determined by the surrounding environment. Suppose that the road use demand is inelastic (with respect to both price and quality). Each firm receives an estimate of the future actual traffic defined as

$$D^E = D^A + \varepsilon,$$

where ε is iid with zero mean, and bidders believe that the average of the bidders' traffic forecasts is a good estimate of the future actual traffic (a standard assumption in common-value models; e.g., see Bikhchandani, and Riley 1991; Bulow, Huang, and Klemperer 1999; Goeree and Offerman 2003). In addition assume that rational bidders believe that the variance of ε is increasing in the number of bidders. Each firm chooses then a strategic traffic forecast D^S such as

$$D^S = D^E + s.$$

As we noted in the section 10.2, the strategic bias s depends on the number of bidders, the degree of common uncertainty, and the likelihood of renegotiation. So we have

$$s = f(NB, CU, PR),$$

where *NB* is the number of bidders, *CU* the level of common uncertainty, and *PR* the likelihood of renegotiation.

Given D^S, each firm chooses the toll $p = g(D^S)$ with $g' < 0$. As in the previous section, g is the same for each firm and given ex ante. We then have $p = g(D^E + f(NB, CU, PR))$.

The net present value can be written as

$$NPV = -\int_{tt}^{t0} I_t e^{-rt} dt + \int_{t0}^{tf} [p_t D_t^A (p_t) - C(D_t^A)] e^{-rt} dt, \tag{1}$$

where I is the initial investment and C the operation and maintenance costs.

As already discussed, we assume that the main strategic variable is the demand, so that costs do not matter. Within this framework, only the gross benefit matters, which is

$$B = \int_{t0}^{tf} [p_t D_t^A] e^{-rt} dt. \tag{2}$$

However, at the bidding stage, the demand included in the financial model is D^S. Thus, given r and B, the only way to reduce the price (toll) included in the bid is to increase the traffic forecast. The probability of winning can be then written as

$$P_{win} = P(D_i^S \geq D_j^S \ \forall j), \tag{3}$$

where i and $j, j \in 1, \ldots, NB-1$ index the bidders.

10.3.3 Number of Bidders and Traffic Forecast Deviation

Let the forecast error e be the difference between the traffic forecast included in the bid and the actual traffic. So we have $e = \varepsilon + s$. The winner's forecast error can then be written as

$$e_i \mid D_i^S > D_j^S \qquad \forall j \neq i = D_i^S - \frac{1}{N} \sum D_j^S. \tag{4}$$

As the variance of ε is increasing in the number of bidders, then $e_i \mid D_i^b > D_j^b \ \forall j \neq i$ is strictly increasing in the number of bidders:

$$e_i \mid D_i^S > D_j^S \qquad \forall j \neq i = k(NB),\ k' > 0, \tag{5}$$

Provided that the probability of winning the auction for the bidder i is proportional to her own forecast D_i^S and inversely proportional to other bidders' forecasts $D_j^S \forall j$, we have

$$Pr(D_i^S > D_j^S \ \ \forall j \neq i) = h(D_i^S, D_j^S \ \ \forall j \neq i), \tag{6}$$

where

$$\frac{\partial h}{\partial D_i^S} > 0, \quad \frac{\partial h}{\partial NB} < 0.$$

The expected forecast error is then

$$E(e_i) = k(NB)h(D_i^S, D_j^S \ \forall j \neq i), \tag{7}$$

Since bidders are risk neutral, they want the expected forecast error to be constant, let us say equal to e_i^*. Thus, as the number of bidders increases, the probability of winning the bid has to decrease as much as the error term increases. Nevertheless, we assume that the impact of the increase in the number of bidders is weaker on the probability of winning than on the error term. This assumption seems realistic as we can expect a high variance of traffic forecasts due to the magnitude of traffic uncertainty. In this case an increase in the error term is not fully compensated by the decrease in the probability of winning. That is,

$$-\frac{\partial h}{\partial NB} < \frac{\partial k}{\partial NB}.$$

Thus bidders have to decrease their traffic forecast to keep the expected forecast error constant. This is the internalization of the winner's curse, which leads us to the following proposition:

Proposition 1 *The greater the number of bidders, the more likely bidders will be conservative to correct for traffic overestimation. So*

$$\frac{\partial D_i^S}{\partial NB} < 0.$$

10.3.4 Number of Bidders and Level of Common Uncertainty

Let us now consider the internalization of the winner's curse relative to the degree of common uncertainty. We assume that the higher the common uncertainty, the higher is the variance of bids, that is,

$$\frac{\partial \mathrm{Var}(D^S)}{\partial CU} > 0. \tag{8}$$

Here the winning expected forecast error is a strictly increasing, concave function of the common uncertainty (*CU*). We can write this winning forecast error as

$$e_i \mid D_i^S > D_j^S \quad \forall j \neq i = k(NB, CU), \tag{9}$$

where

$$\frac{\partial k}{\partial NB} > 0, \quad \frac{\partial k}{\partial CU} > 0, \quad \frac{\partial k^2}{\partial^2 NB} < 0, \quad \frac{\partial k^2}{\partial^2 CU} < 0.$$

The expected forecast error is then

$$E(e_i) = k(NB, CU)h(D_i^S, D_j^S \ \forall j \neq i). \tag{10}$$

Equations (8) and (10) indicate that an increase in the common uncertainty can have two counteracting effects on bids. First, since the variance increases with the common uncertainty, the winning bid is an increasing function of the common uncertainty (equation 8). Second, in order to keep the expected error constant, bidders should revise their bids (forecasts) downward (equation 10), meaning that bidders will have to further downgrade their forecasts when the uncertainty goes higher.

To see the interaction between the common uncertainty and the number of bidders, we repeat the same exercise as in the previous section, and find that the higher the common uncertainty, the more bidders will internalize the winner's curse as the number of bidders increases:

$$\frac{\partial}{\partial CU} \frac{\partial D_i^S}{\partial NB} < 0.$$

This leads us to the following proposition:

Proposition 2 *The greater the degree of common uncertainty, the more likely bidders will be conservative as competition gets fiercer.*

10.3.5 Number of Bidders and Renegotiation

As we noted above, toll road concessions deal with a high incidence of renegotiation. This can impact the behavior of bidders. They might anticipate a future renegotiation that will induce them ex ante to increase their expected forecast error to the limit of the outcome they expect of the renegotiation. In other words, some dynamic concerns are now involved in the bidding behavior.

Suppose that the benefit from a renegotiation (BR) can be written in terms of its equivalent in traffic. We can write the expected benefit from the renegotiation as the benefit (BR) multiplied by the probability of renegotiation (PR).

$E(BR) = BR{*}PR,$

where

$BR = j^{-1}(s_{BR}), j' > 0.$

Here s_{BR} is the overestimation relative to the benefit of the renegotiation. The expected error due to the possibility of renegotiation can be written as

$$E^{R}(e_{i}) = E(e_{i}) + E(s_{BR}). \tag{11}$$

Assuming that the probability of renegotiation is not correlated with the number of bidders or the common uncertainty, we can write

$$E^{R}(e_{i}) = h(D_{i}^{S}, D_{j}^{S}\ \forall j \neq i)k(NB, CU) + E(s_{BR}). \tag{12}$$

Or, more generally, we can rewrite the error term as

$$e_{i}^{R} = k(NB, CU, BR, PR), \tag{13}$$

where

$$\frac{\partial k}{\partial BR} > 0$$

and

$$\frac{\partial k}{\partial PR} > 0.$$

Then, as the probability of renegotiation increases, an increase in the number of bidders has a weaker impact on the correction of traffic forecast overestimation, that is,

$$\frac{\partial}{\partial PR}\frac{\partial D_{i}^{S}}{\partial NB} > 0.$$

This leads to the following proposition:

Proposition 3 *The higher the likelihood of contract renegotiation, the less likely bidders will be conservative as the number of bidders increases.*

In the reminder of this chapter, we empirically test these three predictions of the model. In other words, we want first to test whether overall bidders in such auctions are cognizant of the winner's curse, that is, whether their correction for the overestimation of future traffic becomes larger as the number of bidders increases. Second, we test whether bidders are more or less cognizant of the winner's curse according to the projects' differing levels of common-value components. Third, we investigate the magnitude of the internalization of the winner's curse in function of the likelihood of renegotiation.

10.4 Data on Road Concession Contract Auctions

We constructed a dataset consisting of 49 toll road concession contracts (highways, bridges, and tunnels). They are from Australia, Brazil, Canada, Chile, France, Germany, Hungary, Israel, Jamaica, Portugal, South Africa, Thailand, and United Kingdom. The bidding procedure is the same for all these concession contracts. The oldest auctions in the sample were awarded in 1989, whereas the latest was in 2003.[7] Table 10.1 shows the distribution by country and by year. For this study, a French concessionaire agreed—under the condition that the data remain confidential—to provide access to its internal records containing data included in their winning bids on the traffic forecasts, the construction costs, the length of the facility, the contract duration, and the number of bidders involved in these bids. All the other data used in this study come from the scientific and professional press. As far as we know, this database is the most exhaustive on toll road concession auctions.

Clearly, the lack of data homogeneity is an important point of concern with this database. However, there is no country that displays a large enough number of toll road concessions to enable us to focus our analysis only on one country. Because we also do not—cannot—account for all elements that differ between auctions, we think that if such unobserved factors do not impact bidding behavior in the same way, the more countries we consider, the lower the likelihood that such factors impact bidding behavior in the same sense, and then the greater the probability that their overall impact is null.

10.4.1 Dependent Variable: Traffic Forecast Deviation

We have data on the traffic forecasts included in the bids submitted by the winning bidders, and on the actual traffic coming from traffic

Table 10.1
Toll road concessions by country and by year

	1989	1990	1991	1992	1993	1994	1995	1996	1997	1998	1999	2000	2001	2002	2003	Total
Australia							1								1	2
Brazil						1	3		1							5
Canada					1						1					2
Chile				1		1	2	1								5
France		1							1				2			4
Germany								1			1					2
Hungary						2										2
Israel											1					1
Jamaica													1			1
Portugal						1				2	2	2	2	1		10
RS[a]										7						7
South Africa									1							1
Thailand	1															1
United Kingdom	1		1	1				1			1			1		6
Total	2	1	1	2	1	5	6	3	3	9	6	2	5	2	1	49

a. RS refers to Rio Grande do Sul, the Brazilian southernmost state. It is presented as a different country because its concessions program as well as its regulatory regime are completely independent.

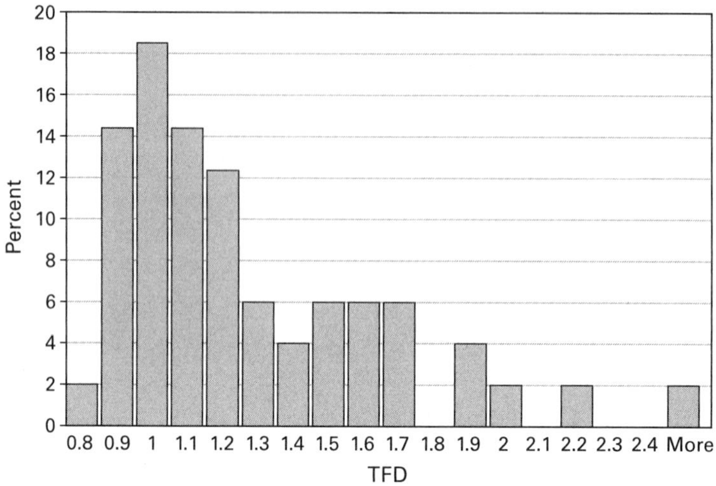

Figure 10.2

counts. We will call the average ratio between them the*traffic forecast deviation (TFD)*. Thus we will define our dependent variable as

$$TFD = \frac{1}{n}\sum_{t=t_0}^{t_0+n-1}\frac{forecast_t}{actual_t}. \tag{14}$$

where $actual_t$ is the actual traffic observed in year t, $forecast_t$ is the traffic forecast for the year t, and n is the number of years for which we could calculate this deviation. As data availability varies across projects, the variable *TFD* used in the regressions is the average deviation for the period for which we have both data on forecast and actual traffic. This period ranges up to 7 years. We take the average *TFD* because it captures the fact that bidders can manipulate the traffic forecasts at the opening of the facility or the traffic growth forecasts, or both. Thus a positive impact on this variable would imply more aggressive bidding behavior, and a negative impact on this variable would imply more conservative bidding behavior.

Figure 10.2 gives the distribution of this TFD variable in the sample. One aspect of this contractual record calls for immediate attention: the prevalence of traffic overestimation, since the average deviation is 1.25 (i.e., an average overestimation of 25 percent).

10.4.2 Explanatory Variables

The propositions to be tested formulated above suggest three main factors that can influence the bidding behavior: the number of bidders,

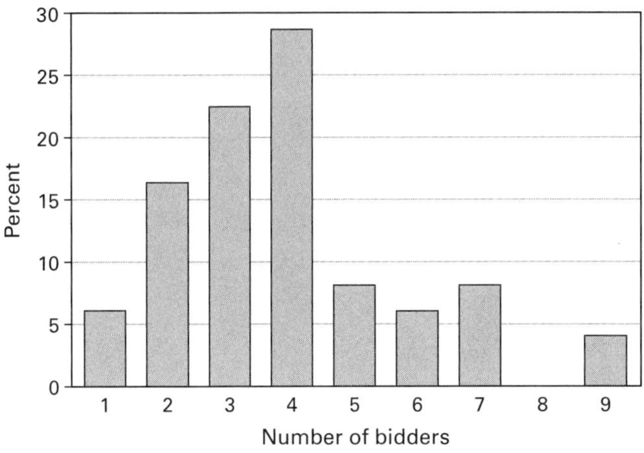

Figure 10.3
Number of bidders

the degree of common uncertainty, and the likelihood of contract renegotiation. The actual number of bidders accounts for the level of competition (it represents the number of bidders that bid after the prequalification stage). Figure 10.3 shows the distribution of the number of bidders in our sample.[8]

The descriptive statistics in table 10.2 indicate that on average there were 3.9 bidders per contract, ranging from 1 to 9 bidders across contracts. The hypothesis is that bidders will be more conservative, the larger the number of bidders; in other words, we expect a negative impact of the *NUMBER OF BIDDERS* variable on our *TFD* variable.

The theoretical literature on auctions suggests that the internalization of the winner's curse should be more pronounced in auctions where there is greater common uncertainty. As we explained above, to examine the potential differences in the effect of the competition across projects, we need to look at the existence of a public information release on the future traffic forecast and at the physical length of facilities being auctioned. So we include in our regressions the dummy variable *PUBLICINFO* and the variable *LENGTH*, reflecting the length of the facility in kilometers. The prediction is that each of these variables, interacted with the number of bidders, will have a positive impact on the traffic forecast deviation.[9]

To take into account the reputation effect of the procuring authority, as would complement the release of her traffic forecast, we interacted the variable *PUBLICINFO* both with the number of bidders and the

Table 10.2
Data definitions and descriptive statistics

Variable	Mean	Median	SD	Min	Max	Definition
TFD	1.25	1.10	0.45	0.80	3.40	Ratio forecast / actual traffic
NB	3.92	4.00	1.89	1.00	9.00	Number of bidders for the contract
Length	107.09	96.00	113.00	0.50	510.00	Length of the facility (km)
Civil law	0.73	1.00	0.45	0	1	1 if the legal framework of the country in question is civil law; 0 otherwise
HIC	0.53	1.00	0.50	0	1	1 if the country in question is a high income country; 0 otherwise
Public information	0.49	0	0.50	0	1	1 if the procuring authority released its own traffic forecast prior to bidding; 0 otherwise
Government learning	2.53	1.00	3.05	0	10	Number of concessions the public authority had awarded before the present project
Trend	9.20	8.00	3.43	3.00	17.00	
Left	0.49	0	0.50	0	1	1 if the procuring authority in question is left-wing; 0 otherwise
Repeated contract	0.49	0	0.87	0	1	1 if the procuring authority and the winning bidder had contracted together at least once before the present project; 0 otherwise
Duration	356.88	348.00	179.96	180.00	1,164.00	Delay between the completion of the construction and the end of the concession (months)
Investment	445.77	259.00	430.26	10.00	1,554.00	Total construction costs (MEuro)

GOVLEARN variable, which reflects the experience of the procuring authority in awarding concession contracts.

On the likelihood of contractual renegotiation, Guasch, Laffont, and Straub (2003) develop a model to accommodate renegotiations initiated by firms. This provides them with a set of predictions for the probabilities of renegotiation of concession contracts. They stress the importance of having a regulator in place and an experienced procuring authority to prevent renegotiations, the necessity to consider the fragility of price caps, the relevance of economic shocks and political cycles, as well as the importance of good institutions (bureaucracy, rule of law, control of corruption) to reduce the incidences of renegotiations. Given the specificity of toll road concession contracts—absence of a regulator in most countries, all price-cap contracts, and consortia composed most of time of both local and foreign companies—we introduced three variables to capture the reliability of contract enforcement. The first is the variable *GOVLEARN*, which reflects the experience of the procuring authority in awarding concession contracts. As a large number of prior concessions should decrease the probability of renegotiation, we can expect a negative impact of this variable interacted with the number of bidders variable on our dependent *TFD* variable.

The second proxy for the likelihood of renegotiation is the variable *HIGH INCOME COUNTRY* developed by the World Bank (2006). As pointed out by Laffont (2005), the prediction is that wealthier countries have more money to finance the functioning of the enforcement mechanism than poorer countries. In other words, the government's "tolerance for renegotiation" depends on the investment in enforcement. This is why we can expect stronger institutional frameworks in wealthier countries and hence lower probabilities of contractual renegotiation in such countries. The hypothesis is therefore that greater numbers of bidders for projects taking place in wealthier countries will more likely lead to more conservative bidding behavior at equilibrium than in poorer countries, that is, to a negative impact of the crossed variable *HIC*NUMBER OF BIDDERS* on our *TFD* dependent variable (highlighting a greater internalization of the winner's curse in wealthier countries).

However, as we discussed above, renegotiations occur in developed countries, though at lower incidences. The legal system should then serve as a useful guide for the probability of enforcing the agreed-upon contract. There has been increased attention from economists and legal scholars directed to the question of which legal frameworks best promote economic growth and stability. Some have suggested that common law regimes outperform civil code regimes throughout the world (La Porta et al. 1998). More specifically, institutional features that traditionally characterize a common law regime make it more difficult to renegotiate than under civil law systems. The reason is that in civil law countries, legislation is seen as the primary source of law. Thus, by default, courts base their judgments on the provisions of codes and statutes, on which decisions in particular cases are to be based. Courts thus have to reason extensively on the basis of general rules and principles of the code, often drawing analogies from statutory provisions to fill lacunae and to achieve coherence. By contrast, in the common law system, cases are the primary source of law, whereas statutes are only seen as incursions into the common law and thus interpreted narrowly.

According to these features of the different legal regimes, we assume that the likelihood of renegotiation is higher in civil law regimes and expect therefore a lower winner's curse effect in civil law countries, that is, a positive impact of the variable *CIVILLAW* interacted with the number of bidders on our *TFD* dependent variable.

The variables used in our estimations are summarized in table 10.2.

10.5 Econometric Results

To test our three theoretical predictions, we performed log-log regressions.[10] Ten specifications—which we abusively refer to as "model" in the following for simplicity—were estimated. We first analyzed the overall impact of number of bidders on bidding behavior (model 1). We then examined the effects of the winner's curse on contract auctions with differing levels of common-value components (models 2 to 6). Last, we identified, in models 7 to 10, if the theoretical effects still hold when we control for the fact that bidders can adapt their behavior to the institutional environment.[11] The results are reported in table 10.3.

The first striking result is that the number of bidders drives the value of bidders' tenders. Model 1 shows that there is a negative impact of fiercer competition on the traffic forecast deviation variable. This result corroborates our proposition 1 (at 1 percent significance level). It shows that bidders are more conservative the more bidders there are for the project.

We also observe that the internalization of the winner's curse is larger for projects with greater common uncertainty. In fact the public release of information prior to bidding has a positive impact on the traffic forecast deviation variable when interacted with the number of bidders variable. This is consistent with the theory, and highlights that one way to hinder the internalization of the winner's curse by bidders is to reduce the information dispersion on the contract valuation by giving more contract information. Such uncertainty effects at the bidding stage on the valuation of a contract have been hitherto ignored. Furthermore we find that the impact of the public release of information on bidding behavior is not stronger when accounting for procuring authority's experience, in contrast to Yin (2006).

Similarly we observe that while the direct impact on the TFD variable of the length variable is negative—which implies that a weaker degree of common uncertainty leads to a forecast error reduction that more than compensates for the increase in the aggressive bidding behavior (i.e., the effect captured by equation 5 is stronger than the one captured by equation 6)—the variable *LENGTH* interacted with the number of bidders variable has a positive and significant impact on the traffic forecast deviation (even if the direct impact of the number of bidders variable is negative). Thus, when compared to projects for which the size of the facility is smaller (i.e., when compared to more uncertain projects), bidders on lengthier projects are less cognizant of the winner's curse.

These results confirm that the larger the size of the common-value component, the more bidders become cognizant of the winner's curse when competition increases. This finding corroborates our proposition 2.

Results of models 7 to 10 show that the internalization of the winner's curse by bidders is significantly higher when bidders expect a low likelihood of renegotiation. In particular, as predicted, model 7 indicates that the effect of the variable *GOVLEARN*, interacted with the number of bidders, is negative, though nearly insignificant, on the TFD variable. This may corroborate the result of Guasch (2004) of a negative impact of the experience of the public authority on the probability of renegotiation. The impact of the variable *CIVIL LAW* interacted with the number of bidders is positive on the traffic forecast deviation, implying that bidders anticipate a higher likelihood of renegotiation in civil law countries and therefore are less prone to internalize the winner's curse when bidding in such countries. This result, in contrast to what is often recommended, favors the approach that consists in relying on long concession-specific documents in an attempt to make the con-

Table 10.3
Econometric results

	(1)	(2)	(3)	(4)	(5)	(6)	(7)	(8)	(9)	(10)	(11)	(12)	(13)
number of bidders (NB)	−0.220	−0.257	−0.373	−0.261	−0.678	−0.660	−0.682	−0.711	−0.863	−0.873	−0.979	−1.016	−0.175
	(−2.87)	(−3.33)	(−3.29)	(−3.36)	(−2.41)	(−2.43)	(−2.45)	(−2.72)	(−2.94)	(−3.17)	(−3.45)	(−3.42)	(−2.60)
Publicinf			−0.284										
			(−1.39)										
Publicinf*NB		0.110	0.305										
		(1.92)	(2.01)										
Publicinf* Govlearn*NB				0.039		0.041							
				(1.90)		(2.14)							
Length					−0.182	−0.170	−0.198	−0.238	−0.207	−0.257	−0.289	−0.307	
					(−2.36)	(−2.28)	(−2.58)	(−3.23)	(−2.71)	(−3.48)	(−3.77)	(−3.82)	
Length*NB					0.103	0.089	0.119	0.134	0.113	0.144	0.161	0.168	
					(1.68)	(1.50)	(1.93)	(2.31)	(1.88)	(2.48)	(2.74)	(2.72)	
Govlearn*NB							−0.014			−0.004	0.006	0.005	
							(−1.49)			(−0.36)	(0.51)	(0.36)	
HIC*NB								−0.159		−0.138	−0.148	−0.143	
								(−2.93)		(−2.16)	(−2.32)	(−1.72)	

Table 10.3 (Continued)

	(1)	(2)	(3)	(4)	(5)	(6)	(7)	(8)	(9)	(10)	(11)	(12)	(13)
Civillaw*NB									0.131	0.117	0.104	0.116	
									(1.82)	(1.71)	(1.52)	(1.48)	
Repeated											−0.132	−0.138	
											(−1.47)	(−1.49)	
Investment												0.01	
												(0.25)	
Duration												−0.07	
												(−0.56)	
Left												−0.057	
												(−0.68)	
Trend												−0.11	
												(−1.02)	
Constant	0.452	0.435	0.609	0.474	1.229	1.194	1.266	1.453	1.381	1.570	1.767	2.457	0.383
	(4.37)	(4.31)	(3.79)	(4.67)	(3.48)	(3.51)	(3.63)	(4.33)	(3.90)	(4.62)	(4.83)	(2.99)	(4.21)
R^2	0.149	0.212	0.244	0.210	0.299	0.365	0.333	0.414	0.348	0.452	0.476	0.499	0.130
Adjusted R^2	0.131	0.178	0.194	0.176	0.252	0.308	0.272	0.360	0.289	0.373	0.386	0.351	0.110
N	49	49	49	49	49	49	49	49	49	49	49	49	47

Note: t-Statistics are in parentheses.

tract as complete as possible, that is, to include every possible contingency to avoid leaving room for ex post renegotiations.

Finally, when we proxied for the likelihood of renegotiation by the countries' level of income, we observe a negative impact of the *HIC* variable as competition gets fiercer on the traffic forecast deviation, implying that bidders are more cognizant of the winner's curse in wealthier countries, that is, in countries in which the probability of renegotiation is lower. These results are consistent with our proposition 3 and hence confirm the need to improve the theoretical framework by considering the transaction as a whole, that is, considering the impact of not only the ex ante but also the ex post conditions on bidding behavior.

10.6 Robustness Analysis

One shortcoming of our work is that the true number of bidders may be unobserved and/or endogenously determined. Porter and Zona (1993) show that bid rigging can occur in construction contract auction settings. This may question our results. However, toll road concession contracts are long-term contracts, and as Chong (2007) shows, collusion is hardly sustainable when contracts are long-term contracts. Furthermore any bid rigging or collusion that may occur would tend to mitigate the internalization of the winner's curse by bidders. But we still find statistical evidence of such an internalization.

It might further be argued that our results are influenced by outliers. To test the robustness of our results to outliers, we excluded from the sample the *TFD* maximum and minimum observations (model 13).

Much of the empirical work on auctions encounters the problem of an endogenous number of bidders. Auction bidders are likely to have been attracted by some aspect of the contract that is not captured in the other regressors or is unobservable to the econometrician. If this unobserved feature is correlated with the traffic forecast deviation, we need to instrument for the number of bidders. Nevertheless, employing a potentially weak instrument may not yield more accurate estimates. Furthermore, because our dependent variable is not the bid (or the price) itself but the traffic forecast deviation, the potentiality of unobservable determinants of traffic forecast deviation is weak. However, to account for this bias, we introduced additional control variables. These are reputation effects, the duration of contract, the total construction costs, the political ideology of the public procuring authority and a trend variable.[12]

So far we have assumed that the auction setting is static whereas auctions for toll road concessions are dynamic(Jofre-Bonet and Pesendorfer 2003). More specifically, repeated interactions render reputational effects important in this toll road concession setting (Athias and Saussier 2007). In fact many of the concessionaires in these auctions bid on many contracts over time. Because the potential loss of future bidding eligibility can counteract concessionaires' incentives to submit opportunistic bids with high traffic forecasts, we introduced the dummy variable *REPEATED* as a control variable. This variable takes the value 1 if the procuring authority and the winning bidder had contracted together at least once before.

The *DURATION* variable, defined as the number of months between the completion of the infrastructure construction and the end of the concession, captures the increasing uncertainty associated with long time horizons in forecasting future traffic growth. The hypothesis is that a longer concession period increases uncertainty, leading to greater forecast errors in traffic growth.

The amount invested—measured in terms of total construction costs—may affect the importance candidates give to the production of better traffic forecasts and also the bidders' determination to win the auction. We capture this effect in the control variable *INVESTMENT*.

It is possible that differences in political ideology (e.g., left- or right-leaning public authorities) help determine the number of bidders. Often private companies show a lack of interest in bidding for contracts when the procuring authority belongs to a particular political party (Athias and Saussier 2007). We capture this effect in the control variable *LEFT*. We further include in the regressions a *TREND* variable so as to control for a temporal evolution of the traffic forecast practices for toll road concessions.

Model 11 shows that the results remain unaltered when controlling for dynamic considerations. While the variable *REPEATED* is weakly significant (15 percent significance level) and has a negative effect on the TFD—suggesting that reputational effect might play a role in such settings—*HIC* and *CIVILLAW* variables interacted with the number of bidders variable are still significant and of the expected sign (the impact of the legal regime is, however, less significant).

Model 12 shows that the results are not affected by the introduction of all the other additional control variables and that none of these variables is significant. Including control variables proved to neither diminish the coefficient of the competition, uncertainty, and institutional variables, nor their sign and significance. In addition model 13 clearly shows that our results were not driven by the outliers.

Although our sample is nonrandom in the sense that we only have observations for which all information was available (especially regarding the traffic forecast), a sample selection bias is not a concern because our observations (and the observations we do not have) do not follow any selection rule; in other words, the function parameters of traffic forecast deviation are expected to be completely independent of the parameters of the function determining the probability of entrance into the sample. We could also suppose that a country fixed-effect do exist. However, our within-country samples are not sufficiently large to introduce country fixed-effects.

Finally, to test the robustness of our results, we performed some tests on the normality of the residuals. Using the Shapiro–Wilk test, we tested the null hypothesis that the sample came from a normally distributed population. In the Shapiro–Wilk test for normality, the p-value is based on the assumption that the distribution is normal. In our case, the p-value turned out to be extremely large (0.93), so we cannot reject the hypothesis that residuals are normally distributed.

10.7 Conclusions

This chapter presents results from our study of the impact of uncertainty and opportunistic renegotiations on bidding behavior in toll infrastructure concession contracts auctions. We first reviewed what the economic theory says about this topic and the peculiarities of such auctions, leading to the formulation of our three propositions. We tested these propositions using unique data gathered from a variety of sources. We showed that bidders bid less aggressively in toll road concession auctions when they expect more competition. We also found, in line with the theory, that the internalization of the winner's curse by bidders is larger for projects for which the common uncertainty is greater. Thus we pointed out the bid effects of uncertainty over the valuation of a contract. We also showed that in concession contracts, bidders bid more strategically in weaker institutional frameworks or in civil law countries where renegotiations are easier. These results suggest the necessity to improve the current theoretical framework for procurement policy and regulation by taking into account the impact of prospective later profitable renegotiation on equilibrium bidding behavior. In other words, our results show that the classical assumption of auction models that bidders are able to commit to bidding promises is not adequate. The theoretical framework should be extended to include the impact of not only the ex ante but also the ex post conditions on bidding behavior.

The policy implication of our results is not straightforward, however. While we find that asymmetric information overturns the common economic wisdom that more competition is always desirable, we also observe a systematic traffic overestimation due to methodological and behavioral sources. The short-term policy implication of our results therefore fits the standard view: governments should restrict entry, or favor negotiation over auction, in toll road concession auctions to encourage aggressive bidding. By contrast, the long-term policy implication of our results is that governments should consider keeping the procedure as open as possible to the extent that the internalization of the winner's curse by bidders reduces the systematic traffic overestimation and then reduces the likelihood that the procuring authority will have to renegotiate the contract, once the bidding competitors are gone. Additionally we find that bidders less internalize the winner's curse when procuring authorities release publicly their own traffic forecast prior to bidding. Thus procuring authorities interested in more aggressive bidding should consider releasing contract information to reduce information dispersion in toll road auction settings.

Notes

We gratefully acknowledge comments and suggestions from Claude Abraham, David Azema, Steven Berry, Luis Cabral, Eduardo Engel, Antonio Estache, Philip Haile, Gabriel Jacondino, Rui Manteigas, Rui Montero, Homero Neves, Charles Paradis, Vincent Piron, Maher Said, Stéphane Saussier, Karl Schlag, Jose Vassallo, Anne Yvrande, and participants at the CESifo workshop on The Economics of Infrastructure Provisioning: The (Changing) Role of the State, Venice, July 26–27 2013.

1. Maskin and Tirole (2008: 413) define a public–private partnership as "A long-term development and service contract between government and private partner. The government typically engages its partner both to develop the project and to operate and service it. The partner may bear substantial risk and even raise private finance. Its revenue derives from some combination of government payments and user fees."

2. We could assume that unbiased estimations are symmetrically distributed around the zero error, as assumed by many authors (Quinet 1998; Trujillo, Quinet, and Estache 2002; Standard and Poor's 2005). However, certain influential characteristic of transport forecasts suggest this assumption to be wrong. By influential characteristic, we mean that the forecast itself determines whether the forecast is tested. In other words, this means

that projects are not launched when the forecast is too low. Statistically unbiased influential forecasts should therefore appear optimistic because some forecasts remain untested. This effect could be called the "survivor's curse" because there are forecasts only for survivor projects, namely for projects for which there are already some positive error forecasts. Thus, while the bias (expected error) across all forecasts is zero, the bias for tested forecasts is positive. Survivors tend therefore to be disappointed (Ehrman and Shugan 1995). As a consequence the mere analysis of error's distributions does not allow any inferences about the bidders' strategy (Nunez 2007).

3. As first demonstrated by Milgrom and Weber (1982) for symmetric common-value environments, the information revealed publicly by losing bidders' exits in an ascending auction reduces both the severity of the winner's cruse and the informational rents obtained by the winner, leading to higher expected revenues than with a first-price sealed-bid auction.

4. This effect was questioned by Kagel and Levin (1986). They show that in presence of a winner's curse (i.e., bidders do not internalize the winner's curse), providing public information generates lower average winning bids and reduces seller's revenues. To the extent that the magnitude of the winner's curse decreases as the common uncertainty concerning the value of the auction decreases, public information will result in a downward revision in the most optimistic bidder's valuation of the auction. They point out that the differential response to public information conditional on the presence or absence of a winner's curse has practical implications that have largely gone unrecognized in the literature.

5. This was also a way for us to check the robustness of the results obtained with the public release of information criterion, since the public release of information can affect the number of bidders (if bidders base their decision to submit a bid on this type of information), implying that the coefficient of the *PUBLICINFO* variable crossed with the number of bidders may be biased.

6. Discussions with experts (from France, Chile, and Spain) and some independent regulatory authorities (Brazil, Portugal) also corroborate this assumption.

7. Our data do not include contracts after 2003. We need the facility to be built and to observe the actual traffic for few years after the opening of the facility in order to be able to capture the fact that bidders can manipulate traffic forecasts not only at the opening of the facility but also the traffic growth forecasts.

8. As can be noticed here, for some auctions only one bidder submitted a tender after the prequalification stage. We nevertheless take into account these auctions because the tendering was competitive.

9. IWe can expect the 2008 financial crisis to constrain the demand and hence increase the degree of common uncertainty over the future traffic, and so lead to less aggressive bidding behavior.

10. By this transformation, we reduce heteroscedasticity, and this allows a convenient interpretation of results that can be read directly as elasticities. The results are the same when the variables are not converted into logarithms, and also when the estimation method is maximum likelihood.

11. Because the public release of information can affect the number of bidders, we introduced the institutional variables only in the model with the length variable as a proxy for uncertainty, as it is truly exogenous.

12. Due to our limited number of observations, we could not introduce a country fixed effect.

References

Athey, Susan, and Philip A. Haile. 2007. Nonparametric approaches to auctions. In J. J. Heckman and E. Leamer, eds., *Handbook of Econometrics*, vol. 6. Amsterdam: Elsevier, 3847–3925.

Athias, Laure, and Stéphane Saussier. 2007. Un partenariat public privé rigide ou flexible? Théorie et application aux concessions routières à péage. *Revue Economique* 58 (3): 565–76.

Bikhchandani, Sushil, and John G. Riley. 1991. Equilibria in open common value auctions. *Journal of Economic Theory* 53 (1): 101–30.

Bulow, Jeremy, Ming Huang, and Paul Klemperer. 1999. Toeholds and takeovers. *Journal of Political Economy* 107 (3): 427–54.

Chong, Eshien. 2007. Collusion in auctions and contractual length: A theoretical analysis with an application to the French water sector. Mimeo.

De Silva, Dakshina, Timothy Dunne, Anuruddha Kankanamge, and Georgia Kosmopoulou. 2008. The impact of public information on bidding in highway procurement auctions. *European Economic Review* 52 (1): 150–81.

Ehrman, Chaim M., and Steven M. Shugan. 1995. The forecaster's dilemma. *Marketing Science* 24 (2): 123–47.

Engel, Eduardo, Ronald Fischer, and Alexander Galetovic. 2003. Privatizing highways in Latin America: Fixing what went wrong. *Journal of LACEA* 4: 129–58.

Engel, Eduardo, Ronald Fischer, and Alexander Galetovic. 2006a. Privatizing highways in the United States. *Review of Industrial Organization* 29: 27–53.

Engel, Eduardo, Ronald Fischer, and Alexander Galetovic. 2006b. Renegotiation without holdup: Anticipating spending and infrastructure concessions. Working paper 12399. NBER.

Engel, Eduardo, Ronald Fischer, and Alexander Galetovic. 2013. The basic public finance of public–private partnerships. *Journal of the European Economic Association* 11 (1): 83–111.

Estache, Antonio. 2006. PPI partnerships vs. PPI divorces in ldcs. *Review of Industrial Organization* 29 (1): 3–26.

Flyvbjerg, Bent, Nils Bruzelius, and Werner Rothengatter. 2003. *Megaprojects and Risk: An Anatomy of Ambition*. Cambridge, UK: Cambridge University Press.

Goeree, Jacob, and Theo Offerman. 2003. Competitive bidding in auctions with private and common values. *Economic Journal* 113 (489): 598–613.

Gomez-Ibanez, José A., and John R. Meyer. 1993. *Going Private: The International Experience with Transport Privatization*. Washington, DC: Brookings Institution.

Guasch, Luis J. 2004. *Granting and renegotiating infrastructure concessions: Doing it right. Report*. World Bank Institute.

Guasch, Luis J., *Jean-Jacques Laffont, and Stephane Straub.* 2003. *Renegotiation of concession contracts in Latin America.Discussion papers.* Edinburgh School of Economics, University of Edinburgh.

Guasch, Luis J., Jean-Jacques Laffont, and Stephane Straub. 2007. Concessions of infrastructure in Latin America: Government-led renegotiation. *Journal of Applied Econometrics* 22 (7): 1267–94.

Jofre-Bonet, Mireia, and Martin Pesendorfer. 2003. Estimation of a dynamic auction game. *Econometrica* 71 (5): 1443–89.

Kagel, John H., and Dan Levin. 1986. The winner's curse and public information in common value auctions. *American Economic Review* 76 (5): 894–920.

La Porta, Rafael, Florencio Lopez de Silanes, Andrei Shleifer, and Robert W. Vishny. 1998. Law and finance. *Journal of Political Economy* 106 (6): 1113–55.

Laffont, Jean-Jacques. 1997. Game theory and empirical economics: The case of auction data. *European Economic Review* 41: 1–35.

Laffont, Jean-Jacques. 2005. *Regulation and Development.* Collection Frederico Caffe Lectures. Cambridge, UK: Cambridge University Pres.

Maskin, Eric, and Jean Tirole. 2008. Public–private partnerships and government spending limits. *International Journal of Industrial Organization* 26 (2): 412–20.

Milgrom, Paul R., and Robert J. Weber. 1982. A theory of auctions and competitive bidding. *Econometrica* 50 (5): 1089–1122.

Nunez, Antonio. 2007. Sources of errors and biases in traffic forecasts for toll road concessions. PhD thesis, University of Lyon.

Porter, Robert H., and John D. Zona. 1993. Detection of bid rigging in procurement auctions. *Journal of Political Economy* 101 (3): 518–38.

Quinet, Emile. 1998. *Principes d'économie des transports.* Paris: Economica.

Schafer, Andreas. 2000. Regularities in travel demand: An international perspective. *Journal of Transportation and Statistics* 3 (3): 1–32.

Spulber, Daniel F. 1990. Auctions and contract enforcement. *Journal of Law Economics and Organization* 6:325–344.

Standard and Poor's. 2005. *Traffic forecasting risk in start-up toll facilities. Technical Report.* London: Standard and Poor's.

Standard and Poor's. 2005. *Traffic forecasting risk study update 2005-through ramp-up and beyond. Technical Report.* London: Standard and Poor's.

Trujillo, Lourdes, Emile Quinet, and Antonio Estache. 2002. Dealing with demand forecast games in transport privatization. *Transport Policy* 9: 325–34.

Yin, Pai-Ling. 2006. Information dispersion and auction prices. Working paper 02–024. Stanford Institute for Economic Policy Research.

11 Electoral Cycles and Renegotiation of Transport Infrastructure Concession Contracts

Julio C. Aguirre

11.1 Introduction

In the 1980s several Latin American countries implemented drastic political and economic reforms. One of the key elements of these reforms was the privatization of a majority of public utilities. This led to the involvement of the private sector in the construction and operation of public utilities under governmental regulation through the supervision of such contracts.

There is an extensive literature on the renegotiation of concession contracts that assesses the determinants of renegotiation, focusing on contractual clauses such as regulatory mechanisms, award criteria, and number of bidders in the auction of contracts, but there are few studies of the relationship between electoral cycles and renegotiation of contracts. This relationship is the topic of this chapter in which I apply quarterly times-series and hazard models to assess the relationship between electoral cycles and contract renegotiation.

Using a database of 27 transport infrastructure concession contracts from Peru (table 11.1) awarded since 1999, I find that the timing of national elections (i.e., the electoral cycles) significantly affects the incidence (and re-incidence) of the renegotiation of contracts. My results are robust to the inclusion of quarter periods both within and out of the electoral year period, and also to controlling for some contractual features (including the designing of the contracts and the manner in which they were bid).

My intention is to provide a perspective on the importance of institutional and regulatory supervision of transport infrastructure concession contracts in order to minimize political influences in contractual stability.

Table 11.1
Concessions of Peruvian transport infrastructure supervised by OSITRAN

Infrastructure	Year signed
Airports	
1. Jorge Chávez International Airport	2001
2. First group of regional airports (Iquitos, Pucallpa, Trujillo, Tarapoto, Cajamarca, Tumbes, Anta, Chachapoyas, Talara, Piura, Chiclayo y Pisco)	2006
3. Second group of regional airports (Andahuaylas, Ayacucho, Juliaca, Arequipa, Puerto Maldonado y Tacna) y Tacna)	2011
Roads	
4. IIRSA-North (Multimodal Amazon North Axis: Paita—Yurimaguas)	2005
5. Road Network No. 5 (Ancón—Huacho—Pativilca)	2003
6. Road Network No. 6 (Puente Pucusana—Cerro Cerro Azul—Ica)	2005
7. Sun Highway (Trujillo—Sullana)	2009
8. IIRSA South T5 (Azángaro—Juliaca; Puerto de Matarani and Ilo)	2007
9. IIRSA South T4 (Azángaro—Inambari)	2005
10. IIRSA South T3 (Inambari—Iñapari)	2005
11. IIRSA South T2 (Urcos—Inambari)	2005
12. IIRSA South T1 (Marcona—Urcos)	2007
13. Buenos Aires—Canchaque	2007
14. New Road (Mocupe—Cayaltí—Oyotún)	2009
15. Road Network 4 (Pativilca—Santa—Trujillo and Puerto Salaverry—Empalme R01N)	2009
16. Road Section: Chancay Roundabout/road/DV Pasamayo—Huaral—Acos	2009
17. IIRSA Center, Section 2	2010
18. Road Network DV Quilca, DV Arequipa (Reparticion) - DV Matarani—DV Moquegua—DV Ilo—Tacna—La Concordia*	2012
Railways	
19. Central Railway	1999
20. South and Southeast Railway	1999
21. Electric train—Line 1, Lima (Villa El Salvador—Av. Grau—San Juan de Lurigancho)	2011
Ports	
22. Matarani Port Terminal	1999
23. Muelle Sur New Container Port Terminal	2006
24. Paita Port Terminal	2009
25. Mineral Shipment Terminal	2011
26. Multipurpose North Terminal in the Port Terminal of Callao	2011
27. New Yurimaguas—Nueva Reforma Port Terminal	2011

Source: Online portal of OSITRAN: http://www.ositran.gob.pe/0/home.aspx.
Note: *Granted but not signed to date.

In the Peruvian case the institutional framework in the field of transport infrastructure includes four principal public institutions. The public agency in charge of designing the concession contracts, PROINVERSION, coordinates with the Ministry of Transportation and Communications (MTC) and the Ministry of Economy and Finance (MEF) the technical transport infrastructure needs for the country (roads, airports, ports, and railroads) and the economic feasibility of each such infrastructure (e.g., public–private partnerships). The contract is awarded to a private operator through a tendering process, delivered also by PROINVERSIÓN. After the signing of the concession contract by the private operator and the state (MTC), the transport infrastructure regulator (OSITRAN) steps in and begins supervising the contract for effective compliance.

The institutional framework before 1999 led to increased deployment of independent regulators with regulatory contracts in different countries (in that contracts supervised by independent regulators were thought to be sustainable and the integrity of the independent regulators to be intact; Eberhard 2007). A full analysis of the addenda of concession contracts in Peru in fact shows that as renegotiations had grown with each government (8, 24, and 37 modifications during Fujimori, Toledo, and Garcia mandates, respectively),[1] there are suggestions of political influences affecting contractual stability. I therefore consider a proxy variable for the election process.

For instance, the autonomy of the regulators could be questioned because every five years the Board of Director is changed subsequent to the election of the President of the Republic. The selection of these Board members is in two stages. In the first stage, an academic institution reviews the technical and academic qualifications of the candidates. In the second stage, a short list of the best three candidates is proposed to the elected President of the Republic, who then makes the final decision.[2] With regard to contracts, my results show that during electoral periods the rate of renegotiation rises (figures 11.1 and 11.2), likely due to the weakened autonomy of the regulatory body.

While no contract is perfect, it is essential to be aware of any imperfections of transaction costs (Coase 1937; Williamson 1995) that could set off the need to renegotiate.[3] Although ideally a renegotiation of a contract would result in a better contract that has a positive effect on social welfare, in reality frequent changes to contracts instead go against social interests, such as to extract extra rents for the firm signing the concession contract (contracts are even auctioned with a view toward

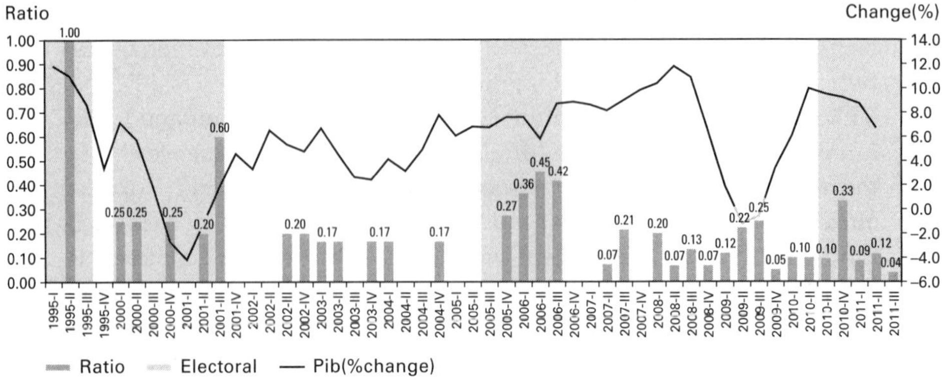

Figure 11.1
Incidence of renegotiation and quarterly electoral cycles

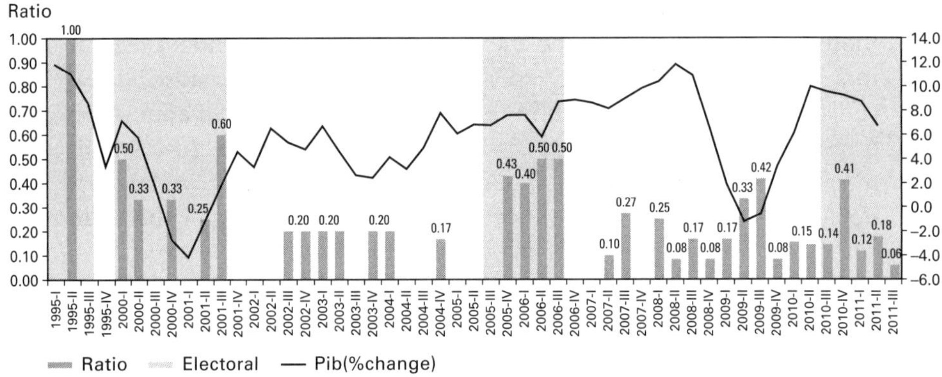

Figure 11.2
Re-incidence of renegotiation and quarterly electoral cycles

renegotiations of the terms in the future), an electoral advantage for the government (promising benefits to voters), and mutual benefits (capture and/or corruption features).

According to the Peru´s transport infrastructure regulator, OSITRAN, the main justifications for amendments to infrastructure concession contracts are (1) the need to modify technical details as work progresses, which represents 47 percent of renegotiation cases, and entails additional investments for the construction of the infrastructure to proceed; (2) loss of "funding" and "assets of the concession," each at 10 percent, whereby banks may limit financial support and hold up the construction of the infrastructure or threaten to seize ownership and management of the concession; (3) "budget difficulties," which represent 8 percent of the renegotiations (and are related to public–private partnership highway concessions), necessitating upgrades of the initial budgets (as developed based on preliminary studies before a concession is approved) for additional works and new traffic flow conditions of roads; (4) "payments to the concession operator" and "extension of the duration of the contract," each at 6 percent, whereby the operator recognizes that the needed additional work could affect the duration terms of the contract; (5) "land expropriation" and "completion of the contract" disputes, each at 5 percent; (6) arbitrage disputes, at 4 percent; (7) "tariffs settings" and "retribution to the state," each at 3 percent; and, (8) "others" categories, including modifications to the first technical design and to salaries, insurance, and guarantees.

Repeated renegotiation of contracts is not beneficial from an institutional perspective (Guasch 2004). Of the current 26 transport infrastructure concession contracts supervised by Peru's regulator authority (table 11.1), OSITRAN, 20 have been modified (76 percent) with 78 addendums (up to April 2013), and the average time from award to first renegotiation is 1.82 years.[4] According to the World Bank, Peru has the highest rate of renegotiation in the Latin America region (*El Comercio* (Lima), May 3, 2011).

In section 11.2, I consider the literature and theoretical framework; in section 11.3, I discuss the data, methodology, and results; and in section 11.4, I provide some concluding remarks.

11.2 Literature and Theoretical Framework

The conceptual framework in the procurement and renegotiation literature deals with transaction costs and asymmetric information topics, which are relevant in developing economies because of difficulties the governments face in enforcement.[5] As a consequence the degree of government commitment influences the probability of renegotiation.

The theory of transaction costs (Coase 1937; Williamson 1985) emphasizes the high costof designing complete contracts, to avoid unforeseen contingencies. The theory of asymmetric information (Laffont and Maskin 1982; Myerson 1982) focuses on the adverse selection problem (ex ante, during the signing of a concession contract, the existence of private information about its type: higher/lower productivity) and the moral hazard problem (ex post, in the implementation of the contract, the possession of private information under the operator's control: higher/lower effort to reduce costs) presence in incomplete contracts.[6]

My analyses are based on the regulation model of Guasch et al. (2006). In particular, using their model allows one to arrive at a probability measure of renegotiation,[7] $\Pr(renegotiation) = (1-v)(1-\pi(x^E))$, where the right side is the government´s "tolerance for renegotiation," which depends on x^E; this is the investment in enforcement as understood to be due to a regulatory agency. In consequence the regulatory agency could be constrained by politics and state capture, thus affecting social welfare. Then, empirically, the probability of renegotiation would be expected to be affected by the results of recent elections (Guasch et al. 2008).

Using this model, Guasch et al. (2003, 2006, 2008) and Guasch (2003, 2004) find that conditions conducive to renegotiations include a mix of contract stipulations, regulatory settings, and economic shocks. Renegotiations were most likely to take place during recessions or after devaluations, and after elections when concessions are awarded by the president-elect's Board put in place in the regulatory agency and regulated by a price cap mechanism and each contract's minimum income guarantee. These authors showed that when investment is present, the incidence of renegotiation is reduced, but in a poor institutional environment (captured by an index of bureaucratic quality) renegotiations increase. In particular, these authors used a probit analysis and a dummy variable to indicate if the year was an election year, in order to capture the behavior of a new administration in honoring the contract signed by a previous administration. They find that electoral cycles had a marginal effect of 3 to 5 percent on the probability of renegotiation.[8]

Alternatively, in my study of the Peruvian transport infrastructure concession contracts, I use quarterly time series to assess how electoral timing affects the speed of contract renegotiations in terms of over a monthly timeframe. I take a broad theoretical and/or empirical perspective and consider the literature on the determinants of renegotiations of concession contracts in terms of the relationship between election cycles and modification of concession contracts. In this regard my study also contributes to the discussion of how the relation between electoral cycles and renegotiation can be motivated more on political interests than technical features. Indeed, according to Transparency International (2006):

> ... political corruption is often associated to the electoral cycle and relates primarily to election funding .... Political corruption often manifests itself as lobbying or as extortion, but also through *revolving door* moves of senior politicians directly into high business positions, often in companies whose activities were previously regulated or controlled by the same politician.

Corruption has thus been observed to be linked to public procurement during the stage of contract design, specifically, when contract renegotiation is permitted or performed introducing substantial changes in the bidding process.

In my study I likewise attempt to determine whether capture, corruption, or populism interests during electoral periods can affect the stability of concession contracts. In the literature, for example, De Brux et al. (2011) analyze the renewals and contract renegotiations in the case of car parks in France. They argue that during the renegotiation the discretionary power of the authority determines the type of contract signed (Delegate Management contract or Public Procurement contract). If the parties are satisfied when the contracts are signed, the probability of contract renewal will be greater than if the parties are adversarial. The study found, among other things, that (1) the speed of the first renegotiation, understood as a proxy of private contractual opportunism (as interpreted by Guasch 2004), decreases the likelihood of renewal and (2) electoral cycle (the change of mayor in the final year of the contract) reduces the likelihood of renewal, as could be due to the change of authority, be it change of party or an impending breach.

Because of the limited information available on money transfers from the government to the utility companies, I do not analyze whether renegotiations lead to welfare losses. Some authors have analyzed the relationship between electoral cycles and the public budget. For instance, Schady (2000) uses province-level data on monthly expenditures, socioeconomic indicators, and electoral outcomes to assess political influences on the timing and geographic distribution of FONCODES[9] expenditures in Peru between 1991 and 1995. Schady (2000) concludes that FONCODES projects were directed at provinces in which the marginal political effect of expenditures was likely to be the greatest. Mejía et al. (2008) explore the factors that explain budgetary allocations for road infrastructure in Colombia during the first Uribe administration. They find evidence suggesting the predominance of political criteria and that technical criteria did not play a role in decisions on investment in road infrastructure. This supports the hypothesis that spending on road infrastructure is a populist measure, since those municipalities in which Uribe-sponsored Consejos Comunales met received an additional \$14.1 million in comparison to municipalities where such meetings did not take place.

11.3 Data, Methodology, and Results

Taking into consideration the review of the literature on this subject published thus far, in my study I use quarterly time-series and hazard analysis in an attempt to show that electoral cycles affect the rate of renegotiation of concession contracts.

11.3.1 Quarter-Yearly Time-Series Analysis

I use 75 observations (quarters-yearly) from 27 contracts signed between 1994 and 2013 (first quarter) administered by the Peruvian regulator, OSITRAN.[10] To test the hypothesis that the electoral timing affects the incidence (and re-incidence) of renegotiation, I estimate the following equation:

$$\begin{aligned} \textit{Incidence of renegotiation}_t = \alpha_t + \theta \textit{Quarter}_t + \gamma\, \textit{Electoral cycle}_t \\ + \beta \textit{GDP}_t + \varepsilon_t\,, \end{aligned} \tag{1}$$

where *Incidence of renegotiation* is measured as the ratio number of modified concession contracts in the quarter-yearly t to stock of concession contracts (modified and unmodified) supervised by OSITRAN in the quarter-yearly t; γ is the parameter of interest for the dummy *Electoral cycle* taking the value 1 if the quarter-yearly t is an electoral period (between the July and September quarter to between the April and June quarter);[11] *GDP* is the current quarter-yearly gross domestic product (percentage change), and ε is the error term. I also include four quarter-yearly dummies *within* the electoral period and two quarter-yearly dummies, each one *out of* the electoral period (one dummy before the July to September quarter and the other one after the April to June quarter). Then I regress the same explanatory variables on the dependent variable *Re-incidence of renegotiation,* which is measured as the number of concession contracts modified more than once in the quarter-yearly t to the stock of concession contracts already modified supervised by OSITRAN in the quarter-yearly t. The summary statistics are reported in table 11.2.

The series used in these estimations are stationary according to standard unit root tests.[12] To control for heteroscedasticity and serial correlation, I use the Newey–West test to compute the standard errors.[13]

Table 11.2
Summary statistics

	Mean	Standard deviation	Observations
Incidence of renegotiation[+]	0.102	0.166	75
Re-incidence of renegotiation[+]	0.107	0.168	75
Quarter-yearly gross domestic product (percentage change) [+]	5.343	3.927	75

Notes: (+) Quarter-yearly data for transport infrastructure concession contracts of Peru, for the period July to September 1994 to end of March 2013; (++) Quarter-yearly data is only available until July to September 2011.

Column 1 of tables 11.3 and 11.4 reports the estimates of equation (1).[14] The coefficient for the electoral cycle is positive and statistically significant. The value of the coefficient implies an increase of incidence and re-incidence of renegotiations of 11.2 and 11.8 percent, respectively, during an electoral period. Also column 2 of tables 11.3 and 11.4 shows that results are robust to including the GDP, as political considerations (Guasch et al. 2008).

Additional Examinations

In order to ensure that the results have a causal interpretation, I explored many alternative specifications. Columns 3 to 6 of tables 11.3 and 11.4 include the coefficients of the first three quarter-yearly dummies *within* the electoral period renegotiation. The coefficient on the electoral cycle remains positive and statistically significant, except on the fourth quarter-yearly dummy (April to June), suggesting that the electoral quarter-yearly period, when the election process (on April) occurs, increases the incidence and re-incidence of renegotiations on 29.7 and 30.0 percent, respectively.

In addition, I evaluated if the effect of the electoral cycle extends beyond the electoral period, a quarter-yearly previous the beginning and a quarter-yearly after the ending of the electoral period. Columns 7 and 8 of tables 11.3 and 11.4 show that the coefficient on both quarter-yearly dummies each one *out of* the electoral period (one dummy before the July to September quarter and the other one after the April to June quarter) are not statistically significant. As column 9 of tables 11.3 and 11.4 shows, the simultaneous inclusion of controls and dummies reinforce the positive effect of the electoral cycle on the incidence

Table 11.3
Effects of electoral cycles on the incidence of renegotiation

	Dependent variable: incidence of renegotiation								
	(1)	(2)	(3)	(4)	(5)	(6)	(7)	(8)	(9)
Electoral quarter	0.112**	0.108**	0.162**	0.112*	0.122*	0.0328	0.105*	0.123**	0.343**
	(0.0556)	(0.0524)	(0.0637)	(0.0667)	(0.0664)	(0.0394)	(0.0529)	(0.0516)	(0.145)
GDP		0.00406	0.00396	0.0041	0.0041	0.00465	0.00418	0.00306	0.00356
		(0.00544)	(0.00541)	(0.00553)	(0.00539)	(0.00474)	(0.00548)	(0.00541)	(0.00478)
D1 *within* electoral period			-0.219***						-0.386**
			(0.0664)						(0.148)
D2 *within* electoral period				-0.0187					-0.236
				(0.0975)					(0.164)
D3 *within* electoral period					-0.0588				-0.266
					(0.0939)				(0.162)
D4 *within* electoral period						0.297**			
						(0.147)			
D. *ex ante out of* electoral period							-0.045		-0.029
							(0.0276)		(0.0265)
D. *ex post out of* electoral period								0.202	0.2
								(0.135)	(0.139)
Constant	0.0720***	0.0513	0.0519	0.0512	0.0511	0.0484	0.0532	0.0417	0.0409
	(0.0158)	(0.0339)	(0.0338)	(0.0344)	(0.0338)	(0.0312)	(0.0343)	(0.0299)	(0.0273)
Observations	75	75	75	75	75	75	75	75	75
R-squared	0.09	0.099	0.188	0.1	0.106	0.262	0.102	0.174	0.368

Notes: Newey–West heteroscedasticity—and autocorrelation- consistent standard errors are in the parenthesis. All models are estimated by OLS. D1 to D4 and D. are dummy variables.*Significant at the 10 percent level; **significant at the 5 percent level; ***significant at the 1 percent level.

Table 11.4
Effects of electoral cycles on the re-incidence of renegotiation

	Dependent variable: re-incidence of renegotiation								
	(1)	(2)	(3)	(4)	(5)	(6)	(7)	(8)	(9)
Electoral quarter	0.118**	0.114**	0.170***	0.117*	0.130*	0.0382	0.111**	0.130**	0.352**
	(0.0561)	(0.0527)	(0.0636)	(0.0662)	(0.0668)	(0.0413)	(0.0532)	(0.0519)	(0.14)
GDP		0.0042	0.00409	0.00421	0.00424	0.00479	0.0043	0.00319	0.00367
		(0.00556)	(0.00555)	(0.00565)	(0.0055)	(0.00486)	(0.0056)	(0.00554)	(0.0049)
D1 *within* electoral period			-0.226***						-0.394***
			(0.0673)						(0.143)
D2 *within* electoral period				-0.0107					-0.232
				(0.103)					(0.163)
D3 *within* electoral period					-0.0635				-0.272*
					(0.0935)				(0.157)
D4 *within* electoral period						0.300**			
						(0.142)			
D. *ex ante out of* electoral period							-0.0423		-0.0261
							(0.0314)		(0.0309)
D. *ex post out of* electoral period								0.204	0.202
								(0.133)	(0.137)
Constant	0.0751***	0.0538	0.0544	0.0538	0.0536	0.0508	0.0556	0.0441	0.0433
	(0.0161)	(0.035)	(0.035)	(0.0354)	(0.0348)	(0.0323)	(0.0354)	(0.0312)	(0.0288)
Observations	75	75	75	75	75	75	75	75	75
R-squared	0.098	0.107	0.199	0.107	0.114	0.269	0.11	0.181	0.376

Notes: Newey–West heteroscedasticity—and autocorrelation consistent standard errors are in the parenthesis. All models are estimated by OLS. D1 to D4 and D. are dummy variables.*Significant at the 10 percent level; **significant at the 5 percent level; ***significant at the 1 percent level.

and impact of re-contract renegotiation, 34.3 and 35.2 percent, respectively.

The results in column 6 of tables 11.3 and 11.4 give the correlation between electoral cycle and the incidence and re-incidence of renegotiations of concession contracts. This is significant only during the electoral period, mainly during the last quarter-yearly of that period when election is in process. The numerical result appears to support the theoretical result of Guasch et al. (2003), which is that political cycles are likely to cause renegotiations when government accepts renegotiation of concessions contracts for firms with which its interests are aligned.

11.3.2 Hazard Analysis

For the hazard of renegotiation, I use survival analysis to model the time elapsed between the granting of a concession contract and its renegotiation. A nonnegative random variable T is defined here as the duration between the granting of a contract and its renegotiation. Let us define the probability that a concession contract that has occupied a (unmodified) state for a time t leaves it in the short interval of length dt after t. The probability that such a contract leaves the state within an interval dt at or after t is $P(t \leq T < t+dt \mid T \geq t)$, where the conditioning event that $T \geq t$ is just the event that the state is still occupied at t, and has not left before then. Dividing this probability by dt, I get the average probability of leaving per unit time period over a short time interval after t, and by considering this average over shorter and shorter intervals, the hazard function takes the form

$$\theta(t) = \lim_{dt \to 0} \frac{P(t \leq T < t+dt \mid T \geq t)}{dt} = \frac{f(t)}{1-F(t)} = \frac{f(t)}{S(t)}, \tag{2}$$

which is the instantaneous rate of leaving per unit time period at t.[15]

The expression $\theta(t)dt$ can be interpreted as the probability of exit from the unmodified state in the short interval of length dt after t, conditional on the state being occupied at t. It is also perfectly sensible to talk about the probability of exit in the short interval of length dt after t *without* the condition $T \geq t$, but this is a quite different concept from the hazard function. The hazard function gives the probability that a contract will be modified at its twentieth month of operation whereas the unconditional concept gives the probability that a concession contract will be modified at the twentieth month of operation. In terms of relative frequencies, for example, $\theta(20)dt$ gives the proportion of a twenty-month operating contract that is modified within dt at its twentieth month of operation. The unconditional concept gives the proportion of contracts modified within dt at the twentieth month of operation.

Let the duration distribution function be $P(T < t) = F(t),\ t \geq 0$, at the point t, and the associated probability density function be $f(t) = dF(t)/dt$. $f(t)$is sometimes known as the unconditional failure rate. Survival analysis makes use of the complement to the cumulative distribution function and is written as $S(t) = 1 - F(t) = P(T \geq t)$. That is, the survival function that gives the contract's probability of survival remains unmodified to t, and also can be expressed as[16]

$$S(t) = \exp\left\{-\int_0^t \theta(s)ds\right\}, \tag{3}$$

and, from (1) and (2) as

$$f(t) = \theta(t)\exp\left\{-\int_0^t \theta(s)ds\right\}. \tag{4}$$

For a parametric estimation, I introduced regressors (time-invariant and time-variant covariates) as relevant characteristics (covariates) from the concession contracts data, into the hazard function. Thus at t this is defined as being conditional on the value of X:

$$\theta(t;x) = \lim_{dt \to 0} \frac{P(t \leq T < t + dt \mid T \geq t, x)}{dt} = \frac{f(t;x)}{S(t;x)} = \exp\left\{-\int_0^t \theta(s;x)ds\right\} \tag{5}$$

with time-invariant covariates and

$$\theta(t;X(t)) = \lim_{dt \to 0} \frac{P(t \leq T < t + dt \mid T \geq t, X(t+dt))}{dt} = \exp\left\{-\int_0^t \theta(s;X(s)ds\right\} \tag{6}$$

with time-variant covariates.

Even if an underlying duration is properly viewed as being continuous, measurements are necessarily discrete. When measurements are fairly precise, it is sensible to treat the durations as continuous random variables. But when the measurements are coarse—for example, monthly or even weekly—it can be important to account for the discreteness of the estimation (Wooldridge 2010).

Thus, for the parametric estimation, I estimated a discrete-time model based on Jenkins's (1995, 2005) "easy estimation" methods, applying a standard binary dependent variable model, in which for each concession contract there were as many data rows as there were time intervals at risk of the event occurring for each contract. If concession contract *i*'s survival time is censored, the binary dependent variable is equal to 0 for all *i*'s spell months; if contract *i*'s survival time is not censored, the binary dependent variable is equal to 0 for all but the last of *i*'s spell months (month 1, …, T_{i-1}) and equal to 1 for the last month (month T_i). Thus I used a panel dataset in which each cross-sectional observation was a vector of binary responses with covariates. Because of the sequential nature of the data, the time-varying covariates could be easily introduced (Wooldridge 2010).

The discrete-time models were estimated by maximum likelihood,[17] and I used a discrete-time proportional hazard model (i.e., a complementary log-log) and a nonproportional hazard specification "logistic" model. The hazard model with time-invariant can be written as $\theta(t;x) = k(x)\lambda_0(t)$, where $k(\cdot) > 0$ is a positive function of x and $\lambda_0(t) > 0$ is the baseline hazard. This is common to all the concession contracts. Individual hazard functions differ proportionately based on the function $k(x)$ of observed covariates (explanatory variables described above). $k(\cdot)$ can be parameterized as $k(x) = \exp(x\beta)$, where β is the vector of parameters I am interested in. Thus $\log\theta(t;x) = z(t) = x\beta + \log\lambda_0(t)$ and β_j measure the semielasticity of the hazard with respect to x_j.[18] I used the complementary log-log ("cloglog") discrete-time hazard function, $p(t)$, where

$$\log[-\log(1-p(t))] = z(t) \Rightarrow p(t) = 1 - \exp[-\exp(z(t))]. \tag{7}$$

The cloglog has the property that the resulting model is a discrete-time counterpart of an underlying continuous-time proportional hazard model (Prentice and Gloeckler 1978).

The available dataset for the hazard exercise includes 26 contracts data—3 airports, 14 roads, 3 railways, and 6 ports—regulated and supervised by OSITRAN and granted between 2003 and 2011 (table 11.1), totaling 522 observations (right censoring).[19]

For the explanatory variables, in order to capture the relationship between electoral cycles and the hazard of renegotiation, I used a dummy variable that takes the value of 1 if the month belongs to an electoral period and 0 otherwise. I expected to find a positive relationship.

In addition I considered as covariates other explanatory variables (some similar to those used by Guasch 2004 in his probit analysis), given that many renegotiations in short periods of time could be also explained by (1) the designing stage of the contract, when the mechanism of regulation of the transport infrastructure (a dummy variable 1 if a price cap scheme with RPI-X is considered and 0 otherwise) and a percentage of land area are allocated to the operator (a dummy variable 1 if 100 percent of land was allocated to the operator before subscription of the contract and 0 otherwise); (2) the awarding stage of the concession process, when a number of firms compete in the auction and meet the awarding criteria (taking 1 if the selection criteria implied an economic transfer from the firm to the government and 0 otherwise); and (3) institutional and economic conjectural factors regarding the experience and the squared experience of the regulator measured in years at the month of renegotiation and the monthly gross domestic production percentage change (to account for a possible impact of economic cycles). I also introduced dummy transport sectors (railways, airport, port and roads).

I expected that the hazard of renegotiations would increase if the mechanism of regulation did not consider productivity gains (price cap without RPI-X)[20] and if land was not fully granted to the winning bidder. Summary statistics on these variables show that frequent renegotiations occurred mostly in the case of contracts with a price cap without the RPI-X schemes and a percentage of allocated land to the operator below 100 percent (table 11.5). Likewise I expected a negative impact of *bidders* because a competitive process (more than one bidder) gives the contract to the efficient firm,[21] reducing the rate of renegotiation), and a positive impact when the award *criteria* imply an economic transfer, since a firm that could not fulfill the contract may bid the higher offer (the winner curse). The descriptive data show that frequent renegotiations occurred mostly when the auction was not competitive (few bidders pursuing the concession contract) and the criteria of selection in the auction implied a monetary transfer (lowest subsidy and/or a canon as the highest periodical payment from the concessionaire to the government).

Last, I expected that the more experienced regulator could limit the incidence of renegotiation and that the monthly gross domestic production percentage change would account for the influence of the economic cycle on the moral hazard of renegotiation.[22]

In table 11.6 I report the estimates of the discrete-time complementary log-log model (equation 7) concerning the transport sector

Table 11.5
Summary statistics of explanatory variables

Variable		Modified No	Modified Yes
Mechanism of regulation	RPI-X		4 (23.53)
	No RPI-X	4 (100.00)	13 (76.47)
Percentage of lands given to the operator	<100	4 (100.00)	11 (64.71)
	100		6 (35.29)
	1	1 (25.00)	11 (64.71)
	2		4 (23.53)
Bidders	3		2 (11.76)
	4	1 (25.00)	
	5	1 (25.00)	
	10	1 (25.00)	
Selection	No transfer	4 (100.00)	3 (17.65)
criteria	Transfer		14 (82.35)
Regulatory experience (years)	mean	12.25	7.53
Electoral	No		6 (35,29)
	Yes		11 (64,71)

Notes: The last column describes how many contracts were (and not) modified (in general over the 21 concession contracts analyzed). The sum of values in each block is equal to the number of observations. Percentages in relation to the total of a column are shown in parenthesis.

dummies. In column 1 the coefficient on the electoral cycles shows that during an electoral period the moral hazard of renegotiation of transport concession contracts had an increase of 5.23 percent.

The remaining columns of table 11.6 show the effects of the electoral cycle with alternative specifications; note that this increases the moral hazard of renegotiation of contracts by 3.3 to 5.3 percent. The magnitudes are similar to those found by Guasch (2004). Indeed the results remained unchanged when I considered the mechanism of regulation and the percentage of land area allocated to the operator before subscription of the contract (columns 2, 3, and 4), or the number of firms competing in the auction and the awarding criteria (columns 5, 6, and 7), or the experience and squared experience of the regulator and monthly gross domestic production percentage change (columns 8, 9, 10, and 11). In particular, besides the electoral cycle, the mechanism of regulation, the percentage of land allocated to the firm before subscription of the contract, the number of bidders, the award criteria and the

Table 11.6
Marginal effects of explanatory variables on hazard of renegotiation

	Dependent variable: Hazard of renegotiation											
	(1)	(2)	(3)	(4)	(5)	(6)	(7)	(8)	(9)	(10)	(11)	(12)
electoral	0.0523***	0.0407**	0.0494**	0.00617**	0.0378**	0.0384**	0.0341**	0.0334*	0.0529***	0.0338*	0.00393*	0.00119
	(0.0196)	(0.0170)	(0.0211)	(0.00309)	(0.0163)	(0.0174)	(0.0161)	(0.0172)	(0.0201)	(0.0176)	(0.00212)	(0.000901)
Mechanism		-0.244		-1.000***							-1.000***	-1.000
of regulation		(0.180)		(6.24e-05)							(5.49e-05)	(0.000)
land			0.0525	1.000***							1.000***	0.998***
			(0.0509)	(4.94e-05)							(4.70e-05)	(0.0230)
bidders					-0.00843***		-0.00543				-0.000760	-0.000203
					(0.00308)		(0.00391)				(0.000702)	(0.000188)
criteria						0.0283**	0.0144				0.00171	-0.000154
						(0.0114)	(0.0127)				(0.00203)	(0.000377)
expreg								0.0103**		0.0105**		0.000597
								(0.00523)		(0.00472)		(0.000517)
expreg2								-0.000696**		-0.000704**		-3.72e-05
								(0.000335)		(0.000319)		(3.34e-05)
pibvar									-0.000544	-6.70e-05		
									(0.00184)	(0.000581)		
lnj	0.0143**	0.0153***	0.0131**	0.00249***	0.0108*	0.0135**	0.0113*	0.0120**	0.0143**	0.0120**	0.00194**	0.000552
	(0.00622)	(0.00557)	(0.00585)	(0.000875)	(0.00562)	(0.00651)	(0.00598)	(0.00605)	(0.00618)	(0.00608)	(0.000874)	(0.000571)
Dummies sector	Yes	Yes	Yes	Yes	Yes	Yes	Yes	Yes	Yes	Yes	Yes	Yes
Observations	522	522	522	522	522	522	522	522	522	522	522	522

Notes: Standard errors in parenthesis clustered at transport sector level (ports, airports, roads and railroads). The model estimated is the complementary log-log model. * Significant at the 10 percent level; ** significant at the 5 percent level; *** significant at the 1 percent level.

regulator´s experience have statistically significant effects and the expected signs on the hazard of renegotiation of transport concession contracts.

11.4 Conclusion and Discussion

I applied quarter-yearly time-series and duration analyses on a database of 26 concession contracts transport infrastructure to identify whether electoral cycles have an effect on the renegotiation of contracts.

In this chapter I report the results. I found the incidence and re-incidence of renegotiation of concession contracts to increase during election periods. The results are robust to the inclusion of coefficients of quarter-yearly dummies *within* the electoral period renegotiation and quarter-yearly dummies *out of* the electoral period (one dummy before the July–September quarter and the other one after the April–June quarter). I also ran a survival analysis for reassurance that the electoral cycle has an effect on the hazard of renegotiation of concession contracts. The results turned out to be statistically significant when I considered covariates such as the mechanism of regulation, the percentage of land allocated to the firm before subscription of the contract, the number of bidders, the award criteria, and the regulator´s experience.

Following Montesinos and Saavedra (2012), the results reveal an imperfection of concession contracts and suggest a change of criteria for the future design of contracts That is, both intrinsic (i.e., mechanism of regulation, the percentage of land allocated to the firm before subscription of the contract, the number of bidders, the award criteria) and extrinsic (the regulator´s experience, the economic environment, the election process) aspects of a contract should be reviewed carefully in order to not affect its stability.

Some inferences from my results are as follows: renegotiations seem to be influenced by electoral votes for a certain candidate or party (or populism) and/or by corruption or capture by interest groups. So there is political risk to the extent to which government interests are aligned with those of the private operator. Further work on such influence would need to consider actual political changes. Likely asymmetries will appear depending on whether the previous government cared more or less for the rents of a firm than its successor (Aubert and Laffont 2004).

However, even I need more accurate data to investigate such potential underlying factors. I only considered results that suggest a weaknesses or vulnerability in the institutional strength of Peru's regulatory framework, but this leaves the door open to political influences or interest groups pressures, as may ultimately affect the welfare of society due to the temporary instability of negotiated contracts.

Any influence of election cycles on the renegotiation of contracts would ultimately affect the expected results of ex ante competition through the granting of the contracts, as a strategy to generate rents ex post. In consequence a policy measure that prevents political influence on the technical decisions of regulatory bodies could be implemented by moving elections of presidents or directors of these regulatory bodies to a time period that does not coincide with the presidential elections of the country. A good discussion is provided by Gabillon and Martirmort (2004) on how the design of credible monetary institutions can ensure economic stability. In the principal–agent literature, the inflationary bias due to the time inconsistency of monetary policy has been shown to be preventable by delegating the implementation of contracts to a central banker who is separate from the government party. This party separation is often considered the main ingredient of the central bank´s independence from the political sphere because it can shield monetary policy from the day-to-day influence of political authorities and from fluctuations in the preferences of the political principals.

Presently I can only prove my results intuitively rather than empirically. As I mentioned in this chapter, Guasch (2004) and Guasch et al. (2003) come closest to providing an empirical estimation of the main determinants of renegotiation of concession contracts in Latin America and the Caribbean. Their studies show the renegotiation of concession contracts to be higher (in the order) in the sectors of water and sanitation (74.4 percent), transportation (54.7 percent), and energy (9.7 percent), in Mexico, Brazil, Argentina, Colombia, Chile, Dominican Republic, Peru, Honduras, Guatemala, Venezuela, Trinidad and Tobago, Costa Rica, Panama, and Uruguay, which together have almost 30 percent of concession contracts in the Latin America region. They find the election process to be a determinant of the renegotiation of concession contracts, and this creates an interesting opportunity for future research that would control for political parties.

Notes

Julio C. Aguirre, Universidad del Pacífico (Peru), aguirre_jc@up.edu.pe. I thank Martin Rossi for useful comments and suggestions and acknowledge the invaluable help of Francisco Taquiri and Gian Carlos Silva. Also special acknowledge to CESifo Group Munich´s sponsorship for presentation of this chapter at the CESifo Venice Summer Institute workshop on "The Economics of Infrastructure Provisioning: The (Changing) Role of the State" in July 2013.

1. According to information provide by Legal Area of OSITRAN.

2. For the 2011 presidential elections, two forerunner candidates asked the outgoing government to postpone the election of the Board of Director of Regulators until after the presidential election, to be one of them who choose the authority (*El Comercio* (Lima), June 3, 2011). In 2012, after two consecutive contests, it was the elected President of the Board of Transportation regulator. The first-best two candidates in the two first rounds were set aside despite the fact that they fulfilled the technical and academic qualifications necessary to such functions.

3. It is not possible for contracting parties to define ex ante or predict all the possible contingencies that may occur after the signing of a contract. Moreover, even if this were possible, it would be very expensive to explicitly write all such contingencies into a contract and to expect that courts or officials would be able to check all actions under each contingency in order to enforce them (Tirole 1999).

4. Guasch (2004) found that renegotiation incidence and average time until renegotiation in the transport sector in Latin America and the Caribbean was 55 percent and 3.12 years, respectively.

5. The 2014 World Development Report (World Bank 2013) and the Global Competitiveness Report 2014 (from the Global Economic Forum) locate Peru in the latter relative position regarding institutional requirements.

6. See Guasch (2004) for details on the theoretical foundations of renegotiation.

7. The formal and extended development of this model can be found in Guasch et al. (2006).

8. The author uses a database over more than 1,000 concession contracts in various countries in Latin America and the Caribbean in the water, transport, energy, and telecom sectors over the period 1985 to 2000.

9. FONCODES, the Fund for Cooperation in Social Development, was created by President Alberto Fujimori in 1981.

10. The dataset is available by request.

11. In Peru the elections always occur in April (every five years). However, the campaigns of political parties usually begin a half year before the elections.

12. According to the augmented Dickey–Fuller test statistic, the null hypothesis that the series has unit root is rejected. All results are as mentioned but none shown were available from the author upon request.

13. I set the lag truncation value at 4, rejecting the null hypothesis that the series are heteroscedastic and serial correlated.

14. The results remain robust when I do not consider a road concession contract awarded in 1994, 4 years before the creation of the regulator (OSITRAN).

15. Equation (1) can be understood as $\theta(t) = Risk = P(Failure)/P(Survival)$, where *Failure* is the unconditional probability that an event will occur, *Survival* is the probability that "up until now" the event has not yet occurred, and *Risk* is the conditional failure rate—given the event has not yet occurred, what are the chances that it will occur? [https://www.iser.essex.ac.uk/resources/survival-analysis-with-stata, date accessed: June 12, 2011].

16. For the detailed mathematical derivation of the moral hazard and survival functions in nonparametric and parametric estimations see Lancaster (1990) and Jenkins (2005).

17. See Jenkins (1995) and Wooldridge (2010) for the construction of the likelihood function.

18. If x_j is the log of an underlying variable, say x_j=log(z_j), β_j is the elasticity of the hazard with respect to z_j.

19. This means that at the time of observation, in those cases where renegotiations had not yet occurred, the total time between entry and exit from the state is unknown.

20. Regarding this variable, Guasch (2004) considers price cap versus rate of return (e.g., a proxy of allocation of risks) rather than a price cap with or without RPI-X schemes. Guasch finds that the probability of renegotiation increases when a price cap mechanism is used.

21. Instead of number of bidders, Guasch (2004) considers the "type of award criteria": competitive process vs. noncompetitive process (direct adjudication or bilateral negotiations). He finds that competitive process increases the probability of renegotiations.

22. Guasch (2004) considers both the rate of growth of GDP and the evolution of real exchange rate as a proxy of macroeconomic shocks. I only consider the former.

References

Aubert, C., and J.-J. Laffont. 2004. Political renegotiation of regulatory contracts. Mimeo. Toulouse.

Coase, R. 1937. The nature of the firm. *Economica 4: 386–405. Reprinted in Oliver E. Williamson and Sidney Winter, eds., 1991. The Nature of the Firm: Origins, Evolution, Development. New York: Oxford University Press, 18–33.*

De Brux, J., J. Beuve, and S. Saussier. 2011. Renegotiations and contract renewals in public private agreements—An empirical analysis. http://chaire-eppp.org/EPPP-annual-conference-2011/program. Accessed April 4, 2011.

Eberhard, A. 2007. Infrastructure regulation in developing countries: An exploration of hybrid and transitional models. Working paper 4. Public–Private Infrastructure Advisory Facility.

El Comercio (Lima), May 3, 2011, B-1.

El Comercio (Lima), June 3, 2011, B-13.

http://www.ositran.gob.pe/repositorioaps/0/0/jer/presentacion_revista/Revista%20 6%20completa.pdf#page=122. Accessed April 2, 2011.

Gabillon, E., and D. Martirmort. 2004. The benefits of central bank's political independence. *European Economic Review* 48: 353–78.

Guasch, J. L. 2003. Infrastructure concessions in Latin America and the Caribbean: The renegotiation issue and its determinants. *Infrastructure and Financial Markets Review* 9 (2): 1–6.

Guasch, J. L. 2004. *Granting and Renegotiating Infrastructure Concessions: Doing It Right.* Washington, DC: World Bank.

Guasch, J. L., J.-J. Laffont, and S. Straub. 2003. Renegotiation of concession contracts in Latin America. Policy Research working paper 3011. Washington, DC: World Bank.

Guasch, J. L., J.-J. Laffont, and S. Straub. 2006. Renegotiation of concession contracts: A theoretical approach. *Review of Industrial Organization* 29 (1): 55–73.

Guasch, J. L., J.-J. Laffont, and S. Straub. 2008. Renegotiation of concession contracts in Latin America: Evidence from the water and transport sectors. *International Journal of Industrial Organization* 26 (2): 421–42.

Jenkins, S. 1995. Easy estimation methods for discrete-time duration models. *Oxford Bulletin of Economics and Statistics* 57 (1): 129–36.

Jenkins, S. 2005. Survival analysis with Stata: Module EC968. University of Essex Summer School. https://www.iser.essex.ac.uk/resources/survival-analysis-with-stata.

Laffont, J. J., and E. Maskin. 1982. The theory of incentives: An overview. In W. Hildenbrand, ed., *Advances in Economic Theory.* Cambridge,: Cambridge University Press, 31–94.

Lancaster, T. 1990. *The Econometric Analysis of Transition Data.* Cambridge, UK: Cambridge University Press.

Mejía, L. B., F. Botero, and J.C. Rodríguez. 2008. Paving roads with votes? Budgetary Allocations for Road Infrastructure Projects in Colombia, 2002–2006. *Colombia Internacional* (68): 14–42.

Myerson, R. 1982. Optimal coordination mechanisms in generalized principal-agent problems. *Journal of Mathematical Economics* 10: 67–81.

Montesinos, J., and E. Saavedra. 2012. Algunos alcances en torno a la institucionalidad y renegociación de concesiones en la infraestructura de transporte de uso público en Perú. Universidad Alberto Hurtado. Mimeo.

Prentice, R. L., and J. C. Gloeckler. 1978. Regression analysis of grouped survival data with application to breast cancer data. *Biometrics* (34), 57–67. Cited in Jenkins (1995).

Schady, N. R. 2000. The Political Economy of Expenditures by the Peruvian Social Fund (FONCODES), 1991–95. *American Political Science Review* 94 (2): 289–304.

Tirole, J. 1999. Incomplete Contracts: Where Do We Stand? *Econometrica* 67(4): 741–81.

Transparency International. (2006). Handbook for Curbing Corruption in Public Procurement. http://archive.transparency.org/regional_pages/asia_pacific/newsroom/news_archive2/handbook_for_curbing_corruption_in_public_procurement_2006. Accessed 05 May 2011.

Williamson, O. 1985. *The Economic Institutions of Capitalism*. New York, NY: The Free Press.

Wooldridge, J. M. 2010. *Econometric Analysis of Cross Section and Panel Data*, 2nd ed. Cambridge: MIT Press.

World Bank. 2013. *World Development Report 2014: Risk and Opportunity—Managing Risk for Development*. Washington, DC: World Bank.

12 Strengthening Transport Infrastructure Connectivity Policies for Inclusive and Sustainable Asia

Biswa Nath Bhattacharyay

12.1 Introduction

The Asia-Pacific region (henceforth Asia) is the world's largest (26 million square kilometers) and most populous continent with 4.1 billion habitants in mid-2009 (UN ESCAP 2009). The region accounts for more than 60 percent of the world's population and 30 percent of the world's total land area (ADB 2007). Its economy today is almost equal to the economies of Europe and North America, and in recent years Asia has consistently recorded the world's highest economic growth rates. The Asia-Pacific region is vast and socioeconomically diverse. Its economies are of various sizes in terms of per capita income and in various stages of economic development, and they differ in population density, natural resources, access to suppliers and global markets, institutional capacity, financial sector, and culture among many other things.

One big factor behind the high growth in Asia during the past two decades was rapid infrastructure development that increased connectivity and enhanced the formation of East Asian production networks and supply chains, making Asia a factory of the world. As a result poverty has been significantly reduced, though Asia still houses more than two-thirds of the world's poor (UN ESCAP, ADB, and UNDP 2010). That is to say, the rapid growth has not been adequately inclusive, creating higher disparities in income and other non-income or social benefits among households and businesses within each country as well as across the region. Additionally the provision of basic services in improving the quality of life has remained highly diverse across Asian countries. There is therefore reason to believe that the existing development gap among Asian countries could cause future instability in the region, as witnessed in the Middle East and North Africa in recent times.

Asia's economic activities in manufacture and exports include business offices, industrial production facilities, and financial markets that are highly integrated with the rest of the world, especially with advanced economies. For example, Germany, the leading exporter among advanced economies, recently had to reduce (0.6 percent in July compared to June 2013) the average selling prices of its export products in view of a slowdown of the Chinese economy.

Although Asia has experienced significant infrastructure growth, the state of infrastructure in terms of quality and quantity is not uniform across Asia; infrastructure varies from country to country as well as within countries. Rapid economic growth, increasing population, rapid urbanization, poor maintenance, rising middle class, and depletion of resources are exerting visible pressure on the existing infrastructure.

The expansion of Asia's sophisticated production networks and the competitiveness of its trade depend on maintaining cost-effective, reliable, and well-integrated infrastructure networks in transport, energy, and telecommunications. The inadequacies in the pattern and nature of Asia's infrastructure development already show that poor networks can hinder growth, reduce competitiveness, be a major obstacle to poverty reduction, and thus engender instability and discord.

To maximize the region's growth potential, it is important that the Asian economies have adequate networks of quality infrastructure. Among the infrastructure, transport can have a big impact on poverty and economic integration. Roads, railways, airways, and waterways, for example, are vital to trade in connecting communities, as well as providing access to employment and to health and education services. Access to basic infrastructure thus can raise the quality of life of a population, particularly of the rural poor.

For Asian transport networks to become proficient, "hard" physical infrastructure within and across countries will need to be supported by "soft" infrastructure—a framework consisting of policies, regulations, governance, systems and procedures, knowledge and capacity, strategies, and institutions that facilitate economic development. Although financing needs of soft infrastructure may be much lower than that of hard infrastructure, soft infrastructure has more complexity and requires more time for development.

Nevertheless, the financing of large transport infrastructure can be a huge challenge at the national and regional levels for countries with inadequate financial savings and reserves, such as Indonesia, India, and Vietnam. This chapter examines the transport financing needs for 32 Asian economies at the national and regional levels up to 2020 and as well as their financing gaps.

This chapter focuses on how effective transport connectivity can work to enable inclusive and sustainable economic growth, trade integration, and connectivity, namely in the form of soft infrastructure consisting of appropriate policies, regulations, systems and procedures, knowledge, technical capacity, financing, and institutions. This chapter presents the concept, roles, benefits, and challenges of transport connectivity in Asia. The chapter also examines the major challenges and prospects of the effective transport infrastructure financing and suggests appropriate policies, mechanisms, and sources of financing at the national and regional levels. Effective policies and strategies are crucial for the financing of transport infrastructure, particularly in attracting the private sector. An empirical analysis is used to measure the impact of institutional governance on national and regional infrastructure across various subregions (i.e., Central Asia, Southeast Asia, South Asia, and Northeast Asia). Last, the chapter suggests a policy framework for seamless, inclusive, and sustainable transport connectivity in Asia.

Section 12.2 considers the concept, benefits, and challenges of transport connectivity. Section 12.3 discusses the necessary contributions of policies, institutions, and regulations in effective transport development. Section 12.4 focuses on government oversight in cost-effective and quality infrastructure development. Section 12.5 discusses effective financing measures, and section 12.6 the issue of inclusive and transport infrastructure, including some of the empirical evidence. The last section addresses the challenges and the prospect of utilizing policies, institutions, and regulations in achieving inclusive, sustainable, and seamless transport connectivity. This section also develops a policy matrix for Asian transport connectivity.

12.2 Transport Infrastructure Connectivity: Role, Benefits, Concept, and Challenges

12.2.1 Role and Benefits of Effective Transport Network

A transport network is effective if it is accessible, timely, inclusive, sustainable, seamless (fully connected and integrated), cost effective, safe, and affordable. Ensuring the effectiveness of a transport network requires both hard (e.g., roads, railways, waterways, airports, and seaports) and soft infrastructure (e.g., policies, regulations, governance, systems and procedures, knowledge and learning capacity of people, and local and regional institutions). A well-developed hard transport infrastructure is supported by adequate soft infrastructure that can:

- strengthen connectivity within national and regional levels;
- facilitate trade and economic integration;
- narrow development gaps among people of different social groups, communities, and countries;
- promote inclusive growth by providing economic opportunities to the poor, disadvantaged, and isolated people and communities;
- ensure environmentally and socially sustainable growth; and
- facilitate the provision of quality basic services at an affordable price.

Enhanced connectivity not only advances trade and economic integration and growth, it benefits the individual household (ADB, JBIC, and World Bank 2005). Improved connectivity minimizes information asymmetry and communication gaps, balances disparities among people, and helps in conflict avoidance and mitigation. Connectivity brings prosperity across communities, regions and classes of people whereas lack of connectivity can create desperation, conflict, tensions, and isolation. Where access to resources and basic services is lacking, such as in remote areas, desperation and tension can arise among the people living there. Connectivity at the national and cross-border levels that improves access to resources and services can work as "bridge for peace" (DFID 2005).

Asia has been experiencing reduced export demand from advanced economies because of slow growth or recessions in advanced economies and various restrictions to address the adverse impact of 2007–2008 financial crisis. Asia is therefore now in a position that it must focus on increased transport connectivity at the national, subregional, and regional levels to promote investments in the region, to enhance trade and economic integration, and to rebalance its growth toward regional demand. Investments in national infrastructure need to be coordinated through regional cooperation for enhancing cross-border connectivity.

Nevertheless, the building of massive infrastructure is expensive. It will also have profound implications for environment and climate changes at the national, regional, and global levels. To remain competitive and at the same time ensure sustainable growth, Asia will therefore need to build efficient and environmentally sustainable seamless transport connections within countries, the region, and with the rest of the world.

In developing national and regional infrastructure, Asia will likely abate the effects of the recent economic and financial crises for a number of reasons:

- Regional infrastructure enhances competitiveness and productivity, which could hasten economic recovery and sustain growth in the medium to long term.
- An improved standard of living could eliminate poverty due to isolated living conditions and provide the people connections to major economic centers and markets, thus narrow the development gap among Asian economies.
- Environmental sustainability could result from the trade of environmentally friendly energy resources across borders.
- The increased regional demand and intraregional trade could accelerate regional trade and economic cooperation and integration and thus rebalance Asia's and world economic growth.

Infrastructure can be national or regional in nature. Box 12.1 provides a definition of regional infrastructure.

12.2.2 Concept of Connectivity

The ASEAN Connectivity Master Plan (ASEAN 2010) is a recent attempt at visualizing a broad network of connectivity and all its components. Connectivity as a concept can address the competitiveness and resilience of a region and efficiently bring people, goods, services, ideas, innovation, knowledge, technology, and capital close together. Connectivity can include foundational support and facilitative means to establish the necessary socioeconomic, political-security and knowledge-cultural pillars for achieving an integrated, sustainable, prosperous, and harmonious region. The major components of connectivity are as follows:

1. Physical connectivity
- Transport
- Energy
- Information and communications technology (ICT)

Box 12.1
Defining regional infrastructure

Regional infrastructure projects are defined as projects that involve physical construction works and/or coordinated policies and procedures spanning two or more countries. Infrastructure projects within each country can have significant cross-border impacts satisfying one or more of the following criteria: (1) planning and implementation that involves cooperation and coordination between two or more countries; (2) as per the predetermined plan, significant sales of goods or services across regional borders amounting to at least 20 percent or more of the total sales; (3) construction of specific infrastructure, such as a road, a bridge, or a tunnel located on or largely on the territory of a country near the border in order to link the country to the network of a neighboring country or a third country.

Sources: Bhattacharyay (2008) and ADB/ADBI (2009).

2. Soft connectivity
- Trade (goods and services) liberalization, promotion, and facilitation
- Investment and financial sector liberalization, promotion, and facilitation
- Agreements/arrangements on mutual recognition of standards, quality, and systems
- Regional connecting infrastructure (e.g., transport, energy, and telecommunications) agreements
- Harmonized or standardized cross-border systems and procedures
- Capacity and institutional building programs
- Research and development, ideas, innovation, knowledge, and technology networks

3. People-to-people, institution-to-institution, and knowledge connectivity
- Educational, commercial, and cultural networks
- Civil society, NGO, public, and private sector networks
- Tourism and hospitality network

Where these concerns compete in meeting extensive infrastructure requirements, they will be addressed by maintaining a concept of "seamless, sustainable transport connectivity" that is sensitive to the impact on the local, national, and global environment (see box 12.2 for definition).

Box 12.2
Defining a seamless sustainable transport connectivity

Seamless sustainable transport connectivity refers to:

- Connected regions that are physically, economically, and financially integrated by efficient and environment-friendly or sustainable (green) infrastructure networks in transport so as to promote trade and investments within the region and with global markets, widen access to markets and public services and thereby promote inclusive and sustainable economic growth and reduce poverty.
- Expanding, deepening, and increasing the efficiency of regional production networks and supply chains due to streamlining of policies, systems, and procedures, such as customs levies and other bureaucratic impediments.
- Developing efficient regional financial markets that channel savings from Asia and the rest of the world into productive transportation investments throughout the region.
- Efficient and seamless connections across Asia and with the rest of the world to create a more competitive, prosperous, and integrated region, and to take advantage of Asia's enormous untapped economic potential.

Source: Adapted from Bhattacharyay (2010a).

12.3 Policies, Institutions, and Regulations in Effective Transport Development

The development and expansion of infrastructure networks depend on clear policies and effective regulatory arrangements (ADB, JBIC, and World Bank 2005). Governments are the key players in formulating infrastructure-related policies, rules and regulations, institutional arrangements, even if they are informal, and they provide the required coordination and related support in developing national and cross-border infrastructure networks (Schiavo-Campo and Sundaram 2000).

For infrastructure policies, regulations, and institutions to be effective, the major components of soft infrastructure would include the following:

1. Coordination, cooperation, and collaboration among agencies and stakeholders
2. Identification and prioritization of projects
3. Standardization of regulatory policies and legal frameworks and systems and procedures

4. Strengthening of capacity building initiatives
5. Management of social and environmental issues
6. Promotion of cost-effective designs and quality materials
7. Involvement of private sector and innovative financing mechanisms (ADB/ADBI 2009)

The components 1 to 5 are discussed below. Issues relating to governance and financing will be discussed in separate sections.

12.3.1 Coordination, Cooperation, and Collaboration

Coordination and collaboration among various agencies and the stakeholders in the implementation of infrastructure projects can be challenging. At the national level, such coordination would be effected between different agencies responsible for the planning, development, and execution of the infrastructure; local, provincial, and central governments, sectoral agencies could be involved. For subregional and regional infrastructure projects, intergovernmental as well as interagency coordination within and among the participating countries would be required. As there are many subregional infrastructure programs with overlapping country membership in Asia, there is a need for pan-Asia level coordination among public and private sector of participating countries, subregional programs, and infrastructure financing institutions. There is a need to formulate a framework for pan-Asian infrastructure cooperation, coordination, and partnership through a Pan-Asian Infrastructure Forum (PAIF). The objective of the proposed PAIF is to coordinate and integrate the ongoing subregional infrastructure programs and projects in Asia (ADB/ADBI 2009). Since the PAIF can be expected to bring the major stakeholders in Asia together, it could include a forum for consensus building, prioritization, and coordination of regional infrastructure-related initiatives as well as for developing harmonized standards for systems and procedures, and likewise for a legal and regulatory framework across the region.

Coordination of the preparation and implementation of transport policies even at the national level often proves to be challenging, particularly because it involves so many planning and implementing agencies and stakeholders with different priorities, systems, and cultures. For example, although Japan has a sophisticated transport system through which it operates a complex network of roads and railways, both national and local transport policy-making in Japan faces certain challenges that arise from the "fragmented approach to policy development, implementation, and operation" (Enoch and Nakamura 2007). For smaller, least developed economies such as Bangladesh, lack of coordination has often led to a piecemeal approach, making many transport projects inconsistent and economically irrational (Ali 2011).

In India there is increasing coordination in the transport sector due to an improved government structure (Raghuram and Rangaraj 2006), but coordination between national and state governments remains problematic and complicated (Wang and Chen 2010). Table 12.1 shows the complexities involved in the planning, financing, implementation, and overall supervision and regulation of transport projects by sectors in India, the third largest economy in Asia.

Similarly in the People's Republic of China (PRC), the largest economy of Asia with immense needs for transport sector development, the institutional setup for infrastructure policy-making, financing, and implementation involves several players at the central, provincial, and local levels (see table 12.2). At the national level there is a need to set up a high-level infrastructure committee chaired by the Prime Minister or a senior Minister. This committee will facilitate the coordination among various agencies and stakeholders and undertake an integrated and comprehensive infrastructure planning of various infrastructure sectors.

Infrastructure links between subregions of Asia such as between Southeast, Central, East, and South Asia are being realized through several major regional and subregional initiatives with overlapping country membership. A list of subregional infrastructure initiatives is presented below:

1. Asian Land Transport Infrastructure Development Project (ALTID)
2. Association of South-East Asian Nations (ASEAN)
3. Brunei Darussalam Indonesia Malaysia the Philippines–East ASEAN Growth Area (BIMP-EGA),
4. Bay of Bengal Initiative for Multi-Sectoral Technical and Economic Cooperation (BIMSTEC)
5. Central Asia Regional Economic Cooperation (CAREC)
5. Greater Mekong Subregion (GMS)
6. Indonesia-Malaysia-Thailand–Growth Triangle (IMT-GT)
7. Mekong-Ganga Cooperation Initiative (MGC)
8. South Asian Association for Regional Cooperation (SAARC)
9. South Asia Subregional Economic Cooperation (SASEC)

Table 12.1
Who does what in Indian transport projects?

Infrastructure sector	Planning	Financing	Implementation	Overall supervision/ regulation
National highways	Planning Commission of India	Ministry of Shipping, road transport and highways (MSRTH)	National highways authority of India (NHAI)	MSRTH/ NHAI
State highways, district roads, village and other roads	State governments/ Ministry of Rural Development (MORD)	MSRTH/ insignificant private financing	State governments/ MORD	State governments/ MORD
Railways	Ministry of Railways/ Indian Railways (IR)	Government of India/ insignificant private financing	Ministry of Railways/IR	Ministry of Railways/IR
Ports	National government (major ports)/ state governments (minor ports)	Government of India	National government (major ports)/state governments (non-major ports)	National government (major ports)/state governments (non-major ports)
Airports	Ministry of Civil Aviation/ Airports Authority of India (AAI)	Government of India/ limited private investment	AAI	Ministry of Civil Aviation

Source: Based on the discussion of India's transport sector by Wang and Chen (2010)

10. Subregional Economic Cooperation in South and Central Asia (SECSCA)
11. Greater Tumen Initiative (GTI)

Under Pan-Asian initiatives, ALTID such as the Asian Highway (AH) and Trans-Asian Railway (TAR) have been implemented as part of subregional and national programs. Table 12.3 summarizes major regional and subregional land and maritime transportation projects in Asia. As discussed earlier, PAIF can coordinate national and subregional infrastructure connectivity programs to achieve a seamless pan-Asian connectivity.

Table 12.2
Infrastructure project planning, financing, and implementation process in PRC

Infrastructure sector	Planning	Financing	Implementation
National arterial expressway	Ministry of Communication (MOCm) and National Development Reform Corporation (NDRC)	Ministry of Communication	Provincial Departments of Communications
Provincial highways	Provincial Department of Communications	Provincial governments	Provincial Departments of Communications
National railways	Ministry of Railways (MOR) and NDRC	Ministry of Railways	Ministry of Railways
Local railways	Provincial governments	Provincial governments	Provincial governments
Power plants	Central government (indicative master planning only)	Power Enterprise	Power Enterprise
Power transmission	Central government (indicative master planning only)	China Power Grid Company and China Southern Grid Company	China Power Grid Company and China Southern Grid Company
Urban water supply and sanitation	Municipal government	Municipal government and urban companies	Municipal government and urban companies
Urban bus transport	Municipal government	Municipal government and bus transport companies	Municipal government and bus transport companies
Urban mass rail transit system	Municipal government (subject to approval of NDRC	Municipal government	Municipal government

Source: Adapted from Liu (2005)

Due to the diversity of Asian economies, many overlapping subregional institutions are not operating at the same speeds and the same multiple objectives—and thus address issues at different levels and by different measures. The number of participating countries has varied from 3 to 16 countries. Most subregional institutions are informal (except ASEAN and SAARC) without any legal binding or enforcement capacity. Even formal ASEAN follows non-interference, sovereignty, incrementalism, and consensual decision-making. Most operate at summit/ministerial level—some at senior officials' level. Most take advisory, and regulatory, modalities. Asia needs formal and strong institutions

Table 12.3
Major regional and subregional land transportation projects in Asia

Region/ subregion	Particular	Projects	Main coordinating bodies	Status[a]
Asia	ALTID	• Asian highway	UNESCAP	Ongoing
Asia	ALTID	• Trans-Asian railway	UNESCAP	Ongoing
Southeast Asia	GMS	• 3 economic corridors	ADB and GMS Secretariat	Partly completed
	ASEAN	• 1 highway corridor • 1 rail corridor	ASEAN Secretariat	Ongoing
	IMT-GT	• 5 economic connectivity corridors	IMT-GT Secretariat[#]	Ongoing
	BIMP-EAGA	• Air and maritime connectivity projects	BIMP-EAGA Secretariat[#]	Ongoing
South Asia	SAARC	• 10 road corridors • 5 rail corridors • 10 inland/maritime gateways • 7 aviation gateways	SAARC Secretariat	Proposed[b]
	SASEC	• 1 road corridor • 1 rail link	ADB	Ongoing
	BIMSTEC	• 1 highway corridor	Member countries[#]	Proposed[b]
Central Asia	SECSCA	• 2 road corridors	ADB	Ongoing
	CAREC	• 6 road corridors	ADB and CAREC Secretariat	Ongoing

Sources: ADB/ADBI (2009) and individual subregional programs websites
Notes: Asian Land Transport Infrastructure Development (ALTID); IMIT-GT: Indonesia-Malaysia–Thailand Growth Triangle; BIMP-EAGA: Brunei Darussalam Indonesia Malaysia the Philippines–East ASEAN Growth Area; CAREC: Central Asia Regional Economic Cooperation; SECSCA: Subregional Economic Cooperation in South and Central Asia; BIMSTEC: Bay of Bengal Initiative for Multi-Sectoral Technical and Economic Cooperation; SASEC: South Asia Subregional Economic Cooperation. SAARC: South Asian Association for Regional Cooperation; ASEAN: Association of Southeast Asian Nations; GMS: Greater Mekong Subregion.
a. As of July 31, 2009.
b. Feasibility studies supported by ADB.

with (1) explicit treaty-based legally binding rules and (2) regulations with compliance monitored by a standing body or secretariat.

The many overlapping infrastructure institutions and initiatives are alone good reason to set up a Pan-Asia Infrastructure Forum (PAIF). This organization would be responsible for regional-level infrastructure planning, strategy, and implementation.

12.3.2 Identification and Prioritization of Projects

Identification, prioritization, and preparation of viable transport projects would allow for both maintenance of existing infrastructure and developing new projects. In the case of a transport facility, even when well-built, it may not be used by the people unless it meets their needs, and therefore its stakeholders should participate in the process of identifying and prioritizing transport projects at the sub-national, national, and cross-border levels (UNESCAP 2008). Appropriate cost and benefit analysis needs to be performed not only for the present generation but also for the future generation.

Japan provides a good example of identification and prioritization of transport projects: its road and rail (both regular and high-speed) networks have been developed keeping in mind the need for multimodal and mass transit facilities for this small but densely populated country with a high concentration of economic activities.

Because of its huge geographical and demographic size, rapidly booming economy, and increasing urbanization, national transport priorities in PRC have focused on a multi-modal system of roads, railways, airways, and harbor networks. However, in order to make it inclusive, PRC needs to connect its rural areas and hinterland with it major economic centers. Initiatives have been taken to connect the villages with cities. Major cities are also connected through a robust 80,000 km railway network, with 6,920 km of high-speed lines in operation (AFP 2010). The government envisions expanding the high-speed railway network to cover 16,000 km by 2020 and provide access to more than 90 percent of the population (*Financial Times* 2010). Together with domestic infrastructure, PRC has also participated in the development of regional transport connectivity through the PRC–ASEAN networks (Kunming–Bangkok highway, Nanning–Singapore economic corridor, etc.), Xinjiang–Central Asia road, PRC–Russia road and railway network, PRC–Pakistan Karakoram highway, and so on.

Based on the demand and supply situation of the Indian transport sector, the prioritization of projects in this fast developing South Asian economy is increasingly being shaped by the following features: increasing share of road transport, increasing urbanization, increasing personalized transport, increasing commercial orientation of infrastructure development, increasing sensitivity to public costs, increasing coordination through the governmental structure, and increasing move toward a supply chain perspective (Raghuram and Rangaraj 2006).

The GMS members, recognizing the economic benefits of increased trade and economic development through connectivity, have enhanced three economic corridors, connecting east and west, north and south and the southern region. The growth from the early 1990s to the mid-2000s shows economic benefits of greater connectivity. From 1992 to 2005 total exports increased by more than threefold while interregional trade increased by more than twelve times. Aside from trade in goods, tourism also bloomed where annual tourist arrivals doubled in the decade 1995 to 2005. Meanwhile net FDI inflows to the GMS rose from about $3 billion in 1992 to about $5.5 billion in 2005 (excluding inflows to the PRC and Myanmar).

For subregional and regional connectivity, a priority should be interregional integration to link landlocked and underdeveloped countries and regions. The Lao PDR has already benefited significantly from integration with its neighbors. Nepal, another landlocked country, shares borders with India and PRC and connectivity would regionally and globally integrate Nepal's markets. The addition of Myanmar is crucial to the link connecting East Asia and South Asia. Moreover in India a "chicken neck" corridor (located in Bangladesh) separates the seven northeastern states from its central provinces and business centers. A connectivity between India and Bangladesh would significantly improve the mobility of goods and people by shortening the distance from Assam to Kolkata port by 60 percent. This way the regional connectivity would also enhance national connectivity.

As proposed in ADB/ADBI (2009), Asia needs to set up an Asian Infrastructure Financing Fund (AIFF) that can identify and prepare priority bankable projects pipeline through a project development mechanism or framework. The AIFF would serve to mobilize regional and international funds (public and private) and finance bankable projects for national and regional connectivity.

12.3.3 Legal and Regulatory Frameworks

Baumol (1967), Posner (1974), Peltzman (1976), and Stigler (1971) have discussed theoretically and empirically the role and impact of economic regulation in the economy and for specific industries. The same authors have presented case studies in the transport industry that include airline, road transport (e.g., trucking and taxi), railways, and shipping. These transport industries are traditionally heavily regulated.

Baumol (1967) presented his public interest theory with a view toward regulation as necessary to overcome market failure or irregularities of companies and industries. Posner (1974) argued against this theory that regulation should instead correct inefficient or inequitable market practices of companies and industries. He proposed his own capture theory whereby regulation would serve the demands of interest groups struggling among themselves to maximize the incomes of their members.

Stigler (1971) had some years earlier proposed an economic theory of regulation that explains (1) who (among citizens) would receive the benefits (through transfer of wealth) or burdens of a regulation, (2) what form a regulation should take, and (3) what impact a regulation would have on the allocation of resources. Mainly economic regulation would protect and provide benefits to the general public (or a large group of the affected public) from adverse impacts of an economic or business development such as infrastructure. Petzman (1976) later formalized the Stigler's model and offered some suggestions as to how a price-output structure could emerge out of regulation.

Effective regulations can ensure efficiency in achieving cost-effective infrastructure, as in the case of public utilities. Regulation is often necessary to effectively manage industries operating as natural monopolies and oligopolies. Therefore, to create effective transport networks, countries need first to strengthen their existing legal and regulatory frameworks; they need to create laws and regulation to ensure inclusive, sustainable, adequate, affordable, safe, and accessible transport networks. Asian countries further need to establish independent infrastructure regulatory bodies for effective regulation. For example, for the Indian railways sector the planning and implementing agencies are also the regulatory and supervisory body (see tables 12.1 and 12.2).

Harmonization of regulatory and legal frameworks is necessary for cross-border transport projects to operate efficiently. There is a need to formulate a cross-border transport agreement among neighboring countries. A good example of cross-border transport agreement (CBTA) is the 2003 Greater Mekong Regions (GMS), a CBTA involving six countries, namely Cambodia, China, Myanmar, Lao PDR, Thailand, and Vietnam in 2003. The main objective of the CBTA is to enhance soft infrastructure, particularly cross-border policy, regulatory, and legal frameworks, for more effective cross-border movement of people, goods, and services. This will complement the large investment in physical infrastructure that should increase economic connectivity (a detailed discussion is available in ADB 2006).

In the case of India and Bangladesh, these countries have a bilaterally agreed protocol for their inland waterways but lack harmonization of customs procedures and standards, so the restriction on the movement of vessels makes the protocol not so useful (ADB/ADBI 2009). Often the regulatory offices in developing countries, particularly in Asia, are small, understaffed, and very expensive to operate (Stone 2008).

The priority areas to strengthen laws and regulations concern (1) issues of safety; (2) encouragement of private investment, privatization, and public–private partnerships (PPP); (3) making transport services and utility affordable and accessible; (4) transparent and effective processes of land acquisitions; (5) emission control; (6) energy efficiency; (7) reducing transport demand; (8) improvements to rural and urban transport; (9) tourism; and (10) foreign investment.

12.4 Governance for Cost-Effective and Quality Infrastructure Development

In many developing countries, where laws are not properly enforced or institutions are weak, it is difficult to implement a project without serious problems arising (ADB/ADBI 2009). For transport projects (as well as other infrastructure projects) the lack of government regulations or their effective implementation can result in delay and onsite alterations to design and construction details, and cost overruns leading to failure projects (Tanzi and Davoodi 1998).

Autonomy, transparency, accountability, decision-making, and decision tools are all critical for ensuring good governance for developing efficient, sustainable, and inclusive infrastructure projects (ADB 1995, 2006; ADB/ADBI 2009).

In this section I analyze the impact of government institutions on national and regional infrastructure across the subregions in Asia using an econometric analysis. My sample consists of 30 Asian economies and my econometric analysis is intended to measure the effectiveness of subregional institutions developing under various subregional infrastructure projects (Central Asia, Southeast Asia, South Asia, and Northeast Asia). As there is no widely accepted definition of either subregion or regional governance, the measurement of implementation effectiveness provides, at least partially, an indication of governance over regional infrastructure.

The governance indicators were calculated from the World Governance Indicators (WGI) of the World Bank Institute (WBI) for countries in the four Asian subregions (Central Asia, South Asia, Southeast Asia, and Northeast Asia), and then estimated was the impact of national governance on an index of six key physical infrastructure indicators (roadways, railways, airports, seaports, telecommunications, and electricity). WGI has six components: Voice and Accountability, Political Stability and Lack of Violence, Government Effectiveness, Regulatory Quality, Rule of Law, and Control of Corruption.[1] I used a composite indicator based on these six indicators. The base year of all variables was 2006 (unless otherwise noted).

The results demonstrated that the coefficients of governance for all the six infrastructure indicators have had positive signs. In terms of impact, government effectiveness was found to be highest whereas for voice and accountability the impact was lowest. Subregional governance for Northeast Asia and Southeast Asia was found to be strong for all six indicators, but most of the estimated coefficients of regional governance in Central and South Asia showed negative signs. This may suggest that these two subregions did not experience any positive impact due to their quality of governance on their regional infrastructure, indicating that adequate improvements have not been done in their national and regional governance to enhance regional infrastructure. Table 12.4 summarizes the regression results for composite governance. Overall, the study suggests that governance influences the development of regional infrastructure in the Asian region, but that, ceteris paribus, countries (e.g., in Northeast Asia) with improved governance had more regional infrastructure development (De and Bhattacharyay 2010).

12.5 Issues Concerning Effective Financing

Financing huge infrastructure needs of Asia at the national and regional level is a considerable challenge, particularly for those countries with high fiscal deficits. In this section I discuss the various sources and instruments for financing national and pan-Asian connectivity.

An integrated Asian financial market could directly enhance cross-border capital and utilize Asia's robust savings and foreign exchange

Table 12.4
Regression results from composite governance index

	National	Regional
Ln per capita income	2.226***	2.611***
	(3.845)	(4.709)
Trade	0.009**	0.010*
	(2.066)	(2.571)
Ln population	0.609**	0.631**
	(3.617)	(4.114)
PPI	0.014	0.065
	(0.342)	(1.629)
Governance (national)	0.293*	
	(1.828)	
Governance (regional), of which		
Central Asia		-0.047
		(-0.381)
South Asia		-0.110
		(-0.501)
Southeast Asia		0.338*
		(1.464)
Northeast Asia		0.759**
		(2.780)
Mean VIF	2.67	2.29
White test, chi^2 (*p*-value)#	21.24 (0.383)	30.00 (0.414)
Observations	30	30
Adjusted *R*-squared	0.860	0.883

Source: De and Bhattacharyay (2010)

Notes: #Cameron and Trivedi's decomposition of IM-test (checking homoscedasticity). $VIF (variance inflation factors) to check multicollinearity. ***, **, * indicate significance at 1 percent, 5 percent, and 10 percent levels; *t*-values are in parentheses.

reserve for national and regional infrastructure investments. A pan-Asia comprehensive investment treaty similar to the ASEAN Comprehensive Investment Agreement (ACIA) would work to promote free movement of cross-border investments for infrastructure.

12.5.1 National and Regional Transport Connectivity Financing Needs in Asia

A big challenge in transport infrastructure development is mobilizing adequate funds. In order to develop appropriate policy and planning as well as to identify appropriate financing sources, it is important to first assess the magnitude of both financing needs and financing gaps.

Table 12.6 provides a breakdown of financing requirements for national transport connectivity in Asia by selected countries. Total national transport infrastructure needs for 2010 to 2020 is $2.6 trillion or $236 billion per year. South Asian countries are expected to see half of their total infrastructure investment needs being diverted to the transportation sector, amounting to about $1.1 trillion. In absolute terms, the top five countries with the largest transport needs are PRC, India, Indonesia, Bangladesh, and Pakistan. It is notable that landlocked countries in East Asia (e.g., Lao PDR) and small island nations (Pacific Islands) are also projected to invest a large portion of their infrastructure funds to improve their transport connectivity, compared to countries in the Central Asian region.

The national infrastructure needs of Asian countries for 2010 to 2020 are huge and vary significantly across countries, as high as 12 percent of GDP in Mongolia and as low as 0.58 percent in Kazakhstan (table 12.5). Total investments required to meet demand for the identified 1,202 regional projects are estimated at approximately US$320 billion, with an average infrastructure investment need of about US$29 billion per year for the period 2010 to 2020 (for details see Bhattacharyay 2010b). Of this total, the needed investment in transport projects is $229 billion (or 20.8 billion per year) during 2010 to 2020 which accounts for about 70 percent of total need (table 12.6).

12.5.2 Infrastructure Financing Gap

The major sources of infrastructure financing is central government spending. Table 12.7 shows central government spending on physical infrastructure (e.g., energy, transport, telecommunications, water, and sanitation) in 2011 and 2012 and per year transport financing needs for the period 2010 to 2012 as well as financing gap. The financing gap is estimated by subtracting per year transport needs (2010 to 2012) from the central government spending in 2011. It is assumed that all central government spending will be used for transport development only. Despite this assumption, most Asian economies have a huge financing gap for transport infrastructure. The total financing gap for all kinds of infrastructure could be much higher.

12.5.3 Potential Sources of Financing

Major potential sources for infrastructure financing include:

1. Public funding
2. Pan-Asian and subregional infrastructure funds

Table 12.5
Estimated transport infrastructure investment needs for national connectivity, 2010 to 2020

Country	Transport investment (% of GDP)	Transport investment per year (US$ billions)
Central Asia	1.86	9.515
Afghanistan	6.21	1.238
Armenia	1.20	0.132
Azerbaijan	0.60	0.311
Georgia	1.20	0.170
Kazakhstan	0.58	0.973
Kyrgyz Rep.	3.94	0.237
Pakistan	2.65	5.201
Tajikistan	3.30	0.212
Uzbekistan	2.65	1.025
East and South East Asia	1.61	144.576
Cambodia	4.43	0.618
PRC	1.39	102.395
Indonesia	3.88	25.701
Lao PDR	10.62	0.807
Malaysia	1.94	4.966
Mongolia	12.04	0.819
Myanmar	2.70	0.882
Philippines	2.30	4.401
Thailand	0.58	1.857
Vietnam	2.07	2.544
South Asia	5.55	108.729
Bangladesh	4.92	5.607
Bhutan	2.84	0.056
India	5.67	100.702
Nepal	1.65	0.253
Sri Lanka	4.23	2.128
The Pacific	2.60	0.401
Fiji	1.01	0.036
Kiribati	5.17	0.007
PNG	3.30	0.291
Samoa	3.33	0.016
Solomon Is.	3.50	0.026
Timor-Leste	0.00	0.0
Tonga	2.29	0.006
Vanuatu	2.92	0.020
Total Asia	2.30	263.689

Sources: Bhattacharyay (2010b) and Centennial Group Holdings (2009)

Table 12.6
Investment needs for identified pipeline infrastructure by regional/subregional, 2010 to 2020 (US$ millions)

Regional/subregional program	Transport			
	Airport/seaport	Rail	Road	Total
AH	-	-	17,425.00	17,425.00
TAR	-	107,469.00	-	107,469.00
ACP	51,446.00	-	-	51,446.00
CAREC	1,347.70	5,131.30	12,932.90	29,337.00
GMS	200	1,523.00	3,972.00	5,858.00
ASEAN	-	16,800.00	-	16,800.00
BIMP-EAGA	-	-	-	-
SASEC	-	-	-	203
Other[a]	-	-	-	89.5
Total	52,993.70	130,923.30	34,329.90	228,627.40

Source: Bhattacharyay (2010a)
Note: ASEAN—Association of South-East Asian Nations; BIMP-EAGA—Brunei Darussalam–Indonesia–Malaysia–Philippines East ASEAN Growth Area; SASEC—South Asia Subregional Economic Council
a. Includes projects connecting East/Southeast–Central–South Asia that do not explicitly fall under a subregional program.

3. Multilateral development banks and bilateral agencies
4. Capital markets, namely local currency bond markets
5. Regional infrastructure companies for financing specific sectors
6. Sovereign wealth funds
7. Asian infrastructure currency unit-based bonds

Public funding has been the major financing source for infrastructure projects. Following the 2008 financial crisis, Asian economies responded with economic stimulus packages to increase domestic demand and to mitigate crisis impacts (table 12.8). A major share of these packages usually goes into public infrastructure projects, including transport projects. At G20[2] meetings and APEC[3] meetings governments were asked to increase infrastructure financing in order to kick-start the falling worldwide economic growth (G20 2010).

Asian connectivity can be supported by creating a Pan-Asian and/or a number of subregional infrastructure funds. An Asian infrastructure financing bank (AIFB) could be created with capital coming from governments, multilateral development banks (MDBs), developed countries, bilateral agencies, private sectors, sovereign wealth funds,

Table 12.7
Transport financing gap in Asian economies (US$ billions), 2011

	Physical infrastructure spending in 2011	Transport financing needs (from table 12.5)	Financing gap
Country/region (1)	2011	Yearly average during 2010–2020	(2) – (1)
Central and West Asia	4.97	9.515	4.545
Armenia	0.09	0.132	0.042
Azerbaijan	0.47	0.311	-0.159
Georgia	0.41	0.170	-0.24
Kazakhstan	*3.77*	0.973	-2.797
Kyrgyz Republic	0.09	0.237	0.147
Tajikistan	0.14	0.212	0.072
East and Southeast Asia	19.48	144.576	125.096
Cambodia	0.01	0.618	0.608
Indonesia	*4.03*	25.701	21.671
Malaysia	6.57	4.966	-1.604
Philippines	3.49	4.401	0.911
Thailand	5.32	1.857	-3.463
China, People's Republic of	*50.62*	102.395	51.775
Mongolia	0.35	0.819	0.469
South Asia	37.00	108.729	71.729
Bangladesh	*1.27*	5.607	4.337
Bhutan	0.11	0.056	-0.045
India	*32.55*	100.702	68.152
Nepal	0.54	0.253	-0.287
Sri Lanka	2.36	2.128	-0.232
Pacific Islands	0.09	0.401	0.311
Fiji, Republic of	*0.02*	0.036	0.016
Kiribati	*0.01*	0.007	-0.003
Papua New Guinea	*0.03*	0.291	0.261
Samoa	0.03	0.016	-0.014

Sources: Author's calculation based on Asian Development Bank (ADB); key indicators for Asia and the Pacific 2013, www.adb.org/statistics
Note: In italics are estimates based on the previous year's growth.

Table 12.8
Infrastructure investment in the stimulus packages of the major Asian economies (US$ billions)

Country	Total fiscal stimulus	Infrastructure component	Infrastructure as percent of total stimulus	Infrastructure type
PRC	600.0	275.0	45.80%	Railways, airports, electrical transmission technology, expressways, telecommunications technologies, rural roads, electricity, gas, water, and irrigation projects
India	60.0	33.5	55.80%	Highway, port, and power sectors
Indonesia	7.7	1.3	16.90%	Communications and transport infrastructure, rural infrastructure, and development of ports, and shipping industry
Vietnam	8.0	4.8	60.00%	Infrastructure spending
Thailand	46.7	30.6	65.50%	Water resource development and road construction in villages and rural areas along with transport, logistics, energy, and telecom improvements
Malaysia	2.0	0.2	8.50%	Low- and medium-cost housing, upgrade, repair, and maintenance of police stations and army camps, and public and basic infrastructure project maintenance
ROK	11.0	3.2	29%	Roads, universities, schools, hospitals
Japan	$154.55	16+	10%+	Yen 1.6 trillion for fostering environmentally friendly technologies, including plans to provide cheaper solar power to homes. Up to $2,500 as tax breaks to consumers on purchases of "green" cars; subsidies of 5% on energy efficient televisions and other appliances.

Sources: Author's estimations from data in Kang (2010), Sugimoto (2010), Kumar and Soumya (2010), Patunru and Zetha (2010), Nguyen, Nguyen, and Nguyen (2010), Jitsuchon (2010), World Bank (2009), FAITC (2009), Alibaba.com (2008), IFCE (2009), Economy Watch (2010), Tabuchi (2009), and ADB (2009a).
Note: PRC: People's Republic of China; ROK: Republic of Korea

Islamic funds, and pension funds. International bodies with experience in developing and financing infrastructure in Asia, such as the ADB, would be the ideal managers of these funds. AIFB could focus on developing regional or cross-border infrastructure. Additionally subregional projects could be financed by initiatives such as the proposed ASEAN Infrastructure Fund established in 2011. Recently China has even proposed and now established an Asian infrastructure investment bank in the line of the proposed AIFB (Banyan 2013).

Multilateral development banks (MDBs), such as the ADB and the World Bank, and bilateral agencies, such as Japan International Cooperation Agency (JICA), are important sources of infrastructure financing. These institutions are in a position to reduce the financing gaps from their own resources and to mobilize long-term funds through capital markets, explicit guarantees, and special co-financing arrangements. MDBs could promote private financing by introducing public–private partnership (PPP) projects and assisting host countries to improve business environments.

The development of bond markets, particularly local currency bond markets, could help reduce foreign currency risks and minimize maturity mismatches. The Asian Bond Market Initiative (ABMI), which was introduced in 2003, is an ASEAN+3 initiative that aims to develop efficient bond markets in Asia, enabling the private and public sectors to raise capital and to undertake long-term investments without currency and maturity risks. Such initiatives could encourage the utilization of Asia's savings and foreign exchange reserves for Asia's infrastructure development, which is long term in nature.

Another option is to have regional companies manage and finance regional infrastructure projects. These companies could be owned by Asian governments, relevant regional public sectors, and private sector firms that have adequate expertise in infrastructure development. They could raise funds from capital markets through equity or infrastructure bonds. The sale of public-sector companies' shares throughout the region would deepen equity markets and provide a needed outlet for household savings and institutions' investment funds.

Another potential source of funding for Asian cross-border infrastructure investment is sovereign wealth fund (SWF) derived from each country's central bank reserves. Due to the infrastructure projects' size, its long-term horizon, competitive returns, and investment guarantees, SWFs can be a good source of funding.

Table 12.9
Types of risk and mitigating instruments

Risk	Instrument
Exchange risk	Exchange rate guarantees; currency baskets
Inflation risk	Inflation-linked instruments
Commodity price risk	Commodity price-linked instruments
Credit risk	Credit guarantees
Demand (traffic) risk	Demand (traffic) guarantees
Economic risk	GDP-linked instruments

Source: Bhattacharyay (2010b)

12.5.4 Potential Infrastructure Financing Instruments

Major potential infrastructure financing instruments include:

1. Guaranteed and linked bonds
2. Islamic financial market instruments
3. Public–private partnerships and privatization
4. Asian infrastructure currency unit-based bonds

Transport infrastructure projects could be financed by instruments such as guaranteed bonds to protect investors from various risks (e.g., fluctuating exchange rates and inflation), insulate borrowers from negative changes in servicing costs, and customize the features of loans to fit the specific needs of lenders and borrowers. New innovative instruments should be created for different classes of borrowers who are facing different types of risks and concerns (see table 12.9).

Islamic financial markets could be an instrument for infrastructure funding. Islamic bonds (*sukuks*) from the Islamic Development Bank (IDB) as well as from financial markets in the Middle East and Malaysia could serve the purpose. However, access to Islamic finance basically limited to some Muslim communities for basic banking services. Increasing the access to these funds therefore remains a challenge. Another issue that needs to be addressed is the lack of standardization of instruments due to varying *Shariah* (Islamic law) interpretations and the fact that financing infrastructure projects tend to evolve sharing the profit or loss on specific projects.

Improvements in the transport sector will require nothing less than huge public and private sector investments, although the public sector is still expected to shoulder the bulk of the required financing. Historically public–private partnerships (PPPs) have played an important role in funding infrastructure in various regions. From 1990 to 2008 the total private investment committed to infrastructure amounted to US$1,640 billion for the world and US$472 billion for Asia-Pacific (WB 2011). Top recipient countries (in terms of value) in Asia during that period were India, PRC, Malaysia, Indonesia, and the Philippines. This important contribution is growing as it is anticipated that private sector will cover about 40 percent of the needed funding.

Restructuring of public sector utilities like transport and logistics services is of particular importance. In this regard countries need to strengthen the processes, systems, and procedures, as well as policies and regulation for effective privatization of public-sector infrastructure companies.

In Japan an important source of infrastructure investment comes from the so-called private finance initiative (PFI), which was enacted through a law in 1999. Under the PFI schemes the private sector is given the option for constructing, maintaining, and managing public facilities, including transport facilities such as roads, railroads, harbors, and airports. A case in point is the 2003 expansion of Tokyo Haneda International Airport, which was financed through such PFI scheme. It shows that private investments can be a good and competent source of infrastructure financing. To secure private investments, it is necessary to create clear and transparent rules and regulations and also a good business environment so that the investments are attractive to the private sector (Invest Japan 2003).

Lengthy executions of transport projects can subject investors to exchange rate risks. Such risk could be minimized through the creation of Asian infrastructure currency unit (AICU) based bonds consisting of a basket of Asian and non-Asian advanced economies' currencies. An AICU is simply an accounting mechanism equal to a weighted measure of Asian currencies and dependent on de facto relative stability among Asian currencies. Weights of the selected currencies in the basket would be based on such factors as gross domestic product (GDP), international reserves, trade, and demand for these currencies.

12.5.5 Land Acquisition

Oppositions of community and nongovernmental organizations to land acquisition for public transport (and other infrastructure) projects is a common phenomenon in almost all the Asian countries. This challenge can often discourage private-sector participation in infrastructure development and delay the implementation of projects. While there are specific laws relating to acquiring land for public infrastructure in most of the countries, the processes in many countries have been subjected to criticism due to lack of transparency in the acquisition process and particularly compensation. Large Asian economies such as India and Indonesia face the problem of lack of coordination and harmonization of laws and regulations, particularly in terms of compensation between the central and provincial/local governments. Some Asian countries have developed more sophisticated procedures.

In Japan acquisitions are managed through the Japan Organization for Land Acquisition and Compensation, whose "[p]urposes of the [o]rganization is to cooperate in land acquisition or land use by the public enterprises undertaking public projects like road construction, embankment, etc. through research, study and calculate on compensation in order to compensate appropriately and fairly" (Ogasawara and Yamashita 2010). However, the notion of consensus-building for acquisition is largely absent in most Asian economies. In order to minimize the detrimental effects arising from land acquisition related problems, appropriate policies and regulations for effective decision-making should be developed through proper consensus building.

12.6 Transport Infrastructure Connectivity for Promoting Inclusive, and Sustainable Growth

According to World Bank (2009), a growth that is broad-based across sectors, and inclusive of the large part of the country's labor force, is an inclusive growth. The importance of infrastructure development for low-income countries (LICs) is reflected in G20's recently concluded *Seoul Development Consensus for Shared Growth;* the consensus recognized infrastructure as one of its nine key pillars of the action plan.

Examples from many Asian economies confirm the impact of infrastructure connectivity in general and transport connectivity in particular on poverty reduction (ADBI/ADB 2009). In an earlier study of ADB (2004), households with better access to roads and electricity in India had low poverty rates, which is the same in the case of other countries such as Lao PDR (Warr 2005; Menon and Warr 2008) and Vietnam (Glewwe et al. 2002). Rural roads have a significant impact on the welfare of the poor because these roads facilitate the day-to-day life of the people—farm-to-market transport of goods, school attendance of children, access to medical services, and so on. However, rural roads across Asia are in such bad condition as to impede attempts at poverty reduction and inclusive growth for the rural poor (Pernia 2011).

Besides the construction of adequate transport connectivity, the rising income in many countries could contribute to overall poverty reduction, though at the same time the income rise could lead to rising disparities (ADB 2007). Infrastructure, in general, and transport connectivity, in particular, can positively contribute in mitigating such disparities: the price and income effects arising from reduced travel costs and time can create jobs and raise income, thus facilitate the reduction of exclusion from markets and social amenities (Hansen 2010). However, because poverty and income inequality in Asia are disproportionately concentrated in rural areas, lagging regions and isolated communities within a country, and in landlocked countries, appropriate policies, regulations and institutions are required to address these specific areas/regions and countries, groups and communities.

12.6.1 Leading and Lagging Regions

Although Asian economies have been experiencing rapid growth for a couple of decades, many of these countries are virtually divided into two different world: some regions within these countries are characterized by rapid economic growth, fast urbanization, and integration with the world economy; while there are also lagging rural regions where people basically rely on agriculture or informal activities (Ahmed 2008). For example, in 2009 the per capita annual disposable income of urban households in PRC was 17,174.7 Yuan while for rural households it was a meager 5,153.2 Yuan (China Statistical Yearbook 2010). Similarly, as observed by Ahmed and Ghani (2008), during the period from 1993 to 2004, the leading states of India (Andhra Pradesh, Gujarat, Haryana, Karnataka, Kerala, Maharashtra, Punjab, Tamil Nadu, and West Bengal) grew at twice the rate of the lagging states (Bihar, Madhya Pradesh, Orissa, Rajasthan, and Uttar Pradesh). Such within-country regional disparities exist in almost all the countries in the Asian region.

Some regions are geographically advantageous because of their proximity to rivers, ocean coasts, airports, and so on, all of which facilitate economic activities. The presence of human-made infrastructure facilitates economic interactions in other regions. For a variety of reasons, including the absence of geographical advantages and human-made infrastructure, the lagging regions are unable to connect with national, or regional, or global markets. These isolated regions fall in

Box 12.3
Anhui integrated transport sector improvement project

Anhui is the least developed province in central PRC. Poverty incidence in Anhui is concentrated in several areas, including the flood-prone, populous Huaibei Plain and the remote and isolated mountainous area of the Dabie Mountain. Inadequate transport accessibility has limited the social and economic development of these areas. The ADB project, approved in 2009, was devised to reduce intra- and inter-provincial disparities. The plan is (1) to strategically integrate the Anhui province with more prosperous neighboring provinces of China to the east, thus to support trade and socioeconomic integration and expand access to economic activities and opportunities; (2) to facilitate more balanced development of all types of road networks toward an improved quality of life across the province, particularly in poverty-prone areas; and (3) to improve transport accessibility and connectivity through an integrated network of local roads connected to the trunk highway system and to major business centers, counties, and townships.

Source: Hansen (2010).

with an increasing trend in income inequality. In order to make growth more inclusive, transport policy should be formulated to connect lagging regions with leading regions. For example, a network of local roads connected to a highway system linking a lagging region to neighboring economic centers or more advanced regions would provide economic opportunities to the poor region. Local and rural roads should be prioritized to facilitate rural people's access to educational and health facilities and other services (Hansen 2010). Box 12.3 describes such an ADB-funded transport improvement project in PRC's Anhui province.

12.6.2 Landlocked Countries

Landlocked countries without direct access to seaports are particularly challenged by barriers to the mobility of their people, goods, and services. Inadequate transport connectivity thus blocks their development. Policies to connect landlocked countries with neighboring countries through transport corridors would address the needs of such disadvantaged countries where the incidence of poverty is often high. In Asia there are 12 landlocked countries. Nepal, a low-income landlocked country in South Asia, shares borders with India and PRC. The presence of these two economically giant neighbors suggests that transport corridors connecting Nepal with India and China could significantly increase mobility of goods and foster trade with Nepal, thereby creating economic opportunities for the country's poor. Additionally the transport of goods from Nepal would be much easier if Nepal could ship their goods through the short transit from India to Bangladesh and then use port facilities in Bangladesh. Lao PDR, the only landlocked country in East Asia, has successfully initiated measures to promote its regional connectivity with neighboring countries (as discussed in the next subsection).

12.6.3 Sustainable Infrastructure Connectivity: Impact on Environment and the Need for Green Transport

Perhaps the most important regional challenge to connectivity in general, and for Asian transport infrastructure in particular, is the issue of energy security—ensuring the access of reliable, adequate, and affordable energy supplies. However, energy production and consumption are also the leading sources of pollution and greenhouse gas emissions. According to International Energy Agency (IEA), in its report on the World Energy Outlook (WEO) for 2009, fossil fuels remain the main sources of primary energy worldwide, accounting for more than three-quarters of the overall increase in energy use between 2007 and 2030. Oil demand (excluding biofuels) is projected to grow by 1 percent each year on average over the projection period, from 85 million barrels per day in 2008 to 105 million barrels per day in 2030. Transport projects, by default, are energy consuming and so are often seriously detrimental to the environment. In this regard transportation sector accounts for 97 percent of the increase in oil use (IEA 2009).

Transportation is thus becoming the fastest growing major contributor to global pollution and climate change, accounting for 23 percent of energy-related CO_2 emissions. If there are no changes in investment strategies and policies, experts foresee a three- to fivefold increase in CO_2 emissions from transportation in Asian countries by 2030, compared to that in 2000 (ADB 2010a). This gives us an indication not only of increasing volume of energy being consumed for road, rail, and air transportation but also of the broader issues of energy security, particularly environment-friendly or green energy supply and managing energy demand through energy efficiency.

While it is important to have quality transport infrastructure, it should be noted that energy production and consumption by this sector has negative externalities, most significant of which is increased carbon dioxide emissions causing adverse environmental impact and climate change. Emissions from fuel consumption by the transport sector has been a major contributor to the increase in emission of greenhouse gases (GHGs) that are harmful not only to the local population but can cause long-term effects such as global warming and climate change.

The total per capita carbon dioxide emissions for the consumption of energy for Asian countries increased significantly over the period of 1998 to 2008 (table 12.11). The pollution has had indirect costs on health and productivity. In addition the construction of a large number of power plants and hydro dams as well as coal-mining operations has displaced local populations, bringing on their resettlement and loss of livelihood.

As a result most Asian countries are presently adopting policies and regulations for making their transport sector more environmentally sustainable, but this may still not be enough. In the PRC new legislations have been passed that encourage the adoption of more energy-efficient technology for burning coal and for using petroleum-derived fuels for transport. The Chinese government has also enacted new taxes on transport fuels, and its 11th five-year plan, set forth in 2006, defined new limits on energy use. Its automobile fuel-efficiency standards, at least as stipulated in government regulations, are now ahead of those in most countries, notably in the United States (Harris 2008). In 2009, in the context of international talks to combat climate change, the PRC announced its target to reduce GHG emissions 40 to 45 percent per unit of GDP by 2020 from the 2005 levels—a very ambitious target given the need for continued economic growth and increased living standards (Wong and Bradsher 2009). The Chinese government has set a goal of reducing the country's energy intensity by 20 percent during the current five-year plan. The measures now envisioned include adopting stricter, high-efficiency building codes, and higher fuel efficiency standards for vehicles, shuttering subscale capacity in energy-intensive sectors, and stepping up investments in renewable energy.

Japan has an emission reduction target of 6 percent compared to 1990 emission levels. Japan's plan for reducing CO_2 emissions includes a package of measures for freight shipping sector, such as (IEA 1991):

1. Increasing modal shift from trucks to rail for shipments longer than 500 km from 40 to 50 percent through better facilities, and new terminals
2. Improving technical efficiency of each mode

3. Reducing inland transport distances through construction of eight new regional gateway ports for containers
4. Improving truck load factors by at least 3 percent
5. Increasing use of trailers and larger trucks, involving deregulation of gross vehicle weight from 20 tons to a maximum of 25 tons for heavy-duty trucks and 20 tons to 28 tons for semi-trailers

In India successive governments have been aware of the need to create more economical and energy-efficient modes of transportation to cater to the needs of a growing population. At the Copenhagen Summit in December 2009, India declared its intention to reduce the country's emission intensity of GDP by 20 to 25 percent from the 2005 level. In July 2010, India's Ministry of Urban Development launched a novel Rs 1,400 Crore (approximately US$300 million) green urban transport project called the Sustainable Urban Transport Project (SUTP), with the support from the Global Environment Facility (GEF), the World Bank, and UNDP.

In August 2008, the Republic of Korea President Lee Myung-bak announced low-carbon green-growth (LCGG) as a national development paradigm, which is being promoted as a growth strategy combined with a job-creation policy. The LCGG strategy involves three strategic factors for sustainable growth. First is sound economic growth with minimal use of energy and resources; second is reduced CO_2 emissions and environmental pollution with the same energy and resource use; third is the creation of new growth through research and development in green technologies, with an aim of achieving early dominance in international markets (Yun 2010).

12.7 Policies for Seamless, Sustainable, and Inclusive Transport Connectivity

Seamless, inclusive, and sustainable transport connectivity in Asia could potentially strengthen trade and economic integration, narrow the development gap, stimulate inclusive and sustainable growth, and ensure access to basic services. The first objective is to develop national infrastructure networks that connect interiors to economic centers, border, and ports within countries though transport-cum-economic corridors. Subsequent to this, there would be development of subregional infrastructure networks that connect neighboring countries within subregions. Last, pan-Asian infrastructure networks would be constructed that connect subregions to each other and so achieve pan-Asian transport connectivity.

As I have argued above, the development of effective transport connectivity requires not only hard infrastructure but also soft infrastructure. Without appropriate policies, regulations, and institutions, connectivity at the national and subregional/regional levels is likely to be haphazard, limited, sporadic, and ultimately ineffective (ADB/ADBI 2009). The financing requirements for hard infrastructure at the national and subregional levels are huge and appropriate financial mechanisms and innovative instruments and policies that can attract funding from the private sector are crucial. The cost of developing and implementing soft infrastructure is not significant but can make hard infrastructure work effectively.

12.7.1 Transport Plans in Asia

Uncoordinated and piecemeal approach to transport connectivity at the national level has generally been a common feature in many countries of developing Asia. Policies, institutions, and regulations should be considered within these countries' longer term strategic frameworks. The priorities for national infrastructure networks are to connect regions within countries to each country's economic centers, borders, and ports. These transport priorities are listed in table 12.10 for the major Asian countries.

The less-developed Asian countries need to establish integrated long-term national transport plans together with transport policy frameworks with sufficient laws, regulations, and institutions. Multilateral development banks (MDBs) can assist these countries in developing capacity and knowledge. A national level transport coordinating committee under the guidance of the Prime Minister's or President's office with representation of concerned institutions and agencies will need to be established to monitor the planning, coordination, and implementation of the transport plan.

These Asian countries can learn from the examples of more advanced economies such as Japan and the Republic of Korea. Of course, laws and regulations should be updated in accordance with each country's needs. For example, in Japan, its sophisticated transport strategy was complemented in 2003 by new laws related to passenger transport. Since 2003 Japan has either amended or established a set of laws related to public transport (Morichi 2007). Table 12.11 summarizes these new laws.

Table 12.10
Transport priorities in selected Asian countries

Country	Transport priorities
China	High-speed rail networks—plans to spend approx. $120 billion for 42 lines by 2012 Transport roads especially in the interiors, to build service sector and integrate the domestic economy Increased use of natural gas as transport fuel
India	Public transport improvements—mass-transit, bus rapid-transit, nonmotorized transport, car-free development, etc. Improvement in transport connectivity; transit oriented development; comprehensive mobility plans
Korea	Low-carbon–green growth (LCGG) national development paradigm—adoption of green technology
Indonesia	Promotion of sustainable transport infrastructure; public transport development
Philippines	Intermodal initiatives, shifting of road investments to regions with less density and lower road quality
Japan	Intelligent transportation system, and integrated modes of transport system Reducing CO_2 emissions by improving technical efficiency, increasing modal shift from truck to rail, increased use of water-transport, increasing truck-load factor by 3%+

Source: Bhattacharyay (2012)

As shown in table 12.3, Asia has undertaken several regional and subregional initiatives or institutions that connect neighboring countries within subregions, and these projects are informal in nature. However, these institutions have no financing capability to fund these projects, . The GMS and CAREC projects have been especially effective. Cooperation among the subregions, particularly in South and East Asia, is still fragile. These subregions can learn from the experiences of GMS and CAREC projects. In the long term the Asian economies will need to adopt a pan-Asian approach for connecting the subregions in a move toward a pan-Asian connectivity. In this regard operationalizing the existing pan-Asian projects, under the programs of Asian Highway and Trans Asian Railway, remains crucial. At the same time, domestic and cross-country transport-cum-economic corridors connecting cities and business centers should be developed. This would facilitate the formation of new cities, industrial clusters and the creation of new business and economic activities. Asian countries need to develop a comprehensive plan that can cater to the specific needs of the Asian region.

The European Union has the most sophisticated institutional framework for regional infrastructure, and Asia can draw important lessons from it. The institutional framework offered by the European Commission and the European Investment Bank (EIB) in facilitating and enabling the development of the Trans-European Networks (TENs) has been vital for EU transport, energy, and telecommunications infrastructure connectivity. A comprehensive agenda coupled with strong supranational institutions has ensured effective implementation of the TENs agreements (Van der Geest and Nunez-Ferrer 2008). Within the Asian context, multilateral development banks (MDBs) such as ADB and PAIF can play the coordinating role in forging the convergence of interests of Asian countries (ADB/ADBI 2009). In developing Asian connectivity, Asia needs formal and strong institutions with legally binding regulations and their compliance monitored by a standing body or secretariat for Asian infrastructure development.

12.7.2 Policy for Seamless, Inclusive and Sustainable Transport Connectivity

This chapter has outlined the need and means for strengthening policy, regulation, and institutions for effective transport infrastructure development in Asia. The financing need for soft infrastructure is much lower than that for hard infrastructure, but it is more complex and time-consuming. Asian countries will need to strengthen their soft infrastructure to make their existing hard infrastructure, as well as new hard infrastructure, cost effective. Asian countries should give immediate attention to developing polices, capable institutions, laws, regulations, and coherent plans at the national and subregional levels for their transport projects—to ensure "win-win" outcomes—and to managing negative socioeconomic impacts.

Tables 12.12 to 12.16 outline the major themes, challenges, policy options, and expected results of developing seamless, inclusive, and sustainable transport networks within and among the Asian economies.

I believe that it is possible for Asia to have a peaceful, prosperous, integrated, and inclusive economy and society through improved infrastructural connectivity. Comprehensive infrastructure plans and strategies at the national, subregional, and regional levels could reduce any negative social and environmental impacts of infrastructure projects and more inclusively distribute benefits among citizens, subregions, and countries (Bhattacharyay et al. 2012).

Table 12.11
Laws related to passenger transport in Japan

	Related all modes	Aviation	Railways	Cars and roads	Sightseeing
Development of infrastructure	○ Law for the Priority Planning for Development of the Social Infrastructure (2003)	○ Law for Developing Haneda International Airport (2004)	○ Law for Improving Convenience of Urban Rail Transport (2005)	▲ National Expressway Law (2003)	
Safety	○ Law for Improving Transport Safety (2006)	▲ Law for the Development of Airport (2003) ▲ Air Transport Law (2003) ▲ Air Transport Law (2005)		▲ Road Traffic Law (2004) ▲ Road Transport Law (2006) ▲ Road Traffic Law (2007)	
Improvement of utility	○ The Law for Promoting Barrier-free Transport and Facilities for the Elderly and the Disabled (2006)			▲ Road Transport Law (2006)	▲ Travel Agency Law (2004)
Restructuring public sector		○ Law for Privatizing Narita International Airport Public Corporation (2003)		○ Law for the Privatization of Japan Highway Public Corporation (2004)	

Table 12.11 (Continued)

	Related all modes	Aviation	Railways	Cars and roads	Sightseeing
Better utilization of rural public transport	○ Law for Better Utilization of Rural Public Transport (2007)			▲ Law for Optimizing Operation of Taxi Business (2007) ▲ Road Transport Law (2002)	
Tourism					▲ Guide-Interpreter Business Law, and Law for Inviting Foreign Tourists (2005) ○ The Tourism Nation Promotion Act (2006)

Source: Morichi (2007)
Note: A sign before a law name means as follows: ○:Newly established in 2003 to 2007; ▲:Amendment in 2003 to 2007.

Table 12.12
Policy matrix for inclusive Asian transport connectivity

Major challenges	Policy options	Expected outcome
• Continuing growth and development • Creating new economic opportunities • Spreading the benefits of growth to remote and disadvantaged communities and regions • Break the hold of chronic poverty • Narrowing down the development gap, particularly between the urban and the rural communities and across regions and countries	• Urban–rural linkages through transport corridors for developing economic opportunities in the hinterland • Connecting lagging regions with cities and economic centers • Regional (along with national) connectivity for remote and isolated communities • Prioritization of economical/affordable and safe mass transit options (e.g., public bus transport, underground subway and railway) • Developing an optimal integrated multimodal transport network in urban areas	Affordable transport, creating business opportunities, better access to markets, poverty reduction and inclusive growth and development within and across countries/regions

Table 12.13
Policy matrix for sustainable Asian transport connectivity

Major challenges	Policy options	Expected outcome
Dealing with detrimental consequences of infrastructure development on the environment	• Incorporating environmental issues within transport development policies, and address transport issues within the ambit of environmental goals • Coordinating transport and energy issues in a coherent manner through an integrated energy and transport policy • Developing a long-term transport plan • Strategies for low-carbon transport (for example, high speed and regular trains instead of energy-inefficient air cargos) • Focus on sustainable mobility and transport demand management • Cross-border/regional initiatives for knowledge sharing and sustainable practices • Application of advanced technologies, such as the intelligent transport system (ITS), to assist in the management of large public transport networks, and for dissemination of information of train and bus arrival, • Capacity building for developing and maintaining environment-friendly transport systems	Environmentally sustainable green growth at the national and regional levels.

Table 12.14
Policy matrix for seamless Asian regional connectivity

Major challenges	Policy options	Expected outcome
• Promoting regional integration and cooperation for increasing trade and development • Providing access to landlocked and remote countries/ regions and lagging regions within a country • Exploit the geographical advantages to facilitate connectivity	• Developing a long-term national, subregional and Asian connectivity plan (e.g., ASEAN connectivity Master Plan) • Identification and prioritization of projects with proper cost–benefit analysis • Harmonization of regulatory and legal frameworks, standards, systems, and procedures at the national, subregional, and regional level • Fostering knowledge, best practices, technology, and capacity building • Comprehensive multilateral instrument that covers all the relevant aspect of cross-border transport facilitation (e.g., goods and movement of people), similar to GMS Cross-Border Transport Agreement	Increased regional trade, investment, tourism, through increased mobility of people, goods, capital and services, and investment

Table 12.15
Policy matrix for effective and adequate financing for Asian transport connectivity

Major challenges	Policy options	Expected outcome
How to effectively finance national and regional transport projects	• Appropriate policies, laws, and regulations for attracting private sector participation through PPP and for effective privatization • A pan-Asia comprehensive investment treaty similar to the ASEAN Comprehensive Investment Agreement (ACIA) • Identifying and utilizing potential mix of financing • Public funding: economic stimulus packages • Pan-Asian and subregional infrastructure funds • Strengthening multilateral development banks and bilateral donors; establishing new banks and funds • Capital markets: local currency bond markets • Regional infrastructure companies for financing specific sectors • Sovereign wealth funds • Developing potential infrastructure financing instruments • Guaranteed and linked bonds • Mobilizing funds from Islamic financial markets • Public–private partnerships • Asian infrastructure currency unit-based bond • Islamic financing instruments	Guaranteed, predictable, cost-effective and sustainable financing for infrastructure projects

Table 12.16
Policy matrix for good governance in implementation, coordination, and institutions for Asian connectivity

Major challenges	Policy options	Expected outcome
Ensuring good governance, laws, and regulations for efficient, sustainable, and inclusive transport infrastructure projects at the national and regional levels	• Improving infrastructure coordination at the national level: establishing a high level national infrastructure coordination committee • Improving infrastructure coordination at the subregional and regional levels: developing a pan-Asian Infrastructure Forum • Ensuring accountability of the officials • Allowing civil society and other stakeholders to participate in decision-making process • Applying laws, regulations, and policies fairly and consistently to ensure predictability: • Ensuring transparency of laws, regulations, and policies, and that information is available for public • Effective and transparent procurement policy • Developing competition policy • Strengthening investment protection law • Effective land acquisition laws and regulation • Creating for common and harmonized Asian transport statistics	Infrastructure projects achieve quality and cost-effectiveness, effective use of resources, and productive infrastructure investments

Notes

The author thanks Joachim Sedlmeir for useful comments on the earlier version of the chapter. The chapter was prepared when the author was an Advisor of Asian Development Bank.

1. See World Bank Governance Indictors, World Bank website at http://info.worldbank.org/governance/wgi/index.aspx#home

2. The G20 is the premier forum for its members' international economic cooperation and decision-making. The G20 members are Argentina, Australia, Brazil, Canada, China, France, Germany, India, Indonesia, Italy, Japan, Republic of Korea, Mexico, Russia, Saudi Arabia, South Africa, Turkey, United Kingdom, United States, and European Union.

3. APEC is the premier Asia-Pacific economic forum to support sustainable economic growth and prosperity in the Asia-Pacific region. Its members are Australia, Brunei Darussalam, Canada, Chile, People's Republic of China, Hong Kong, China, Indonesia, Japan, Republic of Korea, Malaysia, Mexico, New Zealand, Papua New Guinea, Peru, Philippines, Russia, Singapore, Chinese Taipei, Thailand, United States, and Vietnam.

References

Ahmed, S. 2008. *South Asia: Can Regional Cooperation End Poverty?* Washington, DC: World Bank.

Asian Development Bank (ADB). 1995. *Governance: Sound Development Management*. Manila: ADB.

Asian Development Bank (ADB). 2004. *Responding to the Priorities of the Poor: A Pacific Strategy for the Asian Development Bank, 2005–2009*. Manila: ADB.

Asian Development Bank (ADB). 2006. *Greater Mekong Subregion: Regional Cooperation Strategy and Program*. Manila: ADB.

Asian Development Bank (ADB). 2007. *ADB's Infrastructure Operations—Responding to Client Needs*. Manila: ADB.

Asian Development Bank (ADB). 2009a. *Asian Development Bank Outlook 2009*. Manila: ADB.

Asian Development Bank (ADB) / Asian Development Bank Institute (ADBI). 2009. *Infrastructure for a Seamless Asia*. Tokyo: ADBI.

Asian Development Bank (ADB), Japan Bank for International Cooperation (JBIC), World Bank (WB). 2005. *Connecting East Asia: A New Framework for Infrastructure*. Washington, DC: World Bank.

Agence France-Presse (AFP). 2010. China to invest billions in new high-speed rail. AFP July 28, 2010.

Ahmed, S. 2008. *South Asia: Can Regional Cooperation End Poverty*. Washington, DC: World Bank.

Ahmed, S., and E. Ghani. 2009. *Accelerating Growth and Job Creation in South Asia*. Oxford: Oxford University Press.

Ali, T. 2011. Transport infrastructure: Altering its skewed pattern. *Daily Star,* March 31, 2011. http://www.thedailystar.net/suppliments/2011/anniversary/part6/pg6.htm.

Association of Southeast Asian Nations (ASEAN). 2009. Fact sheet. http://www.aseansec.org/19166.htm. Accessed November 4, 2010.

Association of Southeast Asian Nations (ASEAN). 2010. Master plan on Asian connectivity. http://www.aseansec.org/documents/MPAC.pdf. Accessed December 7, 2010.

Banyan, 2013, An Asian infrastructure bank: Only connect. October 4. *Economist*, http://www.economist.com/blogs/analects/2013/10/asian-infrastructure-bank-1 accessed 8 September 2014.

Baumol, William J. 1967. *Welfare Economics and the Theory of the State*, 2nd ed. Cambridge: Harvard University Press.

Bhattacharyay, B., M. Kawai, and R. Nag. 2012. *Infrastructure for Asian Connectivity.* Cheltenham, UK: Elgar/Asian Development Bank Institute.

Bhattacharyay, B. 2012. Seamless sustainable transport connectivity in Asia and the Pacific: Prospects and challenges. *International Economics and Economic Policy,* vol. 9 (no. 2).

Bhattacharyay, B. 2010a. Institutions for Asian connectivity. Working paper 220. ADBI, Tokyo.

Bhattacharyay, B. 2010b. Financing Asia's infrastructure: Modes of development and integration of Asian financial markets. Working paper 229. ADBI, Tokyo.

Bhattacharyay, B. 2008. *Demand for regional infrastructure in Asia and the Pacific: 2010–2020. Paper prepared for ADB/ADBI Flagship Study, "Infrastructure for a Seamless Asia*. ADBI, Tokyo.

Centennial Group Holdings. 2009. *Estimating Infrastructure Demand for Asia and the Pacific 2010–2020. ADBI commissioned report*. Tokyo: ADBI.

China Statistical Yearbook. 2010. Beijing: China Statistical Press.

De, P., and B. Bhattacharyay. 2010. Does governance matter for efficient regional infrastructure development in Asia? Unpublished paper. TADBI, Tokyo.

Department for International Development (DFID). 2005. Provision of Infrastructure in post conflict situations. June. London.

Economy Watch. 2010. South Korea economic stimulus. http://www.economywatch.com/economic-stimulus/world-economic-stimulus/south-korea.html. Accessed August 23, 2010.

Enoch, M., and H. Nakamura. 2007. Transport policy and organization in Japan. *Transport Reviews* 28 (2): 159–80.

Financial Times. 2010. Beijing reviews high-speed rail plans. November 7. http://www.ft.com/cms/s/0/2a109764-eaa8-11df-b28d-00144feab49a.html#axzz14rVT0ars. Accessed November 9, 2010.

Foreign Affairs and International Trade Canada (FAITC). 2009. Worldwide inventory of infrastructure spending plans. January 21, 2009. http://www.international.gc.ca/canadexport/articles/90121h.aspx. Accessed January 28, 2010.

G20. 2010. Seoul Summit Leaders' Declaration. http://www.g20.org/Documents2010/11/seoulsummit_declaration.pdf. Accessed January 4, 2011.

Glewwe, P., M. Gragnolati, and H. Zaman. 2002. Who gained from Vietnam's boom in the 1990s? *Economic Development and Cultural Change* 50 (4): 773–792.

Hansen, S. 2010. ADB's contribution to inclusive growth in transport and energy projects. Sustainable development working paper 13. ADB, Manila.

Harris P. , G. 2008. China's road to destruction: Following the West on global warming. *Global Asia* 3 (4).

International Energy Agency (IEA). 2009. World Energy Outlook (WEO). http://www.iea.org/weo/2009.asp. Accessed August 16, 2010.

Invest Japan. 2003. Special feature: Japan's private finance initiative on the move. Invest Japan 2. http://www.jetro.go.jp/en/invest/reports/newsletter/pdf/ij_02.pdf. Accessed April 2, 2011.

Jitsuchon, S. 2010. Fiscal policy issues in Thailand after the current economic crisis. Paper presented before Conference on Global Financial and Economic Crisis Fiscal Policy Issues after the Crisis. Asian Development Bank Institute, Tokyo, January 19, 2010.

Kang, J. 2010. Meeting the challenges of financial crisis—China's practice: From developing countries' prospective. Paper presented before Conference on Global Financial and Economic Crisis Fiscal Policy Issues after the Crisis. Asian Development Bank Institute, Tokyo, January 19, 2010.

Kumar, R., and A. Soumya. 2010. Fiscal policy issues for India after the current crisis. Paper presented before Conference on Global Financial and Economic Crisis Fiscal Policy Issues after the Crisis. Asian Development Bank Institute, Tokyo, January 19, 2010.

Liu, Z. 2005. Background paper prepared for the East Asia and Pacific Infrastructure Study commissioned by ADB, JBIC, and the World Bank. http://siteresources.worldbank.org/INTEAPINFRASTRUCT/Resources/855084-1137106254308/China.pdf. Accessed March 22, 2011.

Menon, J., and P. Warr. 2008. Roads and poverty: A general equilibrium analysis for Lao PDR. In D. H. Brooks and J. Menon, eds., *Infrastructure and Trade in Asia*. Cheltenham, UK: Elgar.

Morichi, S. 2007. Update on Japanese Transport Policy. Presentation before Urban Sustainability Conference, Berlin, on September 12.

Nguyen, N. A., D. N. Nguyen, and T. Nguyen. 2010. Current global crisis, fiscal stimulus package and implication for Viet Nam. Paper presented before Conference on Global Financial and Economic Crisis Fiscal Policy Issues after the Crisis. Asian Development Bank Institute, Tokyo, January 19, 2010.

Ogasawara, K., and Y. Yamashita. 2010. Land acquisition for public use. In *Japan-System and Current Situation*. http://www.hosyoukikou.jp/zisyukenkyu/CONTENTS/2010JICA.pdf. Accessed April 3, 2011.

Patunru, A. A., and E. Zetha. 2010. Indonesia's savior: Fiscal, monetary, trade, or luck? Paper presented before Conference on Global Financial and Economic Crisis Fiscal Policy Issues after the Crisis. Asian Development Bank Institute, Tokyo, January 19, 2010.

Peltzman, S. 1976. Toward a more general theory of regulation. *Journal of Law and Economics* 19 (2).

Pernia, E. M. 2011. Discussion in Session 3: Improving infrastructure policy and regulation in Asia. Conference on Infrastructure for Inclusive Growth and Poverty Reduction. ADB, Manila, April 14–15, 2011.

Posner, R. A. 1974. Theories of economic regulation. *Bell Journal of Economics and Management Science* 5 (2).

Raghuram, G., and N. Rangaraj. 2006. *Synthesis report on strengthening policy reforms for transport infrastructure development*. IIMA, Ahmedabad.

Schiavo-Campo, Salvatorc, and Pachampet Sundaram. 2000. To serve and to preserve: Improving public administration. In *A Competitive World*. Manila: ADB.

Stone, S. 2008. Asia's infrastructure challenges: Issues of institutional capacity. Working paper 26. ADBI, Tokyo.

Stigler, G. J. 1971. The theory of economic regulation. *Bell Journal of Economics and Management Science* 2 (1): 3–21.

Sugimoto, K. 2010. A study on fiscal policy challenges in Japan. Paper presented before Conference on Global Financial and Economic Crisis Fiscal Policy Issues after the Crisis. Asian Development Bank Institute, Tokyo, January 19, 2010.

Tabuchi, H. 2009. Japan Drafts $154.4 billion Stimulus, New York Times, April 9, Available at: http://www.nytimes.com/2009/04/09/business/global/09yen.html accessed 23 August, 2010.

Tanzi, V., and H. Davoodi. 1998. Corruption, public investment and growth. In H. Shibatu and T. Ihori, eds., *The Welfare State, Public Investment and Growth*. Tokyo: Springer-Verlag.

United Nations Economic and Social Commission for Asia and the Pacific (UN ESCAP). 2008. Economic cooperation and regional integration in the Greater Mekong subregion. Working paper 02/08. UNESCAP, Bangkok.

United Nations Economic and Social Commission for Asia and the Pacific (UN ESCAP). 2009. *Population data sheet*. Bangkok.

United Nations Economic and Social Commission for Asia and the Pacific, Asian Development Bank (ADB) and United Nations Development Programme (UNDP). 2010. *Paths to 2015 MDG priorities in Asia and the Pacific: Asia-Pacific. MDG Report 2010/11*. New York: United Nations.

Van der Geest, W., and J. Nunez-Ferrer. 2008. *Appropriate financial instruments for public private partnerships to boost cross-border infrastructure projects: EU experience. Background paper prepared for the study Infrastructure and Regional Cooperation*. ADBI, Tokyo.

Wang, H., and Z. G. Chen. 2010. Assessment of the regulatory frameworks, policies and institutions of cross-border infrastructure projects in developing Asia. Discussion paper. ADBI Flagship Study on Infrastructure and Regional Cooperation.

Warr, P. 2005. Road development and poverty reduction: The case of Lao PDR. Discussion paper 25. ADBI, Tokyo.

Wong, E., and K. Bradsher. 2009. China Joins U.S. in pledge of hard targets on emissions. *New York Times*, November 26, 2009. http://www.nytimes.com/2009/11/27/science/earth/27climate.html. Accessed April 7, 2011.

World Bank. 2009. What is inclusive growth? Note prepared by PRMED Policy Advisory Group. http://siteresources.worldbank.org/INTDEBTDEPT/Resources/468980-1218567884549/WhatIsInclusiveGrowth20081230.pdf. Accessed May 17, 2011.

World Bank. 2011. Private Participation in Infrastructure (PPI) Project Database. Washington, DC. http://ppi.worldbank.org/.

World Bank, 2009. World Development Indicators. Washington, DC.

Yun, Sun-Jin. 2010. Not so green: South Korea's growth strategy. *Global Asia* 5 (2): 86–89.

IV Sectors: Energy, Telecommunication, Water

13 "New" Models of Public Ownership in Energy

Michael Pollitt

This chapter is motivated by the following question: What is the optimal ownership form in a particular country at a particular time? By "ownership form," we are primarily thinking about the extent to which ownership is private or public. This is a long-standing debate in the literature and has both theoretical and empirical aspects to it. A general conclusion for the energy sector is that the theoretical arguments are fairly nuanced and not definitive, and hence it is important to consider carefully the empirical evidence on the subject (Pollitt 1995).

The energy sector—which we take to consist of the oil, gas, coal, and electricity industries—has been in the vanguard of the privatization and market liberalization process globally (see Pollitt 2012). Ginglinger and Megginson (2010) report that for the period 1977 to 2004 petroleum industry and utility industry[1] privatizations constituted one-third of all European privatization revenue. However, despite a massive increase in private ownership and the move to create competitive gas and electricity markets in many countries, public ownership remains globally very significant. National Oil Companies in the Middle East dominate global oil (and gas) production. State ownership of coal remains significant in the largest coal market, China. Forty two of 46 leading countries still have substantial state ownership within their electricity sectors.[2] In the downstream gas sector, 20 out of 46 leading countries have public ownership in the largest gas distribution company.[3] Meanwhile some countries at the vanguard of market liberalization of energy markets have combined the introduction of competitive electricity and gas markets with continuing public ownership of significant parts of their energy assets (e.g., Norway, Australia, and New Zealand).

The starting point for my discussion is a referee report I received from an organizational behavior journal on a paper entitled "New Models of Public Ownership in Energy," now published as Brophy

Haney and Pollitt (2013). A reviewer—while rejecting the paper—commented that economists seem "to believe in the fact that changing organisational form changes delivery, which is an assumption that organisational and policy scholars have proved wrong a while ago." Economists "also defend ... organisational innovation, without this to be clearly warranted or justified." This is an interesting comment given that academic economists and policy makers continue to disagree among themselves about the importance of ownership and few would regard the question of ownership as being a settled question. Economists would also, surely, take issue with the suggestion that innovation in ownership (or in any aspect of economic organization) is unlikely, especially in the face of continuing technologically and policy induced changes in the energy sector.

This chapter revisits this debate about ownership in the modern context in which the energy sector finds itself, where policy makers across the world want some combination of secure, low carbon, and cheap energy. These three objectives together form the energy "trilemma," which it currently seems impossible to solve.

The chapter proceeds as follows. First, I summarize the empirics of ownership in the energy sector. Second, I consider the close links between public policy and public ownership in energy. Third, I note the problems of public ownership. Fourth, I discuss the other factors that interact with ownership to determine performance outcomes in energy. Fifth, I explore the "new" public ownership issues in energy, starting with a discussion on continuing public ownership despite mass privatization of energy assets. Sixth, I consider what the elements of a "general" theory of public ownership might look like, before returning to the question of does ownership form actually matter anymore in the energy sector?

13.1 Empirical Evidence on Ownership in Energy

Regarding the empirical evidence on the efficacy of different ownership forms, in Pollitt (2012) I suggest that there are four ways in which to measure the impact of privatization (i.e., the change from public to private ownership). First, performance metric regressions examine the impact of privatization/liberalization variables on panel data of performance (e.g., Steiner 2001). Second, statistical tests of before and after performance use a *t*-test for significant differences in performance metrics before and after privatization (following D'Souza and

Megginson 1999). Third, social cost–benefit analyses of reform (following Jones et al. 1990) look at reform as an investment that has costs and benefits. Fourth, macro studies of reform attempt to find impacts using general equilibrium models of the economy. These studies track the impact on GDP of lower prices and costs in reformed industries (e.g., Chisari et al. 1999).

In Pollitt (2012) I review the literature on the liberalization impacts in oil, upstream gas and coal, downstream gas, and electricity and draw a number of conclusions based on the available literature. In general, evidence from public–private cooperative comparisons of energy companies is mixed, though possibly slightly favoring private ownership. There are issues about selection bias, both in comparisons (the most efficient public firms remain in public sector) and in assessing ownership change (the most inefficient get privatized). It is not clear that it is merely reorganization/strategic focus that brings efficiency benefits rather than the form of the change. Separating ownership effects and more general liberalization effects (which includes the introduction of competition and independent regulation) is very difficult in most cases. However, the evidence on the impact of ownership change is generally in favor of privatization being positive for efficiency.

13.2 Public Policy and Public Ownership

The rational case for public ownership in energy sees ownership as a means to end, where public ownership offers better prospects of achieving government policy objectives for the energy sector. Economists might point out that in theory any policy objective should be capable of being decentralized to the private sector under an appropriately specified contract, but that clearly involves an assumption that such a 'near' perfect contract exists (see Laffont and Tirole 1993 for an extended discussion on this theme).

Whatever the productive efficiency reasons for private ownership, there are legitimate distributional concerns around energy that are to do with ultimate impact on both the average and the distribution of real household income. Public ownership may thus be motivated by political concerns about affordability, energy security, environmental objectives, promotion of capital investment, industrial policy, corporate turnarounds, and energy transitions. In this section I discuss how each of these policy objectives can provide a reason for public ownership.

Affordability concerns may lead to public ownership in order to gain control of both consumer and producer surplus. Public monopolies can keep unit prices down and extend access cheaply, often by price discrimination. Windfall profits caused by increases in the marginal wholesale price of energy can be recycled via lower bills, lower taxes, or higher public expenditure. Not only might this moderate the average price effect, but it might smooth prices and dampen the degree of pass through of international commodity prices into domestic energy bills. Public ownership may directly address public concern about energy prices, the legitimacy of energy profits, the capture of the value of natural resources, high salaries in the energy sector (of senior utility executives, whose pay may go up because of the impact of resource windfalls on corporate profits), and the option value of control of the "commanding heights" of economy.

Energy security is often a political concept caught up with the natural political desire for "national" control of strategic assets. Public ownership may therefore be seen as beneficial to national security. This is often most manifest in the oil and gas sector where there is a worry about continuity of supply, in the event of a geopolitical problem involving the foreign owners. Public ownership could be seen as an insurance policy against economic shocks coming via energy quantities or prices. However, geopolitical risks are inherently difficult to quantify because quantification can be only about known threats and be systemic in nature. For economists energy security is about the value of lost energy supply versus the cost, which gives rise to an optimal degree of energy security. This can be decentralized via proper pricing of lost load, but often politicians seem unwilling to rely on an appropriate price mechanism to address this notion of energy security. In the international relations literature, energy security is often wrapped up with managing energy dependency and reducing dependence on imported fuels and technology. Thus public ownership, to the extent that it allows departure from the normal least-cost purchasing rules of the market, may be used to favor the development of sources of energy that are seen to reduce energy dependence (e.g., state investment in hydro or nuclear power).

Environmental objectives toward energy are several and include safety management, preferences over the siting of energy facilities on the basis of local impacts, as well as the reduction of local pollution of water and soil resources and air quality impacts. Historically the need to manage local environment in cities has promoted municipal ownership; for example, see Lazear (2004) who writes about US local public ownership. Large impact projects such as hydro schemes require public authority and involve nonmarket objectives such as local employment (e.g., the Tennessee Valley Authority in US electricity). Local objections to energy projects are often disproportionate to the national value of project and are often inflamed by private ownership and, hence, need national political support if they are to go ahead (e.g., LNG facilities). The general reluctance to use market approaches to the environment, promotes public ownership. The public sector can also better accept difficult to quantity long-term environment liabilities (e.g., nondiversifiable insurance fund type risks for nuclear).

Promotion of investment in energy may be a key political priority. This is particularly true in developing countries where the government may want to extend access to cheaper sources of energy, such as via electrification of poorer households who are not able to pay the full cost of connection. This may provide a reason for state ownership of utilities in electricity and in gas. On the energy production side, the capital requirements of individual energy sector projects are very large and have traditionally been reasons for state ownership. Of the ten largest individual energy projects (from $28bn to $116bn) recently listed by CNN Money, 8 have state company involvement.[4] Historically the French nuclear power program (1975–1999) cost an estimated $330bn (in 2008 money).[5] It is not clear that the private sector alone can easily handle these sorts of large nondiversifiable risk projects.

Industrial policy toward the energy sector may be an important driver of state ownership. This is often related to energy security above. Energy is an important sector in the economy in terms of investment (up to 30 percent of industrial investment) and GDP (up to 10 percent). Energy imports are an important part of the balance of payments. Thus promoting jobs and growth in the sector is seen to be politically important. The distribution of jobs also important, some jobs can be targeted on poorer/more remote regions (e.g., offshore wind in the United Kingdom may promote jobs in poorer northern port towns and cities). Public ownership may also be motivated by the promotion of local technology procurement, use of indigenous hydro/coal resources and the desire to maintain local employment (especially in the coal industry). Public utilities are important within the sector as procurers of technology and significant in supply chain, and public ownership may give governments more control over this. Public ownership can allow lower prices for favored parts of energy intensive industry.[6] When economies are growing rapidly in their early industrialization, anticipatory energy investment may be important, but difficult, given the risks, for the private sector.

Turnarounds may be a key reason for public ownership, even in advanced countries that usually favor private ownership in energy. The periodic financial failure of private energy companies will naturally give rise to some public ownership in order to maintain continuity of supply. This was recently illustrated by the government takeover of the electricity company TEPCO in Japan in order to effect financial and managerial reorganization. This is a general feature of government ownership. Many firms have been owned, at least for a period, because of failure in private sector. The spectacular examples in the United Kingdom (with dates of most recent state ownership) are Rolls Royce Aero-engines (1971–1987), British Aerospace (1977–1985), British Energy (2002–2008), and the Royal Bank of Scotland (2008–). Each was taken over to avoid the high societal transaction costs of failure and because of the difference between public and private discount rates (private and public NPVs diverge significantly).

Energy transitions also provide a reason for public ownership. The private sector is good at the managed adaption to changing relative prices of energy over the long run as new technologies emerge (see Fouquet and Pearson 2006). However, when a rapid transition is required, this may provide a rationale for state ownership, such as the need to rapidly reorganize the sector in times of war. The prospect of imminent catastrophic climate change might provide a similar rationale for state intervention to reorganize the energy sector toward low carbon production and away from fossil fuels. Historically the public sector played a key role (Chick 2007) in the extension of local coverage to give 100 percent access to electricity and gas and the extension of national transmission grids to promote the exploitation of economies of scale at large power plants. This is because of the large capital requirements (in the face of negative cash flow) and the need to standardize provision (in the face of national priorities) and the potential for the stranding of existing investments.

13.3 Problems of Public Ownership

The preceding section provided strong motivations for public ownership in the pursuit of public policy objectives in the energy sector. The key question for public ownership is whether it can actually deliver the objectives set for it. While the public interest in energy is understandable, a reliance on state or municipally owned entities to act in the public interest requires this to be a concept capable of being sufficiently well defined. Other public entities, other than publicly owned energy companies, may be more capable of delivering the objectives (e.g., a local development authority promoting jobs in remote regions, national university funding for energy research). Indeed there are good theoretical reasons to be cautious about public ownership in energy.

Public ownership is an inherently inflexible form of ownership in that while private firms can be reorganized reasonably quickly (via internal management change or external takeover), public ownership may exhibit slowness to adapt to less obvious changes in circumstances, especially given limits to the political saliency of the management of a particular public firm. However, public ownership *may* allow easier mobilization of assets in the face of radical external challenges. This is likely happen where there is an inability to contractually specify the nature of the challenge (Laffont and Tirole 1993). The private sector as a group (rather than specific firms) has the means to mobilize assets quickly.

Private ownership in the absence of competition can be a vehicle for corruption. Lazear (2004) discusses municipalization as the solution to the local corruption inherent in unregulated private ownership of utilities in the early twentieth century in the United States. However, competition (and private ownership) is generally thought to be good for reducing corruption (Ades and DiTella 1999).

Regulatory capture (Stigler 1971) is clearly is a problem for regulated private entities, capable of buying off public officials. Regulatory capture is also a significant problem for publicly owned firms tied in to particular suppliers, technologies, and the like. Scandal undermines trust in any existing ownership form and is often illegal. However, uncompetitive market structures—such as monopoly public ownership—can make destabilizing corruption more likely.

Meanwhile private ownership has other potentially valuable benefits. Private firms are good at exhibiting a customer service focus (e.g., the UK electricity firm PowerGen following privatization as described in Litwin et al. 1996). Large, often multinational, private firms are especially in developing countries relatively committed to the professionalism of staff and merit- (and diversity-) based recruitment. Private firms are more usually committed to continuous learning and open to periodic reorganizations, especially of staff and finances. They are less likely to exhibit biases to particular suppliers or technology (as witnessed by the immediate diversification of asset portfolios and suppliers following the privatization of many energy firms). Indeed there is a healthy focus on finance within private firms, and an unwillingness to tolerate loss-making businesses. Private firms may be more tolerant of the failure of individual projects, more likely to incentivize initiative and risk-taking and more willing to make midterm adjustments to projects to make them a financial success. This makes private firms more likely to adopt profitable new innovations or seek out low-cost innovation.

Pryke (1981: 36) in his classic study of the nationalized industries in Great Britain noted the large labor productivity gap between state owned British electricity sector and US investor-owned utilities that existed by 1978 and 1979. He found that US power plants used 70 percent less labor per unit of output, while in distribution US private firms used 30 to 40 percent less labor per unit of output than in Britain. These differences reflected superior technology, work organization, and worker motivation in the United States.

Behind these differences between public and private firm characteristics lie the incentive structures on which both types of firms are based. Laffont and Tirole (1993) focus on the principal–agent problem and ownership. The nature of the incentive problem is an important distinction between public and private sector. A key issue is the limits—caps on pay and collars on punishment—that the public ownership puts on incentives to pursue efficiency, accept risk, and look out for new business opportunities. This is also about the type of individual who works in the public or private sectors. Public and private ownership may select different employee types (see Spence 1973). This can vary among countries according to the perception of the public sector (e.g., in France publicly owned firms may attract higher quality employees than would be the case in the United States) and the reality of private sector (e.g., the private sector might be seen to be corrupt in Russia, but highly ethical in the United Kingdom, with consequent effects on its attractiveness to high productivity–high integrity individuals; see Jones and Pollitt 1996).

13.4 Beyond Just Ownership

In considering optimal ownership arrangements, it is important to consider the context in which public or private ownership sits. Public ownership may be more attractive when combined with certain other important features of an economy. We discuss how the level of development, technology, inertia, competition, and regulation may influence the optimal ownership form in a given country at a given point in time.

13.4.1 Level of Development

Budget constraints, especially when other sources of tax revenue are limited, may mean there is pressure to privatize profitable energy assets. This is especially true for middle income countries as GDP growth rates slow (e.g., Argentina at the start of the 1990s). Civil service competence, which affects the ability of the state to run public enterprises or regulate private entities, may be a key factor in the efficacy of privatization. The level of prices, combined with the ubiquity of the product, determines financial viability in the private sector. It is easier to privatize the energy sector if prices are already at market levels and household access is relatively well developed. If prices are being held below these levels or there is a requirement for continued subsidies to extend access, then public ownership may be attractive. The capacity of private sector to manage large firms effectively requires minimum levels of trust (La Porta et al. 1997) that may not exist in some developing countries.

13.4.2 Technology

General purpose technologies (e.g., combined cycle gas turbine—CCGT—power plants) at small scale or in large markets favor private ownership. Large site specific technologies (e.g., large dams) in small markets favor public ownership. Technical progress toward smaller scale technologies and in external governance of assets favors private ownership with independent regulation (e.g., CCGTs in technology and independent system operators in governance). Both the perception and the reality of the existence of economies of scale and scope interact to favor public ownership. The creation of global markets for gas and coal reduces the significance of national economies of scale and scope, while the widespread understanding that electricity generation and retailing can be competitive undermines the case for monopoly public ownership.

13.4.3 Inertia

In determining the optimal ownership form, starting points matter and lead to persistence of ownership forms (e.g., the United States has always had widespread private ownership of energy assets whereas China has not). This is important because ownership change is costly and risky and should therefore not be entered into lightly. Ownership change takes several years to pay off (e.g., Newbery and Pollitt 1997 on the CEGB privatization in the United Kingdom). Political decisions to change ownership can only be taken periodically and are often tied to decisions on other/related policies such as on the fiscal position (Italian energy asset privatizations in 1992) or privatizations/nationalizations in other sectors (the UK privatization of electricity in 1990, within the context of the 1979 to 1996 privatization program).

13.4.4 Competition

Firm-level competition is beneficial because of its long-run impact on innovation and productivity. Competition in energy necessarily involves some private ownership, even if only as new private entrants take market share from public incumbents. Competition usually undermines the rationale for public ownership over time. Genuine competition and public ownership can coexist, as in the New Zealand and Norwegian electricity markets, but it is unusual, and associated with advanced forms of governance of public ownership and part private ownership.

13.4.5 Independent Regulation

Independent regulation of privatized electricity and gas assets is necessary to promote competition, to ensure nondiscriminatory access to networks, and to regulate network charges. Effective independent regulation necessarily promotes entry and the reduction in the significance of public ownership in the competitive segments of the energy industry. Publicly owned firms can be subject to independent incentive-based regulation, but this is usually problematic because of the inability to impose effective financial penalties on public company shareholders (e.g., as in the case of the Office of Rail Regulation, which regulates the publicly owned rail track monopoly, Network Rail, in the United Kingdom).

> In the end, what matters is how the combination of ownership and regulation under private ownership compares with ownership and (implicit or explicit) regulation in the public sector.
>
> Vickers and Yarrow (1991: 116).

13.5 Explaining Continuing Public Ownership

Brophy Haney and Pollitt (2013) discuss why more/continuing public ownership might be justified, especially in the light of the nature of the world economy since the global financial crisis in 2008. Following the theoretical literature noted in table 13.1, they conclude that increased concerns about social welfare (Laffont and Tirole 1993), lower growth, high social discount rates, and lower social weight on profits leads to more public ownership (Gilbert and Newbery 1994). If consumer choice is seen to be ineffective, and because there are noncontractible concerns about security of supply, there will be more public procurement (Hart et al. 1997), and at times of rising legal and political risks, there will be more public ownership (Grimsey and Lewis 2002).

There is also, independent of the financial crisis, a renewed focus on other public policy objectives in energy, which, as discussed in section 13.3, may increase the likelihood of public ownership. Factors behind this include *energy security concerns* rising due to the rise of China in demand, Russia in gas supply, and the increasing share of oil coming from the Middle East; *environmental objectives related to climate change,* and the need to decarbonize electricity sector; and *affordability issues coming back on agenda* after the prolonged rise in commodity prices since 2003. This has led to pressure for re-reform of liberalized energy sectors (e.g., UK Electricity Market Reform).

The key factors at work in this changing environment can be summarized as being related to social welfare priorities (e.g., increased concern for inequality within society), capital requirements (e.g., for large low-carbon investments), and risk allocation (e.g., increased political and legal risks). Figure 13.1 illustrates the key factors at work, all of which may be changing in ways that favor public ownership.

Ownership forms evolve. New forms of 'public' ownership may be capable of delivering public policy objectives in energy. Brophy Haney and Pollitt (2013) define public ownership broadly. Their definition of public ownership encompasses all types of companies that essentially restrict ownership and control rights in ways broadly similar to traditional state-owned enterprises and municipal-owned utilities. Thus public "ownership" can take a number of forms, including mutual ownership, consumer trusts, state ownership, and municipal ownership. Public "organization" may involve cooperation with the private sector and between multiple public bodies. The choice is no longer, simply, between full state ownership and full private ownership.

Table 13.1
Theory of public versus private ownership

Focus	Literature	Private ownership (or PPP) more beneficial/likely	Public ownership more beneficial/likely
Public vs. private ownership	Laffont and Tirole 1993	Capital market monitoring Lack of soft budget constraints Lack of expropriation of investments Precise objectives Lack of vulnerability to lobbying	Target social welfare Resolve principal–agent problems
Appropriation of private firm investments by regulators	Gilbert and Newbery 1994	Demand expected to be high Cost advantage higher Cost of capital lower	High discount rates Low social weight on profits Higher probability of low demand
Public–private partnerships	Hart et al. 1997	If there is strong competition for service supply Consumer choice and reputation loss effective in punishing underperformance	If there is serious risk of noncontractible quality loss Consumer choice and reputation loss ineffective in punishing underperformance
Risk allocation	Grimsey and Lewis 2002 World Bank risk allocation toolkit (www.worldbank.org)	Economic and financing risks Construction risks Operational risks Commercial risks	Political risks Legal risks

Source: Brophy Haney and Pollitt (2013: 3)

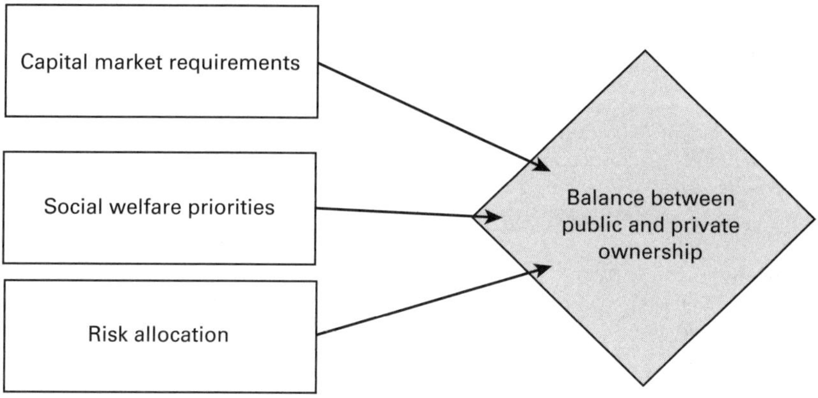

Figure 13.1
Summary factors affecting the balance between public and private ownership
Source: Brophy Haney and Pollitt (2013: 6)

Some examples of modern public "organization" in the upstream energy sector are given in table 13.2. This sector is competitive in the sense that multiple firms can coexist in the market, but even here we observe public-sector involvement in order to address the issues raised by high capital requirements on individual projects, social welfare priorities, and the need to ensure appropriate risk allocation.

Within the downstream energy sector, there are some interesting examples of modern public ownership that address capital requirements, social welfare priorities, and risk issues.

In New Zealand, Electric Power Boards (EPBs) were restructured in the early 1990s as consumer trusts, installing and managing network assets on behalf of consumers. All consumers served by the boards at the time of restructuring were deemed to own the EPBs.

In Great Britain, Aberdeen Heat and Power Ltd (AH&P) was established in 2002 as a not-for-profit company owned in full by Aberdeen City Council. The company was set up to manage Combined Heat and Power (CHP) district heating schemes in the city.

Mutual Energy Northern Ireland, a company limited by guarantee, owns the Moyle electricity Interconnector between Northern Ireland and Scotland, the Scotland to Northern Ireland gas pipeline (SNIP), and the Belfast gas transmission line. It is essentially "owned" by members for the long-term benefit of energy consumers. The Moyle interconnector was the first asset acquired by the company in 2003. The purchase value of the assets was £351m.

Table 13.2
Examples of modern public ownership of upstream energy assets

Asset	Owners	Share	Ownership
Middelgrunden offshore wind farm —*Denmark*	Wind turbine cooperative	50%	Private partnership—8,650 members
	Dong Energy	50%	74% state-owned utility (remainder energy cooperatives)
Olkiluoto 3 nuclear power plant—*Finland*	PVO	60.2%	Several companies in pulp and paper industry; municipalities; municipally owned utilities
	Fortum	25%	51% state-owned stock-market-listed utility
	Oy Mankala AB	8.1%	Subsidiary of a utility owned by the city of Helsinki
	EPV	6.6%	Regional energy procurement company owned by 21 local utilities, mainly municipally owned
Quintero LNG Terminal—*Chile*	BG Group, share acquired by Enagas (Spain) April 2012	40%	Publicly listed on London Stock Exchange
	ENAP	20%	State-owned oil and gas company
	Endesa Chile	20%	Private power generator
	Metrogas	20%	Private gas distributor
Mejillones LNG Terminal—*Chile*	GDF Suez	50%	Multinational publicly listed energy company
	Codelco	50%	State-owned copper company

Source: Brophy Haney and Pollitt (2013: 10)

13.6 Toward a General Theory of Public Ownership

In developing a "general" theory of ownership, I return to my starting question: What is the "optimal" form of ownership in a particular country at a particular time? "Optimal" is defined in the conventional sense of maximizing social welfare. However, the empirical question that is potentially testable is slightly different: What determines the actual patterns of ownership in a particular country at a particular time?

On the basis of the previous discussion I would suggest that there are a number of important of sets of explanatory variables to be included in such an empirical model. These include variables that measure national income, technology, social preferences, institutional endowments, and shocks.

13.6.1 National Income and Macroeconomics

On one hand, low-income countries with undiversified sources of imported energy, concerned about geopolitics, are likely to favor public ownership. On the other hand, rich countries with a high degree of integration into world markets but more concerned about geopolitics might also exhibit more public ownership, relative to their level of development. The government's fiscal position and the significance of the role of public firms in state finances might determine the willingness to privatize publicly owned energy assets.

13.6.2 Technology

One would expect that the use of gas in electricity generation would be positive for private ownership in electricity. Dependency on nuclear and large-scale hydro would be positive for public ownership.

13.6.3 Societal Preferences

National attitudes should be significant in determining the degree of public ownership at any point in time. Thus public opinion on distributional issues (particularly toward key socioeconomic groups), on the efficacy of interventionist solutions and on the desirability of state control would seem to be important.

13.6.4 Institutional Endowments

A sophisticated tax and benefit system gives rise to the ability to more effectively separate equity and efficiency concerns and to redistribute private energy sector gains. This should favor private ownership. The national capacity to establish effective market and regulatory institutions, the quality of regulation and policy-making, and the ability to selectively intervene when necessary allow private regulated ownership to be a good alternative to public ownership.

13.6.5 Events/Shocks

Private sector firms can and do fail, as part of the competitive process and the nature of the operation of the market. Corruption and/or mismanagement scandals undermine support for private ownership and invite public ownership. Commercial shocks (e.g., British Energy facing a collapse in cash flow) may require periods of public ownership for some assets, to allow social beneficial reorganization to occur.

Clearly, societal preferences and institutional endowments are key, as in all development and economic organization questions. Technology is also an important driver in facilitating ownership change. It has the capacity to radically upset existing ownership patterns, as in telecoms. However, income has nonlinear effects and is an interaction term with some of the other variables (e.g., technology). We also need to include time in a model. Lags are likely to be long and variable due to the political cycle in each country and the saliency of other political priorities. All this feels inherently difficult to model given the sample size is limited to 200 countries.

Coming back to the question of "optimal" ownership arrangements, several questions remain.

Can all the genuine (as opposed to mythical) political concerns about energy be decentralized to private entities at reasonable cost and acceptable levels of political oversight? Put another way, is selective intervention more or less costly (or more or less efficacious) under different configurations of ownership?

How do we know that ownership makes a difference? This is difficult because the counterfactual is usually unobservable, except in a small number of cases where there are matched firms operating in the same environment (e.g., following Boardman et al. 2009 on railway privatization in Canada where there were two identical railways, one of which was privatized and one of which was not).

If firms are publicly owned, are societies more or less worried about their performance? That is to say, are policy concerns endogenous to ownership? For example, society may be less concerned about nuclear safety or energy security if assets are publicly owned, independently of objective measurement. This raises the issue of whether society's valuation of outcomes is a function of ownership, and hence the subjective evaluation of the performance of a particular ownership arrangement is itself subject to status quo bias.

Finally, it is worth reconsidering the issue of how to measure the benefits of different forms of ownership. Indeed the benefits of ownership may be not so obvious. Romer (1994) suggested that measures of the benefits of free trade may be underestimated when measured conventionally in terms of cost/price changes. He pointed out that it was necessary to measure the large benefit in variety and quality that resulted from trade (e.g., as exemplified by the near complete collapse of East German industry following reunification). Thus "optimal" ownership may be less about unit cost and more about customer/community satisfaction with the arrangements; reduction in fear of energy bills; release of leadership/political resources to other sectors; expansion of the single market, more generally, across a wider range of economic activity (e.g., within the European Union or the United States); the capacity of the private sector to innovate and adapt to changing political and economic circumstances and to avoid big mistakes. Some of these are analytically tractable (e.g., the fear of bills), but others are not (e.g., avoidance of big mistakes, since the counterfactual is not observable).

13.7 Conclusions

Economists (not organization theorists) continue to think ownership is important (that is why we are writing this book). Fundamentally economists believe that different ownership forms imperfectly compete against each other. They do this on the basis of relative inadequacy (i.e., market vs. government failure). In theory and practice, different ownership forms can achieve similar performance outcomes, and often there are examples of equally effective public and private organizations in the same industry. However, that does not mean that there are not systematic advantages of one ownership form over another.

The public policy interest in energy is the underlying motivator of continuing public ownership in the energy sector. If public policy did not have significant interests in energy security, in the promotion of decarbonization/renewables, and if energy costs were not an important and volatile part of the cost of living, there would be little appetite for public ownership of energy assets. Continuing/increasing public ownership in energy may be encouraged by current/rising concerns about security, affordability, and the environment.

As I have discussed, competition, regulation, level of development, technology, and inertia all contribute to explaining actual ownership of energy assets and the role of ownership in the achievement of public policy objectives. Meanwhile optimal forms and levels of public ownership for a society are driven by income, technology, preferences, and institutional endowments.

There does seem to be innovation within the continuing, new, and emerging forms of public ownership that exist. In particular, mixed ownership forms, mutual ownership, and not-for-profit organizations are gaining prominence in the energy industry. Given the dynamism of ownership forms and the continuing coexistence of varied forms of ownership, it would seem to be the case that there is *still* a role for analyzing the efficacy of different ownership arrangements in meeting societal objectives for energy policy.

Notes

I wish to thank CESifo for their encouragement to contribute to this volume. I also acknowledge without implication the contribution of Aoife Brophy to earlier work in this area and the helpful comments of participants at the CESifo Summer Institute in Venice, July 26–27, 2013.

1. This would mainly be electricity and gas, with some water, privatizations.

2. Source: OECD International Regulation Database, 2013 statistics. Available at: http://www.oecd.org/economy/growth/indicatorsofproductmarketregulationhomepage.htm, accessed April 22, 2015.

3. Source: OECD International Regulation Database, 2013 statistics. Available at http://www.oecd.org/economy/growth/indicatorsofproductmarketregulationhomepage.htm, accessed April 22, 2015.

4. See http://money.cnn.com/gallery/news/economy/2012/08/27/expensive-energy-projects/index.html

5. Grubler (2010).

6. One justification for this might be to avoid marking up energy input prices above their marginal cost, when energy is an intermediate good within an industrializing economy. However, this is to ignore the fact that energy is usually sold on two-part prices, where the per unit charge may be marginal cost.

References

Ades, A., and R. Di Tella. 1999. Rents, competition and corruption. *American Economic Review* 89 (4): 982–93.

Boardman, A., C. Laurin, M. A. Moore, and A. R. And Vining. 2009. The privatization of Canadian railways. *Canadian Public Policy* 35 (1): 59–83.

Brophy Haney, A., and M. Pollitt. 2013. New models of public ownership in energy. *International Journal of Applied Economics* 27 (2): 174–92.

Chick, M. 2007. *Electricity and Energy Policy in Britain, France and the United States since 1945*. Cheltenham, UK: Elgar.

Chisari, O., A. Estache, and C. Romero. 1999. Winners and losers from the privatization and regulation of utilities: Lessons from a general equilibrium model of Argentina. *World Bank Economic Review* 13 (2): 357–78.

D'Souza, J., and W. L. Megginson. 1999. The financial and operating performance of privatized firms during the 1990s. *Journal of Finance* 54 (4): 1397–1438.

Fouquet, R., and P. J. G. Pearson. 2006. Seven centuries of energy services: The price and use of light in the United Kingdom (1300–2000). *Energy Journal* 27 (1): 139–77.

Gilbert, R. J., and D. M. Newbery. 1994. The Dynamic Efficiency of Regulatory Constitutions. *Rand Journal of Economics* 25 (4): 538–54.

Ginglinger, E., and W. Megginson. 2010. The evidence on privatization around the world. *Bankers, Markets and Investors* (Sep/Oct, issue 108): 56–66.

Grimsey, Darrin, and Mervyn K. Lewis. 2002. Accounting for public private partnerships. *Accounting Forum* 26 (3): 245–70.

Grubler, A. 2010. The costs of the French nuclear scale up: A case of negative learning by doing. *Energy Policy* 38 (9): 5174–88.

Hart, O., A. Shleifer, and R. W. Vishny. 1997. The proper scope of government: Theory and application to prisons. *Quarterly Journal of Economics* 112 (4): 1127–58.

Jones, L. P., P. Tandon, and I. Vogelsang. 1990. *Selling Public Enterprises: A Cost–Benefit Methodology*. Cambridge: MIT Press.

Jones, I. W., and M. G. Pollitt. 1996. Economics, ethics and integrity in business. *Journal of General Management* 21 (3): 30–47.

Laffont, J.-J., and J. Tirole. 1993. *A Theory of Incentives in Procurement and Regulation*. Cambridge: MIT Press.

La Porta, R., F. Lopez-de-Silanes, A. Shleifer, and R. W. Vishny. 1997. Trust in large organizatons. *American Economic Review* 87 (May): 33–38.

Lazear, E. 2004. Public ownership in the American city. In A. E. Schwartz, ed., *City Taxes, City Spending: Essays in Honor of Dick Netzer*. Cheltenham, UK: Elgar,130–62.

Litwin, G., J. Bray, and K. L. Brook. 1996. *Mobilising the Organisation: Bringing Strategy to Life*. Hemel Hempstead, UK: Prentice Hall.

Newbery, D. M. G., and M. Pollitt. 1997. Restructuring and privatisation of the CEGB—Was it worth it? *Journal of Industrial Economics* 45 (3): 269–304.

Pollitt, M. G. 1995. *Ownership and Performance in Electric Utilities*. Oxford: Oxford University Press.

Pollitt, M. 2012. The role of policy in energy transitions: Lessons from the energy liberalisation era. *Energy Policy* 50 (Nov): 128–37.

Pryke, R. 1981. *The Nationalised Industries—Policies and Performance since 1968*. Oxford: Robertson.

Romer, P. 1994. New goods, old theory, and the welfare costs of trade restrictions. *Journal of Development Economics* 43 (1): 5–38.

Spence, M. 1973. Job market signaling. *Quarterly Journal of Economics* 87 (3): 355–74.

Steiner, F. 2001. Regulation, industry structure and performance in the electricity supply industry. *OECD Economic Studies* 32 (1): 143–82.

Stigler, G. 1971. The theory of economic regulation. *Bell Journal of Economics* 2: 3–21.

Vickers, J., and G. Yarrow. 1991. Economic perspectives on privatization. *Journal of Economic Perspectives* 5 (2): 111–32.

14 Network Regulation through Ownership Structure: An Application to the Electric Power Industry

Federico Boffa and Lynne Kiesling

14.1 Introduction

In network industries such as electricity, telecommunications, and railroads, the physical network infrastructure has typically been owned and operated by a single vertically integrated firm, with the physical network as only one part of the value chain. Granted an exclusive franchise over a particular service territory, this firm typically faced economic regulation and an obligation to serve all customers at just and reasonable prices in return for this monopoly.

However, economic dynamism and technological change have transformed the underlying cost structure of the traditional natural monopoly, and have made some or all of the transactions in this vertical value chain market based, or potentially market based. In telecommunications this transformation has been the most dramatic, with cellular technology making the physical wires infrastructure contestable, to the extent that many customers now have only mobile phone service.

In electric power, both electricity generation and the retail sale of electric service are technically competitive or potentially competitive (even if not legally competitive in a particular jurisdiction); only the wires component of the value chain can be described as having any of the features of a natural monopoly. The policy approach to this transition has been to implement open-access wires pricing and to retain economic regulation (either rate of return or price cap, depending on the jurisdiction) of the wires company. As unbundling and liberalization in the electricity industry have proceeded around the world, economists, regulators, and industry participants have recommended and implemented changes to regulatory institutions to enable market-based transactions, particularly in generation and wholesale markets and to a lesser extent in retail competition and unbundling the retail energy sales transaction from the wires rental transaction. Yet the wires transaction, the transportation of the electric power to end-use customers, essentially remains governed by traditional economic regulation and cost-based rate-making.

Two fundamental problems arise in natural monopoly and its regulation. The incentives for monopoly behavior inherent in the sole ownership of assets with economies of scale and asset specificity can lead to high prices, reduced output, and deadweight loss; this problem has traditionally led to rate-of-return regulation of network infrastructure industries in the United States. However, such regulation itself poses a problem due to the dispersed and private nature of information and knowledge, and the resulting impossibility of (first-best) optimal regulation. The inability of regulators to observe actual operating costs can lead to distorted incentives, and a regulated environment can also lead to deadweight loss.

A century of experience with such regulatory institutions has revealed several problems with them and the perverse incentives that they can create.[1] First, cost-based rate determination does not provide incentives to minimize costs or to maximize value; it gives the firm an incentive to overstate costs, or to incur more costs to increase the rate base. Even regulatory ex post prudence review of costs is problematic, because it presents the firm with regulatory uncertainty to manage and can make the firm more risk averse and resistant to costs incurred from, for example, implementing new technology or unfamiliar innovations. Second, the information asymmetry between the firm and the regulator means that the regulator cannot observe actual costs, reinforcing the perverse incentives inherent in cost-based rate determination. Third, economic regulation complicates the firm's incentives to invest. The incentive to incur more costs is consistent with increased investment incentives, but if the rate of return or the price cap is set too low, the firm faces reduced investment incentives. The effect that regulation has on the firm's investment incentives depends heavily on the institutional design details and their implementation. Finally, the exclusive franchise right limits the ability of innovations and new technologies, such as distributed generation, to enter and compete with the wires. In situations where policy makers are concerned about insufficient investment in wires (e.g., as in the United States today), this effect is particularly problematic in that such innovations would reduce the constraints on the wires network in the face of increasing demand for electric power service.

The incentive problems inherent in economic regulation of a monopoly wires firm raise a question: Is there an alternative institutional arrangement to sole ownership that may have fewer incentive problems than regulation and possibly lead to better outcomes? This chapter explores one such arrangement—a competitive joint venture—that allows for distributed ownership of the physical infrastructure. In this competitive joint venture (CJV), competing downstream retailers own shares in the physical assets of the wires' distribution company, in proportion to the market shares they achieve in the retail sales of electricity service to end-use customers. This ownership rule provides the wires' owners with a direct incentive to control costs and avoid monopoly pricing of the wires' service, since such decisions would reduce their ability to compete downstream for retail customers. Thus ownership of CJV wires can link the competitive retail sector with the wires sector, enabling us to exploit the benefits of retail competition in the least competitive portion of the value chain. In this chapter we present a model that shows how such an institutional arrangement can generate superior outcomes relative to traditional regulation. This ownership alternative is a hybrid between market institutions facilitating inter-firm contracts and hierarchical governance structures disciplining intra-firm transactions. Ownership of CJV wires combines "single-firm"—or in this context network-internalizing—production and operations with competition at other vertical stages in the supply chain. The existence of scale economies and subadditivity of costs does not necessitate a single *owner* of the network; we exploit that feature to explore outcomes when competing retailers are shareholder-owners of the wires' CJV.

Why explore a CJV ownership structure? Joint ventures have been useful organizational arrangements in several industries, including infrastructure industries. They enable the partners to share costs and risks, to consolidate excess capacity, and to optimize capacity utilization and investment in a new capacity. In many ways joint ventures can harness the cartel-formation incentives in oligopolistic industries to counter the negative consequences of overinvestment in the presence of economies of scale in infrastructure industries. As Stuckey noted in his work on joint ventures in the aluminum industry, "[c]ollective rationality requires that the group-imposed constraints be managed to optimize the group's performance. The major thrust of studies of oligopolies has been to identify the factors that explain how successful a group of oligopolists will be in achieving collective rationality, or, put another way, how well they manage strategic interdependence" (1983, p. 187). Joint ventures thus can provide a credible means of enforcing output and investment agreements.

From a regulation theory perspective, a CJV model provides an alternative institutional framework to the conventional regulatory approaches to infrastructure questions. Natural monopoly regulation presumes sole ownership of infrastructure assets with economies of scale and asset specificity, but that sole ownership is not necessary. The joint venture structure shifts the focus of analysis to questions of ownership rights and use rights that undergird the presence (or absence) of investment incentives, and away from questions of incremental improvements to information-constrained regulatory institutions. Furthermore, by making retailers both owners of wires and buyers of wire services, it harnesses the beneficial tension between buyers and sellers, leading to our theoretical result that the CJV generates efficient access pricing of wires. We also obtain that result because of the competitive nature of the structure—the inability of any firm or coalition of firms to erect entry barriers reduces the ability of incumbent owners to cartelize the joint venture and raise access prices.

We consider the competitive joint venture to be conceptually similar to Gale's (1994) "cost center" cotenancy. However, while in Gale's model production is overseen by an independent manager, implying a form of separation between ownership and control, here we treat ownership and control as in the hands of the shareholders, with two distinctive features:

- Ownership rights in the network result from the market share each firm has on the downstream end-use customer market.
- Control is exerted according to a predetermined institutional mechanism.

We argue that the CJV ownership structure presents efficiency benefits, both static and dynamic, relative to natural monopoly regulation. In a static framework, this institution performs as well as a Demsetz auction.[2] When quality considerations are introduced, however, the CJV institution performs better than the Demsetz auction.

In section 14.2 we describe the CJV ownership structure and couch it in the existing literature and illustrations of joint ventures in practice. In section 14.3 we present a model of how competition in the retail market can be used to achieve competitive prices and efficient short-term investments in the upstream distribution service market. The regulator merely enforces rules governing CJV ownership of the distribution company. This is because this institution does not require the use of public funds, as is the case in other proposed regulatory regimes. Every period, the wires company is owned by the competing retailers in proportion to their market shares. As an interesting policy implication, under the aforementioned circumstances, the mechanism leads to efficiency, a property that can be particularly desirable for countries that have not completed their process of opening the electricity distribution sector to competition. Section 14.4 extends the model in several directions, to include heterogeneity in the retail activity costs, alienability of ownership rights, collusive prospects, and quality decisions. Section 14.5 concludes.

14.2 Competitive Joint Venture Ownership

Consider a CJV structure in which competing retailers own shares in the existing capacity of the distribution wires network. Each member's ownership share is determined by the distribution of markets shares among the retailers in the downstream market.

Capacity expansion within the wires network can be accomplished by any member or group of members who invest to expand capacity. The resulting capacity use rights then belong to those members who funded the capacity expansion and are not shared among all CJV participants. Furthermore the CJV members cannot block an outsider (e.g., a retail entrant) from expanding network capacity, and thereby becoming a member of the CJV. Thus existing members cannot erect entry or expansion barriers. The CJV members share distribution operations and management.[3]

14.2.1 Literature Review

Two streams of literature are relevant for this analysis. The first such stream of literature addresses cotenancy arrangements specifically: relevant works that address theory, law, and experimental testing of the use of cotenancy institutions. These cotenancy institutions have similar foundations to the common-pool resource governance institutions that Ostrom (1990) found and analyzed as shared irrigation network infrastructure. Ostrom's analysis showed that infrastructure commons, in which defining and enforcing property rights is costly, used emergent governance institutions to define and enforce use rights within the commons. The second, the traditional optimal regulation literature, analyzes how regulators should exploit the instruments in their hands—both in terms of information and in terms of extent of their power—in order to maximize total welfare.

Gale (1994) considers a noncooperative joint venture of firms that associate in order to exploit the economies of scale of joint production, and the possibility of using unexploited capacity of their CJV partners. Gale finds that under a use-or-lose clause, the CJV mechanism leads to efficiency because the use-or-lose clause induces cost revelation. His argument, common to all of the papers described here, is that the CJV exploits the economies of scale of joint production, but each firm involved in it is independent, and sets the price independently. In Gale's model the operations and management of the CJV rest in an independent entity established by the CJV partners. Alger and Toman (1990) analyze a natural gas network cotenancy in which an integrated "smart market" outperformed other market institutions. The market institution tested there, a continuous real-time uniform double auction, provides transparent price information for both gas and transportation at each node in the network to all participants; not surprisingly, such an institution leads to rapid price convergence and robust trading to capture the internodal arbitrage opportunities. The treatment variable was the cotenancy of use rights on the pipeline network (vs. a monopoly network link); an important feature of cotenancy in this analysis was the ability of agents to sell or lease their use rights to other agents without their fellow cotenants blocking the transaction. In these experiments the cotenancy ownership structure increased overall efficiency, reduced pipeline prices paid by buyers, and increased prices received by natural gas sellers. Cotenancy ownership of the parts of the network that would otherwise be monopoly links reduced the expression of market power in the pricing of those links, which is the primary reason for the increase in overall efficiency.

The literature on optimal regulation falls into two categories. Bayesian regulation models view the regulator as a Bayesian statistician having prior knowledge about cost and demand functions, expressed by a probability distribution. The regulator then designs a reimbursement scheme that maximizes total (or consumer) welfare under the constraint of decentralized information. The main papers in this stream of literature (Laffont and Tirole 1990; Baron and Myerson 1979; Sappington 1983) find optimal incentive mechanisms that while minimizing the informational rent left to the monopolists, in general, cannot attain the first-best level of welfare that could be achieved under perfect information. Furthermore Koray and Saglam (2005) suggest that the Bayesian regulator will itself require oversight because his beliefs may be manipulatable, and such manipulation may not be detected because the regulator's beliefs are not common knowledge.

Non-Bayesian regulation models (the second category) do not impose informational requirements on the regulator. Institutional mechanisms in non-Bayesian models work regardless of how much the regulator knows about the firm's cost and demand structure.

In that tradition Demsetz (1968) proves that first-best static efficiency can be achieved by auctioning the monopoly franchise rights, and by allocating the right to manage the monopoly to the firm offering to sell the product at the lowest price. Despite its efficiency properties, two issues arise with Demsetz's auction. First of all, having enough firms taking part in the auction to ensure the prevalence of the competitive outcome is important but not assured. Second, Demsetz's auction achieves static efficiency, but it does not perform well in terms of dynamic efficiency. Indeed, given that the regulator, in the absence of information, is unable to measure quality, and given that the firm performing an investment will not necessarily enjoy its full future benefit (it can be replaced by one of the competitors in future auctions), there is a tendency toward underinvestment both in quality-enhancing, and in cost-reducing activities. The static efficiency achieved in a Demsetz auction forms one of the benchmarks against which we will evaluate the performance of the CJV as a regulatory institution[4].

14.2.2 The Use of CJVs in Other Industries

CJV ownership as a regulatory institution has been advocated by economists in a variety of models and applications, particularly in vertical network industries with shared upstream infrastructure, such as electricity, natural gas, and railroads. Joint ventures enable the partners to share costs and risks in the face of uncertainty, often in industries in which the partners must incur large fixed costs ex ante. In infrastructure industries, and particularly in network industries, joint ventures provide both static and dynamic efficiency benefits by enabling partners to manage excess capacity, capacity utilization, and capacity investment. The "competitive" component of the CJV provides pricing discipline by harnessing the downstream competition among the partners. Our model applies to vertical joint ventures, in which downstream firms join to manage an upstream sector characterized by economies of scale.

Alger (1998) argues for using open ownership and competitive rules as opposed to common carriage for the New Zealand natural gas pipeline industry; this model involves open ownership so that anyone may purchase long-term rights to capacity at prices within regulatory constraints, owners must have undivided common interest in shared facilities and it may be possible for owners to establish a total owned capacity which is artificially below physical capacity. Competitive rules would involve owners independently marketing services while paying regulated prices that just cover variable cost, a use it or lose it rule regarding available capacity and establishment of an operator who is independent of any user and who is charged to act neutrally with respect to all owners. These are the rules that may be applied generally for industries exhibiting networks where some activities are competitive and others natural monopolies; therefore they apply to the electricity, telecommunications, airlines, and railways industries as much as they apply to natural gas industries.

Doane and Spulber (1994) look at the effects of open-access transportation on the organizational structure of natural gas in 1980s. They find that open access integrated regional wellhead markets into a national competitive market for natural gas. They also find that incentives for long-term contracts between pipelines and producers are removed by introducing open-access competitive buying and selling of gas at the wellhead.

Vertical competitive joint ventures, usually organized in the legal form of cooperatives, are also extremely common in the agricultural sector, and particularly in the wine sector. In general, they are established to share common inputs. The advantage of this organization is twofold. They exploit scale economies in the provision of upstream inputs, and they involve downstream firms in the management of the upstream facility. This structure ensures a lower input price as well as a closer control on the input quality level. In many cases agricultural vertical joint ventures return surplus income (revenue over expenses and investment) to members in proportion to their use or patronage of the cooperative, and not proportionate to their investment or ownership share. This profit-sharing institution is similar to the institutional design characterized in our model, in which firms are entitled to a share of profit equal to their share of downstream sales. However, firms in wine cooperatives are usually rather small. In contrast, downstream firms in network industries may be larger entities with some degree of market power, facing more complex incentives than those faced by wine cooperatives.

Other industries in which CJV ownership, that is, vertical joint venture, is used to structure transactions include aluminum manufacturing (Stuckey 1983), pharmaceutical research and development, computer memory chip production, and oil pipelines. In these industries joint ventures serve to decrease upstream costs while retaining economies of scale, using contracts to define use rights and to govern the sharing of benefits and of maintenance costs and investment. The prevalent concentration in the aluminum industry suggests its similarity with the downstream sector of network industries.[5]

14.3 A Model of CJV Distribution Wires Ownership

14.3.1 Assumptions

Consider a stylized electricity market with an upstream distribution company and a workably competitive downstream retail sector. There are N firms operating downstream competing in prices.

The single wire company operates at a fixed cost F and at a null marginal cost. Each retailer incurs a cost c for any unit of electricity she acquires, comprising of the sum of the wholesale energy price, assumed to be linear, and of the access charge paid to the distribution company $a(Q)$.[6] The retailer's cost function is then $C_D(Q) = cQ + a(Q)$.

We assume that all the retailers provide a homogeneous good[7] and are constrained to charging linear prices.[8] Consumers are homogeneous. Each consumer is assumed to have an inelastic demand in the relevant range of prices[9] and buys from the retailer charging the lowest price. The aggregate demand in the relevant range of prices is then Q. The demand and the cost structures in the market are common knowledge.

Our model further assumes a credible regulatory environment in which ownership rights, use rights, and the governance and price determination mechanisms in the CJV are enforceable. This institutional environment is known to both the CJV partner firms and the end-use retail customers, who choose accordingly.

The structural regulation imposed by the regulator involves each of the downstream firms owning a share of the upstream firm proportional to its share in the final product market. The time line is the following. First, every period, each retailer proposes to each of the consumers a linear price p that *cannot* be contingent on the access price charged by the distribution company (it may be dependent on the wholesale price, but for simplicity we assume it is not). Second, consumers choose their retailer for the whole period in order to maximize their utility. Third, market share, and consequently ownership share of the upstream firm is determined. Fourth, the access price a is determined by the retailer with the highest ownership share in the CJV. The fact that the same parties compete downstream, while cooperating in the upstream firm, may generate incentives that could lead to inefficient discrimination among downstream firms. In order to avoid these potential inefficiencies, the regulator does not allow the upstream firm to price-discriminate among the downstream firms. Fifth, electricity is traded.

Observe that this CJV governance ties the retailer's choice of retail price and the incentive to gain market share to their ability to choose the upstream access price, and to their upstream profit as well. Also, under the current institutional design, the retailer is now both a customer and a shareholder in the wires company because of its CJV ownership structure. This situation creates a potentially beneficial conflict of interests. On one hand, the firm would like the access price as low as possible as a wires service purchaser; on the other hand, as an owner, the firm prefers an high access price to gain more profit. Furthermore the ownership share of the wires company is determined by the market share in the retail sector. The retailer is driven to lower its cost not only, as usual, to increase his share in the retail market but also to increase his ownership stake in the wires company. Thus we have three driving forces of prices beyond the standard ones. The retailer has an incentive to lower prices in order to gain a larger share in the distribution company. Also she has an incentive to lower the access charges in her role of client of the distribution company. However, in her role of owner of the distribution company, she has an interest to increase the prices in order to increase her profits. Furthermore all N retailers face these complex incentives, and they interact both as competitors and as CJV partners.

Notice, finally, that the length of period t should be selected appropriately. The time period should not be too short, in order to avoid the emergence of excessive transaction costs for customers, due to the high informational load, and to avoid too much adjustment costs for the frequent changes in upstream ownership. It should not be too long either, in order to provide firms and customers with the possibility to adapt in a dynamic market.

14.3.2 Results

The retailers' profits are composed of profit resulting from the retail activity and profit resulting from the ownership share in the wires company. Total profit in the wires company is given by

$$\pi_U = aQ - F.$$

It follows that the profit share of a retailer i in the wire company is

$$\pi_U^i = \frac{q_i}{Q}(aQ - F).$$

The profit originating in the retail activity for retailer i is instead

$$\pi_D^i = p_i q_i - cq_i - aq_i.$$

It follows that total profit for firm i under this market design is given by

$$\pi^i = p_i q_i - cq_i - aq_i + \frac{q_i}{Q}(aQ - F). \tag{1}$$

We can now show that retailer's profit does not depend on the access price charged by the wire company.

Proposition 1 *Under the CJV institution, retailer's profit is independent of the access price a charged by the wires company.*

Proof Rearranging (1), we obtain

$$\pi^i = p_i q_i - cq_i - \frac{Fq_i}{Q},$$

which does not depend on a.■

The intuition for the result is quite transparent. In its role of customer of the wire company, each retailer i sees the access charge as a cost, which lowers its profit by aq_i. In its role of wire company owner, however, i earns exactly the same amount, aq_i. This result, which depends on the decision-making institutions of the CJV, is crucial for the analysis.

Prior to the analysis of the equilibrium price in the CJV game, we briefly examine social efficiency. In this setting, with a constant marginal cost c for the generation and the retail activity and increasing returns in the distribution company, the (second-best) maximization of consumer surplus involves charging at average cost, that is, $P = c + (F/Q)$. The next proposition illustrates the equilibrium price that prevails in the CJV game.

Proposition 2 *In the CJV game: (i) in equilibrium, every consumer pays a unit price equal to the average cost* $P = c + (F/Q)$*; (ii) consumer surplus is maximized.*

Proof Suppose, on one hand, by contradiction, that $P > c + (F/Q)$. Then a firm i' would find it profitable to lower prices to $c + (F/Q) < P' < P$. It would serve the whole market and would still gain positive profit. Suppose, on the other hand, that $P < c + (F/Q)$. The firm charging that price is incurring losses and would do better by not serving its customers.■

Finally, if $P < c + (F/Q)$, no firm i' has an incentive to offer $P' < P$, as it would incur losses; if indeed i' offered $P' < P$, it would serve no market. In equilibrium, $P = c + (F/Q)$, and consumer surplus is maximized.

Even Demsetz's procurement auction, previously discussed, possesses similar properties and yields static efficiency. As we will see later, however, our CJV mechanism has more desirable features than a Demsetz auction in a dynamic setting, generating efficient pricing as well as surplus maximization.

This model possesses several similarities to Gale's open ownership model. Indeed here the only role of the CJV firm is setting an access price. It does not have to purchase inputs, nor bear maintenance costs or investment costs of any kind.[10]

Given the allocation rule for the profit, that it is distributed proportionally among shareholders based on downstream market share, this model and the open ownership model do not differ substantially from each other. However, the institutional mechanism that regulates the two is different. In the traditional form of cotenancy, such as the one Gale envisages, all parties buy the right to access the wires, and the firm is managed by an independent manager, whose incentives are left unspecified; hence there it is unclear why the manager would behave in a way consistent with profit maximization. Our model specifies an institution driving the agents' actions and allows them to achieve the desired outcome in an incentive-compatible manner.

14.4. Extensions

14.4.1 Heterogeneity in the Retail Activity Cost

We now assume that retailers have varying degrees of efficiency. Heterogeneity in efficiency may also result from differences in prices charged by the generators to the retailers or, naturally, also from variations in managerial skills. The marginal cost for retailer *i* is then denoted as c_i. Classify the firms in decreasing order of efficiency, and denote as c_1 the most efficient firm, c_2 the second most efficient, and so on. Differences in costs do not change the nature of the results. It is indeed possible to show the following:

Proposition 3 *Equilibrium in the CJV game has* $c_1 + (F/Q) < P < c_2 + (F/Q)$.

Proof By contradiction, assume first that the equilibrium price P' is such that $P' > c_2 + (F/Q)$. Then there exists at least one retailer i with $c_i < P'$ who has an incentive to deviate, by slightly undercutting P′, thereby serving the entire market. $P' > c_2 + (F/Q)$ thus cannot be an equilibrium.

Assume now that $P' < c_1 + (F/Q)$. Then the retailer naming P' is losing money and would be better off by not serving any customers. Hence he has a profitable deviation.

Any P in the interval $c_1 + (F/Q) < P < c_2 + (F/Q)$ can be supported as an equilibrium. Assume that all retailers charge $P + \varepsilon$, while the most efficient retailer charges P. Under such a circumstance there is no profitable deviation for any retailers. The most efficient firm serves the whole market, and the prevailing price is that of the second most efficient firm.■

The standard Bertrand intuition applies in this case as well. Observe that a similar argument could be developed for the case of heterogeneity in the management cost of the upstream distribution company.

14.4.2 Alienability of Ownership Rights

Up to this point we have assumed the inalienability of the ownership rights. Now we assume that the upstream ownership rights may be transferred. Assume that all retailers but the most efficient one have the same marginal cost for the retail activity, while the most efficient retailer has $\underline{c}$. Further assume that all retailers but one have the same upstream management cost $\overline{F}$, while one retailer has better specific upstream managerial skills and is able to manage the upstream firm at a cost $\underline{F}$. Notice that the retailer with higher efficiency in the retail activity and the one with higher efficiency in managing the upstream wire company may potentially be two different entities.

If the institutional design yielded an efficient outcome, the most efficient retailer would be involved in the retail activity, with a cost $\underline{c}$, the wire company would be managed by the retailer with the most skills in the managerial activity, with a total cost for the upstream activity of $\underline{F}$. The total industry cost is then $\underline{F}+\underline{c}Q$. Maximization of consumer surplus subject to the break-even constraint involves average cost pricing, hence $p=\underline{c}+(\underline{F}/Q)$.

If we include an ownership share trade stage in the CJV mechanism (after the ownership shares allocation, and before the actual production), then the potential gains from trade could be exploited, and productive efficiency achieved. While we do not wish to delve into the institutional details of the trade stage, we observe here that trading ownership rights in this context is possible and welfare enhancing.

14.4.3 Collusion

We now examine the performance of the mechanism in terms of collusion. While the CJV mechanism may raise doubts about a possible increase in the incentives for a collusive behavior among downstream firms as a result of their additional layer of interaction, we demonstrate here that this is not the case if we employ a standard model of tacit collusion.

Consider again homogeneous retailers with a common constant marginal cost c for the provision of the retail activity, and a common fixed cost F for the management of the upstream wire company.

Proposition 4 *Both under the CJV mechanism and under a Demsetz auction followed by downstream competition, retailers tacitly collude on the monopoly price if and only if* $\delta>(N-1)/N$. *Hence the two institutions have the same performance in terms of collusive behavior.*

Proof If retailers were competing only in the downstream stage, and the upstream wire company were managed via Demsetz auction (with a per unit access price of F/Q), the retailers' monopoly profit per period would equal $(p^{mon}Q-F)/N$. A deviation would yield $p^{mon}Q-F$. Hence the (standard) individual rationality constraint for the sustainability of tacit collusion would yield

$$\frac{[p^{mon}-c-(F/Q)]Q}{N(1-\delta)} > \left(p^{mon}-c-\frac{F}{Q}\right)Q. \blacksquare$$

It follows that

$$\delta > \frac{N-1}{N}.$$

Under the CJV agreement, the profit from collusion is given by $\pi^i = [Q(p^{mon}-c)/N] - FQ/N$. The deviation profit is represented by $(p^{mon}-c)Q - F$. The constraint is exactly identical to the situation of upstream Demsetz auction followed by downstream retail competition.

14.4.4 Quality

Here we discuss the properties of the CJV mechanism when electricity can be provided at different quality levels, and compare those properties to the performance of a Demsetz auction. We consider the case where the quality choice (e.g., voltage) depends only on the distribution company. Quality is appreciated by the customers but comes at a cost. The efficient level of quality results from the trade-off between the benefits and costs of quality.

The Demsetz auction can deal with quality in two different ways. The first is that the auctioneer sets some quality standards that the bidding firms have to conform to. For such procedure to yield an efficient outcome, the Demsetz auctioneer is required to know the demand function (in particular, the consumers' preference for quality), as well as to be able to monitor *ex post* the quality level, and to enforce it. In this case, the CJV would have the substantial advantage that it does not impose any information requirements on the regulator.

A second way to deal with quality is to run the Demsetz auction ignoring quality, thereby awarding the franchise to the company that proposes to sell at the lowest price. If price is the only relevant variable, and quality is costly, the winning firm will offer the least possible level of quality. On the contrary, under the CJV agreement, any individual retailer involved in the joint venture (i.e., any retailer with a positive market share), has the incentive to choose quality optimally. In particular, any retailers would have the incentive to choose quality as a vertically integrated monopolist would do. After Spence (1975), we know that under the reasonable assumption that the marginal valuation of quality is weakly decreasing with output (i.e., consumers whose willingness to pay for the product is lower also have a lower valuation for quality), the vertically integrated monopolist will provide a positive quality level, yet lower than the socially optimal one. Hence the quality level provided by the vertically integrated monopolist is higher than the one prevailing in the Demsetz auction, yet lower than the socially optimal one. It follows that even under these reasonable assumptions, the CJV mechanism outperforms the Demsetz auction in terms of total welfare.

14.5 Conclusion

As Vernon Smith observed nearly twenty years ago, "… if the company shares the capacity of a transmission line, then it can either use it, sublet it, or sell it. If just one line with excess capacity exists, then a potential user has two or more owners with whom he or she can bargain. Consequently competition in a market for rights can exist even where only one physical producing unit exists. Scale economies in production need not have anything to do with monopoly in ownership and control. This institution is particularly important in understanding future possibilities for deregulating transmission and distribution" (1988, p. 19).

In keeping with that observation, the CJV institution analyzed here comprises two rules: an ownership rule and a wires access price determination rule. These rules exploit the beneficial tensions that arise because the agents in the CJV are both buyers and sellers, and they thus represent the derived demand for wires service from the downstream retail customers. We find that in a model implementing this CJV structure, it can achieve first-best static efficiency; this result suggests that the CJV could be an institutional alternative to a Demsetz franchise auction.

Our contribution in this chapter is the proposal and analysis of a specific institution, competitive joint venture ownership of a wires network, as an alternative to natural monopoly regulation. Unlike earlier work examining such an institution, we focus on the beneficial incentive alignment of the CJV within a vertical framework.

One important policy implication to arise out of this institutional alternative is the change in the role of the regulator. Rather than serving as an ex ante authority to certify prudent costs and use those costs to determine prices, with a CJV ownership institution the regulator's role becomes ex post market and contract monitoring and enforcement. This shift enables the regulatory institution to circumvent the information asymmetry problem facing the regulator in its ex ante price determination role, as well as shifting the focus of price determination to market processes, and in so doing shifting the focus of price determination from costs to the juxtaposition of costs and value. Thus the CJV ownership structure mitigates the information asymmetry that the Bayesian regulation literature addresses. Some of the existing works on CJVs in infrastructure have pointed out that the scale benefits of network infrastructure do not necessitate monopoly ownership (e.g., see Gale 1994; Smith 1988). This CJV institution suggests that the combination of a competitive downstream retail market and a market for use and control rights on the upstream infrastructure can generate beneficial results, without the onerous information requirements that traditional regulatory institutions impose.

Notes

We would like to thank Ron Braeutigam, Fabio Braggion, Carlo Scarpa, Jim Dana, Reinout DeBock, Ivan Fau, Jean-Michel Glachant, David Haddock, Jakub Kastl, John Panzar, Martin Peski, Salvatore Piccolo, David Porter, Stephen Rassenti, Vernon Smith, Michael Whinston, Dean Williamson, Samantha Zyontz, conference participants at the 2013 CESifo Conference on "The Economics of Infrastructure Provisioning," seminar participants at the Interdisciplinary Center for Economic Science at George Mason University and at the Property and Environment Research Center, and conference participants at the 2006 International Society for New Institutional Economics meetings for their helpful comments. We are very grateful to Zahra Siddique and Kristle Cortes Romero for valuable research assistance, and to the Searle Fund for Policy Research at Northwestern University and the International Foundation for Research in Experimental Economics for supporting this research. 1. See Laffont and Tirole (1993) for a thorough analysis of these issues and an extensive literature review. See also Beard, Kaserman, and Mayo (2001), who show that an upstream monopolist has an incentive for downstream vertical integration regardless of whether or not the monopolist is regulated; however, regulation creates a perverse incentive for the monopolist to degrade the quality of the good it provides to downstream firms.

2. For a setting in which a similar production joint venture agreement outperforms upstream second-best pricing (with downstream Cournot competition), in terms of static efficiency, see Boffa and Panzar (2012).

3. For an extended description of the CJV institution, see Kiesling (2008).

4. See also Williamson (1976) for a seminal related analysis.

5. Current arrangements in the UK railways and electricity sectors, however, are slightly different than our proposed mechanism. Indeed, while they operate on a network industry, they usually do not involve shared ownership of the network. In the electricity sector, the JVs do not involve shared ownership nor shared management of the network (which instead is owned and operated by the National Grid), and they are limited to the generation and to the supply segments. In the railways sector, JVs may involve shared management of the network (e.g., see the Serco-Abellio JV), but the companies involved in it also

cooperate in the downstream sector of train operation. In our proposed CJV mechanism, firms are instead sharing the network ownership while competing downstream.

6. We neglect other costs, such as the cost to access the transmission network.

7. An extension could consist in examining a differentiated product environment, in which electricity may come at different quality levels.

8. This simplifying assumption does not affect the results.

9. Formally, each consumer has a demand of the form

$$D_i(p) = \begin{cases} q_i & \text{for } P \leq c + \dfrac{C_U(Q)}{Q} + R, \\ 0 & \text{for } P > c + \dfrac{C_U(Q)}{Q} + R, \end{cases}$$

where $R>0$, and $Q = \sum q_i$.

10. Clearly, a real-world CJV implementation would be likely to involve both maintenance and investment functions.

References

Alger, Dan. 1998. Open ownership, not common carriage. Working paper. New Zealand Institute for the Study of Competition and Regulation.

Alger, Dan, and Michael A. Toman. 1990. Market-based regulation of natural gas pipelines. *Journal of Regulatory Economics* 2 (3): 263–80.

Baron, David P., and Roger B. Myerson. 1982. Regulating a monopolist with unknown cost. *Econometrica* 50: 911–30.

Beard, T. Randolph, David Kaserman, and John Mayo. 2001. Regulation, vertical integration and sabotage. *Journal of Industrial Economics* 49: 319–34.

Boffa, Federico, and John Panzar. 2012. Bottleneck co-ownership as a regulatory alternative. *Journal of Regulatory Economics* 41 (2): 201–15.

Demsetz, Harold. 1968. Why regulate utilities? *Journal of Law and Economics* 11: 55–66.

Doane, Michael J., and Daniel F. Spulber. 1994. Open access and evolution of the U.S. spot market for natural gas. *Journal of Law and Economics* 37 (2): 477–517.

Gale, Ian. 1994. Price competition in noncooperative joint ventures. *International Journal of Industrial Organization* 12 (1): 53–69.

Joskow, Paul L. 1997. Restructuring, competition and regulatory reform in the U.S. electricity sector. *Journal of Economic Perspectives* 11 (3): 119–38.

Kiesling, L. Lynne. 2008. *Deregulation, Innovation, and Market Liberalization: Electricity Restructuring in a Constantly Evolving Environment*. London: Routledge.

Koray, Semih, and Ismail Saglam. 2005. The need for regulating a Bayesian regulator. *Journal of Regulatory Economics* 28: 5–21.

Laffont, Jean-Jacques, and Jean Tirole. 1993. *A Theory of Incentives in Procurement and Regulation*. Cambridge: MIT Press.

Laffont, Jean-Jacques, and Jean Tirole. 1990. The regulation of multiproduct firms: Part I: Theory. *Journal of Public Economics* 43 (1): 1–36.

Ostrom, Elinor. 1990. *Governing the Commons*. Cambridge, UK: Cambridge University Press.

Sappington, David. 1983. Optimal regulation of a multiproduct monopoly with unknown technological capabilities. *Bell Journal of Economics* 14 (2): 453–63.

Smith, Vernon. 1988. Electric power deregulation: Background and prospects. *Contemporary Policy Issues* 6: 1–24.

Spence, Michael. 1975. Monopoly, quality, and regulation. *Bell Journal of Economics* 6 (2): 417–29.

Stuckey, John Allan. 1983. *Vertical Integration and Joint Ventures in the Aluminum Industry*. Cambridge: Harvard.

Williamson, Oliver E. 1976. Franchise bidding for natural monopolies in general and with respect to CATV. *Bell Journal of Economics* 7 (1): 73–104.

15 Fixed Broadband and Economic Growth: Industry-Level Evidence from the OECD

Stephan Fretz

15.1 Introduction

With the rise of the Internet, information exchange has undergone a fundamental transformation over the last two decades. A key enabler of this process was the deployment of fixed broadband infrastructure at the end of the 1990s and beginning of the new millennium. Broadband infrastructure is commonly defined as a fixed line with a download bandwidth of 256 kbit/s or more. Today the average advertised download speed in the OECD has reached 40 Mbit/s, and penetration ranges from 10 subscriptions per 100 inhabitants in Turkey, to 40 in Switzerland.

While the impact on individuals' lives is beyond debate, the identification of broadband's impact on output and productivity has proved challenging. A number of empirical studies have tried to estimate the magnitude of broadband's impact on economic output variables over the last years. Overall, the results are "not quite conclusive," as the International Telecommunication Union ITU (2012: 2) states in a recent literature survey. Studies conducted at the macro level generally report a positive impact on GDP per capita, but estimates differ considerably across studies.[1] Evidence from industry- and firm-level analyses is even weaker, with the majority of studies finding no positive effect of broadband on productivity.[2] Given the multitude of methodologies applied and research challenges involved, these discrepancies do not come as a surprise; they demonstrate the need for a better understanding of the role of broadband in economic growth.

Meanwhile policy makers almost unanimously continue to advocate further government efforts to foster the rollout of broadband technologies. The European Commission (2012: 13–14), for instance, states that innovation triggered by broadband may create two million additional jobs by 2020. In the United States, President Barack Obama has promoted the construction of a nationwide broadband network as a way to "strengthen our economy and put more Americans back to work" (White House 2012).

Against this backdrop, the question whether broadband stimulates growth—and if so, how and under what conditions—remains an important issue. The literature offers a broad list of ways how broadband may have led to a rise in output or productivity (see section 15.2). Interestingly, to date, these channels have largely remained untested.

In this chapter I investigate three potential growth channels of broadband infrastructure based on productivity data at the industry level. My approach rests on the assumption that not all industries benefited from broadband in the same way. For each potential growth channel, I expect a different set of industries to have been more likely to realize productivity gains than others.

For my analysis, I rely on an empirical strategy that is inspired by the seminal paper by Rajan and Zingales (1998). In their "financial dependence and growth" analysis, they highlight the importance of a well-functioning financial system for economic growth. They show that industries that are strongly dependent on external finance grow disproportionally faster in countries with a more developed financial system. Analogously, I examine broadband dependence and test whether industries with strong broadband dependence increased their productivity overproportionally, either directly after broadband introduction or as broadband diffusion progressed.

I proxy broadband dependence in three ways, each of which addresses a different potential growth channel. First, broadband dependence is measured as share of IT employees in an industry before broadband rollout, accounting for the fact that industries with a high IT intensity were best positioned to realize substantial productivity enhancements from broadband. Second, broadband dependence is proxied by the research and development (R&D) intensity of an industry prior to broadband rollout. This definition could be particularly relevant if the innovation-enhancing effect of broadband (e.g., in the form of knowledge spillovers within and across firms) was the main growth driver. Third, broadband dependence is proxied by the share of high-skilled workers in an industry. According to the literature on skill-biased technological change, high-skilled workers may have benefited most from broadband-related technologies.[3]

The sample analyzed in this chapter consists of 21 OECD countries for which industry-level data on real value added and the number of persons engaged are available from the EU KLEMS database. The observation period ranges from 1996, the year before the first OECD countries in the sample began to deploy broadband, until before the beginning of the financial crisis (2006).

Consistently across specifications, I find no evidence that broadband led to overproportional productivity growth in broadband-dependent industries. Rather, in contrast, broadband seems to have fostered productivity growth in industries that traditionally had a low level of R&D intensity.

More generally, the findings suggest that the deployment of broadband across the OECD did not lead to substantial productivity improvements at the industry level. Further research will be required to identify the circumstances under which broadband still contributes to economic growth.

The remainder of this chapter is structured as follows. Section 15.2 discusses the nature of broadband's likely impact on productivity in light of existing firm-level evidence. Section 15.3 presents the empirical strategy inspired by Rajan and Zingales (1998). Section 15.4 introduces the data and provides background on the broadband dependence measures. Section 15.5 reports the results of the broadband dependence analysis. Section 15.6 concludes.

15.2 Nature of Broadband's Impact on Growth

The nature of broadband's impact on productivity and output is still little understood. Did the impact primarily materialize in the form of productivity increases among early adopting companies? Or did the effect only kick in once a large enough portion of the population had adopted broadband? Was it a one-time increase in output—or does broadband also fuel growth in the long run, thanks to a positive effect on innovation?

Deriving answers to these and related questions is challenging, given that there are a multitude of channels via which broadband may have affected productivity growth:[4] directly through cheaper and faster information exchange, process automation (e.g., e-procurement and e-sales), or offshoring, and indirectly by strengthening the allocative efficiency thanks to increased market transparency and competition,[5] or by fostering innovation. The last channel points to the potential role of broadband as a general purpose technology. Broadband-based applications may increase the overall stock of knowledge in the economy and at the same time lower the transaction costs for individual firms to make use of this knowledge (Prieger 2012).

For my analysis, particularly the question whether the impact materialized at the time of broadband introduction or only gradually as diffusion progressed, is crucial. Figure 15.1 depicts the two stylized patterns.

15.2.1 Impact of Broadband Introduction

The first pattern, displayed in panel a of figure 15.1, shows an impact of broadband introduction on productivity that materializes shortly after broadband becomes available in a country. Such an impact contour would be relevant if broadband led to productivity increases among early adopting companies, and later penetration among the broader business world and population had no substantial impact on productivity.

Companies tend to adopt new technologies faster than households. According to Eurostat, by 2006, broadband adoption in the euro area had reached 77 percent among companies, but only 31 percent among households. Still there are several factors that may preclude a substantial effect on productivity during the initial years after broadband becomes available: companies may have ongoing contracts with existing suppliers, face barriers in adjusting their workforce due to labor market regulations, or require time to adjust their internal business processes. Offshoring certain functions (e.g., call centers) to other countries may take even longer. Moreover these internal changes typically come at a cost, which may depress productivity in the short run (Basu and Fernald 2006). Finally, companies may also adopt a "wait-and-see" attitude until the benefits of the new technologies become apparent (Sadowski, Maitland, and van Dongen 2002). For potential gains resulting from broadband's role as a general purpose technology, which may lead to an increase in the innovation rate of the economy in the long run, the time lag might be even greater. The OECD (2008) notes that for the general purpose technologies electricity and steam, it took several decades before the growth effects unfolded.

The empirical evidence for a positive impact of broadband on productivity shortly after the introduction is weak. Bertschek, Cerquera, and Klein (2011) report that during the early phase of broadband deployment in Germany, from 2001 to 2003, broadband had no impact

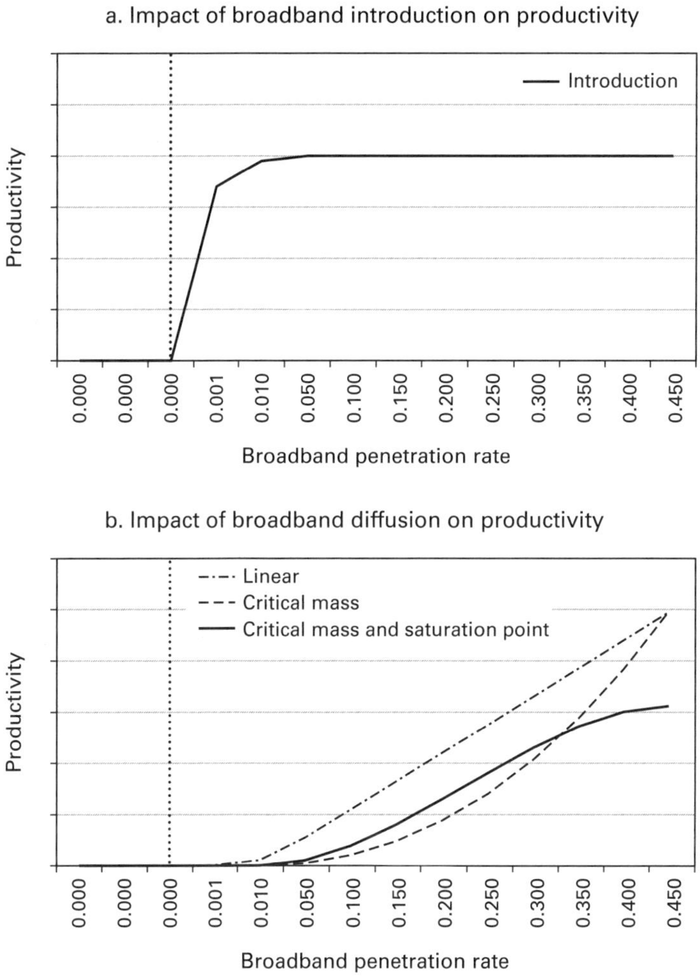

Figure 15.1
Stylized shapes of potential broadband impact

on the labor productivity of firms. Broadband did, however, positively affect innovation activity and thus could have had positive effects on productivity in the long run.

Similarly Colombo, Croce, and Grilli (2013) report that the effects of broadband access and broadband applications on the productivity of small- and medium-sized enterprises in Italy over the period 1998 to 2004 generally have been very small. The authors only find positive effects for certain advanced broadband applications in combination with specific organizational changes. In contrast, the adoption of basic broadband applications such as e-mail did not have a positive effect on productivity.

Therefore, overall, it seems more likely that broadband-related productivity increases among firms materialized only gradually and with a time lag of several years.[6]

15.2.2 Impact of Broadband Diffusion

Panel b of figure 15.1 depicts a pattern where the impact of broadband is related to broadband diffusion. In this case the deployment of broadband infrastructure does not have an immediate impact on productivity; it only gradually leads to higher productivity once penetration increases. The relationship between the impact and the penetration rate can take various forms. In the simplest case, the impact increases linearly as diffusion progresses. However, as has been argued in the literature (see ITU 2012), the impact may also be characterized by a critical mass threshold and/or saturation point. The critical mass threshold represents a minimum penetration rate that needs to be reached in order for the broadband to yield a sizable effect. In the figure that threshold would be at around 10 subscriptions per 100 inhabitants. The saturation point denotes a diffusion level after which incremental increases in broadband penetration do not result in higher output. This may be due to the fact that late adopters of broadband are likely to realize a smaller benefit from broadband than early adopters (Gillett et al. 2006). In the figure the saturation point would be reached at approximately 40 subscriptions per 100 inhabitants.

A recent literature review by the International Telecommunications Union ITU (2012) suggests that broadband diffusion might indeed influence the magnitude of broadband's impact on growth. In particular, broadband seems to contribute more to economic growth in countries with higher broadband diffusion (see Koutroumpis 2009).

The published broadband penetration rate relates to the total number of broadband subscriptions by businesses and households in the economy. In the year when broadband was introduced in a particular OECD country, broadband adoption was typically well below 1 subscriber per 100 inhabitants. It seems unlikely that at this low penetration level, broadband would have made a fundamental difference. Moreover households typically adjust their behavior only incrementally, and not in a disruptive manner. E-commerce, for instance, did not replace traditional retail sales from one day to the next. Rather, it led to a gradual shift across the different sales channels.

Also for the period following the initial rollout years, empirical evidence for a positive impact of broadband on firm productivity is relatively weak. Haller and Lyons (2012), for instance, look at a sample of 2,200 manufacturing firms in Ireland over the period 2002 to 2009 and do not find a statistically significant impact on the productivity of firms from broadband adoption.

In 2008 the UK Office for National Statistics published a report, funded by Eurostat, that linked data from different surveys across 13 European countries on information and communication technologies (ICT) use by businesses. The results for the impact of broadband use on firm productivity are rather inconclusive. Franklin (2008), for instance, shows that within the manufacturing sector of most European countries, the share of a firm's workers with access to high-speed Internet in 2004 is positively correlated with the level of total factor productivity. However, this correlation does not necessarily imply a causal relationship.

In the same report van Leeuwen and Farooqui (2008) analyze the impact of different ICT variables on firm productivity for the Netherlands and the United Kingdom. In a simultaneous equation model the different ICT variables are allowed to affect both the stock of ICT capital and total factor productivity. The results suggest that broadband use is positively associated with ICT capital, but not with total factor productivity.

The only firm-level study that shows a strong positive impact of broadband is the one by Grimes, Ren, and Stevens (2012). These authors compare firms with and without broadband access in New Zealand in 2006 using propensity score matching and report that productivity was 7 to 10 percent higher in firms using broadband.

In my analysis, I test for both potential impact shapes, for an effect shortly after introduction and for a gradual effect that rose as diffusion progressed. The empirical strategy is explained in the next section.

15.3 Empirical Strategy

Rajan and Zingales (1998) show that industries that are more dependent on external finance grow disproportionally faster in countries with well-developed financial systems. In their research setup they exploit the fact that financial dependence varies across industries, whereas the quality of a financial system differs across countries.

I apply an approach similar to theirs to investigate the effects of broadband infrastructure on productivity growth. Specifically, I construct an interaction term between broadband penetration at the country level and broadband dependence at the industry level. Broadband dependence is defined in three ways: first, as share of IT employees as percent of total employees in the industry (IT dependence); second, as share of R&D expenditures as percent of total value added (R&D dependence); and third, as share of high-skilled workers (high-skill dependence). For each industry, broadband dependence is held constant across countries. All measures are derived from values in the United States in 1997 (start of broadband deployment), under the assumption that before the introduction of broadband the US economy was a leading economy in terms of IT adoption, R&D activity, and the prevalence of high-skilled workers. Using values prior to the rollout ensures that the analysis is not confounded by potential effects broadband had on the industry structure (e.g., offshoring of certain activities). The dependent variable is growth in productivity, defined as real value added (VA) per worker.

Each of the three broadband dependence measures investigates a different way broadband could have spurred growth. A statistically significant positive coefficient for the IT dependence interaction term, for instance, would suggest that broadband led to substantial productivity improvements among firms with a strong reliance on IT. A positive coefficient for the R&D dependence interaction term would imply that industries with a focus on innovation benefited most from broadband. According to Koutroumpis (2009: 471–72), broadband "guarantees the provision of information and decreases search and transaction times," thus enhancing the capabilities of workers and fostering the communication between companies. Such a reduction in the cost of information exchange could have had a positive impact on innovation and knowledge spillovers across firms. Finally, a positive coefficient for the high-skill dependence interaction term would indicate that broadband's impact mainly accrued in industries with a large share of high-skilled workers, confirming findings by, for example, Forman, Goldfarb, and Greenstein (2012) and Atasoy (2013) that the Internet had a skill-biased impact similar to earlier generations of information technologies.

The approach of exploiting within-country differences across industries not only allows us to identify whether broadband seems to have had a positive impact on productivity. It also provides insights into which channel produced such a potential growth effect. Moreover, thanks to the inclusion of fixed effects, the approach should be less prone to omitted variable bias or model misspecification than other estimation strategies (see Rajan and Zingales 1998: 563).

The approach rests on the assumption that the impact of broadband differs across industries according to a certain characteristic (i.e., broadband dependence, defined in any of the proposed ways). As a consequence I would not be able to detect a potential growth effect if the impact were the same across all industries (which seems unlikely given existing evidence[7]), or if it were not related to any of the characteristics used as proxy for broadband dependence.

To capture the different impact shapes presented in section 15.2, I apply two different empirical specifications: the first focusing on the potential short-term impact of broadband introduction, and the second testing for a gradual impact related to the broadband penetration rate.

15.3.1 Impact of Broadband Introduction

The analysis of a short-term impact of broadband introduction on productivity is challenging given that all countries introduced broadband within a short period of time (i.e., between 1997 and 2000). Moreover there is some uncertainty around the true introduction year for certain countries (due to limited data availability and some pre-launches in certain regions within countries), and in 2001 the burst of the dot-com bubble led to a decrease in productivity that was not entirely driven by fundamentals but also included a cyclical component. Nonetheless, one can make the following conjecture: if broadband's main impact materialized shortly after introduction, one should see a difference in productivity growth of broadband-dependent industries between early and late adopters in particular during the period 1996 to 2000 when the rollout of broadband started.

The empirical specification closely follows Rajan and Zingales (1998) but uses growth of productivity rather than output as dependent variable. In contrast to Rajan and Zingales, I do not include the lagged industry share as additional explanatory variable besides fixed effects and the interaction term, given that productivity growth is not necessarily linked to the industry share.

The cross-sectional growth regression equation reads as follows:

$$\Delta \ln Prod_{j,i} = constant + \beta(YBBI_i * BBDep_j) + \delta_i + \rho_j + \varepsilon_{j,i},$$

where $\Delta \ln Prod_{j,i}$ is the growth of value added per worker in industry j in country i over the period when broadband rollout started across the OECD (i.e., 1996 to 2000). $(YBBI_i * BBDep_j)$ is my variable of interest, the interaction between the year of broadband introduction at the country level and broadband dependence at the industry level. In the event of a sizable short-term effect of broadband on productivity in broadband-dependent industries, this interaction term may be expected to have a statistically significant, negative coefficient. In contrast to the second specification, the identification exploits differences in the timing of broadband rollout rather than changes in the broadband penetration rate. δ_i and ρ_j are a set of country and industry dummies, and $\varepsilon_{j,i}$ denotes the country-industry-specific error term.

15.3.2 Impact of Broadband Diffusion

The empirical specification for a potential gradual impact is also inspired by Rajan and Zingales (1998), but I use a panel rather than a cross-sectional setup. The panel specification accounts for the fact that broadband penetration increased strongly over the observation period, and potential productivity increases might have been related to this rise in broadband diffusion rather than to differences in the level of broadband penetration across countries. I include country-year-specific fixed effects to control for any economy-wide shocks that affected all industries in a similar way in a given year (e.g., cyclical fluctuations). The country-year fixed effects also capture the part of broadband's effect on productivity that was uniform across the economy. Note that this specification is very flexible in that it does not require broadband's impact on productivity to have been linear, nor the same across countries. It thus would also capture a potential critical mass threshold or saturation point. Similar to the original Rajan and Zingales setup, the broadband penetration rate only enters the regression equation as part of the interaction term, testing whether productivity grew more in industries with strong broadband dependence as broadband diffusion progressed.

The panel regression equation reads as follows:

$$\Delta \ln Prod_{j,i,t} = constant + \beta(BB_{i,t} * BBDep_j) + \delta_{i,t} + \rho_{j,i} + \varepsilon_{j,i,t},$$

where $\Delta \ln Prod_{j,i,t}$ is the growth rate of value added per worker in industry j in country i in year t. $(BB_{i,t} * BBDep_j)$ is my variable of interest, the interaction between broadband penetration at the country level and broadband dependence at the industry level. $\delta_{i,t}$ is a set of country-specific year fixed effects that capture shocks that are common to all industries in a country, in particular, the business cycle. $\rho_{j,i}$ is a full set of country-industry dummies, which account for the fact that the productivity growth trend may differ across industries and countries. Differences may, for instance, arise between manufacturing and services, more and less developed OECD countries, and due to country-specific factors affecting certain industries (e.g., regulation). $\varepsilon_{j,i,t}$ denotes the error term.

15.4 Data

15.4.1 Broadband Penetration Data

I used data on broadband penetration from the World Bank World Development Indicators. The broadband penetration rate is defined as fixed broadband Internet subscriptions per 100 people, that is, "the number of broadband subscribers with a digital subscriber line, cable modem, or other high-speed technology" per 100 inhabitants (see http://data.worldbank.org/indicator/IT.NET.BBND.P2). For the first years, I supplemented the World Bank data with data from the OECD fixed (wired) broadband penetration historical time series (June 2010). For each analysis, I used the earliest penetration data that are available in either of the two databases.

Figure 15.2 shows that during the observation period 1997 to 2006, broadband penetration differed strongly across the 21 OECD countries in our sample.[8] By the year 2000 all countries in the sample had started to deploy broadband, but only in 2005 did the last country (Greece) reach a penetration level of at least 1 subscription per 100 inhabitants. South Korea was the clear leader in terms of broadband adoption between 2000 and 2004.

15.4.2 Industry-Level Economic Data

Industry-level data on value added and employment come from the "EU KLEMS Growth and Productivity Accounts: November 2009 Release" and cover 21 OECD countries. Luxembourg is excluded from the analysis due to its small size and strong focus on financial services. Data are available through 2006 or 2007. The only exception is Canada where I have to rely on data from the March 2008 release that covers the period until 2004.

To calculate value added in real 2005 USD, I use the following variables: gross value added at current basic prices in local currency (VA),

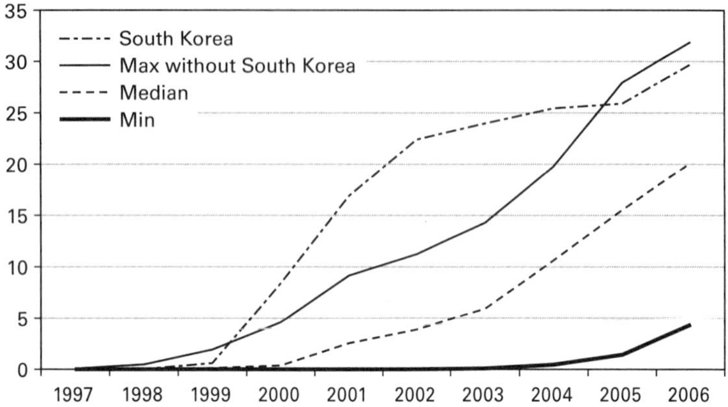

Figure 15.2
Broadband subscriptions per 100 inhabitants in the OECD country sample, 1997 to 2006
Source: Data from the World Bank World Development Indicators and the OECD fixed (wired) broadband penetration historical time series (June 2010).

gross value added price indexes (VA_P), and average exchange rates for year 2005 from Global Insight and Oanda. For Canada, value added is expressed in real 2004 USD terms. The number of workers in an industry is measured as number of persons engaged (EMP).

15.4.3 Broadband Dependence Data

As mentioned above, I define the degree of broadband dependence of an industry in three different ways. First, I approximate broadband dependence by an industry's dependence on IT, measured as share of IT workers as percent of total workers in the industry in the United States in 1997 (i.e., starting year of US broadband deployment). Atkinson and Stewart (2012: 19) write that "the number of IT workers in non-IT industries is a good proxy to measure the extent to which traditional industries are making use of IT." Using the values before the rollout of broadband, this definition of broadband dependence characterizes industries that were likely to benefit from broadband early in the adoption process in the form of productivity enhancements. The data come from the US Bureau of Labor Statistics.

Second, I use an industry's R&D intensity as a proxy for its broadband dependence. The R&D intensity of an industry is measured as share of R&D expenditures as percent of industry value added in the United States in 1997. This definition accounts for the fact that

Table 15.1
Correlations between broadband dependence measures

	IT dependence	R&D dependence	High-skill dependence
IT dependence	1.00		
R&D dependence	0.4336 (0.0438)	1.00	
High-skill dependence	0.4688 (0.0078)	0.4259 (0.0690)	1.00

Note: Not all broadband dependence measures cover the same set of industries. IT dependence and high-skill dependence cover 31, R&D dependence 21 industries. p-values are in parentheses.
Source: Data for the United States in 1997 from the US Bureau of Labor Statistics (IT dependence), OECD STAN database (R&D dependence), and the EU KLEMS March 2008 release (High-skill dependence).

broadband could have facilitated the exchange of information and ideas and thus could have particularly benefited innovation-driven industries. The data come from the OECD STAN database.

Third, I use the share of high-skilled workers in the United States in 1997, taken from the EU KLEMS March 2008 release. Given its potential complementarity to human capital, broadband would have been particularly beneficial for industries with a large share of high-skilled employees.

Table 15.1 contains the correlations between the different broadband dependence measures. Strong correlations would undermine the analysis in the sense that the different proxies for broadband dependence would measure more or less the same. The correlation matrix shows that this is not the case. The correlations between IT, R&D, and high-skill dependence measures are all below 0.5.

15.5 Results

15.5.1 Impact of Broadband Introduction

Table 15.2 provides the results of my testing for the potential short-term impact of broadband introduction. The dependent variable is the four-year productivity growth between 1996 and 2000, calculated as the difference in the log real value added per worker. The interaction term is constructed as a product of broadband dependence at the industry level and the year of broadband introduction at the country level. In the case of a positive short-term impact in broadband-dependent

Table 15.2
Impact of broadband introduction

Dependent variable: Change in log real VA per worker, 1996 to 2000			
	(1) IT	(2) R&D	(3) High-skill
Year of BB intro * IT dep.	0.00737 (0.0108)		
Year of BB intro * R&D dep.		0.00102 (0.00461)	
Year of BB intro * High-skill dep.			0.00176 (0.00156)
Country fixed effects	Yes	Yes	Yes
Industry fixed effects	Yes	Yes	Yes
Constant	-0.604 (0.946)	-2.836 (13.05)	-47.53 (42.29)
Observations	630	438	648
R-squared	0.063	0.085	0.063

Note: Robust standard errors, clustered at the country level, are in parentheses; *** $p < 0.01$, ** $p < 0.05$, * $p < 0.1$.

industries shortly after broadband introduction, the interaction term would be expected to be negative—indicating that broadband-dependent industries grew disproportionally slower in countries that introduced broadband only with a delay.

The results provide no evidence for such a short-term impact. The coefficients for all three interactions are not statistically different from zero, and the point estimates are even positive. This finding is in line with the firm-level studies mentioned in section 15.2, which found no effect on firm productivity in the initial years after broadband introduction.

Table 15.3 shows that the finding does not substantially change if the analysis is conducted for manufacturing and services (excluding utilities) separately. Only the interaction term for the share of high-skilled workers in the services regression is statistically significant—yet again has a positive sign. The coefficient suggests that in countries that introduced broadband comparably late, industries with a large share of high-skilled workers experienced disproportionate productivity growth.

How to interpret this finding? It seems unlikely that the positive interaction term in fact reflects a positive impact of broadband on

Table 15.3
Impact of broadband introduction for manufacturing and services

Dependent variable: Change in log real VA per worker, 1996 to 2000						
	(1)	(2)	(3)	(4)	(5)	(6)
	IT		R&D		High-skill	
	Manu.	Serv.	Manu.	Serv.	Manu.	Serv.
Year of BB intro * IT dep.	-0.00241 (0.0402)	0.00676 (0.00518)				
Year of BB intro * R&D dep.			0.00282 (0.00460)	-0.0705 (0.108) .		
Year of BB intro * High-skill dep.					-0.000203 (0.00476)	0.00188** (0.000873)
Country fixed effects	Yes	Yes	Yes	Yes	Yes	Yes
Industry fixed effects	Yes	Yes	Yes	Yes	Yes	Yes
Constant	0.333 (3.485)	-0.992 (0.792)	-7.839 (13.00)	10.55 (16.13)	5.632 (128.8)	-39.30** (18.25)
Observations	315	294	273	144	315	312
R-squared	0.120	0.146	0.146	0.203	0.120	0.135

Note: Robust standard errors, clustered at the country level, are in parentheses; *** $p < 0.01$, ** $p < 0.05$, * $p < 0.1$.

the productivity growth of high-skilled service workers among broadband latecomers. In countries that introduced broadband in later years, in particular 1999 and 2000, the effect had even less time to materialize. However, services with a high share of skilled workers, such as financial intermediation, may have overproportionally increased their productivity in these countries independent of broadband deployment.

An alternative interpretation: that the outperformance of services with a large share of high-skilled workers among broadband latecomers actually reflects the outperformance of industries with many low-skilled workers in early adopting countries. The service industries with the lowest share of high-skilled workers are privately employed persons, the sale and repair of motor vehicles, hotels and restaurants, transport and storage, and retail trade. Potentially these industries experienced disproportional productivity gains, not only thanks to broadband but also in the form of cyclical effects due to the dot-com economy boom in the late 1999s. For the analysis the year 2000 seems to play a crucial role: for a similar analysis with ending year 1999 or 2001 over 3 respectively 5 years, the coefficient turns negative and loses its statistical significance.

More research will be required to understand the impact of broadband on specific service industries in more detail. However, overall, the short-term broadband dependence analysis in the spirit of Rajan and Zingales provides little evidence for a sizable impact of broadband on productivity growth during the initial years following its introduction. Broadband-dependent industries—according to any of the three definitions—did not experience overproportional growth in countries that introduced broadband relatively early.

15.5.2 Impact of Broadband Diffusion

Table 15.4 provides the main results for the broadband diffusion panel analysis. The dependent variable is the annual growth of real value added per worker. Columns 1, 3, and 5 include the interaction term of the current period; Columns 2, 4, and 6 allow for a lag of one year.

None of the interaction terms are statistically significant, thus again providing no evidence for an outperformance of IT, R&D, or high-skill intensive industries as broadband penetration progressed over the period 1997 to 2006.

Potentially the impact of broadband was different for manufacturing and services. For instance, R&D dependence might have been more relevant for manufacturing than services. Table 15.5 presents results for manufacturing and services (excluding utilities) separately.

The results provide little evidence for potential impact heterogeneity. Only the interaction between broadband penetration and R&D dependence for manufacturing shows a significant, yet negative coefficient. The negative interaction suggests that as broadband diffusion progressed, manufacturing industries with larger R&D intensity experienced slower productivity growth compared to industries with a smaller dependence on R&D. Services seem to have followed a similar trend, with a negative point estimate that is even larger in magnitude and that almost reaches the 10 percent significance level (p-value of 0.145). A potential interpretation for this finding could be that broadband helped increase productivity in industries that traditionally were *not* strong in innovation, namely through the reorganization of business processes.

Table 15.4
Impact of broadband diffusion

Dependent variable: Annual growth of real VA per worker, panel 1997 to 2006						
	(1)	(2)	(3)	(4)	(5)	(6)
	IT		R&D		High-skill	
BB penetration * IT dep.	-2.94e-05 (6.41e-05)					
Lag BB penetration * IT dep.		-1.68e-05 (8.33e-05)				
BB penetration * R&D dep.			-1.29e-05 (1.84e-05)			
Lag BB penetration * R&D dep.				-5.62e-06 (2.36e-05)		
BB penetration * High-skill dep.					-9.98e-06 (6.89e-06)	
Lag BB penetration * High-skill dep.						-1.15e-05 (9.06e-06)
Country-industry fixed effects	Yes	Yes	Yes	Yes	Yes	Yes
Country-year fixed effects	Yes	Yes	Yes	Yes	Yes	Yes
Constant	0.0156*** (0.00546)	0.0213*** (0.00267)	0.0176** (0.00754)	0.0256*** (0.00648)	0.0147*** (0.00558)	0.0246*** (0.00313)
Observations	6,240	6,240	4,344	4,344	6,418	6,418
R-squared	0.049	0.049	0.065	0.065	0.049	0.049
Number of country-industries	630	630	438	438	648	648

Note: Robust standard errors, clustered at the country-industry level, are in parentheses; *** $p < 0.01$, ** $p < 0.05$, * $p < 0.1$.

Table 15.5
Impact of broadband diffusion for manufacturing and services

Dependent variable: Annual growth of real VA per worker, panel 1997 to 2006

	(1)	(2)	(3)	(4)	(5)	(6)
	IT		R&D		High-skill	
	Manu.	Serv.	Manu.	Serv.	Manu.	Serv.
BB penetration * IT dep.	0.000182 (0.000181)	-4.94e-05 (6.43e-05)				
BB penetration * R&D dep.			-4.57e-05** (2.07e-05)	-0.000419 (0.000286)		
BB penetration * High-skill dep.					7.56e-06 (2.59e-05)	-6.74e-06 (5.70e-06)
Country-industry fixed effects	Yes	Yes	Yes	Yes	Yes	Yes
Country-year fixed effects	Yes	Yes	Yes	Yes	Yes	Yes
Constant	0.0164 (0.0104)	0.0169*** (0.00309)	0.0233** (0.0117)	0.0181*** (0.00364)	0.0169 (0.0111)	0.0147*** (0.00346)
Observations	3,120	2,912	2,704	1,432	3,120	3,090
R-squared	0.095	0.075	0.109	0.133	0.095	0.078
Number of country-industries	315	294	273	144	315	312

Note: Robust standard errors, clustered at the country-industry level, are in parentheses; *** $p < 0.01$, ** $p < 0.05$, * $p < 0.1$.

15.6 Conclusion

In recent years several authors have tried to quantify the impact of fixed broadband on economic growth. The findings of these studies at the macro, industry, and firm levels remain inconclusive, however. Estimates vary from zero effect to sizeable impact on the level or growth rate of output per capita. Moreover the analyses do not provide insights into the growth channels at work.

In this chapter I investigate three potential channels for how broadband could have led to growth. The analysis is based on industry-level productivity data for a sample of 21 OECD countries during the period

1997 to 2006. I rely on an empirical strategy inspired by Rajan and Zingales (1998), where identification of the growth effect of broadband rests on the assumption that the magnitude of the impact differed across industries based on their degree of broadband dependence. I use IT intensity, R&D intensity, and the share of high-skilled workers to proxy for an industry's broadband dependence and test for two different impact patterns: a potential impact shortly after broadband introduction that would have been triggered by early adopting companies, and a more gradual effect that rose as broadband was adopted among firms and households across the broader economy.

Consistently across specifications, the results suggest that broadband-dependent industries did *not* experience overproportional productivity growth during the early years when broadband was rolled out across the OECD. In contrast, I find some evidence that broadband could have fostered productivity growth in industries that traditionally had a low level of R&D intensity, in particular, within manufacturing.

The findings cast doubt on some of the growth-enhancing effects of broadband reported in studies at the macro level. They also confirm the results of existing firm-level studies, which generally find no substantial productivity benefits from the use of broadband. In consequence it seems likely that a sizable portion of broadband's welfare gains has accrued to individuals in the form of higher consumer surplus (thanks to online search, price comparison websites, etc.), which is not captured by traditional output or productivity statistics.

Further research will be required to identify the conditions under which broadband indeed leads to measurable productivity gains, both in manufacturing and in services. Recently Forman, Goldfarb, and Greenstein (2012) have shown that the introduction of advanced Internet applications among businesses in the United States during 1995 to 2000 had a heterogeneous effect on regional wages: only 6 percent of counties experienced an increase in wages, whereas the other 94 percent do not seem to have benefited. The counties with wage growth were typically characterized by a combination of high income, education, population, and IT intensity levels. Potentially similar complementarities may be at work between broadband and the productivity growth in industries.

Until these channels and interactions are better understood, claims regularly made by policy makers that higher broadband penetration directly translates into higher productivity or output should be treated with caution.

Notes

I thank Hugo Brito, James E. Prieger, Jan Mischke, Jörg Schläpfer, Joachim Sedlmeir, Rudi Stracke, Uwe Sunde, Matthijs de Zwaan, as well as participants of the 4th Workshop on the Economics of ICTs in Évora (Portugal), the Spring Meeting of Young Economists in Aarhus (Denmark), the CESifo Venice Summer Institute in San Servolo (Italy), and the Graseck Seminar of the LMU Munich (Germany) for helpful comments and suggestions. I am also grateful to CESifo for providing financial support.

1. See Koutroumpis (2009), Qiang, Rossotto, and Kimura (2009), Czernich et al. (2011), Thompson and Garbacz (2011), or Ng, Lye, and Lim (2013) for studies conducted at the country level, and Gillett et al. (2006), Del Bo and Florio (2012), or Forman, Goldfarb, and Greenstein (2012) for analyses at the community or regional level. For a more detailed review of the literature and the main research challenges, see ITU (2012). Holt and Jamison (2009) provide a survey of the studies focusing on the US experience.

2. The main findings from firm-level studies are summarized in section 15.2. For studies focusing on industries, see, for example, Crandall, Lehr, and Litan (2007), Bartelsman (2008), Kolko (2010, 2012), or Heger, Rinawi, and Veith (2011).

3. For a general introduction to skill-biased technological change, see Acemoglu (2009, ch. 15); for evidence on broadband's complementarity with human capital, see, for example, Forman, Goldfarb, and Greenstein (2012) or Atasoy (2013).

4. See also OECD (2008) and ITU (2012) for a discussion of different channels through which broadband's effect may have materialized.

5. Jensen (2007) provides a stark example of how communication technologies may improve market efficiency by analyzing the impact of mobile phones on the fishing industry in the Indian state Kerala. Ater and Orlov (2012) show how the Internet transformed the mode of competition in the airline industry.

6. Brynjolfsson and Hitt (2003) provide evidence for such time lags when analyzing the productivity impact of computerization.

7. In a review of the literature on broadband's impact on employment, the ITU (2012: 14) notes that "research is starting to pinpoint different employment effects by industry sector."

8. Australia, Austria, Belgium, Canada, Czech Republic, Denmark, Finland, France, Germany, Greece, Hungary, Ireland, Italy, Japan, South Korea, Netherlands, Portugal, Spain, Sweden, the United Kingdom, and the United States.

References

Acemoglu, D. 2009. *Introduction to Modern Economic Growth*. Princeton: Princeton University Press.

Atasoy, H. 2013. The effects of broadband Internet expansion on labor market outcomes. *Industrial and Labor Relations Review* 66 (2): 315–45.

Ater, I., and E. Orlov. 2012. The effect of the Internet on product quality in the airline industry. Mimeo. Tel Aviv University and Compass Lexecon.

Atkinson, R. D., and L. A. Stewart. 2012. The 2012 state new economy index: Benchmarking economic transformation in the states. Report. Information Technology and Innovation Foundation.

Bartelsman, E. J. 2008. ICT impacts: From micro to macro. In M. Franklin, P. Stam, and T. Clayton, eds., *Information Society: ICT Impact Assessment by Linking Data from Different Sources*. Final report. Eurostat Agreement 49102.2005.017–2006.128. London: UK Office for National Statistics, 255–79.

Basu, S., and J. Fernald. 2006. Information and communications technology as a general-purpose technology: Evidence from U.S. industry data. Working paper 2006–29. Federal Reserve Bank of San Francisco.

Bertschek, I., D. Cerquera, and G. J. Klein. 2011. More bits—more bucks? Measuring the impact of broadband internet on firm performance. Discussion paper 66–587. Zentrum für Europäische Wirtschaftsforschung (ZEW).

Brynjolfsson, E., and L. M. Hitt. 2003. Computing productivity: Firm-level evidence. *Review of Economics and Statistics* 85 (4): 793–808.

Colombo, M. G., A. Croce, and L. Grilli. 2013. ICT services and small businesses' productivity gains: An analysis of the adoption of broadband internet technology. *Information Economics and Policy* 25 (3): 171–89.

Crandall, R., W. Lehr, and R. Litan. 2007. *The Effects of Broadband Deployment on Output and Employment: A Cross-sectional Analysis of U.S. Data. Issues in Economic Policy 6*. Washington, DC: Brookings Institution.

Czernich, N., O. Falck, T. Kretschmer, and L. Woessmann. 2011. Broadband infrastructure and economic growth. *Economic Journal* 121 (552): 505–32.

Del Bo, C. F., and M. Florio. 2012. Infrastructure and growth in a spatial framework: Evidence from the EU regions. *European Planning Studies* 20 (8): 1393–1414.

European Commission. 2012. Single market act II: Together for new growth. Communication from the Commission to the European Parliament, the Council, the European Economic and Social Committee and the Committee of the Regions. October 3.

Forman, C., A. Goldfarb, and S. Greenstein. 2012. The Internet and local wages: A puzzle. *American Economic Review* 102 (1): 556–75.

Franklin, M. 2008. Productivity and core ICT metrics at firm level. In M. Franklin, P. Stam, and T. Clayton, eds., *Information Society: ICT Impact Assessment by Linking Data from Different Sources*. Final report. Eurostat Agreement 49102.2005.017–2006.128. London: UK Office for National Statistics, 94–119.

Gillett, S. E., W. H. Lehr, C. A. Osorio, and M. A. Sirbu. 2006. Measuring the economic impact of broadband deployment. Final report. National Technical Assistance, Training, Research, and Evaluation Project 99–07–13829. Economic Development Administration, US Department of Commerce.

Grimes, A., C. Ren, and P. Stevens. 2012. The need for speed: Impacts of Internet connectivity on firm productivity. *Journal of Productivity Analysis* 37 (2): 187–201.

Haller, S. A. and S. Lyons. 2012. Broadband adoption and firm productivity: Evidence from Irish manufacturing firms. Discussion paper 42626. Munich Personal RePEc Archive.

Heger, D., M. Rinawi, and T. Veith. 2011. The effect of broadband infrastructure on entrepreneurial activities: The case of Germany. Discussion paper 11–081. Zentrum für Europäische Wirtschaftsforschung (ZEW).

Holt, L., and M. A. Jamison. 2009. Broadband and contributions to economic growth: Lessons from the U.S. experience. *Telecommunications Policy* 33 (10–11): 575–81.

ITU. 2012. The impact of broadband on the economy. Research to date and policy issues. Broadband series. International Telecommunication Union.

Jensen, R. 2007. The digital provide: Information (technology), market performance, and welfare in the South Indian fisheries sector. *Quarterly Journal of Economics* 122 (3): 879–924.

Kolko, J. 2010. Does broadband boost local economic development? Report. Public Policy Institute of California.

Kolko, J. 2012. Broadband and local growth. *Journal of Urban Economics* 71 (1): 100–13.

Koutroumpis, P. 2009. The economic impact of broadband on growth: A simultaneous approach. *Telecommunications Policy* 33 (9): 471–85.

Ng, T. H., C. T. Lye, and Y. S. Lim. 2013. Broadband penetration and economic growth in ASEAN countries: a generalized method of moments approach. *Applied Economics Letters* 20 (9): 857–62.

OECD. 2008. Broadband and the economy. Ministerial background report, dsti/iccp/ie(2007)3/final. Organisation for Economic Co-operation and Development.

Prieger, J. 2012. The economic benefits of mobile broadband. Working paper 38. School of Public Policy, Pepperdine University.

Qiang, C. Z.-W., C. M. Rossotto, and K. Kimura. 2009. Economic impacts of broadband. In *Information and Communications for Development 2009: Extending Reach and Increasing Impact: Part I*. Washington, DC: World Bank, 35–50.

Rajan, R. G., and L. Zingales. 1998. Financial dependence and growth. *American Economic Review* 88 (3): 559–86.

Sadowski, B., C. Maitland, and J. van Dongen. 2002. Strategic use of the Internet by small- and medium-sized companies: An exploratory study. *Information Economics and Policy* 14 (1): 75–93.

Thompson, H. G., and C. Garbacz. 2011. Economic impacts of mobile versus fixed broadband. *Telecommunications Policy* 35 (11): 999–1009.

van Leeuwen, G., and S. Farooqui. 2008. ICT investment and productivity. In M. Franklin, P. Stam, and T. Clayton, eds., *Information Society: ICT Impact Assessment by Linking Data from Different Sources*. Final report. Eurostat Agreement 49102.2005.017–2006.128. London: UK Office for National Statistics, 163–87.

White House. 2012. We can't wait: President Obama signs executive order to make broadband construction faster and cheaper. Press release, June 13.

16 Providing and Financing a Municipal Infrastructure: Water and Sanitation Investments in Milan, 1888 to 1924

Olivier Crespi Reghizzi

16.1 Introduction

For the past ten years much attention has been given by international institutions and donors to the issue of sustainable financing for drinking water and waste water sanitation infrastructure. Through various working panels, such as panel Camdessus and panel Gurria (Van Hofwegen 2006; Winpenny 2003), many international institutions have shifted their official position from "full-cost recovery," based only on rates (to be paid by users), to a "sustainable cost recovery" paradigm, where part of the costs would be covered by taxpayers.[1] This shift led to the Istanbul 2009 World Water forum and then to OECD publications (OECD 2009) clarifying these concepts and suggesting a coherent terminology on costs and financing sources known as the "3T's" (tariffs, taxes, and transfers).

The water industry is highly capital intensive and requires huge lump-sum investments, particularly in the early phase of infrastructure expansion, which is where many developing countries are today (see chapter 1 in this volume). Historically how to finance water investments has frequently been a big concern.

The provision of water and sewer systems (WSS) in Italy (and in Europe) has been mainly at the municipal level. This chapter studies how the water and sanitation infrastructure was started, financed, and expanded by Italian municipalities, and focuses on the special case of Milan's water and sanitation service. Water and sanitation in Milan is indeed very much a municipal story. The chapter traces Milan's WSS from its genesis as a "modern" service in 1888 to the year 1924,[2] using the municipality's yearly financial report[3] as the main data source. By providing a historical context and outlining past solutions to financing challenges, this chapter aims to contribute to the present policy debate on water and sanitation infrastructure financing.

In the second half of the nineteenth century Milan faced a demographic revolution driven by massive flows of immigrants. At Italy's unification in 1861, Milan had only 196,109 inhabitants. With the arrival of large industries[4] came immigration from rural areas, and Milan's population grew massively. Already by 1911 there were more inhabitants in Milan (590,000) than in Turin (427,106) and Rome (511,076), and the population gap with Naples (678,091) was much smaller than in 1861. By 1931 Milan had a highest population (992,036) of all Italian cities except Rome (1,008,083).

Such huge demographic growth was accompanied by spontaneous and unruly urban expansion in the outer limits of the city. All changed in 1889 when a city development masterplan (*Piano regolatore*), designed by the engineer Cesare Beruto, was approved by the Italian Parliament, four years after it was adopted by the City Council in 1886.[5] By 1899 the rapid demographic growth and urban development made it critically clear that construction of a modern water and sanitation system could no longer be postponed.

How did Milan manage to finance such a costly infrastructure? To tackle such a question the Italian municipal fiscal *regime* is described (section 16.2) with a detailed account of Milan's municipality financial constraints. Land value capture tools are given a special attention to show why they failed to have a major role in Milan's urban infrastructure financing unlike the case of Paris (sections 16.2.2 and 16.2.3).

Section 16.3 focuses on the water and sanitation infrastructure brought to completion and estimates the total amounts invested in water and sanitation in Milan, at more than 300 million 1924 Italian lira. This is the order of magnitude of the whole 1921 municipal budget. The major financing tool implemented to cover the huge investment in the short run was repayable financing, as shown in section 16.4. What the borrowing regime of Italian municipalities was like is then discussed in sections 16.4.1 and 16.4.2, the deficit financing tools implemented in Milan in sections 16.4.3 and 16.4.4.

Section 16.5 focuses on how the water services were charged to users over time, namely who were the final payers (e.g., users or taxpayers). Section 16.6 describes the financial flows of the water and sanitation services based on data from yearly municipal financial reports, showing how tariff revenues were covering full service costs. Inflationary effects on the long-term debt are considered as well (section 16.6.4). And a basic overlapping generations model is applied to explore how the infrastructure costs were allocated among the various generations (section16.6.5).

16.2 Municipal Finance

16.2.1 Intergovernmental Financial Relations in Italy

The financial organization of the newly born Italian state was gradually set up between 1861 and 1876. During this time the *imposta di ricchezza mobile* (income tax on all revenues except from property), which was previously in place in the *Regno di Sardegna,* was extended to all of Italy (Legge 1840 del 14 Luglio 1864). It was a nonprogressive income tax on all incomes except those deriving from landownership, which were taxed through the *imposta sui terreni* (land property tax) and *imposta sui fabbricati* (buildings property tax) (Legge n°2136 del 26 Gennaio 1865).

The Italian state became heavily centralized, and municipalities (*comuni*) were under the tight control of the prefect (*prefetto*) who was both the government's representative and the head of the county's (*provincia*) administration[6] (Cassar and Creaco 2007: 713–15). Intergovernmental relations were also centralized through various Acts, particularly the 1859 *Rattazzi* Decree (Regio Decreto 23 Ottobre 1859 n°3702) and the 1865 Act (Legge n° 2248 20 Marzo 1865). Municipal expenses were accordingly classified as compulsory (*spese obbligatorie*) and optional (*spese facoltative).* The municipalities could undertake optional expenses only after they had covered all compulsory expenses. However, the distinction between the two categories was quite arbitrary, and among the compulsory expenses[7] there were some expenses that, by definition, should have been under the central government's responsibility: "primary education, national defense, elections costs, prisons."[8] Furthermore the fact that the optional expenses (e.g., public works and infrastructure) were disincentivized was particularly a problem.

Municipal revenues were authorized to come from three sources: (1) nonfiscal sources (e.g., tariff revenues from municipal services including water and sanitation), (2) autonomous taxes, and (3) piggyback taxes (additional levies on national taxes—called *sovraimposta).* No recurrent transfers from the central government were in place (except minor transfers).

The *dazio di consumo* (excise duty) was the major municipal fiscal revenue. However, a ceiling on the *dazio di consumo* was fixed by the 1865 Act to prevent excessive taxation on low-income people (Cassar and Creaco 2007: 716). In Italy the excise duty was both a central and local tax. Municipalities were authorized to set piggyback duties on goods already taxed by the central state's excise duty and were authorized to create autonomous excise duties only on goods with a minor fiscal yield (Volpi 1959: 16). Progressively the municipalities' share of the excise duties revenues increased as the other fiscal sources were reduced.[9] However, excise duty revenues were fully given to municipalities starting only in 1923 (Volpi 1959: 20)

If total revenues coming from both nonfiscal sources and autonomous fiscal revenues were not sufficient to cover the compulsory expenses, municipalities could ask to be authorized to set piggyback taxes on national taxes (income tax, land property tax, and building property tax). The piggyback taxes had to weigh similarly on the three taxes (Cassar and Creaco 2007: 716).

The fiscal regime of municipalities had some weak points, which put the municipalities in an uneasy financial situation. A first weakness was that the central state and the municipalities were sharing the same fiscal revenues. Thus fiscal competition took place between the two levels of the state. On one hand, even if the legislator had thought of the *sovraimposte* as the revenue of last resort, municipalities considered *sovraimposte* as an ordinary fiscal source (Fraschini 1991: 26). They even preferred to increase *sovraimposte* rather than set autonomous taxes, since *sovraimposte* were less visible and could easily be hidden behind the central state mask (Locatelli 2010: 13; Cassar and Creaco 2007: 717). On the other hand, the central state, which was additionally facing a tight financial situation, progressively limited the municipalities' fiscal autonomy (Marongiu 2001: 19) while extending the list of compulsory expenses of the municipalities, as stated by Luigi Einaudi: "The central state kept confiscating municipal revenues while it transferred new expenses to municipalities."[10]

Some minor modifications to the municipalities' fiscal regime were approved in 1898, 1908, and 1915. As compared with intergovernmental relations in Italy over the 80 years between 1861 and 1941, a major issue of those early years appears to have been that transfers between the central state and the municipalities were not taking place and that the ratio of own tax revenues to total spending was very high (including both autonomous and nonautonomous tax revenues). According to

Marongiu, "before WWI fiscal decentralization was much more significant than in all the rest of the 20th century."[11] Surprisingly, no equalizing mechanism was in place in the newly formed country with such major geographical variability between the north and the south (Giarda 2005) that low municipal revenues were not always able to deliver public services (Fraschini 1991: 27).

As the responsibility for many public services was gradually given over to municipalities (increasing their compulsory expenses) while their fiscal autonomy was reduced, the average income-to-expenses ratio progressively fell from more than 100 percent in 1866 to 1868 to 94 percent in 1899, 89 percent in 1907, and 79.81 percent in 1912 (Cassar and Creaco 2007: 721). Yet municipal budgets had to be balanced (including the debt service) in order to be approved, and the solution often came from repayable finance, as will be discussed in section 16.4.

16.2.2 Taxing (or Not Taxing) Land Added Value

During the forty years under study, massive urban expansion took place in Milan. Within the framework of the various city development masterplans, large investments were allocated by municipalities to build basic infrastructure for water and sanitation. These investments had the effect of significantly increasing the value of nearby properties.

According to value capture theory, urban infrastructure can be financed endogenously if the local authorities are able to design institutional mechanisms that can capture the added value created by urban growth. In other words, through a value capture financing scheme a public administration can monetize a part of the positive externalities of an infrastructure project (Brugnoli 2010: 15). The number of ways to accomplish land added value is shown in table 16.1. This section focuses on the mandatory fiscal tools used in Italy and section 16.2.3 on implemented policies (or nonimplemented policies) in Milan.

In Italy the principle that "those who retrieved some earnings from an infrastructure should give a contribution to the betterment costs" had been included in the June 25, 1865, Act on expropriation for public utility (Marongiu 2001: 86). Other Acts approved in those years for specific urban transformation also espoused this principle. However, contrary to what was enforced at that time in other countries (England, Prussia, and United States), an Act allowing to systematically capture a share of property value increases did not exist in Italy in the nineteenth century.

Table 16.1
Value capture financing tools

Capture from (who is the payer?)	Voluntary tools	Mandatory tools	Comments
Developers	Joint development	Development exaction and impact fees Public land acquisitions and resale	Expansion areas / integrated urban renovation operation
The community[60]	No	Betterment levies General infrastructure tax on land value gains	Built-up areas
Within	Internalization (integrated urban developer)	No	

Source: Based on concepts from various sources (ReUrba 2006; Peterson 2009; Brugnoli 2010)

In 1904 a tax on buildable land areas was approved in Italy.[12] The 1904 Act was nevertheless designed to encourage building activity rather than capture a share of the property value increases.[13] Indeed the idea of allowing local authorities to control land rent had not yet been probed (Dorigati and Molon 1982: 184). As late as 1914, Milan's municipal administration was still asking for a legislative Act allowing it to capture property value increases due to upgrades to the municipal infrastructure, since the tax on building areas was found not to be sufficient to capture in full the land value increases (Sai et al. 1970: 229–30).

Not only did Italy not manage to design an adequate tax to collect a share of the property value increases but also the property tax provided for by the 1865 Act was not scrupulously collected because the tax base (property values) was not kept up to date (Dorigati and Molon 1982: 263).[14] While a general property value review was made in 1870, and then again in 1890, the partial property value reviews implemented after 1910 (according to the 1865 Act) were not sufficient to modify the tax base (Sai et al. 1970: 229–30). Consequently Italy was unable to implement a tax system that would effectively capture land value, be it through betterment levies or through a general tax on property value increases.

16.2.3 Land Acquisitions and Resale Policy in Milan

As the previous section showed, tax tools in Italy could not sufficiently capture a share of the property value increases created by the expanded municipal infrastructure. Many other value capture instruments do exist. One that had been ambitiously implemented within the same decades in Paris under Haussmann's watch consisted in a municipal policy of land acquisition and resale (Peterson 2009; Marchand 1993; Marchand 2011; Crespi Reghizzi 2012). To what extent could such a value capture instrument be implemented in Milan? This section focuses on such a question.

Prior to and in parallel with the Beruto masterplan, a large urban transformation operation was undertaken in areas close to the castle (Foro Buonaparte–Castello–Arena–Arco della Pace) following a decision to move the Piazza d'Armi (military area).[15] To carry through the operation, the municipality obtained the castle and the former military area from the central state; in turn it had to give the new Piazza d'armi area to the state plus a 3 million lira grant to contribute to the barracks' construction. At first, land market prices in the two areas were very different: 8 lira/m^2 in the castle area and 2.70 lira/m^2 in the new Piazza d'armi area. In exchange for the area given to the state, the municipality obtained from the *Società Fondiaria* land to build new streets and urban services. All the 182,000 m^2 available for building were sold to the banker Giovanni Marsaglia in 1886 for 11 million lira (60 lira/m^2) (de Finetti 2002: 352). The operation was entirely profitable and gave significantly large additional revenue to the municipal budget. Unfortunately, such an operation was the exception. The city could have invested profits obtained from this operation to buy land at low price in the periphery to sell afterward at higher market prices and so fuel a revolving mechanism (de Finetti 2002: 352). Instead, the Beruto city development masterplan chose not to pursue such policy.

A municipal policy of land acquisitions and resale consists in owning or "acquiring lands near by an infrastructure project and then sell it on completion of the project" (Peterson 2009: 41). A key issue in implementing such a policy is the expropriation power held by the municipal authorities. Expropriation policies can be classified in three categories: (1) expropriations limited to new streets, (2) expropriations undertaken not only for street areas but also to build collective facilities (schools, public gardens, etc.), and (3) expropriations authorized mostly to finance urbanization costs through the selling of land or buildings at higher market value once the urban infrastructures are constructed.

According to Campos Venuti (1986: 12) the first version of the Beruto masterplan clearly fit the second policy category. It proposed a street network of widely meshed large blocks, and its second version proposed a much denser mesh of smaller blocks more favorable to real estate speculation. The first Beruto masterplan was never approved. The second masterplan was implemented, and the much smaller blocks were clearly less constraining for the landowning bourgeoisie. As Beruto himself states: "[the] small blocks are due to the real estate speculation's interests."[16] Through the implementation of the second version of the Beruto masterplan, Milan's municipality agreed to absorb all the infrastructure costs without managing to involve the private operators in the financing process (Boriani 1982: 59).

Until the early years of the twentieth century, value capture policies could not be extensively implemented in Italy due to the weak available legislative tools on expropriation (1865 Pisanelli Act on expropriations and 15 Gennaio 1885 Act on Naples urban renewal). In 1907 the city of Rome was given authorization to expropriate landowners in order to capture land value.[17] In Milan's City Council the opposition asked the majority to rule on a similar expropriation power in order to force landowners to contribute to the financing of the city's infrastructure (Dorigati and Molon 1982: 185). However, the necessary expropriation power (e.g., to build social housing) was not granted to the city of Milan until the approval of the *Piano di ampliamento* in 1912.

Between 1905 and 1912 a small-scale value capture policy based on land acquisition of larger areas surrounding the new streets was undertaken in eight districts developed in the framework of "integrated urban operation of housing and collective services"(Boriani 1982: 83). The policy proposed by engineer Cesare Saldini and adopted by mayor Cesare Ponti consisted in buying expansive areas of the city (de Finetti 2002: 343) that could be sold by the municipality at much higher value.[18]

This land acquisition policy was nevertheless found to be insufficient as indicated by the 1907 opposition to the 70 million lira loan with the *Cassa Depositi e Prestiti*. Mr. Bottini (representing the opposition) argued that "the city government (*Giunta*) is planning too little land acquisitions to obtain significant added value."[19] Council member Morpurgo countered that a more ambitious land acquisition policy allowing the city to capture land added value more extensively would require the city to contract a much larger loan, which was not possible because the revenues from the additional tax (*sovrimposta*) were not high enough.

As the debate points out, in addition to powerful expropriation legislative means, the capacity to mobilize quickly large amounts of money was key to implementing ambitious land value capture policies. Under Haussmann's plan in Paris, considerable expropriation tools were given to the municipality, which in turn incurred massive debt to finance its urban transformation with very large land expropriations (Pinkney 1955, 1957, 1958; Marchand 2011; Crespi Reghizzi 2012). In Milan, in contrast, these two essential conditions were not met: available expropriation tools were weak and the borrowing policy was too prudent. In fact only two urban value capture operations were undertaken, in 1885 (in the Foro Buonaparte area) and in 1905 (in accord with Saldini–Ponti adopted policy). With the exception of these two urban operations, value capture was not implemented in financing Milan's urban infrastructure, and in particular its water and sanitation infrastructure.

16.2.4 Milan's Municipality: Financial Constraints

In the second half of the nineteenth century Milan's tight financial constraints primarily reflected the general state of Italian municipal finances (see section 16.2.1). Italy's fiscal autonomy had progressively been weakened by various national decrees, and the list of municipal compulsory expenses was growing. Additionally the rapid urban and demographic growth required huge municipal investments to establish modern infrastructure.

After Italy's unification, it was usual at that time for Italian municipalities to depend on excise duties as the main source of revenue (Sai et al. 1970: 26). At that time Milan's municipality administrative area was quite small (area 1 + area 2 in figure 16.1) and limited by the "Spanish walls" (*le mura spagnole* or *bastioni*), as circled on the map. The mainly rural area outside the Spanish walls was under the administrative authority of the rural municipality of I Corpi Santi (just outside the circle on the map). Looking farther away from the I Corpi Santi the administrative fragmentation appears even larger. In 1861 a total of 30 municipalities existed within the present-day bounds of Milan's municipality (Buzzi Donato 1969: 5).

Besides the fragmentation problem in the administration of Milan's municipality, there was the problem of fiscal opportunism in manufacturing activities settling in the I Corpi Santi area, which was not subjected to the excise duties.[20] Although the city's administrative area grew significantly after 1873 with the annexation of I Corpi Santi, at

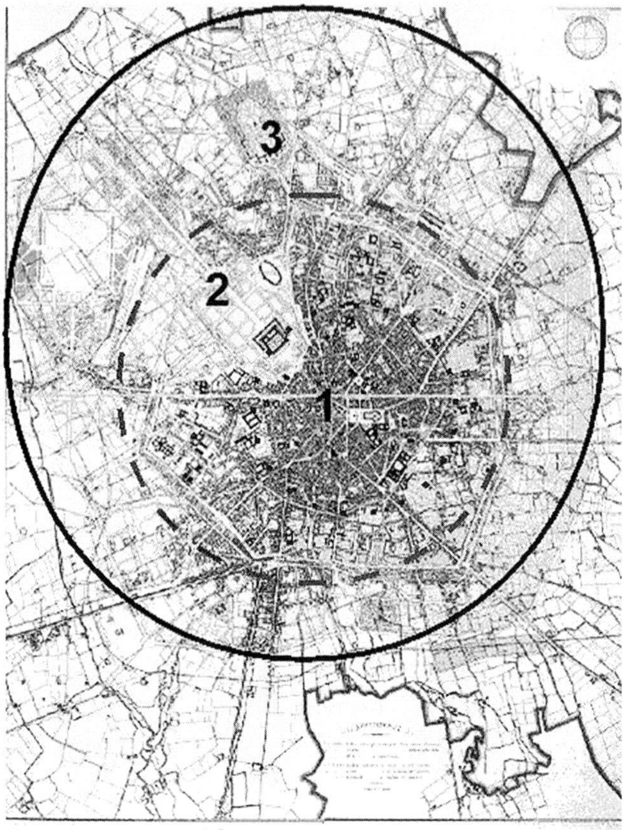

Figure 16.1
Beruto city development masterplan
Source: Adapted from Beruto (1885)

first things did not change much from a fiscal point of view because the annexed areas were exonerated from paying the excise duties.[21] I Corpi Santi residents were subjected only to the *Imposta sulla minuta vendita,* and as such, each resident was subjected to less than a third of the tax paid by a resident of the inner area (Volpi 1959: 23).

Circumstances changed only in 1898 with the abolition of the excise-duty physical barrier that separated the inner and outer parts of the city. Excise duties now started to be collected in the entire city but only on certain large consumptions goods (beverages, meat, forage, and building material), thus creating a "virtual barrier" (Volpi 1959: 24).

Table 16.2
Milan's municipal budget balance / imbalance

	Fiscal revenues	Nonfiscal revenues[61]	Total ordinary revenue[62]	Ordinary expenses	Ordinary budget balance	Extraordinary expenses	Total budget balance
	(1)	(2)	(3)	(4)	(5)=(3)-(4)	(6)	(7)=(3)-(4)-(6)
1888			18.4	16.9	1.5	24.56	-23.06
1898	15.3	2.9	19.5	17.9	1.6	10.6	-9
1903	20.8	4.8	27.2	22.2	5	5.4	-0.4
1908	27.6	8.9	38.8	34	4.8	14.6	-9.8
1913	35.4	12.1	53.3	43.2	10.1	13.58	-3.48
1918	44.2	14.47	66.1	62.7	3.4	20	-16.6
1921	155.9	32.3	200.8	185.6	15.2	102.2	-87

Source: Adapted from Sai et al. (1970: 232) and municipal yearly financial reports
Note: All figures in million Italian lira

Nevertheless, thanks to the 1898 fiscal reform, Milan's municipal budget managed to balance or to have only a minor imbalance from 1900 to 1905. Between 1904 and 1908 Milan experienced major demographic and urban growth (the built area increased from 10.2 to 15.5 thousands of square meters). Public services and public networks now demanded more massive investment due to the rapid urban transformation. In 1906, and more so again in 1908 (due to the international exhibition costs), the municipal budgets closed with significant imbalances (Volpi 1959: 27). During WWI, municipal expenditures (particularly investment in infrastructure) dropped significantly but increased steeply after the war (Volpi 1959: 28). The other part of the equation, namely deficit financing, was used for capital expenditures as well as for the eventual imbalances due to routine expenses, as will be discussed in section 16.4.

16.3 Investing in a Modern Water and Sanitation Service

16.3.1 Far-off Water versus Water from beneath the City?

Milan is located in the middle of the *Pianura Padana* lowlands (Po River Plain) with no river flowing through the city. A system of canals (called *navigli*) had been built over the centuries for navigation purposes. These canals enabled water to be channeled to the city.

In the second half of the nineteenth century there was still no modern water supply system in Milan. Water from the *navigli* was used for all nondrinking purposes while drinking water came from private shallow wells (Bigatti 1997: 29), since the city lies on an abundant aquifer. Many wells were excavated down to 6- to 7-m depths, and a few were bore holed down to 10- to 12-m depths (ATO Città di Milano 2007: 78). Water was made available in large quantities, and some buildings had pumps installed that could bring water up to the second floor (Colombo 1984: 119).

Through the 1870s, however, groundwater quality started to deteriorate and many scientific studies showed a connection between the water pollution and the quantity of waste water discharged in the ground, which was significantly increasing due to the extraordinary urban growth (Colombo 1984: 119). Through the years the scientific and decision-making circles became progressively aware that the vicious spiral of waste water polluting the aquifer from which water was withdrawn had to be interrupted.[22] According to the *water quantity paradigm* (Barraqué 2003) that was mainstream at that time in Western Europe, clean water should be brought to the city from faraway sources. In line with that thought, a call for water supply projects was launched in 1881 by the Milan municipality. This occasioned not only an opportunity to find the best way to deliver far-off water to the city but also to "allow the European monetary markets to provide capital to build such an infrastructure."[23]

Among the twelve projects in the 1881 competition, the Milan municipal commission ranked first a project by the *Società Italiana condotte d'acqua* (linked to the *Banco di Roma)* and a contract was signed. The project planned to channel spring water from the nearby Brembo River; the water was to reach Milan through a 45-km gravity aqueduct plus a 25-km pressure pipeline. A public utility declaration from the Ministry of Public Works was needed to allow the land expropriation and start the project. The inhabitants of the Brembo Valley fiercely opposed the project.[24] Many people and institutions took part in contesting the project, as Colombo (1984: 120) reports. In 1885 the ministry ended up not awarding the *Società Italiana condotte d'acqua* the public utility project.[25]

After Milan's municipality terminated the contract with the *Società Italiana condotte d'acqua,* it launched in 1887 a new call for projects, with many more stipulations than in the first competition. Mainstream thinking had changed over time, and spring water was no longer a priori preferred to groundwater. Twenty-two projects were in the competition and evaluated by the municipal commission, which in the end was unable to make a choice.

16.3.2 Launching the Water Service

In July 1888 the City Council chose to experiment with a water supply pilot project that had been designed by Felice Poggi, an engineer in the municipal technical department (*ufficio tecnico comunale*). The project called for a few deep boreholes to be drilled, a pumping station to be installed, and a 1-km pipeline to be laid underground (Comune di Milano 1888).

In the second half of 1888, two pilot boreholes were made close to the Arena (reaching, respectively, 146.43 and 81.75 m in depth), and in 1889, a steam engine pumping station was installed (140 liter/s of discharge). Roughly 1,200 m of pipelines were laid in order to supply water to the *Piazza Castello–Foro Buonaparte–Via Dante* residential area recently built. The pilot project met success, and an investment plan was approved by the City Council in 1890, going further in the choice of underground water, which was no longer considered a temporary solution.

Thanks to its location on an abundant aquifer, the city of Milan was able to make the sound decision of building only basic water infrastructure (wells, pumps, and pipelines). This way the Milan municipality was able to stay free from the central government's authorization, which would have been compulsory had a distant water source been chosen. Additionally the chosen technical solution had the great advantage of being flexible and gradual in its implementation. Investments in the water infrastructure could be implemented step by step as the number of subscriptions to the water service increased (Bigatti 2000: 222).

As a result many different wells and pumping stations were progressively built, totalizing 331 wells and 17 pumping stations by 1927, with a total nominal discharge capacity of 5,830 liter/s. There was little need for storage units because the abundant aquifer alone provides massive natural water storage just below the city. Only two relatively small reservoirs (1,200 m^3 each) were placed in 1889 and in 1896 inside two of the towers of the Milan castle (*Castello Sforzesco*) near the first pumping station (Municipio di Milano 1907a: 28).

16.3.3 Launching the Sanitation Service

Although various canals and sewers existed already in 1868 in Milan, they had been built randomly street by street with no systemic vision.[26] The first sewer masterplan for the city of Milan was approved that year and implemented very slowly over ten years with only 3.5 km constructed by 1878.

The 1868 masterplan designed a sewer network within Milan historical center. In those years, however, Milan's size was continually expanding. In order to control the urban expansion, in January 1886 a town development masterplan (*Piano regolatore* Beruto) was approved by the City Council. A sanitation masterplan was needed too, and in 1888 a specific sanitation office was created within the municipal technical department with the mission of designing a new sewer masterplan for the city (Municipio di Milano 1890a).

A masterplan was approved by the City Council in 1890. It was designed to serve a 2,830-hectare area with a combined sewer network. The project was based on a 963,265 population count made by the Beruto masterplan and on a household water consumption of 100 liter/person/day. The city was divided in four water collection areas. Three areas would discharge waste water through three major sewers (*Gentilino, Vigentino,* and *Nosedo),* all reaching the *Roggia Vettabbia* River while a fourth area would discharge water into the *Lambro Meridionale* River. Because Milan's ground is naturally sloping from north to south, only free flow gravity sewers were built, as there was no need of pumping stations for waste water. For centuries waste water collected by the Milan's canals (*navigli*) had been channeled through the *Roggia Vettabbia* and had irrigated large farming areas downstream of Milan (called *marcite*).[27] The 1890 sanitation project was clearly planned to respect the waste water disposal practice of farming. The sewer masterplan included 355 km of small section sewers (called *canali*), 30 km of major sewer, and 42 km of secondary sewers to be built or renovated.

Minor modifications to the 1890 Poggi sanitation masterplan were presented through an alternative plan in 1897. A new sanitation masterplan designed by Poggi was approved much later by the City Council in 1911 (Poggi 1911). Its intention was to extend the sewer to new areas where the city was expanding (*Zona di ampliamento).* The various sanitation masterplans were not limited to the administrative area of Milan and the sewer system was designed to collect waste water from a larger area. Such a design did not imply, however, that the city of Milan would finance the sewer infrastructure for the municipalities at its fringes. Poggi suggested that agreements on sewer usage be signed with such bordering municipalities if they chose not to be absorbed by Milan (Poggi 1911: 690). Poggi's suggestion proved to be right; in 1923 Milan would annex eleven previously independent municipalities.[28] A new sanitation masterplan was drafted the next year by Giuseppe Codara in 1924.[29]

One could wonder why so many plans were necessary within so short a time frame. The reason is given by Poggi himself (Poggi 1911: 7): the city had outgrown the sewer infrastructure of the 1889 masterplan; the sewer system had to be enlarged to meet the needs of a growing number of buildings and an influx of population from outlying areas.

To be sure, it was not easy to expand the sewer system as fast as the urban transformation was taking place (Gentile, Brown, and Spadoni 1990: 102). By the end of 1905 only 151 km of sewers had been completed and only 3,950 buildings were connected to the sewers. Between 1888 and 1905 an average of 7.4 km of sewers per year had been built. Such a slow rhythm of work calls for some explanation. On one hand, the work was complicated by the fact that it was necessary to lower the water table before digging the sewers (Municipio di Milano 1907a). On the other hand, there were still some doubts on some technicalities of the project, and in 1898 a study commission was asked to study and give advice.

Last, the work was slowed by the difficulty to reach an agreement with the farmers' irrigation consortium downstream of Milan (*Consorzio Vettabbia*) where Milan's waste water was supposed to be discharged and used for irrigation. It was only in 1905 and 1906 that such agreements were signed, respectively, with the *Consorzio Vettabbia* and the *Consorzio Redefosso*. Even by 1906 the total discharge capacity of the major sewers (Gentilino, Vigentino, Nosedo, and a few smaller ones) was still not large enough to channel all the water in case of large rains. Nevertheless, the acquisition and planned improvements of the Redefosso canal (thanks to the 1906 agreement with the *Consorzio Redefosso*) would help increase the maximum discharge capacity of the whole sewer system (Municipio di Milano 1907a).

After 1906 work sped up significantly, as the figures at the end of 1910 show: 261 km of sewer were connected to 6,500 buildings. Subsequently Poggi's 1911 masterplan extended the sewers further to the city's outskirts, reaching the impressive length of 509 km in 1927 with

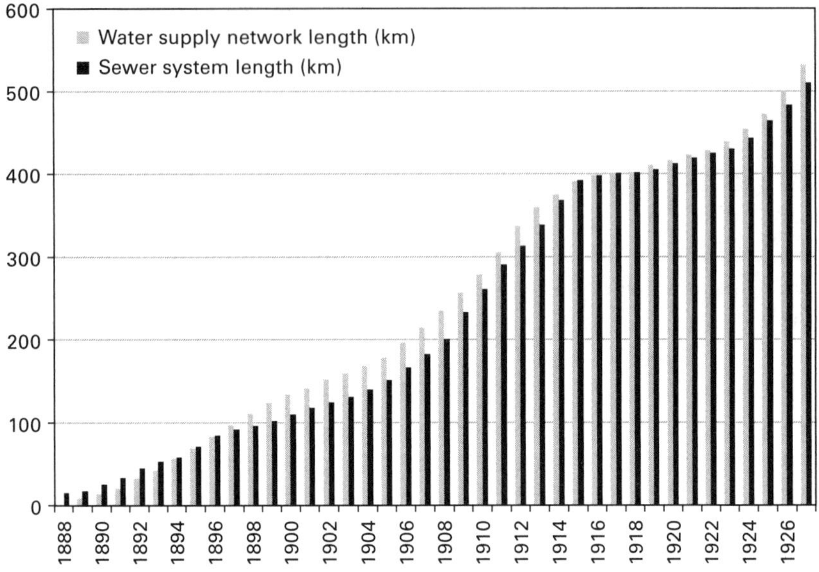

Figure 16.2
Milan's water supply and sewer networks length, 1888 to 1927

the additional 13,760 buildings connected representing roughly 77 percent of Milan's houses according to Bigatti (1997: 223).

16.3.4 Investments Amounts

Within nearly forty years between 1888 and 1926, major water and sanitation infrastructure was built in Milan. By 1926 the water supply and sewer networks reached lengths of 531 and 509 km, respectively (figure 16.2). Each year roughly 13 km of water supply and sewer network were laid down over those forty years.

According to the annual city financial report (*Conto Consuntivo*) capital expenditures in water and sanitation infrastructure added up to total amounts of 79.9 and 227.2 million Italian lira, respectively (expressed in 1924 value). Unquestionably sanitation infrastructure incurred costs nearly three times greater than water supply costs. On average, the annual capital expenditures in water and sanitation in those years were 2.1 and 6.1 million lira, respectively (expressed in 1924 value). The total invested amount of more than 300 million lira (1924 value) represents the same order of magnitude as Milan's whole 1921 municipal budget.

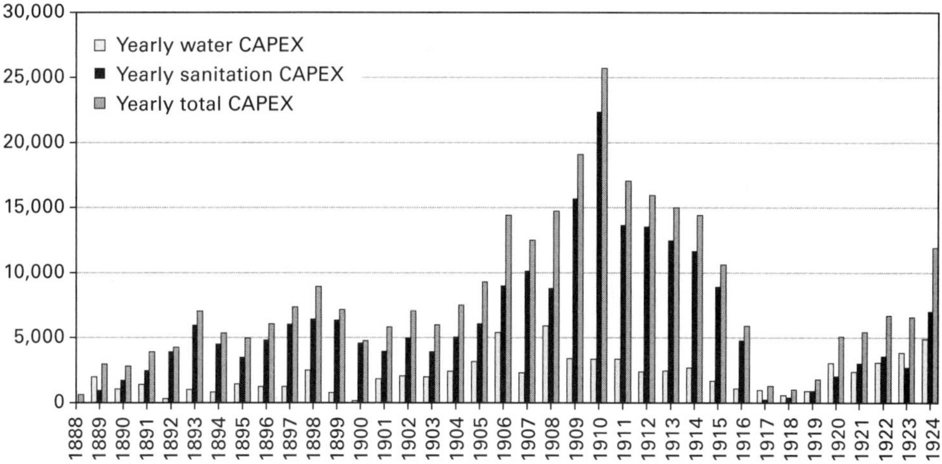

Figure 16.3
Yearly CAPEX in water and sanitation, 1888 to 1924 (thousand lira 1924 value)
Source: Adapted from *Conto consuntivo dell'anno* (various years)

As figure 16.3 shows, investment peaked from 1905 to the start of WWI. In those years the major investments in the sewer network were undertaken not only for hygiene reasons but also to fight underemployment (Sai et al. 1970: 261). During the war the investments nearly came to a standstill. Public works started up again after the war in 1919 and 1920 (Sai et al. 1970: 227).

16.3.5 Water and Sanitation Infrastructure in the Context of Urban Transformation

Key to the expansion of water supply and sewer networks, as was dictated, at least in part, by a number of city development masterplans, was a phase of massive urban expansion and transformation that took place in Milan. The city's urban expansion not only disrupted the networks' topography but also their expansion pace. This much is evident as early as a municipal report of April 1890,[30] which argues that a 2.7 million lira amount is urgently needed for water and sanitation investments because "they are essential to the street works already approved and under implementation in 1890–1891."[31]

One year later a more urgent report (Municipio di Milano 1891a: 26) states that "the realization of the sewers cannot be postponed … [but] should be implemented jointly with the city development masterplan. … since drainage is essential for both the new streets and buildings."[32] It adds that "priority in extending the water supply network is given to the streets having a sewer or to those where ... where at least a single subscription to the water service can be forecast in the first year."[33]

Given the close relation of water and sanitation infrastructure to the city masterplan's development on a technical base, it might be worthwhile to compare their relative investment amounts. At first, expenses dedicated to refurbishing streets and areas according to the *Piano regolatore* were much higher than water and sanitation capital expenditures, but after 1893 to 1894 water and sanitation expenditures (particularly the latter) got higher as figure 16.4 shows. Note that total sanitation capital expenditures over the fifteen years of available data (1897, 1898, and 1899 data are missing), when inflated to 1924 Italian lira (112 million lira), are alone nearly as high as the costs due to the *Piano regolatore* (138 million). If we add up water capital expenditures (43 million lira) to sanitation expenditures, their total cost (156 million lira) is even far greater than all the moneys spent on the *Piano regolatore*'s implementation. Even if we cannot be sure that expenses were always accounted for correctly and ignore whatever hidden cross-subsidies between the two accounting sections might have taken place, we should assume that the order of magnitude to be correct. As a rule, water and sanitation infrastructure represent an essential part of urban transformation and can weigh financially roughly the same as an entire transformation of urban streets.

16.4 Municipal Repayable Finance

Recall from section 16.2 the investments in water and sanitation infrastructure undertaken in Milan in the 1888 to 1924 time frame. The total investment amounted to 96.5 million lira (nominal values) or 307 million lira (inflated to 1924 Italian lira value). This section discusses the financing tools implemented to mobilize such a massive amount of money.

16.4.1 Italian Municipalities Borrowing Constraints

The Acts of 1859 and 1865 (section 16.2.1) called for the municipal budget to be balanced. Debt, however, could be part of the solution not only to finance capital expenditures (investments) but also to cover ordinary budget imbalances. The debt issued by Italian municipalities in those years can be classified (1) as budget imbalance loans, in

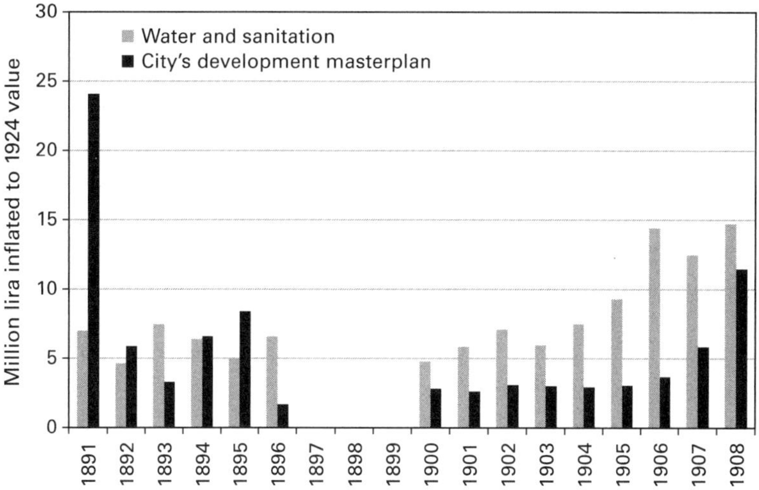

Figure 16.4
Water and sanitation expenditures as compared with urban transformation capital expenditures (in million lira, inflated to 1924 values using ISTAT serie storiche—Tavola 21.6.1)

municipalities with a very low income population and little economic development (resulting in very low fiscal revenues); (2) as loans to resolve temporary imbalances due to external factors (economic crisis, war, etc.); and (3) as loans to finance major capital expenditures needed in municipalities facing a fast economic development (Dorigati and Molon 1982: 187).

According to the 1865 Act (*Legge comunale e provinciale—articolo 137*), approval by the county administration (*provincia)* was required for a municipality to contract any debt. No approval by the Italian Parliament was needed. A municipality could borrow if the two following limitation were abided by (1) a fifth of the ordinary revenues of the municipality had to be higher than the interest costs[34] on the first year of amortization and (2) the revenue from the additional tax on properties had to be high enough to cover the debt service over the payback duration years. In subsequent years progressively more constraints were set by law: the 1870 Act[35] limited the bonus–lots amounts on municipal bonds;[36] then the 1874 Act[37] established some limits on the obligatory expenses. Later the 1880 Depretis reform project (which was not approved in the end) sought to limit municipal loans to not more than a tenth of the ordinary municipal revenues or no larger than 100,000 lira; any greater amount would have to be authorized by a specific act by the Italian parliament (Bufalini and Cavagna Sangiuliani di Gualdana 1881: 29).

16.4.2 Municipal Lending Institutions in Italy

The municipalities could choose between directly issuing municipal bonds and obtaining bank loans. Of the different financial institutions operating in the latter category as lenders there were the *Cassa Depositi e Prestiti*, the various *Casse di Risparmio*, the various *Banche Popolari*, and the standard commercial banks.

The *Cassa Depositi e Prestiti* (CDP) came into existence in 1850 in the *Regno di Sardegna* based on the French *Caisse des depots et consignations.* In 1863, after unification, the CDP extended its activity to all of Italy. Municipalities and other local authorities could contract loans with CDP both for capital expenditures and for debt consolidation (debt previously contracted). Debt consolidation loans surpassed capital expenditures (CAPEX) between 1875 and 1923 except during the 1883 to 1895 years (Della Torre 2001: 20). Loans offered by CDP to municipalities had low interest rates and no commission fees. Payback durations were initially quite short (10 years allowed in 1863) but longer payback durations were authorized afterward (25 years allowed in 1875 and even much longer later). At first the CDP demanded no collaterals except enrollment within the municipal budget plan. However, because some municipalities were negligent in repaying their debts, particularly in southern Italy, after 1875 additional municipal taxes on properties were required as collateral for CDP loans.[38] Furthermore the interest amount could not be higher than a fifth of the municipal revenues.[39] These two conditions limited the municipalities' borrowing power and partially excluded some municipalities from accessing CDP loans, but this way the CDP was protected from insolvency (Conte 2001: 121).

In 1875, a major reform allowed the CDP to collect savings using the countrywide post office network. Thus the CDP started to have more funds available for municipalities than it had before the 1875 reform. After 1880, total loans from CDP to municipalities in fact rose higher than those from all other banks (Della Torre 2001: 20). The trend rose even steeper after 1896[40] when a special financial vehicle (*Sezione autonoma di credito comunale e provinciale—SACCP)* was created within CDP to channel additional money from the market to local authorities (Conte 2001: 141–42).

Other major lenders to local authorities were the various *Casse di Risparmio* created in Italy in the early nineteenth century. Among them, the *Cassa di Risparmio di Milano,* which was created in 1823, had a major role in channeling private savings to municipal budgets. The *Cassa di Risparmio di Milano* opened local branches all over the Lombardy region and was later renamed *Cassa di Risparmio delle Provincie Lombarde* (*CARIPLO*). As will be discussed in the next section, CARIPLO became a major lender to Milan's municipality and held, as collateral, municipal properties through its mortgage loans (*credito fondiario*).

After the 1875 CDP reform, the *Casse di Risparmio* met with competition from the CDP and the postal offices network. CDP had a fiscal advantage because its loans were not subject to the *imposta di ricchezza mobile.*[41] Nevertheless, the total savings collected by postal offices were much lower than those collected by the *Casse di Risparmio* network.[42] This is particularly notable in Lombardy where the CARIPLO was very well established (Della Torre 2001: 30–31).

Until the end of the nineteenth century the total release of municipal bonds[43] appears to be the principal borrowing tool of Italian municipalities (two-thirds of total municipal debt in 1877, half in 1896, and a sixth in 1911). The twentieth century marked the turning point in the choice of borrowing tools by municipalities that contracted loans either with the CDP (including the special vehicle SACCP) or with other financial institutions instead of issuing bonds. Some data further show that loans from SACCP-CDP were frequently issued to consolidate previous debts and thus convert municipal bonds in CDP loans (della Torre 2003: 23, 33).

16.4.3 Milan's Municipal Debt

The principal financial institutions operating as mediators in Milan's municipal debt and all the bonds and loans used by Milan's municipality are summarized in table 16.3. As a rule, debt was centrally managed to fund municipal needs and imbalances as a whole. Only in a few cases was debt contracted to cover sector-specific needs, with the two prominent examples being the 1899 CARIPLO loan for the Simplon railway tunnel and loans for the hydroelectric power plants.

Long-Term and Short-Term Debt

Debt was contracted both with long-term and short-term payback durations. Long-term debt was contracted at fixed interest rates with

Table 16.3
Milan's municipality loans and bonds, 1854 to 1922

	Nominal amount (million Italian lira)	Nominal interest rate (%)	Expiry date	Lender	Main scope	Comment
1854	5,840,000 svanziche	5	1899			
1861	10		1916			Draw emission
1866	5		1921			Draw emission
1886	80	4	1960	bond emission		
1890	8			CARIPLO		2 bank accounts of 4 million lira each
1897	15		1960	bond emission		
1899		4.75	1933	CARIPLO	Simplon railway tunnel	
1901	1		1902		sanitation	Short-term
1905	16		1908			bank account
1907	10					10 milions (3 in *buoni fruttiferi* and 7 with CARIPLO for the 1907 budget deficit)
1906–1907	70	4–3.9	1963	CDP	buildings, electricity, tramways, sanitation, water	17 million al 4%; 53 million al 3.9%
1910	8	4	1960	*CARIPLO*	Power plants	
1909–1910	4.676			various banks	hydropower in Valtellina	Short-term promissory note

Table 16.3 (Continued)

	Nominal amount (million Italian lira)	Nominal interest rate (%)	Expiry date	Lender	Main scope	Comment
1912			1961–1966	CNP	Pensions of the former municipal employees	CNP = *Cassa Nazionale Previdenza*
1914	4.6	4	1963	CDP	hydropower in Valtellina	To convert the 1909 short-term promissory notes
1914	3.5	4	1963	CDP	istituti alta coltura	
1915	1.65	2	1950	CDP	River Olona	
1916	20	5	1921	bond emission	ordinary budget imbalance	
1917	1.5			BPM		Checking account—allowing to wait for the disbursement of the 1914 power plant loan
1919	50	4	1960	bond emission		
1920	40	3%	1955	CDP		Sez autonoma per credito comunale e provinciale,
1920	36	3%	1956	CDP		Sez autonoma per credito comunale e provinciale,
1921	25	5%	1956	CDP		First draft of a total 120 million loan
1921	8			CARIPLO		
1922	8				Power plants	

Source: Based on the *Atti del Municipio di Milano* (various years)
Note: In gray, loans and bonds with which water infrastructure was financed at least partially.

very long payback periods (from 35 to 50 years for the CDP loans up to 75 years for the 1886 bond emission; see table 16.3). From time to time Milan's municipality was forced to revert to short-term debt as a temporary solution. In issuing long-term debt, the municipality had to comply with borrowing limits (section 16.4.1) and short-term debt was occasionally used to bypass these limits. For example, after the 1897 bond emission, Milan's municipality could not acquire anymore debt until 1902 because the yearly budget surplus did not cover any additional debt service. In 1901 a total amount of 1 million lira of six-month municipal debt certificates were issued at a 4.5 percent interest rate and discounted by the Banca Popolare di Milano, the Banca Commerciale Italiana, and another bank. The short-term debt was urgently needed for some sanitation investments and would be converted to a longer term debt, which was possible after 1902 (Atti del Municipio di Milano 1900–1901: 341).

Another explanation for the short-term debt could be CDP's lengthy administrative approval process for long-term loans. The municipality used short-term debt in 1909 to 1910 and in 1917 to fund hydropower plants in *Valtellina*. The 1909 to 1910 promissory notes (*Vaglia cambiari*) were issued while the municipality waited for the long-term loan from CDP, which was finally approved in 1914. However, the funds from the 1914 CDP loan were still not available in 1917 (due to credit restriction during the war). The Milan municipality had to open a short-term "negative" checking account (*conto corrente*) with the Banca Popolare di Milano.

Loans or Bonds

As already mentioned, in the early twentieth century the Italian municipalities subscribing loans preferred financial intermediation rather than issuing municipal bonds (section 16.4.1). Milan's municipality too in the new century chose to borrow mainly through loans with financial institutions (mainly with the CDP) rather than issuing more municipal bonds as in 1886 and 1897. Indeed the conditions offered by CDP were especially attractive for financing the public works that required time spread disbursements for various reasons: (1) better fiscal conditions,[44] (2) better interest rates, (3) time spread according to the pace of work, (4) long duration (fifty years), (5) possibility to get a lower interest rate on postponed disbursements in accord with a decrease in the reference interest rate taking place (Municipio di Milano 1907a: viii).

Financial Institutions

Among the financial institutions, the CDP became the first borrowing option for Milan's municipality in the early twentieth century because it offered better conditions. The second-best option for the municipality was CARIPLO, which demanded municipal properties as collateral.[45] The second-best option was selected when no additional taxes on properties could be used as collateral for a CDP loan. The availability of CARIPLO funds was limited too, and Milan's municipality could not access all the funds and leave nothing available for other Lombardy's municipalities (Atti del Municipio di Milano 1918–1919: 361, 457). As a last resort the municipality would borrow through the Banca Popolare di Milano (BPM) or through the standard commercial banks.[46]

Financial Engineering

A few available municipal bonds emissions were often depended on to convert previously contracted debts to longer durations.[47] Most of the issued bonds and loans had very long maturities. According to some authors, savers in those years were trusting long-term investments, thanks to the comforting effect of the gold standard. In retrospect, however, those savers lost most of their money as the great inflation of 1910 to 1930 curbed severely, in real terms, the profitability of their investments (the key effect of which are discussed in section 16.6.4; section 16.6 will sketch the cost-sharing effects of these mechanisms in the long run, and who was the end-payer *in fine* in those schemes).

Municipal bonds were issued with lots and premiums (*emissione a premi*). The draw calendar was defined at the emission and generally capital payback was not at all linear. For example, according to the 1886 bond emission conditions, 157 bonds (*cartelle*) were to be paid back the first year and 4,419 on the last year meaning 126,500 lira to reimburse the first year and 3,683,000 to pay back in the last year (Atti del Municipio di Milano 1889–1890). Interests were to be paid each term. In the 1897 emission the nominal value of the bonds had a large range (5,000 lira, 1,000 lira, 500 lira, 100 lira) adapted to various kinds of subscribers. Bonds were written in Italian, in French, and in German and were purchasable on various foreign financial exchanges (Paris, Geneva, Bern, Lyon, and Bruxelles) showing that Milan's municipality had the ambition of collecting capital abroad also thanks to the *Union Latine,* which was created in 1865.

16.4.4 Financing Tools for Water and Sanitation Infrastructure

The previous section gave an overview of the financing tools (bonds, loans, credit lines, etc.) used by Milan's municipality in the forty years of this chapter's time frame. Unfortunately, it is not possible to give full details and figures as to the financing tools specifically used to finance water and sanitation infrastructure because loans and bonds were financing Milan's municipal budget as a whole and only in a few cases are there available detailed reports written to justify a loan's approval by the City Council.

However, after 1911 the water and sanitation accounting sections (*Allegato B)* within the city financial report include the re-invoicing of the debt service (interests on the capital invested in the water and sanitation service). Three sources of funding are mentioned: (1) the municipal bonds (*Prestito Unificato* issued in 1886, 1897, and 1919),[48] (2) the 1906 to 1907 loan with the *Cassa Depositi e Prestiti,* and (3) extraordinary credits on the municipal budget.

As was noted in section 16.2.3, only two major urban value capture operations were undertaken in 1885 (*Foro Buonaparte* area) and in 1905 (*Saldini–Ponti* policy). With the exception of these two urban operations, value capture mechanisms did not play a big role in financing Milan's urban infrastructure, including the water and sanitation.

16.5 Water Tariffs, Sanitation Levies, and Connection Policy

As in most European cities, in Milan the water and sanitation service was considered an industrial and commercial service from which revenues could be collected. While water was billed according to volume-indexed rates (section 16.5.1) through collective meters (one meter per block of flats), users were not charged a sanitation bill but a sanitation levy (section 16.5.2).

As Massarutto points out, "it is often a pure terminological convention that of considering revenues either as direct charges or taxation. What really matters is who pays, for what purpose and how much" (Massarutto 2002: 25; see also Massarutto 2007). In my analysis I adopt the classical 3T's approach (OECD 2009); the reader might find interesting to compare the OECD 3T's with the approach suggested by Santandrea, Bailey, and Giorgino (chapter 4 in this volume). Following Massarutto (2002), the main distinction, I focus on is the one between revenues endogenous to WSS (tariff according to the OECD) and ordinary fiscal revenues exogenous to the service (taxes). I then treat Milan's sanitation levy as an endogenous revenue contributing to the "tariff" component of the 3T's rather than to the "tax" (section 16.6).

A key consideration in the initial phase of a network is the connection policy, namely how fast can it service an increasing number of new users. This is particularly tricky for the sanitation service for which users have a very limited willingness to pay because its positive externalities are not individually perceived. Is the connection made compulsory? Or is it encouraged using economic incentives? Section 16.5.3 analyses the connection policy applied in Milan (compulsory connection fees or not) and the pace of subscriptions obtained.

16.5.1 Water

The first set of rules for the water supply service was approved in 1894 (Municipio di Milano 1907b). Water tariffs were slightly volume regressive in order to encourage consumption (table 16.5). An annual fee had to be paid depending on the diameter of the installed meter (table 16.4). Milan's water tariff was in 1903 lower than in many other big Italian cities: 0.25 lira/m^3 in Naples, 0.23 lira/m^3 in Torino, 0.30 lira/m^3 in Verona, 0.25 to 0.30 lira/m^3 in Bologna, 0.27 lira/m^3 in Bergamo, and 0.40 lira/m^3 in Firenze (Bigatti 1997: 113).

In 1907, a new water service set of rules (Municipio di Milano 1907c) was approved with a simpler pricing system (two consumption blocks instead of the six previously applied). The discounted social tariff (previously reserved to houses inhabited by the working class and hydraulic force usage) was extended to social housing and charities. The new tariff was supposed to give slightly lower revenues to the municipality. However, a billing of a minimum consumption per term was made compulsory in order to guarantee a minimum "floor" revenue.

In 1912, a new and very regressive four-block tariff was approved in order to discourage the growing trend of private well drilling. Those private initiatives were source of concern due to the uncontrolled hygienic conditions of the water delivered. Nevertheless, the threat to municipal water revenues was not an issue at that time (Atti del Municipio di Milano 1919–1920: 736).

After WWI, in 1919, a tariff increase was needed because operational costs had increased along with a growth of energy prices and a reduction of working hours from 12 to 8 hours a day. At first it was thought that a four-block tariff would suffice, but then it was decided to go back

Table 16.4
Meter rental fees

Diameter (mm)	1884 rules	1907 rules	1912 rules	1920 rules	1929 rules[63]
	(lira/year)	(lira/quarter)			
7–13	6	Nd	5	7	nd
15	7,20	1,80	10	15	nd
20	9,60	2,40	15	22.50	64
25	10,80	2,70	20	30	160
30	12	5	25	37	180
40	15	3,65	30	45	200
50	18	4,5	35	60	300
80	30	12 + 25 (intake fee)	40	75	400
100	36	15 + 50 (intake fee)	50	100	600
150	nd	18 + 75 (intake fee)	75	150	800

Source: Based on 1884 and 1907 data from Municipio di Milano (1907b); 1912 and 1920 data from Atti del Municipio di Milano (1919–1920: 736); 1929 data from Comune di Milano (1935)

Table 16.5
Milan's water tariff evolution (all values in lira/ m^3)

	1894	1907 and 1920	1912	1929
Minimum unitary price (high consumption block)	0.15	0.15	0.08	0.15
Maximum unitary price (low consumption block)	0.20	0.18	0.10	0.35
Discounted social price	No	0.10	0.06	0.25–0.20

Note: More details in Crespi Reghizzi (2013)

to the 1907 two-block tariff, which could be more easily understood and accepted by the users and moreover would guarantee larger revenues to the municipality (Atti del Municipio di Milano 1919–1920: 736). The fixed part of the tariff to be paid every three months was significantly increased. In 1929, a new tariff was approved with a further increase to the 1920 tariff. While information on the 1929 tariff increase amount is lacking, it can easily be surmized that a massive increase was unavoidable due to the high inflationary times of the 1920s.

16.5.2 Sanitation

The first regulations concerning sanitation service fees were approved by Milan's City Council on June 5, 1888, and initially only for the houses of the *Foro Buonaparte* and *Via Dante* areas, which were the first to be connected.[49] Over the years the same regulations were applied to all buildings connected to the sewer system. The 1888 Act stipulated a *una tantum* connection fee of 35 lira per meter of length of the front of the building. The payment could be divided into installments over five years, amounting to 8.08 lira per year. An additional yearly amount of 0.07 lira per m^2 of total surface of the building was to contribute to the operational costs. It is explicitly written that those contributions were far below the operational and capital expenditures (Atti del Municipio di Milano 1893–1894: 355).

Strictly speaking, the first set of sanitation service regulations was approved by the City Council in 1894 (Atti del Municipio di Milano 1893–1894: 355). Both the connection fee and the yearly contributions were modified to encourage hygienic improvements in the houses connected to the sewer system. To such a purpose, sanitation fees would be set higher for high-income earners than for middle-income earners, who in turn would pay more than a low-income houseowner.[50]

In 1907, the sanitation regulations were revised to collect more revenue for the sanitation service. In 1920, the sanitation regulations were revised once more and the fees significantly raised because "although the sanitation system was put in place mainly for hygienic reasons, the building owners are getting so many benefits from the sewer system that it makes sense to ask them a larger contribution" (Atti del Municipio di Milano 1919–1920: 920). Indeed after WWI the financial constraints of the municipality tightened so much that all sources of revenues were carefully reviewed in order to balance the municipal budget. It was necessary to raise the sanitation yearly revenues from the previous 1 million lira to 4 million lira in order to meet the operational expenditures (1 million lira) and the debt service on the invested capital (4 millions) (Atti del Municipio di Milano 1919–1920: 921).

16.5.3 Connection Policy

In the 1891 and 1907 water service regulations, users were not charged any *una tantum* water connection fee as long as the water meter could be installed right at the entrance of their private properties. However,

Table 16.6
1919 water connection fees

Diameter	Connection fee (lira)
Up to 15 mm	50
20–40 mm	100
50 mm	200
Over 50 mm	To be discussed case by case

Source: Based on on Atti del Municipio di Milano (1919–1920: 919)

the full installations cost of the pipeline in the private property (upstream or downstream of the water meter) was charged to the user.

Connections could be requested by either the owner or the tenant. The tenant, however, had to obtain a waiver from the owner. A deposit of 25 lira was added if the connection was not requested by the building owner. In 1919 additional water connection fees were applied in order to increase the water service revenues (table 16.6).

Although users did not pay to connect to the water service until 1919, a sanitation connection fee was considered by the 1888 City Council charged with the setting of fees. Six years later, an 1894 sanitation regulation forbade the construction of cesspools in all houses being built on streets with existing sewer pipelines and made it compulsory for new houses to be connected to the sewer system. Previously constructed houses were given a six-year deadline to connect to the sewer system. If they connected before the deadline, they were exonerated from paying the yearly sanitation fee for the first six years. Then the 1907 regulations shortened the exoneration from six to two years because "now the connection to the sewer system is not anymore seen as a constraint and is instead asked by the building owners themselves."[51] In 1920 the exoneration period was shortened again, to one year.

At first the pace of connection was slow. In 1897, there were approximately 8,000 houses in Milan of which only 21 percent were connected to the water supply and only 15 percent to the sewer system. In a fifteen-year interval up to WWI, the water connections rose significantly to 81 percent of houses connected to the drinking water network and 77 percent to the sewer system (Bigatti 2000: 223). In 1926 the percentages slightly dropped to 72.6 percent of houses connected to the drinking water network. These percentages, however, conceal the fact that access to the water service was not equally spread among the social

Table 16.7
Percentage of houses without drinking water, latrine, or bathroom in Milan in 1926

	Low-income/working class	Other	Total
Flat without drinking water	56.7	24.65	37.42
Flat without latrine and water	68.54	34.37	48
Flat without bathroom	94.1	64.84	76.5

Source: Based on Buzzi Donato (1969: 22)
Note: Percentage are expressed in total number of houses inhabited by each category (working class and others, respectively).

classes. Only 43.7 percent of the low-income working-class houses were connected to the water network in contrast to 75.25 percent among the houses of other social classes (table 16.7). Such variability among social classes in access to hygienic conditions confirms the sharp inequality in living conditions that Milan's urban "fast and furious" urban development spawned.

16.6 Financial Flows of the Water and Sanitation Services

The previous section discussed how water and sanitation revenues were collected. In this section the overall financial flows pertaining to Milan's water and sewer system are considered. Because water and sanitation services were municipally managed, their budget was part of the city's general budget (the gray shaded area in figure 16.5). The budget data come from various years of the city annual financial report. In my model I adopt the classical 3T's OECD approach (OECD 2009) to analyze the cost sharing between the tariff revenues and the tax revenues. Since, by definition, no "transfers" were in place from the central government, the costs uncovered by tariff revenues were covered by the municipal general budget (tax revenues). Figure 16.5 and table 16.8 summarize the model.

16.6.1 Data from the Municipal Budget

The city annual financial report (*Conto consuntivo dell'anno)* included distinct accounting chapters for water and sanitation. The city annual financial report at that time adopted a classic accounting scheme: *Entrata* (revenues) and *Uscita* (expenses), which were subdivided into *ordinarie* (ordinary) and *extraordinarie* (extraordinary) costs. The ordinary expenses represent "operational" expenditures (OPEX) and the extraordinary ones represent "capital" expenditures (CAPEX).

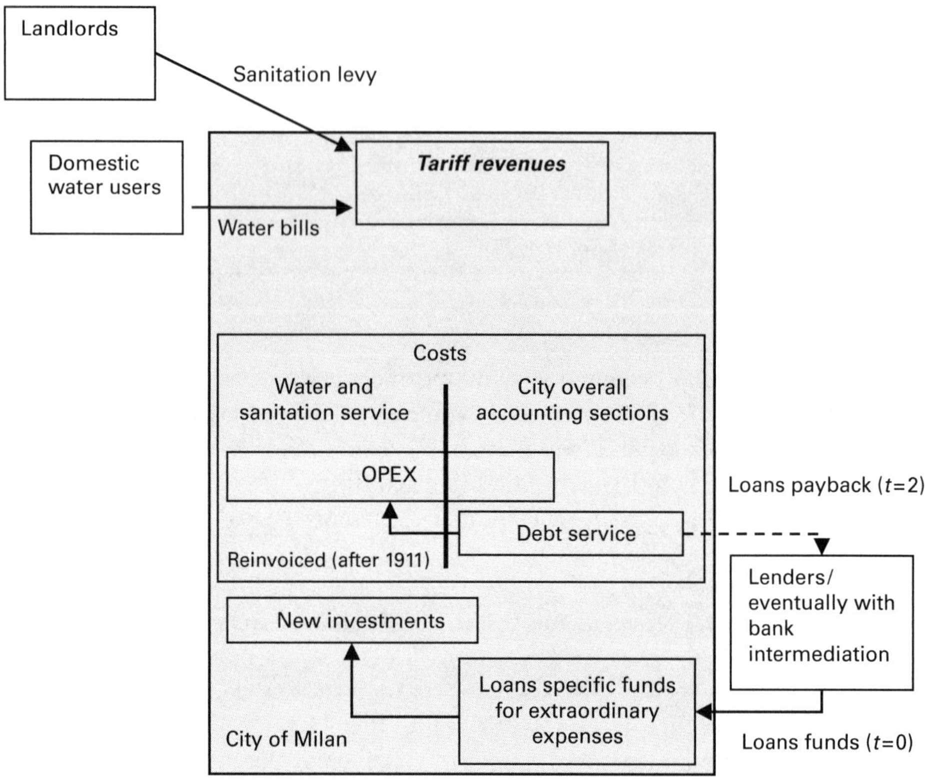

Figure 16.5
Institutional scheme and financial flows of Milan's water and sewer system, 1888 to 1924

Revenues coming from "tariffs" in those years were from household water users through water billing and from landlords paying a sanitation levy. As was discussed in section 16.5, such a levy might be considered, for the purpose of this analysis, as revenue endogenous to the WSS contributing to the "tariff" part of the revenue. Additional revenue came from the *una tantum* connection fees for the sanitation service and included the water service use after 1920 (section 16.5.3). Although the WSS had distinct accounting sections, it did not have distinct budget and accounts. All revenue flowed into the water and sanitation general municipal budget and was not directly channeled to the WSS. Separate data are available on tariff revenues for the water and sanitation services. I have excluded from the water tariff the internal billing for water consumption by municipal buildings.

Table 16.8
Water, sanitation accounting scheme, and model, 1888 to 1924

Cost classification	Accounting entries in use	Content's description	Approach in model
OPEX	Internal OPEX: Data in the water and sanitation ordinary expenses chapters	Energy, Most salaries of the technical staff Ordinary maintenance expenses	Summarized from the existing data in the water and sanitation ordinary expenses chapters
	External OPEX: Within other chapters of the city financial report, unknown for the 1888–1910 years, mentioned distinctly and reinvoiced after 1911	Management and office clerk salaries Paper, office lighting and heating, Cars	Unknown for the 1888–1910, mentioned distinctly and reinvoiced after 1911
Debt service	In the city overall debt service chapter, partially reinvoiced to the water and sanitation chapters after 1911		Estimated through our debt amortization model
New investments	In the water, sanitation and canals extraordinary expenses chapters—each loan has its own extraordinary expenses accounting fund		New investments were paid by extraordinary expenses funds coming from the contracted loans. They are taken into account only through the debt service model.

On the costs side there were three main categories: operational expenditures (OPEX), the debt service, and new investments expenditures (capital expenditures—CAPEX). At first only a fraction of operational expenditures was accounted for in the water and sanitation chapter of the city financial report (energy, most salaries of the technical staff, and ordinary maintenance expenses). Because some of the expenses (management and office clerk salaries, paper, office lighting and heating, cars) were mixed in the various overall chapters of the city budget, I will refer to these as OPEX external costs. Only after 1911 (Atti del Municipio 1912–1913) did operational expenses include a re-invoicing of the expenses previously mixed in other accounting chapters.

The debt service expenditures were accounted for in a general expenses chapter. Before 1911 no reference was made to debt service in the water and sanitation accounting chapters. After 1911 debt service expenses were partially re-invoiced in the water and sanitation accounting chapters (data on the debt service figures re-invoiced to water and sanitation accounts in 1911, 1914, 1917, 1920, 1922, and 1924 are available in Crespi Reghizzi 2013).

16.6.2 Evidence on OPEX Costs Recovery

Revenues, OPEX, and gross profit (expressed as the difference between revenues and OPEX) are reported in table 16.9. Moreover figure 16.6 shows the percentage of the yearly OPEX costs covered by tariff revenues.

As is clear from the data, until 1899, "tariff" revenues were not even sufficient to cover the OPEX costs for water and for sanitation even without considering "hidden subsidies" (water and sanitation OPEX external costs). By definition, costs uncovered by "tariff" revenues are covered by the city general budget, meaning "tax" revenues according to the OECD definition. After 1899, "tariff" revenues covered OPEX costs for both water and sanitation (which did not include OPEX external costs at that time).

I suspect that such a threshold was reached in 1899 when some economies of scale were reached because of the increased number of users (translating into more revenue) in front of nearly constant or decreasing operational expenditures. Indeed tariff revenue increased because (1) the quantity of water metered and billed doubled from 1.17 to 2.42 million m^3, (2) the number of private water meters reached 2,538, and (3) the number of buildings connected to sanitation and paying the sanitation levy kept on growing (142 connected in 1893, then 227 connected in 1894, and 464 connected in 1895).[52]

Revenue from the sanitation service was always lower than that of the water service, which is not surprising. In turn sanitation operational expenditures were very low (much lower than water OPEX) because the sewer system was gravity based and no waste water treatment was in place.

16.6.3 Capital Expenditures and Estimated Debt Service

As in many infrastructure sectors, water and sanitation are industries where capital expenditures dominate operational expenditures. Capital expenditures were financed mainly through debt, as explained in the

Table 16.9
Revenues, OPEX, and gross profit of Milan's WSS, 1890 to 1924 (all values in lira)

	Water			Sanitation			Total		
Years	Revenues	OPEX	Gross profit	Revenues	OPEX	Gross profit	Revenues	OPEX	Gross profit
1890	12,497	31,631	-19,134	2,748	1,939	809	15,245	33,570	-18,325
1891	34,122	34,518	-396	4,524	9,825	-5,301	38,646	44,343	-5,697
1892	57,860	57,446	414	14,626	14,625	1	72,486	72,071	415
1893	78,581	78,485	96	16,927	17,406	-479	95,508	95,891	-383
1894	114,460	115,767	-1,307	22,000	28,413	-6,413	136,460	144,180	-7,720
1895	144,004	144,086	-82	28,272	31,264	-2,992	172,276	175,350	-3,074
1896	181,980	197,496	-15,516	55,392	61,298	-5,906	237,372	258,794	-21,422
1897	252,618	288,143	-35,525	59,334	72,425	-13,091	311,952	360,568	-48,616
1898	330,156	334,414	-4,258	76,166	97,717	-21,551	406,322	432,131	-25 809
1899	445,379	378,423	66,956	87,694	54,317	33,377	533,073	432,740	100,333
1900	525,637	329,848	195,789	139,630	46,805	92,825	655,251	376,653	288,614
1901	586,443	174,193	412,250	149,743	59,221	90,522	729,586	233,414	502,772
1902	722,846	210,884	511,962	173,102	71,696	101,406	895,948	282,580	613,368
1903	839,869	222,653	617,216	205,275	71,311	133,964	1,045,144	293,964	751,180
1904	1,042,030	253,373	788,657	294,598	69,995	224,603	1,302,694	323,368	1,013,260
1905	1,132,347	364,402	767,945	328,035	87,683	240,352	1,460,382	452,085	1,008,297
1906	1,476,819	452,031	1,024,788	390,594	77,034	313,560	1,867,413	529,065	1,338,348
1908	1,948,968	627,934	1,321,034	489,603	151,599	338,004	2,438,571	779,533	1,659,038
1911	2,779,809	683,808	2,096,001	756,006	204,000	552,006	3,535,815	887,808	3,535,815
1914	2,721,329	893,361	1,827,968	821,386	261,861	559,525	3,542,715	1,155,222	2,387,493
1917	3,588,139	1,341,658	2,246,481	951,254	210,614	740,640	4,539,394	1,552,272	2,987,121
1920	6,350,218	3,308,380	3,041,838	2,039,236	1,127,133	912,103	8,389,454	4,435,513	3,953,941
1923	9,618,500	4,869,846	4,748,654	3,105,251	1,074,720	2,030,531	11,258,501	5,944,566	6,779,185
1924	9,553,103	5,324,441	4,228,662	5,533,857	1,411,629	4,122,228	14,038,096	6,736,070	8,350,890

Source: Data based on *Conto Consuntivo dell'anno* … (various years)

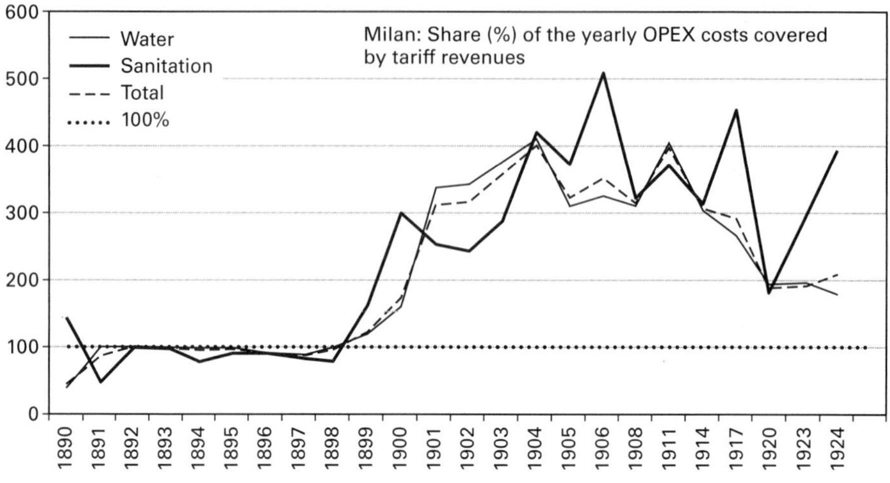

Figure 16.6
Percentage of Milan's WSS yearly OPEX costs covered by tariff revenues

previous sections. What was the return on invested capital given by the available gross profits? Were gross profits high enough to fully cover debt service (capital payback and interests)?

Water, sanitation, and total data are summarized in tables 16.10, 16.11, and 16.12. The first evaluation is the rate of return on the invested capital index computed as the percentage ratio between gross profit and invested capital up to that year. The index is negative before 1899 because gross profit is negative. Concerning water only, after 1901 the rate of return is greater than 10 percent, which might be considered an acceptable figure. The rate of return given by sanitation's gross profits is, in contrast, very low (below 5 percent except for the 1924 value), meaning that the investment costs were huge compared to the profits derived from the service. As a consequence the total rate of return on the investment is low too (never above 10 percent, and above 5 percent only after 1904).

Using this debt model, I attempt to simulate a virtual debt service. My debt service model is fully described in Crespi Reghizzi (2013), and with it I estimate a debt service value (capital payback and interests) based on the following basic assumptions: 4.5 percent interest rate, 50-year payback duration with no grace period, linear amortization, and a disbursement calendar following the capital expenditures calendar. The model is very basic and as such is only able to return an order of magnitude.[53]

Table 16.10
Water service financial flows, 1889 to 1924

Water	(1)	(2)	(3)	(5)	(5) = 100*(3)/(4)	(6)	(7) = (3) − (6)
years	Revenues	OPEX	Gross profit	Invested capital	Return on capital (%)	Debt service	Net profit
1889	2,960	0	0	547,081	0.00	34,955	-34,955
1890	12,497	31,631	-19,134	777,607	-2.46	49,240	-68,374
1891	34,122	34,518	-396	1,085,458	-0.04	68,273	-68,669
1892	57,860	57,446	414	1,155,010	0.04	71,755	-71,340
1893	78,581	78,485	96	1,372,981	0.01	84,687	-84,591
1894	114,460	115,767	-1,307	1,542,981	-0.08	94,348	-95,655
1895	144,004	144,086	-82	1,843,138	0.00	112,200	-112,282
1896	181,980	197,496	-15,516	2,101,730	-0.74	127,117	-142,633
1897	252,618	288,143	-35,525	2,364,558	-1.50	142,072	-177,597
1898	330,156	334,414	-4,258	2,891,144	-0.15	173,698	-177,956
1899	445,379	378,423	66,956	3,053,581	2.19	181,509	-114,553
1900	525,637	329,848	195,789	3,086,801	6.34	180,890	14,899
1901	586,443	174,193	412,250	3,468,554	11.89	202,582	209,668
1902	722,846	210,884	511,962	3,893,542	13.15	226,702	285,260
1903	839,869	222,653	617,216	4,318,496	14.29	250,437	366,779
1904	1,042,030	253,373	788,657	4,835,560	16.31	279,694	508,963
1905	1,132,347	364,402	767,945	5,516,297	13.92	318,978	448,967
1906	1,476,819	452,031	1,024,788	6,696,881	15.30	389,688	635,100
1908	1,948,968	627,934	1,321,034	8,565,922	15.42	496,960	824,074
1911	2,779,809	683,808	2,096,001	10,850,069	19.32	618,214	1,477,787
1914	2,721,329	893,361	1,827,968	12,621,096	14.48	700,919	1,127,049
1917	3,588,139	1,341,658	2,246,481	13,826,663	16.25	743,051	1,503,430
1920	6,350,218	3,308,380	3,041,838	17,265,508	17.62	924,973	2,116,865
1923	9,618,500	4,869,846	4,748,654	26,307,132	18.05	1,450,995	3,297,659
1924	9,553,103	5,324,441	4,228,662	31,189,847	13.56	1,740,301	2,488,361

Note: All data in Italian lira

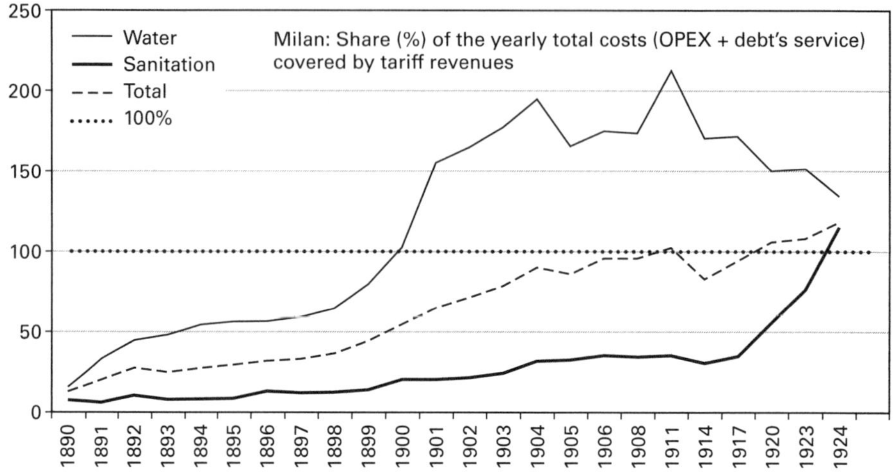

Figure 16.7
Percentage of Milan's WSS yearly total costs (OPEX + debt service) covered by tariff revenues

Figure 16.7 shows the share of the yearly total costs (including the debt service) covered by tariff revenues. Water tariff revenues were high enough to cover operational expenditures (OPEX) and the debt service (after 1899). However, sanitation levy revenues (considered as tariff) were not even sufficient at first to cover OPEX, meaning that sanitation infrastructure was mainly financed by tax revenues.

The water and sanitation infrastructure as a whole was financed by a mix of tax and tariff revenues as the share of the yearly total costs covered by tariff revenues is below 50 percent until 1899, above 70 percent after 1901, and close to 100 percent after 1906. This is also due to the effect of inflation, which in the 1920s absorbed a significant part of the debt service in real terms as discussed next, in section 16.6.4.

16.6.4 Inflation

In the previous section I showed that the debt service stayed fairly constant and so progressively represented a lower percentage of the water and sanitation. Indeed tariff revenues and OPEX expenses increased significantly in those years while the debt service stayed fairly constant. Inflation played a key role in the borrowing–lending relationship in determining *in fine* the cost-sharing equilibrium between the lender and the borrower. In fact all the loans contracted by the city of Milan in those years had a fixed rate and most loans had long

Table 16.11
Sanitation service financial flows, 1889 to 1924

Water	(1)	(2)	(3)	(4)	(5) = 100*(3)/(4)	(6)	(7) = (3) − (6)
years	Revenues	OPEX	Gross profit	Invested capital	Return on capital (%)	Debt service	Net profit
1889	-	-	-	209,200	-	13,404	- 13,404
1890	2,748	1,939	809	592,419	0.14	37,781	- 36,972
1891	4,524	9,825	- 5 301	1,134,189	- 0.47	71,975	- 77,276
1892	14,626	14,625	1	1,989,114	0.00	125,755	- 125,754
1893	16,927	17,406	- 479	3,253,927	- 0.01	205,039	- 205,518
1894	22,000	28,413	- 6,413	4,211,279	- 0.15	263,477	- 269,890
1895	28,272	31,264	- 2,992	4,951,245	- 0.06	307,118	- 310,110
1896	55,392	61,298	- 5,906	5,957,116	- 0.10	367,139	- 373,045
1897	59,334	72,425	- 13,091	7,217,014	- 0.18	442,537	- 455,628
1898	76,166	97,717	- 21,551	8,562,184	- 0.25	522,267	- 543,818
1899	87,694	54,317	33,377	9,874,093	0.34	598,654	- 565,277
1900	139,630	46,805	92,825	10,830,780	0.86	651,091	- 558,266
1901	149,743	59,221	90,522	11,659,016	0.78	694,433	- 603,911
1902	173,102	71,696	101,406	12,691,995	0.80	750,154	- 648,748
1903	205,275	71,311	133,964	13,530,630	0.99	792,488	- 658,524
1904	294,598	69,995	224,603	14,621,523	1.54	850,237	- 625,634
1905	328,035	87,683	240,352	15,932,958	1.51	921,140	- 680,788
1906	390,594	77,034	313,560	17,906,392	1.75	1,033,298	- 719,738
1908	489,603	151,599	338,004	22,231,532	1.52	1,276,213	- 938,209
1911	756,006	204,000	552,006	33,931,109	1.63	1,955,344	- 1,403,338
1914	821,386	261,861	559,525	42,787,900	1.31	2,423,090	- 1,863,565
1917	951,254	210,614	740,640	46,673,265	1.59	2,551,211	- 1,810,571
1920	2,039,236	1,127,133	912,103	49,217,013	1.85	2,587,265	- 1,675,162
1923	3,105,251	1,074,720	2,030,531	58,343,904	3.48	3,030,920	- 1,000,389
1924	5,533,857	1,411,629	4,122,228	65,364,758	6.31	3,428,447	693,781

Note: All data in Italian lira

Table 16.12
Water and sanitation services financial flows, 1889 to 1924

Water	(1)	(2)	(3)	(4)	(5) = 100*(3)/(4)	(6)	(7) = (3) – (6)
years	Revenues	OPEX	Gross profit	Invested capital	Return on capital (%)	Debt service	Net profit
1889	2,960	-	-	756,281	-	48,360	-48,360
1890	15,245	33,570	-18,325	1,370,026	-1.34	87,020	-105,345
1891	38,646	44,343	-5,697	2,219,648	-0.26	140,248	-145,945
1892	72,486	72,071	415	3,144,124	0.01	197,509	-197,094
1893	95,508	95,891	-383	4,626,908	-0.01	289,726	-290,109
1894	136,460	144,180	-7,720	5,754,260	-0.13	357,825	-365,545
1895	172,276	175,350	-3,074	6,794,383	-0.05	419,318	-422,392
1896	237,372	258,794	-21,422	8,058,846	-0.27	494,255	-515,677
1897	311,952	360,568	-48,616	9,581,572	-0.51	584,609	-633,225
1898	406,322	432,131	-25,809	11,453,328	-0.23	695,965	-721,774
1899	533,073	432,740	100,333	12,927,674	0.78	780,163	-679,830
1900	655,251	376,653	288,614	13,917,581	2.07	831,981	-543,367
1901	729,586	233,414	502,772	15,127,569	3.32	897,015	-394,243
1902	895,948	282,580	613,368	16,585,537	3.70	976,856	-363,488
1903	1,045,144	293,964	751,180	17,849,126	4.21	1,042,925	-291,745
1904	1,302,694	323,368	1,013,260	19,457,083	5.21	1,129,931	-116,671
1905	1,460,382	452,085	1,008,297	21,449,254	4.70	1,240,118	-231,821
1906	1,867,413	529,065	1,338,348	24,603,273	5.44	1,422,986	-84,638
1908	2,438,571	779,533	1,659,038	30,797,454	5.39	1,773,173	-114,135
1911	3,535,815	887,808	3,535,815	44,781,179	7.90	2,573,559	962,256
1914	3,542,715	1,155,222	2,387,493	55,408,997	4.31	3,124,008	-736,515
1917	4,539,394	1,552,272	2,987,121	60,499,928	4.94	3,294,262	-307,141
1920	8,389,454	4,435,513	3,953,941	66,482,521	5.95	3,512,238	441,703
1923	11,258,501	5,944,566	6,779,185	84,651,035	8.01	4,481,915	2,297,270
1924	14,038,096	6,736,070	8,350,890	96,554,604	8.65	5,168,748	3,182,142

Source: Author's elaboration, all data in Italian lira

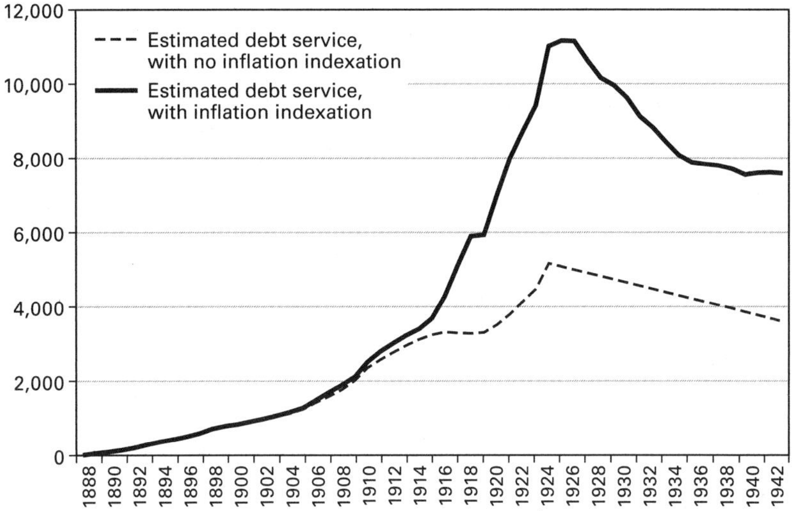

Figure 16.8
Estimated debt service, 1888 to 1944 (in thousand lira), with or without inflation

payback durations between 35 and 75 years. The high inflation rates of 1910 to 1940 had in Italy the effect of absorbing a significant part of the debt's residual burden, transferring it, in the long run, away from the borrower to the "lenders." I show this in figure 16.8, and compare the real debt service with no indexation to inflation and a "virtual" debt service increased by an inflation index[54] as if the interest rate were indexed-linked to inflation. Whereas until 1915 inflation had a minor role (the two curves are very close), after 1916 Italian annual inflation rates increased significantly and debt service indexed to inflation is thus diverted from the curve with no indexation to inflation. The area between the two curves, which is increasing, is a good proxy of the lenders' progressive absorption of a significant part of the debt service in real terms.

As the last column in table 16.13 shows, after 1916 a significant part of the debt's burden was absorbed by the lenders (bond subscribers or instititutional lenders) in real terms. Over the long run, because of inflation a substantial part of the capital costs was diverted from the water sanitation budget.

In section 16.6.4 (table 16.3) I described how investments were financed through fixed-interest loans with CDP. CDP at that time was a state-owned institution channeling savings[55] to the municipalities.

Table 16.13
Total debt service over nine years, with or without inflation

		Debt service		Difference	
		(1)	(2)	(3) = (2) − (1)	(4) = 100*(3)/(2)
From	To	No inflation	With inflation		Percent
1889	1897	2,627.3	2,677.2	49.9	1.9
1898	1906	9,017.9	9,213.9	195.9	2.1
1907	1915	22,399.4	24,365.3	1,965.9	8.1
1916	1924	29,116.9	54,377.7	25,260.8	46.5
1925	1933	43,390.4	91,626.0	48,235.6	52.6
1934	1942	36,351.5	70,519.6	34,168.1	48.5

Note: All values in thousands of Italian lira

But what was the impact of inflation on long-term loans between CDP and Italian municipalities? For sure CDP absorbed a part of investment costs since it was being paid back in lower real terms than were expected. Since CDP was state owned, it can be assumed that from the municipality point of view could be regarded as a transfer in real terms. Going further in that direction, what was the impact of inflation on the financial relations between CDP and the postal savers (or the CDP bond subscribers in the case of SACCP)? Did the CDP absorb the inflation impact since it had to pay higher interest rates to the postal savers? Or was the inflation's burden transferred to the savers (no major change in the interest rate paid to the savers)? These are all key questions to address in further research.

16.6.5 Intergenerational Transfers

Water and sanitation infrastructure has a very long lifetime. Most of the sewer and water network built in Milan in the years 1888 to 1924 is still in use today. Infrastructure can thus be analyzed as capital stock that is progressively built up and passed down to the next generation as legacy. What intergenerational transfers are implied? How is the investment's burden shared between generations?

Nearly half of all infrastructure appear to have been implemented between 1907 and 1915 and a significant fraction between 1898 and 1906 (CAPEX column in table 16.14). A first-level analysis tells us that the 1898 to 1915 generations paid for most of the capital stock.

Table 16.14
CAPEX and debt service's burden on nine years, 1889 to 1942

Years		CAPEX		Debt service
From	To	1924 value	1942 value	1942 value
1889	1897	38,001	75,309	20,749
1898	1906	63,905	117,967	70,947
1907	1915	148,872	241,031	159,666
1916	1924	56,352	75,946	84,247
1925	1933	0	0	70,092
1934	1942	0	0	58,122
Total		307,131	510,253	463,824

Note: All values in thousand Italian lira (1924 or 1942 value)

However, the infrastructure was financed through debt. Thus, by definition, this has the function of spreading the investment costs over many generations. I used such a debt service model to compute the total debt service paid in the six time intervals, each nine years long (four investments phases from 1889 to 1924 and two only debt payback time phases from 1925 to 1942).[56] The debt service results (last column in the table 16.14) show effectively that through deficit financing the investment's burden is better spread over different time phases, unloading on the 1907 to 1915 generations and charging more the 1916 to 1942 generations.

I explore this issue further using a basic overlapping generations model in which each generation is composed of everyone who is born at the same time instead of "everyone who is alive at a given time" (Rosen and Gayer 2010: 466). My model is schematized in table 16.15 and based on the following assumptions:

- Six time periods of 9 years each.
- Investments made only in the first 4 time periods in which debt payback takes place in the last two time periods.
- Each generation alive for 4 time periods, labeled "young," "adult1," "adult2," and "old"
- Seven generations crossing the time frame labeled gen0, gen1, ..., gen6
- In every time period four generations alive so that the burden weighing on each generation is a quarter of the total burden of that time period (as computed in the preceding section)

Table 16.15
Overlapping generations model—schematic view

	1889–1897	1898–1906	1907–1915	1916–1924	1925–1933	1934–1942
Young	gen 3	gen 4	gen 5	gen 6		
Adult 1	gen 2	gen 3	gen 4	gen 5	gen 6	
Adult 2	gen 1	gen 2	gen 3	gen 4	gen 5	gen 6
Old	gen 0	gen 1	gen 2	gen 3	gen 4	gen 5

Table 16.16
Results from the overlapping generations model based on debt service

	1889–1897	1898–1906	1907–1915	1916–1924	1925–1933	1934–1942	Total
gen 0		0	0	0	0	0	5,187
gen 1	5,187	17,737	0	0	0	0	22,924
gen 2	5,187	17,737	39,917	0	0	0	62,841
gen 3	5,187	17,737	39,917	21,062	0	0	83,902
gen 4	0	17,737	39,917	21,062	17,523	0	96,238
gen 5	0	0	39,917	21,062	17,523	14,531	93,032
gen 6	0	0	0	21,062	17,523	14,531	53,115

Note: All data in thousand Italian lira (1942 value)

The model treats the debt service[57] amounts (last column in table 16.14) as input. The results are given in table 16.16 and show that the investment effort is well spread among the generations (particularly among 5 generations from gen 2 to gen 6) such that only the first two generations contribute far less due to the "border effect" of the model.

16.7 Conclusion

At the end of the nineteenth century and in the early decades of the twentieth century, Milan faced a massive economic development crisis due to a hugely increasing populace driven by the migration of workers from the rural areas to the city. The municipality had to find a solution to provide at least the basic infrastructure and services to meet the rapid urban expansion. In particular, the construction of a modern water and sanitation system could no longer be postponed without risking major epidemics and other negative impacts on the health of the populace.

At first, the solution of bringing spring water from the mountains to the city was considered, but it required the support of the central government to bypass the resistance from the Brembo River residents. Such support did not come. Consequently Milan had to chose among local groundwater resources instead of distant springs. In doing so, Milan's municipality would work on a fully autonomous solution that required little approval or support from the central government.

Water and sanitation in Italy has thus turned out to be mainly a municipal story and the Milan's story is perfect example of such a paradigm. To analyze how such an infrastructure was financed, one has first to understand what the financial intergovernmental relations between the municipalities and the central government were like. The newly born Italian state was facing an uneasy financial situation, and in consequence it imposed a tight financial discipline to the municipalities (ordinary budget balance, no transfers from the central government, borrowing constraints). Furthermore, because municipal fiscal revenues relied mainly on non-autonomous fiscal sources shared with the central government, fiscal competition would grow together with a progressive reduction of the fiscal revenues left to municipalities, and so would the compulsory expenses to be made by municipalities increase.

In such a tight financial situation how did Milan's municipality manage to finance a costly water and sanitation infrastructure? The first idea was likely to capture the land added value created by the infrastructure. I showed that this kind of tool had only a small role in the financing of Milan's urban infrastructure because both the legislative (expropriation) and fiscal tools available in Italy were not sufficiently powerful. Milan's municipality was then faced with three choices: postponing the investment, increasing the burden on the present generation, or borrowing and thus to spread the investment costs on future generations. However, postponing the provision of a modern water and sanitation service was truly not an option due to the public health externalities that would have ensued. So the classic public finance dilemma of deficit financing as whether to unburden the present generation in favor of the future generation was in full force.

Indeed, in 1891, Milan's policy makers were already pointing out the implicit intergenerational transfers caused by deficit financing: "To justify a loan, it is not sufficient to tell that public infrastructure will benefit mostly our grandchildren. Since we are confiscating future revenues, we also have to demonstrate that no other infrastructure needs will appear in the future and that we are providing today to all the future needs, including the unpredictable ones."[58] Yet infrastructure deficit financing was not preventable as "it would not be possible to increase taxes to cover each year those expenses. Neither to spread those extraordinary and urgent public works through the years in order to finance them on the yearly budget's surplus would be a sound decision since those works cannot be postponed.[59]

As I have shown, deficit financing (both through bond and loans) was the major financing tool Milan had left to cover the investment costs in the short run. In the end, the combined effect of high inflation and long-term deficit financing at a fixed interest rate would absorb a large part of the investment costs. In Milan, within the time frame of my analysis, debt was paid back both by users (tariff) and by local taxpayers (tax). At that time this was in fact a common policy in most cities in Europe and North America (Millward and Sheard 1995; Millward 2000; Bartlett 2003; Falkus 1977).

In the 1990s, in contrast, the mainstream policy consisted in recovering all costs through tariff revenues only. Although in the last two decades international institutions have softened their position on the issue of full-cost recovery and shifted to "sustainable cost recovery" according to the 3T's paradigm (OECD 2009), often revenues coming from tariffs are still considered more legitimate than the other two T's, as the General Secretary of OECD stated at the last Marseille World Water Forum (Gurria 2012).

The important lesson we have from the financing policies adopted by Western world cities in their nineteenth-century expansion phases should remind us that water and sanitation infrastructure costs can be financed thanks to municipal debt serviced by a mix of tax and tariff revenues and not by tariff alone. A historical perspective is useful to show that each local context and each time period calls for a context-tailored financing policy. A historical analysis can inform today's policies as we learn that a single financing solution fitting all situations does not exist.

Notes

We wish to thank the Paris water operator *Eau de Paris* and the *Agence Nationale de la Recherche* (ANR) through the EAU&3E research project (http://eau3e.hypotheses.org) for their financial support. We also acknowledge CESIFO sponsorship.

1. According to the World Bank, "cost recovery should be sufficient to pay for operations, maintenance and a fair return on capital investment, and provide for this outcome through loan covenants"(Bartlett 2003: 12: quoting a 1993 World Bank report).

2. After 1924 the fascist regime abolished the autonomy of Italian municipalities (*ordinamento podestarile).* In those years Milan municipal budget and reports are no longer available.

3. *Conto consuntivo dell'anno.*

4. Such as Riva in 1889, Carlo Erba in 1892, Tecnomasio Brown Boveri and Breda in 1903, Marelli in 1905, Pirelli, Falck and Alfa Romeo in 1906 (Boriani 1982: 60).

5. The public utility declaration decrees were passed by Parliament on April 29, 1888, and on July 11, 1889.

6. The mayor was formally appointed by the king. The prefect had the power to revoke the mayors' decisions.

7. Maintenance of water supply systems and streets were among the compulsory expenses while all new investments (capital expenditures) were considered as optional expenses.

8. Author's translation of the following Italian text: "*istruzione elementare per i due sessi, guardia nazionale, registri dello stato civile, elezioni, sala d'arresto presso la giudicatura del mandamento e per la custodia del mandamento.*" Art 116 Legge 20 marzo 1865 n° 2248 quoted by (Volpi 1959).

9. A municipality could moreover choose to collect not only its share of the excise duty but also the central government's share on its behalf. In that case the municipality would guarantee fixed revenue (*canone daziario*) to the central government. The amount of such *canone daziario* was judged too high by many municipalities, and special Acts were passed to delay its payment in various installments (Volpi 1959: 20). At the end of the nineteenth century the *canone daziario* amount was frozen and stayed untouched for many years. As a result the central government share of the excise duties fell steadily, leaving most of monies to the municipalities.

10. "*Lo Stato di fronte ai comuni non ha saputo far altro che togliere entrate da una parte e rovesciare su di esse nuove spese generali e non locali*" (L. Einaudi, *Pronunciamento dei comuni* in *Cronache* 1905: vol. 2, p. 203; quoted by Cassar and Creaco 2007).

11. "*Prima della prima guerra si ebbe un decentramento delle entrate quale dopo non si ebbe per tutto il resto del '900*" (Marongiu 1999, 9–15; quoted by Locatelli 2010, 18).

12. *Tassa comunale sulle aree fabbricabili,* approved by Legge n°320 8 luglio 1904.

13. Such a tax was initially conceived for the Rome municipality but then extended to all municipalities who needed to incentivize to build houses. It was to be paid until a building had been completed on the area (Municipio di Milano 1907a).

14. Including the additional tax (*sovraimposta comunale*) on property.

15. This is the same area on which a corruption scandal with mayor Bellinzaghi arose in 1884. The urban operation was implemented in the end after Bellinzaghi quitted. We do not know whether bribery took place on the final deal or not.

16. "*gli isolati piccoli sono il prodotto della speculazione*" (Beruto 1885: 6).

17. Legge 11 luglio 1907 n°502.

18. "The municipality has already bought 1,360,000 square meters of lands for a total cost of 4 and half millions. There will be the need for 400,000 square meters of roads. Water networks, sewers and public lighting will also be required. Alltogether this will sum up to an exected total cost of 3 millions. Thus, 7.5 millions will be required to ensure a 1 million square meter of net built land. There is no doubt that at the end the land value of that areas will be far higher than the total expenses made by the municipality."

Author's translation of the following Italian expression: "*Già a quest'ora sono assicurati al comune 1360 000 mq di aree che costarono, tutte insieme circa 4 millioni e mezzo ; vi si dovranno sistemare a strade circa 400 000 mq; vi si dovranno ativare i pubblici servizi di fognatura, illuminazione, acqua potabile; si dovrà dar loro vita con un pronto allacciamento alla rete tranviaria e tutto cio' richiederà una spesa che si preventive in circa 3 millioni; sono quindi 7,5 millioni all'incirca che si dovranno spendere nel quinquennio, riccorrendo a fondi straordinari, per assicuare al Comune una superficie netta fabbricabile di circa un milione di mq. Non v'ha dubbio che, a sistemazione fatta, il valore di quell'area supererà di gran lunga le spese che il Comune avrà anticipato*"(Municipio di Milano 1905: 32).

19. "*Cosi' la Giunta propone l'acquisto di aree ma in misura troppo limitata per fornire largamente del plus valore e senza un concetto direttivo*" (Atti del Municipio di Milano 1906–1907, Seduta ordinaria del 19 luglio 1907: 572).

20. "It is an excise duty wich pushes out from the city's wall the industries. It is an oppressive regulation which is immoral since it encourages smuggling" "*si tratta di un dazio che bandisce dalla città nostra le industrie, spingendole oltre le mura, vessatorio su mille modi, immorale nelle conseguenze del contrabbando*" (Mussi at the City Council in 1872; quoted by Sai et al. 1970: 32).

21. Two annexations took place in Milan: in 1873 and in 1923. In the last instance 11 other municipalities were annexed, giving to Milan roughly the same size it has nowadays (18,176 ha versus 7,600 ha before 1923) and increasing significantly its population too.

22. "All under the ground! That could be the definition of the sanitation system of our city. And drinking water ? All coming from underground resources! That's the vicious cycle that we should absolutely stop" Authors translation from: "*Tutto all'aves! Si potrebbe dire il sistema di fognatura della città, volendo darne una succinta definizione quantunque esagerata … E l'acqua da bere? Tutta dall'aves! Ecco il ciclo che devesi assolutamente interrompere*" (Felice Poggi; quoted by Colombo 1984: 119).

23. "*Permettendo i mercati monetari europei di associare capitali per l'esecuzione di tal genere di intraprese*" (Municipio di Milano 1881; quoted by Colombo 1984).

24. The Brembo Valley is located in the Bergamo region. It is well known that Bergamo and Milan have a long history of rivalry.

25. "*Lettera del Maggio 1885 in cui il Consiglio Superiore dei Lavori Pubblici rifiuta la dichiarazione di publica utilita per la conduttura d'acqua verso Milano delle sorgenti della Val Brembo*," reported in (Motta 1989).

26. There were 123 canals/sewers, totaling 153 km in 1868 (Gentile, Brown, and Spadoni 1990: 29).

27. There is a historical document (September 28, 1583) providing a technical description of 15 irrigation intakes from the *Roggia Vettabbia*. A copy of the document is available in Gentile et al. (1990: 12).

28. Baggio, Trenno, Musocco, Affori, Niguarda, Greco, Gorla, Crescenzago, Lambrate, Chiaravalle, and Vigentino.

29. The implementation of the new masterplan is outside the time frame of this study.

30. That document was written to justify a 8 million lira *mutuo ipotecario* with the *Cassa di Risparmio delle Provincie Lombarde*.

31. *"Sono richiesti dalle opere di viabilità già deliberate ed iniziate pel biennio 1890–1891"* (Municipio di Milano 1890b: 9).

32. *"L'opera stessa è stata iniziata ed è destinata a svolgersi parallelamente al piano regolatore, del quale è necessario e connesso organismo, dovendosi alle nuove costruzioni e alle nuove vie designare i convenienti provvedimenti di scolo."*

33. *"Si prediligono le vie dove c'è la fognatura o dove ha da essere eseguita. Pero estendere acqua ovunque ci sia la fognatura sarebbe eccessivo, allora si prediligono le vie dove ci dovrebbe essere una richiesta nell'anno."*

34. Including interest costs due to previously contracted loans.

35. Legge 19 luglio 1970 n° 5704.

36. *"Somma riservata a premi non superi 1/5 degli interessi annuali"* (Bufalini and Cavagna Sangiuliani di Gualdana 1881: 205).

37. Legge 14 giugno 1874 n°1961.

38. The municipality would give delegations to the tax collector to payback and amortize the loan as a collateral (*"delegazioni sull'esattore delle imposte dirette"*; Municipio di Milano 1907a).

39. The Milan City Council documents show indeed that these two conditions had to be met to obtain the loan from CDP. This was not straightforward for Milan's municipality since it had already touched the ceiling on the additional tax on properties. A waiver had to be obtained (Municipio di Milano 1907a).

40. Legge 551/1896 and Legge 227/1897.

41. Indeed municipal bonds were subjected to the tax while state bonds were not. This fact was criticized by local authorities (Municipio di Milano 1916). The municipality guaranteed a net interest to the lenders (bond subscribers). Thus the *imposta di richezza mobile* was an additional cost to be paid by the municipality when due.

42. Things changed only after 1925 when new savings products were commercialized by CDP through the postal network (*Buoni Postali Fruttiferi).*

43. In smaller size municipalities Municipal bonds were directly subscribed by local gentry while in larger cities banks were subscribing significant parts of the bonds too (della Torre 2003: 29).

44. CDP was exempted from the *imposta di richezza mobile*. In the previous bond emissions the municipality guaranteed a net interest to the lenders (bond subscribers). Thus the *imposta di richezza mobile* was an additional cost to be paid by the municipality when due.

45. In the framework of a *conto corrente* or a *mutuo ipotecario*.

46. The name of the Banca Commerciale Italiana is quoted as an option too, and some money was borrowed in the short term from the BPM.

47. Holders of the 1882 loan could choose either to be paid back at the nominal value or to subscribe to the 1897 municipal bond emission at a 4 percent interest rate (Atti del municipio di Milano 1895–1896); the payback would stay in effect until 1960.

48. An amount of 15 million lira on the 1886 80 million municipal bond emission was allocated to public works, including water and sanitation investments.

49. A copy of *Regolamento provvisorio per la fognatura del nuovo corso dal Cordusio al Foro Buonaparte ed addiacenze* is provided in Gentile et al. (1990: 90). It made sewer connection compulsory for landowners and gave precise technical guidelines on how to connect properly a private building to the sewer system.

50. "*... coll'intento pero' di facilitare l'attuazione del risanamento domestico, nelle case che maggiormente ne hanno bisogno, proporzionando quindi la misura del corrispettivo per modo che una casa signorile sia chiamata ad un contributo maggiore di quella d'affitto del medio ceto e questa più di una casa d'operai. Per queste ultime si è inoltre creduto opportuno di stabilire norme speciali e facilitazioni a vantaggio dell'igiene* [1894]" (Atti del Municipio di Milano 1893–1894: 355).

51. "*... ora che l'impianto di fognatura non è più considerato come un aggravio, ma insistemente invocato dagli stessi proprietari di case (che possono cosii ridurre i loro stabili in migliori condizioni di affittanza, eliminando in pari tempo le difficoltà e gli inconvenienti dello spurgo dei pozzi neri)*" (Municipio di Milano 1907d: 3).

52. According to the 1894 sanitation rules, buildings connecting to the sewer system were exonerated from paying the sanitation levy for six years (see section16.5.3). Buildings connected in 1893 and 1894 would start to pay the levy in 1899.

53. I also tested the sensitivity of my model to the payback duration with two other hypotheses (35 and 70 years). The results confirm a negative net profit for the water and sanitation service in all years except in the last years.

54. I computed "virtual inflated debt service" as the sum of two elements: capital payback (no inflation on this) and interests that I inflated using an inflation index. The inflation index is equal to 1 in 1988 and comes from ISTAT, serie storica, tavola 21.

55. Collected either through the postal office networks or in the market through bond emissions in the case of the *Sezione Autonoma per il Credito Comunale e Provinciale* (SACCP).

56. The reader should be aware that the debt service model is very basic and cannot fully represent the complexity of loans effectively contracted by the municipality to finance its water and sanitation infrastructure. Still, such a model can help one appreciate the order of magnitude of each generation's contribution.

57. Debt service amounts are computed using CAPEX amounts.

58. Such a position was taken within a report that argued in favor of a fiscal reform of Milan's excise duty system (section 16.2.4). "*a giustificarli [i prestiti] non basta affermare che i vantaggi delle grandi opere pubbliche ridondano in gran parte sui nipoti ; occorre dimostrare che a tempi nuovi non corrispondano nuove aspirazioni, e che noi provvediamo oggi a tutte le aspirazioni anche le non prevedibili di quell'avvenire di cui andiamo man mano confiscando i redditi.*" (Municipio di Milano 1891b: 42).

59. "*Già venne altra volta accennato come non sarebbe praticamente possibile il richiedere ad inasprimenti di tasse o a tasse nuove i mezzi necessari per far fronte annualmente a simili spese. Non si riuscirebbe a nulla di pronto ed efficace. Per l'esecuzione di opere straordinarie ed urgenti ad un tempo come quelle sottoposte al vostro esame, il sistema di provvedervi ripartitamente in una lunghissima serie di anni, si da potervi far fronte con le risorse ordinarie di bilancio, non risponde ai bisogni che le dette opere reclamano, né al loro coordinamento, nè a quell'incremento della vita cittadina che non soffre soverchi ritardi nei miglioramenti di pubblici servizi e nello sviluppo edilizio*" (Municipio di Milano 1907a: v).

60. "The community consists of all property owners in the direct vicinity of the infrastructure (direct beneficiaries)" ReUrba (2006).

61. Nonfiscal revenues are composed of tariff revenues from municipal services: tramways, electricity, water, and sanitation.

62. Total ordinary revenues (column 3) are not only the addition of fiscal and nonfiscal revenues (columns 1 and 3), there is a third addend, not given in the table, which is represented by the *rendite patrimoniali*. Under this category are included: revenues from municipal buildings, revenues from government bonds, and revenues from concessions to private companies (tramways to the Edison Company). I have omitted these revenues from the table because they always amount to minor sums.

63. The 1929 rules refer to an "intake fee" (*canone di presa)* rather than a meter rental fee.

References

Città di Milano, A. T. O. 2007. Piano d'ambito dell'ATO Città di Milano." http://www.atocittadimilano.it/default.asp?pag=23&tipo=9.

Barraqué, Bernard. 2003. The three ages of engineering for the water industry. http://francestanford.stanford.edu/sites/francestanford.stanford.edu/files/Barraque.pdf.

Bartlett, Sarah. 2003. Who pays for water: Cost recovery and user fees in Boston's public water infrastructure 1849 to 1895. http://dspace.mit.edu/bitstream/handle/1721.1/64560/52971451.pdf?sequence=1.

Beruto, Cesare. 1885. Il piano regolatore di Milano. In *Atti del municipio di Milano 1885–1886*, by Municipio di Milano.

Bigatti, Giorgio. 1997. La conquista dell'acqua. Urbanizzazione e approvvigionamento idrico. In Giorgio Bigatti, Andrea Giuntini, Andrea Mantegazza, and Claudia Rotondi, eds., *L'acqua e il gas in Italia: la storia dei servizi a rete delle aziende pubbliche e delle Federgasacqua*. Collana Ciriec di storie d'impresa pubblica e di pubblico interesse. Milano: F. Angeli.

Bigatti, Giorgio. 2000. *La città operosa: Milano nell'Ottocento. Studi e ricerche storiche 254*. Milano: FrancoAngeli.

Boriani, Maurizio. 1982. La costruzione della Milano moderna. In Maurizio Boriani, Remo Dorigati, Valeria Erba, Marina Molon, and Corinna Morandi, eds., *La Costruzione della Milano moderna: Casa e servizi in un secolo di storia cittadina*. Milano: Clup.

Brugnoli, Alberto. 2010. *Finanziamento delle infrastrutture e cattura del valore: Casi, modelli ed esperienze a confronto*. Milano: Guerini e Associati.

Bufalini, Francesco, and Antonio Cavagna Sangiuliani di Gualdana. 1881. *Commento teorico-pratico della legge e del regolamento comunale e provinciale: opera compilata in base alla legislazione, dottrina e giurisprudenza dal 1865 al 1881 coll'aggiunta di tutte le riforme state proposte*. Torino: Augusto Federico Negro. http://archive.org/details/commentoteoricop00bufa.

Buzzi Donato, Alessandro. 1969. Note sullo sviluppo di Milano negli ultimi cento anni. In *Quaderni di documentazione e studio a cura del servizio statistica*. Milano: Comune di Milano.

Campos Venuti, Giuseppe. 1986. Lo sviluppo di Milano dall'Unità d'Italia al secondo dopoguerra. In Giuseppe Campos Venuti, Antonello Boatti, Annapaola Canevari, and Valeria Erba, eds., *Un Secolo di urbanistica a Milano*. Milano: Clup.

Cassar, Silvana, and Salvo Creaco. 2007. Finanza e disavanzi degli enti locali dall'Unificazione al secondo dopoguerra. In Giuseppe De Luca and Angelo Moioli, *Debito pubblico e mercati finanziari in Italia: secoli XIII–XX*. Milano: Franco Angeli

Colombo, Cecilia. 1984. La costruzione della rete dell'acqua potabile a Milano nel primo decennio del Novecento. In Ornella Selvafolta and Aldo Castellano, eds., *Costruire in Lombardia: Rete e infrastrutture territoriali*. Milano: Electa.

Comune di Milano. 1888. *Verbali della seduta del consiglio comunale di Milano del 12, 13 e 14 luglio 1888*.

Comune di Milano. 1935. *Notizie generali sull'acquedotto comunale e descrizione dei nuovi tipi di centrali di pompatura*.

Conte, Leandro. 2001. Amministrare il risparmio: storia della CDP, 1850–1913. In Marcello De Cecco and Gianni Toniolo, eds., *Storia della cassa depositi e prestiti*. Roma: Laterza.

Crespi Reghizzi, Olivier. 2012. The financing history of urban water infrastructures in Paris (1807–1925): Lessons from the past to enlighten present and future challenges? In *Università degli studi di Milano*. http://ideas.repec.org/p/mil/wpdepa/2012-22.html.

Crespi Reghizzi, Olivier. 2013. Providing and financing a municipal infrastructure: A long run analysis of water and sanitation investments in Milan (1888–2000). In Venice: CESIFO Summer Institute. http://www.cesifo-group.de/portal/page/portal/CFP_CONF/CFP_CONF_VSI/VSI%202013/vsi13-eip-Picot/Papers/vsi13_eip_CrespiReghizzi.pdf.

De Finetti, Giuseppe. 2002. *Milano: Costruzione di una citta*. Milano: Hoepli.

Della Torre, Giuseppe. 2003. I finanziamenti agli enti locali nell'Italia liberale, 1864–1915: Disavanzi di bilancio, investimenti in opere pubbliche e gestione del debito pregresso. Punti aperti e primi risultati di un'analisi quantitativa. In *Cassino: Centro Interuniversitario di Ricerca per la Storia Finanziaria Italiana*.

Della Torre, Giuseppe. 2001. Fatti stilizzati per una storia quantitativa della CDP. In Marcello De Cecco and Gianni Toniolo, eds., *Storia della cassa depositi e prestiti*. Roma: Laterza.

Dorigati, Remo, and Marina Molon. 1982. Fabbisogni residenziali, bisogni e modelli insediativi nell'età giolittiana. In Maurizio Boriani, Remo Dorigati, Valeria Erba, Marina Molon, and Corinna Morandi, eds., *La Costruzione della Milano moderna: casa e servizi in un secolo di storia cittadina*. Milano: Clup.

Falkus, Malcolm. 1977. The development of municipal trading in the nineteenth century. *Business History* 19 (2): 134–61. doi:10.1080/00076797700000023.

Fraschini, Angela. 1991. *La finanza comunale in Italia: Uno schema interpretativo*. Milano : FrancoAngeli.

Gentile, Antonio, Maurizio Brown, and Giampiero Spadoni. 1990. *Viaggio nel sottosuolo di Milano tra acque e canali segreti*. Milano: Comune di Milano.

Giarda, Piero. 2005. Decentralization and intergovernmental fiscal relations in Italy: A review of past and recent trends. *Quaderni dell'istituto di economia e finanza*, Università Cattolica del Sacro Cuore edition.

Gurria, Angel. 2012. Remarks by Angel Gurría, OECD Secretary-General, at the Opening Ceremony of the 6th World Water Forum. Presented before the World Water Forum, Marseille, March 13.

Locatelli, Andrea Maria. 2010. *Enti locali e fiscalità nel "900 i cattolici e l"autonomia disconosciuta*. Storia Ricerche. Milano: V&P.

Marchand, Bernard. 1993. *Paris, histoire d'une ville*. Paris: Éditions du Seuil.

Marchand, Bernard. 2011. Le financement des travaux d'Haussmann: Un exemple pour les pays émergents? http://halshs.archives-ouvertes.fr/docs/00/58/34/57/PDF/Haussmann.pdf.

Marongiu, Gianni. 1999. *La riforma dei tributi comunali*. Milano: EGEA.

Marongiu, Gianni. 2001. *Storia dei tributi degli enti locali (1861–2000). Il Diritto tributario commentato, ser. 1*, vol. 92. Padova: CEDAM.

Massarutto, Antonio. 2002. Full-cost recovery and optimal pricing rules for water supply and sewerage. Research report, courtesy of the author.

Massarutto, Antonio. 2007. Water pricing and full cost recovery of water services: Economic incentive or instrument of public finance? *Water Policy* 9 (6): 591. doi:10.2166/wp.2007.024.

Millward, Robert. 2000. The political economy of urban utilities. In Martin Daunton, ed., *1840–1950*. Cambridge, UK: Cambridge University Press, 315–50. http://histories.cambridge.org/extract?id=chol9780521417075_CHOL9780521417075A012.

Millward, Robert, and Sally Sheard. 1995. The urban fiscal problem, 1870–1914: Government expenditure and finance in England and Wales. *Economic History Review* 48 (3): 501–35. doi:10.1111/j.1468-0289.1995.tb01429.x.

Motta, Vittorio. 1989. *L'acquedotto di Milano—Appendice*. Milano: Comune di Milano.

Municipio di Milano. 1881. Sulle proposte condutture di acqua potabile per la città, Relazione della giunta.

Municipio di Milano. 1890a. Progetto per la fognatura generale della città. In *Atti del municipio di Milano 1889–1890*. Milano: Tipografia Luigi di Pirola.

Municipio di Milano. 1890b. Relazione finanziaria e conseguenti proposte—Allegato II. In *Atti del municipio di Milano 1890–1891*. Milano: Pirola.

Municipio di Milano. 1891a. Relazione della commissione nominata dal Consiglio comunale nella seduta del 23 maggio 1891 per lo studio della situazione finanziaria del comune e relative proposte. In *Atti del municipio di Milano 1891–1892*. Milano: Tipografia Luigi di Pirola.

Municipio di Milano. 1891b. Relazione della commissione per lo studio della situazione finanziaria del comune. In *Milano: Atti del municipio di Milano 1891–1892*.

Municipio di Milano. 1905. Relazione della giunta sul bilancio preventivo 1906. In *Atti del municipio di Milano 1905–1906*. Milano: Reggiani.

Municipio di Milano. 1907a. Relazione della giunta municipale sulla proposta di un prestito di 70 milioni da assumersi dal Comune presso la Cassa Depositi e Prestit per acquisti e per opere di indole straordinaria e di pubblica utilità. In *Atti del municipio di Milano 1906–1907*. Milano: Civelli.

Municipio di Milano. 1907b. Norme per il servizio dell'acqua potabile—1894. In *Atti del municipio di Milano 1906–1907*.

Municipio di Milano. 1907c. Norme per il servizio dell'acqua potabile—1907. In *Atti del municipio di Milano 1906–1907*.

Municipio di Milano. 1907d. Progetto di nuovo regolamento per il servizio della fognatura. In *Atti del municipio di Milano 1906–1907*.

Municipio di Milano. 1916. Relazione della giunta municipale per l'emissione di un prestito su obbligazioni per 20 milioni, fruttante 5% interesse al netto di qualsiasi trattenuta presente e futura. In *Atti del municipio di Milano 1916–1917*.

OECD. 2009. *Managing Water for All: An OECD Perspective on Pricing and Financing*. Paris: OECD.

Peterson, George E. 2009. *Unlocking Land Values to Finance Urban Infrastructure*. Public–Private Infrastructure Advisory Facility, Trends and Policy Options 7. Washington, DC: World Bank.

Pinkney, David. 1958. *Napoleon III and the Rebuilding of Paris*. Princeton: Princeton University Press.

Pinkney, David H. 1955. Napoleon III's transformation of Paris: The origins and development of the idea. *Journal of Modern History* 27 (2): 125–34.

Pinkney, David H. 1957. Money and politics in the rebuilding of Paris, 1860–1870. *Journal of Economic History* 17 (01): 45–61. doi:10.1017/S0022050700059866.

Poggi. 1911. Le fognature di Milano. In *Atti del municipio di Milano 1911–1912*. Milano: Vallardi.

ReUrba. 2006. Value oriented planning. http://www.stipo.nl/documenten/998_reurba/2006%20ReUrbA%20final%20Value%20Oriented%20Planning.pdf.

Rosen, Harvey S, and Ted Gayer. 2010. *Public Finance*. Boston: McGraw-Hill/Higher Education.

Sai, Mario, Maria Adele Scala, Luciano Tinelli, and Isabella Superti-Furga. 1970. *3: Il Comune di Milano. Storia amministrativa delle province lombarde*. Milano: Giuffré.

Van Hofwegen, Paul. 2006. *Task Force on Financing Water for All, Enhancing Access to Finance for Local Governments, Financing Water for Agriculture. Chaired by Angel Gurria*. World Water Council.

Volpi, Franco. 1959. *Le finanze comunali di un grande centro urbano: Spese, entrate, disavanzi del Comune di Milano dal 1938 al 1958, nel quadro della situazione e delle prospettive della finanza locale in Italia. Istituto Giangiacomo Feltrinelli. Centro di studi e ricerche sulla struttura economica italiana 3*. Milano: Feltrinelli.

Winpenny, James. 2003. *Report of the World Panel on Financing Water Infrastructure. Chaired by Michel Camdessus*. World Water Council.

Contributors

Julio C. Aguirre, Universidad del Pacífico (Peru)

Laure Athias, University of Lausanne, IDHEAP

Stephen J. Bailey, Glasgow Caledonian University

Sumedha Bajar, Institute for Social and Economic Change (India)

Biswa Nath Bhattacharyay, Asian Development Bank (formerly)

Federico Boffa, Free University of Bolzano

Olivier Crespi Reghizzi, CIRED, AgroParisTech and CERTET, Bocconi University

Daniel Danau, Université de Caen Basse-Normandie

Sumit S. Deole, University of Halle-Wittenberg

Balázs Égert, Organisation for Economic Co-operation and Development (OECD)

Massimo Florio, University of Milan

Stephan Fretz, University of St. Gallen

Asmae El Gallaa, Aix Marseille School of Economics (AMSE)

Marco Giorgino, Politecnico di Milano

Hugh Goldsmith, European Investment Bank

Nico Grove, Institute for Infrastructure Economics and Management (IEM)

Klaus Markus Hofmann, Deutsche Bahn AG, NETWORK Institute

Lynne Kiesling, Northwestern University

Johann Kranz, Georg-August-University of Göttingen

Antonio Nunez, University of Lyon

Arnold Picot, Ludwig-Maximilians-Universität Munich

Michael Pollitt, Judge Business School, University of Cambridge

Martina Santandrea, Politecnico di Milano

Stéphane Straub, Toulouse School of Economics

Annalisa Vinella, Università degli Studi di Bari "Aldo Moro"

Index